A Note from the Authors

You are about to embark on an amazing journey of discovery. The study of life ⟨⟩ workings of cells to the complex interactions of entire ecosystems, through th⟨⟩ in DNA to the ways genetic information evolves over time. At the same time that our understanding of biology is growing in leaps and bounds, so too are great insights into how learners acquire new knowledge and skills. We are thrilled to join Scott Freeman on *Biological Science*, a book dedicated to active, research-based learning and to exploring the experimental evidence that informs what we know about biology. The next few pages highlight the features in this book and in MasteringBiology® that will help you succeed.

From left to right: Michael Black, Emily Taylor, Jon Monroe, Lizabeth Allison, Greg Podgorski, Kim Quillin

To the Student: How to Use This Book

New chapter-opening Roadmaps visually group and organize information to help you anticipate key ideas as well as recognize meaningful relationships and connections between them.

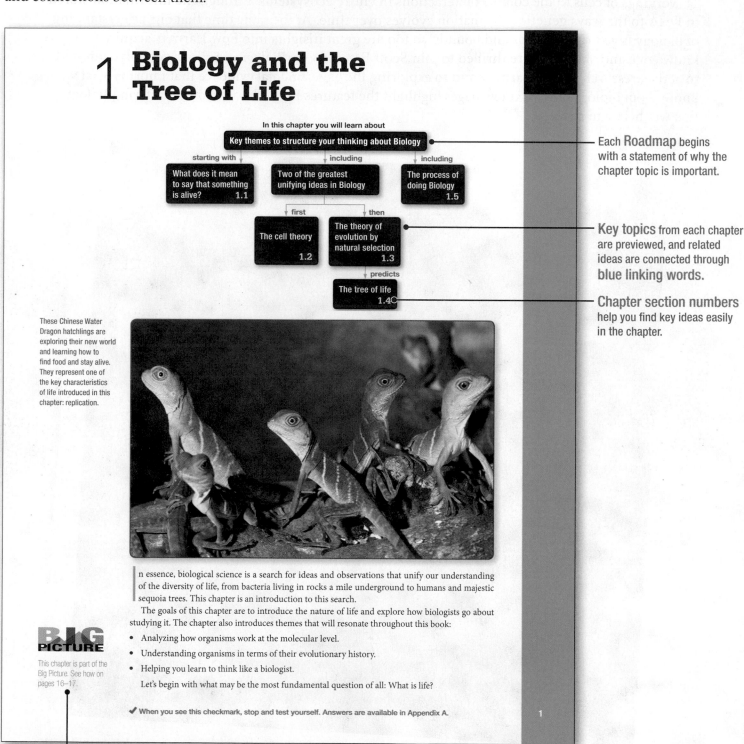

1 **Biology and the Tree of Life**

In this chapter you will learn about

Key themes to structure your thinking about Biology

starting with | *including* | *including*

What does it mean to say that something is alive? **1.1**

Two of the greatest unifying ideas in Biology

The process of doing Biology **1.5**

first | *then*

The cell theory **1.2**

The theory of evolution by natural selection **1.3**

predicts

The tree of life **1.4**

Each **Roadmap** begins with a statement of why the chapter topic is important.

Key topics from each chapter are previewed, and related ideas are connected through **blue linking words**.

Chapter section numbers help you find key ideas easily in the chapter.

These Chinese Water Dragon hatchlings are exploring their new world and learning how to find food and stay alive. They represent one of the key characteristics of life introduced in this chapter: replication.

BIG PICTURE

This chapter is part of the Big Picture. See how on pages 16–17.

In essence, biological science is a search for ideas and observations that unify our understanding of the diversity of life, from bacteria living in rocks a mile underground to humans and majestic sequoia trees. This chapter is an introduction to this search.

The goals of this chapter are to introduce the nature of life and explore how biologists go about studying it. The chapter also introduces themes that will resonate throughout this book:

- Analyzing how organisms work at the molecular level.
- Understanding organisms in terms of their evolutionary history.
- Helping you learn to think like a biologist.

Let's begin with what may be the most fundamental question of all: What is life?

✔ When you see this checkmark, stop and test yourself. Answers are available in Appendix A.

1

Big Picture Concept Maps are referenced on the opening page of related chapters, pointing you to summary pages that help you synthesize challenging topics.

Big Picture Concept Maps integrate visuals and words to help you synthesize information about challenging topics in biology that span multiple chapters and units.

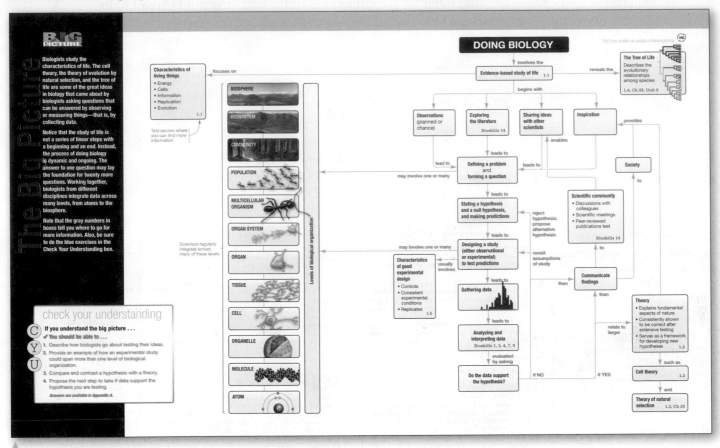

Three New Big Picture topics have been added to the Fifth Edition:

- NEW! Doing Biology
- NEW! The Chemistry of Life
- Energy for Life
- Genetic Information
- Evolution
- NEW! Plant and Animal Form and Function
- Ecology

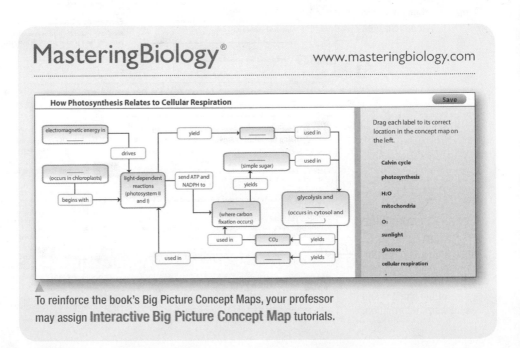

To reinforce the book's Big Picture Concept Maps, your professor may assign **Interactive Big Picture Concept Map** tutorials.

Practice for success on tests and exams

Intertwined color-coded "active learning threads" are embedded in the text. The gold thread helps you to identify important ideas, and the blue thread helps you to test your understanding.

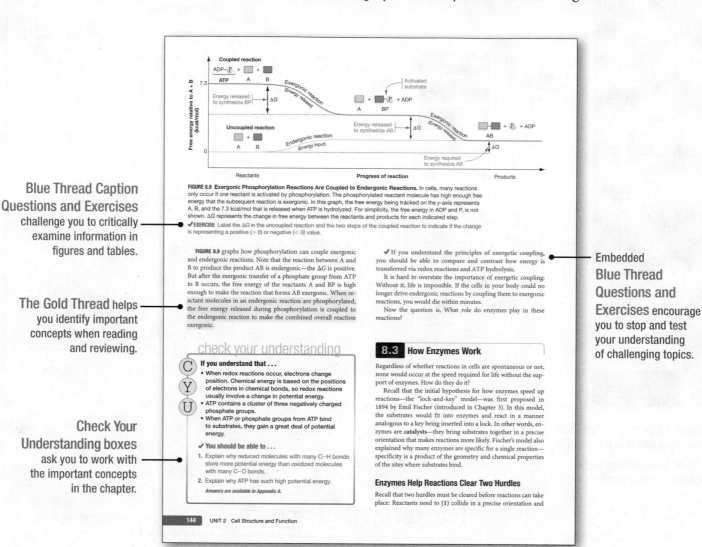

FIGURE 8.9 Exergonic Phosphorylation Reactions Are Coupled to Endergonic Reactions. In cells, many reactions only occur if one reactant is activated by phosphorylation. The phosphorylated reactant molecule has high enough free energy that the subsequent reaction is exergonic. In this graph, the free energy being tracked on the *y*-axis represents A, B, and the 7.3 kcal/mol that is released when ATP is hydrolyzed. For simplicity, the free energy in ADP and P$_i$ is not shown. ΔG represents the change in free energy between the reactants and products for each indicated step.

✔ **EXERCISE** Label the ΔG in the uncoupled reaction and the two steps of the coupled reaction to indicate if the change is representing a positive (> 0) or negative (< 0) value.

Blue Thread Caption Questions and Exercises challenge you to critically examine information in figures and tables.

The Gold Thread helps you identify important concepts when reading and reviewing.

FIGURE 8.9 graphs how phosphorylation can couple exergonic and endergonic reactions. Note that the reaction between A and B to produce the product AB is endergonic—the ΔG is positive. But after the exergonic transfer of a phosphate group from ATP to B occurs, the free energy of the reactants A and BP is high enough to make the reaction that forms AB exergonic. When reactant molecules in an endergonic reaction are phosphorylated, the free energy released during phosphorylation is coupled to the endergonic reaction to make the combined overall reaction exergonic.

✔ If you understand the principles of energetic coupling, you should be able to compare and contrast how energy is transferred via redox reactions and ATP hydrolysis.

It is hard to overstate the importance of energetic coupling: Without it, life is impossible. If the cells in your body could no longer drive endergonic reactions by coupling them to exergonic reactions, you would die within minutes.

Now the question is, What role do enzymes play in these reactions?

Embedded Blue Thread Questions and Exercises encourage you to stop and test your understanding of challenging topics.

check your understanding

If you understand that . . .

(C) (Y) (U)

• When redox reactions occur, electrons change position. Chemical energy is based on the positions of electrons in chemical bonds, so redox reactions usually involve a change in potential energy.

• ATP contains a cluster of three negatively charged phosphate groups.

• When ATP or phosphate groups from ATP bind to substrates, they gain a great deal of potential energy.

✔ **You should be able to . . .**

1. Explain why reduced molecules with many C–H bonds store more potential energy than oxidized molecules with many C–O bonds.

2. Explain why ATP has such high potential energy.

Answers are available in Appendix A.

Check Your Understanding boxes ask you to work with the important concepts in the chapter.

8.3 How Enzymes Work

Regardless of whether reactions in cells are spontaneous or not, none would occur at the speed required for life without the support of enzymes. How do they do it?

Recall that the initial hypothesis for how enzymes speed up reactions—the "lock-and-key" model—was first proposed in 1894 by Emil Fischer (introduced in Chapter 3). In this model, the substrates would fit into enzymes and react in a manner analogous to a key being inserted into a lock. In other words, enzymes are **catalysts**—they bring substrates together in a precise orientation that makes reactions more likely. Fischer's model also explained why many enzymes are specific for a single reaction—specificity is a product of the geometry and chemical properties of the sites where substrates bind.

Enzymes Help Reactions Clear Two Hurdles

Recall that two hurdles must be cleared before reactions can take place: Reactants need to (1) collide in a precise orientation and

8.2 Nonspontaneous Reactions May Be Driven Using Chemical Energy

• Redox reactions transfer energy by coupling exergonic oxidation reactions to endergonic reduction reactions.

• High-energy C–H bonds may be formed during the reduction step of a redox reaction when an H$^+$ is combined with a transferred electron.

• The hydrolysis of ATP is an exergonic reaction and may be used to drive a variety of cellular processes.

• When a phosphate group from ATP is added to a substrate that participates in an endergonic reaction, the potential energy of the substrate is raised enough to make the reaction exergonic and thus spontaneous.

✔ You should be able to explain what energetic coupling means, and why life would not exist without it.

8.3 How Enzymes Work

• Enzymes are protein catalysts. They speed reaction rates but do not affect the change in free energy of the reaction.

• The structure of an enzyme has an active site that brings sub-

End-of-Chapter Blue Thread Exercises, integrated in the chapter summary, help you review the major themes of the chapter and synthesize information.

• Protein cleavage and phosphorylation are examples of how enzymes may be regulated by modifying their primary structure.

✔ You should be able to compare and contrast the effect of allosteric regulation versus phosphorylation on enzyme function.

8.5 Enzymes Can Work Together in Metabolic Pathways

• In cells, enzymes often work together in metabolic pathways that sequentially modify a substrate to make a product.

• A pathway may be regulated by controlling the activity of one enzyme, often the first in the series of reactions. Feedback inhibition results from the accumulation of a product that binds to an enzyme in the pathway and inactivates it.

• Metabolic pathways were vital to the evolution of life, and new pathways continue to evolve in cells.

✔ You should be able to predict how the removal of the intermediate in a two-step metabolic pathway would affect the enzymatic rates of the first and last.

 www.masteringbiology.com

1. MasteringBiology Assignments

Identify gaps in your understanding, then fill them

The Fifth Edition provides many opportunities for you to test yourself and offers **helpful learning strategies.**

Analyze: Can I recognize underlying patterns and structure?

Evaluate: Can I make judgments on the relative value of ideas and information?

Create: Can I put ideas and information together to generate something new?

Apply: Can I use these ideas in the same way or in a new situation?

Understand: Can I explain this concept in my own words?

Remember: Can I recall the key terms and ideas?

◀ **Bloom's Taxonomy** describes six learning levels: Remember, Understand, Apply, Analyze, Evaluate, and Create. Questions in the book span all levels, including self-testing at the higher levels to help you develop higher-order thinking skills that will prepare you for exams.

Steps to Building Understanding
Each chapter ends with three groups of questions that build in difficulty:

✓ **TEST YOUR KNOWLEDGE**

Begin by testing your basic knowledge of new information.

✓ **TEST YOUR UNDERSTANDING**

Once you're confident with the basics, demonstrate your deeper understanding of the material.

✓ **TEST YOUR PROBLEM-SOLVING SKILLS**

Work towards mastery of the content by answering questions that challenge you at the highest level of competency.

BIOSKILL 16 using Bloom's taxonomy

Most students have at one time or another wondered why a particular question on an exam seemed so hard, while others seemed easy. The explanation lies in the type of cognitive skills required to answer the question. Let's take a closer look.

NEW! BioSkill Covering Bloom's Taxonomy helps you to recognize question types using the Bloom's cognitive hierarchy, and it provides specific strategies to help you study for questions at all six levels.

Answer Appendix Includes Bloom's Taxonomy Information
Answers to all questions in the text now include the Bloom's level being tested. You can simultaneously practice assessing your understanding of content and recognizing Bloom's levels. Combining this information with the guidance in the BioSkill on Bloom's Taxonomy will help you form a plan to improve your study skills.

▶

✓ **Test Your Problem-Solving Skills**

13. *analyze* A scientific theory is not a guess—it is an idea whose validity can be tested with data. Both the cell theory and the theory of evolution have been validated by large bodies of observational and experimental data.
14. *apply* If all eukaryotes living today have a nucleus, then it is logical to conclude that the nucleus arose in a common ancestor of all eukaryotes, indicated by the arrow you should have added to the figure. See **FIGURE A1.2.** If it had arisen in a common ancestor of Bacteria or Archaea, then species in those groups would have had to lose the trait—an unlikely event.
15. *evaluate* The data set was so large and diverse that it was no longer reasonable to argue that noncellular life-forms would be discovered. **16.** *apply* b

---

MasteringBiology®
www.masteringbiology.com

NEW! End-of-chapter questions from the book are now available for your professor to assign as homework in MasteringBiology.

Practice scientific thinking and scientific skills

A unique emphasis on the process of scientific discovery and experimental design teaches you how to think like a scientist as you learn fundamental biology concepts.

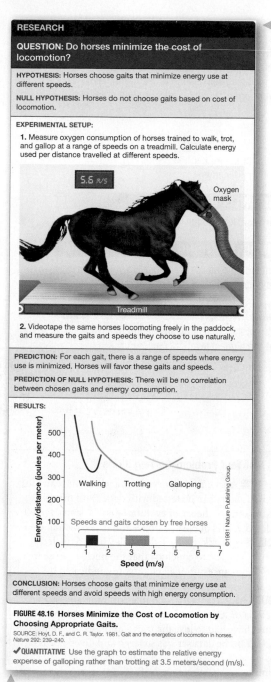

RESEARCH

QUESTION: Do horses minimize the cost of locomotion?

HYPOTHESIS: Horses choose gaits that minimize energy use at different speeds.

NULL HYPOTHESIS: Horses do not choose gaits based on cost of locomotion.

EXPERIMENTAL SETUP:

1. Measure oxygen consumption of horses trained to walk, trot, and gallop at a range of speeds on a treadmill. Calculate energy used per distance travelled at different speeds.

5.6 m/s

Oxygen mask

Treadmill

2. Videotape the same horses locomoting freely in the paddock, and measure the gaits and speeds they choose to use naturally.

PREDICTION: For each gait, there is a range of speeds where energy use is minimized. Horses will favor these gaits and speeds.

PREDICTION OF NULL HYPOTHESIS: There will be no correlation between chosen gaits and energy consumption.

RESULTS:

©1981 Nature Publishing Group

Energy/distance (joules per meter) vs Speed (m/s)

Walking Trotting Galloping

Speeds and gaits chosen by free horses

CONCLUSION: Horses choose gaits that minimize energy use at different speeds and avoid speeds with high energy consumption.

FIGURE 48.16 Horses Minimize the Cost of Locomotion by Choosing Appropriate Gaits.
SOURCE: Hoyt, D. F., and C. R. Taylor. 1981. Gait and the energetics of locomotion in horses. Nature 292: 239–240.

✔**QUANTITATIVE** Use the graph to estimate the relative energy expense of galloping rather than trotting at 3.5 meters/second (m/s).

All of the Research Boxes cite the original research paper and include a question that asks you to analyze the design of the experiment or study.

▶ **Research Boxes** explain how research studies are designed and give you additional practice interpreting data. Each Research Box consistently models the scientific method, presenting the research question, hypotheses, experimental setup, predictions, results, and conclusion. 15 Research Boxes are new to the Fifth Edition.

MasteringBiology®
www.masteringbiology.com

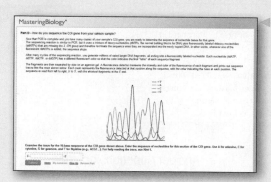

▶ **NEW! Solve It Tutorials** are available for homework assignments in MasteringBiology and give you an opportunity to work like a scientist through a simulated investigation that requires you to analyze and interpret data.

Experimental Inquiry Tutorials based on some of biology's most seminal experiments give you a chance to analyze data and the reasoning that led scientists from the data to their conclusions.

Experimental Inquiry tutorial topics include:

- What Can You Learn About the Process of Science from Investigating a Cricket's Chirp?
- Which Wavelengths of Light Drive Photosynthesis?
- What Is the Inheritance Pattern of Sex-Linked Traits?
- Does DNA Replication Follow the Conservative, Semiconservative, or Dispersive Model?
- How Do Calcium Ions Help to Prevent Polyspermy During Egg Fertilization?

- Did Natural Selection of Ground Finches Occur When the Environment Changed?
- What Effect Does Auxin Have on Coleoptile Growth?
- What Role Do Genes Play in Appetite Regulation?
- Can a Species' Niche Be Influenced by Interspecific Competition?
- What Factors Influence the Loss of Nutrients from a Forest Ecosystem?

Build important skills scientists use to perform, evaluate, and communicate scientific research.

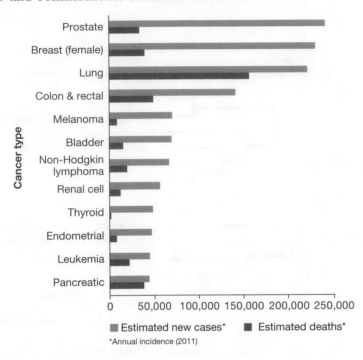

■ Estimated new cases*   ■ Estimated deaths*

*Annual incidence (2011)

NEW! Graphs and tables now include their data sources, emphasizing the research process that leads to our understanding of biological ideas.

FIGURE 4.13 Cancers Vary in Type and Severity.
DATA: The website of the National Cancer Institute (http://www.cancer.gov), Common Cancer Types, November 2010.

✔ **QUANTITATIVE** Which extinction event ended the era of the dinosaurs 65 million years ago? About what percentage of families went extinct?

NEW! Quantitative questions are identified throughout the text, helping you practice computational problem solving and data analysis.

Expanded BioSkills Appendix helps you build skills that will be important to your success in biology. At relevant points in the text, you'll find references to the BioSkills appendix that will help you learn and practice foundational skills.

BioSkills Topics include:

- The Metric System and Significant Figures
- Some Common Latin and Greek Roots Used in Biology
- Reading Graphs
- Using Statistical Tests and Interpreting Standard Error Bars
- Combining Probabilities

- Using Logarithms
- Reading a Phylogenetic Tree
- Reading Chemical Structures
- Separating and Visualizing Molecules
- Separating Cell Components by Centrifugation
- Biological Imaging: Microscopy and X-ray Crystallography

- Cell and Tissue Culture Methods
- Model Organisms
- NEW! Primary Literature and Peer Review
- Making Concept Maps
- NEW! Using Bloom's Taxonomy

MasteringBiology®
www.masteringbiology.com

You can access self-paced BioSkills activities in the Study Area, and your instructor can assign additional activities in MasteringBiology.

Visualize biology processes and structures

A carefully crafted visual program helps you gain a better understanding of biology through accurate, appropriately detailed figures.

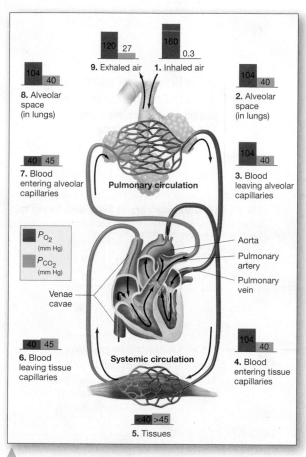

Informative figures help you think through complex biological processes in manageable steps.

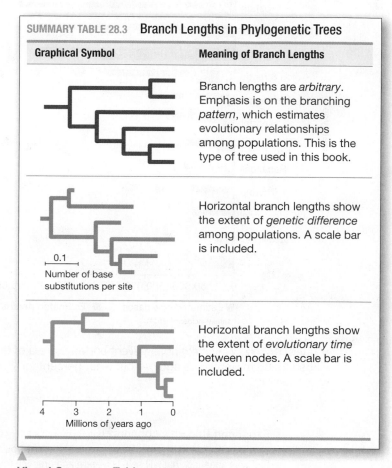

Visual Summary Tables pull together important information in a format that allows for easy comparison and review.

Instructor and Student Resources

For Instructors

Instructor Resource DVD-ROM
978-0-321-86112-2 • 0-321-86112-4

Everything you need for lectures in one place, including video segments that demonstrate how to incorporate active-learning techniques into your own classroom. Enhanced menus make locating and assessing the digital resources for each chapter easy. The Instructor Resource CD/DVD-ROM includes PowerPoint® Lecture Outlines that integrate figures and animations for classroom presentations. All textbook figures, art, and photos are in JPEG format, and all PowerPoint slides and JPEGs have editable labels. Over 300 Instructor Animations accurately depict complex topics and dynamic processes described in the book.

Instructor Guide (Download only)
Available in the instructor resource area of MasteringBiology.®

TestGen® (Download only)
All of the exam questions in the Test Bank have been peer reviewed and student tested, providing questions that set the standard for quality and accuracy. To improve the Test Bank, Metadata from MasteringBiology users has been incorporated directly into the software. Test questions that are ranked according to Bloom's taxonomy and improved TestGen® software makes assembling tests that much easier.

For Students

Study Guide
978-0-321-85832-0 • 0-321-85832-8

The Study Guide presents a breakdown of key biological concepts, difficult topics, and quizzes to help students prepare for exams. Unique to this study guide are four introductory, stand-alone chapters that introduce students to foundational ideas and skills necessary for classroom success: Introduction to Experimentation and Research in the Biological Sciences, Presenting Biological Data, Understanding Patterns in Biology and Improving Study Techniques, and Reading and Writing to Understand Biology. "Looking Forward" and "Looking Back" sections help students make connections across the chapters instead of viewing them as discrete entities.

Practicing Biology: A Student Workbook
978-0-321-88647-7 • 0-321-88647-X

This workbook focuses on key ideas, principles, and concepts that are fundamental to understanding biology. A variety of hands-on activities such as mapping and modeling suit different learning styles and help students discover which topics they need more help on. Students learn biology by doing biology. An instructors guide can be downloaded from the Instructor Area of MasteringBiology.

MasteringBiology®

www.masteringbiology.com

MasteringBiology is an online homework, tutorial, and assessment system that delivers self-paced tutorials that provide individualized coaching, focus on your course objectives, and respond to each student's progress. The Mastering system helps instructors maximize class time with customizable, easy-to-assign, and automatically graded assessments that motivate students to learn outside of class and arrive prepared for lecture. MasteringBiology is also available with a complete Pearson eText edition of *Biological Science*.

Highlights of the Fifth Edition Item Library include:

* **NEW! assignment options** include Solve It activities, end-of-chapter problems, and questions that accompany new BioSkills and new Big Picture Interactive Concept Maps.
* **NEW! "best of" homework pre-built assignments** help professors assign popular, key content quickly, including a blend of tutorials, end-of-chapter problems, and test bank questions.

* *Get Ready for Biology* and Chemistry Review **assignment options** help students get up to speed with activities that review chemistry, mathematics, and basic biology.

MasteringBiology® Virtual Labs

978-0-321-88644-6 • 0-321-88644-5

MasteringBiology: Virtual Labs is an online environment that promotes critical-thinking skills using virtual experiments and explorations that might be difficult to perform in a wet-lab environment due to time, cost, or safety concerns. MasteringBiology: Virtual Labs offers unique learning experiences in the areas of microscopy, molecular biology, genetics, ecology, and systematics.

For more information, please visit www.pearsonhighered.com/virtualbiologylabs

Scott Freeman • Lizabeth Allison • Michael Black • Kim Quillin

Biological Science

Custom Edition for Northern Arizona University

Taken from:
Biological Science, Fifth Edition
by Scott Freeman, Lizabeth Allison, Michael Black, Greg Podgorski,
Kim Quillin, Jon Monroe, and Emily Taylor

Cover Art: Courtesy of Photodisc/Getty Images.

Taken from:

Biological Science, Fifth Edition
by Scott Freeman, Lizabeth Allison, Michael Black, Greg Podgorski, Kim Quillin, Jon Monroe, and Emily Taylor
Copyright © 2014, 2011, 2008 by Pearson Education, Inc.
Boston, Massachusetts 02116

This special edition published in cooperation with Pearson Learning Solutions.

Pearson Learning Solutions, 501 Boylston Street, Suite 900, Boston, MA 02116
A Pearson Education Company
www.pearsoned.com

Printed in the United States of America

8 9 10 11 V011 19 18 17 16 15

000200010271800580

MC

ISBN 10: 1-269-46055-2
ISBN 13: 978-1-269-46055-2

Detailed Contents

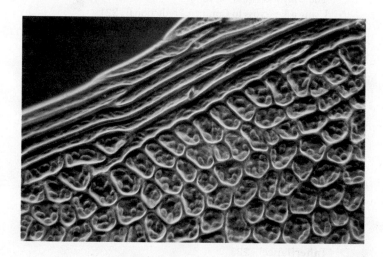

About the Authors

A Letter from Scott:

I started working on *Biological Science* in 1997 with a simple goal: To help change the way biology is taught. After just shy of 20,000 hours of work on four editions of this text, that goal still gets me out of bed in the morning. But instead of focusing my energies on textbook writing, I've decided to devote myself full-time to research on student learning and developing new courses for undergraduate and graduate students at the University of Washington.

So with this edition I am passing the torch—to an all-star cast of leading scientists and educators who have enthusiastically taught from, and contributed to, previous editions of *Biological Science*. Working with them, I have seen the new team bring their passion, talent, and creativity to the book, with expertise that spans the breadth of the life sciences. Just as important, they work beautifully together because they think alike. They are driven by a shared concern for student learning, a commitment to the craft of writing, and a background in evidence-based teaching.

These pages provide a brief introduction to Liz Allison, Michael Black, Greg Podgorski, Kim Quillin, Jon Monroe, and Emily Taylor. As a group, they've built on the book's existing strengths and infused this edition with fresh energy, perspective, and ideas. I'm full of admiration for what they have accomplished, and excited about the impact this edition will have on biology students from all over the world.—*Scott Freeman*

Scott Freeman received a Ph.D. in Zoology from the University of Washington and was subsequently awarded an Alfred P. Sloan Post-doctoral Fellowship in Molecular Evolution at Princeton University. He has done research in evolutionary biology on topics ranging from nest parasitism to the molecular systematics of the blackbird family and is coauthor, with Jon Herron, of the standard-setting undergraduate text *Evolutionary Analysis*. Scott is the recipient of a Distinguished Teaching Award from the University of Washington and is currently a Senior Lecturer in the UW Department of Biology, where he teaches introductory biology for majors, a writing-intensive course for majors called The Tree of Life, and a graduate seminar in college science teaching. Scott's current research focuses on how active learning affects student learning and academic performance.

Lizabeth A. Allison is professor and chair of the Biology Department at the College of William & Mary. She received her Ph.D. in Zoology from the University of Washington, specializing in molecular and cellular biology. Before coming to William & Mary, she spent eight years as a faculty member at the University of Canterbury in New Zealand. Liz teaches introductory biology for majors and upper-division molecular biology courses. She has mentored graduate students and more than 80 undergraduate research students, many of them coauthoring papers with her on intracellular trafficking of the thyroid hormone receptor in normal and cancer cells. The recipient of numerous awards, including a State Council for Higher Education in Virginia (SCHEV) Outstanding Faculty Award in 2009, Liz received one of the three inaugural Arts & Sciences Faculty Awards for Teaching Excellence in 2011, and a Plumeri Award for Faculty Excellence in 2012. In addition to her work on this text, she is author of *Fundamental Molecular Biology*, now in its second edition.
Lead Author; Chapter 1 and BioSkills
laalli@wm.edu

Michael Black received his Ph.D. in Microbiology & Immunology from Stanford University School of Medicine as a Howard Hughes Predoctoral Fellow. After graduation, he studied cell biology as a Burroughs Wellcome Postdoctoral Fellow at the MRC Laboratory of Molecular Biology in Cambridge, England. His current research focuses on the use of molecules to identify and track the transmission of microbes in the environment. Michael is a professor of Cell & Molecular Biology at California Polytechnic State University in San Luis Obispo, where he teaches introductory and advanced classes for majors in cell biology and microbiology. In addition to his teaching and research activities, Michael serves as the director of the Undergraduate Biotechnology Lab, where he works alongside undergraduate technicians to integrate research projects and inquiry-based activities into undergraduate classes.
Chapters 2–12, 36, and 51
mblack@calpoly.edu

Greg Podgorski received his Ph.D. in Molecular and Cellular Biology from Penn State University and has been a postdoctoral fellow at the Max Plank Institute for Biochemistry and Columbia University. His research interests are in biology education, developmental genetics, and computational biology. Greg's most recent work has been in mathematical modeling of how patterns of different cell types emerge during development and how tumors recruit new blood vessels in cancer. Greg has been teaching at Utah State University for more than 20 years in courses that include introductory biology for majors and for nonmajors, genetics, cell biology, developmental biology, and microbiology, and he has offered courses in nonmajors biology in Beijing and Hong Kong. He's won teaching awards at Utah State University and has been recognized by the National Academies as a Teaching Fellow and a Teaching Mentor.

Chapters 13–24

greg.podgorski@usu.edu

Jon Monroe is professor of Biology at James Madison University in Harrisonburg, Virginia. Jon completed his undergraduate work in Botany at the University of Michigan and his graduate work in Plant Physiology at Cornell University. He began his current position after a postdoc in biochemistry at Michigan State University. He currently teaches Plant Biology, and Cell and Molecular Biology. Jon's interest in plants is broad, ranging from systematics and taxonomy to physiology and biochemistry. His research, mostly with undergraduates, uses Arabidopsis thaliana to study the functions of a family of β-amylase genes in starch metabolism. Jon has been active in promoting undergraduate research through his work with the American Society of Plant Biologists (ASPB) and the Council on Undergraduate Research. He has received ASPB's Excellence in Teaching award and James Madison University Alumni Association's Distinguished Faculty Award.

Chapters 29–32; 37–41

monroejd@jmu.edu

Kim Quillin received her B.A. in Biology at Oberlin College *summa cum laude* and her Ph.D. in Integrative Biology from the University of California, Berkeley (as a National Science Foundation Graduate Fellow). Kim has worked in the trenches with Scott Freeman on every edition of *Biological Science*, starting with the ground-up development of the illustrations in the first edition in 1999 and expanding her role in each edition, always with the focus of helping students to think like biologists. Kim currently teaches introductory biology at Salisbury University, a member of the University System of Maryland, where she is actively involved in the ongoing student-centered reform of the concepts-and-methods course for biology majors. Her current research focuses on the scholarship of teaching and learning with an emphasis on measuring science process skills and the advantages and pitfalls of active multimedia learning.

Chapters 25–28; 33–35; 48; 52–57

kxquillin@salisbury.edu

Emily Taylor earned a B.A. in English at the University of California, Berkeley followed by a Ph.D. in Biological Sciences from Arizona State University, where she conducted research in the field of environmental physiology as a National Science Foundation Graduate Research Fellow. She is currently an associate professor of Biological Sciences at the California Polytechnic State University in San Luis Obispo, California. Her student-centered research program focuses on the endocrine and reproductive physiology of free-ranging reptiles, especially rattlesnakes. She teaches numerous undergraduate and graduate courses, including introductory biology, anatomy and physiology, and herpetology, and received the California Faculty Association's Distinguished Educator Award in 2010 and Cal Poly's Distinguished Teaching Award in 2012. Her revision of Unit 8 is her first foray into textbook writing.

Chapters 42–50

etaylor@calpoly.edu

Preface to Instructors

The first edition of *Biological Science* was visionary in its unique emphasis on the process of scientific discovery and experimental design—teaching how we know what we know. The goal was for students not only to learn the language of biology and understand fundamental concepts but also to begin to apply those concepts in new situations, analyze experimental design, synthesize results, and evaluate hypotheses and data—to learn how to think like biologists. Each edition since has proudly expanded on this vision. The Fifth Edition is no exception.

A team of six dedicated teacher-scholars has joined Scott to build on and refine the original vision, and by so doing, make the book an even better teaching and learning tool. The pace of biological discovery is rapid, and with each novel breakthrough it becomes even more challenging to decide what is essential to include in an introductory biology text. Pulling together an author team with firsthand expertise from molecules to ecosystems has ensured that the content of the Fifth Edition reflects cutting-edge biology that is pitched at the right level for introductory students and is as accurate and as exciting as ever for instructors and students alike.

New findings from education research continue to inform and inspire the team's thinking about *Biological Science*—we know more today than ever before about how students learn. These findings demand that we constantly look for new ways to increase student engagement in the learning process, and to help instructors align course activities and learning goals with testing strategies.

The New Coauthors

The new coauthor team brings a broad set of talents and interests to the project, motivated by a deep commitment to undergraduate teaching, whether at a small liberal arts college or a large university. Kim Quillin has been a partner in this textbook in every edition. For the Fifth Edition, she revised chapters across three units in addition to spearheading the continued effort to enhance the visual-teaching program. Michael Black, Greg Podgorski, Jon Monroe, and Emily Taylor, who served as unit advisors on the Fourth Edition, were already familiar with the book. And most of the authorial team have been avid users of previous editions for many years.

Core Values

Together, the coauthor team has worked to extend the vision and maintain the core values of *Biological Science*—to provide a book for instructors who embrace the challenge of boosting students to higher levels of learning, and to provide a book for

students that helps them each step of the way in learning to think like scientists. Dedicated instructors have high expectations of their students—the Fifth Edition provides scaffolding to help students learn at the level called for by the National Academy of Sciences, the Howard Hughes Medical Institute, the American Association of Medical Academies, and the National Science Foundation.

What's New in This Edition

The Fifth Edition contains many new or expanded features, all of them targeted at ways to help students learn to construct their own knowledge and think like biologists.

- **Road Maps** The new Road Maps at the beginning of each chapter pair with the Big Picture concept maps introduced in the Fourth Edition. Together they help students navigate chapter content and see the forest for the trees. Each Road Map starts with a purpose statement that tells students what they can expect to learn from each chapter. It then goes on to visually group and organize information to help students anticipate key ideas as well as recognize meaningful relationships and connections between the ideas.

- **The Big Picture** Introduced in the Fourth Edition, Big Picture concept maps integrate words and visuals to help students synthesize information about challenging topics that span multiple chapters and units. In response to requests from instructors and students, three new Big Pictures focused on additional tough topics have been added: Doing Biology, The Chemistry of Life, and Plant and Animal Form and Function. In addition, the Ecology Big Picture is completely revised to reflect changes to that unit.

- **New Chapters** Two new chapters are added to better serve instructors and students. Chapter 11, Energy and Enzymes: An Introduction to Metabolic Pathways. This chapter consolidates these critical topics in a place where students and instructors need it most—right before the chapters on cellular respiration and photosynthesis.

- **New BioSkills** Instructors recognize that biology students need to develop foundational science skills in addition to content knowledge. While these skills are emphasized throughout the book, *Biological Science*, beginning with the Third Edition, has provided a robust set of materials and activities to guide students who need extra help. To promote even fuller use of this resource, the BioSkills are now updated, expanded, and reorganized. New in this edition are a discussion of significant figures within the BioSkills on the Metric

System, and two new BioSkills on Primary Literature and Peer Review and Using Bloom's Taxonomy. BioSkills are located in Appendix B, and practice activities can be assigned online in MasteringBiology®.

- **Promotion of Quantitative Skills** Reports like *Biology 2010, Scientific Foundations for Future Physicians*, and *Vision and Change* all place a premium on quantitative skills. To infuse a quantitative component throughout the text, new and existing quantitative questions are flagged in each chapter to encourage students to work on developing their ability to read or create a graph, perform or interpret a calculation, or use other forms of quantitative reasoning.

- **Bloom's Taxonomy** In the Fifth Edition, all questions in the text are assigned a Bloom's Taxonomy level to help both students and instructors understand whether a question requires higher-order or lower-order cognitive skills. Questions span all six Bloom's levels. (Bloom's levels are identified in Appendix A: Answers.) The coauthors were trained by experts Mary Pat Wenderoth and Clarissa Dirks[1] to ensure we followed a process that would result in high inter-rater reliability—or agreement among raters—in assigning Bloom's levels to questions. The new BioSkill, Using Bloom's Taxonomy, explains the six Bloom's levels to students and offers a practical guide to the kinds of study activities best suited for answering questions at each level.

- **Expanded Emphasis on "Doing Biology"** A constant hallmark of this text is its emphasis on experimental evidence—on teaching how we know what we know. To reflect the progress of science, in the Fifth Edition, the coauthor team replaced many experiments with fresh examples and added new Research Boxes. And as noted earlier, they added a new Big Picture on Doing Biology, focusing on the process of science and the organizational levels of biology. Data sources are now cited for all graphs and data tables to model the importance of citing data sources to students. Updated Research Box questions continue to encourage students to analyze some aspect of experimental design. Also new to this edition is a BioSkill on Primary Literature and Peer Review.

- **Art Program** The art program is further enhanced in this edition by the addition of more illustrated summary tables. These tables make subject areas more accessible to visual learners and reinforce key concepts of the chapter.

Updated Blue Thread Scaffolding

In the Third and Fourth editions of *Biological Science*, a metacognitive tool was formulated as the now popular feature known as "Blue Thread"—sets of questions designed to help students identify what they do and don't understand. The fundamental idea is that if students really understand a piece of information or a concept, they should be able to do something with it.

In the Fifth Edition, the Blue Thread is revised to reflect changes in chapter content, and to incorporate user feedback. Blue-Thread questions appear in the following locations:

- **In-text "You should be able to's"** offer exercises on topics that professors and students have identified as the most difficult concepts in each chapter.

- **Caption questions and exercises** challenge students to examine the information in a figure or table critically—not just absorb it.

- **Check Your Understanding boxes** present two to three tasks that students should be able to complete in order to demonstrate a mastery of summarized key ideas.

- **Chapter summaries** include "You should be able to" problems or exercises related to each key concept.

- **End-of-chapter** questions are organized in three levels of increasing difficulty so students can build from lower to higher-order cognitive questions.

Integration of Media

The textbook continues to be supported by MasteringBiology®, the most powerful online homework, tutorial, and assessment system available. Tutorials follow the Socratic method, coaching students to the correct answer by offering feedback specific to a student's misconceptions as well as providing hints students can access if they get stuck. Instructors can associate content with publisher-provided learning outcomes or create their own. Content highlights include the following:

- **NEW! Solve It Tutorials** These activities allow students to act like scientists in simulated investigations. Each tutorial presents an interesting, real-world question that students will answer by analyzing and interpreting data.

- **Experimental Inquiry Tutorials** The call to teach students about the process of science has never been louder. To support such teaching, there are 10 interactive tutorials on classic scientific experiments—ranging from Meselson–Stahl on DNA replication to the Grants' work on Galápagos finches and Connell's work on competition. Students who use these tutorials should be better prepared to think critically about experimental design and evaluate the wider implications of the data—preparing them to do the work of real scientists in the future.

- **BioFlix® Animations and Tutorials** BioFlix are movie-quality, 3-D animations that focus on the most difficult core topics and are accompanied by in-depth, online tutorials that provide hints and feedback to guide student learning. Eighteen BioFlix animations and tutorials tackle topics such as meiosis, mitosis, DNA replication, photosynthesis, homeostasis, and the carbon cycle.

[1] Crowe, A., C. Dirks, and M. P. Wenderoth. 2008. Biology in Bloom: Implementing Bloom's Taxonomy to enhance student learning in biology. *CBE–Life Sciences Education* 7: 368–381.

- **NEW! End-of-Chapter Questions** Multiple choice end-of-chapter questions are now available to assign in MasteringBiology.

- **Blue-Thread Questions** Over 500 questions based on the Blue-Thread Questions in the textbook are assignable in MasteringBiology.

- **Big Picture Tutorials** Interactive concept map activities based on the Big Picture figures in the textbook are assignable in MasteringBiology, including tutorials to support the three new Big Pictures: Doing Biology, The Chemistry of Life, and Plant and Animal Form and Function.

- **BioSkills Activities** Activities based on the BioSkills content in the textbook are assignable in MasteringBiology, including activities to support the new BioSkills on Primary Literature and Peer Review and Using Bloom's Taxonomy.

- **Reading Quiz Questions** Every chapter includes reading quiz questions you can assign to ensure students read the textbook and understand the basics. These quizzes are perfect as a pre-lecture assignment to get students into the content before class, allowing you to use class time more effectively.

Serving a Community of Teachers

All of us on the coauthor team are deeply committed to students and to supporting the efforts of dedicated teachers. Doing biology is what we love. At various points along our diverse paths, we have been inspired by our own teachers when we were students, and now are inspired by our colleagues as we strive to become even better teacher-scholars. In the tradition of all previous editions of *Biological Science*, we have tried to infuse this textbook with the spirit and practice of evidence-based teaching. We welcome your comments, suggestions, and questions.

Thank you for your work on behalf of your students.

Content Highlights of the Fifth Edition

As discussed in the preface, a major focus of this revision is to enhance the pedagogical utility of *Biological Science*. Another major goal is to ensure that the content reflects the current state of science and is accurate. The expanded author team has scrutinized every chapter to add new, relevant content, update descriptions when appropriate, and adjust the approach to certain topics to enhance student comprehension. In this section, some of the key content improvements to the textbook are highlighted.

Chapter 1 Biology and the Tree of Life A concept map summarizing the defining characteristics of life is added. The process of doing biology coverage is expanded to include discussion of both experimental and descriptive studies, and more rigorous definitions of the terms hypothesis and theory.

Chapter 2 Inside the Cell Several new electron micrographs were selected to more clearly illustrate cell component structure and function. A new figure is added to better depict the pulse–chase assay used to identify the secretory pathway. Coverage of nuclear transport is expanded to differentiate between passive diffusion and active nuclear import. Updated content emphasizes the role of the cytoskeleton in localizing organelles, and how polarity of microtubules and microfilaments influences their growth rate.

Chapter 3 Lipids, Membranes, and the First Cells New content on lipid and membrane evolution and the proposed characteristics of the first protocell is introduced. The aquaporin and potassium channel figures are updated; how key amino acids serve as selectivity filters is now highlighted.

Chapter 4 The Cell Cycle A new figure helps explain the pulse–chase assay for identifying phases of the cell cycle. Content is added to the text and to a figure that illustrates the similarities between chromosome segregation in eukaryotes and prokaryotes. A revised description of anaphase emphasizes how microtubule fraying at the kinetochore can drive chromosome movement. The explanation of how phosphorylation and dephosphorylation turns on MPF activity is updated to reflect current research.

Chapter 5 Nucleic Acids and the RNA World New experimental results concerning the synthesis of nucleotides and nucleic acids in a prebiotic environment are discussed. The section on the RNA world is expanded to include the artificial evolution of a novel ribozyme involved in nucleotide synthesis.

Chapter 6 DNA and the Gene: Synthesis and Repair A new research figure is added that focuses on the relationship between telomere length and senescence in cultured somatic cells.

Chapter 7 How Genes Work Coverage of the evolving concept of the gene and of different types of RNA is expanded. A figure showing the karyotype of a cancer cell is revised to improve clarity.

Chapter 8 Transcription, RNA Processing, and Translation The sections on transcription in bacteria and eukaryotes are now separated, and content on charging tRNAs was moved to a new section. The discussion of translation is reorganized, first to emphasize the process in bacteria and then to highlight differences in eukaryotes.

Chapter 9 Protein Structure and Function The chapter is reorganized to emphasize the link between structure and function, from amino acids to folded proteins. Updated content illustrates that protein shapes are flexible and dynamic, and may remain incompletely folded until the protein interacts with other molecules or ions. Details of how enzymes work were moved to Chapter 10.

Chapter 10 Energy and Enzymes: An Introduction to Pathways This new chapter pulls together concepts in energy, chemical reactions, and enzymes that previously were covered in three different chapters. Oxidation and reduction reactions are emphasized to prepare students for Chapters 13 and 14. The energetics behind ATP hydrolysis and its role in driving endergonic reactions is discussed, and figures are revised to better illustrate the process. Updated content on enzyme regulation and a new process figure show a model for how metabolic pathways may have evolved.

Chapter 11 Meiosis To improve the flow of the chapter, the section on advantages of sexual reproduction was moved to before mistakes in meiosis. The discussion of the role and timing of crossing over during meiosis I is updated. A new study that supports the hypothesis that sex evolved in response to the selective pressure of pathogens is introduced.

Chapter 12 Mendel and the Gene Material on gene linkage is revised to emphasize the importance of genetic mapping. A new matched set of figures on pedigree analysis brings together the various modes of transmission that were previously shown in four individual figures. A new summary table on characteristics of different patterns of inheritance is added.

Chapter 13 Cellular Respiration and Fermentation Two new summary tables for glycolysis and the citric acid cycle are added that provide the names of the enzymes and the reaction each catalyzes. New content is introduced to propose a connection between the universal nature of the proton motive force and the story of the chemical evolution of life.

Chapter 14 Photosynthesis More extensive comparison between the chemical reactions in mitochondria and chloroplasts is added. A new figure is introduced to illustrate noncyclic electron flow in the context of the thylakoid membrane. Greater emphasis is placed on the number of ATPs and NADPHs required for each cycle of carbon fixation and reduction.

Appendix D Water and Carbon: The Chemical Basis of Life A stronger emphasis on chemical evolution is threaded throughout the chapter to bring chemistry to life for the student reader. Two prominent models for chemical evolution are introduced; the historic Miller prebiotic soup experiment was moved here. Advanced discussion of energy and chemical reactions was moved to a new chapter (see Chapter 10).

Appendix E An Introduction to Carbohydrates The molecular basis for resistance of structural polymers, such as cellulose, to degradation is clarified. A new research box illustrates the role of carbohydrates in cellular recognition and attachment using the egg and sperm of mice as a model system.

Acknowledgments

Reviewers

The peer review system is the key to quality and clarity in science publishing. In addition to providing a filter, the investment that respected individuals make in vetting the material—catching errors or inconsistencies and making suggestions to improve the presentation—gives authors, editors, and readers confidence that the text meets rigorous professional standards.

Peer review plays the same role in textbook publishing. The time and care that this book's reviewers have invested is a tribute to their professional integrity, their scholarship, and their concern for the quality of teaching. Virtually every paragraph in this edition has been revised and improved based on insights from the following individuals.

Tamarah Adair, *Baylor University*
Sandra D. Adams, *Montclair State University*
Marc Albrecht, *University of Nebraska at Kearney*
Larry Alice, *Western Kentucky University*
Leo M. Alves, *Manhattan College*
David R. Angelini, *American University*
Dan Ardia, *Franklin & Marshall College*
Paul Arriola, *Elmhurst College*
Davinderjit K. Bagga, *University of Montevallo*
Susan Barrett, *Wheaton College*
Donald Baud, *University of Memphis*
Vernon W. Bauer, *Francis Marion University*
Robert Bauman, *Amarillo College*
Christopher Beck, *Emory University*
Vagner Benedito, *West Virginia University*
Scott Bingham, *Arizona State University*
Stephanie Bingham, *Barry University*
Wendy Birky, *California State University, Northridge*
Jason Blank, *California Polytechnic State University*
Kristopher A. Blee, *California State University, Chico*
Margaret Bloch-Qazi, *Gustavus Adolphus College*
Lanh Bloodworth, *Florida State College at Jacksonville*
Catherine H. Borer, *Berry College*
James Bottesch, *Brevard Community College*
Jacqueline K. Bowman, *Arkansas Tech University*
John Bowman, *University of California, Davis*
Chris Brochu, *University of Iowa*
Matthew Brown, *Dalhousie University*
Mark Browning, *Purdue University*
Carolyn J. W. Bunde, *Idaho State University*
David Byres, *Florida State College at Jacksonville*
Michael Campbell, *Penn State Erie*
Manel Camps, *University of California, Santa Cruz*
Geralyn M. Caplan, *Owensboro Community and Technical College*
Richard Cardullo, *University of California, Riverside*

David Carlini, *American University*
Dale Casamatta, *University of North Florida*
Deborah Chapman, *University of Pittsburgh*
Joe Coelho, *Quincy University*
Allen Collins, *Smithsonian Museum of Natural History*
Robert A. Colvin, *Ohio University*
Kimberly L. Conner, *Florida State College at Jacksonville*
Karen Curto, *University of Pittsburgh*
Clarissa Dirks, *Evergreen State College*
Peter Ducey, *SUNY Cortland*
Erastus Dudley, *Huntingdon College*
Jeffrey P. Duguay, *Delta State University*
Tod Duncan, *University of Colorado, Denver*
Joseph Esdin, *University of California, Los Angeles*
Brent Ewers, *University of Wyoming*
Amy Farris, *Ivy Tech Community College*
Bruce Fisher, *Roane State Community College*
Ryan Fisher, *Salem State University*
David Fitch, *New York University*
Elizabeth Fitch, *Motlow State Community College*
Michael P. Franklin, *California State University, Northridge*
Susannah French, *Utah State University*
Caitlin Gabor, *Texas State University*
Matthew Gilg, *University of North Florida*
Kendra Greenlee, *North Dakota State University*
Patricia A. Grove, *College of Mount Saint Vincent*
Nancy Guild, *University of Colorado, Boulder*
Cynthia Hemenway, *North Carolina State University*
Christopher R. Herlihy, *Middle Tennessee State University*
Kendra Hill, *South Dakota State University*
Sara Hoot, *University of Wisconsin, Milwaukee*
Kelly Howe, *University of New Mexico*
Robin Hulbert, *California Polytechnic State University*
Rick Jellen, *Brigham Young University*
Russell Johnson, *Colby College*
William Jira Katembe, *Delta State University*
Elena K. Keeling, *California Polytechnic State University*
Jill B. Keeney, *Juniata College*
Greg Kelly, *University of Western Ontario*
Scott L. Kight, *Montclair State University*
Charles Knight, *California Polytechnic State University*
Jenny Knight, *University of Colorado, Boulder*
William Kroll, *Loyola University Chicago*
Dominic Lannutti, *El Paso Community College*
Brenda Leady, *University of Toledo*
David Lindberg, *University of California, Berkeley*
Barbara Lom, *Davidson College*
Robert Maxwell, *Georgia State University*
Marshall D. McCue, *St. Mary's University*
Kurt A. McKean, *SUNY Albany*
Michael Meighan, *University of California, Berkeley*
John Merrill, *Michigan State University*

Richard Merritt, *Houston Community College*
Alan Molumby, *University of Illinois at Chicago*
Jeremy Montague, *Barry University*
Chad E. Montgomery, *Truman State University*
Kimberly D. Moore, *Lone Star College System, North Harris*
Michael Morgan, *Berry College*
James Mulrooney, *Central Connecticut State University*
John D. Nagy, *Scottsdale Community College*
Margaret Olney, *St. Martin's University*
Nathan Okia, *Auburn University at Montgomery*
Robert Osuna, *SUNY Albany*
Daniel Panaccione, *West Virginia University*
Stephanie Pandolfi, *Michigan State University*
Michael Rockwell Parker, *Monell Chemical Senses Center*
Lisa Parks, *North Carolina State University*
Nancy Pelaez, *Purdue University*
Shelley W. Penrod, *Lone Star College System, North Harris*
Andrea Pesce, *James Madison University*
Raymond Pierotti, *University of Kansas*
Melissa Ann Pilgrim, *University of South Carolina Upstate*
Paul Pillitteri, *Southern Utah University*
Debra Pires, *University of California, Los Angeles*
P. David Polly, *Indiana University, Bloomington*
Vanessa Quinn, *Purdue University North Central*
Stacey L. Raimondi, *Elmhurst College*
Stephanie Randell, *McLennan Community College*
Marceau Ratard, *Delgado Community College*
Flona Redway, *Barry University*
Srebrenka Robic, *Agnes Scott College*
Dave Robinson, *Bellarmine University*
George Robinson, *SUNY Albany*
Adam W. Rollins, *Lincoln Memorial University*
Amanda Rosenzweig, *Delgado Community College*
Leonard C. Salvatori, *Indian River State College*
Dee Ann Sato, *Cypress College*
Leena Sawant, *Houston Community College*
Jon Scales, *Midwestern State University*
Oswald Schmitz, *Yale University*
Joan Sharp, *Simon Fraser University*
Julie Schroer, *North Dakota State University*
Timothy E. Shannon, *Francis Marion University*
Lynnette Sievert, *Emporia State University*
Susan Skambis, *Valencia College*
Ann E. Stapleton, *University of North Carolina, Wilmington*
Mary-Pat Stein, *California State University, Northridge*
Christine Strand, *California Polytechnic State University*
Denise Strickland, *Midlands Technical College*
Jackie Swanik, *Wake Technical Community College*
Billie J. Swalla, *University of Washington*
Zuzana Swigonova, *University of Pittsburgh*
Briana Timmerman, *University of South Carolina*
Catherine Ueckert, *Northern Arizona University*
Sara Via, *University of Maryland, College Park*
Thomas J. Volk, *University of Wisconsin–La Crosse*
Jeffrey Walck, *Middle Tennessee State University*
Andrea Weeks, *George Mason University*
Margaret S. White, *Scottsdale Community College*
Steven D. Wilt, *Bellarmine University*
Candace Winstead, *California Polytechnic State University*
James A. Wise, *Hampton University*

Correspondents

One of the most enjoyable interactions we have as textbook authors is correspondence or conversations with researchers and teachers who take the time and trouble to contact us to discuss an issue with the book, or who respond to our queries about a particular data set or study. We are always amazed and heartened by the generosity of these individuals. They care, deeply.

Lawrence Alice, *Western Kentucky University*
David Baum, *University of Wisconsin–Madison*
Meredith Blackwell, *Louisiana State University*
Nancy Burley, *University of California, Irvine*
Thomas Breithaupt, *University of Hull*
Philip Cantino, *Ohio University*
Allen Collins, *Smithsonian Museum of Natural History*
Robert Full, *University of California, Berkeley*
Arundhati Ghosh, *University of Pittsburgh*
Jennifer Gottwald, *University of Wisconsin–Madison*
Jon Harrison, *Arizona State University*
David Hawksworth, *Natural History Museum, London*
Jim Herrick, *James Madison University*
John Hunt, *University of Exeter*
Doug Jensen, *Converse College*
Scott Kight, *Montclair State University*
Scott Kirkton, *Union College*
Mimi Koehl, *University of California, Berkeley*
Rodger Kram, *University of Colorado*
Matthew McHenry, *University of California, Irvine*
Alison Miyamoto, *California State University, Fullerton*
Sean Menke, *Lake Forest College*
Rich Mooi, *California Academy of Sciences*
Michael Oliver, *MalawiCichlids.com*
M. Rockwell Parker, *Monell Chemical Senses Center*
Andrea Pesce, *James Madison University*
Chris Preston, *Monterey Bay Aquarium Research Institute*
Scott Sakaluk, *Illinois State University*
Kyle Seifert, *James Madison University*
Jos Snoeks, *Royal Museum for Central Africa*
Jeffrey Spring, *University of Louisiana*
Christy Strand, *California Polytechnic State University, San Luis Obispo*
Torsten Struck, *University of Osnabrueck, Germany*
Oswald Schmitz, *Yale University*
Ian Tattersal, *American Museum of Natural History*
Robert Turgeon, *Cornell University*
Tom Volk, *University of Wisconsin–La Crosse*
Naomi Wernick, *University of Massachusetts, Lowell*

Supplements Contributors

Instructors depend on an impressive array of support materials—in print and online—to design and deliver their courses. The student experience would be much weaker without the study guide, test bank, activities, animations, quizzes, and tutorials written by the following individuals.

Brian Bagatto, *University of Akron*
Scott Bingham, *Arizona State University*
Jay L. Brewster, *Pepperdine University*

Mirjana Brockett, *Georgia Institute of Technology*
Warren Burggren, *University of North Texas*
Jeff Carmichael, *University of North Dakota*
Tim Christensen, *East Carolina University*
Erica Cline, *University of Washington—Tacoma*
Patricia Colberg, *University of Wyoming*
Elia Crisucci, *University of Pittsburgh*
Elizabeth Cowles, *Eastern Connecticut State University*
Clarissa Dirks, *Evergreen State College*
Lisa Elfring, *University of Arizona, Tucson*
Brent Ewers, *University of Wyoming*
Rebecca Ferrell, *Metropolitan State University of Denver*
Miriam Ferzli, *North Carolina State University*
Cheryl Frederick, *University of Washington*
Cindee Giffen, *University of Wisconsin–Madison*
Kathy M. Gillen, *Kenyon College*
Linda Green, *Georgia Institute of Technology*
Christopher Harendza, *Montgomery County Community College*
Cynthia Hemenway, *North Carolina State University*
Laurel Hester, *University of South Carolina*
Jean Heitz, *University of Wisconsin–Madison*
Tracey Hickox, *University of Illinois, Urbana–Champaign*
Jacob Kerby, *University of South Dakota*
David Kooyman, *Brigham Young University*
Barbara Lom, *Davidson College*
Cindy Malone, *California State University, Northridge*
Jim Manser, retired, *Harvey Mudd College*
Jeanette McGuire, *Michigan State University*
Mark Music, *Indian River State College*
Jennifer Nauen, *University of Delaware*
Chris Pagliarulo, *University of California, Davis*
Stephanie Scher Pandolfi, *Michigan State University*
Lisa Parks, *North Carolina State University*
Debra Pires, *University of California, Los Angeles*
Carol Pollock, *University of British Columbia*
Jessica Poulin, *University at Buffalo, the State University of New York*
Vanessa Quinn, *Purdue University North Central*
Eric Ribbens, *Western Illinois University*
Christina T. Russin, *Northwestern University*
Leonard Salvatori, *Indian River State College*
Joan Sharp, *Simon Fraser University*
Chrissy Spencer, *Georgia Institute of Technology*
Mary-Pat Stein, *California State University, Northridge*
Suzanne Simon-Westendorf, *Ohio University*
Fred Wasserman, *Boston University*
Cindy White, *University of Northern Colorado*
Edward Zalisko, *Blackburn College*

Book Team

Anyone who has been involved in producing a textbook knows that many people work behind the scenes to make it all happen. The coauthor team is indebted to the many talented individuals who have made this book possible.

Development editors Mary Catherine Hager, Moira Lerner-Nelson, and Bill O'Neal provided incisive comments on the revised manuscript. Fernanda Oyarzun and Adam Steinberg used their artistic sense, science skills, and love of teaching to hone the figures for many chapters.

The final version of the text was copyedited by Chris Thillen and expertly proofread by Pete Shanks. The final figure designs were rendered by Imagineering Media Services and carefully proofread by Frank Purcell. Maureen Spuhler, Eric Schrader, and Kristen Piljay researched images for the Fifth Edition.

The book's clean, innovative design was developed by Mark Ong and Emily Friel. Text and art were skillfully set in the design by S4Carlisle Publishing Services. The book's production was supervised by Lori Newman and Mike Early.

The extensive supplements program was managed by Brady Golden and Katie Cook. All of the individuals mentioned—and more—were supported with cheerful, dedicated efficiency by Editorial Assistant Leslie Allen for the first half of the project; Eddie Lee has since stepped in to skillfully fill this role.

Creating MasteringBiology® tutorials and activities also requires a team. Media content development was overseen by Tania Mlawer and Sarah Jensen, who benefited from the program expertise of Caroline Power and Caroline Ross. Joseph Mochnick and Daniel Ross worked together as media producers. Lauren Fogel (VP, Director, Media Development), Stacy Treco (VP, Director, Media Product Strategy), and Laura ensured that the complete media program that accompanies the Fifth Edition, including MasteringBiology, will meet the needs of the students and professors who use our offerings.

Pearson's talented sales reps, who listen to professors, advise the editorial staff, and get the book in students' hands, are supported by tireless Executive Marketing Manager Lauren Harp and Director of Marketing Christy Lesko. The marketing materials that support the outreach effort were produced by Lillian Carr and her colleagues in Pearson's Marketing Comunications group. David Theisen, national director for Key Markets, tirelessly visits countless professors each year, enthusiastically discussing their courses and providing us with meaningful editorial guidance.

The vision and resources required to run this entire enterprise are the responsibility of Vice President and Editor-in-Chief Beth Wilbur, who provided inspirational and focused leadership, and President of Pearson Science Paul Corey, who displays unwavering commitment to high-quality science publishing.

Becky Ruden recruited the coauthor team, drawing us to the project with her energy and belief in this book. The editorial team was skillfully directed by Executive Director of Development Deborah Gale. Finally, we are deeply grateful for three key drivers of the Fifth Edition. Project Editor Anna Amato's superb organizational skills and calm demeanor assured that all the wheels and cogs of the process ran smoothly to keep the mammoth project steadily rolling forward. Supervising Development Editor Sonia DiVittorio's deep expertise, creative vision, keen attention to detail, level, and clarity, and inspiring insistence on excellence kept the bar high for everyone on every aspect of the project. Lastly, Senior Acquisitions Editor Michael Gillespie's boundless energy and enthusiasm, positive attitude, and sharp intellect have fueled and united the team and also guided the book through the hurdles to existence. The coauthor team thanks these exceptional people for making the art and science of book writing a productive and exhilarating process.

1 Biology and the Tree of Life

In this chapter you will learn about

Key themes to structure your thinking about Biology

starting with

What does it mean to say that something is alive? 1.1

including

Two of the greatest unifying ideas in Biology

first

The cell theory 1.2

then

The theory of evolution by natural selection 1.3

predicts

The tree of life 1.4

including

The process of doing Biology 1.5

These Chinese water dragon hatchlings are exploring their new world and learning how to find food and stay alive. They represent one of the key characteristics of life introduced in this chapter—replication.

In essence, biological science is a search for ideas and observations that unify our understanding of the diversity of life, from bacteria living in rocks a mile underground to humans and majestic sequoia trees. This chapter is an introduction to this search.

The goals of this chapter are to introduce the nature of life and explore how biologists go about studying it. The chapter also introduces themes that will resonate throughout this book:

This chapter is part of the Big Picture. See how on pages 16–17.

- Analyzing how organisms work at the molecular level.

- Understanding organisms in terms of their evolutionary history.

- Helping you learn to think like a biologist.

Let's begin with what may be the most fundamental question of all: What is life?

✔ When you see this checkmark, stop and test yourself. Answers are available in Appendix A.

1.1 What Does It Mean to Say That Something Is Alive?

An **organism** is a life-form—a living entity made up of one or more cells. Although there is no simple definition of life that is endorsed by all biologists, most agree that organisms share a suite of five fundamental characteristics.

- *Energy* To stay alive and reproduce, organisms have to acquire and use energy. To give just two examples: plants absorb sunlight; animals ingest food.

- *Cells* Organisms are made up of membrane-bound units called cells. A cell's membrane regulates the passage of materials between exterior and interior spaces.

- *Information* Organisms process hereditary, or genetic, information encoded in units called genes. Organisms also respond to information from the environment and adjust to maintain stable internal conditions. Right now, cells throughout your body are using information to make the molecules that keep you alive; your eyes and brain are decoding information on this page that will help you learn some biology, and if your room is too hot you might be sweating to cool off.

- *Replication* One of the great biologists of the twentieth century, François Jacob, said that the "dream of a bacterium is to become two bacteria." Almost everything an organism does contributes to one goal: replicating itself.

- *Evolution* Organisms are the product of evolution, and their populations continue to evolve.

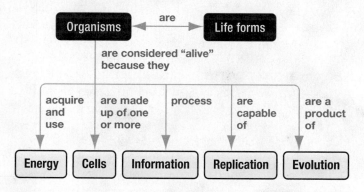

You can think of this text as one long exploration of these five traits. Here's to life!

1.2 The Cell Theory

Two of the greatest unifying ideas in all of science laid the groundwork for modern biology: the cell theory and the theory of evolution by natural selection. Formally, scientists define a **theory** as an explanation for a very general class of phenomena or observations that are supported by a wide body of evidence. The cell theory and theory of evolution address fundamental questions: What are organisms made of? Where do they come from?

When these concepts emerged in the mid-1800s, they revolutionized the way biologists think about the world. They established two of the five attributes of life: Organisms are cellular, and their populations change over time.

Neither insight came easily, however. The cell theory, for example, emerged after some 200 years of work. In 1665 the Englishman Robert Hooke devised a crude microscope to examine the structure of cork (a bark tissue) from an oak tree. The instrument magnified objects to just 30× (30 times) their normal size, but it allowed Hooke to see something extraordinary. In the cork he observed small, pore-like compartments that were invisible to the naked eye. Hooke coined the term "cells" for these structures because of their resemblance to the cells inhabited by monks in a monastery.

Soon after Hooke published his results, a Dutch scientist named Anton van Leeuwenhoek succeeded in developing much more powerful microscopes, some capable of magnifications up to 300×. With these instruments, van Leeuwenhoek inspected samples of pond water and made the first observations of a dazzling collection of single-celled organisms that he called "animalcules." He also observed and described human blood cells and sperm cells, shown in **FIGURE 1.1**.

In the 1670s an Italian researcher who was studying the leaves and stems of plants with a microscope concluded that plant tissues were composed of many individual cells. By the early 1800s, enough data had accumulated for a German biologist to claim that *all* organisms consist of cells. Did this claim hold up?

All Organisms Are Made of Cells

Advances in microscopy have made it possible to examine the amazing diversity and complexity of cells at higher and higher magnifications. Biologists have developed microscopes that are tens of thousands of times more powerful than van Leeuwenhoek's and have described over a million new species. The basic conclusion made in the 1800s remains intact, however: All organisms are made of cells.

The smallest organisms known today are bacteria that are barely 200 nanometers wide, or 200 *billionths* of a meter. (See **BioSkills 1** in Appendix B to review the metric system and its prefixes.[1]) It would take 5000 of these organisms lined up side by side to span a millimeter. This is the distance between the smallest hash marks on a metric ruler. In contrast, sequoia trees can be over 100 meters tall. This is the equivalent of a 20-story building. Bacteria and sequoias are composed of the same fundamental building block, however—the cell. Bacteria consist of a single cell; sequoias are made up of many cells.

Today a **cell** is defined as a highly organized compartment that is bounded by a thin, flexible structure called a plasma membrane and that contains concentrated chemicals in an aqueous (watery) solution. The chemical reactions that sustain life take place inside cells. Most cells are also capable of reproducing by dividing—in effect, by making a copy of themselves.

The realization that all organisms are made of cells was fundamentally important, but it formed only the first part of the cell

---

[1]BioSkills are located in the second appendix at the back of the book. They focus on general skills that you'll use throughout this course. More than a few students have found them to be a life-saver. Please use them!

(a) van Leeuwenhoek built his own microscopes—which, while small, were powerful. They allowed him to see, for example . . .

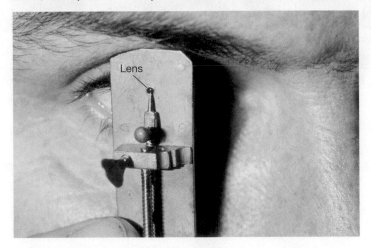

(b) . . . human blood cells (this modern photo was shot through one of van Leeuwenhoek's original microscopes) . . .

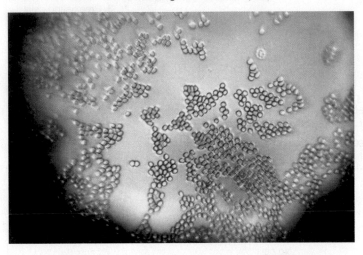

(c) . . . and animal sperm (drawing by van Leeuwenhoek of canine sperm cells on left, human on right).

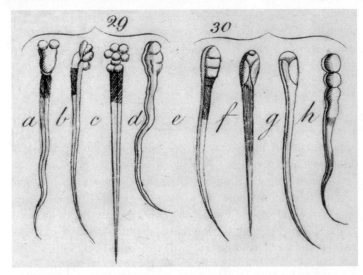

FIGURE 1.1 Van Leeuwenhoek's Microscope Made Cells Visible.

theory. In addition to understanding what organisms are made of, scientists wanted to understand how cells come to be.

Where Do Cells Come From?

Most scientific theories have two components: The first describes a pattern in the natural world; the second identifies a mechanism or process that is responsible for creating that pattern. Hooke and his fellow scientists articulated the pattern component of the cell theory. In 1858, a German scientist named Rudolph Virchow added the process component by stating that all cells arise from preexisting cells.

The complete **cell theory** can be stated as follows: All organisms are made of cells, and all cells come from preexisting cells.

Two Hypotheses The cell theory was a direct challenge to the prevailing explanation of where cells come from, called spontaneous generation. In the mid-1800s, most biologists believed that organisms could arise spontaneously under certain conditions. For example, the bacteria and fungi that spoil foods such as milk and wine were thought to appear in these nutrient-rich media of their own accord—springing to life from nonliving materials. In contrast, the cell theory maintained that cells do not spring to life spontaneously but are produced only when preexisting cells grow and divide. The all-cells-from-cells explanation was a **hypothesis:** a testable statement to explain a phenomenon or a set of observations.

Biologists usually use the word theory to refer to proposed explanations for broad patterns in nature and prefer hypothesis to refer to explanations for more tightly focused questions. A theory serves as a framework for the development of new hypotheses.

An Experiment to Settle the Question Soon after Virchow's all-cells-from-cells hypothesis appeared in print, a French scientist named Louis Pasteur set out to test its predictions experimentally. An experimental **prediction** describes a measurable or observable result that must be correct if a hypothesis is valid.

Pasteur wanted to determine whether microorganisms could arise spontaneously in a nutrient broth or whether they appear only when a broth is exposed to a source of preexisting cells. To address the question, he created two treatment groups: a broth that was not exposed to a source of preexisting cells and a broth that was.

The spontaneous generation hypothesis predicted that cells would appear in both treatment groups. The all-cells-from-cells hypothesis predicted that cells would appear only in the treatment exposed to a source of preexisting cells.

FIGURE 1.2 (on page 4) shows Pasteur's experimental setup. Note that the two treatments are identical in every respect but one. Both used glass flasks filled with the same amount of the same nutrient broth. Both were boiled for the same amount of time to kill any existing organisms such as bacteria or fungi. But because the flask pictured in Figure 1.2a had a straight neck, it was exposed to preexisting cells after sterilization by the heat treatment. These preexisting cells are the bacteria and fungi that cling to dust particles in the air. They could drop into the nutrient broth because the neck of the flask was straight.

In contrast, the flask drawn in Figure 1.2b had a long swan neck. Pasteur knew that water would condense in the crook of the swan neck after the boiling treatment and that this pool of water

QUESTION: Do cells arise spontaneously or from other cells?

SPONTANEOUS GENERATION HYPOTHESIS: Cells arise spontaneously from nonliving materials.

ALL-CELLS-FROM-CELLS HYPOTHESIS: Cells are produced only when preexisting cells grow and divide.

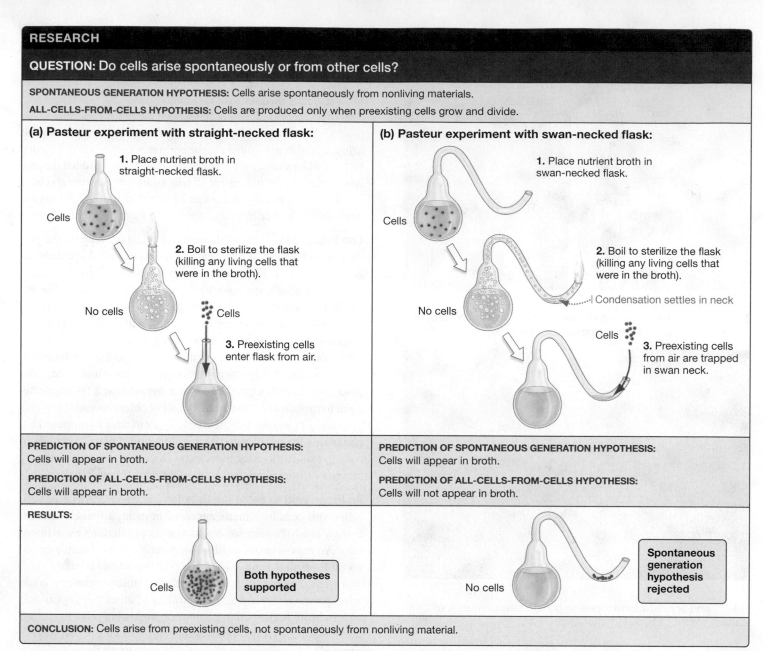

(a) Pasteur experiment with straight-necked flask:

1. Place nutrient broth in straight-necked flask.

Cells

2. Boil to sterilize the flask (killing any living cells that were in the broth).

No cells   Cells

3. Preexisting cells enter flask from air.

(b) Pasteur experiment with swan-necked flask:

1. Place nutrient broth in swan-necked flask.

Cells

2. Boil to sterilize the flask (killing any living cells that were in the broth).

No cells   Condensation settles in neck

Cells

3. Preexisting cells from air are trapped in swan neck.

PREDICTION OF SPONTANEOUS GENERATION HYPOTHESIS: Cells will appear in broth.

PREDICTION OF ALL-CELLS-FROM-CELLS HYPOTHESIS: Cells will appear in broth.

RESULTS:

Cells   Both hypotheses supported

PREDICTION OF SPONTANEOUS GENERATION HYPOTHESIS: Cells will appear in broth.

PREDICTION OF ALL-CELLS-FROM-CELLS HYPOTHESIS: Cells will not appear in broth.

No cells   Spontaneous generation hypothesis rejected

CONCLUSION: Cells arise from preexisting cells, not spontaneously from nonliving material.

FIGURE 1.2 The Spontaneous Generation and All-Cells-from-Cells Hypotheses Were Tested Experimentally.

✔ **QUESTION** What problem would arise in interpreting the results of this experiment if Pasteur had (1) put different types of broth in the two treatments, (2) heated them for different lengths of time, or (3) used a ceramic flask for one treatment and a glass flask for the other?

would trap any bacteria or fungi that entered on dust particles. Thus, the contents of the swan-necked flask were isolated from any source of preexisting cells even though still open to the air.

Pasteur's experimental setup was effective because there was only one difference between the two treatments and because that difference was the factor being tested—in this case, a broth's exposure to preexisting cells.

One Hypothesis Supported And Pasteur's results? As Figure 1.2 shows, the treatment exposed to preexisting cells quickly filled with bacteria and fungi. This observation was important because it showed that the heat sterilization step had not altered the nutrient broth's capacity to support growth.

The broth in the swan-necked flask remained sterile, however. Even when the flask was left standing for months, no organisms appeared in it. This result was inconsistent with the hypothesis of spontaneous generation.

Because Pasteur's data were so conclusive—meaning that there was no other reasonable explanation for them—the results persuaded most biologists that the all-cells-from-cells hypothesis was correct. However, you will see that biologists now have evidence that life did arise from nonlife early in Earth's history, through a process called chemical evolution (Chapters 3, 5, 9, App. D, E).

The success of the cell theory's process component had an important implication: If all cells come from preexisting cells, it follows that all individuals in an isolated population of single-celled organisms are related by common ancestry. Similarly, in you and most other multicellular individuals, all the cells present are descended from preexisting cells, tracing back to a fertilized egg. A fertilized egg is a cell created by the fusion of sperm and egg—cells that formed in individuals of the previous generation. In this way, all the cells in a multicellular organism are connected by common ancestry.

The second great founding idea in biology is similar, in spirit, to the cell theory. It also happened to be published the same year as the all-cells-from-cells hypothesis. This was the realization, made independently by the English scientists Charles Darwin and Alfred Russel Wallace, that all species—all distinct, identifiable types of organisms—are connected by common ancestry.

1.3 The Theory of Evolution by Natural Selection

In 1858 short papers written separately by Darwin and Wallace were read to a small group of scientists attending a meeting of the Linnean Society of London. A year later, Darwin published a book that expanded on the idea summarized in those brief papers. The book was called *The Origin of Species*. The first edition sold out in a day.

What Is Evolution?

Like the cell theory, the theory of evolution by natural selection has a pattern and a process component. Darwin and Wallace's theory made two important claims concerning patterns that exist in the natural world.

1. Species are related by common ancestry. This contrasted with the prevailing view in science at the time, which was that species represent independent entities created separately by a divine being.

2. In contrast to the accepted view that species remain unchanged through time, Darwin and Wallace proposed that the characteristics of species can be modified from generation to generation. Darwin called this process descent with modification.

Evolution is a change in the characteristics of a population over time. It means that species are not independent and unchanging entities, but are related to one another and can change through time.

What Is Natural Selection?

This pattern component of the theory of evolution was actually not original to Darwin and Wallace. Several scientists had already come to the same conclusions about the relationships between species. The great insight by Darwin and Wallace was in proposing a process, called **natural selection,** that explains *how* evolution occurs.

Two Conditions of Natural Selection Natural selection occurs whenever two conditions are met.

1. Individuals within a population vary in characteristics that are **heritable**—meaning, traits that can be passed on to offspring.

A **population** is defined as a group of individuals of the same species living in the same area at the same time.

2. In a particular environment, certain versions of these heritable traits help individuals survive better or reproduce more than do other versions.

If certain heritable traits lead to increased success in producing offspring, then those traits become more common in the population over time. In this way, the population's characteristics change as a result of natural selection acting on individuals. This is a key insight: Natural selection acts on individuals, but evolutionary change occurs in populations.

Selection on Maize as an Example To clarify how selection works, consider an example of **artificial selection**—changes in populations that occur when *humans* select certain individuals to produce the most offspring. Beginning in 1896, researchers began a long-term selection experiment on maize (corn).

1. In the original population, the percentage of protein in maize kernels was variable among individuals. Kernel protein content is a heritable trait—parents tend to pass the trait on to their offspring.

2. Each year for many years, researchers chose individuals with the highest kernel protein content to be the parents of the next generation. In this environment, individuals with high kernel protein content produced more offspring than individuals with low kernel protein content.

FIGURE 1.3 shows the results. Note that this graph plots generation number on the *x*-axis, starting from the first generation (0 on the graph) and continuing for 100 generations. The average percentage of protein in a kernel among individuals in this population is plotted on the *y*-axis.

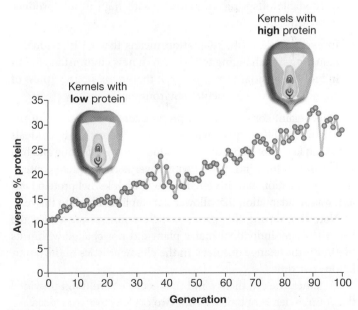

FIGURE 1.3 Response to Selection for High Kernel Protein Content in Maize.

DATA: Moose, S. P., J. W. Dudley, and T. R. Rocheford. 2004. *Trends in Plant Sciences* 9: 358–364; and the Illinois long-term selection experiment for oil and protein in corn (University of Illinois at Urbana–Champaign).

To read this graph, put your finger on the x-axis at generation 0. Then read up the y-axis, and note that kernels averaged about 11 percent protein at the start of the experiment. Now read the graph to the right. Each dot is a data point, representing the average kernel protein concentration in a particular generation. (A generation in maize is one year.) The lines on this graph simply connect the dots, to make the pattern in the data easier to see. During a few years the average protein content goes down, because of poor growing conditions or chance changes in how the many genes responsible for this trait interact. However, at the end of the graph, after 100 generations of selection, average kernel protein content is about 29 percent. (For more help with reading graphs, see **BioSkills 3** in Appendix B.)

This sort of change in the characteristics of a population, over time, is evolution. Humans have been practicing artificial selection for thousands of years, and biologists have now documented evolution by *natural* selection—where humans don't do the selecting—occurring in thousands of different populations, including humans. Evolution occurs when heritable variation leads to differential success in reproduction.

✔ **QUANTITATIVE** If you understand the concepts of selection and evolution, you should be able to describe how protein content in maize kernels changed over time, using the same x-axis and y-axis as in Figure 1.3, when researchers selected individuals with the *lowest* kernel protein content to be the parents of the next generation. (This experiment was actually done, starting with the same population at the same time as selection for high protein content.)

Fitness and Adaptation   Darwin also introduced some new terminology to identify what is happening during natural selection.

- In everyday English, fitness means health and well-being. But in biology, **fitness** means the ability of an individual to produce viable offspring. Individuals with high fitness produce many surviving offspring.

- In everyday English, adaptation means that an individual is adjusting and changing to function in new circumstances. But in biology, an **adaptation** is a trait that increases the fitness of an individual in a particular environment.

Once again, consider kernel protein content in maize: In the environment of the experiment graphed in Figure 1.3, individuals with high kernel protein content produced more offspring and had higher fitness than individuals with lower kernel protein content. In this population and this environment, high kernel protein content was an adaptation that allowed certain individuals to thrive.

Note that during this process, the amount of protein in the kernels of any individual maize plant did not change within its lifetime—the change occurred in the characteristics of the population over time.

Together, the cell theory and the theory of evolution provided the young science of biology with two central, unifying ideas:

1. The cell is the fundamental structural unit in all organisms.

2. All species are related by common ancestry and have changed over time in response to natural selection.

check your understanding

If you understand that . . .

- Natural selection occurs when heritable variation in certain traits leads to improved success in reproduction. Because individuals with these traits produce many offspring with the same traits, the traits increase in frequency and evolution occurs.
- Evolution is a change in the characteristics of a population over time.

✔ **You should be able to . . .**

Using the graph you just analyzed in Figure 1.3, describe the average kernel protein content over time in a maize population where *no* selection occurred.

Answers are available in Appendix A.

1.4 The Tree of Life

Section 1.3 focuses on how individual populations change through time in response to natural selection. But over the past several decades, biologists have also documented dozens of cases in which natural selection has caused populations of one species to diverge and form new species. This divergence process is called **speciation.**

Research on speciation has two important implications: All species come from preexisting species, and all species, past and present, trace their ancestry back to a single common ancestor.

The theory of evolution by natural selection predicts that biologists should be able to construct a **tree of life**—a family tree of organisms. If life on Earth arose just once, then such a diagram would describe the genealogical relationships between species with a single, ancestral species at its base.

Has this task been accomplished? If the tree of life exists, what does it look like?

Using Molecules to Understand the Tree of Life

One of the great breakthroughs in research on the tree of life occurred when American biologist Carl Woese (pronounced *woze*) and colleagues began analyzing the chemical components of organisms as a way to understand their evolutionary relationships. Their goal was to understand the **phylogeny** of all organisms—their actual genealogical relationships. Translated literally, phylogeny means "tribe-source."

To understand which organisms are closely versus distantly related, Woese and co-workers needed to study a molecule that is found in all organisms. The molecule they selected is called small subunit ribosomal RNA (rRNA). It is an essential part of the machinery that all cells use to grow and reproduce.

Although rRNA is a large and complex molecule, its underlying structure is simple. The rRNA molecule is made up of sequences of four smaller chemical components called ribonucleotides. These ribonucleotides are symbolized by the letters A, U, C, and G. In rRNA, ribonucleotides are connected to one another linearly, like the boxcars of a freight train.

Analyzing rRNA Why might rRNA be useful for understanding the relationships between organisms? The answer is that the ribonucleotide sequence in rRNA is a trait that can change during the course of evolution. Although rRNA performs the same function in all organisms, the sequence of ribonucleotide building blocks in this molecule is not identical among species.

In land plants, for example, the molecule might start with the sequence A-U-A-U-**C**-G-A-G (**FIGURE 1.4**). In green algae, which are closely related to land plants, the same section of the molecule might contain A-U-A-U-**G**-G-A-G. But in brown algae, which are not closely related to green algae or to land plants, the same part of the molecule might consist of A-**A**-A-U-**G**-G-A-**C**.

The research that Woese and co-workers pursued was based on a simple premise: If the theory of evolution is correct, then rRNA sequences should be very similar in closely related organisms but less similar in organisms that are less closely related. Species that are part of the same evolutionary lineage, like the plants, should share certain changes in rRNA that no other species have.

To test this premise, the researchers determined the sequence of ribonucleotides in the rRNA of a wide array of species. Then they considered what the similarities and differences in the sequences implied about relationships between the species. The goal was to produce a diagram that described the phylogeny of the organisms in the study.

A diagram that depicts evolutionary history in this way is called a phylogenetic tree. Just as a family tree shows relationships between individuals, a phylogenetic tree shows relationships between species. On a phylogenetic tree, branches that share a recent common ancestor represent species that are closely related; branches that don't share recent common ancestors represent species that are more distantly related.

The Tree of Life Estimated from Genetic Data To construct a phylogenetic tree, researchers use a computer to find the arrangement of branches that is most consistent with the similarities and differences observed in the data.

Although the initial work was based only on the sequences of ribonucleotides observed in rRNA, biologists now use data sets that include sequences from a wide array of genetic material. **FIGURE 1.5** shows a recent tree produced by comparing these sequences. Because this tree includes such a diverse array of

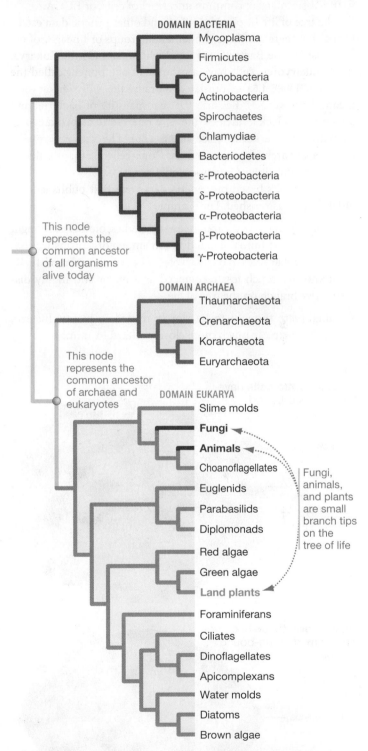

FIGURE 1.5 The Tree of Life. A phylogenetic tree estimated from a large amount of genetic sequence data. The three domains of life revealed by the analysis are labeled. Common names are given for lineages in the domains Bacteria and Eukarya. Phyla names are given for members of the domain Archaea, because most of these organisms have no common names.

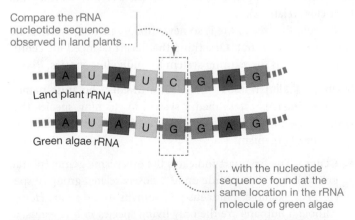

FIGURE 1.4 RNA Molecules Are Made Up of Smaller Molecules. A complete small subunit rRNA molecule contains about 2000 ribonucleotides; just 8 are shown in this comparison.

✔ **QUESTION** Suppose that in the same section of rRNA, molds and other fungi have the sequence A-U-A-U-G-G-A-C. Are fungi more closely related to green algae or to land plants? Explain your logic.

species, it is often called the universal tree, or the tree of life. (For help in learning how to read a phylogenetic tree, see **BioSkills 7** in Appendix B.) Notice that the tree's main node is the common ancestor of all living organisms. Researchers who study the origin of life propose that the tree's root extends even further back to the "*last universal common ancestor*" of cells, or **LUCA.**

The tree of life implied by rRNA and other genetic data established that there are three fundamental groups or lineages of organisms: **(1)** the Bacteria, **(2)** the Archaea, and **(3)** the Eukarya. In all **eukaryotes,** cells have a prominent component called the nucleus (**FIGURE 1.6a**). Translated literally, the word eukaryotes means "true kernel." Because the vast majority of bacterial and archaeal cells lack a nucleus, they are referred to as **prokaryotes** (literally, "before kernel"; see **FIGURE 1.6b**). The vast majority of bacteria and archaea are unicellular ("one-celled"); many eukaryotes are multicellular ("many-celled").

When results based on genetic data were first published, biologists were astonished. For example:

- Prior to Woese's work and follow-up studies, biologists thought that the most fundamental division among organisms was between prokaryotes and eukaryotes. The Archaea were virtually unknown—much less recognized as a major and highly distinctive branch on the tree of life.

- Fungi were thought to be closely related to plants. Instead, they are actually much more closely related to animals.

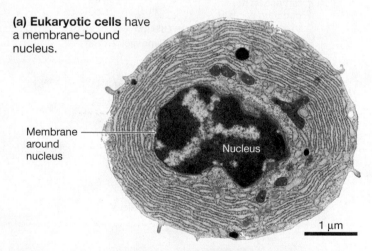

(a) Eukaryotic cells have a membrane-bound nucleus.

Membrane around nucleus

Nucleus

1 μm

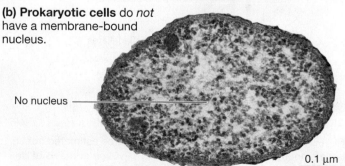

(b) Prokaryotic cells do *not* have a membrane-bound nucleus.

No nucleus

0.1 μm

FIGURE 1.6 Eukaryotes and Prokaryotes.

✔**QUANTITATIVE** How many times larger is the eukaryotic cell in this figure than the prokaryotic cell? (Hint: Study the scale bars.)

- Traditional approaches for classifying organisms—including the system of five kingdoms divided into various classes, orders, and families that you may have learned in high school—are inaccurate in many cases, because they do not reflect the actual evolutionary history of the organisms involved.

The Tree of Life Is a Work in Progress   Just as researching your family tree can help you understand who you are and where you came from, so the tree of life helps biologists understand the relationships between organisms and the history of species. The discovery of the Archaea and the accurate placement of lineages such as the fungi qualify as exciting breakthroughs in our understanding of evolutionary history and life's diversity.

Work on the tree of life continues at a furious pace, however, and the location of certain branches on the tree is hotly debated. As databases expand and as techniques for analyzing data improve, the shape of the tree of life presented in Figure 1.5 will undoubtedly change. Our understanding of the tree of life, like our understanding of every other topic in biological science, is dynamic.

How Should We Name Branches on the Tree of Life?

In science, the effort to name and classify organisms is called **taxonomy.** Any named group is called a **taxon** (plural: **taxa**). Currently, biologists are working to create a taxonomy, or naming system, that accurately reflects the phylogeny of organisms.

Based on the tree of life implied by genetic data, Woese proposed a new taxonomic category called the **domain.** The three domains of life are the Bacteria, Archaea, and Eukarya.

Biologists often use the term **phylum** (plural: **phyla**) to refer to major lineages within each domain. Although the designation is somewhat arbitrary, each phylum is considered a major branch on the tree of life. Within the lineage called animals, biologists currently name 30–35 phyla—each of which is distinguished by distinctive aspects of its body structure as well as by distinctive gene sequences. For example, the mollusks (clams, squid, octopuses) constitute a phylum, as do chordates (the vertebrates and their close relatives).

Because the tree of life is so new, though, naming systems are still being worked out. One thing that hasn't changed for centuries, however, is the naming system for individual species.

Scientific (Latin) Names   In 1735, a Swedish botanist named Carolus Linnaeus established a system for naming species that is still in use today. Linnaeus created a two-part name unique to each type of organism.

- *Genus*   The first part indicates the organism's **genus** (plural: **genera**). A genus is made up of a closely related group of species. For example, Linnaeus put humans in the genus *Homo*. Although humans are the only living species in this genus, at least six extinct organisms, all of which walked upright and made extensive use of tools, were later also assigned to *Homo*.

- *Species*   The second term in the two-part name identifies the organism's species. Linnaeus gave humans the species name *sapiens*.

An organism's genus and species designation is called its **scientific name** or Latin name. Scientific names are always italicized. Genus names are always capitalized, but species names are not—as in *Homo sapiens*.

Scientific names are based on Latin or Greek word roots or on words "Latinized" from other languages. Linnaeus gave a scientific name to every species then known, and also Latinized his own name—from Karl von Linné to Carolus Linnaeus.

Linnaeus maintained that different types of organisms should not be given the same genus and species names. Other species may be assigned to the genus *Homo*, and members of other genera may be named *sapiens*, but only humans are named *Homo sapiens*. Each scientific name is unique.

Scientific Names Are Often Descriptive Scientific names and terms are often based on Latin or Greek word roots that are descriptive. For example, *Homo sapiens* is derived from the Latin *homo* for "man" and *sapiens* for "wise" or "knowing." The yeast that bakers use to produce bread and that brewers use to brew beer is called *Saccharomyces cerevisiae*. The Greek root *saccharo* means "sugar," and *myces* refers to a fungus. *Saccharomyces* is aptly named "sugar fungus" because yeast is a fungus and because the domesticated strains of yeast used in commercial baking and brewing are often fed sugar. The species name of this organism, *cerevisiae*, is Latin for "beer." Loosely translated, then, the scientific name of brewer's yeast means "sugar-fungus for beer."

Scientific names and terms often seem daunting at first glance. So, most biologists find it extremely helpful to memorize some of the common Latin and Greek roots. To aid you in this process, new terms in this text are often accompanied by a translation of their Latin or Greek word roots in parentheses. (A glossary of common root words with translations and examples is also provided in **BioSkills 2** in Appendix B.)

check your understanding

C Y U

If you understand that . . .

- A phylogenetic tree shows the evolutionary relationships between species.
- To infer where species belong on a phylogenetic tree, biologists examine genetic and other characteristics of the species involved. Closely related species should have similar characteristics, while less closely related species should be less similar.

✔ **You should be able to . . .**

Examine the following rRNA ribonucleotide sequences and draw a phylogenetic tree showing the relationships between species A, B, and C that these data imply:

Species A: A A C T A G C G C G A T

Species B: A A C T A G C G C C A T

Species C: T T C T A G C G G T A T

Answers are available in Appendix A.

1.5 Doing Biology

This chapter has introduced some of the great ideas in biology. The development of the cell theory and the theory of evolution by natural selection provided cornerstones when the science was young; the tree of life is a relatively recent insight that has revolutionized our understanding of life's diversity.

These theories are considered great because they explain fundamental aspects of nature, and because they have consistently been shown to be correct. They are considered correct because they have withstood extensive testing.

How do biologists go about testing their ideas? Before answering this question, let's step back a bit and consider the types of questions that researchers can and cannot ask.

The Nature of Science

Biologists ask questions about organisms, just as physicists and chemists ask questions about the physical world or geologists ask questions about Earth's history and the ongoing processes that shape landforms.

No matter what their field, all scientists ask questions that can be answered by observing or measuring things—by collecting data. Conversely, scientists cannot address questions that can't be answered by observing or measuring things.

This distinction is important. It is at the root of continuing controversies about teaching evolution in publicly funded schools. In the United States and in Turkey, in particular, some Christian and Islamic leaders have been particularly successful in pushing their claim that evolution and religious faith are in conflict. Even though the theory of evolution is considered one of the most successful and best-substantiated ideas in the history of science, they object to teaching it.

The vast majority of biologists and many religious leaders reject this claim; they see no conflict between evolution and religious faith. Their view is that science and religion are compatible because they address different types of questions.

- Science is about formulating hypotheses and finding evidence that supports or conflicts with those hypotheses.

- Religious faith addresses questions that cannot be answered by data. The questions addressed by the world's great religions focus on why we exist and how we should live.

Both types of questions are seen as legitimate and important.

So how do biologists go about answering questions? After formulating hypotheses, biologists perform experimental studies, or studies that yield descriptive data, such as observing a behavior, characterizing a structure within a cell by microscopy, or sequencing rRNA. Let's consider two recent examples of this process.

Why Do Giraffes Have Long Necks? An Introduction to Hypothesis Testing

If you were asked why giraffes have long necks, you might say based on your observations that long necks enable giraffes to reach food that is unavailable to other mammals. This hypothesis is expressed in African folktales and has traditionally been accepted by many biologists. The food competition hypothesis is so plausible, in fact, that for decades no one thought to test it.

In the mid-1990s, however, Robert Simmons and Lue Scheepers assembled data suggesting that the food competition hypothesis is only part of the story. Their analysis supports an alternative hypothesis—that long necks allow giraffes to use their heads as effective weapons for battering their opponents, and that longer-necked giraffes would have a competitive advantage in fights.

Before exploring these alternative explanations, it's important to recognize that hypothesis testing is a two-step process:

Step 1 State the hypothesis as precisely as possible and list the predictions it makes.

Step 2 Design an observational or experimental study that is capable of testing those predictions.

If the predictions are accurate, the hypothesis is supported. If the predictions are not met, then researchers do further tests, modify the original hypothesis, or search for alternative explanations. But the process does not end here. Biologists also talk to other researchers. Over coffee, at scientific meetings, or through publications, biologists communicate their results to the scientific community and beyond. (You can see the Big Picture of the process of doing biology on pages 16–17.)

Now that you understand more about hypothesis testing, let's return to the giraffes. How did biologists test the food competition hypothesis? What data support their alternative explanation?

The Food Competition Hypothesis: Predictions and Tests The food competition hypothesis claims that giraffes compete for food with other species of mammals. When food is scarce, as it is during the dry season, giraffes with longer necks can reach food that is unavailable to other species and to giraffes with shorter necks. As a result, the longest-necked individuals in a giraffe population survive better and produce more young than do shorter-necked individuals, and average neck length of the population increases with each generation.

To use the terms introduced earlier, long necks are adaptations that increase the fitness of individual giraffes during competition for food. This type of natural selection has gone on so long that the population has become extremely long necked.

The food competition hypothesis makes several explicit predictions. For example, the food competition hypothesis predicts that:

- neck length is variable among giraffes;

- neck length in giraffes is heritable; and

- giraffes feed high in trees, especially during the dry season, when food is scarce and the threat of starvation is high.

The first prediction is correct. Studies in zoos and natural populations confirm that neck length is variable among individuals.

The researchers were unable to test the second prediction, however, because they studied giraffes in a natural population and were unable to do breeding experiments. As a result, they simply had to accept this prediction as an assumption. In

(a) Most feeding is done at about shoulder height.

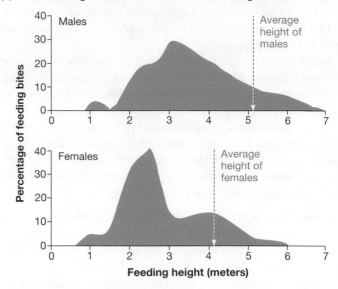

(b) Typical feeding posture in giraffes

FIGURE 1.7 Giraffes Do Not Usually Extend Their Necks Upward to Feed.

DATA: Young, T. P., L. A. Isbell. 1991. *Ethology* 87: 79–89.

general, though, biologists prefer to test every assumption behind a hypothesis.

What about the prediction regarding feeding high in trees? According to Simmons and Scheepers, this is where the food competition hypothesis breaks down.

Consider, for example, data collected by a different research team on the amount of time that giraffes spend feeding in vegetation of different heights. **FIGURE 1.7a** plots the height of vegetation versus the percentage of bites taken by a giraffe, for males and for females from the same population in Kenya. The dashed line on each graph indicates the average height of a male or female in this population.

Note that the average height of a giraffe in this population is much greater than the height where most feeding takes place. In this population, both male and female giraffes spend most of their feeding time eating vegetation that averages just 60 percent of their full height. Studies on other populations of giraffes, during both the wet and dry seasons, are consistent with these data. Giraffes usually feed with their necks bent (**FIGURE 1.7b**).

These data cast doubt on the food competition hypothesis, because one of its predictions does not appear to hold. Biologists have not abandoned this hypothesis completely, though, because feeding high in trees may be particularly valuable during extreme droughts, when a giraffe's ability to reach leaves far above the ground could mean the difference between life and death. Still, Simmons and Scheepers have offered an alternative explanation for why giraffes have long necks. The new hypothesis is based on the mating system of giraffes.

The Sexual Competition Hypothesis: Predictions and Tests Giraffes have an unusual mating system. Breeding occurs year round rather than seasonally. To determine when females are coming into estrus or "heat" and are thus receptive to mating, the males nuzzle the rumps of females. In response, the females urinate into the males' mouths. The males then tip their heads back and pull their lips to and fro, as if tasting the liquid. Biologists who have witnessed this behavior have proposed that the males taste the females' urine to detect whether estrus has begun.

Once a female giraffe enters estrus, males fight among themselves for the opportunity to mate. Combat is spectacular. The bulls stand next to one another, swing their necks, and strike thunderous blows with their heads. Researchers have seen males knocked unconscious for 20 minutes after being hit and have cataloged numerous instances in which the loser died. Giraffes are not the only animals known to fight in this way—male giraffe weevils also use enormously long necks to fight for mating rights.

These observations inspired a new explanation for why giraffes have long necks. The sexual competition hypothesis is based on the idea that longer-necked giraffes are able to strike harder blows during combat than can shorter-necked giraffes. In engineering terms, longer necks provide a longer "moment arm." A long moment arm increases the force of an impact. (Think about the type of sledgehammer you'd use to bash down a concrete wall—one with a short handle or one with a long handle?)

The idea here is that longer-necked males should win more fights and, as a result, father more offspring than shorter-necked males do. If neck length in giraffes is inherited, then the average neck length in the population should increase over time. Under the sexual competition hypothesis, long necks are adaptations that increase the fitness of males during competition for females.

Although several studies have shown that long-necked males are more successful in fighting and that the winners of fights gain access to estrous females, the question of why giraffes have long necks is not closed. With the data collected to date, most biologists would probably concede that the food competition hypothesis needs further testing and refinement and that the sexual competition hypothesis appears promising. It could also be true that both hypotheses are correct. For our purposes, the important take-home message is that all hypotheses must be tested rigorously.

In many cases in biological science, testing hypotheses rigorously involves experimentation. Experimenting on giraffes is difficult. But in the case study considered next, biologists were able to test an interesting hypothesis experimentally.

How Do Ants Navigate? An Introduction to Experimental Design

Experiments are a powerful scientific tool because they allow researchers to test the effect of a single, well-defined factor on a particular phenomenon. Because experiments testing the effect of neck length on food and sexual competition in giraffes haven't been done yet, let's consider a different question: When ants leave their nest to search for food, how do they find their way back?

The Saharan desert ant lives in colonies and makes a living by scavenging the dead carcasses of insects. Individuals leave the burrow and wander about searching for food at midday, when temperatures at the surface can reach 60°C (140°F) and predators are hiding from the heat.

Foraging trips can take the ants hundreds of meters—an impressive distance when you consider that these animals are only about a centimeter long. But when an ant returns, it doesn't follow the same long, wandering route it took on its way away from the nest. Instead, individuals return in a straight line (**FIGURE 1.8**).

Once individuals are close to the nest, they engage in a characteristic set of back-and-forth U-turns until they find their nest hole. How do they do know how far they are from the nest?

The Pedometer Hypothesis Early work on navigation in desert ants showed that they use the Sun's position as a compass—meaning that they always know the approximate direction of the nest relative to the Sun. But how do they know how far to go?

After experiments had shown that the ants do not use landmarks to navigate, Matthias Wittlinger and co-workers set out to test a novel idea. The biologists proposed that Saharan desert ants know how far they are from the nest by integrating information from leg movements.

According to this pedometer hypothesis, the ants always know how far they are from the nest because they track the number

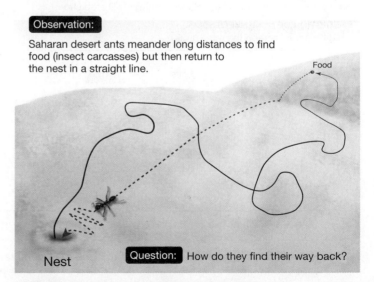

Observation:

Saharan desert ants meander long distances to find food (insect carcasses) but then return to the nest in a straight line.

Food

Question: How do they find their way back?

Nest

FIGURE 1.8 Navigation in Foraging Desert Ants.

of steps they have taken and their stride length. The idea is that they can make a beeline back toward the burrow because they integrate information on the angles they have traveled *and* the distance they have gone—based on step number and stride length.

If the pedometer hypothesis is wrong, however, then stride length and step number should have no effect on the ability of an ant to get back to its nest. This latter possibility is called a **null hypothesis.** A null hypothesis specifies what should be observed when the hypothesis being tested isn't correct.

Testing the Hypothesis To test their idea, Wittlinger's group allowed ants to walk from a nest to a feeder through a channel—a distance of 10 m. Then they caught ants at the feeder and created three test groups, each with 25 individuals (**FIGURES 1.9** and **1.10**):

- *Stumps* By cutting the lower legs of some individuals off, they created ants with shorter-than-normal legs.

- *Normal* Some individuals were left alone, meaning that they had normal leg length.

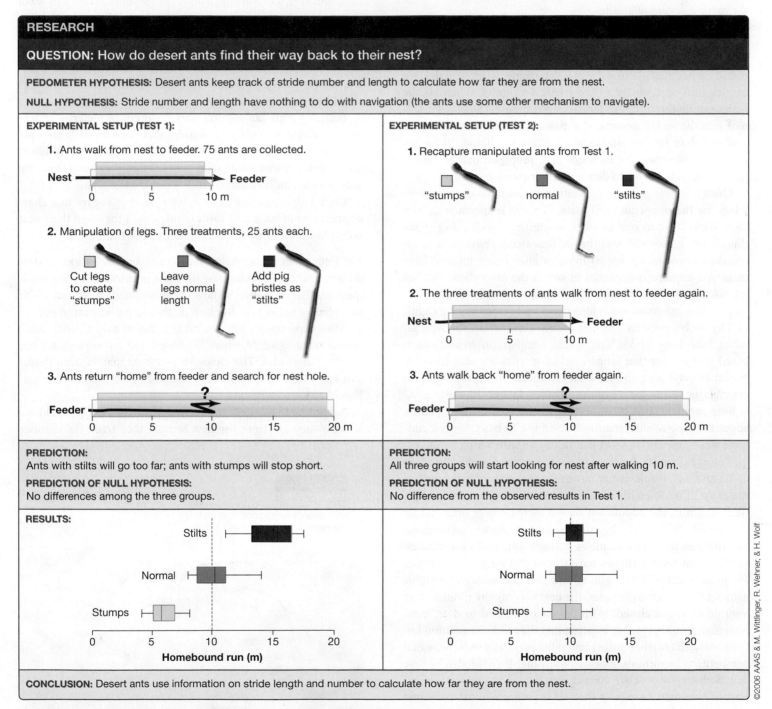

RESEARCH

QUESTION: How do desert ants find their way back to their nest?

PEDOMETER HYPOTHESIS: Desert ants keep track of stride number and length to calculate how far they are from the nest.

NULL HYPOTHESIS: Stride number and length have nothing to do with navigation (the ants use some other mechanism to navigate).

EXPERIMENTAL SETUP (TEST 1):

1. Ants walk from nest to feeder. 75 ants are collected.

Nest ——→ Feeder
0   5   10 m

2. Manipulation of legs. Three treatments, 25 ants each.

Cut legs to create "stumps"   Leave legs normal length   Add pig bristles as "stilts"

3. Ants return "home" from feeder and search for nest hole.

Feeder   ?
0   5   10   15   20 m

EXPERIMENTAL SETUP (TEST 2):

1. Recapture manipulated ants from Test 1.

"stumps"   normal   "stilts"

2. The three treatments of ants walk from nest to feeder again.

Nest ——→ Feeder
0   5   10 m

3. Ants walk back "home" from feeder again.

Feeder   ?
0   5   10   15   20 m

PREDICTION:
Ants with stilts will go too far; ants with stumps will stop short.

PREDICTION OF NULL HYPOTHESIS:
No differences among the three groups.

PREDICTION:
All three groups will start looking for nest after walking 10 m.

PREDICTION OF NULL HYPOTHESIS:
No difference from the observed results in Test 1.

RESULTS:

Stilts / Normal / Stumps
Homebound run (m)
0   5   10   15   20

Stilts / Normal / Stumps
Homebound run (m)
0   5   10   15   20

CONCLUSION: Desert ants use information on stride length and number to calculate how far they are from the nest.

FIGURE 1.9 An Experimental Test: Do Desert Ants Use a "Pedometer"?

SOURCE: Wittlinger, M., R. Wehner, and H. Wolf. 2006. The ant odometer: Stepping on stilts and stumps. *Science* 312: 1965–1967.

✔**QUESTION** What is the advantage of using 25 ants in each group instead of just one?

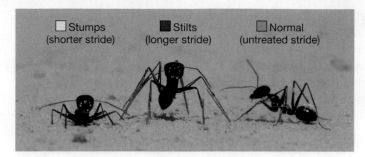

Stumps (shorter stride)　Stilts (longer stride)　Normal (untreated stride)

FIGURE 1.10 Manipulation of Desert Ant Stride Length.

- *Stilts* By gluing pig bristles onto each leg, the biologists created ants with longer-than-normal legs.

Next they put the ants in a different channel and recorded how far they traveled in a direct line before starting their nest-searching behavior. To see the data they collected, look at the graph on the left side of the "Results" section in Figure 1.9.

- *Stumps* The ants with stumps stopped short, by about 5 m, before starting to search for the nest opening.
- *Normal* The normal ants walked the correct distance—about 10 m.
- *Stilts* The ants with stilts walked about 5 m too far before starting to search for the nest opening.

To check the validity of this result, the researchers put the test ants back in the nest and recaptured them one to several days later, when they had walked to the feeder on their stumps, normal legs, or stilts. Now when the ants were put into the other channel to "walk back," they all traveled the correct distance—10 m—before starting to search for the nest (see the graph on the right side of the "Results" section in Figure 1.9).

The graphs in the "Results" display "box-and-whisker" plots that allow you to easily see where most of the data fall. Each box indicates the range of distances where 50 percent of the ants stopped to search for the nest. The whiskers indicate the lower extreme (stopping short of the nest location) and the upper extreme (going too far) of where the ants stopped to search. The vertical line inside each box indicates the median—meaning that half the ants stopped above this distance and half below. (For more details on how biologists report medians and indicate the variability and uncertainty in data, see **BioSkills 4** in Appendix B.)

Interpreting the Results The pedometer hypothesis predicts that an ant's ability to walk home depends on the number and length of steps taken on its outbound trip. Recall that a prediction specifies what we should observe if a hypothesis is correct. Good scientific hypotheses make testable predictions—predictions that can be supported or rejected by collecting and analyzing data. In this case, the researchers tested the prediction by altering stride length and recording the distance traveled on the return trip. Under the null hypothesis in this experiment, all the ants—altered and unaltered—should have walked 10 m in the first test before they started looking for their nest.

Important Characteristics of Good Experimental Design In relation to designing effective experiments, this study illustrates several important points:

- It is critical to include **control** groups. A control checks for factors, other than the one being tested, that might influence the experiment's outcome. In this case, there were two controls. Including a normal, unmanipulated individual controlled for the possibility that switching the individuals to a new channel altered their behavior. In addition, the researchers had to control for the possibility that the manipulation itself—and not the change in leg length—affected the behavior of the stilts and stumps ants. This is why they did the second test, where the outbound and return runs were done with the same legs.

- The experimental conditions must be as constant or equivalent as possible. The investigators used ants of the same species, from the same nest, at the same time of day, under the same humidity and temperature conditions, at the same feeders, in the same channels. Controlling all the variables except one—leg length in this case—is crucial because it eliminates alternative explanations for the results.

- Repeating the test is essential. It is almost universally true that larger sample sizes in experiments are better. By testing many individuals, the amount of distortion or "noise" in the data caused by unusual individuals or circumstances is reduced.

✔ If you understand these points, you should be able to explain: (1) What you would conclude if in the first test, the normal individual had not walked 10 m on the return trip before

check your understanding

If you understand that . . .

- Hypotheses are proposed explanations that make testable predictions.
- Predictions describe observable outcomes of particular conditions.
- Well-designed experiments alter just one condition—a condition relevant to the hypothesis being tested.

✔ You should be able to . . .

Design an experiment to test the hypothesis that desert ants feed during the hottest part of the day because it allows them to avoid being eaten by lizards. Then answer the following questions about your experimental design:

1. How does the presence of a control group in your experiment allow you to test the hypothesis?

2. How are experimental conditions controlled or standardized in a way that precludes alternative explanations of the data?

Answers are available in Appendix A.

looking for the nest; and (2) What you would conclude if the stilts and stumps ants had not navigated normally during the second test.

From the outcomes of these experiments, the researchers concluded that desert ants use stride length and number to measure how far they are from the nest. They interpreted their results as strong support for the pedometer hypothesis.

The giraffe and ant studies demonstrate a vital point: Biologists practice evidence-based decision making. They ask questions about how organisms work, pose hypotheses to answer those questions, and use experimental or observational evidence to decide which hypotheses are correct.

The data on giraffes and ants are a taste of things to come. In this text you will encounter hypotheses and research on questions ranging from how water gets to the top of 100-meter-tall sequoia trees to how the bacterium that causes tuberculosis has become resistant to antibiotics. As you work through this book, you'll get lots of practice thinking about hypotheses and predictions, analyzing the nature of control treatments, and interpreting graphs.

A commitment to tough-minded hypothesis testing and sound experimental design is a hallmark of biological science. Understanding their value is an important first step in becoming a biologist.

CHAPTER 1 REVIEW

For media, go to MasteringBiology

If you understand . . .

1.1 What Does It Mean to Say That Something Is Alive?

- There is no single, well-accepted definition of life. Instead, biologists point to five characteristics that organisms share.

✔ You should be able to explain why the cells in a dead organism are different from the cells in a live organism.

1.2 The Cell Theory

- The cell theory identified the fundamental structural unit common to all life.

✔ You should be able to describe the evidence that supported the pattern and the process components of the cell theory.

1.3 The Theory of Evolution by Natural Selection

- The theory of evolution states that all organisms are related by common ancestry.

- Natural selection is a well-tested explanation for why species change through time and why they are so well adapted to their habitats.

✔ You should be able to explain why the average protein content of seeds in a natural population of a grass species would increase over time, if seeds with higher protein content survive better and grow into individuals that produce many seeds with high protein content when they mature.

1.4 The Tree of Life

- The theory of evolution predicts that all organisms are part of a genealogy of species, and that all species trace their ancestry back to a single common ancestor.

- To construct this phylogeny, biologists have analyzed the sequences in rRNA and in an array of genetic material found in all cells.

- A tree of life, based on similarities and differences in these molecules, has three fundamental lineages, or domains: the Bacteria, the Archaea, and the Eukarya.

✔ You should be able to explain how biologists can determine which of the three domains a newly discovered species belongs to by analyzing its rRNA.

1.5 Doing Biology

- Biology is a hypothesis-driven, experimental science.

✔ You should be able to explain (1) the relationship between a hypothesis and a prediction and (2) why experiments are convincing ways to test predictions.

MB MasteringBiology

1. **MasteringBiology Assignments**

   Tutorials and Activities An Introduction to Graphing; Experimental Inquiry: What Can You Learn about the Process of Science from Investigating a Cricket's Chirp?; Introduction to Experimental Design; Levels of Life Card Game; Metric System Review; The Scientific Method

   Questions Reading Quizzes, Blue-Thread Questions, Test Bank

2. **eText** Read your book online, search, take notes, highlight text, and more.

3. **The Study Area** Practice Test, Cumulative Test, BioFlix® 3-D Animations, Videos, Activities, Audio Glossary, Word Study Tools, Art

You should be able to . . .

1. Anton van Leeuwenhoek made an important contribution to the development of the cell theory. How?
   a. He articulated the pattern component of the theory—that all organisms are made of cells.
   b. He articulated the process component of the theory—that all cells come from preexisting cells.
   c. He invented the first microscope and saw the first cell.
   d. He invented more powerful microscopes and was the first to describe the diversity of cells.

2. What does it mean to say that experimental conditions are controlled?
   a. The test groups consist of the same individuals.
   b. The null hypothesis is correct.
   c. There is no difference in outcome between the control and experimental treatment.
   d. All physical conditions except for one are identical for all groups tested.

3. The term *evolution* means that _____ change through time.

4. What does it mean to say that a characteristic of an organism is heritable?
   a. The characteristic evolves.
   b. The characteristic can be passed on to offspring.
   c. The characteristic is advantageous to the organism.
   d. The characteristic does not vary in the population.

5. In biology, to what does the term *fitness* refer?

6. Could *both* the food competition hypothesis and the sexual competition hypothesis explain why giraffes have long necks? Why or why not?
   a. No. In science, only one hypothesis can be correct.
   b. No. Observations have shown that the food competition hypothesis cannot be correct.
   c. Yes. Long necks could be advantageous for more than one reason.
   d. Yes. All giraffes have been shown to feed at the highest possible height and fight for mates.

7. What would researchers have to demonstrate to convince you that they had discovered life on another planet?

8. What did Linnaeus's system of naming organisms ensure?
   a. Two different organisms never end up with the same genus and species name.
   b. Two different organisms have the same genus and species name if they are closely related.
   c. The genus name is different for closely related species.
   d. The species name is the same for each organism in a genus.

9. What does it mean to say that a species is adapted to a particular habitat?

10. Explain how selection occurs during natural selection. What is selected, and why?

11. The following two statements explain the logic behind the use of molecular sequence data to estimate evolutionary relationships:

    "If the theory of evolution is true, then rRNA sequences should be very similar in closely related organisms but less similar in organisms that are less closely related."

    "On a phylogenetic tree, branches that share a recent common ancestor represent species that are closely related; branches that don't share recent common ancestors represent species that are more distantly related."

    Is the logic of these statements sound? Why or why not?

12. Explain why researchers formulate a null hypothesis in addition to a hypothesis when designing an experimental study.

13. A scientific theory is a set of propositions that defines and explains some aspect of the world. This definition contrasts sharply with the everyday usage of the word theory, which often carries meanings such as "speculation" or "guess." Explain the difference between the two definitions, using the cell theory and the theory of evolution by natural selection as examples.

14. Turn back to the tree of life shown in Figure 1.5. Note that Bacteria and Archaea are prokaryotes, while Eukarya are eukaryotes. On the simplified tree below, draw an arrow that points to the branch where the structure called the nucleus originated. Explain your reasoning.

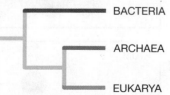

BACTERIA

ARCHAEA

EUKARYA

15. The proponents of the cell theory could not "prove" that it was correct in the sense of providing incontrovertible evidence that all organisms are made up of cells. They could state only that all organisms examined to date were made of cells. Why was it reasonable for them to conclude that the theory was valid?

16. Some humans have heritable traits that make them resistant to infection by HIV. In areas of the world where HIV infection rates are high, are human populations evolving? Explain your logic.
    a. No. HIV infection rates would not affect human evolution.
    b. Yes. The heritable traits that confer resistance to HIV should increase over time.
    c. No. The heritable traits that confer resistance to HIV should decrease over time.
    d. Yes. The heritable traits that confer resistance to HIV should decrease over time.

BIG PICTURE

Biologists study the characteristics of life. The cell theory, the theory of evolution by natural selection, and the tree of life are some of the great ideas in biology that came about by biologists asking questions that can be answered by observing or measuring things—that is, by collecting data.

Notice that the study of life is not a series of linear steps with a beginning and an end. Instead, the process of doing biology is dynamic and ongoing. The answer to one question may lay the foundation for twenty more questions. Working together, biologists from different disciplines integrate data across many levels, from atoms to the biosphere.

Note that the gray numbers in boxes tell you where to go for more information. Also, be sure to do the blue exercises in the Check Your Understanding box.

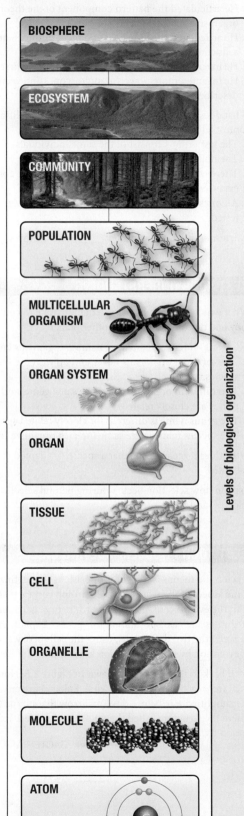

Characteristics of living things
- Energy
- Cells
- Information
- Replication
- Evolution

1.1

focuses on

Text section where you can find more information

BIOSPHERE

ECOSYSTEM

COMMUNITY

POPULATION

MULTICELLULAR ORGANISM

ORGAN SYSTEM

Scientists regularly integrate across many of these levels

ORGAN

TISSUE

CELL

ORGANELLE

MOLECULE

ATOM

Levels of biological organization

check your understanding

If you understand the big picture . . .

✔ **You should be able to . . .**

1. Describe how biologists go about testing their ideas.

2. Provide an example of how an experimental study could span more than one level of biological organization.

3. Compare and contrast a hypothesis with a theory.

4. Propose the next step to take if data support the hypothesis you are testing.

Answers are available in Appendix A.

C
Y
U

DOING BIOLOGY

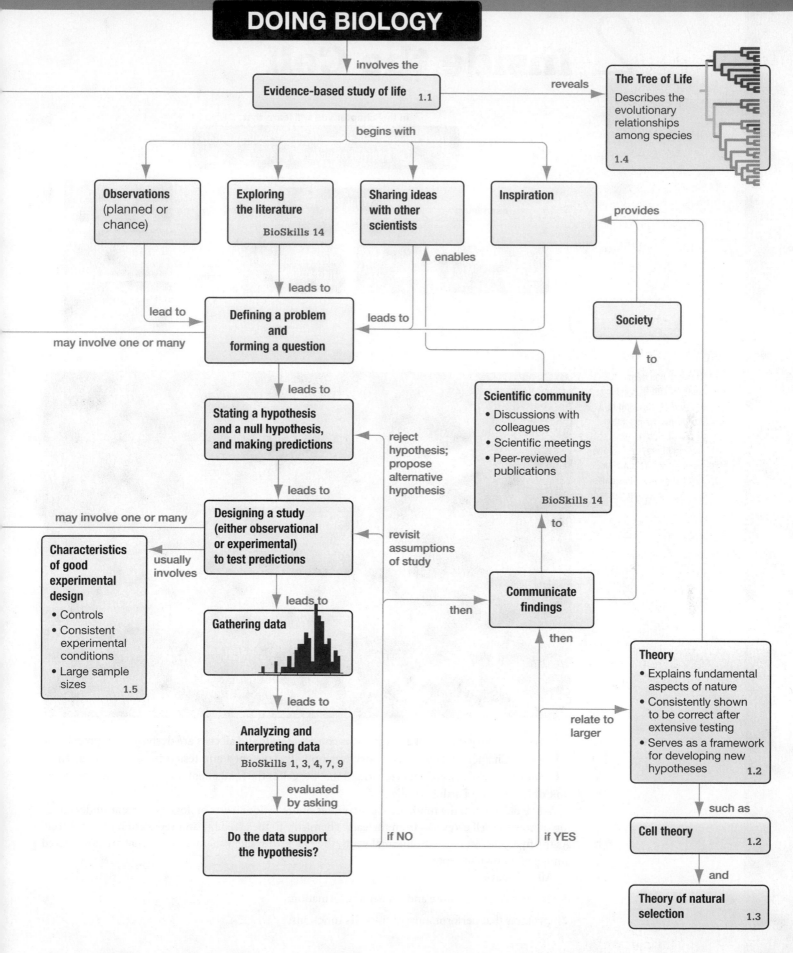

Evidence-based study of life 1.1
— involves the →

reveals →
The Tree of Life
Describes the evolutionary relationships among species
1.4

begins with

Observations (planned or chance)

Exploring the literature
BioSkills 14

Sharing ideas with other scientists

Inspiration

provides

lead to

may involve one or many

leads to

Defining a problem and forming a question
← leads to
enables

Society
to

leads to

Stating a hypothesis and a null hypothesis, and making predictions
← reject hypothesis; propose alternative hypothesis

Scientific community
• Discussions with colleagues
• Scientific meetings
• Peer-reviewed publications
BioSkills 14

leads to

Characteristics of good experimental design
• Controls
• Consistent experimental conditions
• Large sample sizes
1.5

may involve one or many

usually involves

Designing a study (either observational or experimental) to test predictions
← revisit assumptions of study

to

leads to

Gathering data
then → **Communicate findings**
then

leads to

Theory
• Explains fundamental aspects of nature
• Consistently shown to be correct after extensive testing
• Serves as a framework for developing new hypotheses
1.2

relate to larger

Analyzing and interpreting data
BioSkills 1, 3, 4, 7, 9

evaluated by asking

such as

Do the data support the hypothesis?
if NO   *if YES*

Cell theory 1.2

and

Theory of natural selection 1.3

17

2 Inside the Cell

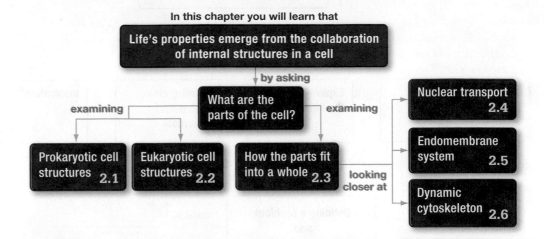

In this chapter you will learn that

Life's properties emerge from the collaboration of internal structures in a cell

by asking

What are the parts of the cell?

examining

Prokaryotic cell structures 2.1

Eukaryotic cell structures 2.2

How the parts fit into a whole 2.3

examining

Nuclear transport 2.4

looking closer at

Endomembrane system 2.5

Dynamic cytoskeleton 2.6

This cell has been treated with fluorescing molecules that bind to its fibrous cytoskeleton. Microtubules (large protein fibers) are yellow; actin filaments (smaller fibers) are blue. The cell's nucleus has been stained green.

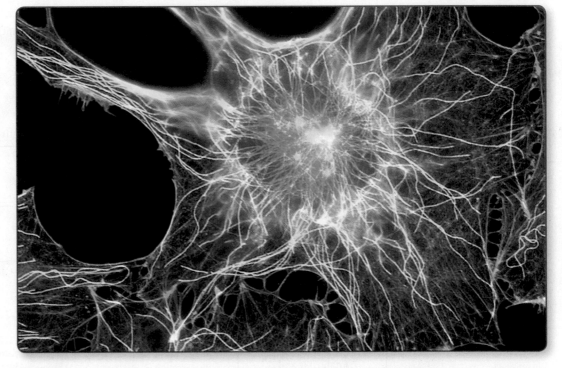

The cell theory states that all organisms consist of cells and all cells are derived from preexisting cells (Chapter 1). Since this theory was initially developed and tested in the 1850s, an enormous body of research has confirmed that the cell is the fundamental structural and functional unit of life. Life on Earth is cellular.

We've delved into the fundamental attributes of life by looking at biologists' current understanding of how the cell evolved—from the early chemistry to the assembly and replication of a protocell. As the first cells left the hydrothermal vents, they took with them characteristics that are now shared among all known life-forms.

All cells have

1. nucleic acids that store and transmit information;

2. proteins that perform most of the cell's functions;

✔ When you see this checkmark, stop and test yourself. Answers are available in Appendix A.

3. carbohydrates that provide chemical energy, carbon, support, and identity; and

4. a plasma membrane, which serves as a selectively permeable membrane barrier.

Thanks to the selective permeability of phospholipid bilayers and the activity of membrane transport proteins, the plasma membrane creates an internal environment that differs from conditions outside the cell. Our task now is to explore the structures inside the cell to understand how the properties of life emerged from the combination of these characteristics.

Let's begin by analyzing how the parts inside a cell function individually and then exploring how they work as a unit. This approach is analogous to studying individual organs in the body and then analyzing how they work together to form the nervous system or digestive system. As you study this material, keep asking yourself some key questions: How does the structure of this part or group of parts correlate with its function? What problem does it solve?

2.1 Bacterial and Archaeal Cell Structures and Their Functions

Cells are divided into two fundamental types called eukaryotes and prokaryotes (see Chapter 1). This division is mostly based on cell **morphology** ("form-science")—eukaryotic cells have a membrane-bound compartment called a nucleus, and prokaryotic cells do not.

But according to **phylogeny** ("tribe-source"), or evolutionary history, organisms are divided into three broad domains called (1) Bacteria, (2) Archaea, and (3) Eukarya. Members of the Bacteria and Archaea are prokaryotic; members of the Eukarya—including algae, fungi, plants, and animals—are eukaryotic.

A Revolutionary New View

For almost 200 years, biologists thought that prokaryotic cells were simple in terms of their morphology and that there was little structural diversity among species. This conclusion was valid at the time, given the resolution of the microscopes that were available and the number of species that had been studied.

Things have changed. Recent improvements in microscopy and other research tools have convinced biologists that prokaryotic cells, among which bacteria are the best understood, possess an array of distinctive structures and functions found among millions of species. This conclusion represents one of the most exciting discoveries in cell biology over the past 10 years.

To keep things simple at the start, though, **FIGURE 2.1** offers a low-magnification, stripped-down diagram of a bacterial cell.

Prokaryotic Cell Structures: A Parts List

The labels in Figure 2.1 highlight the components common to all or most bacteria studied to date. Let's explore these elements one by one, and also look at more specialized structures found in particular species, starting from the inside and working out.

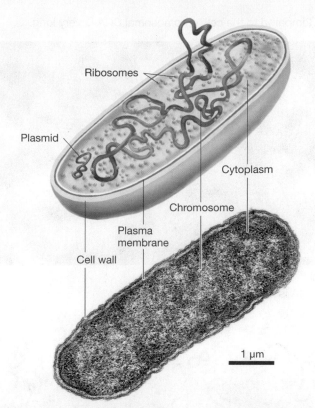

FIGURE 2.1 Overview of a Prokaryotic Cell. Prokaryotic cells are identified by a negative trait—the absence of a membrane-bound nucleus. Although there is wide variation in the size and shape of bacterial and archaeal cells, they all contain a plasma membrane, a chromosome, and protein-synthesizing ribosomes.

The Chromosome Is Organized in a Nucleoid The most prominent structure inside a bacterial cell is the **chromosome.** Most bacterial species have a single, circular chromosome that consists of a large DNA molecule associated with a small number of proteins. The DNA molecule contains information, and the proteins provide structural support for the DNA.

Recall that the information in DNA is encoded in its sequence of nitrogenous bases. Segments of DNA that contain information for building functional RNAs, some of which may be used to make polypeptides, are called **genes** (Chapter 5). Thus, chromosomes contain DNA, which contains genes.

In the well-studied bacterium *Escherichia coli*, the circular chromosome would be over 1 mm long if it were linear—500 times longer than the cell itself (**FIGURE 2.2a**; see page 20). This situation is typical in prokaryotes. To fit into the cell, the DNA double helix coils on itself with the aid of enzymes to form a compact, "supercoiled" structure. Supercoiled regions of DNA resemble a rubber band that has been held at either end and then twisted until it coils back upon itself.

The location and structural organization of the circular chromosome is called the **nucleoid** (pronounced *NEW-klee-oyd*). The genetic material in the nucleoid is often organized by clustering loops of DNA into distinct domains, but it is not separated from the rest of the cell interior by a membrane. The functional role of this organization of the bacterial chromosome and how it changes over time is currently the subject of intense research.

(a) Compared to the cell, chromosomal DNA is very long.

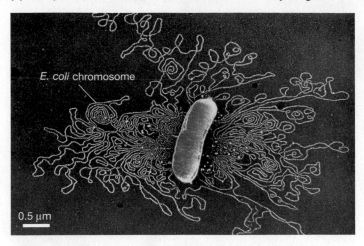

(b) DNA is packaged by supercoiling.

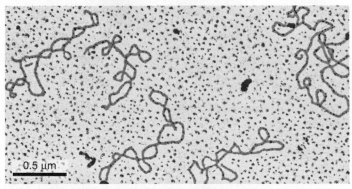

FIGURE 2.2 Bacterial DNA Is Supercoiled. (a) The chromosomes of bacteria and archaea are often over 1000 times the length of the cell, as shown in this micrograph of *E. coli* that has been treated to release its DNA. To fit inside cells, this DNA must be highly compacted by supercoiling. **(b)** A colorized electron micrograph showing the effect of supercoiling on the DNA of isolated plasmids.

In addition to one or more chromosomes, bacterial cells may contain from one to about a hundred small, usually circular, supercoiled DNA molecules called **plasmids** (**FIGURE 2.2b**). Plasmids contain genes but are physically independent of the cellular chromosome. In many cases the genes carried by plasmids are not required under normal conditions; instead, they help cells adapt to unusual circumstances, such as the sudden presence of a poison in the environment. As a result, plasmids can be considered auxiliary genetic elements.

Ribosomes Manufacture Proteins **Ribosomes** are observed in all prokaryotic cells and are found throughout the cell interior. It is not unusual for a single cell to contain 10,000 ribosomes, each functioning as a protein-manufacturing center.

Ribosomes are complex structures composed of large and small subunits, each of which contains RNA and protein molecules. Biologists often refer to ribosomes, along with other multicomponent complexes that perform specialized tasks, as "macromolecular machines." (Chapter 8 analyzes the structure and function of ribosomes in detail.)

Photosynthetic Species Have Internal Membrane Complexes In addition to the nucleoid and ribosomes found in all bacteria and archaea studied to date, it is common to observe extensive internal membranes in prokaryotes that perform photosynthesis. Photosynthesis is the suite of chemical reactions responsible for converting the energy in sunlight into chemical energy stored in sugars.

The photosynthetic membranes observed in prokaryotes contain the enzymes and pigment molecules required for these reactions to occur and develop as infoldings of the plasma membrane. In some cases, vesicles pinch off as the plasma membrane folds in. In other cases, flattened stacks of photosynthetic membrane remain connected to the plasma membrane, like those shown in **FIGURE 2.3**. The extensive surface area provided by these internal membranes makes it possible for more photosynthetic reactions to occur and thus increases the cell's ability to make food.

Organelles Perform Specialized Functions Recent research indicates that several bacterial species have internal compartments that qualify as **organelles** ("little organs"). An organelle is a membrane-bound compartment inside the cell that contains enzymes or structures specialized for a particular function.

Bacterial organelles perform an array of tasks, including

- storing calcium ions or other key molecules;

- holding crystals of the mineral magnetite, which function like a compass needle to help cells sense a magnetic field and swim in a directed way;

- organizing enzymes responsible for synthesizing complex carbon compounds from carbon dioxide; and

- sequestering enzymes that generate chemical energy from ammonium ions.

The Cytoskeleton Structures the Cell Interior Recent research has also shown that bacteria and archaea contain long, thin fibers that serve a variety of roles inside the cell. All bacterial species,

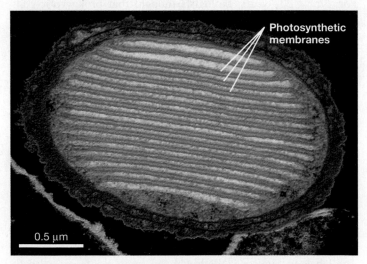

Photosynthetic membranes

FIGURE 2.3 Photosynthetic Membranes in Bacteria. The green stripes in this photosynthetic bacterium are membranes that contain the pigments and enzymes required for photosynthesis. This photo has been colorized to enhance the membranes.

for example, contain protein fibers that are essential for cell division to take place. Some species also have protein filaments that help maintain cell shape. Protein filaments such as these form the basis of the **cytoskeleton** ("cell skeleton").

The discovery of bacterial cytoskeletal elements is so new that much remains to be learned. Currently, researchers are working to understand how the different cytoskeletal elements enable cells to divide and if they play a role in organizing the cell interior into distinctive regions.

The Plasma Membrane Separates Life from Nonlife The plasma membrane consists of a phospholipid bilayer and proteins that either span the bilayer or attach to one side. Inside the membrane, all the contents of a cell, excluding the nucleus, are collectively termed the **cytoplasm** ("cell-formed").

Because all archaea and virtually all bacteria are unicellular, the plasma membrane creates an internal environment that is distinct from the outside, nonliving environment. The combined effect of a lipid bilayer and membrane proteins prohibits the entry of many substances that would be dangerous to life while allowing the passage of molecules and ions required for life (see Chapter 3).

The Cell Wall Forms a Protective "Exoskeleton" Because the cytoplasm contains a high concentration of solutes, in most habitats it is hypertonic relative to the surrounding environment. When this is the case, water enters the cell via osmosis and makes the cell's volume expand. In virtually all bacteria and archaea, this pressure is resisted by a stiff **cell wall.**

Bacterial and archaeal cell walls are a tough, fibrous layer that surrounds the plasma membrane. In prokaryotes, the pressure of the plasma membrane against the cell wall is about the same as the pressure in an automobile tire.

The cell wall protects the organism and gives it shape and rigidity, much like the exoskeleton (external skeleton) of a crab or insect. In addition, many bacteria have another protective layer outside the cell wall that consists of lipids with polysaccharides attached. Lipids that contain carbohydrate groups are termed **glycolipids.**

External Structures Enable Movement and Attachment Besides having a cell wall to provide protection, as just described, many bacteria also interact with their environment via structures that grow from the plasma membrane. The flagella and fimbriae shown in **FIGURE 2.4** are examples that are commonly found on bacterial surfaces.

Bacterial **flagella** (singular: **flagellum**) are assembled from over 40 different proteins at the cell surface of certain species. The base of this structure is embedded in the plasma membrane, and its rotation spins a long, helical filament that propels cells through water. At top speed, flagellar movement can drive a bacterial cell through water at 60 cell lengths per second. In contrast, the fastest animal in the ocean—the sailfish—can swim at a mere 10 body lengths per second.

Fimbriae (singular: **fimbria**) are needlelike projections that extend from the plasma membrane of some bacteria and promote attachment to other cells or surfaces. These structures are

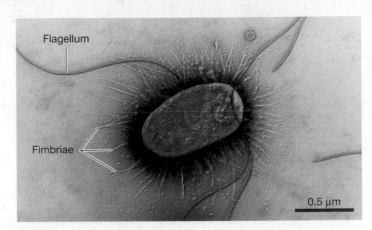

FIGURE 2.4 Extracellular Appendages Found on Bacteria. Some species of bacteria, such as the *E. coli* shown here, assemble large protein structures used for swimming through liquid (flagella) or adhering to surfaces (fimbriae).

more numerous than flagella and are often distributed over the entire surface of the cell. Fimbriae are crucial to the establishment of many infections based on their ability to glue bacteria to the surface of tissues.

The painting in **FIGURE 2.5** shows a cross section of a bacterial cell and provides a close-up view of the internal and external structures introduced in this section. One feature that prokaryotic and eukaryotic cells have in common: They are both packed with dynamic, highly integrated structures.

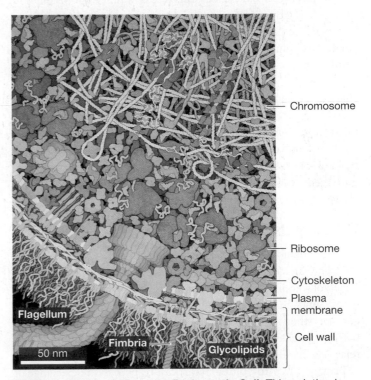

FIGURE 2.5 Close-up View of a Prokaryotic Cell. This painting is David Goodsell's representation of a cross section through part of a bacterial cell. It is based on electron micrographs of bacterial cells and is drawn to scale. Note that the cell is packed with proteins, DNA, ribosomes, and other molecular machinery.

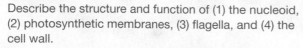
check your understanding

If you understand that . . .

- Each structure in a prokaryotic cell performs a function vital to the cell.

✓ **You should be able to . . .**

Describe the structure and function of (1) the nucleoid, (2) photosynthetic membranes, (3) flagella, and (4) the cell wall.

Answers are available in Appendix A.

2.2 Eukaryotic Cell Structures and Their Functions

The Eukarya includes species that range from microscopic algae to 100-meter-tall redwood trees. Brown algae, red algae, fungi, amoebae, slime molds, green plants, and animals are all eukaryotic. Although multicellularity has evolved several times among eukaryotes, many species are unicellular.

The first thing that strikes biologists about eukaryotic cells is how much larger they are on average than bacteria and archaea. Most prokaryotic cells measure 1 to 10 μm in diameter, while most eukaryotic cells range from about 5 to 100 μm in diameter. A micrograph of an average eukaryotic cell, at the same scale as the bacterial cell in Figure 2.3, would fill this page. For many species of unicellular eukaryotes, this size difference allows them to make a living by ingesting bacteria and archaea whole.

Large size has a downside, however. As a cell increases in diameter, its volume increases more than its surface area. In other words, the relationship between them—the surface-area-to-volume ratio—changes. Since the surface is where the cell exchanges substances with its environment, the reduction in this ratio decreases the rate of exchange: Diffusion only allows for rapid movement across very small distances.

Prokaryotic cells tend to be small enough so that ions and small molecules arrive where they are needed via diffusion. The random movement of diffusion alone, however, is insufficient for this type of transport as the cell's diameter increases.

The Benefits of Organelles

How do eukaryotic cells solve the problems that size can engender? The answer lies in their numerous organelles. In effect, the huge volume inside a eukaryotic cell is compartmentalized into many small bins. Because eukaryotic cells are subdivided, the **cytosol**—the fluid portion between the plasma membrane and these organelles—is only a fraction of the total cell volume. This relatively small volume of cytosol reduces the effect of the total cell surface-area-to-volume ratio with respect to the exchange of nutrients and waste products.

Compartmentalization also offers two key advantages:

1. Incompatible chemical reactions can be separated. For example, new fatty acids can be synthesized in one organelle while

SUMMARY TABLE 2.1 **How Do the Structures of Prokaryotic and Eukaryotic Cells Differ?**

	Bacteria and Archaea	Eukaryotes
Location of DNA	In nucleoid (not membrane bound); plasmids also common	Inside nucleus (membrane bound); plasmids extremely rare
Internal Membranes and Organelles	Extensive internal membranes only in photosynthetic species; limited types and numbers of organelles	Large numbers of organelles; many types of organelles
Cytoskeleton	Limited in extent, relative to eukaryotes	Extensive—usually found throughout volume of cell
Overall Size	Usually small relative to eukaryotes	Most are larger than prokaryotes

excess or damaged fatty acids are degraded and recycled in a different organelle.

2. Chemical reactions become more efficient. First, the substrates required for particular reactions can be localized and maintained at high concentrations within organelles. Second, if substrates are used up in a particular part of the organelle, they can be replaced by substrates that have only a short distance to diffuse. Third, groups of enzymes that work together can be clustered within or on the membranes of organelles instead of floating free in the cytosol. When the product of one reaction is the substrate for a second reaction catalyzed by another enzyme, clustering the enzymes increases the speed and efficiency of both reaction sequences.

If bacteria and archaea can be compared to small, specialized machine shops, then eukaryotic cells resemble sprawling industrial complexes. The organelles and other structures found in eukaryotes are analogous to highly specialized buildings that act as administrative centers, factories, transportation corridors, waste and recycling facilities, warehouses, and power stations.

When typical prokaryotic and eukaryotic cells are compared, four key differences, identified in **TABLE 2.1**, stand out:

1. Eukaryotic chromosomes are found inside a membrane-bound compartment called the **nucleus.**

2. Eukaryotic cells are often much larger than prokaryotes.

3. Eukaryotic cells contain extensive amounts of internal membrane.

4. Eukaryotic cells feature a particularly diverse and dynamic cytoskeleton.

Eukaryotic Cell Structures: A Parts List

FIGURE 2.6 provides a simplified view of a typical animal cell and a plant cell. The artist has removed most of the cytoskeletal elements

(a) Generalized animal cell

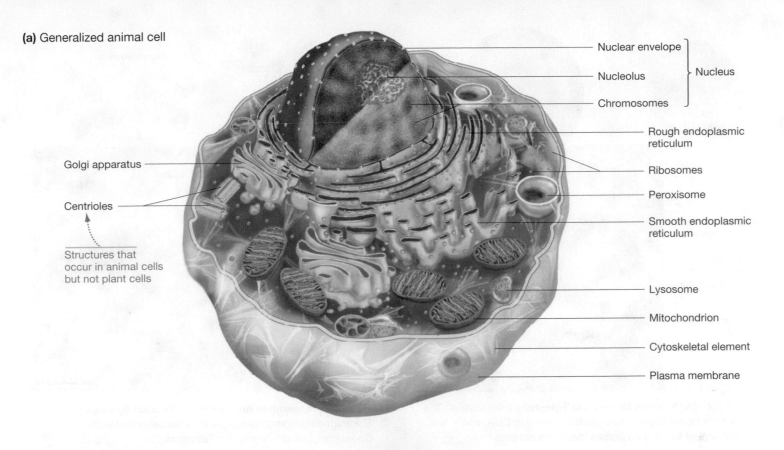

Nuclear envelope ⎤
Nucleolus ⎬ Nucleus
Chromosomes ⎦

Rough endoplasmic reticulum

Ribosomes

Peroxisome

Smooth endoplasmic reticulum

Golgi apparatus

Centrioles

Structures that occur in animal cells but not plant cells

Lysosome

Mitochondrion

Cytoskeletal element

Plasma membrane

(b) Generalized plant cell

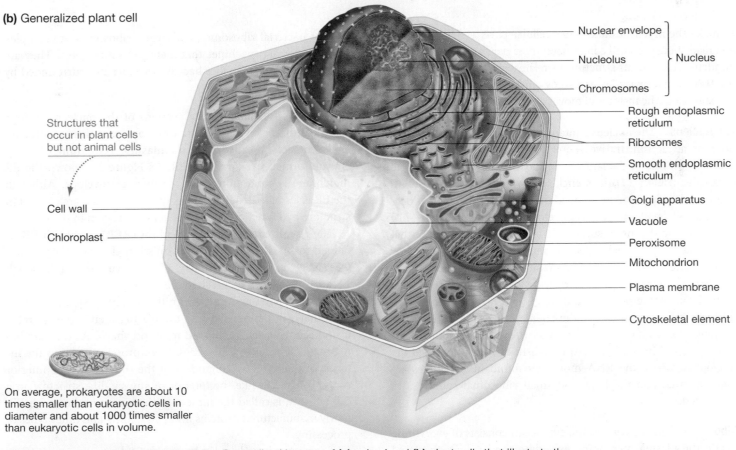

Nuclear envelope ⎤
Nucleolus ⎬ Nucleus
Chromosomes ⎦

Rough endoplasmic reticulum

Ribosomes

Smooth endoplasmic reticulum

Structures that occur in plant cells but not animal cells

Golgi apparatus

Vacuole

Cell wall

Peroxisome

Chloroplast

Mitochondrion

Plasma membrane

Cytoskeletal element

On average, prokaryotes are about 10 times smaller than eukaryotic cells in diameter and about 1000 times smaller than eukaryotic cells in volume.

FIGURE 2.6 Overview of Eukaryotic Cells. Generalized images of **(a)** animal and **(b)** plant cells that illustrate the cellular structures in the "typical" eukaryote. The structures have been color-coded for clarity. Compare with the prokaryotic cell, shown at true relative size at bottom left.

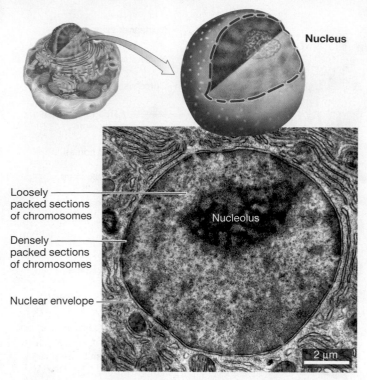

Nucleus

Loosely packed sections of chromosomes

Densely packed sections of chromosomes

Nuclear envelope

Nucleolus

2 µm

FIGURE 2.7 The Nucleus Stores and Transmits Information. The genetic, or hereditary, information is encoded in DNA, which is a component of the chromosomes inside the nucleus.

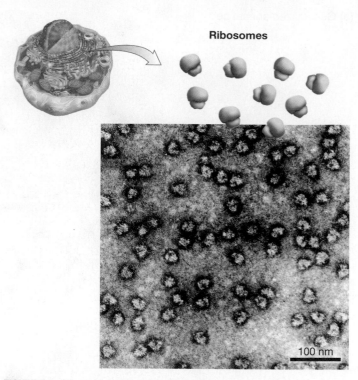

Ribosomes

100 nm

FIGURE 2.8 Ribosomes Are the Site of Protein Synthesis. Eukaryotic ribosomes are larger than bacterial and archaeal ribosomes, but similar in overall structure.

to make the organelles and other cellular parts easier to see. As you read about each cell component in the pages that follow, focus on identifying how its structure correlates with its function. Then use **TABLE 2.2** (see page 29) as a study guide. As with bacterial cells, let's start from the inside and move to the outside.

The Nucleus The nucleus contains the chromosomes and functions as an administrative center for information storage and processing. Among the largest and most highly organized of all organelles (**FIGURE 2.7**), it is enclosed by a unique structure—a complex double membrane called the **nuclear envelope**. As Section 2.4 will detail, the nuclear envelope is studded with pore-like openings, and the inside surface is linked to fibrous proteins that form a lattice-like sheet called the **nuclear lamina**. The nuclear lamina stiffens the structure and maintains its shape.

Chromosomes do not float freely inside the nucleus—instead, each chromosome occupies a distinct area, which may vary in different cell types and over the course of cell replication. The nucleus also contains specific sites where gene products are processed and includes at least one distinctive region called the **nucleolus,** where the RNA molecules found in ribosomes are manufactured and the large and small ribosomal subunits are assembled.

Ribosomes In eukaryotes, the cytoplasm consists of everything inside the plasma membrane excluding the nucleus. Scattered throughout this cytoplasm are millions of ribosomes (**FIGURE 2.8**).

Like bacterial ribosomes, eukaryotic ribosomes are complex macromolecular machines that manufacture proteins. They are not classified as organelles because they are not surrounded by membranes.

Endoplasmic Reticulum The portions of the nuclear envelope extend into the cytoplasm to form an extensive membrane-enclosed factory called the **endoplasmic reticulum** (literally, "inside-formed-network"), or ER. As Figure 2.6 shows, the ER membrane is continuous with the nuclear envelope. Although the ER is a single structure, it has two regions that are distinct in structure and function. Let's consider each region in turn.

The **rough endoplasmic reticulum (RER),** or **rough ER,** is named for its appearance in transmission electron micrographs (see **FIGURE 2.9**, left). The knobby-looking structures in the rough ER are ribosomes that attach to the membrane.

The ribosomes associated with the rough ER synthesize proteins that will be inserted into the plasma membrane, secreted to the cell exterior, or shipped to an organelle. As they are being manufactured by ribosomes, these proteins move to the interior of the sac-like component of the rough ER. The interior of the rough ER, like the interior of any sac-like structure in a cell or body, is called the **lumen.** In the lumen of the rough ER, newly manufactured proteins undergo folding and other types of processing.

The proteins produced in the rough ER have a variety of functions. Some carry messages to other cells; some act as membrane

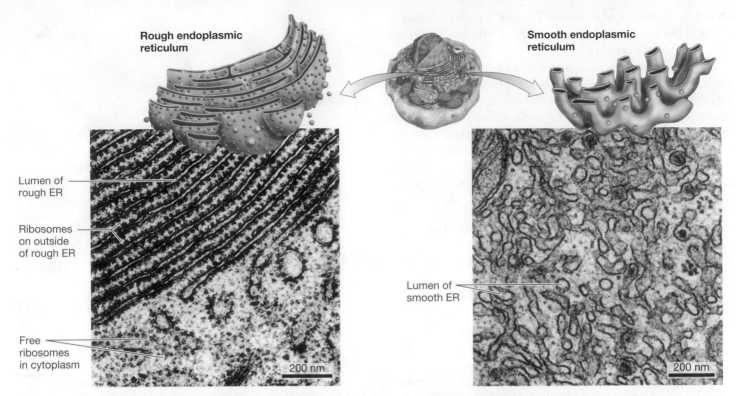

Rough endoplasmic reticulum

Smooth endoplasmic reticulum

Lumen of rough ER

Ribosomes on outside of rough ER

Free ribosomes in cytoplasm

200 nm

Lumen of smooth ER

200 nm

FIGURE 2.9 The Endoplasmic Reticulum Is a Site of Synthesis, Processing, and Storage. The ER is continuous with the nuclear envelope and possesses two distinct regions: on the left, the rough ER is a system of membrane-bound sacs and tubules with ribosomes attached; on the right, the smooth ER is a system of membrane-bound sacs and tubules that lacks ribosomes.

transport proteins or pumps; others are enzymes. The common theme is that many of the rough ER products are packaged into vesicles and transported to various distant destinations—often to the surface of the cell or beyond.

In electron micrographs, parts of the ER that are free of ribosomes appear smooth and even. Appropriately, these parts of the ER are called the **smooth endoplasmic reticulum (SER)**, or **smooth ER** (see **FIGURE 2.9**, right).

The smooth ER contains enzymes that catalyze reactions involving lipids. Depending on the type of cell, these enzymes may synthesize lipids needed by the organism or break down lipids and other molecules that are poisonous. For example, the smooth ER is the manufacturing site for phospholipids used in plasma membranes. In addition, the smooth ER functions as a reservoir for calcium ions (Ca^{2+}) that act as a signal triggering a wide array of activities inside the cell.

The structure of the endoplasmic reticulum correlates closely with its function. The rough ER has ribosomes and functions primarily as a protein-manufacturing center; the smooth ER lacks ribosomes and functions primarily as a lipid-processing center.

Golgi Apparatus In many cases, the products of the rough ER pass through the Golgi apparatus before they reach their final destination. The **Golgi apparatus** consists of discrete flattened, membranous sacs called **cisternae** (singular: **cisterna**), which are stacked on top of one another (**FIGURE 2.10**). The organelle also

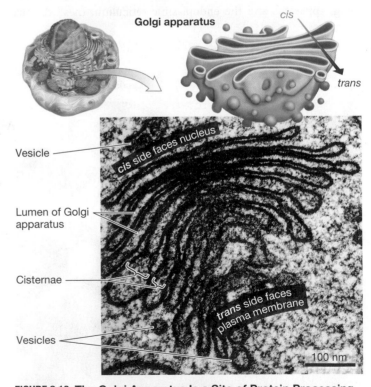

Golgi apparatus

cis

trans

Vesicle

cis side faces nucleus

Lumen of Golgi apparatus

Cisternae

trans side faces plasma membrane

Vesicles

100 nm

FIGURE 2.10 The Golgi Apparatus Is a Site of Protein Processing, Sorting, and Shipping. The Golgi apparatus is a collection of flattened vesicles called cisternae.

has a distinct polarity, or sidedness. The *cis* ("this side") surface is closest to the nucleus, and the *trans* ("across") surface is oriented toward the plasma membrane.

The *cis* side of a Golgi apparatus receives products from the rough ER, and the *trans* side ships them out to other organelles or the cell surface. In between, within the cisternae, the rough ER's products are processed and packaged for delivery. Micrographs often show "bubbles" on either side of the Golgi stack. These are membrane-bound vesicles that carry proteins or other products to and from the organelle. Section 2.5 analyzes the intracellular movement of molecules from the rough ER to the Golgi apparatus and beyond in more detail.

Lysosomes Animal cells contain organelles called **lysosomes** that function as recycling centers (**FIGURE 2.11**). Lysosomes contain about 40 different enzymes, each specialized for hydrolyzing different types of macromolecules—proteins, nucleic acids, lipids, or carbohydrates. The amino acids, nucleotides, sugars, and other molecules that result from acid hydrolysis leave the lysosome via transport proteins in the organelle's membrane. Once in the cytosol, they can be used as sources of energy or building blocks for new molecules.

These digestive enzymes are collectively called acid hydrolases because under acidic conditions (pH of 5.0), they use water to break monomers from macromolecules. In the cytosol, where the pH is about 7.2, acid hydrolases are less active. Proton pumps in the lysosomal membrane maintain an acidic pH in the lumen of the lysosome by importing hydrogen ions.

Even though lysosomes are physically separated from the Golgi apparatus and the endoplasmic reticulum, these various

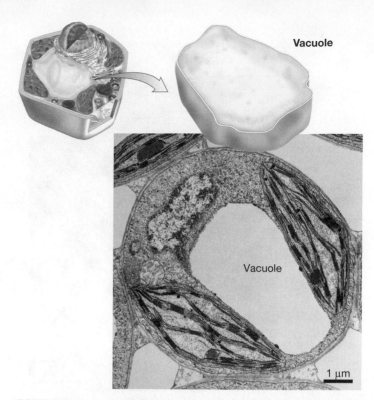

Vacuole

Vacuole

1 μm

FIGURE 2.12 Vacuoles Are Generally Storage Centers in Plant and Fungal Cells. Vacuoles vary in size and function. Some contain digestive enzymes and serve as recycling centers; most are large storage containers.

✔**QUESTION** Why are toxins like nicotine, cocaine, and caffeine stored in vacuoles instead of the cytosol?

organelles jointly form a key functional grouping referred to as the **endomembrane system.** The endomembrane ("inner-membrane") system is a center for producing, processing, and transporting proteins and lipids in eukaryotic cells. For example, acid hydrolases are synthesized in the ER, processed in the Golgi, and then shipped to the lysosome.

Vacuoles The cells of plants, fungi, and certain other groups lack lysosomes. Instead, they contain a prominent organelle called a vacuole. Compared with the lysosomes of animal cells, the **vacuoles** of plant and fungal cells are large—sometimes taking up as much as 80 percent of a plant cell's volume (**FIGURE 2.12**).

Although some vacuoles contain enzymes that are specialized for digestion, most of the vacuoles observed in plant and fungal cells act as storage depots. In many cases, ions such as potassium (K^+) and chloride (Cl^-), among other solutes, are stored at such high concentrations they draw water in from the environment. As the vacuole expands in volume, the cytoplasm pushes the plasma membrane against the cell wall, which maintains the plant cell's shape. In other cells, vacuoles have more specialized storage functions:

- Inside seeds, cells may contain a large vacuole filled with proteins. When the embryonic plant inside the seed begins to grow, enzymes begin digesting these proteins to provide amino acids for the growing individual.

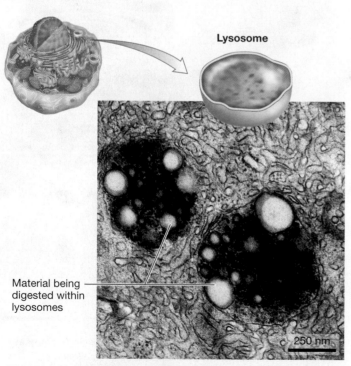

Lysosome

Material being digested within lysosomes

250 nm

FIGURE 2.11 Lysosomes Are Recycling Centers. Lysosomes are usually oval or globular and have a single membrane.

- In cells that make up flower petals or fruits, vacuoles are filled with colorful pigments.

- Elsewhere, vacuoles may be packed with noxious compounds that protect leaves and stems from being eaten by predators. The type of chemical involved varies by species, ranging from bitter-tasting tannins to toxins such as nicotine, morphine, caffeine, or cocaine.

Peroxisomes Virtually all eukaryotic cells contain globular organelles called **peroxisomes** (**FIGURE 2.13**). These organelles have a single membrane and originate as buds from the ER.

Although different types of cells from the same individual may have distinct types of peroxisomes, these organelles all share a common function: Peroxisomes are centers for reduction–oxidation (redox) reactions. (Chapter 10 explains in detail how redox reactions transfer electrons between atoms and molecules.) For example, the peroxisomes in your liver cells contain enzymes that remove electrons from, or oxidize, the ethanol in alcoholic beverages.

Different types of peroxisomes contain different suites of redox enzymes. In the leaves of plants, specialized peroxisomes called **glyoxysomes** are packed with enzymes that oxidize fats to form a compound that can be used to store energy for the cell. But plant seeds have a different type of peroxisome—one that is packed with enzymes responsible for releasing energy from stored fatty acids. The young plant uses this energy as it begins to grow.

In animals and plants, the products of these reactions often include hydrogen peroxide (H_2O_2), which is highly reactive.

If hydrogen peroxide escaped from the peroxisome, it would quickly react with and damage DNA, proteins, and cellular membranes. This event is rare, however, because inside the peroxisome, the enzyme catalase quickly "detoxifies" hydrogen peroxide by catalyzing its oxidation to form water and oxygen. The enzymes found inside the peroxisome make a specialized set of oxidation reactions possible and safe for the cell.

Mitochondria The energy required to build these organelles and do other types of work comes from adenosine triphosphate (ATP), most of which is produced in the cell's **mitochondria** (singular: **mitochondrion**).

As **FIGURE 2.14** shows, each mitochondrion has two membranes. The outer membrane defines the organelle's surface, while the inner membrane is connected to a series of sac-like **cristae.** The solution enclosed within the inner membrane is called the **mitochondrial matrix.** In eukaryotes, most of the enzymes and molecular machines responsible for synthesizing ATP are embedded in the membranes of the cristae or suspended in the matrix (see Chapter 13). Depending on the type of cell, from 50 to more than a million mitochondria may be present.

Each mitochondrion has many copies of a small, circular chromosome that is independent of the nuclear chromosomes. This mitochondrial DNA contains only around 37 genes in most eukaryotes—most of the genes responsible for the function of the organelle reside in the nuclear DNA.

Among the genes present in mitochondrial DNA are those that encode RNAs for mitochondrial ribosomes. These ribosomes are

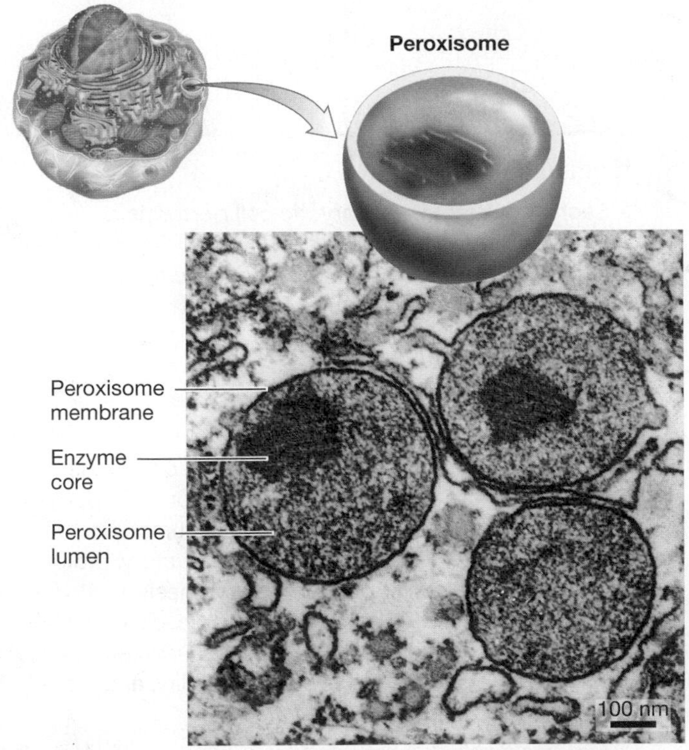

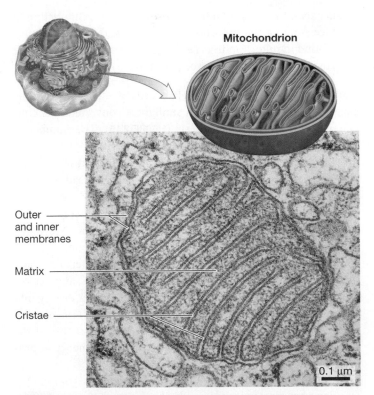

Peroxisome

Peroxisome membrane

Enzyme core

Peroxisome lumen

100 nm

FIGURE 2.13 Peroxisomes Are the Site of Oxidation Reactions. Peroxisomes are globular organelles that are defined by a single membrane.

Mitochondrion

Outer and inner membranes

Matrix

Cristae

0.1 μm

FIGURE 2.14 Mitochondria Are Power-Generating Stations. Mitochondria vary in size and shape, but all have a double membrane with sac-like cristae inside.

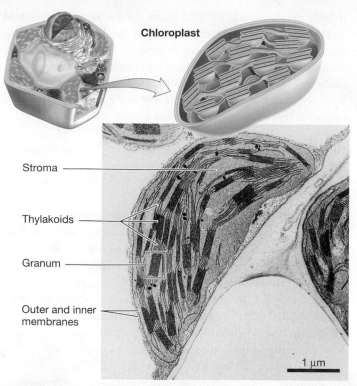

Chloroplast

Stroma

Thylakoids

Granum

Outer and inner
membranes

1 µm

FIGURE 2.15 Chloroplasts Are Sugar-Manufacturing Centers in Plants and Algae. Many of the enzymes and other molecules required for photosynthesis are located in membranes inside the chloroplast. These membranes form thylakoids that consist of discs stacked into grana.

smaller than those found in the cytosol, yet they still function to produce some of the mitochondrial proteins. (Most of the proteins found in mitochondria are produced from ribosomes in the cytosol and imported into the organelle.)

Chloroplasts   Most algal and plant cells possess an organelle called the **chloroplast,** in which sunlight is converted to chemical energy during photosynthesis (**FIGURE 2.15**). The number of chloroplasts per cell varies from none to several dozen.

The chloroplast has a double membrane around its exterior, analogous to the structure of a mitochondrion. Instead of featuring sac-like cristae that connect to the inner membrane, though, the interior of the chloroplast is dominated by a network of hundreds of membrane-bound, flattened, sac-like structures called **thylakoids,** which are independent of the inner membrane.

Thylakoids have stacks, like pancakes, that are called **grana** (singular: **granum**). Many of the pigments, enzymes, and macromolecular machines responsible for converting light energy into chemical energy are embedded in the thylakoid membranes (see Chapter 14). The region outside the thylakoids, called the **stroma,** contains enzymes that use this chemical energy to produce sugars.

Like mitochondria, each chloroplast contains copies of a circular chromosome and small ribosomes that manufacture some, but not all, of the organelle's proteins. Both mitochondria

and chloroplasts also grow and divide independently of cell division through a process that resembles bacterial fission (see Chapter 4).

These attributes are odd compared with those of the other organelles and have led biologists to propose that mitochondria and chloroplasts were once free-living bacteria. According to the **endosymbiosis theory,** the ancestors of modern eukaryotes ingested these bacteria, but instead of destroying them, established a mutually beneficial relationship with them.

Cytoskeleton   The final major structural feature that is common to all eukaryotic cells is the cytoskeleton, an extensive system of protein fibers. In addition to giving the cell its shape and structural stability, cytoskeletal proteins are involved in moving the cell itself and moving materials within the cell. In essence, the cytoskeleton organizes all the organelles and other cellular structures into a cohesive whole. Section 2.6 will analyze the structure and functions of the cytoskeleton in detail.

The Cell Wall   In fungi, algae, and plants, cells possess an outer cell wall in addition to their plasma membrane. The cell wall is located outside the plasma membrane and furnishes a durable, outer layer that provides structural support for the cell. The cells of animals, amoebae, and other groups lack a cell wall—their exterior surface consists of the plasma membrane only.

Although the composition of the cell wall varies among species and even among types of cells in the same individual, the general plan is similar: Rods or fibers composed of a carbohydrate run through a stiff matrix made of other polysaccharides and proteins.

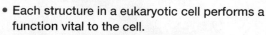
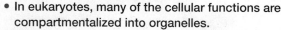

check your understanding

 If you understand that . . .

- Each structure in a eukaryotic cell performs a function vital to the cell.
- In eukaryotes, many of the cellular functions are compartmentalized into organelles.

✔ **You should be able to . . .**

1. Explain how the structure of lysosomes and peroxisomes correlates with their function.

2. In Table 2.2, label each component with one of the following roles: administrative/information hub, power station, warehouse, large molecule manufacturing and shipping facility (with subtitles for lipid factory, protein finishing and shipping line, protein synthesis and folding center, waste processing and recycling center), support beams, perimeter fencing with secured gates, protein factory, food-manufacturing facility, and fatty-acid processing and detox center.

Answers are available in Appendix A.

SUMMARY TABLE 2.2 Eukaryotic Cell Components

Icons Not to Scale		Structure		Function
		Membrane	Components	
	Nucleus	Double ("envelope"); openings called nuclear pores	Chromosomes Nucleolus Nuclear lamina	Information storage and transmission Ribosome subunit assembly Structural support
	Ribosomes	None	Complex of RNA and proteins	Protein synthesis
	Endomembrane system			
	Endoplasmic reticulum: rough	Single; contains receptors for entry of selected proteins	Network of branching sacs Ribosomes associated	Protein synthesis and processing
	Endoplasmic reticulum: smooth	Single; contains enzymes for synthesizing phospholipids	Network of branching sacs Enzymes for synthesizing or breaking down lipids	Lipid synthesis and processing
	Golgi apparatus	Single; contains receptors for products of rough ER	Stack of flattened, distinct cisternae	Protein, lipid, and carbohydrate processing
	Lysosomes	Single; contains proton pumps	Acid hydrolases (catalyze hydrolysis reactions)	Digestion and recycling
	Vacuoles	Single; contains transporters for selected molecules	Varies—pigments, oils, carbohydrates, water, or toxins	Varies—coloration, storage of oils, carbohydrates, water, or toxins
	Peroxisomes	Single; contains transporters for selected macromolecules	Enzymes that catalyze oxidation reactions Catalase (processes peroxide)	Oxidation of fatty acids, ethanol, or other compounds
	Mitochondria	Double; inner contains enzymes for ATP production	Enzymes that harvest energy from molecules to make ATP	ATP production
	Chloroplasts	Double; plus membrane-bound sacs in interior	Pigments Enzymes that use light energy to make sugars	Production of sugars via photosynthesis
	Cytoskeleton	None	Actin filaments Intermediate filaments Microtubules	Structural support; movement of materials; in some species, movement of whole cell
	Plasma membrane	Single; contains transport and receptor proteins	Phospholipid bilayer with transport and receptor proteins	Selective permeability—maintains intracellular environment
	Cell wall	None	Carbohydrate fibers running through carbohydrate or protein matrix	Protection, structural support

2.3 Putting the Parts into a Whole

Within a cell, the structure of each component correlates with its function. In the same way, the overall size, shape, and composition of a cell correlate with its function.

Cells might be analogous to machine shops or industrial complexes, but clothing manufacturing centers are very different in layout and composition from airplane production facilities. How does the physical and chemical makeup of a cell correlate with its function?

Structure and Function at the Whole-Cell Level

Inside an individual plant or animal, cells are specialized for certain tasks and have a structure that correlates with those tasks. For example, the muscle cells in your upper leg are extremely long, tube-shaped structures. They are filled with protein fibers that slide past one another as the entire muscle flexes or relaxes. It is this sliding motion that allows your muscles to contract or extend as you run. Muscle cells are also packed with mitochondria, which produce the ATP required for the sliding motion to occur.

In contrast, nearby fat cells are rounded, globular structures that store fatty acids. They consist of little more than a plasma membrane, a nucleus, and a fat droplet. Neither cell bears a close resemblance to the generalized animal cell pictured in Figure 2.6a.

To drive home the correlation between the overall structure and function of a cell, examine the transmission electron micrographs in **FIGURE 2.16**.

- The animal cell in Figure 2.16a, located in the pancreas, manufactures and exports digestive enzymes. It is packed with rough ER and Golgi, which make these functions possible.

- The animal cell in Figure 2.16b, from the testis, synthesizes and exports the steroid hormone testosterone—a lipid-soluble signal. This cell is dominated by smooth ER, where processing of steroids and other lipids takes place.

- The plant cell in Figure 2.16c, from the leaf of a potato, has hundreds of chloroplasts and is specialized for absorbing light and manufacturing sugar.

- The animal cells in Figure 2.16d come from brown fat. The cells have numerous mitochondria that have been altered so they convert energy stored in fat into heat instead of ATP.

In each case, the types of organelles in each cell and their size and number correlate with the cell's specialized function.

The Dynamic Cell

Biologists study the structure and function of organelles and cells with a combination of tools and approaches. For several decades, a technique called **differential centrifugation** was particularly important because it allowed researchers to isolate particular cell components and analyze their chemical composition. Differential centrifugation is based on breaking cells apart to create a complex mixture and separating components in a centrifuge (see **BioSkills 10** in Appendix B). The individual parts of the cell

(a) Animal pancreatic cell: Exports digestive enzymes.

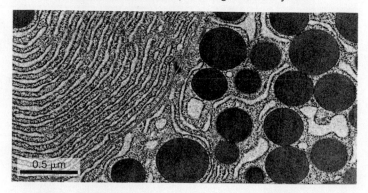

(b) Animal testis cell: Exports lipid-soluble signals.

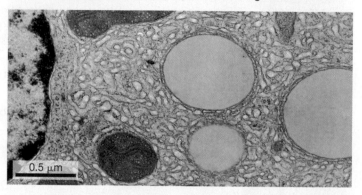

(c) Plant leaf cell: Manufactures ATP and sugar.

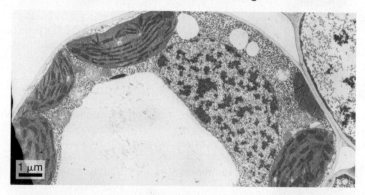

(d) Brown fat cells: Burn fat to generate heat in lieu of ATP.

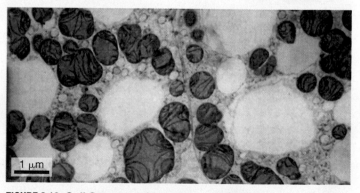

FIGURE 2.16 Cell Structure Correlates with Function.

✓**EXERCISE** In part (a), label the rough ER and the dark, round secretory vesicles. In (b), label the smooth ER. In (c), label the chloroplasts, vacuole, and nucleus. In (d), label the mitochondria.

can then be purified and studied in detail, in isolation from other parts of the cell.

Historically and currently, however, the most important research in cell biology is based on imaging—simply looking at cells. Recent innovations allow biologists to put fluorescing tags or other types of markers on particular cell components and then look at them with increasingly sophisticated light microscopes and electron microscopes. Advances in microscopy provide increasingly high magnification and better resolution.

It's important to recognize, though, that some of these techniques have limitations. Differential centrifugation splits cells into parts that are analyzed independently, and electron microscopy gives a fixed "snapshot" of the cell or organisms being observed. Neither technique allows investigators to explore directly how things move from place to place in the cell or how parts interact. The information gleaned from these techniques can make cells seem static. In reality, cells are dynamic.

The amount of chemical activity and the speed of molecular movement inside cells are nothing short of fantastic. Bacterial ribosomes add up to 20 amino acids per second to a growing polypeptide, and eukaryotic ribosomes typically add 2 per second. Given that there are about 15,000 ribosomes in each bacterium and possibly a million in an average eukaryotic cell, hundreds or even thousands of new protein molecules can be produced each second in every cell. Here are some other remarkable cellular feats:

- In an average second, a typical cell in your body uses an average of 10 million ATP molecules and synthesizes just as many.

- It's not unusual for a cellular enzyme to catalyze 25,000 or more reactions per second; most cells contain hundreds or thousands of different enzymes.

- A minute is more than enough time for each membrane phospholipid in your body to travel the breadth of the organelle or cell where it resides.

- The hundreds of trillions of mitochondria inside you are completely replaced about every 10 days, for as long as you live.

Because humans are such large organisms, it's impossible for us to imagine what life is really like inside a cell. At the scale of a ribosome or an organelle or a cell, gravity is inconsequential. Instead, the dominant forces are the charge- or polarity-based electrostatic attractions between molecules and their energy of motion. At this level, events take nanoseconds, and speeds are measured in micrometers per second. This is the speed of life.

Contemporary methods for studying cells (including some of the imaging techniques featured in **BioSkills 11** in Appendix B) capture this dynamism by tracking how organelles and molecules move and interact over time. The ability to digitize video images of live cells, or take time-lapse photographs of living cells, is allowing researchers to see and study dynamic processes.

The rest of this chapter focuses on this theme of cellular dynamism and movement. Its goal is to put some of the individual pieces of a cell together and ask how they work as systems to accomplish key tasks.

To begin, let's first look at how molecules move into and out of the cell's control center—the nucleus—and then consider how proteins move from ribosomes into the lumen of the rough ER and then to the Golgi apparatus and beyond. The chapter closes by introducing the cytoskeletal elements and their associated motor proteins and how they are used to transport cargo inside the cell or move the cell itself.

2.4 Cell Systems I: Nuclear Transport

The nucleus is the information center of eukaryotic cells—a corporate headquarters, design center, and library all rolled into one. Appropriately enough, its interior is highly organized.

The organelle's overall shape and structure are defined by the mesh-like nuclear lamina. The nuclear lamina provides an attachment point for the chromosomes, each of which occupies a well-defined region in the nucleus.

In addition, specific centers exist where the genetic information in DNA is decoded and processed. At these locations, large suites of enzymes interact to produce RNA messages from specific genes at specific times. Meanwhile, the nucleolus functions as the site of ribosome assembly.

Structure and Function of the Nuclear Envelope

The nuclear envelope separates the nucleus from the rest of the cell. Starting in the 1950s, transmission electron micrographs of cross sections through the nuclear envelope showed that the structure is supported by the fibrous nuclear lamina and bounded by two membranes, each consisting of a lipid bilayer. How does this administrative center communicate with the rest of the cell across the double membrane barrier?

Micrographs like the one in **FIGURE 2.17** (see page 32) show that the nuclear envelope is broken with openings, approximately 60 nanometers (nm) in diameter, called **nuclear pores.** Because these pores extend through both the inner and outer nuclear membranes, they connect the inside of the nucleus with the cytosol. Follow-up research showed that each pore consists of over 50 different proteins. As the diagram on the right side of Figure 2.17 shows, these protein molecules form an elaborate structure called the **nuclear pore complex.**

What substances traverse nuclear pores? Chromosomal DNA clearly does not—it remains in the nucleus as long as the nuclear envelope remains intact. But DNA is used to synthesize RNA inside the nucleus, most of which is exported through nuclear pores to the cytoplasm.

Several types of RNA molecules are produced, each distinguished by size and function. For example, **ribosomal RNAs** are manufactured in the nucleolus, where they bind to proteins to form ribosomes. Molecules called **messenger RNAs (mRNA)** carry the information required to manufacture proteins. Both the newly assembled ribosomes and the mRNAs must be transported from the nucleus to the cytoplasm, where protein synthesis takes place.

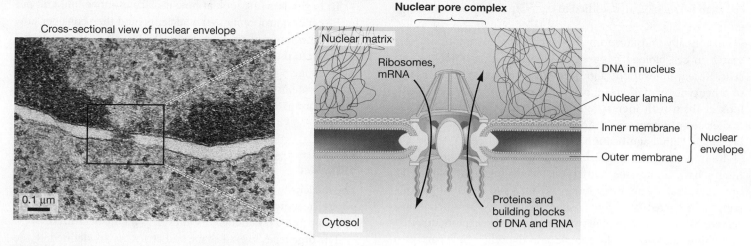

Cross-sectional view of nuclear envelope

Nuclear pore complex

Nuclear matrix

Ribosomes, mRNA

DNA in nucleus

Nuclear lamina

Inner membrane

Outer membrane

Nuclear envelope

0.1 μm

Proteins and building blocks of DNA and RNA

Cytosol

FIGURE 2.17 Structure of the Nuclear Envelope and Nuclear Pore Complex.

Inbound traffic is also impressive. Nucleoside triphosphates that act as building blocks for DNA and RNA enter the nucleus, as do a variety of proteins responsible for copying DNA, synthesizing RNAs, extending the nuclear lamina, or assembling ribosomes.

To summarize, ribosomal subunits and various types of RNAs exit the nucleus; nucleotides and certain proteins enter it. In a typical cell, over 500 molecules pass through each of the 3000–4000 nuclear pores every second. The scale of traffic through the nuclear pores is mind-boggling. How is it regulated and directed?

Experiments in the early 1960s showed that size matters in the passage of molecules through nuclear pores. This conclusion was based on the results from injecting tiny gold particles that varied in diameter and tracking their movement across the pores. In electron micrographs, gold particles show up as defined black dots that can be easily distinguished from cellular structures. Immediately after injection, most of the gold particles were observed in the cytoplasm, and only a few were closely associated with nuclear pores. Ten minutes after injection, only the small particles (< 12.5 nm in diameter) appeared to be distributed throughout both the nucleus and the cytoplasm, and the larger particles were excluded from entering the nucleus.

The fact that the pore opening is almost 5 times larger than this 12.5-nm size limit supports the hypothesis that the nuclear pore complex serves as a gate to control passage through the envelope. If this is the case, then what is required to open these gates so that proteins larger than the size limit, like those responsible for replicating DNA, may pass?

How Do Large Molecules Enter the Nucleus?

It was clear to researchers that size was not the sole factor in selective transport across the nuclear envelope. Certain proteins were concentrated in the nucleus, while others were completely excluded—even if they were similar in size.

A series of experiments on a protein called nucleoplasmin helped researchers understand the nature of nuclear import. Nucleoplasmin is strictly found in the nucleus and plays an important role in the assembly of chromatin. When researchers labeled nucleoplasmin with a radioactive atom and injected it into the cytoplasm of living cells, they found that the radioactive protein was quickly concentrated into the nucleus. Is there a "send-to-nucleus" signal within the nucleoplasmin protein that is responsible for this directed transport?

As shown in **FIGURE 2.18**, the distinctive structure of nucleoplasmin was used to further investigate this process. First, researchers used enzymes called proteases to cleave the core sections of nucleoplasmin from the tails. After separating the tails from the core fragments, they labeled each component with radioactive atoms and injected them into the cytoplasm of different cells.

At various times after the injections, researchers examined the nuclei and cytoplasm of the cells to track down the radioactive label. The results were striking. They found that tail fragments were rapidly transported from the cytoplasm into the nucleus. Core fragments, in contrast, were not allowed to pass through the nuclear envelope and remained in the cytoplasm.

These data led to a key hypothesis: Nuclear proteins are synthesized by ribosomes in the cytosol and contain a "zip code"—a molecular address tag—that marks them for transport through the nuclear pore complex. This zip code allows the nuclear pore complex to open in some way that permits larger proteins and RNA molecules to pass through.

By analyzing different stretches of the tail, the biologists eventually found a 17-amino-acid-long section that had to be present to direct nucleoplasmin to the nucleus. Follow-up work confirmed that other proteins bound for the nucleus, even those expressed by some viruses, have similar amino acid sequences directing their transport. This common sequence came to be called the **nuclear localization signal (NLS)**. Proteins that leave the nucleus have a different signal, required for nuclear export.

QUESTION: Does the nucleoplasmin protein contain a "Send to nucleus" signal?

HYPOTHESIS: Nucleoplasmin contains a discrete "Send to nucleus" signal that resides in either the tail or core region.

NULL HYPOTHESIS: Nucleoplasmin does not require a signal to enter the nucleus, or the entire protein serves as the signal.

EXPERIMENTAL SETUP:

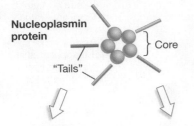

Nucleoplasmin protein

Core

"Tails"

1. Use protease to cleave tails off of nucleoplasmin protein core.

Labeled tails

Labeled cores

2. Attach radioactive labels to protein tails and cores.

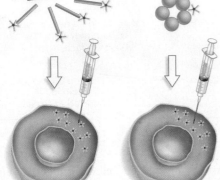

3. Inject labeled tails and cores into cytoplasm of different cells.

4. Wait, then locate labeled fragments ....

PREDICTION:

PREDICTION OF NULL HYPOTHESIS:

RESULTS:

Labeled tail fragments **located in nucleus**

Labeled core fragments still **located in cytoplasm**

CONCLUSION:

FIGURE 2.18 Does the Nucleoplasmin Protein Contain a "Send to Nucleus" Signal?

SOURCES: Mills, A. D., R. A. Laskey, P. Black, et al. 1980. *Journal of Molecular Biology* 139: 561–568; Dingwall, C., S. V. Sharnick, and R. A. Laskey. 1982. *Cell* 30: 449–458.

✔**EXERCISE** Without looking at the text, fill in the prediction(s) and conclusion(s) in this experiment.

More recent research has shown that the movement of proteins and other large molecules into and out of the nucleus is an energy-demanding process that involves special transport proteins. These nuclear transport proteins function like trucks that haul cargo into or out of the nucleus through the nuclear pore complex, depending on whether they have an import or export zip code. Currently, biologists are trying to unravel how all this traffic in and out of the nucleus is regulated to avoid backups and head-on collisions.

✔ If you understand the process of nuclear transport, you should be able to compare and contrast the movement of (1) nucleotides and (2) large proteins through the nuclear pore complex. Which would you expect to require the input of energy?

2.5 Cell Systems II: The Endomembrane System Manufactures, Ships, and Recycles Cargo

The nuclear membrane is not the only place in cells where cargo moves in a regulated and energy-demanding fashion. Most of the proteins found in peroxisomes, mitochondria, and chloroplasts are also actively imported from the cytosol. These proteins contain special signal sequences, like the nuclear localization signal, that target them to the appropriate organelles.

If you think about it for a moment, the need to sort proteins and ship them to specific destinations should be clear. Proteins are produced by ribosomes that are either free in the cytosol or on the surface of the ER. Many of these proteins must be transported to a compartment inside the eukaryotic cell. Acid hydrolases must be shipped to lysosomes and catalase to peroxisomes. To get to the right location, each protein has to have an address tag and a transport and delivery system.

To get a better understanding of protein sorting and transport in eukaryotic cells, let's consider perhaps the most intricate of all manufacturing and shipping complexes: the endomembrane system. In this system, proteins that are synthesized in the rough ER move to the Golgi apparatus for processing, and from there they travel to the cell surface or other destinations.

Studying the Pathway through the Endomembrane System

The idea that materials move through the endomembrane system in an orderly way was inspired by a simple observation. According to electron micrographs, cells that secrete digestive enzymes, hormones, or other products have particularly large amounts of rough ER and Golgi. This correlation led to the idea that these organelles may participate in a "secretory pathway" that starts in the rough ER and ends with products leaving the cell (**FIGURE 2.19**, see page 34). How does this hypothesized pathway work?

Tracking Protein Movement via Pulse–Chase Assay George Palade and colleagues did pioneering research on the secretory

FIGURE 2.19 **The Secretory Pathway Hypothesis.** The secretory pathway hypothesis proposes that proteins intended for secretion from the cell are synthesized and processed in a highly prescribed series of steps. Note that proteins are packaged into vesicles when they move from the RER to the Golgi and from the Golgi to the cell surface.

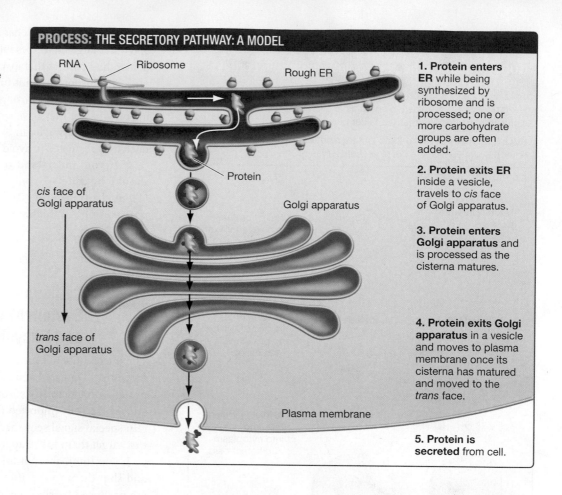

PROCESS: THE SECRETORY PATHWAY: A MODEL

RNA   Ribosome   Rough ER

Protein

cis face of Golgi apparatus

Golgi apparatus

trans face of Golgi apparatus

Plasma membrane

1. **Protein enters ER** while being synthesized by ribosome and is processed; one or more carbohydrate groups are often added.

2. **Protein exits ER** inside a vesicle, travels to *cis* face of Golgi apparatus.

3. **Protein enters Golgi apparatus** and is processed as the cisterna matures.

4. **Protein exits Golgi apparatus** in a vesicle and moves to plasma membrane once its cisterna has matured and moved to the *trans* face.

5. **Protein is secreted** from cell.

pathway using a **pulse–chase experiment** to track protein movement. This strategy is based on two steps:

1. *The "Pulse"* Expose experimental cells to a high concentration of a modified amino acid for a short time. For example, if a cell is briefly exposed to a large amount of radioactively labeled amino acid, virtually all the proteins synthesized during that interval will be radiolabeled.

2. *The "Chase"* The pulse ends by washing away the modified amino acid and replacing it with the normal version of the same molecule. The time following the end of the pulse is referred to as the chase. If the chase consists of unlabeled amino acid, then the proteins synthesized during the chase period will *not* be radiolabeled.

The idea is to mark a population of molecules at a particular interval and then follow their fate over time. This approach is analogous to adding a small amount of dye to a stream and then following the movement of the dye molecules.

To understand why the chase is necessary in these experiments, imagine what would happen if you added dye to a stream continuously. Soon the entire stream would be dyed—you could no longer tell where a specific population of dye molecules were moving.

In testing the secretory pathway hypothesis, Palade's team focused on pancreatic cells that were growing in **culture,** or in vitro.[1] These cells are specialized for secreting digestive enzymes into the small intestine and are packed with rough ER and Golgi.

The basic experimental approach was to pulse the cell culture for 3 minutes with a radiolabeled version of the amino acid leucine, followed by a long chase with nonradioactive leucine (**FIGURE 2.20a**). The pulse produced a population of proteins that were related to one another by the timing of their synthesis. At different points during the chase, the researchers tracked the movement of these proteins by preparing samples of the cells for autoradiography and electron microscopy (see **BioSkills 10** and **11** in Appendix B). The drawings in **FIGURE 2.20b** illustrate what the researchers would have seen in micrographs taken at different times before and after the start of the chase.

Results of the Pulse–Chase Experiment The graph in Figure 2.20b was based on the electron microscopy results, which showed that proteins are trafficked through the secretory pathway in a highly organized and directed manner. Track the movement of proteins through the cell during the chase by covering the graph with a piece of paper and then slowly sliding it off from

[1]The term in vitro is Latin for "in glass." Experiments that are performed outside living organisms are done in vitro. The term in vivo, in contrast, is Latin for "in life." Experiments performed with living organisms are done in vivo.

(a) Setup for a pulse-chase experiment

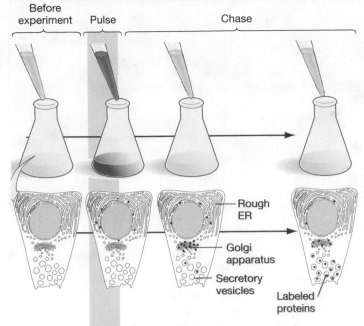

(b) Tracking pulse-labeled proteins during the chase

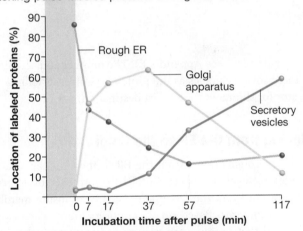

FIGURE 2.20 Tracking Protein Movement in a Pulse–Chase Experiment. Part **(a)** shows how investigators label newly synthesized proteins during the pulse with radioactive amino acids (red). At the start of the chase, this medium is replaced with non-radioactive amino acids (yellow) so only those proteins labeled in the pulse will be tracked. Part **(b)** provides the results of a pulse–chase experiment. The drawings represent micrographs taken that show the radiolabeled proteins (red dots) in the cells. The graph shows the relative abundance of radiolabeled proteins in three different organelles during the chase.

left to right. Notice what is happening to each line at the following three time points:

1. Immediately after the pulse, most of the newly synthesized proteins are inside this cell's rough ER.

2. At 37 minutes into the chase, the situation has changed. Most of the labeled proteins have left the rough ER and entered the

Golgi apparatus, and some of them have accumulated inside structures called secretory vesicles.

3. By the end of the chase, at 117 minutes, most of the labeled proteins have left the Golgi and are either in secretory vesicles or were secreted from the cells.

Over a period of two hours, the labeled population of proteins moved along a defined trail through the rough ER, Golgi apparatus, and secretory vesicles to reach the exterior of the cell. ✔ **QUANTITATIVE** If you understand how the pulse–chase experiment is used to track proteins, use the graph in Figure 2.20b to estimate the time it takes for proteins to pass through the Golgi apparatus.

The results support the hypotheses that a secretory pathway exists and that the rough ER and Golgi apparatus function together as an integrated endomembrane system. Next, let's break this secretory pathway down to examine four of the steps in more detail:

1. How do proteins enter the lumen of the ER?

2. How do the proteins move from the ER to the Golgi apparatus?

3. Once they're inside the Golgi, what happens to them?

4. And finally, how does the Golgi sort out the proteins so each will end up going to the appropriate place?

Entering the Endomembrane System: The Signal Hypothesis

The synthesis of proteins destined to be secreted or embedded in membranes begins in ribosomes free in the cytosol. Günter Blobel and colleagues proposed that at some point these ribosomes become attached to the outside of the ER. But what directs these ribosomes to the ER? The signal hypothesis predicts that proteins bound for the endomembrane system have a molecular zip code analogous to the nuclear localization signal. Blobel proposed that the first few amino acids in the growing polypeptide act as a signal that marks the ribosome for transport to the ER membrane.

This hypothesis received important support when researchers made a puzzling observation: When proteins that are normally synthesized in the rough ER are instead manufactured by isolated ribosomes in vitro—with *no* ER present—they are 20 amino acids longer, on average, than usual.

Blobel seized on these data. He claimed that the extra amino acids are the "send-to-ER" signal, and that the signal is removed inside the organelle. When the same protein is synthesized in vitro, the signal is not removed.

Blobel's group went on to produce convincing data that supported the hypothesis: They identified a sequence of amino acids that will move proteins into the ER lumen, called the **ER signal sequence.**

More recent work has documented the mechanisms responsible for receiving this send-to-ER signal and inserting the

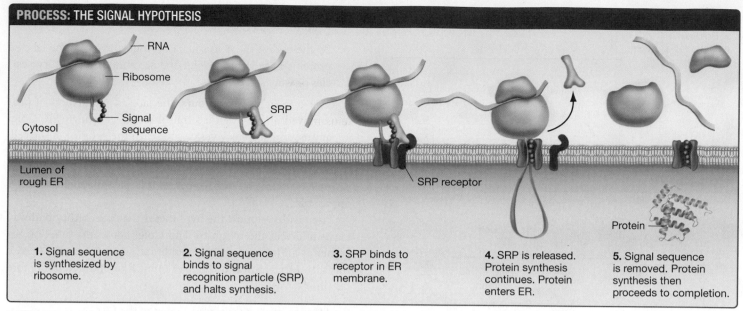

RNA

Ribosome

Signal sequence

Cytosol

SRP

Lumen of rough ER

SRP receptor

Protein

1. Signal sequence is synthesized by ribosome.

2. Signal sequence binds to signal recognition particle (SRP) and halts synthesis.

3. SRP binds to receptor in ER membrane.

4. SRP is released. Protein synthesis continues. Protein enters ER.

5. Signal sequence is removed. Protein synthesis then proceeds to completion.

FIGURE 2.21 The Signal Hypothesis Explains How Proteins Destined for Secretion Enter the Endomembrane System. According to the signal hypothesis, proteins destined for secretion contain a short stretch of amino acids that interact with a signal recognition particle (SRP) in the cytoplasm. This interaction directs the synthesis of the remaining protein into the ER.

protein into the rough ER. **FIGURE 2.21** illustrates the key steps involved.

Step 1 Protein synthesis begins on a free ribosome in the cytosol. The ribosome synthesizes the ER signal sequence.

Step 2 The signal sequence binds to a **signal recognition particle (SRP)**—a complex of RNA and protein. The attached SRP causes protein synthesis to stop.

Step 3 The ribosome + signal sequence + SRP complex moves to the ER membrane, where it attaches to the SRP receptor. Think of the SRP as a key that is activated by an ER signal sequence. The SRP receptor in the ER membrane is the lock.

Step 4 Once the lock (the receptor) and key (the SRP) connect, the SRP is released and protein synthesis continues.

Step 5 The growing protein is fed into the ER lumen through a channel, and the signal sequence is removed.

If the protein will eventually be shipped to the inside of an organelle or secreted from the cell, it is completely transferred into the lumen of the rough ER. If it is an integral membrane protein, part of it remains in the cytosol and rough ER membrane while it is being processed.

Once proteins are inside the rough ER or inserted into its membrane, they fold into their three-dimensional shape with the help of chaperone proteins (see Chapter 9). In addition, proteins that enter the ER lumen interact with enzymes that catalyze the addition of carbohydrate side chains (Figure 2.19). Because carbohydrates are polymers of sugar monomers, the addition of one or more carbohydrate groups is called **glycosylation** ("sugar-together"). The resulting molecule is a **glycoprotein**

("sugar-protein"; see Appendix E). The number and arrangement of these sugars changes as the protein matures, serving as an indicator for shipment to the next destination.

Moving from the ER to the Golgi

How do proteins travel from the ER to the Golgi apparatus? In Palade's pulse–chase experiment, labeled proteins found between the rough ER and the Golgi apparatus were inside membrane-bound structures. Based on these observations, Palade's group suggested that proteins are transported in vesicles that bud off from the ER, move away, fuse with the membrane on the *cis* face of the Golgi apparatus, and dump their cargo inside.

This hypothesis was supported when other researchers used differential centrifugation to isolate and characterize the vesicles that contained labeled proteins. They found that a distinctive type of vesicle carries proteins from the rough ER to the Golgi apparatus. Ensuring that only appropriate cargo is loaded into these vesicles and that the vesicles dock and fuse only with the *cis* face of the Golgi involves a complex series of events and is an area of active research.

What Happens Inside the Golgi Apparatus?

Section 2.2 indicated that the Golgi apparatus consists of a stack of flattened vesicles called cisternae, and that cargo enters one side of the organelle and exits the other. Recent research has shown that the composition of the Golgi apparatus is dynamic. New cisternae constantly form at the *cis* face of the Golgi, while old cisternae break apart at the *trans* face, to be replaced by the cisternae behind it. In this way a new cisterna follows those formed earlier, advancing toward the *trans* face of the Golgi. As it does, it changes in composition and activity through a process called **cisternal maturation.**

By separating individual cisternae and analyzing their contents, researchers have found that cisternae at various stages of maturation contain different suites of enzymes. Many of these enzymes catalyze glycosylation reactions that further modify the oligosaccharides that were attached to the protein in the ER. As the cisternae slowly move from *cis* to *trans*, these enzymes are replaced with those representing more mature cisternae. The result is that proteins are modified in a stepwise manner as they slowly move through the Golgi.

If the rough ER is like a foundry and stamping plant where rough parts are manufactured, then the Golgi can be considered a finishing area where products are polished, painted, and readied for shipping.

How Do Proteins Reach Their Destinations?

The rough ER and Golgi apparatus constitute an impressive assembly line. Certain proteins manufactured by this process remain in these organelles, replacing worn-out resident molecules. But those proteins that are simply passing through as cargo must be sorted and sent to their intended destination as the *trans* cisterna they are in breaks up into vesicles.

How are these finished products put into the right shipping containers, and how are the different containers addressed?

Studies on enzymes that are shipped to lysosomes have provided some answers to both questions. A key finding was that lysosome-bound proteins have a phosphate group attached to a specific sugar subunit on their surface, forming the compound mannose-6-phosphate. If mannose-6-phosphate is removed from these proteins, they are not transported to a lysosome.

This is strong evidence that the phosphorylated sugar serves as a zip code, analogous to the nuclear localization signal and ER signal sequence discussed earlier. Data indicate that mannose-6-phosphate binds to a receptor protein in the membrane of the *trans*-Golgi cisterna. Regions that are enriched with these receptor–cargo complexes will form vesicles that, in turn, have proteins on their cytosolic surfaces that direct their transport and fusion with pre-lysosomal compartments. In this way, the presence of mannose-6-phosphate targets proteins for vesicles that deliver their contents to organelles that eventually become lysosomes.

FIGURE 2.22 presents a simplified model of how cargo is sorted and loaded into specific vesicles that are shipped to different destinations. Each cargo protein has a molecular tag that directs it to particular vesicle budding sites by interacting with receptors in the *trans* cisterna. These receptors, along with other cytosolic proteins that are not shown, direct the transport vesicles to the correct destinations.

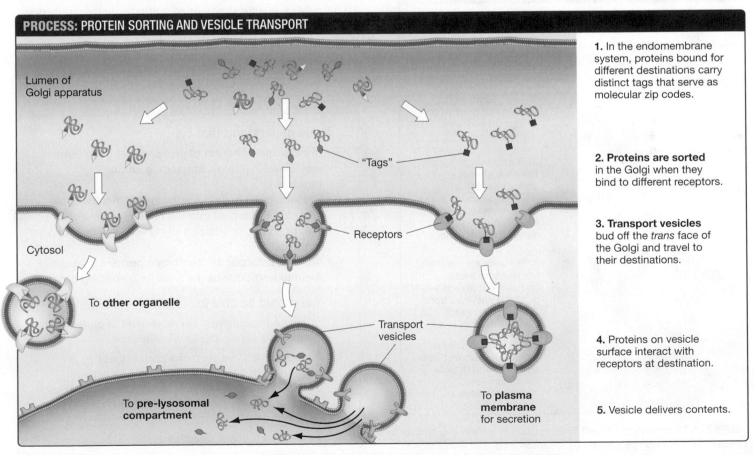

PROCESS: PROTEIN SORTING AND VESICLE TRANSPORT

Lumen of Golgi apparatus

"Tags"

Receptors

Cytosol

To **other organelle**

Transport vesicles

To **pre-lysosomal compartment**

To **plasma membrane** for secretion

1. In the endomembrane system, proteins bound for different destinations carry distinct tags that serve as molecular zip codes.

2. **Proteins are sorted** in the Golgi when they bind to different receptors.

3. **Transport vesicles** bud off the *trans* face of the Golgi and travel to their destinations.

4. **Proteins on vesicle surface interact with receptors at destination.**

5. Vesicle delivers contents.

FIGURE 2.22 In the Golgi Apparatus, Proteins Are Sorted into Vesicles That Are Targeted to a Destination.

In particular, notice that the transport vesicle shown on the right of Figure 2.22 is bound for the plasma membrane, where it will secrete its contents to the outside. This process is called **exocytosis** ("outside-cell-act"). When exocytosis occurs, the vesicle membrane and plasma membrane make contact. As the two membranes fuse, their lipid bilayers rearrange in a way that exposes the interior of the vesicle to the outside of the cell. The vesicle's contents then diffuse into the space outside the cell. This is how cells in your pancreas deliver digestive enzymes to the duct that leads to your small intestine—where food is digested.

Recycling Material in the Lysosome

Now that you have seen how cargo moves out of the cell, let's look at how cargo is brought into the cell. Previously, you learned about how cells import small molecules across lipid bilayers (see Chapter 6), but this is not possible for large molecules like proteins and complex carbohydrates. For these molecules to be recycled and used by the cell, they must first be digested in the lysosome—but how do they get there?

Endocytosis ("inside-cell-act") refers to any pinching off of the plasma membrane that results in the uptake of material from outside the cell. **Receptor-mediated endocytosis** is illustrated in **FIGURE 2.23**. As its name implies, the sequence of events begins when macromolecules outside the cell bind to receptors on the plasma membrane. More than 25 distinct receptors have now been characterized, each specialized for binding to different cargo.

Once receptor binding occurs, the plasma membrane folds in and pinches off to form an endocytic vesicle. These vesicles then drop off their cargo in a transient organelle called the **early endosome** ("inside-body"). The activity of proton pumps in the membrane of this organelle acidifies its lumen, which causes the cargo to be released from their receptors. Many of these emptied cargo receptors are then repackaged into vesicles and returned to the plasma membrane.

As proton pumps continue to lower the early endosome's pH, it undergoes a series of processing steps that cause it to mature into a **late endosome**. The late endosome is the pre-lysosomal compartment introduced earlier (Figure 2.22), where the acid hydrolases from the Golgi apparatus are dropped off. As before, the emptied cargo receptors transported from the Golgi are removed from the late endosome as it matures into a fully active lysosome.

In addition to receptor-mediated endocytosis, the lysosome is involved in recycling material via autophagy and phagocytosis (see **FIGURE 2.24**). During **autophagy** (literally, "same-eating"), damaged organelles are enclosed within an internal membrane and delivered to a lysosome. There the components are digested and recycled. In **phagocytosis** ("eat-cell-act"), the plasma membrane of a cell surrounds a smaller cell or food particle and engulfs it, forming a structure called a phagosome. This structure is delivered to a lysosome, where it is taken in and digested.

Regardless of whether the materials in lysosomes originate via autophagy, phagocytosis, or receptor-mediated endocytosis, the result is similar: Molecules are hydrolyzed. ✔ If you understand the interaction between the endomembrane system

PROCESS: RECEPTOR-MEDIATED ENDOCYTOSIS

Recycling of membrane proteins

Endocytic vesicle

H⁺

Early endosome

H⁺   H⁺

Vesicle from Golgi apparatus

Late endosome

Lysosome

1. Macromolecules outside the cell bind to membrane proteins that act as receptors.

2. The plasma membrane folds in and pinches off to form an endocytic vesicle.

3. The endocytic vesicle fuses with an early endosome, activating protons that lower its pH. Cargo is released and empty receptors are recycled to the surface.

4. The early endosome matures into a late endosome that receives digestive enzymes from the Golgi apparatus.

5. The late endosome matures into a functional lysosome and digests the endocytosed macromolecules.

FIGURE 2.23 Receptor-Mediated Endocytosis Is a Pathway to the Lysosome. Endosomes created by receptor-mediated endocytosis will mature into lysosomes.

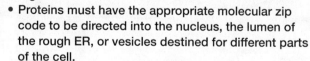

check your understanding

If you understand that . . .

- In cells, the transport of proteins and other large molecules is energy demanding and tightly regulated.
- Proteins must have the appropriate molecular zip code to be directed into the nucleus, the lumen of the rough ER, or vesicles destined for different parts of the cell.
- Vesicles incorporate membrane proteins that direct them to particular target sites for unloading cargo.

✔ **You should be able to . . .**

1. Compare and contrast the movement of proteins into the nucleus versus the ER lumen.

2. Predict the final location of a protein that has been engineered to include an ER signal sequence, mannose-6-phosphate tag, and a nuclear localization signal. Justify your answer by addressing the impact of each signal on its transport.

Answers are available in Appendix A.

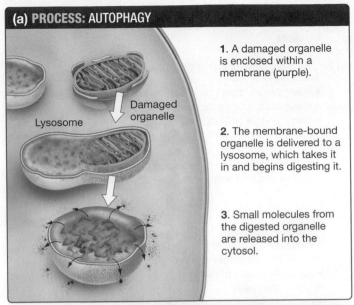

(a) PROCESS: AUTOPHAGY

1. A damaged organelle is enclosed within a membrane (purple).

2. The membrane-bound organelle is delivered to a lysosome, which takes it in and begins digesting it.

3. Small molecules from the digested organelle are released into the cytosol.

Damaged organelle

Lysosome

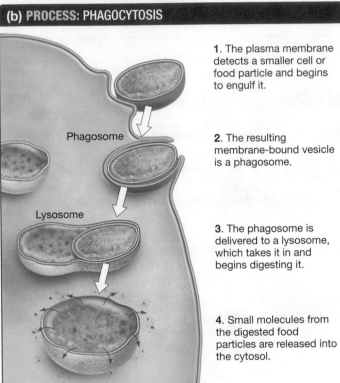

(b) PROCESS: PHAGOCYTOSIS

1. The plasma membrane detects a smaller cell or food particle and begins to engulf it.

2. The resulting membrane-bound vesicle is a phagosome.

3. The phagosome is delivered to a lysosome, which takes it in and begins digesting it.

4. Small molecules from the digested food particles are released into the cytosol.

Phagosome

Lysosome

FIGURE 2.24 Two More Ways to Deliver Materials to Lysosomes. Materials can be transported to lysosomes **(a)** via autophagy or **(b)** after phagocytosis.

and endocytosis, you should be able to predict how the loss of the mannose-6-phosphate receptor would affect receptor-mediated endocytosis.

It is important to note, however, that not all the materials that are surrounded by membrane and taken into a cell end up in lysosomes. In addition to receptor-mediated endocytosis and phagocytosis, small fluid-filled vesicles can be brought into a cell via **bulk-phase endocytosis.** There does not appear to be any cargo selection in bulk-phase endocytosis, and the vesicles are not transported to lysosomes. These tiny vesicles are used elsewhere in the cell and are likely involved in recycling lipids deposited on the plasma membrane during exocytosis.

Throughout this section, vesicles have been key to the transport of cargo. If these transport steps depended on the random movement of diffusion alone, however, then the vesicles and their cargo might never reach their intended destinations. Are there instead defined tracks that direct the movement of these shipping containers? If so, what are these tracks, and what molecule or molecules function to transport the vesicles along them? Let's delve into these questions in the next section.

2.6 Cell Systems III: The Dynamic Cytoskeleton

The endomembrane system may be the best-studied example of how individual organelles work together in a dynamic, highly integrated way. This integration depends in part on the physical relationship of organelles, which is organized by the cytoskeletal system.

The cytoskeleton is a dense and complex network of fibers that helps maintain cell shape by providing structural support. However, the cytoskeleton is not a static structure like the scaffolding used at construction sites. Its fibrous proteins move and change to alter the cell's shape, shift its contents, and even move the cell itself. Like the rest of the cell, the cytoskeleton is dynamic.

As **TABLE 2.3** (see page 40) shows, there are three distinct cytoskeletal elements in eukaryotic cells: actin filaments, intermediate filaments, and microtubules. Recent research has shown structural and functional relationships between these three eukaryotic filaments and cytoskeletal elements in bacteria.

Each of the three cytoskeletal elements found in eukaryotes has a distinct size, structure, and function. Let's look at each one in turn.

Actin Filaments

Sometimes called **microfilaments** because they are the cytoskeletal element with the smallest diameter, **actin filaments** are fibrous structures made of the globular protein actin (Table 2.3). In animal cells, actin is often the most abundant of all proteins—typically it represents 5–10 percent of the total protein in the cell. Each of your liver cells contains about half a billion of these molecules.

Actin Filament Structure A completed actin filament resembles two long strands that coil around each other. Actin filaments form when individual actin protein subunits assemble, or polymerize, from head to tail through the formation of noncovalent bonds.

Because the actin proteins are not symmetrical, this head-to-tail arrangement of actin subunits results in filaments that have two different ends, or polarity. The two distinct ends of an actin filament are referred to as plus and minus ends. The structural difference between these two ends results in different rates of

Filament	Structure	Subunits	Functions
The three types of filaments that make up the cytoskeleton are distinguished by their size, structure, and type of protein subunit.			
Actin filaments (microfilaments)	Strands in double helix 7 nm − end + end	Actin	• maintain cell shape by resisting tension (pull) • move cells via muscle contraction or cell crawling • divide animal cells in two • move organelles and cytoplasm in plants, fungi, and animals
Intermediate filaments	Fibers wound into thicker cables 10 nm	Keratins, lamins, or others	• maintain cell shape by resisting tension (pull) • anchor nucleus and some other organelles
Microtubules	Hollow tube 25 nm − end + end	α- and β-tubulin dimers	• maintain cell shape by resisting compression (push) • move cells via flagella or cilia • move chromosomes during cell division • assist formation of cell plate during plant cell division • move organelles • provide tracks for intracellular transport

assembling new actin subunits: The plus end grows faster than the minus end.

Each filament is generally unstable and will grow or shrink depending on the concentration of free actin subunits. In addition to controlling the availability of free actin, cells regulate the length and longevity of microfilaments via actin-binding proteins that either stabilize or destabilize their structure.

In animal cells, actin filaments are particularly abundant just under the plasma membrane. They are organized into long, parallel bundles or dense, crisscrossing networks in which individual actin filaments are linked to one another by other proteins. The reinforced bundles and networks of actin filaments help stiffen the cell and define its shape.

Actin Filament Function   In addition to providing structural support, actin filaments are involved in movement. In several cases, actin's role in movement depends on the protein myosin. Myosin is a **motor protein**: a protein that converts the potential energy in ATP into the kinetic energy of mechanical work, just as a car's motor converts the chemical energy in gasoline into spinning wheels.

The interaction between actin and myosin is frequently presented in the context of how it produces muscle contraction and movement. For now, it's enough to recognize that when myosin binds and hydrolyzes ATP to ADP, it undergoes a series of shape changes that extends the "head" region, attaches it to actin, and then contracts to pull itself along the actin filament. The shape change of this protein causes the actin and myosin to slide past each other. After repeated rounds of this contraction cycle, the myosin progressively moves toward the plus end of the actin filament (**FIGURE 2.25a**). This type of movement is analogous to an inchworm contracting its body as it moves along a stick.

(a) Actin and myosin interact to cause movement.

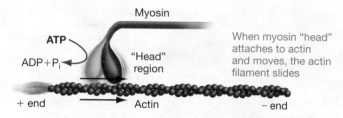

When myosin "head" attaches to actin and moves, the actin filament slides

(b) Examples of movement caused by actin–myosin interactions

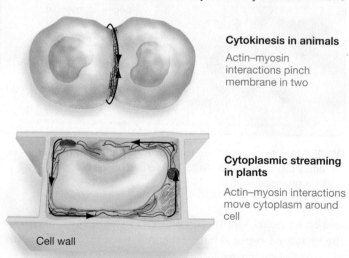

Cytokinesis in animals

Actin–myosin interactions pinch membrane in two

Cytoplasmic streaming in plants

Actin–myosin interactions move cytoplasm around cell

FIGURE 2.25 Many Cellular Movements Are Based on Actin–Myosin Interactions. (a) ATP hydrolysis in the "head" region of myosin causes the protein to attach to actin and change shape. The movement slides the myosin toward the plus end of actin. **(b)** Actin–myosin interactions can divide cells and move organelles and cytoplasm.

As **FIGURE 2.25b** shows, the ATP-powered interaction between actin and myosin is the basis for an array of cell movements:

- **Cytokinesis** ("cell-moving") is the process of cell division. In animals, this occurs by the use of actin filaments that are connected to the plasma membrane and arranged in a ring around the circumference of the cell. Myosin causes the filaments to slide past one another, drawing in the membrane and pinching the cell in two.

- **Cytoplasmic streaming** is the directed flow of cytosol and organelles within plant cells. The movement occurs along actin filaments and is powered by myosin. It is especially common in large cells, where the circulation of cytoplasm facilitates material transport.

In addition, the movement called **cell crawling** occurs when groups of actin filaments grow, creating bulges in the plasma membrane that extend and move the cell. Cell crawling occurs in a wide range of organisms and cell types, including amoebae, slime molds, and certain animal cells.

Intermediate Filaments

Many types of **intermediate filament** exist, each consisting of a different—though similar in size and structure—type of protein (Table 2.3). Humans, for example, have 70 genes that code for intermediate filament proteins. This is in stark contrast to actin filaments and microtubules, which are made from the same protein subunits in all eukaryotic cells.

Moreover, intermediate filaments are not polar; instead, each end of these filaments is identical. They are not involved in directed movement driven by myosin or other motor proteins, but instead serve a purely structural role in eukaryotic cells.

The intermediate filaments that you are most familiar with belong to a family of molecules called the keratins. The cells that make up your skin and line surfaces inside your body contain about 20 types of keratin. These intermediate filaments provide the mechanical strength required for these cells to resist pressure and abrasion. Certain cells in the skin can also produce secreted forms of keratin. Depending on the location of the cell and keratins involved, the secreted filaments form fingernails, toenails, or hair.

Nuclear lamins, which make up the nuclear lamina layer introduced in Section 2.4, also qualify as intermediate filaments. Nuclear lamins form a dense mesh under the nuclear envelope. Recall that in addition to giving the nucleus its shape, they anchor the chromosomes. They are also involved in the breakup and reassembly of the nuclear envelope when cells divide.

Some intermediate filaments project from the nucleus through the cytoplasm to the plasma membrane, where they are linked to intermediate filaments that run parallel to the cell surface. In this way, intermediate filaments form a flexible skeleton that helps shape the cell surface and hold the nucleus in place.

Microtubules

Microtubules are the largest cytoskeletal components in terms of diameter. As Table 2.3 shows, they are assembled from subunits consisting of two polypeptides, called α-tubulin and β-tubulin, that exist as stable protein **dimers** ("two-parts").

Tubulin dimers polymerize from head to tail to form filaments that interact with one another to create relatively large, hollow tubes. Because of this polarity, these microtubules have α-tubulin polypeptides at one end (the minus end) and β-tubulins at the other end (the plus end). Like actin filaments, microtubules are dynamic and grow faster at their plus ends compared with their minus ends.

Microtubules originate from a structure called the **microtubule organizing center (MTOC).** Their plus ends grow outward, radiating throughout the cell. Although plant cells typically have hundreds of sites where microtubules start growing, most animal and fungal cells have just one site that is near the nucleus.

In animals, the microtubule organizing center has a distinctive structure and is called a **centrosome.** As **FIGURE 2.26** shows, animal centrosomes contain two bundles of microtubules called **centrioles.** Although additional microtubules emanate from these structures in animals, they do not grow directly from the centrioles.

(a) In animals, microtubules originate from centrosomes.

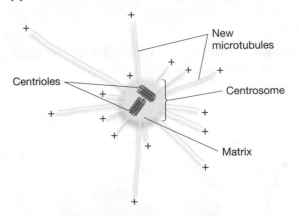

Centrioles
New microtubules
Centrosome
Matrix

(b) Centrioles consist of microtubules.

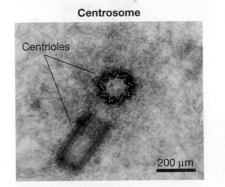

Centrosome

Centrioles

200 μm

Centrioles (oriented at 90° to each other)

Microtubule triplets

FIGURE 2.26 Centrosomes Are a Type of Microtubule-Organizing Center. (a) Microtubule-organizing centers, such as the centrosomes of animal cells, are the sites where new microtubules are made. Microtubules grow from the matrix surrounding the centrioles, and their positive ends point away from the centrosomes. **(b)** The two centrioles inside a centrosome consist of microtubules as triplets arranged in a circle.

In function, microtubules are similar to actin filaments: They provide stability and are involved in movement. Like steel girders in a skyscraper, the microtubules that radiate from an organizing center stiffen the cell by resisting compression forces. Microtubules also provide a structural framework for organelles. If microtubules are prevented from forming, the network-like configuration of the ER collapses and the Golgi apparatus disappears into vesicles.

Microtubules are best known for their role in separating chromosomes during mitosis and meiosis (see Chapters 4 and 11). But microtubules are involved in many other types of cellular movement as well. Let's first consider their role in moving materials inside cells and then explore how microtubules can help cells to swim.

Microtubules Serve as Tracks for Vesicle Transport
Recall from Section 2.5 that vesicles are used to transport materials to a wide array of destinations inside cells. To study how this movement happens, Ronald Vale and colleagues focused on the giant axon, an extremely large nerve cell in squid that runs the length of the animal's body. If the squid is disturbed, the cell signals muscles to contract so it can jet away to safety. The researchers decided to study this particular cell for three reasons.

1. The giant axon is so large that it is relatively easy to see and manipulate.

2. Large numbers of vesicles are transported down the length of the cell. As a result, a large amount of cargo moves a long distance.

3. The researchers found that if they gently squeezed the cytoplasm out of the cell, vesicle transport still occurred in the extracellular cytoplasmic material. This allowed them to do experiments on vesicle transport without the plasma membrane being in the way.

In short, the squid giant axon provided a system that could be observed and manipulated efficiently in the lab. To watch vesicle transport in action, the researchers mounted a video camera to a microscope. As **FIGURE 2.27** shows, this technique allowed them to document that vesicle transport occurred along filamentous tracks.

To identify the filament involved, the biologists measured the diameter of the tracks and analyzed their chemical composition. Both types of data indicated that the tracks consist of microtubules. Microtubules also appear to be required for movement of materials elsewhere in the cell. For instance, if experimental cells are treated with a drug that disrupts microtubules, the movement of vesicles from the rough ER to the Golgi apparatus is impaired.

The general message of these experiments is that transport vesicles move through the cell along microtubules. How? Do the tracks themselves move, like a conveyer belt, or are vesicles carried along on some sort of molecular vehicle?

Motor Proteins Pull Vesicles Along the Tracks
To study the way vesicles move along microtubules, Vale's group took the squid axon's transport system apart and then determined what components were required to put it back together. A simple experiment convinced the group that this movement is an energy-dependent process: If they depleted the amount of ATP in the cytoplasm, vesicle transport stopped.

To examine this process further, they mixed purified microtubules and vesicles with ATP, but no transport occurred. Something had been left out—but what? To find the missing element or elements, the researchers purified one subcellular part after another and added it to the microtubule + vesicle + ATP system.

Through trial and error, and further purification steps, the researchers finally succeeded in isolating a protein that generated vesicle movement. They named the molecule **kinesin,** from the Greek word *kinein* ("to move").

Like myosin, kinesin is a motor protein. Kinesin converts the chemical energy in ATP into mechanical energy in the form of movement. More specifically, when ATP is hydrolyzed by kinesin, the protein moves along microtubules in a directional manner: toward the plus end.

Biologists began to understand how kinesin works when X-ray diffraction studies showed that it has three major regions: a head section with two globular pieces, a tail associated with small polypeptides, and a stalk that connects the head and tail (**FIGURE 2.28a**).

Follow-up studies confirmed that the head region binds to the microtubule while the tail region binds to the transport vesicle. Recent work has shown that kinesin uses these domains to "walk" along the microtubule through a series of conformational changes as it hydrolyzes ATP (**FIGURE 2.28b**). Amazingly, these motors have been found to "walk" up to 375 steps per second.

Cells contain several different versions of the kinesin motor, each specialized for a different role in the cell. If kinesins move

(a) Electron micrograph

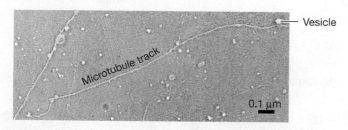

Vesicle

Microtubule track

0.1 μm

(b) Video image

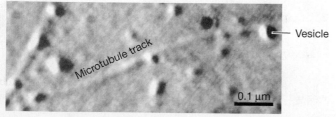

Vesicle

Microtubule track

0.1 μm

FIGURE 2.27 Transport Vesicles Move along Microtubule Track. The images show extruded cytoplasm from a squid giant axon. **(a)** An electron micrograph that allowed researchers to measure the diameter of the filaments and confirm that they are microtubules. In the upper part of this image, you can see a vesicle on a "track." **(b)** A video microscope image using enhanced contrast that allowed researchers to watch vesicles move in real time.

(a) Structure of kinesin

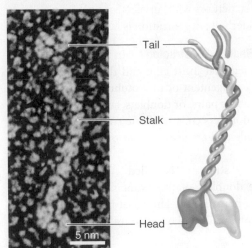

Tail

Stalk

Head

5 nm

(b) Kinesin "walks" along a microtubule track.

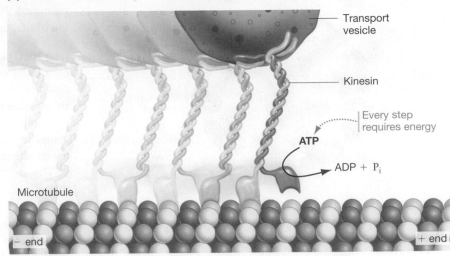

Transport vesicle

Kinesin

Every step requires energy

ATP

ADP + P$_i$

Microtubule

− end

+ end

FIGURE 2.28 Motor Proteins Move Vesicles along Microtubules. (a) Kinesin has three distinct regions. **(b)** The current model depicting how kinesin "walks" along a microtubule track to transport vesicles. The two head segments act like feet that alternately attach, pivot, and release in response to the gain or loss of a phosphate group from ATP.

only toward the plus ends of microtubules, then what is responsible for moving the cargo in the opposite direction? By studying whole-cell locomotion, researchers discovered a motor that could move toward the minus end of microtubules.

Flagella and Cilia: Moving the Entire Cell

Flagella are long, whiplike projections from the cell surface that function in movement. While many bacteria and eukaryotes have flagella, the structure is completely different in the two groups.

- Bacterial flagella are helical rods made of a protein called flagellin; eukaryotic flagella consist of several microtubules constructed from tubulin dimers.

- Bacterial flagella move the cell by rotating the rod like a ship's propeller; eukaryotic flagella move the cell by undulating—they whip back and forth.

- Eukaryotic flagella are surrounded by the plasma membrane and are considered organelles; bacterial flagella are not.

Based on these observations, biologists conclude that the two structures evolved independently, even though their function is similar.

To understand how some cells move, let's focus on eukaryotic flagella. Eukaryotic flagella are closely related to structures called **cilia** (singular: **cilium**), which are short, hairlike projections that are also found in some eukaryotic cells (**FIGURE 2.29**). Flagella are generally much longer than cilia, and the two structures differ in

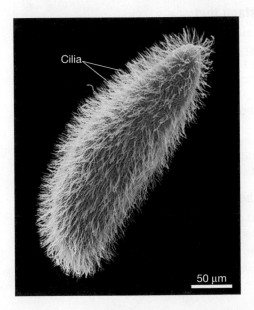

Cilia

50 μm

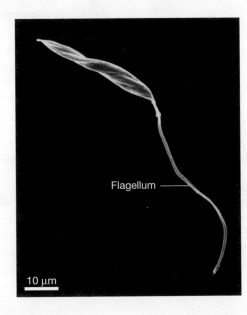

Flagellum

10 μm

FIGURE 2.29 Cilia and Flagella Differ in Length and Number. Cells typically only have 1–4 flagella but may have up to 14,000 cilia. The cells in these scanning electron micrographs have been colorized.

(a) Transmission electron micrograph of axoneme

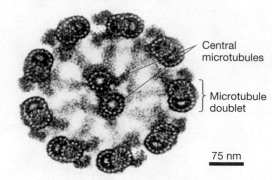

Central microtubules

Microtubule doublet

75 nm

(b) Structure of axoneme

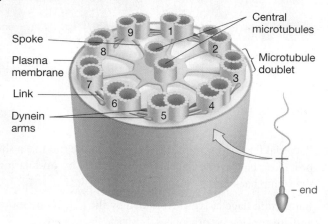

Spoke

Plasma membrane

Link

Dynein arms

Central microtubules

Microtubule doublet

– end

(c) Mechanism of axoneme bending

Microtubule doublet

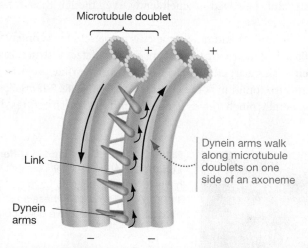

Link

Dynein arms

Dynein arms walk along microtubule doublets on one side of an axoneme

+ ATP: Causes dynein to walk toward minus end and pull toward plus end

FIGURE 2.30 The Structure and Function of Cilia and Flagella.
(a) Transmission electron micrograph of a cross section through an axoneme. **(b)** The microtubules in cilia and flagella are connected by links and spokes, and the entire structure is surrounded by the plasma membrane. **(c)** When dynein arms walk along the microtubule doublets on one side of a flagellum, force is transmitted to these links and spokes, causing the entire axoneme to bend.

✔**QUESTION** If the links and spokes were removed from the microtubule doublets, what would happen to the axoneme after adding ATP?

their abundance and pattern of movement. But when researchers examined the two structures with an electron microscope, they found that their underlying organization is identical.

How are Cilia and Flagella Constructed? In the 1950s, anatomical studies established that most cilia and flagella have a characteristic "9 + 2" arrangement of microtubules. As **FIGURE 2.30a** shows, nine microtubule pairs, or doublets, surround two central microtubules. The doublets consist of one complete and one incomplete microtubule and are arranged around the periphery of the structure.

The entire 9 + 2 structure is called the **axoneme** ("axle-thread"). The nine doublets of the axoneme originate from a structure called the **basal body.** The basal body is identical in structure with a centriole and plays a central role in the growth of the axoneme.

Through further study, biologists gained a more detailed view of the axoneme's structure. Spoke-like proteins connect each doublet to the central pair of microtubules, and molecular links connect the nine doublets to one another (**FIGURE 2.30b**). Each doublet also has a set of arms that project toward an adjacent doublet.

Axonemes are complex. How do their components interact to generate motion?

What Provides the Force Required for Movement? In the 1960s Ian Gibbons began studying the cilia of a common unicellular eukaryote called *Tetrahymena*. Gibbons found that he could isolate axonemes by using a detergent to remove the plasma membrane that surrounds cilia and then subjecting the resulting solution to differential centrifugation. These steps gave Gibbons a cell-free system for studying how the axonemes in cilia and flagella work. He found that the isolated structures would beat only if he supplied them with ATP, confirming that the beating of cilia is an energy-demanding process.

check your understanding

If you understand that . . .

- Each component of the cytoskeleton has a unique structure and set of functions. Actin filaments, intermediate filaments, and microtubules all play a role in structural support. In addition, actin filaments and microtubules work in conjunction with motor proteins to move cytoplasmic materials or the entire cell.
- Most elements of the cytoskeleton are dynamic— they grow and shrink depending on the needs of the cell.

✔ **You should be able to . . .**

Compare and contrast the structure and function of actin filaments, intermediate filaments, and microtubules.

Answers are available in Appendix A.

In another experiment, Gibbons treated the isolated axonemes with a molecule that disrupts interactions between proteins. The resulting axonemes could not beat even after being supplied with ATP. When Gibbons examined them in the electron microscope, he found that the treatment had removed the arms from the doublets. This result suggested that the arms are required for movement. Follow-up work showed that the arms are made of a large protein that Gibbons named **dynein** (from the Greek word *dyne*, meaning "force").

Like myosin and kinesin, dynein is a motor protein that uses ATP to undergo conformational changes. These shape changes move dynein along microtubules toward the minus end. Note that dynein moves in the opposite direction from the kinesin motor, which moves toward the plus end. In the cytoplasm, dynein motors are known to play various roles similar to the other motors, including the transport of vesicles. In the context of the axoneme, however, the outcome of dynein walking in the axoneme is very different.

So what is special about the axoneme? Remember that each of the nine doublets in the axoneme is connected to the central pair of microtubules by a spoke, and all the doublets are connected to each other by molecular links (Figure 2.30b). As a result, the sliding motion produced by dynein walking is constrained—if one doublet slides, it transmits force to the rest of the axoneme via the links and spokes (**FIGURE 2.30c**). If the dynein arms on just one side of the axoneme are activated, then the localized movement results in bending. The bending of cilia or flagella results in a swimming motion.

Scaled for size, flagella-powered swimming can be rapid. In terms of the number of body or cell lengths traveled per second, a sperm cell from a bull moves faster than a human world-record-holder does when swimming freestyle. At the cellular level, life is fast paced.

Taken together, the data reviewed in this chapter can be summed up in six words: Cells are dynamic, highly integrated structures. To maintain the level of organization that is required for life, chemical reactions must take place at mind-boggling speeds. How cells accomplish this feat is taken up elsewhere (see Chapter 10).

CHAPTER 2 REVIEW

 For media, go to MasteringBiology

If you understand . . .

2.1 Bacterial and Archaeal Cell Structures and Their Functions

- There are two basic cellular designs: prokaryotic and eukaryotic. The single defining characteristic that differentiates prokaryotes from eukaryotes is the absence of a nucleus.

- Structures common to most, if not all, prokaryotes are ribosomes, a cell wall, a plasma membrane, an interior cytoskeleton, and a nucleoid.

- Many prokaryotes also possess flagella, fimbriae, and internal membrane structures, some of which are considered organelles.

✓ You should be able to predict what would happen to cells that are exposed to (1) a drug that prevents ribosomes from functioning, (2) an enzyme that degrades the cell wall, or (3) a drug that prevents the assembly of the cytoskeleton.

2.2 Eukaryotic Cell Structures and Their Functions

- Eukaryotic cells are usually much larger and more structurally complex than prokaryotic cells.

- Eukaryotic cells contain numerous specialized organelles, which allow eukaryotic cells to compartmentalize functions and grow to a large size. Organelles common to most, if not all, eukaryotes are as follows:

  1. The nucleus, which contains the cell's chromosomes and serves as its control center.

  2. The endomembrane system, which consists of a diverse group of interrelated organelles, including the endoplasmic reticulum, Golgi apparatus, lysosomes or vacuoles, and endosomes. These organelles work together to synthesize, process, sort, transport, and recycle material.

  3. Peroxisomes, which are organelles where key reactions take place that often result in the generation of toxic by-products. Specialized enzymes are included that safely disarm these by-products soon after they are generated.

  4. Mitochondria and chloroplasts, which have extensive internal membrane systems where the enzymes responsible for ATP generation and photosynthesis reside.

✓ You should be able to predict what would happen to a plant cell that is exposed to (1) a drug that poisons mitochondria, (2) a drug that inhibits catalase in the peroxisome, or (3) a drug that inhibits the formation of centrioles.

2.3 Putting the Parts into a Whole

- Cells have a tightly organized interior, where the presence and quantity of organelles often reflect the function of the cell.

- The activity in a cell illustrates the dynamic nature of life. Organelles and cytosolic proteins continually bustle about with a seemingly nonstop rush hour.

- Much of what is known about cellular activity has come from advances in cell imaging and techniques for isolating cellular components.

✔ You should be able to predict how a liver cell would differ compared with a salivary gland cell in terms of organelles.

2.4 Cell Systems I: Nuclear Transport

- Cells have sophisticated systems for making sure that proteins and other products end up in the right place.

- Traffic across the nuclear envelope occurs through nuclear pores, which contain a multiprotein nuclear pore complex that serves as gatekeeper.

- Small molecules can passively diffuse through the nuclear pore. Larger molecules enter the nucleus only if they contain a specific molecular signal that directs them through the pore via nuclear transport proteins.

✔ You should be able to propose a hypothesis that would address how certain cytoplasmic proteins can be induced to enter the nucleus by either the addition or the removal of phosphates.

2.5 Cell Systems II: The Endomembrane System Manufactures, Ships, and Recycles Cargo

- Molecules synthesized in the ER may be transported as cargo to the Golgi apparatus and then to a number of different sites, depending on the cargo.

- Before products leave the Golgi, they are sorted by their molecular "zip codes" that direct them to specific vesicles. The vesicles interact with receptor proteins at the target location so that the contents are delivered correctly.

- The lysosome is built from enzymes and membranes that are made and processed through the endomembrane system. These organelles are involved in recycling products via autophagy, phagocytosis, and receptor-mediated endocytosis.

✔ You should be able to justify why proteins (see Chapter 9)—and not RNA, DNA, carbohydrates, or lipids—are the molecules responsible for "reading" the array of molecular zip codes in cells.

2.6 Cell Systems III: The Dynamic Cytoskeleton

- The cytoskeleton is an extensive system of fibers that provides (1) structural support and a framework for arranging and organizing organelles and other cell components; (2) paths for moving vesicles inside cells; and (3) machinery for moving the cell as a whole through the beating of flagella or cilia, or through cell crawling.

- Subunits are constantly being added to or removed from cytoskeletal filaments. Actin filaments and microtubules are polarized, meaning different ends of the filaments are designated as plus or minus ends. The plus ends have a higher growth rate than the minus ends.

- Movement often depends on motor proteins, which use chemical energy stored in ATP to change shape and position. Myosin motors move toward the plus ends of actin filaments. Kinesin and dynein motors move along microtubules toward the plus and minus ends, respectively.

- A specific type of dynein is found in the axonemes of eukaryotic cilia and flagella. These motors move microtubules to generate forces that bend the structures and enable cells to swim or generate water currents.

✔ You should be able to predict which of the three motors presented in this section would be responsible for transporting vesicles from the Golgi to the plasma membrane.

(MB) MasteringBiology

1. MasteringBiology Assignments

Tutorials and Activities Cilia and Flagella; Endomembrane System; Exocytosis and Endocytosis; Form Fits Function: Cells; Membrane Transport: Bulk Transport; Prokaryotic Cell Structure and Function; Pulse–Chase Experiment; Review: Animal Cell Structure and Function; Tour of a Plant Cell: Structures and Functions; Tour of an Animal Cell: Structures and Functions; Tour of an Animal Cell: The Endomembrane System; Transport into the Nucleus

Questions Reading Quizzes, Blue-Thread Questions, Test Bank

2. eText Read your book online, search, take notes, highlight text, and more.

3. The Study Area Practice Test, Cumulative Test, BioFlix® 3-D Animations, Videos, Activities, Audio Glossary, Word Study Tools, Art

You should be able to . . .

1. Which of the following accurately describes a difference between prokaryotic and eukaryotic cells?
   a. Prokaryotic cells have fimbriae that allow the cell to swim whereas eukaryotic cells have flagella.
   b. Eukaryotic cells are generally larger than prokaryotic cells.
   c. Eukaryotic cells have organelles.
   d. Prokaryotic cells have nuclei and eukaryotic cells have nucleoids.

2. What are three attributes of mitochondria and chloroplasts that suggest they were once free-living bacteria?

3. Which of the following is *not* true of secreted proteins?
   a. They are synthesized using ribosomes.
   b. They enter the ER lumen during translation.
   c. They contain a signal that directs them into the lysosome.
   d. They are transported between organelles in membrane-bound vesicles.

4. Which of the following results provided evidence of a nuclear localization signal in the nucleoplasmin protein?
   a. The protein was small and easily slipped through the nuclear pore complex.
   b. After cleavage of the protein, only the tail segments appeared in the nucleus.
   c. Removing the tail allowed the core segment to enter the nucleus.
   d. The SRP bound only to the tail, not the core segment.

5. Molecular zip codes direct molecules to particular destinations in the cell. How are these signals read?
   a. They bind to receptor proteins.
   b. They enter transport vesicles.
   c. They bind to motor proteins.
   d. They are glycosylated by enzymes in the Golgi apparatus.

6. How does the hydrolysis of ATP result in the movement of a motor protein along a cytoskeletal filament?

7. Compare and contrast the structure of a generalized plant cell, animal cell, and prokaryotic cell. Which features are common to all cells? Which are specific to just prokaryotes, or just plants, or just animals?

8. Cells that line your intestines are known to possess a large number of membrane proteins that transport small molecules and ions across the plasma membrane. Which of the following cell structures would you expect to be required for this function of the cells?
   a. the endoplasmic reticulum
   b. peroxisomes
   c. lysosomes
   d. the cell wall

9. Most of the proteins that reside in the nucleus possess a nuclear localization signal (NLS), even if they are small enough to pass through the pore complex unhindered. Why would a small protein have an NLS, when it naturally diffuses across the pore without one?

10. Make a flowchart that traces the movement of a secreted protein from its site of synthesis to the outside of a eukaryotic cell. Identify all the organelles that the protein passes through. Add notes indicating what happens to the protein at each step.

11. Although all three cytoskeletal fibers constantly replace their subunits, only actin filaments and microtubules demonstrate differences in the rate of growth between the two ends. What is responsible for this difference, and why is this not observed in intermediate filaments?

12. Describe how vesicles move in a directed manner between organelles of the endomembrane system. Explain why this movement requires ATP.

13. Which of the following cell structures would you expect to be most important in the growth of bacteria on the surface of your teeth?
   a. cell wall
   b. fimbriae
   c. flagella
   d. cilia

14. The enzymes found in peroxisomes are synthesized by cytosolic ribosomes. Suggest a hypothesis for how these proteins find their way to the peroxisomes.

15. Propose an experiment that would determine if the NLS in nucleoplasmin is limited to this protein only or if it could direct other structures into the nucleus.

16. George Palade's research group used the pulse–chase assay to dissect the secretory pathway in pancreatic cells. If they had instead performed this assay on muscle cells, which have high energy demands and primarily consist of actin and myosin filaments, where would you expect the labeled proteins to go during the chase?

3 Lipids, Membranes, and the First Cells

In this chapter you will learn how

Life's defining barrier—the plasma membrane—is built of lipids and proteins

by looking at

Lipid structure and function **3.1**

and how

Lipids spontaneously form bilayers **3.2**

How do substances move across bilayers?

then asking

via

Diffusion and osmosis **3.3**

Membrane proteins **3.4**

A space-filling model of a phospholipid bilayer. In single-celled organisms, this cluster of molecules forms part of the boundary between life (inside the cell) and nonlife (outside the cell)—the cell membrane.

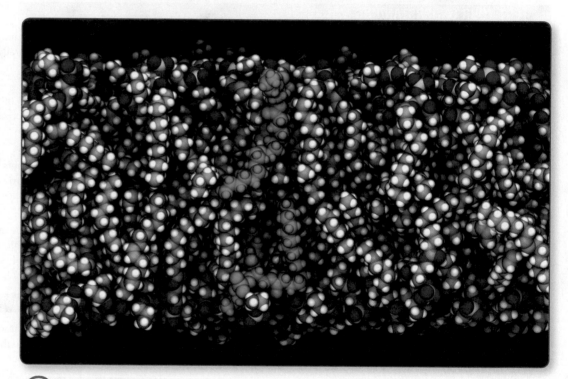

Currently, most biologists support the hypothesis that biological evolution began with a catalytic RNA molecule that could replicate itself. As the offspring of this molecule multiplied, natural selection would have favored the most efficient versions. A second great milestone in the history of life occurred when descendants of these replicators became enclosed within a membrane.

Why is the presence of a membrane so important? The **plasma membrane,** or **cell membrane,** separates life from nonlife. It is a layer of molecules that surrounds the cell interior and separates it from the environment.

- The plasma membrane serves as a selective barrier: It keeps damaging compounds out of the cell and allows entry of compounds needed by the cell.

- Because the plasma membrane sequesters the appropriate chemicals in an enclosed area, reactants collide more frequently—the chemical reactions necessary for life occur much more efficiently.

This chapter is part of the Big Picture. See how on pages 68–69.

✔ When you see this checkmark, stop and test yourself. Answers are available in Appendix A.

While researchers of chemical evolution are currently debating when membranes arose—whether early or late during the emergence of life—there is little argument about the importance of this event. After life secured a membrane, it continued to evolve into an efficient and dynamic reaction vessel—the cell.

How do membranes form? Which ions and molecules can pass through a membrane and which cannot, and why? These are some of the most fundamental questions in all of biological science. Let's delve into them, beginning with the membrane's foundation—lipids.

3.1 Lipid Structure and Function

Lipid is a catchall term for carbon-containing compounds that are found in organisms and are largely nonpolar and hydrophobic—meaning that they do not dissolve readily in water. (Recall from Appendix D that water is a polar solvent.) Lipids do dissolve, however, in liquids consisting of nonpolar organic compounds.

To understand why lipids are insoluble in water, examine the five-carbon compound called isoprene, illustrated in **FIGURE 3.1a**. Note that isoprene consists of carbon atoms bonded to hydrogen atoms. The figure also shows the structural formula of a chain of linked isoprenes, called an isoprenoid.

Molecules that contain only carbon and hydrogen are known as **hydrocarbons.** Hydrocarbons are nonpolar because electrons are shared equally in C−H bonds—owing to the approximately equal electronegativity of carbon and hydrogen. Since these bonds form no partial charges, hydrocarbons are hydrophobic. Thus lipids do not dissolve in water, because they have a significant hydrocarbon component.

Bond Saturation Is an Important Aspect of Hydrocarbon Structure

FIGURE 3.1b gives the structural formula of a **fatty acid,** a simple lipid consisting of a hydrocarbon chain bonded to a carboxyl (−COOH) functional group. Fatty acids and isoprenes are key building blocks of important lipids found in organisms. Just as subtle differences in the orientation of hydroxyls in sugars can lead to dramatic effects in their structure and function, the type of C−C bond used in hydrocarbon chains is a key factor in lipid structure.

When two carbon atoms form a double bond, the attached atoms are found in a plane instead of a three-dimensional tetrahedron. The carbon atoms involved are also locked into place. They cannot rotate freely, as they do in carbon–carbon single bonds. As a result, certain double bonds between carbon atoms produce a "kink" in an otherwise straight hydrocarbon chain (Figure 3.1b, left).

Hydrocarbon chains that consist of only single bonds between the carbons are called **saturated.** If one or more double bonds exist in the hydrocarbon chains, then they are **unsaturated.** The choice of terms is logical. If a hydrocarbon chain does not contain a double bond, it is saturated with the maximum number of hydrogen atoms that can attach to the carbon skeleton. If it is unsaturated, then a C−H bond is removed to form a C=C double bond, resulting in fewer than the maximum number of attached hydrogen atoms.

Foods that contain lipids with many double bonds are said to be polyunsaturated and are advertised as healthier than foods with saturated fats. Recent research suggests that polyunsaturated fats help protect the heart from disease. Exactly how this occurs is under investigation.

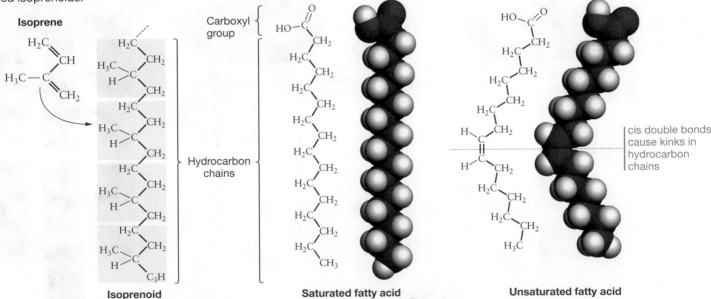

(a) Isoprenes can be linked into chains called isoprenoids.

(b) Fatty acids can be saturated or unsaturated.

Isoprene

Isoprenoid

Carboxyl group

Hydrocarbon chains

Saturated fatty acid

Unsaturated fatty acid

cis double bonds cause kinks in hydrocarbon chains

FIGURE 3.1 Hydrocarbon Structure. (a) Isoprene subunits, like the one shown to the left, can be linked to each other, end to end, to form long hydrocarbon chains called isoprenoids. **(b)** Fatty acids typically contain a total of 14–20 carbon atoms, most found in their long hydrocarbon "tails." Unsaturated hydrocarbons contain carbon–carbon double bonds; saturated hydrocarbons do not.

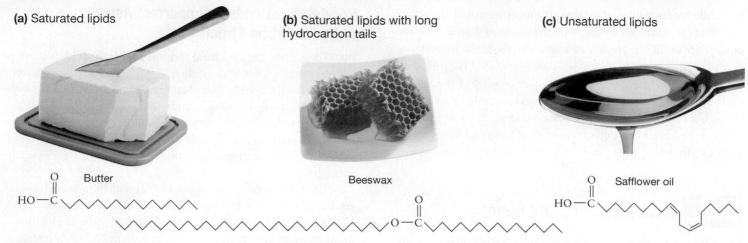

(a) Saturated lipids

(b) Saturated lipids with long hydrocarbon tails

(c) Unsaturated lipids

Butter

Beeswax

Safflower oil

FIGURE 3.2 The Fluidity of Lipids Depends on the Length and Saturation of Their Hydrocarbon Chains. (a) Butter consists primarily of saturated lipids. **(b)** Waxes are lipids with extremely long saturated hydrocarbon chains. **(c)** Oils are dominated by "polyunsaturates"—lipids with hydrocarbon chains that contain multiple C=C double bonds.

Bond saturation also profoundly affects the physical state of lipids. Highly saturated fats, such as butter, are solid at room temperature (**FIGURE 3.2a**). Saturated lipids that have extremely long hydrocarbon tails, like **waxes** do, form particularly stiff solids at room temperature (**FIGURE 3.2b**). Highly unsaturated fats are liquid at room temperature (**FIGURE 3.2c**).

A Look at Three Types of Lipids Found in Cells

Unlike amino acids, nucleotides, and monosaccharides, lipids are characterized by a physical property—their insolubility in water—instead of a shared chemical structure. This insolubility is based on the high proportion of nonpolar C—C and C—H bonds relative to polar functional groups. As a result, the structure of lipids varies widely. For example, consider the most important types of lipids found in cells: fats, steroids, and phospholipids.

Fats **Fats** are nonpolar molecules composed of three fatty acids that are linked to a three-carbon molecule called **glycerol.** Because of this structure, fats are also called triacylglycerols or triglycerides. When the fatty acids are polyunsaturated, they form liquid triacylglycerols called **oils.** In organisms, the primary role of fats is energy storage.

As **FIGURE 3.3a** shows, fats form when a dehydration reaction occurs between a hydroxyl group of glycerol and the carboxyl

(a) Fats form via dehydration reactions.

(b) Fats consist of glycerol linked by ester linkages to three fatty acids.

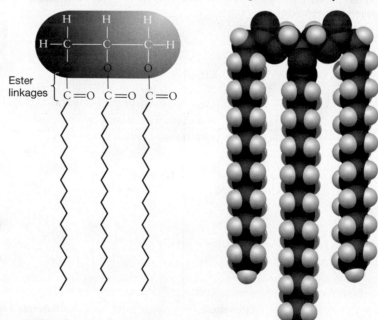

FIGURE 3.3 Fats Are One Type of Lipid Found in Cells. (a) When glycerol and a fatty acid react, a water molecule leaves. The covalent bond that results from this reaction is termed an ester linkage. **(b)** The structural formula and a space-filling model of tristearin, the most common type of fat in beef.

group of a fatty acid. The glycerol and fatty acid molecules become joined by an **ester linkage.** Fats are not polymers, however, and fatty acids are not monomers. As **FIGURE 3.3b** shows, fatty acids are not linked together to form a macromolecule in the way that amino acids, nucleotides, and monosaccharides are.

Steroids Steroids are a family of lipids distinguished by the bulky, four-ring structure shown in orange in **FIGURE 3.4a.** The various steroids differ from one another by the functional groups or side groups attached to different carbons in those hydrophobic rings. The steroid shown in the figure is cholesterol, which has a hydrophilic hydroxyl group attached to the top ring and an isoprenoid "tail" attached at the bottom. Cholesterol is an important component of plasma membranes in many organisms.

Phospholipids Phospholipids consist of a glycerol that is linked to a phosphate group and two hydrocarbon chains of either isoprenoids or fatty acids. The phosphate group is also bonded to a small organic molecule that is charged or polar (**FIGURE 3.4b**).

Phospholipids composed of fatty acids are found in the domains Bacteria and Eukarya; phospholipids with isoprenoid chains are found in the domain Archaea. (The domains of life were introduced in Chapter 1.) In all three domains, phospholipids are crucial components of the plasma membrane.

The lipids found in organisms have a wide array of structures and functions. In addition to storing chemical energy, lipids act as pigments that capture or respond to sunlight, serve as signals between cells, form waterproof coatings on leaves and skin, and act as vitamins used in many cellular processes. The most prominent function of lipids, however, is their role in cell membranes.

The Structures of Membrane Lipids

Not all lipids can form membranes. Membrane-forming lipids have a polar, hydrophilic region—in addition to the nonpolar, hydrophobic region found in all lipids.

To better understand this structure, take another look at the phospholipid illustrated in Figure 3.4b. Notice that the molecule has a "head" region containing highly polar covalent bonds as well as a negatively charged phosphate attached to a polar or charged group. The charges and polar bonds in the head region interact with water molecules when a phospholipid is placed in solution. In contrast, the long hydrocarbon tails of a phospholipid are nonpolar and hydrophobic. Water molecules cannot form hydrogen bonds with the hydrocarbon tail, so they do not interact extensively with this part of the molecule.

Compounds that contain both hydrophilic and hydrophobic elements are **amphipathic** (literally, "dual-sympathy"). Phospholipids are amphipathic. As Figure 3.4a shows, cholesterol is also amphipathic. Because it has a hydroxyl functional group attached to its rings, it has both hydrophilic and hydrophobic regions. ✔ If you understand these concepts, you should be able to look back at Figure 3.1b and explain why fatty acids are also amphipathic.

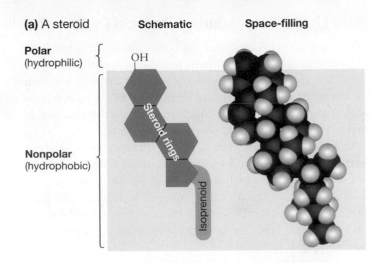

(a) A steroid

Schematic · Space-filling

Polar (hydrophilic) · OH

Steroid rings

Nonpolar (hydrophobic) · Isoprenoid

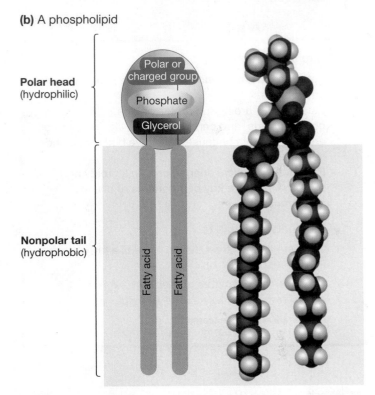

(b) A phospholipid

Polar head (hydrophilic) · Polar or charged group · Phosphate · Glycerol

Nonpolar tail (hydrophobic) · Fatty acid · Fatty acid

FIGURE 3.4 Some Lipids Contain Hydrophilic and Hydrophobic Regions. (a) All steroids have the distinctive four-ring structure shown in orange. Cholesterol has a polar hydroxyl group and an isoprenoid chain attached to these rings. **(b)** Most phospholipids consist of two fatty acid or isoprenoid chains that are linked to glycerol, which is linked to a phosphate group, which is linked to a small organic molecule that is polar or charged.

✔**QUESTION** If cholesterol and phospholipids were in solution, which part of the molecules would interact with water molecules?

The amphipathic nature of phospholipids is far and away their most important feature biologically. It is responsible for life's defining barrier—the plasma membrane. If the membrane defines life, then amphipathic lipids must have existed when life first originated during chemical evolution. Was that possible?

Were Lipids Present during Chemical Evolution?

Like amino acids, nucleic acids, and carbohydrates (Chapters 3–5), there is evidence that lipids were present during chemical evolution. Laboratory experiments have shown that simple lipids, such as fatty acids, can be synthesized from H_2 and CO_2 via reactions with mineral catalysts under conditions thought to be present in prebiotic hydrothermal vent systems (Appendix D).

It is also possible that lipids literally fell from the sky early in Earth's history. Modern meteorites have been found to contain not only amino acids and carbohydrates but also lipids that exhibit amphipathic qualities. For example, lipids extracted from the meteorite that struck Murchison, Australia, in 1969 spontaneously formed lipid "bubbles" that resembled small cells. Why do amphipathic lipids do this?

check your understanding

If you understand that . . .

- Fats, steroids, and phospholipids differ in structure and function.
- Fats and oils are nonpolar; fatty acids, phospholipids, and certain steroids, like cholesterol, are amphipathic because they have both polar and nonpolar regions.
- Fats store chemical energy; certain steroids and phospholipids are key components of plasma membranes.

✔ You should be able to . . .

1. Compare and contrast the structure of a fat, a steroid, and a phospholipid.
2. Based on their structure, explain what makes cholesterol and phospholipids amphipathic.

Answers are available in Appendix A.

3.2 Phospholipid Bilayers

Amphipathic lipids do not dissolve when they are placed in water. Their hydrophilic heads interact with water, but their hydrophobic tails do not. Instead of dissolving in water, then, amphipathic lipids assume one of two types of structures: micelles or lipid bilayers.

- Micelles (**FIGURE 3.5a**) are tiny droplets created when the hydrophilic heads of a set of lipids face the water and form hydrogen bonds, while the hydrophobic tails interact with each other in the interior, away from the water.

- A **lipid bilayer** is created when two sheets of lipid molecules align. As **FIGURE 3.5b** shows, the hydrophilic heads in each layer face the surrounding solution while the hydrophobic tails face one another inside the bilayer. In this way, the hydrophilic heads interact with water while the hydrophobic tails interact with one another.

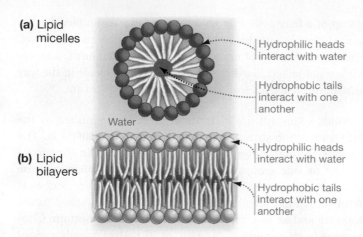

(a) Lipid micelles

Hydrophilic heads interact with water

Hydrophobic tails interact with one another

Water

(b) Lipid bilayers

Hydrophilic heads interact with water

Hydrophobic tails interact with one another

FIGURE 3.5 Lipids Form Micelles and Bilayers in Solution. In **(a)** a micelle or **(b)** a lipid bilayer, the hydrophilic heads of lipids face out, toward water; the hydrophobic tails face in, away from water. Lipid bilayers are the foundation of plasma membranes.

Micelles tend to form from fatty acids or other simple amphipathic hydrocarbon chains. Bilayers tend to form from phospholipids that contain two hydrocarbon tails. For this reason, bilayers are often called phospholipid bilayers.

It's critical to recognize that micelles and phospholipid bilayers form spontaneously—no input of energy is required. This concept can be difficult to grasp because entropy clearly decreases when these structures form. The key is to recognize that micelles and lipid bilayers are much more stable energetically than are independent phospholipids in solution.

Independent lipids are unstable in water because their hydrophobic tails disrupt hydrogen bonds that could otherwise form between water molecules. As a result, the tails of amphipathic molecules are forced together and participate in hydrophobic interactions (introduced in Appendix D). This point should also remind you of the aqueous behavior of hydrophobic side chains in proteins and bases in nucleic acids.

Artificial Membranes as an Experimental System

When phospholipids are added to an aqueous solution and agitated, lipid bilayers spontaneously form small spherical structures. The hydrophilic heads on both sides of the bilayer remain in contact with the aqueous solution—water is present both inside and outside the vesicle. Artificial membrane-bound vesicles like these are called liposomes (**FIGURE 3.6**).

To explore how membranes work, researchers began creating and experimenting with liposomes and planar bilayers—lipid bilayers constructed across a hole in a glass or plastic wall separating two aqueous solutions (**FIGURE 3.7a**). Some of the first questions they posed concerned the permeability of lipid bilayers. The **permeability** of a structure is its tendency to allow a given substance to pass through it.

Using liposomes and planar bilayers, researchers can study what happens when a known ion or molecule is added to one side of a lipid bilayer (**FIGURE 3.7b**). Does the substance cross the

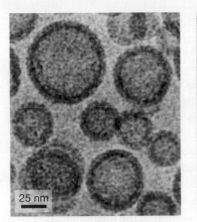

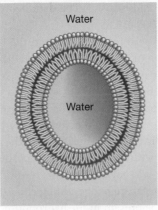

25 nm

FIGURE 3.6 Liposomes Are Artificial Membrane-Bound Vesicles. Electron micrograph of liposomes in cross section (left) and a cross-sectional diagram of the lipid bilayer in a liposome (right).

(a) Planar bilayers: Artificial membranes

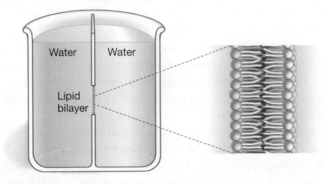

(b) Artificial-membrane experiments

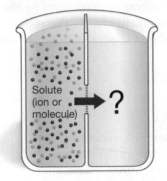

How rapidly can different solutes cross the membrane (if at all) when …

1. Different types of phospholipids are used to make the membrane?

2. Proteins or other molecules are added to the membrane?

FIGURE 3.7 Use of Planar Bilayers in Experiments. (a) The construction of a planar bilayer across a hole in a wall separating two water-filled compartments. **(b)** A wide variety of experiments are possible with planar bilayers; a few are suggested here.

membrane and show up on the other side? If so, how rapidly does the movement take place? What happens when a different type of phospholipid is used to make the artificial membrane? Does the membrane's permeability change when proteins or other types of molecules become part of it?

Biologists describe such an experimental system as elegant and powerful because it gives them precise control over which factor changes from one experimental treatment to the next.

Control, in turn, is why experiments are such an effective way to explore scientific questions. Recall that good experimental design allows researchers to alter one factor at a time and determine what effect, if any, each has on the process being studied (Chapter 1).

Selective Permeability of Lipid Bilayers

When researchers put molecules or ions on one side of a liposome or planar bilayer and measure the rate at which the molecules arrive on the other side, a clear pattern emerges: Lipid bilayers are highly selective.

Selective permeability means that some substances cross a membrane more easily than other substances do. Small nonpolar molecules move across bilayers quickly. In contrast, large molecules and charged substances cross the membrane slowly, if at all. This difference in membrane permeability is a critical issue because controlling what passes between the exterior and interior environments is a key characteristic of cells.

According to the data in **FIGURE 3.8**, small nonpolar molecules such as oxygen (O_2) move across selectively permeable membranes more than a billion times faster than do chloride ions (Cl^-). In essence, ions cannot cross membranes at all—unless they have "help" in the form of membrane proteins introduced later in the chapter. Very small and uncharged molecules such as water (H_2O) can cross membranes relatively rapidly, even if they are polar. Small polar molecules such as glycerol have intermediate permeability.

The leading hypothesis to explain this pattern is that charged compounds and large polar molecules are more stable dissolved in water than they are in the nonpolar interior of membranes. ✔ **If you understand this hypothesis, you should be able to predict where amino acids and nucleotides would be placed in Figure 3.8 and explain your reasoning.**

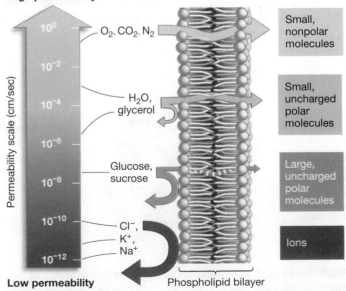

FIGURE 3.8 Lipid Bilayers Show Selective Permeability. Only certain substances cross lipid bilayers readily. Size and polarity or charge affect the rate of diffusion across a membrane.

How Does Lipid Structure Affect Membrane Permeability?

The amphipathic nature of phospholipids allows them to spontaneously form membranes. But not all phospholipid bilayers are the same. The nature of the hydrocarbon tails, in addition to the presence of cholesterol molecules, profoundly influences how a membrane behaves.

Bond Saturation and Hydrocarbon Chain Length Affect Membrane Fluidity and Permeability The degree of saturation in a phospholipid—along with the length of its hydrocarbon tails—affects key aspects of a lipid's behavior in a membrane.

- When unsaturated hydrocarbon tails are packed into a lipid bilayer, kinks created by double bonds produce spaces among the tails. These spaces reduce the strength of the van der Waals interactions (see Chapter 9) that hold the hydrophobic tails together, weakening the barrier to solutes.

- Packed saturated hydrocarbon tails have fewer spaces and stronger van der Waals interactions. As the length of saturated hydrocarbon tails increases, the forces that hold them together also grow stronger, making the membrane even denser.

These observations have profound impacts on membrane fluidity and permeability—two closely related properties. As **FIGURE 3.9** shows, lipid bilayers are more permeable as well as more fluid when they contain short, kinked, unsaturated hydrocarbon tails. An unsaturated membrane allows more materials to pass because its interior is held together less tightly. Bilayers containing long, straight, saturated hydrocarbon tails are much less permeable and fluid. Experiments on liposomes have shown exactly these patterns.

Cholesterol Reduces Membrane Permeability Cholesterol molecules are present, to varying extents, in the membranes of every cell in your body. What effect does adding cholesterol have on a membrane? Researchers have found that adding cholesterol molecules to liposomes dramatically reduces the permeability of lipid bilayers. The data behind this conclusion are presented in **FIGURE 3.10**.

To read the graph in the "Results" section of Figure 3.10, put your finger on the x-axis at the point marked 20°C, and note that permeability to glycerol is much higher at this temperature in membranes that contain no cholesterol versus 20 percent or 50 percent cholesterol. Using this procedure at other temperature points should convince you that membranes lacking cholesterol are more permeable than the other two membranes at every temperature tested in the experiment.

What explains this result? Because the steroid rings in cholesterol are bulky, adding cholesterol fills gaps that would otherwise be present in the hydrophobic section of the membrane.

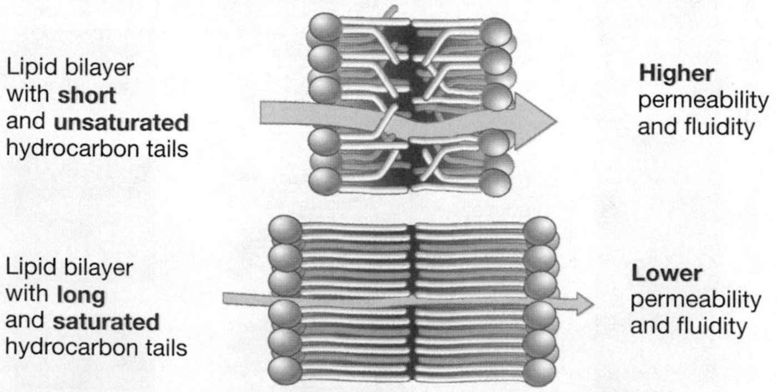

How Does Temperature Affect the Fluidity and Permeability of Membranes?

At about 25°C—or "room temperature"—the phospholipids in a plasma membrane have a consistency resembling olive oil. This fluid physical state allows individual lipid molecules to move laterally within each layer (**FIGURE 3.11**), a little like a person moving about in a dense crowd. By tagging individual phospholipids and following their movement, researchers have clocked average speeds of 2 micrometers (μm)/second at room temperature. At these speeds, a phospholipid could travel the length of a small bacterial cell in a second.

Recall that permeability is closely related to fluidity. As temperature drops, molecules in a bilayer move more slowly. As a result, the hydrophobic tails in the interior of membranes pack together more tightly. At very low temperatures, lipid bilayers even begin to solidify. As the graph in Figure 3.10 indicates, low temperatures can make membranes impervious to molecules that would normally cross them readily. Put your finger on the x-axis of that graph, just about the freezing point

Lipid bilayer with **short** and **unsaturated** hydrocarbon tails

Higher permeability and fluidity

Lipid bilayer with **long** and **saturated** hydrocarbon tails

Lower permeability and fluidity

FIGURE 3.9 Fatty Acid Structure Changes the Permeability of Membranes. Lipid bilayers consisting of phospholipids containing unsaturated fatty acids should have more gaps and be more permeable than those with saturated fatty acids.

QUESTION: Does adding cholesterol to a membrane affect its permeability?

HYPOTHESIS: Cholesterol reduces permeability because it fills spaces in phospholipid bilayers.

NULL HYPOTHESIS: Cholesterol has no effect on permeability.

EXPERIMENTAL SETUP:

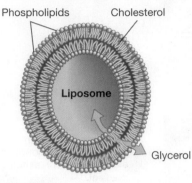

Phospholipids   Cholesterol

Liposome

Glycerol

1. Construct liposomes: Create with no cholesterol, 20% cholesterol, and 50% cholesterol.

2. Measure glycerol movement: Record how quickly glycerol moves across each type of membrane at different temperatures.

PREDICTION: Liposomes with higher cholesterol levels will have reduced permeability.

PREDICTION OF NULL HYPOTHESIS: All liposomes will have the same permeability.

RESULTS:

[Graph: x-axis "Temperature (°C)" 0, 10, 20, 30; y-axis "Permeability of membrane to glycerol". Three curves labeled "No cholesterol", "20% of lipids = cholesterol", "50% of lipids = cholesterol"]

CONCLUSION: Adding cholesterol to membranes decreases their permeability to glycerol. The permeability of all membranes analyzed in this experiment increases with increasing temperature.

FIGURE 3.10 The Permeability of a Membrane Depends on Its Composition.

SOURCE: de Gier, J., et al. (1968). Lipid composition and permeability of liposomes. *Biochimica et Biophysica Acta* 150: 666–675.

✔**QUANTITATIVE** Suppose the investigators had instead created liposomes using phospholipids with fully saturated tails and compared them to two other sets of liposomes where either 20 percent or 50 percent of the phospholipids contained polyunsaturated tails. Label the three lines on the graph above with your prediction for the three different liposomes in this new experiment.

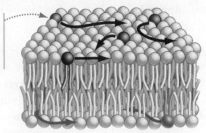

Phospholipids are in constant lateral motion, but rarely flip to the other side of the bilayer

FIGURE 3.11 Phospholipids Move within Membranes. Membranes are dynamic—in part because phospholipid molecules randomly move laterally within each layer in the structure.

of water (0°C), and note that even membranes that lack cholesterol are almost completely impermeable to glycerol. Indeed, trace any of the three lines in Figure 3.10, and as you move to the right (increasing temperature), you also move up (increasing permeability).

These observations on glycerol and lipid movement demonstrate that membranes are dynamic. Phospholipid molecules whiz around each layer, while water and small nonpolar molecules shoot in and out of the membrane. How quickly molecules move within and across membranes is a function of temperature, the structure of hydrocarbon tails, and the number of cholesterol molecules in the bilayer.

3.3 How Molecules Move across Lipid Bilayers: Diffusion and Osmosis

Small uncharged molecules and hydrophobic compounds can cross membranes readily and spontaneously—without an input of energy. The question now is: How is this possible? What process is responsible for movement of molecules across lipid bilayers?

Diffusion

A thought experiment can help explain how substances can cross membranes spontaneously. Suppose you rack up a set of billiard balls in the middle of a pool table and then begin to vibrate the table.

1. Because of the vibration, the billiard balls will move about randomly. They will also bump into one another.

2. After these collisions, some balls will move outward—away from their original position.

3. As movement and collisions continue, the overall or net movement of balls will be outward. This occurs because the random motion of the balls disrupts their original, nonrandom position. As the balls move at random, they are more likely to move away from one another than to stay together.

4. Eventually, the balls will be distributed randomly across the table. The entropy of the billiard balls has increased. Recall that entropy is a measure of the randomness or disorder in

a system (Appendix D). The second law of thermodynamics states that in an isolated system, entropy always increases.

This hypothetical example illustrates how vibrating billiard balls move at random. More to the point, it also explains how substances located on one side of a lipid bilayer can move to the other side spontaneously. All dissolved molecules and ions, or **solutes,** have thermal energy and are in constant, random motion. Movement of molecules and ions that results from their kinetic energy is known as **diffusion.**

A difference in solute concentrations creates what is called a **concentration gradient.** Solutes move randomly in all directions, but when a concentration gradient exists, there is a net movement from regions of high concentration to regions of low concentration. Diffusion down a concentration gradient, or away from the higher concentration, is a spontaneous process because it results in an increase in entropy.

Once the molecules or ions are randomly distributed throughout a solution, a chemical equilibrium is established. For example, consider two aqueous solutions separated by a lipid bilayer. **FIGURE 3.12** shows how molecules that can pass through the bilayer diffuse to the other side. At equilibrium, these molecules continue to move back and forth across the membrane, but at equal rates—simply because they are equally likely to move in any direction. This means that there is no longer a net movement of molecules across the membrane. ✔ If you understand diffusion, you should be able to predict how a difference in temperature across a membrane would affect the concentration of a solute at equilibrium.

Osmosis

What about water? As the data in Figure 3.8 show, water moves across lipid bilayers relatively quickly. The movement of water is a special case of diffusion that is given its own name: **osmosis.** Osmosis occurs only when solutions are separated by a membrane that permits water to cross, but holds back some or all of the solutes—that is, a selectively permeable membrane.

It's important to note that some of the water molecules in a solution are unavailable to diffuse across the membrane. Recall that solutes form ionic or hydrogen bonds with water molecules (Appendix D). Water molecules that are bound to a solute that can't cross the membrane are themselves prevented from crossing.

Only unbound water molecules are able to diffuse across the membrane during osmosis. When these unbound water molecules move across a membrane, they flow from the solution with the lower solute concentration into the solution with the higher solute concentration.

To drive this point home, let's suppose the concentration of a particular solute is higher on one side of a selectively permeable membrane than it is on the other side (**FIGURE 3.13**, step 1). Further, suppose that this solute cannot diffuse through the membrane to establish equilibrium. What happens? Water will move from the side with a lower concentration of solute to the side with a higher concentration of solute (Figure 3.13, step 2). Osmosis dilutes the higher concentration and equalizes the concentrations

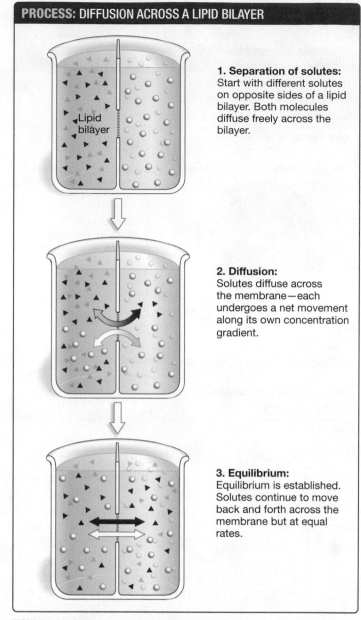

PROCESS: DIFFUSION ACROSS A LIPID BILAYER

1. Separation of solutes: Start with different solutes on opposite sides of a lipid bilayer. Both molecules diffuse freely across the bilayer.

Lipid bilayer

2. Diffusion: Solutes diffuse across the membrane—each undergoes a net movement along its own concentration gradient.

3. Equilibrium: Equilibrium is established. Solutes continue to move back and forth across the membrane but at equal rates.

FIGURE 3.12 Diffusion across a Selectively Permeable Membrane Establishes an Equilibrium.

on both sides. The movement of water is spontaneous. It is driven by the increase in entropy achieved when solute concentrations are equal on both sides of the membrane.

Movement of water by osmosis is important because it can swell or shrink a membrane-bound vesicle. Consider the liposomes illustrated in **FIGURE 3.14**. (Remember that osmosis occurs only when a solute cannot pass through a separating membrane.)

- *Left* If the solution inside the membrane has a lower concentration of solutes than the exterior has, water moves out of the vesicle into the solution outside. The solution inside is said to be **hypotonic** ("lower-tone") relative to the outside of the vesicle. As water leaves, the vesicle shrinks and the membrane shrivels, resulting in lower vesicle firmness.

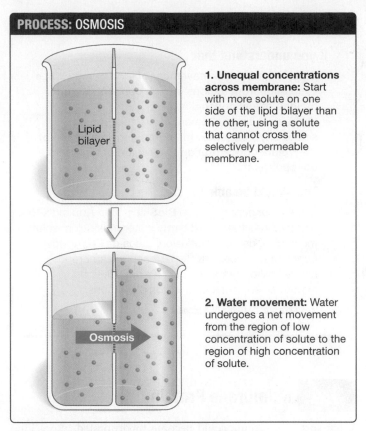

1. Unequal concentrations across membrane: Start with more solute on one side of the lipid bilayer than the other, using a solute that cannot cross the selectively permeable membrane.

Lipid bilayer

Osmosis

2. Water movement: Water undergoes a net movement from the region of low concentration of solute to the region of high concentration of solute.

FIGURE 3.13 Osmosis Is the Diffusion of Water.

✔**QUESTION** Suppose you doubled the number of solute molecules on the left side of the membrane (at the start). At equilibrium, would the water level on the left side be higher or lower than what is shown in the second drawing?

- *Middle* If the solution inside the membrane has a higher concentration of solutes than the exterior has, water moves into the vesicle via osmosis. The inside solution is said to be **hypertonic** ("excess-tone") relative to the outside of the vesicle. The incoming water causes the vesicle to swell and increase in firmness, or even burst.

- *Right* If solute concentrations are equal on both sides of the membrane, the liposome maintains its size. When the inside solution does not affect the membrane's shape, that solution is called **isotonic** ("equal-tone").

Note that the terms hypertonic, hypotonic, and isotonic are relative—they can be used only to express the relationship between a given solution and another solution separated by a membrane. Biologists also commonly use these terms to describe the solution that is exterior to the cells or vesicles.

Membranes and Chemical Evolution

What do diffusion and osmosis have to do with the first membranes floating in the prebiotic soup? Both processes tend to *reduce* differences in chemical composition between the inside and outside of membrane-bound compartments.

If liposome-like structures first arose in the oceans of early Earth, their interiors probably didn't offer a radically different environment from the surrounding solution. In all likelihood, the primary importance of the first lipid bilayers was simply to provide a container for replicating RNA, the macromolecule most likely to have been the first "living" molecule (see Chapter 5). But ribonucleotide monomers would need to be available for these

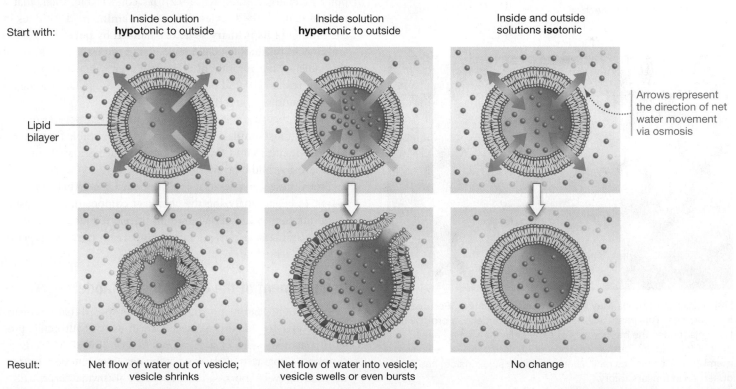

Start with:

Inside solution **hypo**tonic to outside

Inside solution **hyper**tonic to outside

Inside and outside solutions **iso**tonic

Lipid bilayer

Arrows represent the direction of net water movement via osmosis

Result:

Net flow of water out of vesicle; vesicle shrinks

Net flow of water into vesicle; vesicle swells or even bursts

No change

FIGURE 3.14 Osmosis Can Shrink or Burst Membrane-Bound Vesicles.

RNAs to replicate. Can negatively charged ribonucleotides get across lipid bilayers and inside lipid-bounded vesicles?

The answer is yes. Jack Szostak and colleagues first set out to study the permeability of membranes consisting of fatty acids and other simple amphipathic lipids thought to be present in the early oceans. Like phospholipids, fatty acids will spontaneously assemble into lipid bilayers and water-filled vesicles. Their experiments showed that ions, and even ribonucleotides, can diffuse across the fatty acid vesicle membranes—meaning that monomers could have been available for RNA synthesis.

Lending support to this hypothesis, the same minerals found to catalyze the polymerization of RNA from activated nucleotides (see Chapter 5) will also promote the formation of fatty acid vesicles—and in the process, often incorporate themselves and RNA inside. Simple vesicle-like structures that harbor nucleic acids are referred to as **protocells** (**FIGURE 3.15**). Most origin-of-life researchers view protocells as possible intermediates in the evolution of the cell.

Laboratory simulations also showed that free lipids and micelles can become incorporated into fatty acid bilayers, causing protocells to grow. Shearing forces, as from bubbling, shaking, or wave action, cause protocells to divide. Based on these observations, it is reasonable to hypothesize that once replicating RNAs became surrounded by a lipid bilayer, this simple life-form and its descendants would occupy cell-like structures that grew and divided.

Now let's investigate the next great innovation in the evolution of the cell: the ability to create and maintain a specialized internal environment that is conducive to life. What is necessary to construct an effective plasma membrane—one that imports ions and molecules needed for life while excluding ions and molecules that might damage it?

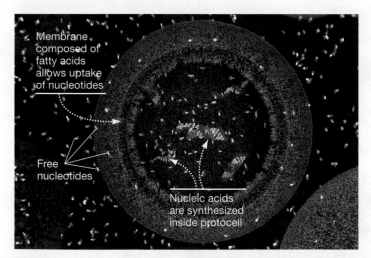

FIGURE 3.15 Protocells May Have Possessed Simple, Permeable Membranes. This image shows a computer model of a protocell. Like this model, the membranes of early cells may have been built of fatty acids. Passive transport of nucleotides across these membranes, as well as replication of nucleic acids inside, has been observed in the laboratory.

If you understand that . . .

- Diffusion is the net movement of ions or molecules in solution from regions of high concentration to regions of low concentration.
- Osmosis is the movement of water across a selectively permeable membrane, from a region of low solute concentration to a region of high solute concentration.

✔ **You should be able to . . .**

Make a concept map (see **BioSkills 15** in Appendix B) that includes the boxed terms water molecules, solute molecules, osmosis, diffusion, areas of high-to-low concentration, selectively permeable membranes, concentration gradients, hypertonic solutions, hypotonic solutions, and isotonic solutions.

Answers are available in Appendix A.

3.4 Membrane Proteins

What sort of molecule could become incorporated into a lipid bilayer and affect the bilayer's permeability? The title of this section gives the answer away. Proteins that are amphipathic can be inserted into lipid bilayers.

Proteins can be amphipathic because their monomers, amino acids, have side chains that range from highly nonpolar to highly polar or charged (see Figure 9.2). It's conceivable, then, that a protein could have a series of nonpolar amino acid residues in the middle of its primary structure flanked by polar or charged amino acid residues (**FIGURE 3.16a**). The nonpolar residues would be stable in the interior of a lipid bilayer, while the polar or charged residues would be stable alongside the polar lipid heads and surrounding water (**FIGURE 3.16b**).

Further, because the secondary and tertiary structures of proteins are almost limitless in their variety, it is possible for proteins to form openings and thus function as some sort of channel or pore across a lipid bilayer.

From these considerations, it's not surprising that when researchers began analyzing the chemical composition of plasma membranes, they found that proteins were often just as common, in terms of mass, as phospholipids. How were these two types of molecules arranged?

Development of the Fluid-Mosaic Model

In 1935 Hugh Davson and James Danielli proposed that cell membranes were structured like a sandwich in which hydrophilic proteins coat both sides of a pure lipid bilayer (**FIGURE 3.17a**). Early electron micrographs of plasma membranes seemed to be consistent with the sandwich model, and for decades it was widely accepted.

(a) Proteins can be amphipathic.

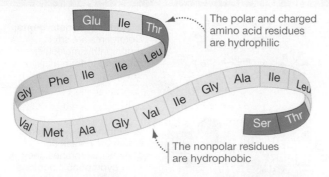

The polar and charged amino acid residues are hydrophilic

The nonpolar residues are hydrophobic

(b) Amphipathic proteins can integrate into lipid bilayers.

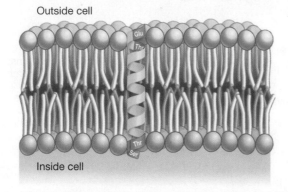

Outside cell

Inside cell

FIGURE 3.16 Amphipathic Proteins Are Anchored in Lipid Bilayers.

(a) Sandwich model

Cell exterior

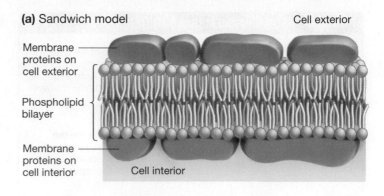

Membrane proteins on cell exterior

Phospholipid bilayer

Membrane proteins on cell interior

Cell interior

(b) Fluid-mosaic model

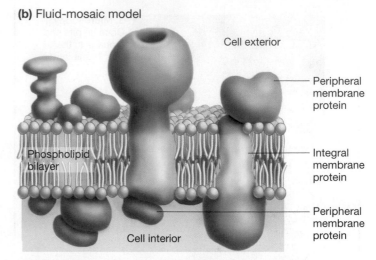

Cell exterior

Peripheral membrane protein

Phospholipid bilayer

Integral membrane protein

Peripheral membrane protein

Cell interior

FIGURE 3.17 Past and Current Models of Membrane Structure Differ in Where Membrane Proteins Reside. (a) The protein-lipid-lipid-protein sandwich model was the first hypothesis for the arrangement of lipids and proteins in cell membranes. **(b)** The fluid-mosaic model was a radical departure from the sandwich hypothesis.

The realization that membrane proteins could be amphipathic, however, led S. Jon Singer and Garth Nicolson to suggest an alternative hypothesis. In 1972, they proposed that at least some proteins span the membrane instead of being found only outside the lipid bilayer. Their hypothesis was called the **fluid-mosaic model** (**FIGURE 3.17b**). Singer and Nicolson suggested that membranes are a mosaic of phospholipids and different types of proteins. The overall structure was proposed to be dynamic and fluid.

The controversy over the nature of the cell membrane was resolved in the early 1970s with the development of an innovative technique for visualizing the surface of plasma membranes. The method is called freeze-fracture electron microscopy because the steps involve freezing and fracturing the membrane before examining it with a **scanning electron microscope (SEM)**, which produces images of an object's surface (see **BioSkills 11** in Appendix B).

As **FIGURE 3.18** (see page 60) shows, the freeze-fracture technique allows researchers to split cell membranes and view the middle of the structure. The scanning electron micrographs that result show pits and mounds studding the inner surfaces of the lipid bilayer. Researchers interpreted these structures as the locations of membrane proteins. As step 4 in the figure shows, the mounds represent proteins that remained attached to one side of the split lipid bilayer and the pits are the holes they left behind.

These observations conflicted with the sandwich model but were consistent with the fluid-mosaic model. Based on these and subsequent observations, the fluid-mosaic model is now widely accepted.

Notice in Figure 3.17b that some proteins span the membrane and have segments facing both the interior and the exterior surfaces. Proteins like these are called **integral membrane proteins,** or **transmembrane proteins.** Proteins that bind to the membrane without passing through it are called **peripheral membrane proteins.**

Certain peripheral proteins are found only on the interior surface of a cellular membrane, while others are found only on the exterior surface. As a result, the interior and exterior surfaces of the plasma membrane are distinct—the peripheral proteins and the ends of transmembrane proteins differ. Peripheral membrane proteins are often attached to transmembrane proteins.

How do these proteins affect the permeability of membranes? The answer to this question starts with an investigation of the structure of proteins involved in the transport of molecules and ions across the plasma membrane.

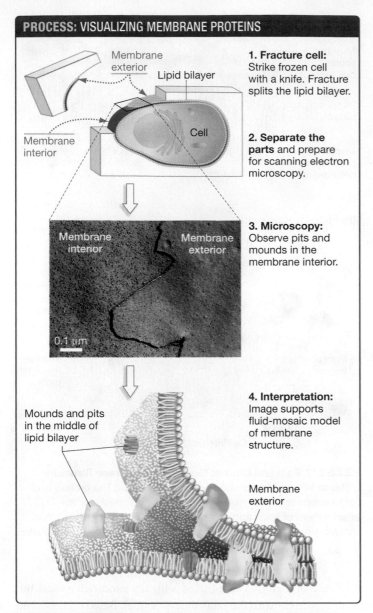

1. **Fracture cell:** Strike frozen cell with a knife. Fracture splits the lipid bilayer.

Membrane exterior
Lipid bilayer
Membrane interior
Cell

2. **Separate the parts** and prepare for scanning electron microscopy.

Membrane interior
Membrane exterior
0.1 μm

3. **Microscopy:** Observe pits and mounds in the membrane interior.

Mounds and pits in the middle of lipid bilayer

4. **Interpretation:** Image supports fluid-mosaic model of membrane structure.

Membrane exterior

FIGURE 3.18 Freeze-Fracture Preparations Allow Biologists to View Membrane Proteins.

✓**QUESTION** What would be an appropriate control to show that the pits and mounds were not simply irregularities in the lipid bilayer caused by the freeze-fracture process?

Systems for Studying Membrane Proteins

The discovery of transmembrane proteins was consistent with the hypothesis that proteins affect membrane permeability. To test this hypothesis, researchers needed some way to isolate and purify membrane proteins.

FIGURE 3.19 outlines one method that researchers developed to separate proteins from membranes. The key to the technique is the use of detergents. A **detergent** is a small amphipathic molecule. When detergents are added to the solution surrounding a lipid bilayer, the hydrophobic tails of the detergent molecule interact with the hydrophobic tails of the lipids and with the

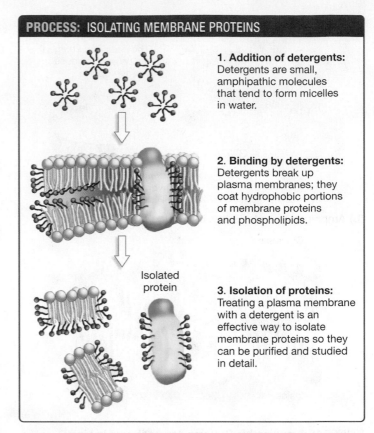

1. **Addition of detergents:** Detergents are small, amphipathic molecules that tend to form micelles in water.

2. **Binding by detergents:** Detergents break up plasma membranes; they coat hydrophobic portions of membrane proteins and phospholipids.

Isolated protein

3. **Isolation of proteins:** Treating a plasma membrane with a detergent is an effective way to isolate membrane proteins so they can be purified and studied in detail.

FIGURE 3.19 Detergents Can Be Used to Isolate Proteins from Membranes.

hydrophobic portions of transmembrane proteins. These interactions displace the membrane phospholipids and end up forming water-soluble detergent–protein complexes that can be isolated.

Since intensive experimentation on membrane proteins began, researchers have identified three broad classes of proteins that affect membrane permeability: channels, carriers, and pumps. Let's consider each class in turn.

Facilitated Diffusion via Channel Proteins

As the data in Figure 3.8 show, ions almost never cross pure phospholipid bilayers on their own. But in cells, ions routinely cross membranes through specialized membrane proteins called **ion channels.**

Ion channels form pores, or openings, in a membrane. Ions move through these pores in a predictable direction: from regions of high concentration to regions of low concentration and from areas of like charge to areas of unlike charge.

In **FIGURE 3.20**, for example, a large concentration gradient favors the movement of sodium ions from the outside of a membrane to the inside. But in addition, the inside of this cell has a net negative charge while the outside has a net positive charge. As a result, the combination of these two factors influences the final concentration of sodium ions inside the cell once equilibrium has been established.

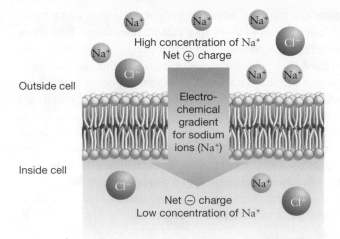

FIGURE 3.20 An Electrochemical Gradient Is a Combined Concentration and Electrical Gradient. Electrochemical gradients are established when ions build up on one side of a membrane.

Ions move in response to a combined concentration and electrical gradient, or what biologists call an **electrochemical gradient.** ✔ If you understand this concept, you should be able to add an arrow to Figure 3.20 indicating the electrochemical gradient for chloride ions.

Is an Ion Channel Involved in Cystic Fibrosis?

To understand the types of experiments that biologists do to confirm that a membrane protein is an ion channel, consider work on the cause of cystic fibrosis.

Cystic fibrosis (CF) is the most common genetic disease in humans of Northern European descent. It affects cells that produce mucus, sweat, and digestive juices. Normally these secretions are thin and slippery and act as lubricants. In individuals with CF, however, the secretions become abnormally concentrated and sticky and clog passageways in organs like the lungs.

Experiments published in 1983 suggested that cystic fibrosis is caused by defects in a membrane protein that allow chloride ions (Cl^-) to move across plasma membranes. It was proposed that reduced chloride ion transport would account for the thick mucus.

How is the transport of chloride ions involved in mucus consistency? Water movement across cell membranes is largely determined by the presence of extracellular ions like chloride. If a defective channel prevents chloride ions from leaving cells, water isn't pulled from cells by osmosis to maintain the proper mucus consistency. In effect, the disease results from the mismanagement of osmosis.

Using molecular techniques introduced in Unit 3, biologists were able to (1) find the gene that is defective in people suffering from CF and (2) use the gene to produce copies of the normal protein, which was called CFTR (short for cystic fibrosis transmembrane conductance regulator).

Is CFTR a chloride channel? To answer this question, researchers inserted purified CFTR into planar bilayers and

RESEARCH

QUESTION: Is CFTR a chloride channel?

HYPOTHESIS: CFTR increases the flow of chloride ions across a membrane.

NULL HYPOTHESIS: CFTR has no effect on membrane permeability.

EXPERIMENTAL SETUP:

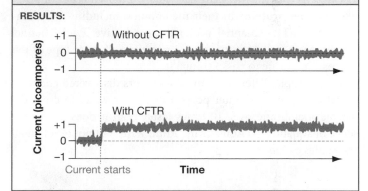

Membrane **without CFTR**

Membrane **with CFTR**

Ion flow?

Ion flow?

1. **Create planar bilayers** with and without CFTR.

2. **Add chloride ions** to one side of the planar bilayer to create an electrochemical gradient.

3. **Record electrical currents** to measure ion flow across the planar bilayers.

PREDICTION: Ion flow will be higher in membrane with CFTR.

PREDICTION OF NULL HYPOTHESIS: Ion flow will be the same in both membranes.

RESULTS:

Without CFTR

With CFTR

Current starts   Time

Current (picoamperes)

CONCLUSION: CFTR facilitates diffusion of chloride ions along an electrochemical gradient. CFTR is a chloride channel.

FIGURE 3.21 Electric Current Measurements Indicate that Chloride Flows through CFTR.

SOURCE: Bear, C. A., et al. (1992). Purification and functional reconstitution of the cystic fibrosis transmembrane conductance regulator (CFTR). *Cell* 68: 809–818.

✔ **QUESTION** The researchers repeated the "with CFTR" treatment 45 times, but recorded a current in only 35 of the replicates. Does this observation negate the conclusion? Explain why or why not.

measured the flow of electric current across the membrane. Because ions carry a charge, ion movement across a membrane produces an electric current.

The graphs in **FIGURE 3.21**, which plot the amount of current flowing across the membrane over time, show the results from this experiment. Notice that when CFTR was absent, no electric current passed through the membrane. But when CFTR was

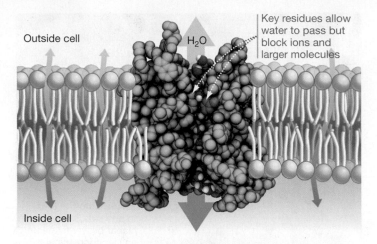

Outside cell

H₂O

Key residues allow water to pass but block ions and larger molecules

Inside cell

FIGURE 3.22 Membrane Channels Are Highly Selective. A cutaway view looking at the inside of a membrane channel, aquaporin. The key residues identified in the space-filling model selectively filter ions and other small molecules, allowing only water (red and white structures) to pass through.

inserted into the membrane, current began to flow. This was strong evidence that CFTR was indeed a chloride ion channel.

Protein Structure Determines Channel Selectivity Subsequent research has shown that cells have many different types of pore-like **channel proteins** in their membranes, including ion channels like CFTR. Channel proteins are selective. Each channel protein has a structure that permits only a particular type of ion or small molecule to pass through it.

For example, Peter Agre and co-workers discovered channels called **aquaporins** ("water-pores") that allow water to cross the plasma membrane over 10 times faster than it does in the absence of aquaporins. Aquaporins admit water but not other small molecules or ions.

FIGURE 3.22 shows a cutaway view from the side of an aquaporin, indicating how it fits in a plasma membrane. Like other channels that have been studied in detail, aquaporins have a pore that is lined with polar functional groups—in this case, carbonyl groups that interact with water. A channel's pore is hydrophilic relative to the hydrophobic residues facing the phospholipid tails of the membrane.

But how can aquaporin be selective for water and not other polar molecules? The answer was found when researchers examined its structure. Key side chains in the interior of the pore function as a molecular filter. The distance between these groups across the channel allows only those substances capable of interacting with all of them to pass through to the other side.

Movement Through Many Membrane Channels Is Regulated Recent research has shown that many aquaporins and ion channels are **gated channels**—meaning that they open or close in response to a signal, such as the binding of a particular molecule or a change in the electrical voltage across the membrane.

As an example of how voltage-gated channels work, **FIGURE 3.23** shows a potassium channel in closed and open configurations. The electrical charge on the membrane is normally negative on the inside relative to the outside, which causes the channel to adopt a closed shape that prevents potassium ions from passing through. When this charge asymmetry is reversed, the shape changes in a way that opens the channel and allows potassium ions to cross. The key point here is that in almost all cases, the flow of ions and small molecules through membrane channels is carefully controlled.

In all cases, however, the movement of substances through channels is passive—meaning it does not require an input of energy. **Passive transport** is powered by diffusion along an electrochemical gradient. Channel proteins simply enable ions or polar molecules to move across lipid bilayers efficiently, in response to

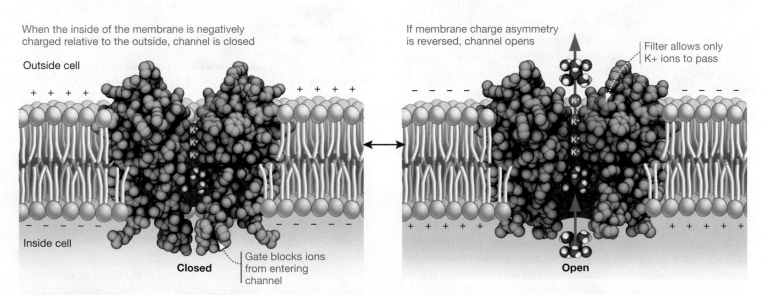

When the inside of the membrane is negatively charged relative to the outside, channel is closed

Outside cell

+ + + +   + + + +

K⁺
K⁺
K⁺

− − − − −   − − − − −

Inside cell

Closed

Gate blocks ions from entering channel

If membrane charge asymmetry is reversed, channel opens

Filter allows only K+ ions to pass

− − − − −   − − − − −

K⁺
K⁺
K⁺
K⁺

+ + + + +   + + + + + +

Open

FIGURE 3.23 Some Membrane Channels Are Highly Regulated. A model of a voltage-gated K⁺ channel in the closed and open configurations. The channel filter displaces water molecules that normally surround the K⁺ ions in an aqueous solution.

an existing gradient. They are responsible for **facilitated diffusion:** the passive transport of substances that otherwise would not cross a membrane readily.

Facilitated Diffusion via Carrier Proteins

Facilitated diffusion can also occur through **carrier proteins**—specialized membrane proteins that change shape during the transport process. Perhaps the best-studied carrier protein is one that is involved in transporting glucose into cells.

The Search for a Glucose Carrier   Next to ribose, the six-carbon sugar glucose is the most prevalent sugar found in organisms. Virtually all cells alive today use glucose as a building block for important macromolecules and as a source of stored chemical energy (Appendix E). But as Figure 3.8 shows, lipid bilayers are only moderately permeable to glucose. It is reasonable to expect, then, that plasma membranes have some mechanism for increasing their permeability to this sugar.

This prediction was supported in experiments on pure preparations of plasma membranes from human red blood cells. These plasma membranes turned out to be much more permeable to glucose than are pure lipid bilayers. Why?

After isolating and analyzing many proteins from red blood cell membranes, researchers found one protein that specifically increases membrane permeability to glucose. When they added this purified protein to liposomes, the artificial membrane transported glucose at the same rate as a membrane from a living cell. This experiment convinced biologists that the membrane protein—now called GLUT-1 (short for glucose transporter 1)—was indeed responsible for transporting glucose across plasma membranes.

How Does GLUT-1 Work?   Recall that proteins frequently change shape when they bind to other molecules and that such conformational changes are often a critical step in their function (Chapter 3). **FIGURE 3.24** illustrates the current hypothesis for how GLUT-1 works to facilitate the movement of glucose. The idea is that when glucose binds to GLUT-1, it changes the shape of the protein in a way that moves the sugar through the hydrophobic region of the membrane and releases it on the other side.

What powers the movement of molecules through carriers? The answer is diffusion. GLUT-1 facilitates diffusion by allowing glucose to enter the carrier from either side of the membrane. Glucose will pass through the carrier in the direction dictated by its concentration gradient. A large variety of molecules move across plasma membranes via specific carrier proteins.

Pumps Perform Active Transport

Diffusion—whether it is facilitated by proteins or not—is a passive process that will move substances in either direction across a membrane to make the cell interior and exterior more similar. But it is also possible for cells to move molecules or ions in a directed manner, often *against* their electrochemical gradient. Accomplishing this task requires an input of energy, because the cell must counteract the decrease in entropy that occurs when molecules or ions are concentrated. It makes sense, then, that transport against an electrochemical gradient is called **active transport.**

In cells, ATP (adenosine triphosphate) often provides the energy for active transport by transferring a phosphate group (HPO_4^{2-}) to an active transport protein called a **pump.** Recall that ATP contains three phosphate groups (Chapter 5), and that phosphate groups carry two negative charges (Appendix D). When a phosphate group leaves ATP and binds to a pump, its negative charges interact with charged amino acid residues in the protein. As a result, the protein's potential energy increases and its shape changes.

The Sodium–Potassium Pump   A classic example of how structural change leads to active transport is provided in the **sodium–potassium pump,** or more formally, Na^+/K^+-ATPase. The Na^+/K^+ part of the name refers to the ions that are transported, ATP indicates that adenosine triphosphate is used, and *–ase* identifies the molecule as an enzyme.

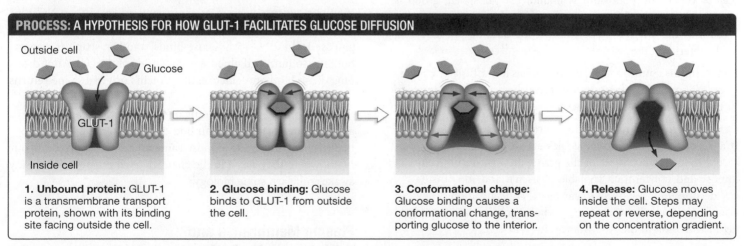

PROCESS: A HYPOTHESIS FOR HOW GLUT-1 FACILITATES GLUCOSE DIFFUSION

Outside cell

Glucose

GLUT-1

Inside cell

1. Unbound protein: GLUT-1 is a transmembrane transport protein, shown with its binding site facing outside the cell.

2. Glucose binding: Glucose binds to GLUT-1 from outside the cell.

3. Conformational change: Glucose binding causes a conformational change, transporting glucose to the interior.

4. Release: Glucose moves inside the cell. Steps may repeat or reverse, depending on the concentration gradient.

FIGURE 3.24 Carrier Proteins Undergo Structural Changes to Move Substances. This model suggests that GLUT-1 binds a glucose molecule, undergoes a conformational change, and releases glucose on the other side of the membrane.

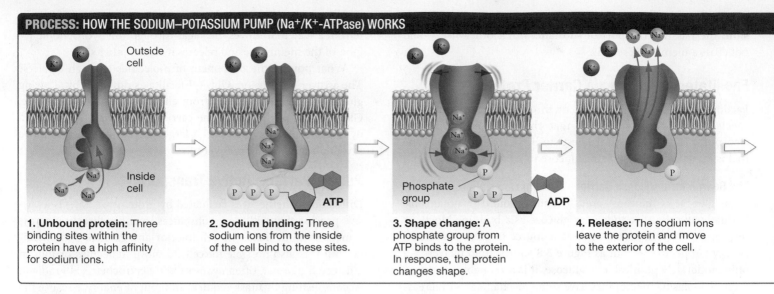

Outside cell

Inside cell

ATP

Phosphate group

ADP

1. Unbound protein: Three binding sites within the protein have a high affinity for sodium ions.

2. Sodium binding: Three sodium ions from the inside of the cell bind to these sites.

3. Shape change: A phosphate group from ATP binds to the protein. In response, the protein changes shape.

4. Release: The sodium ions leave the protein and move to the exterior of the cell.

FIGURE 3.25 The Sodium–Potassium Pump Depends on an Input of Chemical Energy Stored in ATP.

As shown in **FIGURE 3.25**, sodium and potassium ions move in a multistep process:

Step 1 When Na⁺/K⁺-ATPase is in the conformation shown here, binding sites with a high affinity for sodium ions are available.

Step 2 Three sodium ions from the inside of the cell bind to these sites and activate the ATPase activity in the pump.

Step 3 A phosphate group from ATP is transferred to the pump. When the phosphate group attaches, the pump changes its shape in a way that opens the ion-binding pocket to the external environment and reduces its affinity for sodium ions.

Step 4 The sodium ions leave the protein and move to the exterior of the cell.

Step 5 In this conformation, the pump has binding sites with a high affinity for potassium ions facing the external environment.

Step 6 Two potassium ions from outside the cell bind to the pump.

Step 7 When the potassium is bound, the phosphate group is cleaved from the protein and its structure changes in response—back to the original shape with the ion-binding pocket facing the interior of the cell.

Step 8 In this conformation, the pump has low affinity for potassium ions. The potassium ions leave the protein and move to the interior of the cell. The cycle then repeats.

Other types of pumps move protons (H⁺), calcium ions (Ca²⁺), or other ions or molecules across membranes in a directed manner, regardless of the gradients. As a result, cells can import and concentrate valuable nutrients and ions inside the cell despite their relatively low external concentration. They can also expel molecules or ions, even when a concentration gradient favors diffusion of these substances into the cell.

Secondary Active Transport Approximately 30 percent of all the ATP generated in your body is used to drive the Na⁺/K⁺-ATPase

cycle. Each cycle exports three Na⁺ ions for every two K⁺ ions it imports. In this way, the sodium–potassium pump converts energy from ATP to an electrochemical gradient across the membrane. The outside of the membrane becomes positively charged relative to the inside. This gradient favors a flow of anions out of the cell and a flow of cations into the cell.

The electrochemical gradients established by the Na⁺/K⁺-ATPase represent a form of stored energy, much like the electrical energy stored in a battery. How do cells use this energy?

Gradients are crucial to the function of the cell, in part because they make it possible for cells to engage in **secondary active transport**—also known as cotransport. When cotransport occurs, a gradient set up by a pump provides the energy required to power the movement of a different molecule against its particular gradient.

Recall that GLUT-1 facilitates the movement of glucose into or out of cells in the direction of its gradient. Can glucose be moved against its gradient? The answer is yes—a cotransport protein in your gut cells uses the Na⁺ gradient created by Na⁺/K⁺-ATPases to import glucose against its chemical gradient. When Na⁺ ions bind to this cotransporter, its shape changes in a way that allows glucose to bind. Once glucose binds, another shape transports both the sodium and glucose to the inside of the cell. After dropping off sodium and glucose, the protein's original shape returns to repeat the cycle.

In this way, glucose present in the food you are digesting is actively transported into your body. The glucose molecules eventually diffuse into your bloodstream and are transported to your brain, where they provide the chemical energy you need to stay awake and learn some biology.

Plasma Membranes and the Intracellular Environment

Taken together, the selective permeability of the lipid bilayer and the specificity of the proteins involved in passive transport and

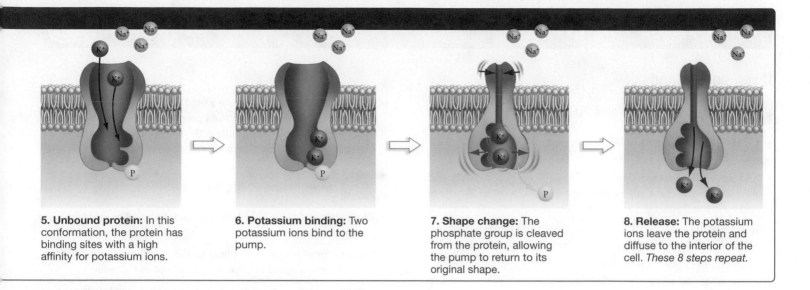

5. Unbound protein: In this conformation, the protein has binding sites with a high affinity for potassium ions.

6. Potassium binding: Two potassium ions bind to the pump.

7. Shape change: The phosphate group is cleaved from the protein, allowing the pump to return to its original shape.

8. Release: The potassium ions leave the protein and diffuse to the interior of the cell. *These 8 steps repeat.*

active transport enable cells to create an internal environment that is much different from the external one (**FIGURE 3.26**).

With the evolution of membrane proteins, the early cells acquired the ability to create an internal environment that was conducive to life—one that contained the substances required for manufacturing ATP and copying ribozymes. Cells with particularly efficient and selective membrane proteins would be favored by natural selection and would come to dominate the population. Cellular life had begun.

Some 3.5 billion years later, cells continue to evolve. What do today's cells look like, and how do they produce and store the chemical energy that makes life possible? Answering these and related questions is the focus of the following unit.

check your understanding

(C)(Y)(U)

If you understand that . . .

- Membrane proteins allow substances that ordinarily do not readily cross lipid bilayers to enter or exit cells.
- Substances may move across a membrane along an electrochemical gradient, via facilitated diffusion through channel or carrier proteins. Or, they may move against a gradient in response to work done by pumps.

✔ **You should be able to . . .**

Explain what is passive about passive transport, active about active transport, and "co" about cotransport.

Answers are available in Appendix A.

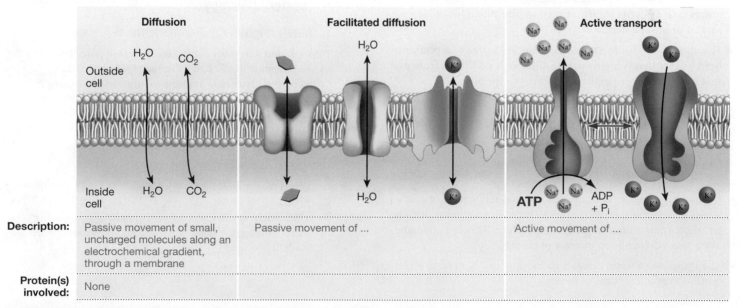

	Diffusion	Facilitated diffusion	Active transport
Description:	Passive movement of small, uncharged molecules along an electrochemical gradient, through a membrane	Passive movement of ...	Active movement of ...
Protein(s) involved:	None		

FIGURE 3.26 Summary of the Passive and Active Mechanisms of Membrane Transport.
✔**EXERCISE** Complete the chart.

If you understand . . .

3.1 Lipid Structure and Function

- Lipids are largely hydrophobic compounds due to their high number of nonpolar C–H bonds.

- The three main types of lipids found in cells are fats, steroids, and phospholipids. These molecules vary considerably in structure and function.

- In hydrocarbon chains, the length and degree of saturation have a profound effect on their physical properties.

- Amphipathic lipids possess a distinct hydrophilic region containing polar or charged groups. Phospholipids have a polar head and a nonpolar tail. The nonpolar tail usually consists of fatty acids or isoprenoids.

✔ You should be able to explain how adding hydrogen (H_2) to vegetable oil, a process called hydrogenation, results in a butter-like solid called margarine.

3.2 Phospholipid Bilayers

- In solution, phospholipids spontaneously assemble into bilayers that can serve as a physical barrier between an internal and external environment.

- Small nonpolar molecules tend to move across lipid bilayers readily; ions cross rarely, if at all.

- The permeability and fluidity of lipid bilayers depend on temperature, on the concentration of steroids, and on the chemical structure of the lipids present, such as the saturation status and length of the hydrocarbon chains. Phospholipids with longer or saturated tails form a dense and highly hydrophobic interior that lowers bilayer permeability, relative to phospholipids containing shorter or unsaturated tails.

✔ You should be able to explain how the structure of a phospholipid bilayer that is highly permeable and fluid differs from one that is highly impermeable and lacking in fluidity.

3.3 How Molecules Move across Lipid Bilayers: Diffusion and Osmosis

- Diffusion is the random movement of ions or molecules owing to their kinetic energy.

- Diffusion can result in the net directional movement of solutes across a membrane, if the membrane separates solutions that differ in concentration, charge, or temperature. This is a spontaneous process driven by an increase in entropy.

- The diffusion of water across a membrane in response to a concentration gradient is called osmosis.

✔ You should be able to imagine a beaker with solutions separated by a planar membrane and then predict what will happen after addition of a solute to one side if the solute (1) crosses the membrane readily or (2) is incapable of crossing the membrane.

3.4 Membrane Proteins

- The permeability of lipid bilayers can be altered significantly by membrane proteins.

- Channel proteins provide pores in the membrane and facilitate the diffusion of specific solutes into and out of the cell.

- Carriers undergo conformational changes that facilitate the diffusion of specific molecules into and out of the cell.

- Pumps use energy to actively move ions or molecules in a single direction, often against the electrical or chemical gradient.

- In combination, the selective permeability of phospholipid bilayers and the specificity of transport proteins make it possible to create an environment inside a cell that is radically different from the exterior.

✔ You should be able to draw and label the membrane of a cell that is placed in a solution containing calcium ions and lactose and show the activity of the following membrane proteins: (1) an H^+ pump that exports protons; (2) a calcium channel; and (3) a lactose carrier. Your drawing should include arrows and labels indicating the direction of solute movement and the direction of the appropriate electrochemical gradients.

MB MasteringBiology

1. MasteringBiology Assignments

Tutorials and Activities Active Transport; Diffusion, Diffusion and Osmosis; Facilitated Diffusion Lipids; Membrane Structure; Membrane Transport: Diffusion and Passive Transport; Membrane Transport: The Sodium–Potassium Pump; Membrane Transport Proteins; Osmosis; Membrane Transport: Cotransport; Osmosis and Water Balance in Cells; Selective Permeability of Membranes

Questions Reading Quizzes, Blue-Thread Questions, Test Bank

2. eText Read your book online, search, take notes, highlight text, and more.

3. The Study Area Practice Test, Cumulative Test, BioFlix® 3-D Animations, Videos, Activities, Audio Glossary, Word Study Tools, Art

You should be able to . . .

1. How is the structure of saturated fats different from that of unsaturated fats?
   a. All of the carbons in the hydrocarbon tails of saturated fats are bonded to one another with double bonds.
   b. Saturated fats have three hydrocarbon tails bonded to the glycerol molecule instead of just two.
   c. The hydrocarbon tails in a saturated fat have the maximum number of hydrogens possible.
   d. Saturated fats have no oxygens present.

2. What distinguishes amphipathic lipids from other lipids?
   a. Amphipathic lipids have polar and nonpolar regions.
   b. Amphipathic lipids have saturated and unsaturated regions.
   c. Amphipathic lipids are steroids.
   d. Amphipathic lipids dissolve in water.

3. If a solution surrounding a cell is hypertonic relative to the inside of the cell, how will water move?
   a. It will move into the cell via osmosis.
   b. It will move out of the cell via osmosis.
   c. It will not move, because equilibrium exists.
   d. It will evaporate from the cell surface more rapidly.

4. When does a concentration gradient exist?
   a. when membranes rupture
   b. when solute concentrations are high
   c. when solute concentrations are low
   d. when solute concentrations differ on the two sides of a membrane

5. What two conditions must be present for the effects of osmosis to occur?

6. In terms of structure, how do channel proteins differ from carrier proteins?

7. If a cell were placed in a solution with a high potassium concentration and no sodium, what would happen to the sodium–potassium pump's activity?
   a. It would stop moving ions across the membrane.
   b. It would continue using ATP to pump sodium out of the cell and potassium into the cell.
   c. It would move sodium and potassium ions across the membrane, but no ATP would be used.
   d. It would reverse the direction of sodium and potassium ions to move them against their gradients.

8. Cooking oil lipids consist of long, unsaturated hydrocarbon chains. Would you expect these molecules to form membranes spontaneously? Why or why not? Describe, on a molecular level, how you would expect these lipids to interact with water.

9. Explain why phospholipids form a bilayer in solution, and why the process is spontaneous.

10. Ethanol (C_2H_5OH) is the active ingredient in alcoholic beverages. Would you predict that this molecule crosses lipid bilayers quickly, slowly, or not at all? Explain your reasoning.

11. Integral membrane proteins are anchored in lipid bilayers. Of the following four groups of amino acids—nonpolar, polar, charged/acidic, charged/basic (see Figure 9.2)—which would likely be found in the portion that crosses the lipid bilayer? Explain your reasoning.

12. Examine the experimental chamber in Figure 3.7a. If the lipid bilayer were to contain the CFTR molecule, what would pass through the membrane if you added a 1-molar solution of sodium chloride on the left side and a 1-molar solution of potassium ions on the right? Assume that there is an equal amount of water on each side at the start of the experiment.

13. In an experiment, you create two groups of liposomes—one made from red blood cell membranes and the other from frog egg cell membranes. When placed in water, those made with red blood cell membranes burst more rapidly than those made from frog membranes. What is the best explanation for these results?
    a. The red blood cell liposomes are more hypertonic relative to water than the frog egg liposomes.
    b. The red blood cell liposomes are more hypotonic relative to water than the frog egg liposomes.
    c. The red blood cell liposomes contain aquaporins, which are not abundant in the frog egg liposomes.
    d. The frog egg liposomes contain ion channels, which are not present in the red blood cell liposomes.

14. When phospholipids are arranged in a bilayer, it is theoretically possible for individual molecules in the bilayer to flip-flop. That is, a phospholipid could turn 180° and become part of the membrane's other surface. From what you know about the behavior of polar heads and nonpolar tails, predict whether flip-flops are frequent or rare. Then design an experiment, using a planar bilayer with one side made up of phospholipids that contain a dye molecule on their hydrophilic head, to test your prediction.

15. Unicellular organisms live in a wide range of habitats, from the hot springs in Yellowstone National Park to the freezing temperatures of the Antarctic. Make a prediction about the saturation status of membrane phospholipids in organisms that live in extremely cold environments versus those that live in extremely hot environments. Explain your reasoning.

16. When biomedical researchers design drugs, they sometimes add methyl (CH_3) groups or charged groups to the molecules. If these groups are not directly involved in the activity of the drug, predict the purpose of these modifications and explain why these strategies are necessary.

THE CHEMISTRY OF LIFE

The first spark of life ignited when simple chemical reactions began to convert small molecules into larger, more complex molecules with novel 3-D structures and activities. According to the theory of chemical evolution, these reactions eventually led to the formation of the four types of macromolecules characteristic of life—proteins, nucleic acids, carbohydrates, and lipids.

As you look through this concept map, consider how the functions of the four types of macromolecules are determined by their structures, and how these structures stem from the chemical properties of the atoms and bonds used to build them.

Note that each box in the concept map indicates the chapters and sections where you can go for review. Also, be sure to do the blue exercises in the Check Your Understanding box below.

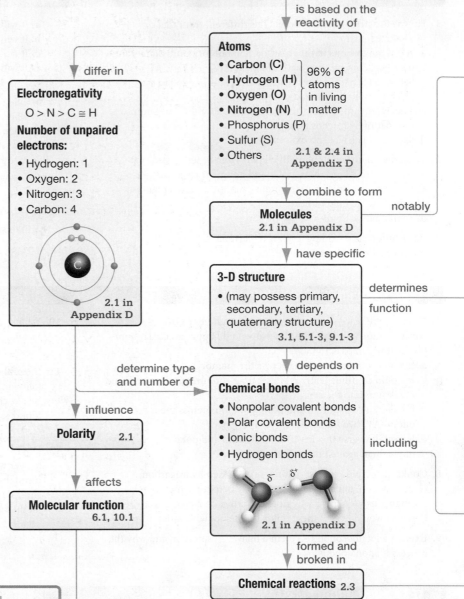

is based on the reactivity of

Atoms
- Carbon (C)
- Hydrogen (H) } 96% of atoms in living matter
- Oxygen (O)
- Nitrogen (N)
- Phosphorus (P)
- Sulfur (S)
- Others   **2.1 & 2.4 in Appendix D**

differ in

Electronegativity

O > N > C ≅ H

Number of unpaired electrons:
- Hydrogen: 1
- Oxygen: 2
- Nitrogen: 3
- Carbon: 4

2.1 in Appendix D

combine to form

notably

Molecules
2.1 in Appendix D

have specific

3-D structure
- (may possess primary, secondary, tertiary, quaternary structure)
3.1, 5.1-3, 9.1-3

determines function

depends on

determine type and number of

Chemical bonds
- Nonpolar covalent bonds
- Polar covalent bonds
- Ionic bonds
- Hydrogen bonds

including

2.1 in Appendix D

influence

Polarity   **2.1**

affects

Molecular function
6.1, 10.1

formed and broken in

Chemical reactions 2.3

as demonstrated by

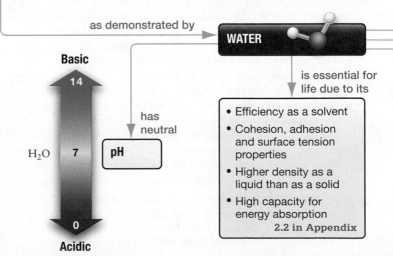

WATER

is essential for life due to its

- Efficiency as a solvent
- Cohesion, adhesion and surface tension properties
- Higher density as a liquid than as a solid
- High capacity for energy absorption
2.2 in Appendix

Basic
14

has neutral

H_2O 7   **pH**

0
Acidic

check your understanding

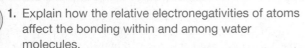

If you understand the big picture . . .
✔ You should be able to . . .

1. Explain how the relative electronegativities of atoms affect the bonding within and among water molecules.

2. Describe the attributes of RNA that make it a candidate for the origin of life. Why isn't DNA considered a candidate?

3. Circle the atoms in amino acids and nucleotides that engage in creating bonds with other monomers.

4. Draw a protein in the lipid bilayer. What role might it play?

Answers are available in Appendix A.

Biological macromolecules

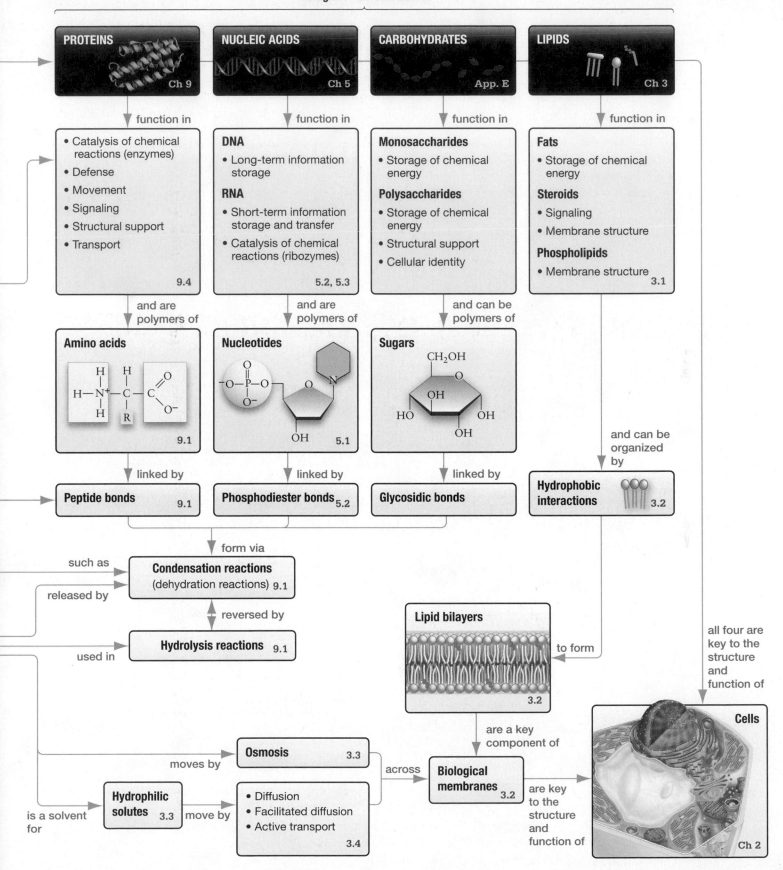

PROTEINS Ch 9

NUCLEIC ACIDS Ch 5

CARBOHYDRATES App. E

LIPIDS Ch 3

function in

function in

function in

function in

PROTEINS
- Catalysis of chemical reactions (enzymes)
- Defense
- Movement
- Signaling
- Structural support
- Transport

9.4

DNA
- Long-term information storage

RNA
- Short-term information storage and transfer
- Catalysis of chemical reactions (ribozymes)

5.2, 5.3

Monosaccharides
- Storage of chemical energy

Polysaccharides
- Storage of chemical energy
- Structural support
- Cellular identity

Fats
- Storage of chemical energy

Steroids
- Signaling
- Membrane structure

Phospholipids
- Membrane structure

3.1

and are polymers of

and are polymers of

and can be polymers of

Amino acids 9.1

Nucleotides 5.1

Sugars

and can be organized by

linked by

linked by

linked by

Peptide bonds 9.1

Phosphodiester bonds 5.2

Glycosidic bonds

Hydrophobic interactions 3.2

form via

such as

Condensation reactions
(dehydration reactions) 9.1

released by

reversed by

Hydrolysis reactions 9.1

used in

Lipid bilayers

3.2

to form

all four are key to the structure and function of

are a key component of

Osmosis 3.3

moves by

across

Biological membranes 3.2

are key to the structure and function of

Cells

Ch 2

Hydrophilic solutes 3.3

move by

- Diffusion
- Facilitated diffusion
- Active transport

3.4

is a solvent for

4 The Cell Cycle

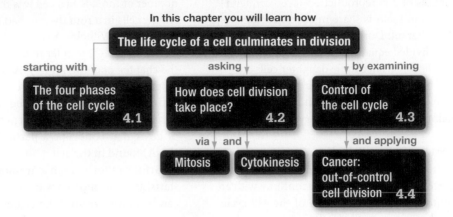

In this chapter you will learn how

The life cycle of a cell culminates in division

starting with

The four phases of the cell cycle 4.1

asking

How does cell division take place? 4.2

by examining

Control of the cell cycle 4.3

via and

Mitosis **Cytokinesis**

and applying

Cancer: out-of-control cell division 4.4

This cell, from a hyacinth plant, is undergoing a type of nuclear division called mitosis. Understanding how mitosis occurs is a major focus of this chapter.

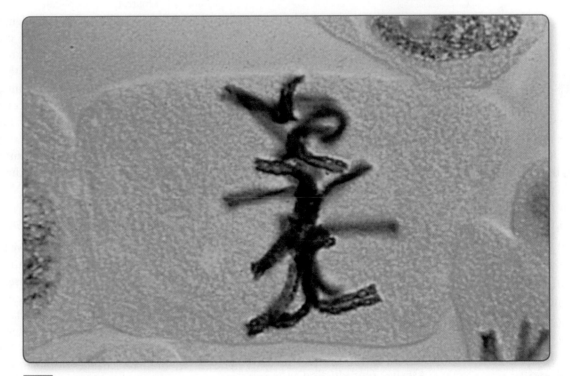

The cell theory maintains that all organisms are made of cells and all cells arise from preexisting cells (Chapter 1). Although the cell theory was widely accepted among biologists by the 1860s, most believed that new cells arose within preexisting cells by a process that resembled the growth of mineral crystals. But Rudolf Virchow proposed that new cells arise by splitting preexisting cells—that is, by **cell division.**

In the late 1800s, microscopic observations of newly developing organisms, or **embryos,** confirmed Virchow's hypothesis. Multicellular eukaryotes start life as single-celled embryos and grow through a series of cell divisions.

Early studies revealed two fundamentally different ways that nuclei divide before cell division: meiosis and mitosis. In animals, **meiosis** leads to the production of sperm and eggs, which are the male and female reproductive cells termed **gametes. Mitosis** leads to the production of all other cell types, referred to as **somatic** (literally, "body-belonging") **cells.**

✔ When you see this checkmark, stop and test yourself. Answers are available in Appendix A.

71

Mitosis and meiosis are usually accompanied by **cytokinesis** ("cell movement")—the division of the cytoplasm into two distinct cells. When cytokinesis is complete, a so-called parent cell has given rise to two daughter cells.

Mitotic and meiotic cell divisions are responsible for one of the five fundamental attributes of life: reproduction (see Chapter 1). But even though mitosis and meiosis share many characteristics, they are fundamentally different. During mitosis, the genetic material is copied and then divided equally between two cells. This is referred to as cellular *replication*, since these daughter cells are genetically identical with the original parent cell. In contrast, meiosis results in daughter cells that are genetically different from each other and that have half the amount of hereditary material as the parent cell.

This chapter focuses on mitotic cell division; meiotic cell division is the subject of the next chapter (Chapter 11). Let's begin with a look at the key events in a cell's life cycle, continue with an in-depth analysis of mitosis and the regulation of the cell cycle, and end by examining how uncontrolled cell division can lead to cancer.

4.1 How Do Cells Replicate?

For life on Earth to exist, cells must replicate. The general requirements for cellular replication are to (1) copy the DNA (deoxyribonucleic acid), (2) separate the copies, and (3) divide the cytoplasm to create two complete cells.

This chapter focuses on eukaryotic cell replication, which is responsible for three key events:

1. *Growth*   The trillions of genetically identical cells that make up your body are the product of mitotic divisions that started in a single fertilized egg.

2. *Wound repair*   When you suffer a scrape, cellular replication generates the cells that repair your skin.

3. *Reproduction*   When yeast cells grow in bread dough or in a vat of beer, they are reproducing by cellular replication. In yeasts and other single-cell eukaryotes, mitotic division is the basis of asexual reproduction. **Asexual reproduction** produces offspring that are genetically identical with the parent.

These events are so basic to life that cell replication has been studied for well over a century. Like much work in biology, the research on how cells divide began by simply observing the process.

What Is a Chromosome?

As studies of cell division in eukaryotes began, biologists found that certain chemical dyes made threadlike structures visible within nuclei. In 1879, Walther Flemming used a dye made from a coal tar to observe these threadlike structures and how they changed in the dividing cells of salamander embryos. The threads

first appeared in pairs just before division and then split to produce single, unpaired threads in the daughter cells. Flemming introduced the term mitosis, from the Greek *mitos* ("thread"), to describe this process.

Others studied the roundworm *Ascaris* and noted that the total number of threads in a cell was the same before and after mitosis. All the cells in a roundworm had the same number of threads.

In 1888 Wilhelm Waldeyer coined the term **chromosome** ("colored-body") to refer to these threadlike structures (visible in the chapter-opening photo). A chromosome consists of a single, long DNA double helix that is wrapped around proteins, called **histones,** in a highly organized manner. DNA encodes the cell's hereditary information, or genetic material. A gene is a length of DNA that codes for a particular protein or ribonucleic acid (RNA) found in the cell.

Before mitosis, each chromosome is replicated. As mitosis starts, the chromosomes condense into compact structures that can be moved around the cell efficiently. Then one of the chromosome copies is distributed to each of two daughter cells.

FIGURE 4.1 illustrates unreplicated chromosomes, replicated chromosomes before they have condensed prior to mitosis, and replicated chromosomes that have condensed at the start of mitosis. Each of the DNA copies in a replicated chromosome is called a **chromatid.** Before mitosis, the two chromatids are joined along their entire length by proteins called cohesins. Once mitosis begins, however, many of these connections are removed except for those at a specialized region of the chromosome called the **centromere.** Chromatid copies that remain attached at their centromere are referred to as **sister chromatids.** Even though a replicated chromosome consists of two chromatids, it is still considered a single chromosome.

Cells Alternate between M Phase and Interphase

The division of eukaryotic cells is like a well-choreographed stage performance. The most visually stimulating part of the show occurs when cells are in their dividing phase, called the **M** (*m*itotic or *m*eiotic) **phase.** With a light microscope, chromosomes can be stained and observed as discrete units only during M phase, when they condense into compact structures.

The rest of the time, the cell is in **interphase** ("between-phase"). No dramatic changes in the nucleus are visible by light microscopy during interphase. The chromosomes uncoil into the extremely long, thin structures shown in Figure 4.1 and are no longer stained as individual threads. However, this does not mean that the cell is idle. Interphase is an active time: The cell is either growing and preparing to divide or fulfilling its specialized function in a multicellular individual. Cells actually spend most of their time in interphase.

The Discovery of S Phase

Once M phase and interphase were identified by microscopy, researchers could start assigning roles to these distinct phases. They could see that the separation of chromosomes and cytokinesis

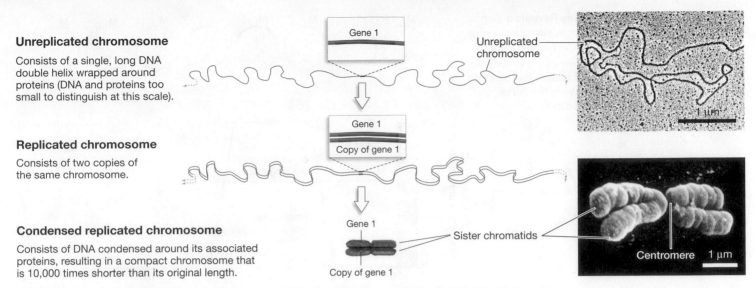

Unreplicated chromosome

Consists of a single, long DNA double helix wrapped around proteins (DNA and proteins too small to distinguish at this scale).

Replicated chromosome

Consists of two copies of the same chromosome.

Condensed replicated chromosome

Consists of DNA condensed around its associated proteins, resulting in a compact chromosome that is 10,000 times shorter than its original length.

Gene 1

Gene 1
Copy of gene 1

Gene 1
Copy of gene 1

Unreplicated chromosome

1 μm

Sister chromatids

Centromere   1 μm

FIGURE 4.1 Changes in Chromosome Morphology. After chromosomes replicate, the two identical copies are attached to each other along their entire length. Early in mitosis, replicated chromosomes condense and sister chromatids remain attached at a region called the centromere.

took place during the M phase, but when are the chromosomes copied?

To answer this question, researchers needed to distinguish cells that were replicating their DNA from those that were not. They were able to do this by adding radioactive phosphorus, in the form of phosphates, to cells. Those cells that were synthesizing DNA would incorporate the radioactive isotope into nucleotides (see Chapter 4 to review where phosphates are in DNA).

The idea was to:

1. label DNA as chromosomes were being copied;

2. wash away any radioactive isotope that hadn't been incorporated and remove RNA, which would also incorporate phosphorus; and then

3. visualize the labeled, newly synthesized DNA by exposing the treated cells to X-ray film. Emissions from radioactive phosphorus create a black dot in the film. This is the technique called autoradiography (see **BioSkills 9** in Appendix B).

In 1951, Alma Howard and Stephen Pelc performed this experiment and looked for cells with black dots—indicating active DNA synthesis—immediately after the exposure to a radioactive isotope ended. They found black dots in some of the interphase cells, but none in M-phase cells. Several years later, these results were verified using radioactive thymidine, which is incorporated into DNA but not RNA. These results were strong evidence that DNA replication occurs during interphase.

Thus, biologists had identified a new stage in the life of a cell. They called it **synthesis (or S) phase.** S phase is part of interphase. Replication of the genetic material is separated, in time, from the partitioning of chromosome copies during M phase.

Howard and Pelc coined the term **cell cycle** to describe the orderly sequence of events that leads a eukaryotic cell through the duplication of its chromosomes to the time it divides.

The Discovery of the Gap Phases

In addition to discovering the S phase, Howard and Pelc made another key observation—not all the interphase cells were labeled. This meant that there was at least one "gap" in interphase when DNA was not being copied.

Howard and Pelc, along with researchers in other labs, followed up on these early results by asking where S phase was positioned in interphase. There were three possible scenarios:

1. The S phase is immediately before M phase, with a single gap between the end of M and start of S phase;

2. the S phase is immediately after M phase, with a gap between the end of S and the start of M phase; or

3. two gaps exist, one before and one after the S phase.

To address which of these models, if any, is correct, many experiments were done using cells in culture. Cultured cells are powerful experimental tools because they can be manipulated much more easily than cells in an intact organism (see **BioSkills 12** in Appendix B). In most of these studies, researchers used cultures that were asynchronous, meaning that the cells were randomly distributed in the cycle.

To understand the value of these asynchronous cultures, imagine the cell cycle were a clock. Every complete rotation around the clock would represent one cell division, and each tick would represent a different point in the cycle. At any given time, an asynchronous culture would have at least one cell present at each of the ticks on the clock. As time passes, these cells would move around this cell-cycle clock at the same rate and in the same direction.

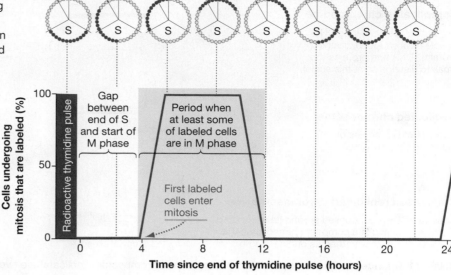

FIGURE 4.2 The Pulse–Chase Assay Reveals a Gap Phase. Cells labeled with radioactive thymidine during the pulse can be tracked during the chase to identify when they enter M phase. In this assay, a gap between the end of S phase and start of M phase was identified based on the delay observed between the pulse and the presence of labeled mitotic cells.

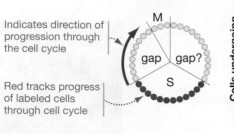

Indicates direction of progression through the cell cycle

Red tracks progress of labeled cells through cell cycle

In one experiment, researchers marked the S-phase cells in a human cell culture by exposing it to radioactively labeled thymidine. A short time later, they stopped the labeling by flooding the solution surrounding the cultured cells with nonradioactive thymidine. This pulse–chase approach (introduced in Chapter 2) labeled only those cells that were in S phase during the radioactive pulse. Imagine these marked cells moving like a hand on the clock that could be tracked as they progressed through the cell cycle.

Once the pulse ended, the researchers analyzed samples of the culture at different times during the chase. For each batch of cells, they recorded how many labeled cells were undergoing mitosis, meaning that the cells that were in S phase during the pulse had entered M phase.

One striking result emerged early on: None of the labeled cells started mitosis immediately. Because the cultures were asynchronous, at least some of the cells must have been at the very end of their S phase when exposed to the pulse. If the S phase had been immediately followed by the M phase, some of these labeled cells would have entered M just as the chase began. Instead, it took several hours before any of the labeled cells began mitosis.

The time lag between the end of the pulse and the appearance of the first labeled mitotic nuclei corresponds to a period between the end of S phase and the beginning of M phase. This gap represents the time when chromosome replication is complete, but mitosis has not yet begun. **FIGURE 4.2** shows how cells labeled with radioactive thymidine can be tracked as they progress through the M phase.

After this result, the possibilities for the organization of the cell cycle were narrowed to either one gap between the end of S and start of M phase, or two gaps that flank the S phase. Which of the models best represents the eukaryotic cell cycle? Once researchers determined the lengths of the S and M phases, they found that the combined time, including the gap between these phases, was still short compared with the length of the cell cycle. This discrepancy represents an additional gap phase that is between the end of M and the start of S phase.

The cell cycle was thus finally mapped out. The gap between the end of M and start of S phase is called the **G₁ phase.** The second gap, between the end of S and start of M phase, is called the **G₂ phase.**

The Cell Cycle

FIGURE 4.3 pulls these results together into a comprehensive view of the cell cycle. The cell cycle involves four phases: M phase and an interphase consisting of the G₁, S, and G₂ phases. In the cycle diagrammed here, the G₁ phase is about twice as long as G₂, but the timing of these phases varies depending on the cell type and growth conditions.

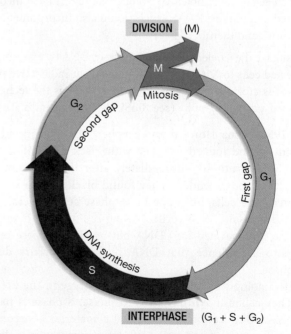

FIGURE 4.3 The Cell Cycle Has Four Phases. A representative cell cycle. The time required for the G₁ and G₂ phases varies dramatically among cells and organisms.

Why do the gap phases exist? Besides needing to copy their chromosomes during interphase, cells also must prepare for division by replicating organelles and increasing in size. Before mitosis can take place, the parent cell must grow large enough to divide into two cells that will be normal in size and function. The two gap phases provide the time required to accomplish these tasks. They allow the cell to complete all the requirements for cell division other than chromosome replication.

Now let's turn to the M phase. Once the genetic material has been copied, how do cells divide it between daughter cells?

4.2 What Happens during M Phase?

The M phase typically consists of two distinct events: the division of the nucleus and the division of the cytoplasm. During cell replication, mitosis divides the replicated chromosomes to form two daughter nuclei with identical chromosomes and genes. Mitosis is usually accompanied by cytokinesis—cytoplasmic division that results in two daughter cells.

FIGURE 4.4 provides an overview of how chromosomes change before, during, and after mitosis and cytokinesis, beginning with a hypothetical plant cell or animal cell in G_1 phase. The first drawing shows a total of four chromosomes in the cell, but chromosome number varies widely among species—chimpanzees and potato plants have a total of 48 chromosomes in each cell; a maize (corn) plant has 20, dogs have 78, and fruit flies have 8.

Eukaryotic chromosomes consist of DNA wrapped around the globular histone proteins. In eukaryotes this DNA–protein material is called **chromatin.** During interphase, the chromatin of each chromosome is in a "relaxed" or uncondensed state, forming long, thin strands (see Figure 4.1, top).

The second drawing in Figure 4.4 shows chromosomes that have been copied before mitosis. Each chromosome now consists of two sister chromatids. Each chromatid contains one long DNA double helix, and sister chromatids represent exact copies of the same genetic information.

At the start of mitosis, then, each chromosome consists of two sister chromatids that are attached to each other at the centromere.

✔ You should be able to explain the relationship between chromosomes and (1) genes, (2) chromatin, and (3) sister chromatids.

Events in Mitosis

As the third drawing in Figure 4.4 indicates, mitosis begins when chromatin condenses to form a much more compact structure. Replicated, condensed chromosomes correspond to the paired threads observed by early biologists.

During mitosis, the two sister chromatids separate to form independent daughter chromosomes. One copy of each chromosome goes to each of the two daughter cells. (See the final drawing in Figure 4.4.) As a result, each cell receives an identical copy of the genetic information that was contained in the parent cell.

Biologists have identified five subphases within M phase based on distinctive events that occur. Interphase is followed by the mitotic subphases of prophase, prometaphase, metaphase, anaphase, and telophase.

Recall that before mitosis begins, chromosomes have already replicated during the S phase of interphase. Now let's look at how cells separate the chromatids in these replicated chromosomes by investigating each subphase of mitosis in turn (**FIGURE 4.5**, on page 76).

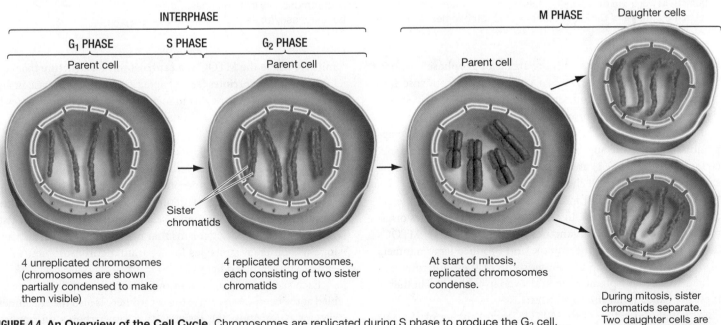

FIGURE 4.4 An Overview of the Cell Cycle. Chromosomes are replicated during S phase to produce the G_2 cell. During M phase, the replicated chromosomes are partitioned to the two daughter cells. Each daughter cell contains the same complement of chromosomes as the parent cell.

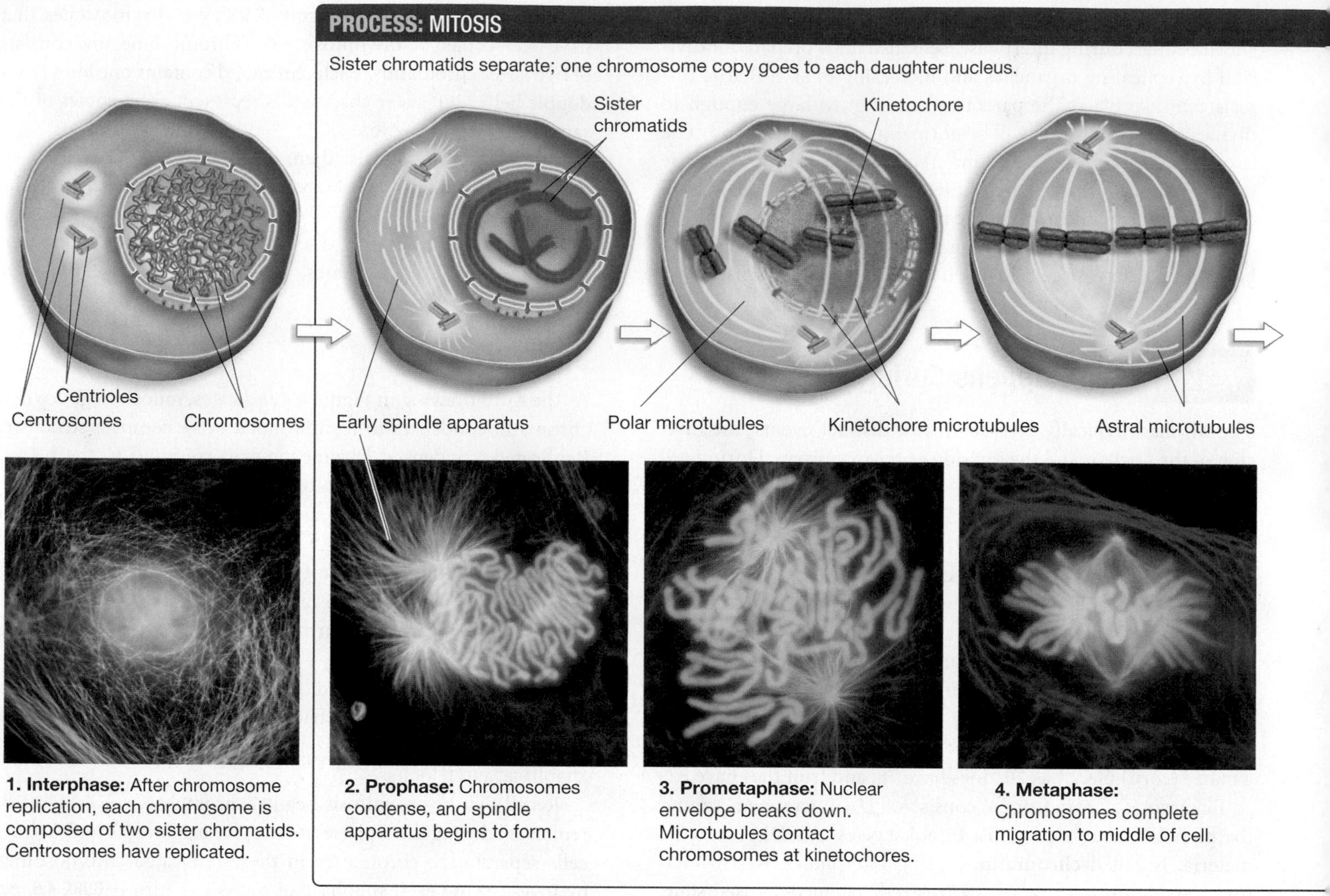

Sister chromatids separate; one chromosome copy goes to each daughter nucleus.

Sister chromatids

Kinetochore

Centrioles
Centrosomes   Chromosomes   Early spindle apparatus   Polar microtubules   Kinetochore microtubules   Astral microtubules

1. **Interphase:** After chromosome replication, each chromosome is composed of two sister chromatids. Centrosomes have replicated.

2. **Prophase:** Chromosomes condense, and spindle apparatus begins to form.

3. **Prometaphase:** Nuclear envelope breaks down. Microtubules contact chromosomes at kinetochores.

4. **Metaphase:** Chromosomes complete migration to middle of cell.

FIGURE 4.5 Mitosis and Cytokinesis. In the micrographs, under the drawings, chromosomes are stained blue, microtubules are yellow/green, and intermediate filaments are red.

✔**QUANTITATIVE:** If the model cell in this figure has x amount of DNA and four chromosomes in its G_1 phase, then what is the amount of DNA and number of chromosomes in (1) prophase; (2) anaphase; (3) each daughter cell after division is complete?

Prophase   Mitosis begins with the events of **prophase** ("before-phase," Figure 4.5, step 2), when chromosomes condense into compact structures. Chromosomes first become visible in the light microscope during prophase.

Prophase is also marked by the formation of the spindle apparatus. The **spindle apparatus** is a structure that produces mechanical forces that (1) move replicated chromosomes during early mitosis and (2) pull chromatids apart in late mitosis.

The spindle consists of microtubules—components of the cytoskeleton (see Chapter 2). In all eukaryotes, microtubules originate from microtubule-organizing centers (MTOCs). MTOCs define the two poles of the spindle and produce large numbers of microtubules. During prophase, some of these microtubules extend from each spindle pole and overlap with one another—these are called **polar microtubules.**

Although the nature of this MTOC varies among plants, animals, fungi, and other eukaryotic groups, the spindle apparatus has the same function. Figure 4.5 illustrates an animal cell undergoing

mitosis, where the MTOC is a **centrosome**—a structure that contains a pair of **centrioles** (see Chapter 2). During prophase in animal cells, the spindle begins to form around the chromosomes by moving centrosomes to opposite sides of the nucleus.

Prometaphase   In many eukaryotes, once chromosomes have condensed, the nuclear envelope disintegrates. Once the envelope has been removed, microtubules are able to attach to chromosomes at specialized structures called **kinetochores.** These events occur during **prometaphase** ("before middle-phase"; see Figure 4.5, step 3). (Organisms that maintain their nuclear envelope use different strategies for separating chromosomes, which will not be discussed here.)

Each sister chromatid has its own kinetochore, which is assembled at the centromere. Since the centromere is also the attachment site for chromatids, the result is two kinetochores on opposite sides of each replicated chromosome. The microtubules that are attached to these structures are called **kinetochore microtubules.**

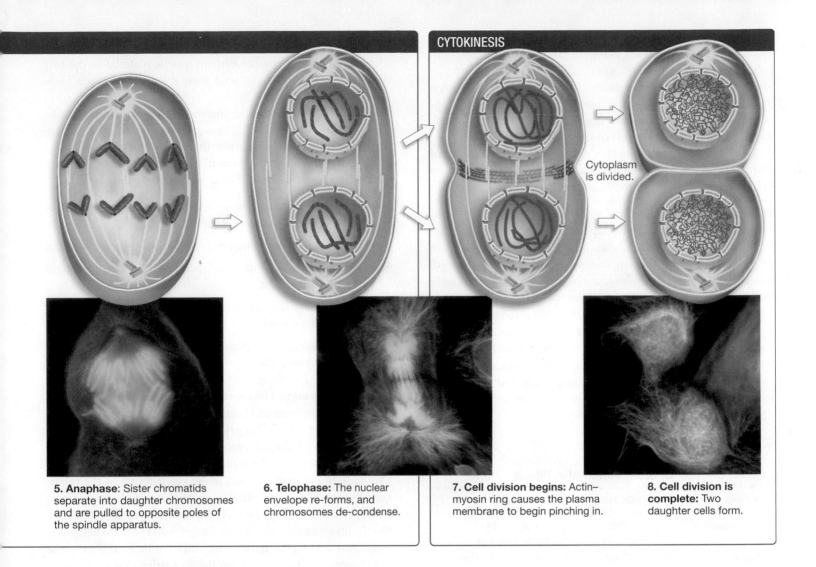

CYTOKINESIS

Cytoplasm is divided.

5. Anaphase: Sister chromatids separate into daughter chromosomes and are pulled to opposite poles of the spindle apparatus.

6. Telophase: The nuclear envelope re-forms, and chromosomes de-condense.

7. Cell division begins: Actin–myosin ring causes the plasma membrane to begin pinching in.

8. Cell division is complete: Two daughter cells form.

Early in mitosis, kinesin and dynein motors are recruited to the kinetochore, where they can "walk" the chromosome up and down microtubules. These motors are thought to be very important in the initial attachment of the kinetochore to the plus end of the microtubule. If these ideas are correct, then the process is similar to the way these motors walk along microtubules during vesicle transport (see Chapter 2).

In all eukaryotes, after the kinetochores have attached to microtubules, chromosomes begin to move to the middle of the cell during prometaphase.

Metaphase Once the kinetochore microtubules have moved all the chromosomes to the middle of the spindle (Figure 4.5, step 4), the mitotic cells enter **metaphase** ("middle-phase"). At this point, the chromosomes are lined up along an imaginary plane between the two spindle poles called the **metaphase plate.**

The formation of the spindle apparatus is now complete. The polar microtubules that extend from each spindle pole overlap in the middle of the cell, thereby forming a pole-to-pole connection. Each chromosome is held by kinetochore microtubules reaching out from opposite poles and exerting the same amount of tension, or pull. The spindle poles are held in place partly because of

astral microtubules that extend from the MTOCs and interact with proteins on the cell membrane.

The alignment of these chromosomes results from the growth and shrinkage of the attached kinetochore microtubules. When chromosomes reach the metaphase plate, the shrinkage of these microtubules at the MTOCs is balanced by slow growth of microtubules at the kinetochores. Since the sister chromatids of each chromosome are connected to opposite poles, a tug of war occurs during metaphase that pulls them in opposite directions.

Anaphase At the start of **anaphase** ("against-phase"), the cohesins that are holding sister chromatids together at the centromeres split (Figure 4.5, step 5). Because the chromatids are under tension, each replicated chromosome is pulled apart to create two independent daughter chromosomes. By definition, this separation of chromatids instantly doubles the number of chromosomes in the cell.

Two types of movement occur during anaphase. First, the daughter chromosomes move to opposite poles via the attachment of kinetochore proteins to the shrinking kinetochore microtubules. Second, the two poles of the spindle are pushed and pulled farther apart. The motor proteins in overlapping polar microtubules push the poles away from each other. Different motors on the membrane walk along on the astral microtubules to pull the poles to opposite sides of the cell.

During anaphase, then, replicated chromosomes split into two identical sets of daughter chromosomes. Their separation to opposite poles is a critical step in mitosis because it ensures that each daughter cell receives the same complement of chromosomes.

When anaphase is complete, two complete collections of chromosomes are fully separated, each being identical with those of the parent cell before chromosome replication.

Telophase   During **telophase** ("end-phase"), the nuclear envelope that dissolved in prometaphase reforms around each set of chromosomes, and the chromosomes begin to de-condense (Figure 4.5, step 6). Once two independent nuclei have formed, mitosis is complete. At this point, most cells will go on to divide their cytoplasm via cytokinesis to form two daughter cells.

TABLE 4.1 summarizes the key structures involved in mitosis.

✔ **After you've studied the table and reviewed Figure 4.5, you should be able to make a table with rows titled (1) spindle apparatus, (2) nuclear envelope, and (3) chromosomes, and columns titled with the five phases of mitosis. Fill in the table by summarizing what happens to each structure during each phase of mitosis.**

SUMMARY TABLE 4.1   **Structures Involved in Mitosis**

Structure	Definition
Chromosome	A structure composed of a DNA molecule and associated proteins
Chromatin	The material that makes up eukaryotic chromosomes; consists of a DNA molecule complexed with histone proteins (see Chapter 19)
Chromatid	One strand of a replicated chromosome, with its associated proteins
Sister chromatids	The two strands of a replicated chromosome. When chromosomes are replicated, they consist of two sister chromatids. The genetic material in sister chromatids is identical. When sister chromatids separate during mitosis, they become independent chromosomes.
Centromere	The structure that joins sister chromatids
Kinetochores	The structures on sister chromatids where microtubules attach
Microtubule-organizing center	Any structure that organizes microtubules (see Chapter 2)
Centrosome	The microtubule-organizing center in animals and some plants
Centrioles	Cylindrical structures that comprise microtubules, located inside animal centrosomes

How Do Chromosomes Move during Anaphase?

The exact and equal partitioning of genetic material to the two daughter nuclei is the most fundamental aspect of mitosis. How does this process occur?

To understand how sister chromatids separate and move to opposite sides of the spindle, biologists have focused on understanding the function of spindle microtubules. How do kinetochore microtubules pull chromatids apart? And how does the kinetochore join the chromosome and microtubules?

Mitotic Spindle Forces   The spindle apparatus is composed of microtubules (see Chapter 2). Recall that:

- microtubules are composed of α-tubulin and β-tubulin dimers,

- microtubules are asymmetric—meaning they have a plus end and a minus end, and

- the plus end is the site where microtubule growth normally occurs while disassembly is more frequent at the minus end.

During mitosis, the microtubules originating from the poles are highly dynamic. Rapid growth and shrinkage ensures that some of the microtubules will be able to attach to kinetochores with their plus ends. Others will be stabilized by different proteins in the cytoplasm and become polar or astral microtubules.

These observations suggest two possible mechanisms for the movement of chromosomes during anaphase. The simplest mechanism would be for microtubules to stop growing at the plus ends, but remain attached to the kinetochore. As the minus ends disassemble at the spindle pole, the chromosome would be reeled in like a hooked fish. An alternative model would have the chromosomes moving along microtubules that are being disassembled at the plus ends at the kinetochore. In this case, the chromosome is like a yo-yo running up a string into your hand.

To test these hypotheses, biologists introduced fluorescently labeled tubulin subunits into prophase or metaphase cells. This treatment made the kinetochore microtubules visible (**FIGURE 4.6**, step 1). Once anaphase began, the researchers marked a region of these microtubules with a bar-shaped beam of laser light. The laser permanently bleached a section of the fluorescently labeled structures, darkening them—although they were still functional (Figure 4.6, step 2).

As anaphase progressed, two things happened: **(1)** The darkened region appeared to remain stationary, and **(2)** the chromosomes moved closer to the darkened regions of the microtubules, eventually overtaking them.

This result suggested that the kinetochore microtubules remain stationary during anaphase, but shorten because tubulin subunits are lost from their plus ends. As microtubule ends shrink back to the spindle poles, the chromosomes are pulled along. But if the microtubule is disassembling at the kinetochore, how does the chromosome remain attached?

Kinetochores Are Linked to Retreating Microtubule Ends   The kinetochore is a complex of many proteins that build a base on the centromere region of the chromosome and a "crown" of fibrous proteins projecting outward. **FIGURE 4.7** shows a current

QUESTION: How do kinetochore microtubules shorten to pull daughter chromosomes apart during anaphase?

HYPOTHESIS: Microtubules shorten at the spindle pole.

ALTERNATIVE HYPOTHESIS: Microtubules shorten at the kinetochore.

EXPERIMENTAL SETUP:

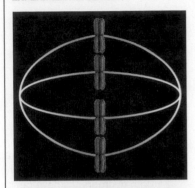

1. Label targets: Use fluorescent labels to make the metaphase chromosomes fluoresce blue and the microtubules fluoresce yellow.

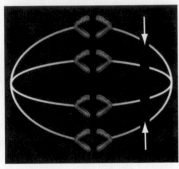

2. Mark microtubules: At the start of anaphase, darken a section of microtubules to mark them without changing their function.

PREDICTION:

PREDICTION OF ALTERNATIVE HYPOTHESIS: Daughter chromosomes will move toward the pole faster than the darkened section.

RESULTS:

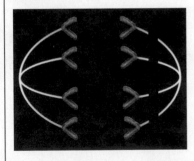

The darkened areas of the microtubules remained stationary as the chromosomes moved through them toward the pole.

CONCLUSION: Kinetochore microtubules shorten at the kinetochore to pull daughter chromosomes apart during anaphase.

FIGURE 4.6 During Anaphase, Microtubules Shorten at the Kinetochore.

SOURCE: Gorbsky, G. J., et al. 1987. Chromosomes move poleward during anaphase along stationary microtubules that coordinately disassemble from their kinetochore ends. *Journal of Cellular Biology* 104: 9–18.

✔**EXERCISE** Complete the prediction for what would occur if chromosome movement were based on microtubules shortening at the spindle pole.

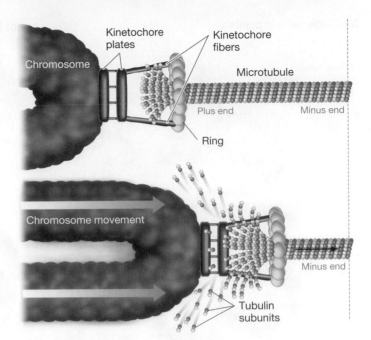

FIGURE 4.7 How Do Microtubules Move Chromosomes during Anaphase? Microtubules are disassembled at the kinetochore during anaphase. In yeast, kinetochore proteins tether the chromosome to a ring that is pushed toward the spindle pole by the fraying plus end of the microtubule.

model for kinetochore structure and function during chromosome movement in anaphase. For simplicity, a yeast kinetochore is shown, which attaches to only one microtubule. (Other eukaryotes can have as many as 30 microtubules attached to each kinetochore.)

Biologists have found that as anaphase gets under way, the plus ends of the kinetochore microtubules begin to fray and disassemble. Fibers that extend from the yeast kinetochore are tethered to this retreating end by attaching to a ring that surrounds the kinetochore microtubule (Figure 4.7, top). As the fraying end widens, its expansion forces the ring, and the attached chromosome, toward the minus end of the microtubule (see Figure 4.7, bottom). The result is that the chromosome is pulled to the spindle pole by the depolymerization of the kinetochore microtubule.

Cytokinesis Results in Two Daughter Cells

At this point, the chromosomes have been replicated in S phase and partitioned to opposite sides of the spindle via mitosis. Now it's time to divide the cell into two daughters that contain identical copies of each chromosome. If these cells are to be viable, however, the parent cell must also ensure that more than just chromosomes make it into each daughter cell.

While the cell is in interphase, the cytoplasmic contents, including the organelles, have increased in number or volume. During cytokinesis (Figure 4.5, steps 7 and 8), the cytoplasm divides to form two daughter cells, each with its own nucleus and complete set of organelles. In most types of cells, cytokinesis directly follows mitosis.

(a) Cytokinesis in plants

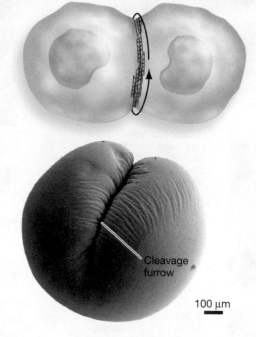

Microtubules direct vesicles to center of spindle where they fuse to divide the cell in two

Microtubule   Cell plate

5 μm

(b) Cytokinesis in animals

Actin–myosin interactions pinch the membrane in two

Cleavage furrow

100 μm

FIGURE 4.8 The Mechanism of Cytokinesis Varies among Eukaryotes. (a) In plants, the cytoplasm is divided by a cell plate that forms in the middle of the parent cell. **(b)** In animals, the cytoplasm is divided by a cleavage furrow. (The cells in both micrographs have been stained or colorized.)

In plants, polar microtubules left over from the spindle help define and organize the region where the new plasma membranes and cell walls will form. Vesicles from the Golgi apparatus carry components to build a new cell wall to the middle of the dividing cell. These vesicles are moved along the polar microtubules via motor proteins. In the middle of what was the spindle, the vesicles start to fuse together to form a flattened sac-like structure called the **cell plate** (**FIGURE 4.8a**). The cell plate continues to grow as new vesicles fuse with it, eventually contacting the existing plasma membrane. When the cell plate fuses with the existing plasma membrane, it divides the cell into two new daughter cells.

In animals and many other eukaryotes, cytokinesis begins with the formation of a **cleavage furrow** (**FIGURE 4.8b**). The furrow appears because a ring of actin filaments forms just inside the plasma membrane, in the middle of what used to be the spindle. Myosin motor proteins bind to these actin filaments and use adenosine triphosphate (ATP) to contract in a way that causes actin filaments to slide (see Chapter 2).

As myosin moves the ring of actin filaments on the inside of the plasma membrane, the ring shrinks in size and tightens. Because the ring is attached to the plasma membrane, the shrinking ring pulls the membrane with it. As a result, the plasma membrane pinches inward. The actin and myosin filaments continue to slide past each other, tightening the ring further, until the original membrane pinches in two and cell division is complete.

The overall process involved in chromosome separation and cytoplasmic division is a common requirement for all living organisms. The mechanisms involved in accomplishing these events, however, vary depending on the type of cell. What about

bacterial cells? How does chromosomal segregation and cytokinesis compare between prokaryotes and eukaryotes?

Bacterial Cell Replication Many bacteria divide using a process called **binary fission.** Recent research has shown that chromosome segregation and cytokinesis in bacterial division is strikingly similar to what occurs in the eukaryotic M phase (**FIGURE 4.9**). As the bacterial chromosome is being replicated, protein filaments attach to the copies and separate them to opposite sides of the cell.

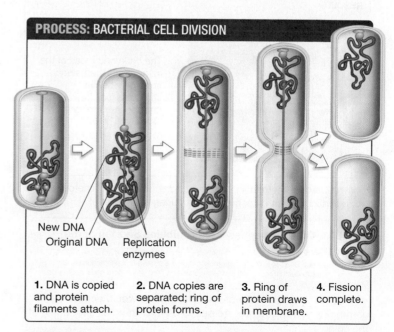

PROCESS: BACTERIAL CELL DIVISION

New DNA
Original DNA   Replication enzymes

1. DNA is copied and protein filaments attach.

2. DNA copies are separated; ring of protein forms.

3. Ring of protein draws in membrane.

4. Fission complete.

FIGURE 4.9 Bacterial Cells Divide but Do Not Undergo Mitosis.

Once the copies of the chromosome have been partitioned to opposite sides of the cell, other filaments, made up of proteins that are similar to eukaryotic tubulin, are responsible for dividing the cytoplasm. These filaments attach to the cell membrane to form a ring between the chromosome copies. A signal from the cell causes the filaments to constrict, drawing in the membrane and eventually cleaving the parent into two genetically identical cells.

Having explored what occurs during cell division, let's focus on how it is controlled in eukaryotes. When does a eukaryotic cell divide, and when does it stop dividing?

check your understanding

If you understand that . . .

- After chromosomes replicate, mitosis separates the copies to generate two nuclei with the same chromosomal complement.
- Microtubules attach to kinetochores and move chromosomes by the addition and subtraction of tubulin dimers.
- Cytokinesis divides the nuclei and cytoplasmic components into two daughter cells that are genetically identical with each other and the parent cell.

✔ You should be able to . . .

1. Draw the mitotic spindle for an animal cell that has two chromosomes in metaphase and label the sister chromatids, kinetochores, centrosomes, and the three types of microtubules.

2. Predict how the inhibition of microtubule motors in a plant cell would affect the activities in M phase.

Answers are available in Appendix A.

4.3 Control of the Cell Cycle

Although the events of mitosis are virtually identical in all eukaryotes, other aspects of the cell cycle vary. In humans, for example, intestinal cells routinely divide more than twice a day to replace tissue that is lost during digestion; mature human nerve and muscle cells do not divide at all.

Most of these differences are due to variation in the length of the G_1 phase. In rapidly dividing cells, G_1 is essentially eliminated. Most nondividing cells, in contrast, are permanently stuck in G_1. Researchers refer to this arrested stage as the G_0 state, or simply "G zero." Cells that are in G_0 have effectively exited the cell cycle and are sometimes referred to as post-mitotic. Nerve cells, muscle cells, and many other cell types enter G_0 once they have matured.

A cell's division rate can also vary in response to changing conditions. For example, human liver cells normally replicate about once per year. But if part of the liver is damaged or lost, the remaining cells divide every one or two days until repair is accomplished. Cells of unicellular organisms such as yeasts, bacteria, or archaeans divide rapidly only if the environment is rich in nutrients; otherwise, they enter a quiescent (inactive) state.

To explain these differences, biologists hypothesized that the cell cycle must be regulated in some way. Cell-cycle control is now the most prominent issue in research on cell division—partly because defects in control can lead to uncontrolled, cancerous growth.

The Discovery of Cell-Cycle Regulatory Molecules

The first solid evidence for cell-cycle control molecules came to light in 1970. Researchers found that certain chemicals, viruses, or an electric shock could fuse the membranes of two mammalian cells that were growing in culture, forming a single cell with two nuclei.

How did cell-fusion experiments relate to cell-cycle regulation? When investigators fused cells that were in different stages of the cell cycle, certain nuclei changed phases. For example, when a cell in M phase was fused with one in interphase, the nucleus of the interphase cell immediately initiated mitosis, even if the chromosomes had not been replicated. The biologists hypothesized that the cytoplasm of M-phase cells contains a regulatory molecule that induces interphase cells to enter M phase.

But cell-fusion experiments were difficult to control and left researchers wondering if it was the nucleus or the cytoplasm that was responsible for the induction. To address this issue, they turned to the South African clawed frog, *Xenopus laevis*.

As an egg of these frogs matures, it changes from a cell called an oocyte, which is arrested in a phase similar to G_2, to a mature egg that is arrested in M phase. The large size of these cells—more than 1 mm in diameter—makes them relatively easy to manipulate. Using instruments with extremely fine needles, researchers could specifically examine the effects of the cytoplasm by pulling a sample from a mature egg or an oocyte and injecting it into another.

When biologists purified cytoplasm from M-phase frog eggs and injected it into the cytoplasm of frog oocytes arrested in G_2, the immature oocytes immediately entered M phase (**FIGURE 4.10**, see page 82). But when cytoplasm from interphase cells was injected into G_2 oocytes, the cells remained in the G_2 phase. The researchers concluded that the cytoplasm of M-phase cells—but not the cytoplasm of interphase cells—contains a factor that drives immature oocytes into M phase to complete their maturation.

The factor that initiates M-phase in oocytes was purified and is now called **M phase–promoting factor,** or **MPF.** Subsequent experiments showed that MPF induces M phase in all eukaryotes. For example, injecting M-phase cytoplasm from mammalian cells into immature frog oocytes results in egg maturation, and human MPF can also trigger M phase in yeast cells.

MPF appears to be a general signal that says "Start M phase." How does it work?

QUESTION: Is M phase controlled by regulatory molecules in the cytoplasm?

HYPOTHESIS: Cytoplasmic regulatory molecules control entry into M phase.

NULL HYPOTHESIS: M-phase regulatory molecules are not in the cytoplasm or do not exist.

EXPERIMENTAL SETUP:

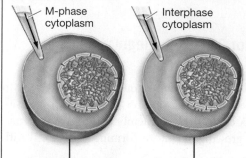

M-phase cytoplasm

Interphase cytoplasm

Microinject cytoplasm from M-phase cell into one frog oocyte and cytoplasm from interphase cell into another frog oocyte.

PREDICTION: Only the oocyte injected with M-phase cytoplasm will begin M phase.

PREDICTION OF NULL HYPOTHESIS: Neither of the frog oocytes will begin M phase.

RESULTS:

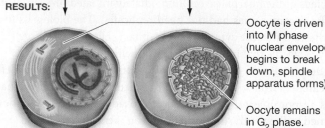

Oocyte is driven into M phase (nuclear envelope begins to break down, spindle apparatus forms).

Oocyte remains in G₂ phase.

CONCLUSION: M-phase cytoplasm contains a regulatory molecule that induces M phase in interphase cells.

FIGURE 4.10 Experimental Evidence for Cell-Cycle Control Molecules. When the cytoplasm from M-phase cells is microinjected into cells in interphase, the interphase chromosomes condense and begin M phase.

SOURCE: Masui, Y., and C. L. Markert. 1971. Cytoplasmic control of nuclear behavior during meiotic maturation of frog oocytes. *Journal of Experimental Zoology* 177: 129–145.

✔**QUESTION** This experiment was done using cells that were undergoing meiosis. What could the investigators do to show that the factor used in meiotic division is the same as used for mitotic division?

MPF Contains a Protein Kinase and a Cyclin   MPF is made up of two distinct polypeptide subunits. One subunit is a protein kinase—an enzyme that catalyzes the transfer of a phosphate group from ATP to a target protein. Recall that phosphorylation may activate or inactivate the function of proteins by changing their shape (Chapter 10). As a result, kinases frequently act as regulatory proteins in the cell.

These observations suggested that MPF phosphorylates proteins that trigger the onset of M phase. But research showed that

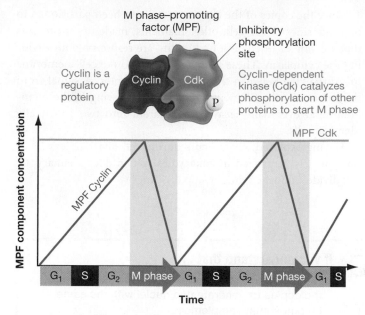

FIGURE 4.11 Cyclin Concentration Regulates the Concentration of the MPF Dimer. Cyclin concentrations cycle in dividing cells, reaching a peak in M phase. The activity of MPF, shown in the blue shaded area, requires both cyclin and Cdk components.

✔**QUESTION** Proteins that degrade cyclin are activated by events that MPF initiates. Why is this important?

the concentration of the protein kinase is more or less constant throughout the cell cycle. How can MPF trigger M phase if the protein kinase subunit is always present?

The answer lies in the second MPF subunit, which belongs to a family of proteins called **cyclins.** Cyclins got their name because their concentrations fluctuate throughout the cell cycle.

As **FIGURE 4.11** shows, the concentration of the cyclin associated with MPF builds during interphase and peaks in M phase. The timing of this increase is important because the protein kinase subunit in MPF is functional only when it is bound to the cyclin subunit. As a result, the protein kinase subunit of MPF is called a **cyclin-dependent kinase,** or **Cdk.**

To summarize, MPF is a dimer consisting of a cyclin and a cyclin-dependent kinase. The cyclin subunit regulates the formation of the MPF dimer; the kinase subunit catalyzes the phosphorylation of other proteins to start M phase.

How Is MPF Turned On?   According to Figure 4.11, the number of cyclins builds up steadily during interphase. Why doesn't this increasing concentration of MPF trigger the onset of M phase?

The answer is that the activity of MPF's Cdk subunit is further regulated by two phosphorylation events. The phosphorylation of one site in Cdk activates the kinase, but when the second site is phosphorylated, it is inactivated. Both these sites are phosphorylated after cyclin binds to the Cdk. This allows the concentration of the dimer to increase without prematurely starting M phase. Late in G₂ phase, however, an enzyme removes the inhibitory phosphate. This dephosphorylation reaction, coupled with the addition of the activating phosphate, changes the Cdk's shape in a way that turns on its kinase activity.

Once MPF is active, it triggers a chain of events. Although the exact mechanisms involved are still under investigation, the result is that chromosomes begin to condense and the spindle apparatus starts to form. In this way, MPF triggers the onset of M phase.

How Is MPF Turned Off? During anaphase, an enzyme complex begins degrading MPF's cyclin subunit. In this way, MPF triggers a chain of events that leads to its own destruction.

MPF deactivation illustrates two key concepts about regulatory systems in cells:

- **Negative feedback** occurs when a process is slowed or shut down by one of its products. Thermostats shut down furnaces when temperatures are high; phosphofructokinase is inhibited by ATP (see Chapter 13); MPF is turned off by an enzyme complex that is activated by events in mitosis.

- Destroying specific proteins is a common way to control cell processes. In this case, the enzyme complex that is activated in anaphase attaches small proteins called ubiquitins to MPF's cyclin subunit. This marks the subunit for destruction by a protein complex called the proteasome.

In response to MPF activity, then, the concentration of cyclin declines rapidly. Slowly, it builds up again during interphase. This sets up an oscillation in cyclin concentration.

✔ If you understand this aspect of cell-cycle regulation, you should be able to explain the relationship between MPF and (1) cyclin, (2) Cdk, and (3) the enzymes that phosphorylate MPF, dephosphorylate MPF, and degrade cyclin.

Cell-Cycle Checkpoints Can Arrest the Cell Cycle

The dramatic changes in cyclin concentrations and Cdk activity drive the ordered events of the cell cycle. These events are occurring in your body right now. Over a 24-hour period, you swallow millions of cheek cells and lose millions of cells from your intestinal lining as waste. To replace them, cells in your cheek and intestinal tissue are making and degrading cyclin and pushing themselves through the cell cycle.

MPF is only one of many protein complexes involved in regulating the cell cycle, however. A different cyclin complex triggers the passage from G_1 phase into S phase, and several regulatory proteins maintain the G_0 state of quiescent cells. An array of regulatory molecules holds cells in particular stages or stimulates passage to the next phase.

To make sense of these observations, Leland Hartwell and Ted Weinert introduced the concept of a **cell-cycle checkpoint.** A cell-cycle checkpoint is a critical point in the cell cycle that is regulated.

Hartwell and Weinert identified checkpoints by analyzing yeast cells with defects in the cell cycle. The defective cells kept dividing under culture conditions when normal cells stopped growing, because the defective cells lacked a specific checkpoint. In multicellular organisms, cells that keep dividing in this way may form a mass of cells called a **tumor.**

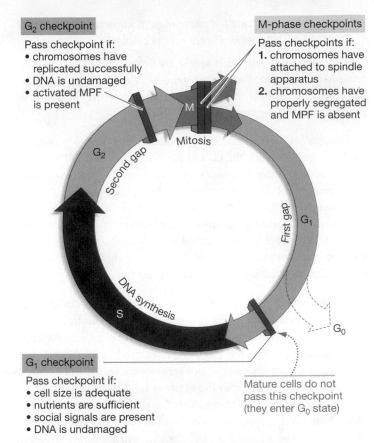

G₂ checkpoint
Pass checkpoint if:
- chromosomes have replicated successfully
- DNA is undamaged
- activated MPF is present

M-phase checkpoints
Pass checkpoints if:
1. chromosomes have attached to spindle apparatus
2. chromosomes have properly segregated and MPF is absent

G₁ checkpoint
Pass checkpoint if:
- cell size is adequate
- nutrients are sufficient
- social signals are present
- DNA is undamaged

Mature cells do not pass this checkpoint (they enter G_0 state)

FIGURE 4.12 The Four Cell-Cycle Checkpoints.

There are distinct checkpoints in three of the four phases of the cell cycle (**FIGURE 4.12**). In effect, interactions among regulatory molecules at each checkpoint allow a cell to "decide" whether to proceed with division or not. If these regulatory molecules are defective, the checkpoint may fail and cells may start dividing in an uncontrolled fashion.

G_1 Checkpoint The first cell-cycle checkpoint occurs late in G_1. For most cells, this checkpoint is the most important in establishing whether the cell will continue through the cycle and divide, or exit the cycle and enter G_0. What determines whether a cell passes the G_1 checkpoint?

- *Size* Because a cell must reach a certain size before its daughter cells will be large enough to function normally, biologists hypothesize that some mechanism exists to arrest the cell cycle if the cell is too small.

- *Availability of nutrients* Unicellular organisms arrest at the G_1 checkpoint if nutrient conditions are poor.

- *Social signals* Cells in multicellular organisms pass (or do not pass) through the G_1 checkpoint in response to signaling molecules from other cells, which are termed social signals.

- *Damage to DNA* If DNA is physically damaged, the protein **p53** activates genes that either stop the cell cycle until the damage can be repaired or cause the cell's programmed, controlled destruction—a phenomenon known as **apoptosis.** In this way, p53 acts as a brake on the cell cycle.

If "brake" molecules such as p53 are defective, damaged DNA remains unrepaired. Damage in genes that regulate cell growth can lead to uncontrolled cell division. Consequently, regulatory proteins like p53 are called **tumor suppressors.**

G₂ Checkpoint The second checkpoint occurs after S phase, at the boundary between the G_2 and M phases. Because MPF is the key signal triggering the onset of M phase, investigators were not surprised to find that it is involved in the G_2 checkpoint.

Data suggest that if DNA is damaged or if chromosomes are not replicated correctly, removal of the inactivating phosphate is blocked. When MPF is not turned on, cells remain in G_2 phase. Cells at this checkpoint may also respond to signals from other cells and to internal signals relating to their size.

M-Phase Checkpoints The final two checkpoints occur during mitosis. The first regulates the onset of anaphase. Cells in M phase will not split the chromatids until all kinetochores attach properly to the spindle apparatus. If the metaphase checkpoint did not exist, some chromosomes might not separate correctly, and daughter cells would receive either too many or too few chromosomes.

The second checkpoint regulates the progression through M phase into G_1. If chromosomes do not fully separate during anaphase, MPF will not decline and the cell will be arrested in M phase. The enzymes that are responsible for cyclin destruction are activated only when all the chromosomes have been properly separated. The presence of MPF activity prevents the cell from undergoing cytokinesis and exiting the M phase.

To summarize, the four cell-cycle checkpoints have the same purpose: They prevent the division of cells that are damaged or that have other problems. The G_1 checkpoint also prevents mature cells that are in the G_0 state from dividing.

Understanding cell-cycle regulation is fundamental. If one of the checkpoints fails, the affected cells may begin dividing in an uncontrolled fashion. For the organism as a whole, the consequences of uncontrolled cell division may be dire: cancer.

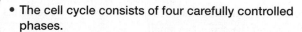

check your understanding

C Y U

If you understand that . . .

- The cell cycle consists of four carefully controlled phases.

✔ **You should be able to . . .**

1. List the phases of the cell cycle, noting where checkpoints occur.

2. Summarize how levels of Cdk and cyclin change over time and how this is related to MPF activity, noting the particular phases that are involved.

Answers are available in Appendix A.

4.4 Cancer: Out-of-Control Cell Division

Fifty percent of American men and 33 percent of American women will develop cancer during their lifetime. In the United States, one in four of all deaths is from cancer. It is the second leading cause of death, exceeded only by heart disease.

Cancer is a general term for disease caused by cells that divide in an uncontrolled fashion, invade nearby tissues, and spread to other sites in the body. Cancerous cells cause disease because they use nutrients and space needed by normal cells and disrupt the function of normal tissues.

Humans suffer from at least 200 types of cancer. Stated another way, cancer is not a single illness but a complex family of diseases that affect an array of organs, including the breast, colon, brain, lung, and skin (**FIGURE 4.13**). In addition, several types of cancer can affect the same organ. Skin cancers, for example, come in multiple forms.

Although cancers vary in time of onset, growth rate, seriousness, and cause, they have a unifying feature: Cancers arise from cells in which cell-cycle checkpoints have failed.

Cancerous cells have two types of defects related to cell division: (1) defects that make the proteins required for cell growth active when they shouldn't be, and (2) defects that prevent tumor suppressor genes from shutting down the cell cycle.

For example, the protein Ras is a key component in signal transduction systems—including phosphorylation cascades that trigger cell growth. Many cancers have defective forms of Ras that do not become inactivated. Instead, the defective Ras constantly sends signals that trigger mitosis and cell division.

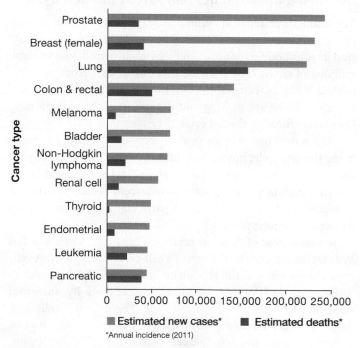

FIGURE 4.13 Cancers Vary in Type and Severity.

DATA: The website of the National Cancer Institute (http://www.cancer.gov), Common Cancer Types, November 2010.

Likewise, a large percentage of cancers have defective forms of the tumor suppressor p53. Instead of being arrested or destroyed, cells with damaged DNA are allowed to continue growing.

Let's review the general characteristics of cancer and then explore how regulatory mechanisms become defective.

Properties of Cancer Cells

When even a single cell in a multicellular organism begins to divide in an uncontrolled fashion, a mass of cells called a tumor may result. If a tumor can be surgically removed without damage to the affected organ, a cure might be achieved. Often, though, surgery doesn't cure cancer. Why?

In addition to uncontrolled replication, cancer cells are invasive—meaning that they are able to spread to adjacent tissues and throughout the body via the bloodstream or the lymphatic vessels, which collect excess fluid from tissues and return it to the bloodstream.

Invasiveness is a defining feature of a **malignant tumor**—one that is cancerous. Masses of noninvasive cells are noncancerous and form **benign tumors.** Some benign tumors are largely harmless. Others grow quickly and can cause problems if they are located in the brain or other sensitive parts of the body.

Cells become malignant and cancerous if they gain the ability to detach from the original tumor and invade other tissues. By spreading from the primary tumor site, cancer cells can establish secondary tumors elsewhere in the body (**FIGURE 4.14**). This process is called **metastasis.**

If metastasis has occurred by the time the original tumor is detected, secondary tumors have already formed and surgical removal of the primary tumor will not lead to a cure. This is why early detection is the key to treating cancer most effectively.

Cancer Involves Loss of Cell-Cycle Control

What causes cancer at the molecular level? Recall that when many cells mature, they enter the G_0 phase—meaning their cell cycle is arrested at the G_1 checkpoint. In contrast, cells that do pass through the G_1 checkpoint are irreversibly committed to replicating their DNA and entering G_2.

Based on this observation, biologists hypothesize that many types of cancer involve defects in the G_1 checkpoint. To understand the molecular nature of the disease, then, researchers have focused on understanding the normal mechanisms that operate at that checkpoint. Cancer research and research on the normal cell cycle have become two sides of the same coin.

Social Control In unicellular organisms, passage through the G_1 checkpoint is thought to depend primarily on cell size and the availability of nutrients. If nutrients are plentiful, cells pass through the checkpoint and divide rapidly.

In multicellular organisms, however, cells divide in response to signals from other cells. Biologists refer to this as *social control* over cell division. The general idea is that individual cells should be allowed to divide only when their growth is in the best interests of the organism as a whole.

(a) Benign tumor

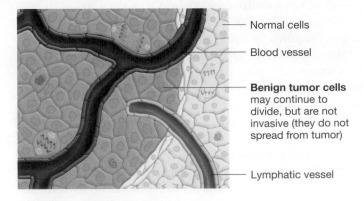

- Normal cells
- Blood vessel
- **Benign tumor cells** may continue to divide, but are not invasive (they do not spread from tumor)
- Lymphatic vessel

(b) Malignant tumor

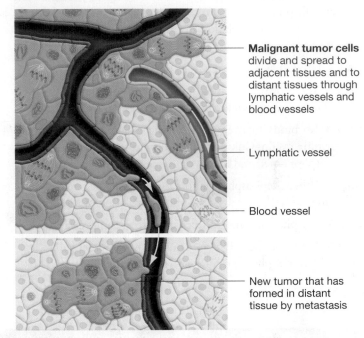

- **Malignant tumor cells** divide and spread to adjacent tissues and to distant tissues through lymphatic vessels and blood vessels
- Lymphatic vessel
- Blood vessel
- New tumor that has formed in distant tissue by metastasis

FIGURE 4.14 Cancers Spread to New Locations in the Body.
(a) Benign tumors grow in a single location. **(b)** Malignant tumors are metastatic—meaning that their cells can spread to distant parts of the body and initiate new tumors. Malignant tumors cause cancer.

Social control of the cell cycle is based on **growth factors**—polypeptides or small proteins that stimulate cell division. Many growth factors were discovered by researchers who were trying to grow cells in culture. When isolated mammalian cells were placed in a culture flask and provided with adequate nutrients, they arrested in G_1 phase. The cells began to grow again only when biologists added **serum**—the liquid portion of blood that remains after blood cells and cell fragments have been removed. Researchers identified growth factors as the components in the serum that were responsible for allowing cells to pass through the G_1 checkpoint.

Cancer cells are an exception. They can often be cultured successfully without externally supplied growth factors. This observation suggests that the normal social controls on the G_1 checkpoint have broken down in cancer cells.

How Does the G₁ Checkpoint Work? In G_0 cells, the arrival of growth factors stimulates the production of a key regulatory protein called E2F. When E2F is activated, it triggers the expression of genes required for S phase.

When E2F is first produced, however, its activity is blocked by a tumor suppressor protein called Rb. **Rb protein** is one of the key molecules that enforces the G_1 checkpoint. It is called Rb because a nonfunctional version was first discovered in children with retinoblastoma, a cancer in the light-sensing tissue, or retina, of the eye.

When E2F is bound to Rb, it is in the "off" position—it can't activate the genes required for S phase. As long as Rb stays bound to E2F, the cell remains in G_0. But as **FIGURE 4.15** shows, the situation changes dramatically if growth factors continue to arrive. To understand how growth factors affect E2F activity, think back to how cells progress from G_2 to M phase. As in passage from G_2 to M phase, phosphorylation of other proteins catalyzed by an activated cyclin–Cdk dimer permits passage from G_1 to S.

Step 1 Growth factors arrive from other cells.

Step 2 The growth factors stimulate the production of E2F and of G_1 cyclins, which are different from those used in MPF.

Step 3 Rb binds to E2F, inactivating it. The G_1 cyclins begin forming cyclin–Cdk dimers. Initially, the Cdk component is phosphorylated and inactive.

Step 4 When dephosphorylation turns on the G_1 cyclin–Cdk complexes, they catalyze the phosphorylation of Rb.

Step 5 The phosphorylated Rb changes shape and releases E2F.

Step 6 The unbound E2F is free to activate its target genes. Production of S-phase proteins gets S phase under way.

In this way, growth factors function as a social signal that says, "It's OK to override Rb. Go ahead and pass the G_1 checkpoint and divide."

How Do Social Controls and Cell-Cycle Checkpoints Fail? Cells can become cancerous when social controls fail—meaning, when cells begin dividing in the absence of the go-ahead signal from growth factors. One of two things can go wrong: The G_1 cyclin is overproduced, or Rb is defective.

When cyclins are overproduced and stay at high concentrations, the Cdk that binds to cyclin phosphorylates Rb continuously. This activates E2F and sends the cell into S phase.

Cyclin overproduction results from (**1**) excessive amounts of growth factors or (**2**) cyclin production in the absence of growth signals. Cyclins are produced continuously when a signaling pathway is defective. Because this pathway includes the Ras protein, it is common to find overactive Ras proteins in cancerous cells.

What happens if Rb is defective? When Rb is missing or does not bind normally to E2F, any E2F that is present pushes the cell through the G_1 checkpoint and into S phase, leading to uncontrolled cell division.

Because cancer is actually a family of diseases with a complex and highly variable molecular basis, there will be no "magic bullet," or single therapy, that cures all forms of the illness. Still, recent progress in understanding the cell cycle and the molecular basis of cancer has been dramatic, and cancer prevention and early detection programs are increasingly effective. The prognosis for many cancer patients is remarkably better now than it was even a few years ago. Thanks to research, almost all of us know someone who is a cancer survivor.

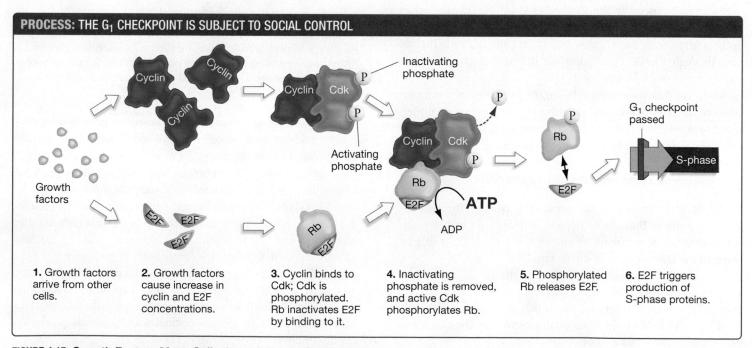

PROCESS: THE G₁ CHECKPOINT IS SUBJECT TO SOCIAL CONTROL

1. Growth factors arrive from other cells.

2. Growth factors cause increase in cyclin and E2F concentrations.

3. Cyclin binds to Cdk; Cdk is phosphorylated. Rb inactivates E2F by binding to it.

4. Inactivating phosphate is removed, and active Cdk phosphorylates Rb.

5. Phosphorylated Rb releases E2F.

6. E2F triggers production of S-phase proteins.

FIGURE 4.15 Growth Factors Move Cells through the G₁ Checkpoint.

If you understand . . .

4.1   How Do Cells Replicate?

- When a cell divides, it must copy its chromosomes, separate the copies, and divide the cytoplasm to generate daughter cells such that each carries the same chromosomal complement as the parent.
- Eukaryotic cells divide by alternating between interphase and M phase.
- Interphase consists of S phase, when chromosomes are replicated, and gap phases called G_1 and G_2, when cells grow and prepare for division.
- Eukaryotic cells divide by cycling through four phases: G_1, S, G_2, and M. Mature cells arrest at G_1 and enter a nonreplicating phase called G_0.

✔ You should be able to explain the roles of each of the four stages of the cell cycle.

4.2   What Happens during M Phase?

- Mitosis and cytokinesis are responsible for the partitioning of chromosomes and division of the parent cell into two daughter cells.
- Mitosis can be described as a sequence of five phases:
  1. *Prophase*   Chromosomes condense. The spindle apparatus begins to form, and polar microtubules overlap each other.
  2. *Prometaphase*   In cells of many organisms, the nuclear envelope disintegrates. Microtubules attach to the kinetochores of chromosomes and begin moving them to the middle of the spindle.
  3. *Metaphase*   All the chromosomes are positioned in the middle of the spindle. The spindle is anchored to the cell membrane by astral microtubules.
  4. *Anaphase*   Sister chromatids are pulled apart by the disassembly of kinetochore microtubules at the kinetochore. The separated chromatids are now daughter chromosomes. The spindle poles are moved farther apart to fully separate the replicated chromosomes.
  5. *Telophase*   Daughter chromosomes are fully separated and are clustered at opposite poles of the spindle. A nuclear envelope forms around each set and the chromosomes de-condense.
- In most cells, mitosis is followed by cytokinesis—division of all cell contents.

✔ You should be able to predict how mitosis would be different in cells where the nuclear envelope remains intact (e.g., yeast).

4.3   Control of the Cell Cycle

- The onset of S and M phases is primarily determined by the activity of protein dimers consisting of cyclin and cyclin-dependent kinases (Cdks).

- Cyclin concentrations oscillate during the cell cycle, regulating the formation of the dimer. The activity of the Cdk is further regulated by addition of a phosphate in its activating site and removal of one from its inhibitory site.
- Progression through the cell cycle is controlled by checkpoints in three phases.
  1. The G_1 checkpoint regulates progress based on nutrient availability, cell size, DNA damage, and social signals.
  2. The G_2 checkpoint delays progress until chromosome replication is complete and any damaged DNA that is present is repaired.
  3. The two M-phase checkpoints will (1) delay anaphase until all chromosomes are correctly attached to the spindle apparatus and (2) delay the onset of cytokinesis and G_1 until all the chromosomes have been properly partitioned.

✔ You should be able to predict what would happen if the kinase that adds the inhibitory phosphates to Cdk were defective.

4.4   Cancer: Out-of-Control Cell Division

- Cancer is characterized by (1) loss of control at the G_1 checkpoint, resulting in cells that divide in an uncontrolled fashion; and (2) metastasis, or the ability of tumor cells to spread throughout the body.
- The G_1 checkpoint depends in part on Rb, which prevents progression to S phase, and G_1 cyclin–Cdk complexes that trigger progression to S phase. Defects in Rb and G_1 cyclin are common in human cancer cells.

✔ You should be able to compare and contrast the effect of removing growth factors from asynchronous cultures of human cells that are normal versus those that are cancerous.

(MB)   **MasteringBiology**

1. **MasteringBiology Assignments**

   Tutorials and Activities Causes of Cancer; Cell Culture Methods; Four Phases of the Cell Cycle; Mitosis (1 of 3): Mitosis and the Cell Cycle; Mitosis (2 of 3): Mechanism of Mitosis; Mitosis (3 of 3): Comparing Cell Division in Animals, Plants, and Bacteria; Mitosis and Cytokinesis Animation; Roles of Cell Division; The Cell Cycle; The Phases of Mitosis

   Questions Reading Quizzes, Blue-Thread Questions, Test Bank

2. **eText** Read your book online, search, take notes, highlight text, and more.

3. **The Study Area** Practice Test, Cumulative Test, BioFlix® 3-D Animations, Videos, Activities, Audio Glossary, Word Study Tools, Art

You should be able to . . .

1. Which statement about the daughter cells following mitosis and cytokinesis is correct?
   a. They are genetically different from each other and from the parent cell.
   b. They are genetically identical with each other and with the parent cell.
   c. They are genetically identical with each other but different from the parent cell.
   d. Only one of the two daughter cells is genetically identical with the parent cell.

2. Progression through the cell cycle is regulated by oscillations in the concentration of which type of molecule?
   a. p53, Rb, and other tumor suppressors
   b. receptor tyrosine kinases
   c. cyclin-dependent kinases
   d. cyclins

3. After the S phase, what comprises a single chromosome?
   a. two daughter chromosomes
   b. a double-stranded DNA molecule
   c. two single-stranded molecules of DNA
   d. two sister chromatids

4. What major events occur during anaphase of mitosis?
   a. Chromosomes replicate, so each chromosome consists of two identical sister chromatids.
   b. Chromosomes condense and the nuclear envelope disappears.
   c. Sister chromatids separate, and the spindle poles are pushed farther apart.
   d. The chromosomes end up at opposite ends of the cell, and two nuclear envelopes form around them.

5. What evidence suggests that during anaphase, kinetochore microtubules shorten at the kinetochore?

6. Under normal conditions, what happens to the cell cycle if the chromosomes fail to separate properly at anaphase?

7. Identify at least two events in the cell cycle that must be completed successfully for daughter cells to share an identical complement of chromosomes.

8. Make a concept map illustrating normal events at the G_1 checkpoint. Your diagram should include p53, DNA damage, Rb, E2F, social signals, G_1 Cdk, G_1 cyclin, S-phase proteins, phosphorylated (inactivated) cyclin–Cdk, dephosphorylated (activated) cyclin–Cdk, phosphorylated (inactivated) Rb.

9. Explain how microinjection experiments supported the hypothesis that specific molecules in the cytoplasm are involved in the transition from interphase to M phase. What was the control for this experiment?

10. Why are most protein kinases considered regulatory proteins?

11. Why are cyclins called cyclins? Explain their relationship to MPF activity.

12. In multicellular organisms, nondividing cells stay in G_0 phase. For the cell, why is it better to be held in G_1 rather than S, G_2, or M phase?
    a. G_1 cells are larger and more likely to perform the normal functions of the cell.
    b. G_1 cells have not replicated their DNA in preparation for division.
    c. G_1 cells are the only ones that do not have their chromatin in a highly condensed state.
    d. MPF is required to enter S phase, so the cell is committed to entering M phase if the cycle moves beyond G_1.

13. **QUANTITATIVE** A particular cell spends 4 hours in G_1 phase, 2 hours in S phase, 2 hours in G_2 phase, and 30 minutes in M phase. If a pulse–chase assay were performed with radioactive thymidine on an asynchronous culture, what percentage of mitotic cells would be radiolabeled after 9 hours?
    a. 0%
    b. 50%
    c. 75%
    d. 100%

14. When fruit fly embryos first begin to develop, a large cell is generated that contains over 8000 nuclei that are genetically identical with one another. What is most likely responsible for this result?

15. What is most likely responsible for the reduction in death rates over the past several years in cancers of the breast and prostate? How is this related to the development of cancer?

16. Cancer is primarily a disease of older people. Further, a group of individuals may share a genetic predisposition to developing certain types of cancer, yet vary a great deal in time of onset—or not get the disease at all. What conclusion could be drawn based on these observations? How does this relate to the requirements for a cell to become cancerous?

5 Nucleic Acids and the RNA World

In this chapter you will learn that

Nucleic acids store the information that encodes life

by asking ↓

What is a nucleic acid? **5.1**

comparing/contrasting

DNA structure and function **5.2**

RNA structure and function **5.3**

and by asking

Could life have evolved from an RNA? **5.4**

specialized for

Stability and storage

Versatility and catalysis

This is part of the sheet-metal-and-wire model that James Watson and Francis Crick used to figure out the secondary structure of DNA. The large "T" stands for the nitrogen-containing base thymine.

This chapter is part of the Big Picture. See how on pages 68–69.

ife began when chemical evolution led to the production of a molecule that could promote its own replication. The nature of this first "living molecule," however, has been the subject of many investigations and heated debates. Even though proteins are the workhorse molecules of today's cells, relatively few researchers favor the hypothesis that life began as a protein molecule. Instead, the vast majority of biologists contend that life began as a polymer called a nucleic acid—specifically, a molecule of ribonucleic acid (RNA). This proposal is called the **RNA world hypothesis.**

The RNA world hypothesis contends that chemical evolution led to the existence of an RNA molecule that could replicate itself. Once this molecule existed, chance errors in the copying process

✔ When you see this checkmark, stop and test yourself. Answers are available in Appendix A.

created variations that would undergo natural selection—the evolutionary process by which individuals with certain attributes are selectively reproduced (see Chapter 1). At this point, chemical evolution was over and biological evolution was off and running.

To test this hypothesis, several groups around the world have been working to synthesize a self-replicating RNA molecule in the laboratory. If they ever succeed, they will have created a life-form in a test tube.

This chapter focuses on the structure and function of nucleic acids. Let's begin with an analysis of nucleic acid monomers and how they are linked together into polymers. Afterwards, you will learn about the experiments used to determine if a nucleic acid could have triggered the evolution of life on Earth.

5.1 What Is a Nucleic Acid?

Nucleic acids are polymers, just as proteins are polymers. But instead of being made up of monomers called amino acids, **nucleic acids** are made up of monomers called **nucleotides.**

FIGURE 5.1a diagrams the three components of a nucleotide: (1) a phosphate group, (2) a five-carbon sugar, and (3) a nitrogenous (nitrogen-containing) base. The phosphate is bonded to the sugar molecule, which in turn is bonded to the nitrogenous base.

The sugar component of a nucleotide is an organic compound bearing reactive hydroxyl (−OH) functional groups. Notice that the prime symbols (') in Figure 5.1 indicate that the carbon being referred to is part of the sugar—not of the attached nitrogenous base. The phosphate group in a nucleotide is attached to the 5' carbon.

Although a wide variety of nucleotides are found in living cells, origin-of-life researchers concentrate on two types: **ribonucleotides,** the monomers of **ribonucleic acid** (**RNA**), and **deoxyribonucleotides,** the monomers of **deoxyribonucleic acid** (**DNA**). In ribonucleotides, the sugar is ribose; in deoxyribonucleotides, it is deoxyribose (*deoxy* means "lacking oxygen"). As **FIGURE 5.1b** shows, these two sugars differ by a single oxygen atom. Ribose has an −OH group bonded to the 2' carbon. Deoxyribose has an H instead at the same location. In both of these sugars, an −OH group is bonded to the 3' carbon.

In addition to the type of sugar, nucleotides also differ in the type of nitrogenous base. These bases, diagrammed in **FIGURE 5.1c**, belong to structural groups called **purines** and **pyrimidines.** The purines are adenine (A) and guanine (G); the pyrimidines are cytosine (C), uracil (U), and thymine (T). Note that the two rings in adenine and guanine are linked together by nine atoms, compared to the six atoms that make a single ring in each pyrimidine. This makes remembering which bases are purines easy, since both adenine and guanine include "nine" in their names.

As Figure 5.1c shows, ribonucleotides and deoxyribonucleotides also differ in one of their pyrimidine bases. Ribonucleotides

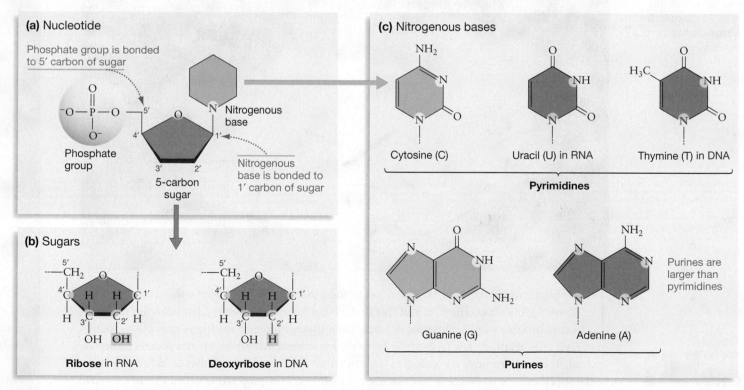

FIGURE 5.1 The General Structure of a Nucleotide. Note that in the bases, the nitrogen that bonds to the sugar is colored blue.

use uracil (U) while deoxyribonucleotides use the closely related base thymine (T).

✔ You should be able to diagram a ribonucleotide and a deoxyribonucleotide. Use a ball for the phosphate group, a pentagon to represent the sugar subunit, and a hexagon to represent the nitrogenous base. Label the 2′, 3′, and 5′ carbons on the sugar molecule, and add the atoms or groups that are bonded to each.

To summarize: After the different sugars and bases are taken into account, eight different nucleotides are used to build nucleic acids—four ribonucleotides (A, G, C, and U) and four deoxyribonucleotides (A, G, C, and T). If nucleic acids played any role in the chemical evolution of life, then at least some of these nucleotides must have been present in the prebiotic oceans. Is there any evidence to suggest that this was possible?

Could Chemical Evolution Result in the Production of Nucleotides?

Based on data from Stanley Miller and researchers who followed (Appendix D), most biologists contend that amino acids could have been synthesized early in Earth's history. The reactions behind the prebiotic synthesis of nucleotides, however, have been more difficult to identify.

Miller-like laboratory simulations have shown that nitrogenous bases and many different types of sugars can be synthesized readily under conditions that mimic the prebiotic soup. In these experiments, almost all the sugars that have five or six carbons—called pentoses and hexoses, respectively—are produced in approximately equal amounts. If nucleic acids were to form in the prebiotic soup, however, ribose would have had to predominate.

How ribose came to be the dominant sugar during chemical evolution (i.e., what selective process was at work) is still a mystery. Origin-of-life researchers refer to this issue as the "ribose problem." Recent work focusing on the conditions that exist in deep-sea hydrothermal vent systems (see Appendix D) may point to a possible solution.

Here's the line of reasoning researchers are currently pursuing: Ribose molecules may have been selectively enriched from the mix of sugars in certain early Earth deep-sea vent systems. In one experiment, researchers simulated the conditions that exist in these vents. Then they tested whether minerals that are predicted to have existed in the vent chimneys are able to bind sugars. What they found was striking—the minerals preferentially bound to ribose over other pentoses and hexoses. Did this occur in the ancient vents? If so, the implications are exciting: A high concentration of ribose would be present in the same deep-sea vent environment where chemical evolution is thought to have taken place.

Despite the observed synthesis of nitrogenous bases and the recent discovery of ribose enrichment, the production of nucleotides remains a serious challenge for the theory of chemical evolution. At this time, experiments that attempt to simulate early

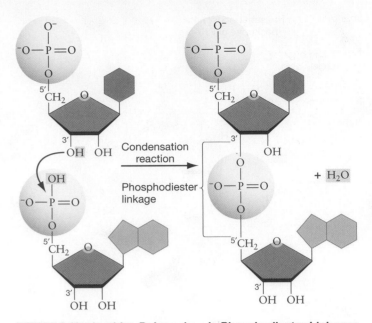

FIGURE 5.2 Nucleotides Polymerize via Phosphodiester Linkages. Ribonucleotides can polymerize via condensation reactions. The resulting phosphodiester linkage connects the 3′ carbon of one ribonucleotide and the 5′ carbon of another ribonucleotide.

Earth environments have yet to synthesize complete nucleotides. But research on this issue continues.

In the meantime, let's consider the next question: Once nucleotides formed, how would they polymerize to form RNA and DNA? This question has an answer.

How Do Nucleotides Polymerize to Form Nucleic Acids?

Nucleic acids form when nucleotides polymerize. As **FIGURE 5.2** shows, the polymerization reaction involves the formation of a bond between a hydroxyl on the sugar component of one nucleotide and the phosphate group of another nucleotide. The result of this condensation reaction is called a **phosphodiester linkage,** or a phosphodiester bond.

A phosphodiester linkage joins the 5′ carbon on the sugar of one nucleotide to the 3′ carbon on the sugar of another. When the nucleotides involved contain the sugar ribose, the polymer that is produced is RNA. If the nucleotides contain the sugar deoxyribose instead, then the resulting polymer is DNA.

DNA and RNA Strands Are Directional **FIGURE 5.3** (see page 92) shows how the chain of phosphodiester linkages in a nucleic acid acts as a backbone, analogous to the peptide-bonded backbone found in proteins.

Like the peptide-bonded backbone of a polypeptide, the sugar-phosphate backbone of a nucleic acid is directional. In a strand of RNA or DNA, one end has an unlinked 5′ phosphate while the other end has an unlinked 3′ hydroxyl—meaning the groups are not linked to another nucleotide. By convention, the

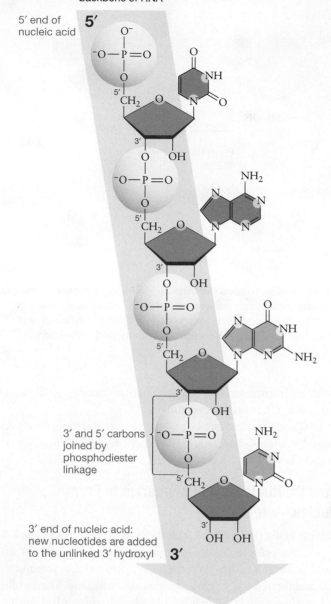

The sugar-phosphate
backbone of RNA

5′ end of nucleic acid

5′

3′ and 5′ carbons joined by phosphodiester linkage

3′ end of nucleic acid: new nucleotides are added to the unlinked 3′ hydroxyl

3′

FIGURE 5.3 RNA Has a Sugar-Phosphate Backbone.

✔**EXERCISE** Identify the four bases in this RNA strand, using Figure 5.1c as a key. Then write down the base sequence, starting at the 5′ end.

sequence of bases found in an RNA or DNA strand is always written in the 5′→3′ direction. (This system is logical because in cells, RNA and DNA are always synthesized in this direction. Bases are added only at the 3′ end of the growing molecule.)

The order of the different nitrogenous bases in a nucleic acid forms the primary structure of the molecule. When biologists write the primary structure of a stretch of DNA or RNA, they simply list the sequence of nucleotides in the 5′→3′ direction, using their single-letter abbreviations. For example, a six-base-long DNA sequence might be ATTAGC. It would take roughly

6 billion of these letters to write the primary structure of the DNA in most of your cells.

Polymerization Requires an Energy Source In cells, the polymerization reactions that join nucleotides into nucleic acids are catalyzed by enzymes. Like other polymerization reactions, the process is not spontaneous. An input of energy is needed to tip the energy balance in favor of the process.

Polymerization can take place in cells because the potential energy of the nucleotide monomers is first raised by reactions that add two phosphate groups to the ribonucleotides or deoxyribonucleotides, creating nucleoside triphosphates.[1] In the case of nucleic acid polymerization, researchers refer to these nucleotides as "activated." **FIGURE 5.4a** shows an example of an activated nucleotide; this molecule is called **adenosine triphosphate,** or **ATP.**

Why do added phosphate groups raise the energy content of a molecule? Recall that phosphates are negatively charged and that like charges repel (Appendix D). Linking two or more phosphates with covalent bonds generates strong repulsive forces. These bonds therefore carry a large amount of potential energy, which can be harvested to power other chemical reactions (**FIGURE 5.4b**). You will see in later chapters that the potential energy stored in ATP is used to drive other cellular activities, independent of nucleotide polymerization.

This is a key point, and one that you will encounter again and again in this text: The addition of one or more phosphate groups raises the potential energy of substrate molecules enough to make an otherwise nonspontaneous reaction possible. (Chapter 10 explains how this happens in more detail.)

Could Nucleic Acids Have Formed in the Absence of Cellular Enzymes? Accumulating data suggest that the answer is yes.

Activation of nucleotides has been observed when prebiotic conditions are simulated experimentally. In a suite of follow-up experiments, researchers have produced RNA molecules by incubating activated nucleotides with tiny mineral particles—in one case, molecules up to 50 nucleotides long were observed. These results support the hypothesis that polymerization of activated nucleotides in the prebiotic world may have been catalyzed by minerals. This model would be in line with the surface metabolism model for chemical evolution (introduced in Appendix D).

More recent work has shown that under certain conditions, up to 100 nucleotides can be linked together, even without first being activated. To accomplish this, heat was introduced as a source of energy and small nonpolar molecules, called lipids, were added to help the monomers interact. This experiment is particularly interesting with respect to the setting for chemical evolution, because both of these factors—heat and lipids—are thought to have been present in prebiotic hydrothermal vents. (The chemical origins and properties of lipids are covered in Chapter 3.)

---

[1]A molecule consisting of a sugar and one of the bases in Figure 5.1c is called a nucleoside (a nucleotide is a sugar, a base, and one or more phosphate groups). Thus, a sugar attached to a base and three phosphate groups is called a nucleoside triphosphate.

(a) ATP is an example of an activated nucleotide.

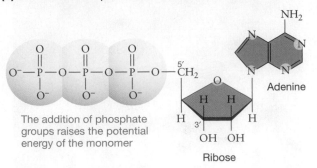

The addition of phosphate groups raises the potential energy of the monomer

Adenine

Ribose

FIGURE 5.4 Activated Monomers Drive Polymerization Reactions. Polymerization reactions are generally nonspontaneous, but those reactions involving nucleoside triphosphates, such as ATP, are spontaneous. The potential energy stored in activated nucleotides is released when the pyrophosphate (PP_i) is removed before the polymerizing condensation reaction shown in Figure 5.2.

(b) Energy is released when phosphates are removed by hydrolysis.

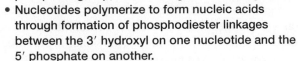
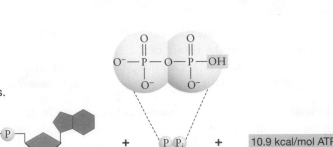

ATP

H_2O

Water

AMP

Inorganic pyrophosphate

10.9 kcal/mol ATP

Energy used to link nucleotide to RNA

Based on these results, there is a strong consensus that if ribonucleotides and deoxyribonucleotides were able to form during chemical evolution, they would be able to polymerize into DNA and RNA. Now, what do these nucleic acids look like, and what can they do?

check your understanding

If you understand that . . .

- Nucleotides are monomers that consist of a sugar, a phosphate group, and a nitrogen-containing base.
- Nucleotides polymerize to form nucleic acids through formation of phosphodiester linkages between the 3′ hydroxyl on one nucleotide and the 5′ phosphate on another.
- During polymerization, nucleotides are added only to the 3′ end of a nucleic acid strand.

✔ **You should be able to . . .**

Draw a simplified diagram of the phosphodiester linkage between two nucleotides, indicate the 5′→3′ polarity, and mark where the next nucleotide would be added to the growing chain.

Answers are available in Appendix A.

5.2 DNA Structure and Function

The primary structure of nucleic acids is somewhat similar to the primary structure of proteins. Proteins have a peptide-bonded backbone with a series of R-groups that extend from it. DNA and RNA molecules have a sugar-phosphate backbone, created by phosphodiester linkages, and a sequence of any of four nitrogenous bases that extend from it.

Like proteins, DNA and RNA also have secondary structure. While the α-helices and β-pleated sheets of proteins are formed by hydrogen bonding between groups in the backbone, the secondary structure of nucleic acids is formed by hydrogen bonding between the nitrogenous bases.

Let's analyze the secondary structure and function of DNA first, and then dig into the secondary structure and function of RNA.

What Is the Nature of DNA's Secondary Structure?

The solution to DNA's secondary structure, announced in 1953, ranks among the great scientific breakthroughs of the twentieth century. James Watson and Francis Crick presented a model for the secondary structure of DNA in a one-page paper published in the scientific journal *Nature*.

Early Data Provided Clues Watson and Crick's finding was a hypothesis based on a series of results from other laboratories. They were trying to propose a secondary structure that could explain several important observations about the DNA found in cells:

- Chemists had worked out the structure of nucleotides and knew that DNA polymerized through the formation of phosphodiester linkages. Thus, Watson and Crick knew that the molecule had a sugar-phosphate backbone.

- By analyzing the nitrogenous bases in DNA samples from different organisms, Erwin Chargaff had established two empirical rules: (**1**) The number of purines in a given DNA molecule is equal to the number of pyrimidines, and (**2**) the number of T's and A's in DNA are equal, and the number of C's and G's in DNA are equal.

- By bombarding DNA with X-rays and analyzing how it scattered the radiation, Rosalind Franklin and Maurice Wilkins had calculated the distances between groups of atoms in the molecule (see **BioSkills 11** in Appendix B for an introduction to this technique, called **X-ray crystallography**). The scattering patterns showed that three distances were repeated many times: 0.34 nanometer (nm), 2.0 nm, and 3.4 nm. Because the measurements repeated, the researchers inferred that DNA molecules had a regular and repeating structure. The pattern of X-ray scattering suggested that the molecule was helical, or spiral, in nature.

Based on this work, understanding DNA's structure boiled down to understanding the nature of the helix involved. What type of helix would have a sugar-phosphate backbone and explain both Chargaff's rules and the Franklin–Wilkins measurements?

DNA Strands Are Antiparallel Watson and Crick began by analyzing the size and geometry of deoxyribose, phosphate groups, and nitrogenous bases. The bond angles and measurements suggested that the distance of 2.0 nm probably represented the width of the helix and that 0.34 nm was likely to be the distance between bases stacked in a spiral.

How could they make sense of Chargaff's rules and the 3.4-nm distance, which appeared to be exactly 10 times the distance between a single pair of bases?

To solve this problem, Watson and Crick constructed a series of physical models like the one pictured in **FIGURE 5.5**. The models allowed them to tinker with different types of helical configurations. After many false starts, something clicked:

- They arranged two strands of DNA side by side and running in opposite directions—meaning that one strand ran in the 5′ → 3′ direction while the other strand was oriented 3′ → 5′. Strands with this orientation are said to be **antiparallel.**

- If the antiparallel strands are twisted together to form a **double helix,** the coiled sugar-phosphate backbones end up on the outside of the spiral and the nitrogenous bases on the inside.

FIGURE 5.5 Building a Physical Model of DNA Structure. Watson (left) and Crick (right) represented the arrangement of the four deoxyribonucleotides in a double helix, using metal plates and wires with precise lengths and geometries.

- For the bases from each backbone to fit in the interior of the 2.0-nm-wide structure, they have to form purine-pyrimidine pairs (see **FIGURE 5.6a**). This is a key point: The pairing allows hydrogen bonds to form between certain purines and pyrimidines. Adenine forms hydrogen bonds with thymine, and guanine forms hydrogen bonds with cytosine (**FIGURE 5.6b**).

- The A-T and G-C bases were said to be complementary. Two hydrogen bonds form when A and T pair, and three hydrogen bonds form when G and C pair. As a result, the G-C interaction is slightly stronger than the A-T bond. In contrast, A-C and G-T pairs allowed no or only one hydrogen bond.

(a) Only purine-pyrimidine pairs fit inside the double helix.

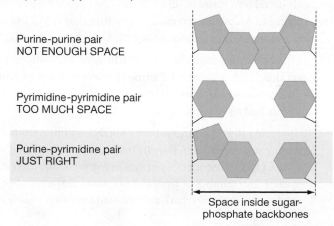

Purine-purine pair
NOT ENOUGH SPACE

Pyrimidine-pyrimidine pair
TOO MUCH SPACE

Purine-pyrimidine pair
JUST RIGHT

Space inside sugar-phosphate backbones

(b) Hydrogen bonds form between G-C pairs and A-T pairs.

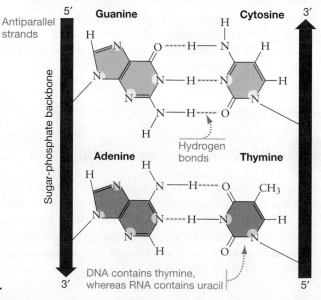

FIGURE 5.6 Complementary Base Pairing Is Based on Hydrogen Bonding.

Watson and Crick had discovered **complementary base pairing.** In fact, the term **Watson–Crick pairing** is now used interchangeably with the phrase complementary base pairing. The physical restraints posed by these interactions resulted in a full helical twist every 10 bases, or 3.4 nm.

The Double Helix **FIGURE 5.7a** shows how antiparallel strands of DNA form when complementary bases line up and form hydrogen bonds. As you study the figure, notice that DNA is put together like a ladder whose ends have been twisted in opposite directions. The sugar-phosphate backbones form the supports of the ladder; the base pairs represent the rungs of the ladder. The twisting allows the nitrogenous bases to line up in a way that makes hydrogen bonding between them possible.

The nitrogenous bases in the middle of the molecule are hydrophobic. This is a key point, because twisting into a double helix minimizes contact between the bases and surrounding water molecules. In addition to hydrogen bonding, van der Waals interactions between the tightly stacked bases in the interior further contribute to the stability of the helix. You see the same forces—hydrogen bonding, hydrophobicity, and van der Waals interactions—play similar roles in protein folding (Chapter 9). But DNA as a whole is hydrophilic and water soluble because the backbones, which face the exterior of the molecule, contain negatively charged phosphate groups that interact with water.

FIGURE 5.7b highlights additional features of DNA's secondary structure. It's important to note that the outside of the helical DNA molecule forms two types of grooves. The larger of the two is known as the major groove, and the smaller one is known as the minor groove. From this figure, you can identify how DNA's secondary structure explains the measurements observed by Franklin and Wilkins.

Since the model of the double helix was published, experimental tests have shown that the hypothesis is correct in almost every detail. To summarize:

- DNA's secondary structure consists of two antiparallel strands twisted into a double helix.

- The molecule is stabilized by hydrophobic interactions in its interior and by hydrogen bonding between the complementary base pairs A-T and G-C.

✔ You should be able to explain why complementary base pairing would not be possible if two DNA strands were aligned in a parallel fashion—instead of the antiparallel alignment shown in Figure 5.6b.

Now the question is, how does this secondary structure affect the molecule's function?

(a) Cartoons of DNA structure

(b) Space-filling model of DNA double helix

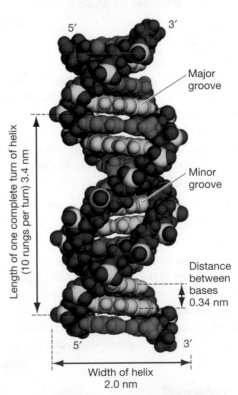

Base pairing

Double helix

Length of one complete turn of helix (10 rungs per turn) 3.4 nm

Major groove

Minor groove

Distance between bases 0.34 nm

Width of helix 2.0 nm

FIGURE 5.7 The Secondary Structure of DNA Is a Double Helix. (a) The cartoons illustrate complementary base pairing and how strands are twisted into a double helix. **(b)** The space-filling model shows tight packing of the bases inside the double helix. The double-helix structure explains the measurements inferred from X-ray analysis of DNA molecules.

DNA Functions as an Information-Containing Molecule

Watson and Crick's model created a sensation for a simple reason: It revealed how DNA could store and transmit biological information. In literature, information consists of letters on a page. In music, information is composed of the notes on a staff. But inside cells, information consists of a sequence of nucleotides in a nucleic acid. The four nitrogenous bases function like letters of the alphabet. A sequence of bases is like the sequence of letters in a word—it has meaning.

In all organisms that have been examined to date, from tiny bacteria to gigantic redwood trees, DNA carries the information required for the organism's growth and reproduction. Exploring how hereditary information is encoded and translated into action is the heart of several later chapters (Chapters 7 and 8).

Here, however, our focus is on how life began. The theory of chemical evolution holds that life began once a molecule emerged that could make a copy of itself. Does the information contained within DNA allow it to be replicated?

Watson and Crick ended their paper on the double helix with one of the classic understatements in the scientific literature: "It has not escaped our notice that the specific pairing we have postulated immediately suggests a possible copying mechanism." Here's the key insight: DNA's primary structure serves as a mold or template for the synthesis of a complementary strand. DNA contains the information required for a copy of itself to be made. **FIGURE 5.8** shows how a copy of DNA can be made by complementary base pairing.

Step 1 Heating or enzyme-catalyzed reactions can cause the double helix to separate.

Step 2 Free deoxyribonucleotides form hydrogen bonds with complementary bases on the original strand of DNA—also called a **template strand.** As they do, their sugar-phosphate groups form phosphodiester linkages to create a new strand—also called a **complementary strand.** Note that the $5' \rightarrow 3'$ directionality of the complementary strand is opposite that of the template strand.

Step 3 Complementary base pairing allows each strand of a DNA double helix to be copied exactly, producing two identical daughter molecules.

DNA copying is the basis for a second of the five characteristics of life (introduced in Chapter 1): replication. But can DNA catalyze the reactions needed to *self*-replicate? In today's cells and in laboratory experiments, the answer is no. Instead, the molecule is copied through a complicated series of energy-demanding reactions, catalyzed by a large suite of enzymes. Why can't DNA catalyze these reactions itself?

Is DNA a Catalytic Molecule?

The DNA double helix is highly structured. It is regular, symmetric, and held together by hydrogen bonding, hydrophobic

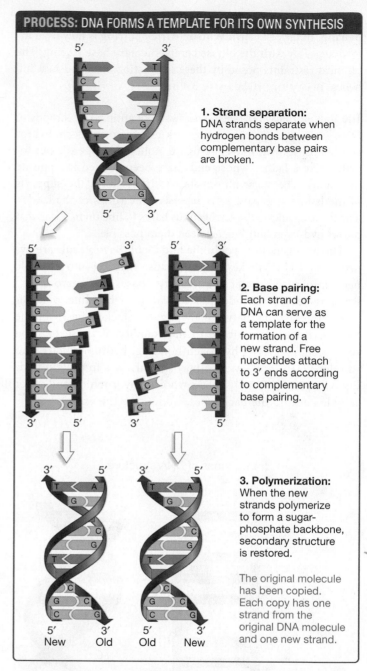

PROCESS: DNA FORMS A TEMPLATE FOR ITS OWN SYNTHESIS

1. Strand separation: DNA strands separate when hydrogen bonds between complementary base pairs are broken.

2. Base pairing: Each strand of DNA can serve as a template for the formation of a new strand. Free nucleotides attach to 3′ ends according to complementary base pairing.

3. Polymerization: When the new strands polymerize to form a sugar-phosphate backbone, secondary structure is restored.

The original molecule has been copied. Each copy has one strand from the original DNA molecule and one new strand.

FIGURE 5.8 Making a Copy of DNA. If new bases are added to each of the two strands of DNA via complementary base pairing, a copy of the DNA molecule can be produced.

✔ **QUESTION** When double-stranded DNA is heated to 95°C, the bonds between complementary base pairs break and single-stranded DNA results. Considering this observation, is the reaction shown in step 1 spontaneous?

interactions, and phosphodiester linkages. In addition, the molecule has few functional groups exposed that can participate in chemical reactions. For example, the lack of a 2′ hydroxyl group on each deoxyribonucleotide makes the polymer much less reactive than RNA, and thus much more resistant to degradation.

Intact stretches of DNA have been recovered from fossils that are tens of thousands of years old. The molecules have the same sequence of bases as the organisms had when they were alive, despite death and exposure to a wide array of pH, temperature, and chemical conditions. DNA's stability is the key to its effectiveness as a reliable information-bearing molecule. DNA's structure is consistent with its function in cells.

The orderliness and stability that make DNA such a dependable information repository also make it extraordinarily inept at catalysis, however. Recall that enzyme function is based on a specific binding event between a substrate and a protein catalyst (Chapter 9). Thanks to variation in reactivity among R-groups in amino acids, and the enormous diversity of shapes found in proteins, a wide array of catalytic activities can be generated. In comparison, DNA's primary and secondary structures are simple. It is not surprising, then, that DNA has never been observed to catalyze any reaction in any organism. Although researchers have been able to construct single-stranded DNA molecules that can catalyze some reactions in the laboratory, the number and diversity of reactions involved is a minute fraction of the activity catalyzed by enzymes.

In short, DNA furnishes an extraordinarily stable template for copying itself and for storing information encoded in a sequence of bases. But owing to its inability to act as an effective catalyst, there is virtually no support for the hypothesis that the first life-form consisted of DNA. Instead, most biologists who are working on the origin of life support the hypothesis that life began with RNA. How does the structure of RNA differ from DNA?

check your understanding

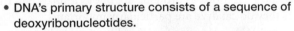

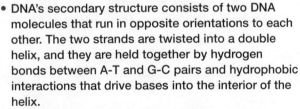

If you understand that . . .

- DNA's primary structure consists of a sequence of deoxyribonucleotides.
- DNA's secondary structure consists of two DNA molecules that run in opposite orientations to each other. The two strands are twisted into a double helix, and they are held together by hydrogen bonds between A-T and G-C pairs and hydrophobic interactions that drive bases into the interior of the helix.
- The sequence of deoxyribonucleotides in DNA contains information. Owing to complementary base pairing, each DNA strand also contains the information required to form its complementary strand.

✔ **You should be able to . . .**

Make a sketch of a double-stranded DNA molecule in the form of a ladder with the sequence of A-G-C-T. Label the 5′ and 3′ ends, the sugar-phosphate backbones, the hydrogen bonds between complementary bases, and the location of hydrophobic interactions.

Answers are available in Appendix A.

The first living molecule would have needed to perform two key functions: carry information and catalyze reactions that promoted its own replication. At first glance, these two functions appear to conflict. Information storage requires regularity and stability; catalysis requires variation in chemical composition and flexibility in shape. How is it possible for a molecule to do both? The answer lies in structure.

Structurally, RNA Differs from DNA

Recall that proteins can have up to four levels of structure. Single-chain proteins possess a primary sequence of amino acids, secondary folds that are stabilized by hydrogen bonding between atoms in the peptide-bonded backbone, and tertiary folds that are stabilized by interactions involving R-groups. Quaternary structure is found in proteins consisting of multiple polypeptides.

DNA has only primary and secondary structure. But RNA, like single-chained proteins, can have up to three levels of structure.

Primary Structure Like DNA, RNA has a primary structure consisting of a sugar-phosphate backbone formed by phosphodiester linkages and, extending from that backbone, a sequence of four types of nitrogenous bases. But it's important to recall two significant differences between these nucleic acids:

1. The sugar in the sugar-phosphate backbone of RNA is ribose, not deoxyribose as in DNA.

2. The pyrimidine base thymine does not exist in RNA. Instead, RNA contains the closely related pyrimidine base uracil.

The first point is critical. Look back at Figure 5.1b and compare the functional groups attached to ribose and deoxyribose. Notice the hydroxyl (−OH) group on the 2′ carbon of ribose. This additional hydroxyl is much more reactive than the hydrogen atom on the 2′ carbon of deoxyribose. When RNA molecules fold in certain ways, the hydroxyl group can attack the phosphate linkage between nucleotides, which would generate a break in the sugar-phosphate backbone. While this −OH group makes RNA much less stable than DNA, it can also support catalytic activity by the molecule.

Secondary Structure Like DNA molecules, most RNA molecules have secondary structure that results from complementary base pairing between purine and pyrimidine bases. In RNA, adenine forms hydrogen bonds only with uracil, and guanine again forms hydrogen bonds with cytosine. (Other, non-Watson–Crick base pairs occur, although less frequently.) Three hydrogen bonds form between guanine and cytosine, but only two form between adenine and uracil.

This hydrogen bonding should seem familiar, since DNA bonds together in a similar manner—so how do the secondary structures of RNA and DNA differ? In the vast majority of cases, the purine and pyrimidine bases in RNA undergo hydrogen

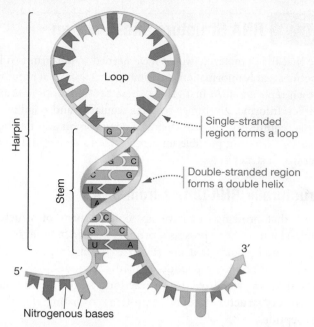

FIGURE 5.9 **Complementary Base Pairing and Secondary Structure in RNA: Stem-and-Loop Structures.** This RNA molecule has secondary structure. The double-stranded "stem" and single-stranded "loop" form a hairpin. The bonded bases in the stem are antiparallel, meaning that they are oriented in opposite directions.

bonding with complementary bases on the *same strand*, rather than forming hydrogen bonds with complementary bases on a different strand, as in DNA.

FIGURE 5.9 shows how within-strand base pairing works. The key is that when bases on one part of an RNA strand fold over and align with ribonucleotides on another part of the same strand, the two sugar-phosphate strands are antiparallel. In this orientation, hydrogen bonding between complementary bases results in a stable double helix.

If the section where the fold occurs includes unpaired bases, then the stem-and-loop configuration shown in Figure 5.9 results. This type of secondary structure is called a **hairpin.** Several other types of RNA secondary structures are possible, each involving a different length and arrangement of base-paired segments.

Like the α-helices and β-pleated sheets observed in many proteins, RNA secondary structures can form spontaneously. They are directed by hydrophobic interactions and stabilized by hydrogen bonding between the bases. Even though hairpins and other types of secondary structure reduce the entropy of RNA molecules, the energy released in these interactions makes the overall process favorable.

Tertiary Structure RNA molecules can also have tertiary structure, which arises when secondary structures fold into more complex shapes. As a result, RNA molecules with different base sequences can have very different overall shapes and chemical properties. RNA molecules are much more diverse in size, shape, and reactivity than DNA molecules are. Structurally and chemically, RNA is intermediate between the complexity of proteins and the simplicity of DNA.

TABLE 5.1 summarizes the similarities and differences in the structures of RNA and DNA.

RNA's Structure Makes It an Extraordinarily Versatile Molecule

In terms of structure, you've seen that RNA is intermediate between DNA and proteins. RNA is intermediate in terms of function as well. RNA molecules cannot archive information nearly as efficiently as DNA molecules do, but they do perform key functions in information processing. Likewise, they cannot catalyze as many reactions as proteins do. But as it turns out, the reactions they do catalyze are particularly important.

In cells, RNA molecules function like a jackknife or a pocket tool with an array of attachments: They perform a wide variety of

SUMMARY TABLE 5.1   **DNA and RNA Structure**

Level of Structure	DNA		RNA	
Primary	Sequence of deoxyribonucleotides; bases are A, T, G, C	5′ A A T G T G C C G 3′	Sequence of ribonucleotides; bases are A, U, G, C	5′ U U A C A C G G C 3′
Secondary	Two antiparallel strands twist into a double helix, stabilized by hydrogen bonding between complementary bases (A-T, G-C) and hydrophobic interactions		Most common are hairpins, formed when a single strand folds back on itself to form a double-helix "stem" and a single-stranded "loop"	
			Folds that form distinctive three-dimensional shapes	Example: tRNA
Tertiary	None*			

*In cells, DNA coils around proteins that bind to the double helix. In many cases the DNA-protein complex folds into highly organized, compact structures. But DNA does not form tertiary structure on its own.

tasks reasonably well. Some of the most surprising results in the last decade of biological science, in fact, involve new insights into the diversity of roles that RNAs play in cells. These molecules process information stored in DNA, synthesize proteins, and defend against attack by viruses, among other things.

Next let's focus on the roles that RNA could have played in the origin of life—as an information-containing entity and as a catalyst.

RNA Is an Information-Containing Molecule

Because RNA contains a sequence of bases analogous to the letters in a word, it can function as an information-containing molecule. And because hydrogen bonding occurs specifically between A-U pairs and G-C pairs in RNA, it is possible for RNA to furnish the information required to make a copy of itself.

FIGURE 5.10 illustrates how the information stored in an RNA molecule can be used to direct its own replication.

First, a complementary copy of the RNA is made when free ribonucleotides form hydrogen bonds with complementary bases on the original strand of RNA—the template strand. As they do, their sugar-phosphate groups form phosphodiester linkages to produce a double-stranded RNA molecule (steps 1 and 2).

To make a copy of the original single-stranded RNA, the hydrogen bonds between the double-stranded product must first be broken by heating or by a catalyzed reaction (step 3). The newly made complementary RNA molecule now exists independently of the original template strand. If steps 1–3 were repeated with the new strand serving as a template (steps 4–6), the resulting molecule would be a copy of the original. In this way, the primary sequence of an RNA serves as a mold.

RNA Can Function as a Catalytic Molecule

In terms of diversity in chemical reactivity and overall shape, RNA molecules are no match for proteins. The primary structure of RNA molecules is much more restricted because RNA has only four types of nucleotides versus the 20 types of amino acids found in proteins. Secondary through tertiary structure is more limited as a result, meaning that RNA cannot form the wide array of catalysts observed among proteins.

But because RNA has a degree of structural and chemical complexity, it is capable of catalyzing a number of chemical reactions. Sidney Altman and Thomas Cech shared the 1989 Nobel Prize in chemistry for showing that catalytic RNAs, or **ribozymes,** exist in organisms.

FIGURE 5.11 (on page 100) shows the structure of a ribozyme Cech isolated from a single-celled organism called *Tetrahymena*. This ribozyme catalyzes both the hydrolysis and the condensation of phosphodiester linkages in RNA. Researchers have since discovered a variety of ribozymes that catalyze an array of reactions in cells. For example, ribozymes catalyze the formation of peptide bonds when amino acids polymerize to form polypeptides. Ribozymes are at work in your cells right now.

The three-dimensional nature of ribozymes is vital to their catalytic activity. To catalyze a chemical reaction, substrates must

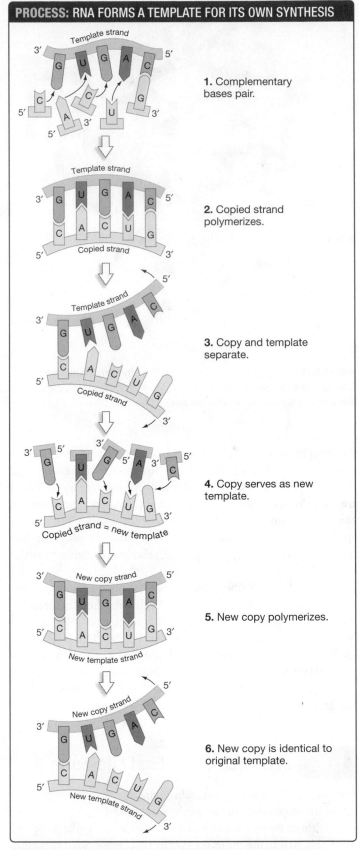

PROCESS: RNA FORMS A TEMPLATE FOR ITS OWN SYNTHESIS

1. Complementary bases pair.
2. Copied strand polymerizes.
3. Copy and template separate.
4. Copy serves as new template.
5. New copy polymerizes.
6. New copy is identical to original template.

FIGURE 5.10 RNA Molecules Contain Information That Allows Them to Be Replicated. For a single-stranded RNA to be copied, it must pass through double-stranded RNA intermediates.

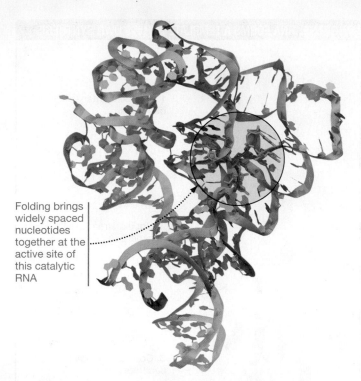

Folding brings widely spaced nucleotides together at the active site of this catalytic RNA

FIGURE 5.11 Tertiary Structure of the *Tetrahymena* Ribozyme. The folded structure brings together bases from distant locations in the primary structure to form the active site.

be brought together in an environment that will promote the reaction. As with protein enzymes, the region of the ribozyme that is responsible for this activity is called the active site. When the *Tetrahymena* ribozyme was compared to protein enzymes that catalyze similar reactions, their active sites were found to be similar in structure. This observation about two very different molecules demonstrates the critical relationship between structure and function

The discovery of ribozymes was a watershed event in origin-of-life research. Before Altman and Cech published their results, most biologists thought that the only molecules capable of catalyzing reactions in cells were proteins. The fact that a ribozyme in *Tetrahymena* catalyzed a condensation reaction raised the possibility that an RNA molecule could make a copy of itself. Such a molecule could qualify as the first living entity. Is there any experimental evidence to support this hypothesis?

5.4 In Search of the First Life-Form

The theory of chemical evolution maintains that life began as a naked self-replicator—a molecule that existed by itself in solution, without being enclosed in a membrane. To make a copy of itself, that first living molecule had to (1) provide a template that could be copied, and (2) catalyze polymerization reactions that would link monomers into a copy of that template. Because RNA is capable of both processes, most origin-of-life researchers propose that the first life-form was made of RNA.

No self-replicating RNA molecules have been discovered in nature, however, so researchers test the hypothesis by trying to simulate the RNA world in the laboratory. The eventual goal is to create an RNA molecule that can catalyze its own replication.

How Biologists Study the RNA World

To understand how researchers go about testing the RNA world hypothesis, consider two recent experiments by researchers in David Bartel's laboratory. In one study, the team attempted to generate an RNA molecule that could catalyze the kind of template-directed polymerization needed for RNA replication—an RNA "replicase." Starting with a ribozyme capable of joining two ribonucleotides together, they generated billions of copies into which random mutations were introduced.

Next they incubated the mutants with free ribonucleotides and began selecting for replicase activity. Molecules that exhibited such activity were isolated and copied. After two weeks and 18 rounds of selection, the team succeeded in isolating a ribozyme that could add 14 nucleotides to an existing RNA strand.

Note that the team's experimental protocol was designed to mimic the process of natural selection introduced in Chapter 1. The population of RNAs from each round had variable characteristics that could be replicated and passed on to the next generation of ribozymes. In addition, the researchers were able to select the most efficient RNAs to be the "parents" of the next generation—and in the process introduce new mutations that potentially could make some of the "offspring" even better ribozymes.

This research created considerable excitement among biologists interested in the origin of life, because adding ribonucleotides to a growing strand is a key attribute of an RNA replicase. However, since the maximum product length generated was less than 10 percent of the ribozyme's own length, an RNA replicase capable of making a full-length copy of itself was far from being discovered. In fact, the difficulty in creating an effective RNA replicase has led many researchers to question the idea of a replicase being the first ribozyme to emerge in the RNA world.

In another study, Bartel's group asked a different question: Would it be possible to select for a ribozyme that could make ribonucleotides? This type of ribozyme is not known to exist in nature but would be a key component in the RNA world.

Recall that the direction of a chemical reaction and how much product it makes is influenced by the amount of reactants present (Appendix D). Since the chemical evolution of nucleotides is thought to have been inefficient, nucleotides would have been a scarce resource on early Earth. Ribozymes that could catalyze the production of nucleotides would be more likely to be copied due to local accumulation of monomers.

Starting with a large pool of randomly generated RNA sequences, the researchers selected for RNAs that could catalyze the addition of a uracil base to a ribose sugar. By round 11, the group had recovered ribozymes that were 50,000 times better at catalyzing the reaction than those found in the fourth round and over 1 million times more efficient than the uncatalyzed reaction. In effect, molecular evolution had occurred in the reaction tubes.

Thanks to similar efforts at other laboratories around the world, biologists have produced an increasingly impressive set of catalytic activities from RNA molecules. The results from each of these studies help clarify our view of what occurred in the RNA world. If a living ribozyme ever existed, then each round of simulated molecular evolution brings us closer to resurrecting it.

The RNA World May Have Sparked the Evolution of Life

Although ribozymes like these lab-generated molecules may have been present in the RNA world, they have not been observed in nature. Of those that have been discovered in modern cells, most play key roles in the synthesis of proteins. This relationship suggests the order of events in chemical evolution—the RNA world preceded proteins.

The evolution of protein enzymes would have marked the end of the RNA world—providing the means for catalyzing reactions necessary for life to emerge in a cellular form. After this milestone, three of the five fundamental characteristics of life (see Chapter 1) were solidly in place:

1. *Information* Proteins and ribozymes were processing information stored in nucleic acids for the synthesis of more proteins.

2. *Replication* Enzymes, and possibly ribozymes, were replicating the nucleic acids that stored the hereditary information.

3. *Evolution* Random changes in the synthesis of proteins, and selective advantages resulting from some of these changes, allowed for the evolution of new proteins and protein families.

If these events occurred in a hydrothermal vent, the molecular assemblages of nucleic acids and proteins would have been constantly fed with thermal and chemical energy. To gain independence from their undersea hatchery, enzymes would have evolved to store this energy as something more portable—carbohydrates. The structure and function of carbohydrates will be the focus of the next chapter.

If you understand . . .

5.1 What Is a Nucleic Acid?

- Nucleic acids are polymers of nucleotide monomers, which consist of a sugar, a phosphate group, and a nitrogenous base. Ribonucleotide monomers polymerize to form RNA. Deoxyribonucleotide monomers polymerize to form DNA.

- Ribonucleotides have a hydroxyl ($-OH$) group on their 2' carbon; deoxyribonucleotides do not.

- Nucleic acids polymerize when condensation reactions join nucleotides together via phosphodiester linkages.

- Nucleic acids are directional: they have a 5' end and a 3' end. During polymerization, new nucleotides are added only to the 3' end.

✔ **You should be able to state what cells do to activate nucleotides for incorporation into a polymer and explain why activation is required.**

5.2 DNA Structure and Function

- DNA's primary structure consists of a sequence of linked nitrogenous bases. Its secondary structure consists of two DNA strands running in opposite directions that are twisted into a double helix.

- DNA is an extremely stable molecule that serves as a superb archive for information in the form of base sequences. It lacks a reactive 2' hydroxyl group, and its secondary structure is stabilized by hydrophobic interactions and hydrogen bonds that form between complementary bases stacked on the inside of the helix.

- DNA is readily copied via complementary base pairing. Complementary base pairing occurs between A-T and G-C pairs in DNA.

- DNA's structural stability and regularity are advantageous for information storage, but they make DNA an ineffective catalyst.

✔ **You should be able to explain why DNA molecules with a high percentage of guanine and cytosine are particularly stable.**

5.3 RNA Structure and Function

- Like DNA, RNA's primary structure consists of a sequence of linked nitrogenous bases. RNA's secondary structure includes short regions of double helices and looped structures called hairpins.

- RNA molecules are usually single stranded. They have secondary structure because of complementary base pairing between A-U and G-C pairs on the same strand.

- Unlike DNA, the secondary structures of RNA can fold into more complex shapes, stabilized by hydrogen bonding, which give the molecule tertiary structure.

- RNA is versatile. The primary function of proteins is to catalyze chemical reactions, and the primary function of DNA is to carry information. But RNA is an "all-purpose" macromolecule that can do both.

✔ **You should be able to explain why many RNA molecules exhibit tertiary structure, while most DNA molecules do not.**

5.4 In Search of the First Life-Form

- To test the RNA world hypothesis, researchers are attempting to synthesize new ribozymes in the laboratory. Using artificial selection strategies, they have succeeded in identifying RNAs that catalyze several different reactions.

- Ribozymes that catalyze reactions necessary for the production of nucleotides may have preceded the evolution of RNA replicases.

✔ You should be able to provide two examples of activities in the RNA world you expect would benefit from catalysis and justify your choices.

 **MasteringBiology**

1. MasteringBiology Assignments

Tutorials and Activities Double Helix; Heritable Information: DNA; Nucleic Acid Building Blocks; Nucleic Acid Structure; Structure of RNA and DNA

Questions Reading Quizzes, Blue-Thread Questions, Test Bank

2. eText Read your book online, search, take notes, highlight text, and more.

3. The Study Area Practice Test, Cumulative Test, BioFlix® 3-D Animations, Videos, Activities, Audio Glossary, Word Study Tools, Art

You should be able to . . .

✓ TEST YOUR KNOWLEDGE
Answers are available in Appendix A

1. What are the four nitrogenous bases found in RNA?
   a. uracil, guanine, cytosine, thymine (U, G, C, T)
   b. adenine, guanine, cytosine, thymine (A, G, C, T)
   c. adenine, uracil, guanine, cytosine (A, U, G, C)
   d. alanine, threonine, glycine, cysteine (A, T, G, C)

2. What determines the primary structure of a DNA molecule?
   a. the sugar-phosphate backbone
   b. complementary base pairing and the formation of hairpins
   c. the sequence of deoxyribonucleotides
   d. the sequence of ribonucleotides

3. DNA attains a secondary structure when hydrogen bonds form between the nitrogenous bases called purines and pyrimidines. What are the complementary base pairs that form in DNA?
   a. A-T and G-C
   b. A-U and G-C
   c. A-G and T-C
   d. A-T and G-U

4. Which of the following rules apply to the synthesis of nucleic acids?
   a. Nucleotides are added to the 5′ end of nucleic acids.
   b. The synthesis of nucleic acids cannot occur without the presence of an enzyme to catalyze the reaction.
   c. Strands are synthesized in a parallel direction such that one end of the double-stranded product has the 3′ ends and other has the 5′ ends.
   d. Complementary pairing between bases is required for copying nucleic acids.

5. Nucleic acids are directional, meaning that there are two different ends. What functional groups define the two different ends of a DNA strand?

6. What is responsible for the increased stability of DNA compared to RNA?

✓ TEST YOUR UNDERSTANDING
Answers are available in Appendix A

7. Explain how Chargaff's rules relate to the complementary base pairing seen in the secondary structure of DNA. Would you expect these rules to apply to RNA as well? Explain why or why not.

8. **QUANTITATIVE** If nucleotides from the DNA of a human were quantified and 30 percent of them consisted of adenine, what percentage of guanine nucleotides would be present?
   a. 20 percent
   b. 30 percent
   c. 40 percent
   d. 70 percent

9. What would be the sequence of the strand of DNA that is made from the following template: 5′-GATATCGAT-3′ (Your answer must be written 5′→3′.) How would this sequence be different if RNA were made from this DNA template?

10. A major theme in this chapter is that the structure of molecules correlates with their function. Explain how DNA's secondary structure limits its catalytic abilities compared with that of RNA. Why is it expected that RNA molecules can catalyze a modest but significant array of reactions?

11. To replicate a ribozyme, a complete complementary copy must be made. Would you expect the double-stranded intermediate to maintain its catalytic activity? Justify your answer with an explanation.

12. Suppose that Bartel's research group succeeded in producing a molecule that could make a copy of itself. Which of the five fundamental characteristics of life (provided in Chapter 1) would support the claim that this molecule is alive?

13. Make a concept map (see **BioSkills 15** in Appendix B) that relates DNA's primary structure to its secondary structure. Your diagram should include deoxyribonucleotides, hydrophobic interactions, purines, pyrimidines, phosphodiester linkages, DNA primary structure, DNA secondary structure, complementary base pairing, and antiparallel strands.

14. Viruses are particles that infect cells. In some viruses, the genetic material consists of two strands of RNA, bonded together via complementary base pairing. Would these antiparallel strands form a double helix? Explain why or why not.

15. Before Watson and Crick published their model of the DNA double helix, Linus Pauling offered a model based on a triple helix. If the three sugar-phosphate backbones were on the outside of such a molecule, would hydrogen bonding or hydrophobic interactions be more important in keeping such a secondary structure together?

16. How would you expect the structure of ribozymes in organisms that grow in very hot environments, such as hot springs or deep-sea vents, to differ from those in organisms that grow in cooler environments?
    a. These ribozymes would have more hairpin secondary structures.
    b. The hairpins would have more G's and C's in the primary structure.
    c. The hairpins would have more A's and U's in the primary structure.
    d. These ribozymes would exhibit no tertiary structure.

6 DNA and the Gene: Synthesis and Repair

In this chapter you will learn how

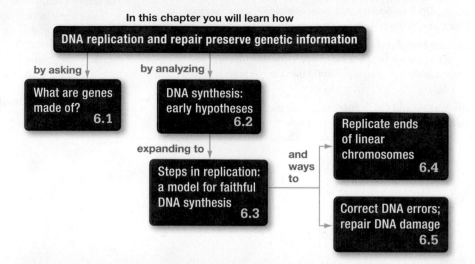

DNA replication and repair preserve genetic information

by asking

What are genes made of? 6.1

by analyzing

DNA synthesis: early hypotheses 6.2

expanding to

Steps in replication: a model for faithful DNA synthesis 6.3

and ways to

Replicate ends of linear chromosomes 6.4

Correct DNA errors; repair DNA damage 6.5

Electron micrograph (with color added) showing DNA in the process of replication. The original DNA double helix (far right) is being replicated into two DNA double helices (on the left). The two helices diverge at the replication fork, which is where DNA synthesis is taking place.

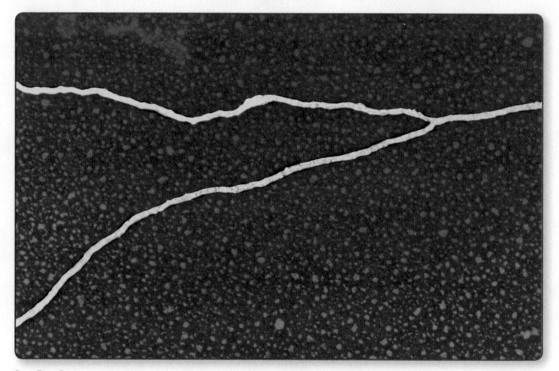

What are genes made of, and how are they copied so that they are faithfully passed on to offspring? These questions dominated biology during the middle of the twentieth century. Since Mendel's time, the predominant research strategy in genetics had been to conduct a series of experimental crosses, create a genetic model to explain the types and proportions of phenotypes that resulted, and then test the model's predictions through reciprocal crosses, testcrosses, or other techniques. This strategy led to virtually all the discoveries of classical genetics, including Mendel's rules, sex linkage, linkage, and quantitative inheritance (see Chapter 12).

The chemical composition and molecular structure of Mendel's hereditary factors—which came to be called genes—remained a mystery for the first half of the twentieth century. Although biologists knew that genes and chromosomes were replicated during the cell cycle, with copies distributed

✔ When you see this checkmark, stop and test yourself. Answers are available in Appendix A.

to daughter cells during mitosis and meiosis (see Chapters 4 and 11), no one had the slightest clue about how the copying occurred.

The goal of this chapter is to explore how researchers solved these mysteries. The results provided a link between two of the five attributes of life (introduced in Chapter 1): processing genetic information and replication.

How are genes copied, so they can be passed on to succeeding generations? Let's begin with studies that identified the nature of the genetic material, then explore how genes are copied during the synthesis phase of the cell cycle, and conclude by analyzing how incorrectly copied or damaged genes are repaired. Once the molecular nature of the gene was known, the nature of biological science changed forever.

6.1 What Are Genes Made Of?

The chromosome theory of inheritance (Chapter 12) proposed that chromosomes contain genes. It had been known since the late 1800s that chromosomes are a complex of DNA and proteins. The question, then, of what genes are made of came down to a simple choice: DNA or protein?

Initially, most biologists backed the hypothesis that genes are made of proteins. The arguments in favor of this hypothesis were compelling. Hundreds, if not thousands, of complex and highly regulated chemical reactions occur in even the simplest living cells. The amount of information required to specify and coordinate these reactions is mind-boggling. With their almost limitless variation in structure and function, proteins are complex enough to contain this much information.

In contrast, DNA was known to be composed of just four types of deoxyribonucleotides (Chapter 5). Early but incorrect evidence suggested that DNA was a simple molecule with some sort of repetitive and uninteresting structure. It seemed impossible that such a simple compound could hold complex information.

DNA or protein? The experiment that settled the question is considered a classic in biological science.

The Hershey–Chase Experiment

In 1952 Alfred Hershey and Martha Chase took up the question of whether genes were made of protein or DNA by studying how a virus called T2 infects and replicates within the bacterium *Escherichia coli*. Nearly 10 years before Hershey and Chase began their study, Oswald Avery and colleagues showed in 1944 that DNA could serve as genetic material, but many scientists remained unconvinced of the finding or its generality. Hershey and Chase knew that T2 infections begin when the virus attaches to the cell wall of *E. coli* and injects its genes into the cell's interior (**FIGURE 6.1a**). These genes then direct the production of a new generation of

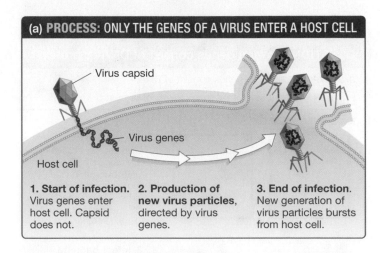

(a) PROCESS: ONLY THE GENES OF A VIRUS ENTER A HOST CELL

Virus capsid

Virus genes

Host cell

1. Start of infection. Virus genes enter host cell. Capsid does not.

2. Production of new virus particles, directed by virus genes.

3. End of infection. New generation of virus particles bursts from host cell.

(b) The virus's capsid stays outside the cell.

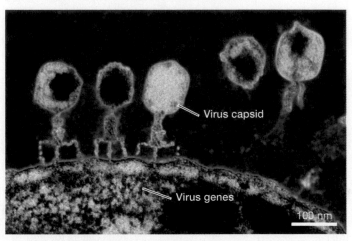

Virus capsid

Virus genes

100 nm

FIGURE 6.1 Viruses Inject Genes into Bacterial Cells and Leave a Capsid Behind. Color has been added to the transmission electron micrograph in (b) to make key structures more visible.

virus particles inside the infected cell, which acts as a host for the virus.

During the infection, the exterior protein coat, or **capsid,** of the original, parent virus is left behind. The capsid remains attached to the exterior of the host cell (**FIGURE 6.1b**). Hershey and Chase also knew that T2 is made up almost exclusively of protein and DNA. Was it protein or DNA that entered the host cell and directed the production of new viruses?

Hershey and Chase's strategy for determining the composition of the viral substance that enters the cell and acts as the hereditary material was based on two biochemical facts: (1) Proteins contain sulfur but not phosphorus, and (2) DNA contains phosphorus but not sulfur.

As **FIGURE 6.2** (see page 106) shows, the researchers began their work by growing viruses in the presence of either a radioactive isotope of sulfur (^{35}S) or a radioactive isotope of phosphorus (^{32}P). Because these isotopes were incorporated into newly synthesized proteins and DNA, this step produced a population of viruses with radioactive proteins and a population with radioactive DNA.

QUESTION: Do viral genes consist of DNA or protein?

DNA HYPOTHESIS: Viral genes consist of DNA.

PROTEIN HYPOTHESIS: Viral genes consist of protein.

EXPERIMENTAL SETUP:

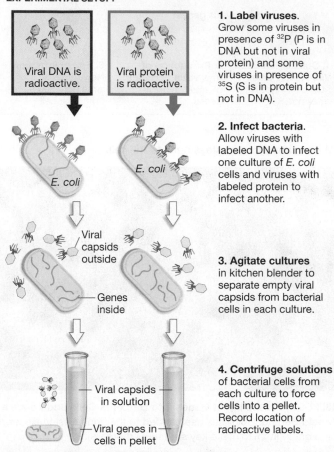

Viral DNA is radioactive.

Viral protein is radioactive.

1. Label viruses. Grow some viruses in presence of ^{32}P (P is in DNA but not in viral protein) and some viruses in presence of ^{35}S (S is in protein but not in DNA).

E. coli

E. coli

2. Infect bacteria. Allow viruses with labeled DNA to infect one culture of *E. coli* cells and viruses with labeled protein to infect another.

Viral capsids outside

Genes inside

3. Agitate cultures in kitchen blender to separate empty viral capsids from bacterial cells in each culture.

Viral capsids in solution

Viral genes in cells in pellet

4. Centrifuge solutions of bacterial cells from each culture to force cells into a pellet. Record location of radioactive labels.

PREDICTION OF DNA HYPOTHESIS: Radioactive DNA will be located within pellet.

PREDICTION OF PROTEIN HYPOTHESIS: Radioactive protein will be located within pellet.

RESULTS:

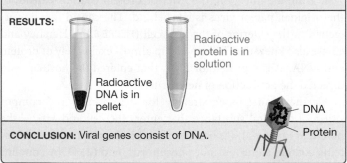

Radioactive protein is in solution

Radioactive DNA is in pellet

DNA

Protein

CONCLUSION: Viral genes consist of DNA.

FIGURE 6.2 Experimental Evidence that DNA Is the Hereditary Material.

SOURCE: Hershey, A. D., and M. Chase. 1952. Independent functions of viral protein and nucleic acid in growth of bacteriophage. *Journal of General Physiology* 36: 39–56.

✔ **QUESTION** What evidence would these investigators have to produce to convince you that the viral capsids were shaken off the bacterial cells by the agitation step?

Hershey and Chase allowed each set of radioactive viruses to infect *E. coli* cells. If genes consist of DNA, then radioactive protein should be found only in the capsids outside the infected host cells, while radioactive DNA should be located inside the cells. But if genes consist of proteins, then radioactive protein—and no radioactive DNA—should be inside the cells.

To test these predictions, Hershey and Chase sheared the capsids off the cells by vigorously agitating each of the cultures in kitchen blenders. When the researchers spun the samples in a centrifuge, the small phage capsids remained in the solution while the cells formed a pellet at the bottom of the centrifuge tube (see **BioSkills 10** in Appendix B to review how centrifugation works).

As predicted by the DNA hypothesis, the biologists found that virtually all the radioactive protein was outside cells in the emptied capsids, while virtually all the radioactive DNA was inside the host cells. Because the injected component of the virus directs the production of a new generation of virus particles, this component must represent the virus's genes.

After these results were published, proponents of the protein hypothesis accepted that DNA, not protein, must be the hereditary material. An astonishing claim—that DNA contained all the information for life's complexity—was correct.

The Secondary Structure of DNA

In 1953, one year after Hershey and Chase's landmark results were published, Watson and Crick proposed a model for the secondary structure of DNA. Recall that DNA is typically double-stranded with each strand consisting of a long, linear polymer made up of monomers called deoxyribonucleotides (Chapter 5).

Each deoxyribonucleotide consists of a deoxyribose sugar, a phosphate group, and a nitrogenous base (**FIGURE 6.3a**). Deoxyribonucleotides link together into a polymer when a phosphodiester bond forms between a hydroxyl group on the 3′ carbon of one deoxyribose and the phosphate group attached to the 5′ carbon of another deoxyribose. The two strands together make up one DNA molecule that functions as the genetic information storage molecule of cells.

As **FIGURE 6.3b** shows, the primary structure of each strand of DNA has two major features: (1) a "backbone" made up of the sugar and phosphate groups of deoxyribonucleotides and (2) a series of bases that project from the backbone. Each strand of DNA has a directionality, or polarity: One end has an exposed hydroxyl group on the 3′ carbon of a deoxyribose, while the other has an exposed phosphate group on a 5′ carbon. Thus, the molecule has distinctly different 3′ and 5′ ends.

As they explored different models for the secondary structure of DNA, Watson and Crick hit on the idea of lining up two of these long strands in opposite directions, or in what is called antiparallel fashion (**FIGURE 6.4a**). They realized that antiparallel strands will twist around each other into a spiral or helix because certain bases fit together snugly in pairs inside the spiral and form hydrogen bonds (**FIGURE 6.4b**). The double-stranded molecule that results is called a **double helix**.

(a) Structure of a deoxyribonucleotide

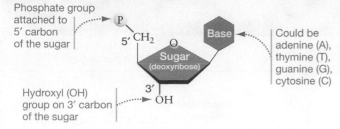

Phosphate group attached to 5′ carbon of the sugar

5′ CH₂

Sugar (deoxyribose)

Base

Could be adenine (A), thymine (T), guanine (G), cytosine (C)

Hydroxyl (OH) group on 3′ carbon of the sugar

3′ OH

(b) Primary structure of DNA

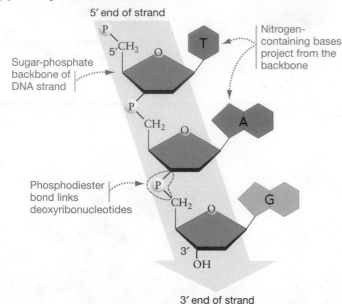

5′ end of strand

Sugar-phosphate backbone of DNA strand

Nitrogen-containing bases project from the backbone

Phosphodiester bond links deoxyribonucleotides

3′ end of strand

FIGURE 6.3 DNA's Primary Structure. (a) Deoxyribonucleotides are monomers that polymerize to form DNA. **(b)** DNA's primary structure is made up of a sequence of deoxyribonucleotides. Notice that the structure has a sugar–phosphate "backbone" with nitrogen-containing bases attached.

✔ **EXERCISE** Write the base sequence of the DNA in part (b), in the 5′ → 3′ direction.

The double-helical DNA is stabilized by hydrogen bonds that form between the bases adenine (A) and thymine (T) and between the bases guanine (G) and cytosine (C), along with hydrophobic interactions that the bases experience inside the helix. Hydrogen bonding of particular base pairs is **complementary base pairing.**

6.2 Testing Early Hypotheses about DNA Synthesis

Watson and Crick realized that the A-T and G-C pairing rules suggested a way for DNA to be copied when chromosomes are replicated during S phase of the cell cycle, before mitosis and meiosis. They suggested that the existing strands of DNA served as a template (pattern) for the production of new strands and that deoxyribonucleotides were added to the new strands according to complementary base pairing. For example, if the template

(a) Complementary base pairing

(b) The double helix

FIGURE 6.4 DNA's Secondary Structure: The Double Helix. (a) DNA normally consists of two strands, each with a sugar–phosphate backbone. Nitrogen-containing bases project from each strand and form hydrogen bonds. Only A-T and G-C pairs fit together in a way that allows hydrogen bonding to occur between the strands. **(b)** Bonding between complementary bases twists the molecule into a double helix.

strand contained a T, then an A would be added to the new strand to pair with that T. Similarly, a G on the template strand would dictate the addition of a C on the new strand.

Complementary base pairing provided a mechanism for DNA to be copied. But many questions remained about how the copying was done.

Three Alternative Hypotheses

Biologists at the time proposed three alternative hypotheses about how the old and new strands might interact during replication:

1. *Semiconservative replication* If the old, **parental strands** of DNA separated, each could then be used as a template for the synthesis of a new, **daughter strand.** This hypothesis is called **semiconservative replication** because each new daughter DNA molecule would consist of one old strand and one new strand.

2. *Conservative replication* If the bases temporarily turned outward so that complementary strands no longer faced each other, they could serve as a template for the synthesis of an entirely new double helix all at once. This hypothesis, called conservative replication, would result in an intact parental

QUESTION: Is replication semiconservative, conservative, or dispersive?

HYPOTHESIS 1:	HYPOTHESIS 2:	HYPOTHESIS 3:
Replication is semiconservative.	Replication is conservative.	Replication is dispersive.

EXPERIMENTAL SETUP:

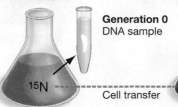 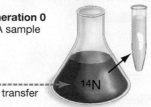 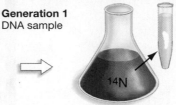 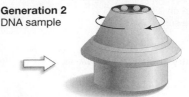

Generation 0
DNA sample

Generation 1
DNA sample

Generation 2
DNA sample

1. Grow *E. coli* cells in medium with ^{15}N as sole source of nitrogen for many generations. Collect sample and purify DNA.

2. Transfer cells to medium containing ^{14}N. After cells divide once, collect sample and purify DNA.

3. After cells have divided a second time in ^{14}N medium, collect sample and purify DNA.

4. Centrifuge the three samples separately. Compare the locations of the DNA bands in each sample.

PREDICTIONS:

Semiconservative replication

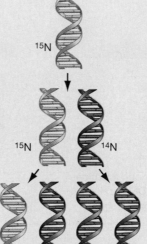

Generation 0

^{15}N

Generation 1

Hybrid   Hybrid

Generation 2

Hybrid ^{14}N Hybrid ^{14}N

After 2 generations:
1/2 low-density DNA (^{14}N)
1/2 intermediate-density DNA (hybrid)

Conservative replication

^{15}N

^{15}N ^{14}N

^{15}N ^{14}N

After 2 generations:
1/4 high-density DNA (^{15}N)
3/4 low-density DNA (^{14}N)

Dispersive replication

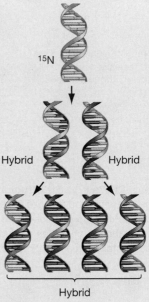

^{15}N

Hybrid   Hybrid

Hybrid

After 2 generations:
All intermediate-density DNA (hybrid)

RESULTS:

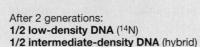
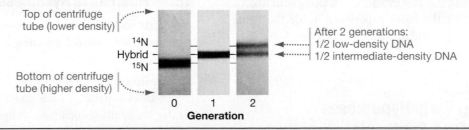

Top of centrifuge tube (lower density)

^{14}N
Hybrid
^{15}N

Bottom of centrifuge tube (higher density)

After 2 generations:
1/2 low-density DNA
1/2 intermediate-density DNA

0   1   2
Generation

CONCLUSION: Data from generation 1 conflict with conservative replication hypothesis. Data from generation 2 conflict with dispersive replication hypothesis. Replication is semiconservative.

FIGURE 6.5 The Meselson–Stahl Experiment.

SOURCE: Meselson, M., and F. W. Stahl. 1958. The replication of DNA in *Escherichia coli*. *Proceedings of the National Academy of Sciences USA* 44: 671–682.

✓**EXERCISE** Meselson and Stahl actually let their experiment run for a fourth generation with cultures growing in the presence of ^{14}N. Explain what data from third- and fourth-generation DNA should look like—that is, where the DNA band(s) should be.

molecule and a daughter DNA molecule consisting entirely of newly synthesized strands.

3. **Dispersive replication**   If the parental double helix were cut wherever one strand crossed over another and DNA was synthesized in short sections by extending each of the cut parental strands to the next strand crossover, then there would be a mix of new and old segments along each replicated molecule. This possibility is called dispersive replication—stretches of old DNA would be interspersed with new DNA down the length of each daughter strand.

Matthew Meselson and Franklin Stahl realized that if they could tag or mark parental and daughter strands of DNA in a way that would make them distinguishable from each other, they could determine whether replication was conservative, semiconservative, or dispersive.

The Meselson–Stahl Experiment

Before Meselson and Stahl could do any tagging to distinguish old DNA from new DNA, they needed to choose an organism to study. They decided to work with the bacterium *Escherichia coli*—the same inhabitant of the human gastrointestinal tract that Hershey and Chase used. Because *E. coli* is small and grows quickly and readily in the laboratory, it had become a favored model organism in studies of biochemistry and molecular genetics. (See **BioSkills 13** in Appendix B for more on *E. coli*.)

Like all organisms, bacterial cells copy their entire complement of DNA, or their **genome,** before every cell division. To distinguish parental strands of DNA from daughter strands when *E. coli* replicated, Meselson and Stahl grew the cells for successive generations in the presence of different isotopes of nitrogen: first ^{15}N and later ^{14}N. Because ^{15}N contains an extra neutron, it is heavier than the normal isotope, ^{14}N.

This difference in mass, which creates a difference in density between ^{14}N-containing and ^{15}N-containing DNA, was the key to the experiment summarized in **FIGURE 6.5**. The logic ran as follows:

- If different nitrogen isotopes were available in the growth medium when different generations of DNA were produced, then the parental and daughter strands would have different densities.

- The technique called density-gradient centrifugation separates molecules based on their density (**BioSkills 10** in Appendix B). Low-density molecules cluster in bands high in the centrifuge tube; higher-density molecules cluster in bands lower in the centrifuge tube.

- When intact, double-stranded DNA molecules are subjected to density-gradient centrifugation, DNA that contains ^{14}N should form a band higher in the centrifuge tube; DNA that contains ^{15}N should form a band lower in the centrifuge tube.

In short, DNA containing ^{14}N and DNA containing ^{15}N should form separate bands. How could this tagging system be used to test whether replication is semiconservative, conservative, or dispersive?

Meselson and Stahl began by growing *E. coli* cells with nutrients that contained only ^{15}N. They purified DNA from a sample of these cells and transferred the rest of the culture to a growth medium containing only the ^{14}N isotope. After enough time had elapsed for these cells to divide once—meaning that the DNA had been copied once—they removed a sample and isolated the DNA. After the remainder of the culture had divided again, they removed another sample and isolated its DNA.

As Figure 6.5 shows, the conservative, semiconservative, and dispersive models make distinct predictions about the makeup of the DNA molecules after replication occurs in the first and second generation. Examine the figure carefully to understand these distinct predictions.

The photograph at the bottom of Figure 6.5 shows the experiment's results. After one generation, the density of the DNA molecules was intermediate. These data suggested that the hypothesis of conservative replication was wrong, since it predicted two different densities in the first generation.

After two generations, a lower-density band appeared in addition to the intermediate-density band. This result offered strong support for the hypothesis that DNA replication is semiconservative. Had dispersive replication occurred, the second generation would have produced only a single, intermediate density band. Each newly made DNA molecule comprises one old strand and one new strand—replication is semiconservative.

6.3   A Model for DNA Synthesis

The DNA inside a cell is like an ancient text that has been painstakingly copied and handed down, generation after generation. But while the most ancient of all human texts contain messages that are thousands of years old, the DNA in living cells has been copied and passed down for billions of years. And instead of being copied by monks or clerks, DNA is replicated by molecular scribes. What molecules are responsible for copying DNA, and how do they work?

Meselson and Stahl showed that each strand of DNA is copied in its entirety each time replication occurs, but how does DNA synthesis proceed? Does it require an input of energy in the form of ATP, or it is spontaneous? Is it catalyzed by an enzyme, or does it occur quickly on its own?

The initial breakthrough on DNA replication came with the discovery of an enzyme called **DNA polymerase,** so named because it polymerizes deoxyribonucleotides into DNA. This protein catalyzes DNA synthesis. Follow-up work showed that there are several types of DNA polymerase. DNA polymerase III, for example, is the enzyme that is primarily responsible for copying *E. coli*'s chromosome before cell division.

FIGURE 6.6 (see page 110) illustrates a critical characteristic of DNA polymerases: They can work in only one direction. DNA polymerases can add deoxyribonucleotides only to the 3′ end of a growing DNA chain. As a result, DNA synthesis always proceeds in the 5′ → 3′ direction. ✔ If you understand this

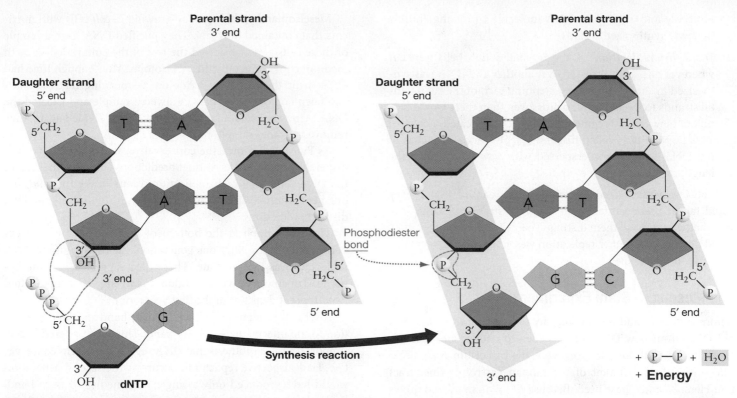

FIGURE 6.6 The DNA Synthesis Reaction. A condensation reaction results in formation of a phosphodiester bond between the 3′ carbon on the end of a DNA strand and the 5′ carbon on an incoming deoxyribonucleoside triphosphate (dNTP) monomer.

concept, you should be able to draw two lines representing a DNA molecule, assign the 3′-to-5′ polarity of each strand, and then label the direction in which DNA synthesis will proceed for each strand.

Figure 6.6 makes another important point about DNA synthesis. You might recall from earlier chapters that polymerization reactions generally are endergonic, meaning they require an input of energy. But for DNA synthesis, the reaction is exergonic (it releases energy) because the monomers that are used in the DNA synthesis reaction are **deoxyribonucleoside triphosphates (dNTPs).** (The N in dNTP stands for any of the four bases found in DNA: adenine, thymine, guanine, or cytosine). Because they have three closely spaced phosphate groups, dNTPs have high potential energy—high enough to make the formation of phosphodiester bonds in a growing DNA strand exergonic as two of the phosphates are cleaved off (see Chapter 10).

How Does Replication Get Started?

Another major insight into the mechanism of DNA synthesis emerged when electron microscopy caught DNA replication in action. As **FIGURE 6.7a** shows, a "bubble" forms when DNA is being synthesized. Initially, the replication bubble forms at a specific sequence of bases called the **origin of replication** (**FIGURE 6.7b**). Bacterial chromosomes have only one origin of replication, and thus a single replication bubble forms. Eukaryotes have multiple origins of replication along each chromosome, and thus multiple replication bubbles (**FIGURE 6.7c**).

DNA synthesis is bidirectional—that is, it occurs in both directions at the same time. Therefore, replication bubbles grow in two directions as DNA replication proceeds.

A specific set of proteins are responsible for recognizing sites where replication begins and opening the double helix at those points. These proteins are activated by the proteins that initiate S phase in the cell cycle (see Chapter 4).

Once a replication bubble opens at the origin of replication, a different set of enzymes takes over to start DNA synthesis. Active DNA synthesis takes place at the replication forks of each replication bubble (shown in Figure 6.7c). The **replication fork** is the Y-shaped region where the parent–DNA double helix is split into two single strands and copied.

How Is the Helix Opened and Stabilized?

A large group of enzymes and specialized proteins converge on the point where the double helix opens. The enzyme called **DNA helicase** breaks the hydrogen bonds between the base pairs. This reaction causes the two strands of DNA to separate. **Single-strand DNA-binding proteins (SSBPs)** attach to the separated strands and prevent them from snapping back into a double helix. Working together, DNA helicase and single-strand DNA-binding proteins open up the double helix and maintain the separation of both strands during copying (**FIGURE 6.8**, step 1).

The "unzipping" process that occurs at the replication fork creates tension farther down the helix. To understand why, imagine what would happen if you started to pull apart the twisted

(a) DNA being replicated

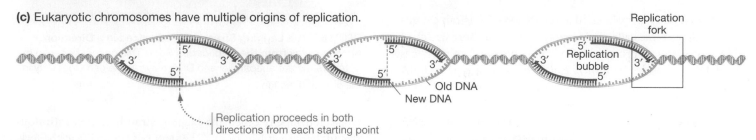

0.25 μm

(b) Bacterial chromosomes have a single origin of replication.

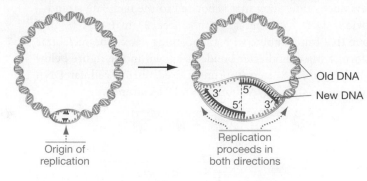

Origin of replication

Old DNA

New DNA

Replication proceeds in both directions

(c) Eukaryotic chromosomes have multiple origins of replication.

Replication fork

Replication bubble

Old DNA

New DNA

Replication proceeds in both directions from each starting point

FIGURE 6.7 DNA Synthesis Proceeds in Two Directions from an Origin of Replication. Color has been added to the micrograph in part (a).

strands of a rope. The untwisting movements at one end would force the intact section to rotate in response. If the intact end of the rope were fixed in place, it would coil on itself in response to the twisting forces. DNA does not become tightly coiled ahead of the replication fork, because the twisting induced by helicase is relaxed by proteins called topoisomerases. A **topoisomerase** is an enzyme that cuts DNA, allows it to unwind, and rejoins it ahead of the advancing replication fork.

Now, what happens once the DNA helix is open?

How Is the Leading Strand Synthesized?

The keys to understanding what happens at the start of DNA synthesis are to recall that DNA polymerase (**1**) works only in the 5′ → 3′ direction and (**2**) requires both a 3′ end to extend from and a single-stranded template. Both of these properties control how synthesis occurs on both template strands of DNA, and as you'll soon see, they significantly complicate copying one of these. The single-stranded template dictates which

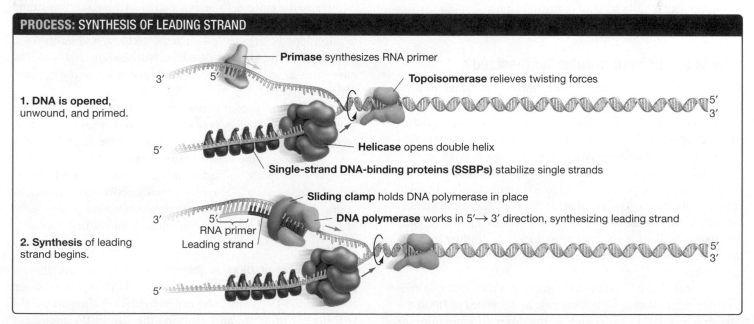

PROCESS: SYNTHESIS OF LEADING STRAND

Primase synthesizes RNA primer

Topoisomerase relieves twisting forces

1. DNA is opened, unwound, and primed.

Helicase opens double helix

Single-strand DNA-binding proteins (SSBPs) stabilize single strands

Sliding clamp holds DNA polymerase in place

DNA polymerase works in 5′→ 3′ direction, synthesizing leading strand

RNA primer
Leading strand

2. Synthesis of leading strand begins.

FIGURE 6.8 Leading-Strand Synthesis.

deoxyribonucleotide should be added next. A **primer**—a strand a few nucleotides long that is bonded to the template strand—provides DNA polymerase with a free 3′ hydroxyl (—OH) group that can combine with an incoming deoxyribonucleotide to form a phosphodiester bond. As shown in the figure below and in Figure 6.8, step 2, primers used during cellular DNA synthesis are short RNA strands, not DNA strands.

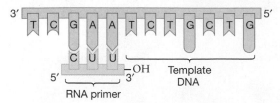

But what adds the primer? Before DNA synthesis can get under way, an enzyme called **primase** synthesizes a short stretch of RNA that acts as a primer for DNA polymerase. The primer is about 10 nucleotides long in *E. coli*. Primase is a type of **RNA polymerase**—an enzyme that catalyzes the polymerization of ribonucleotides into RNA (see Chapter 5 to review RNA's structure). Unlike DNA polymerases, primase and other RNA polymerases do not require a primer to begin synthesis.

Once a primer is present on a single-stranded template, DNA polymerase begins working in the 5′ → 3′ direction and adds deoxyribonucleotides to complete the complementary strand. As Figure 6.8, step 2, shows, DNA polymerase has a shape that grips the DNA strand during synthesis, similar to your hand clasping a rope. Deoxyribonucleotide addition is catalyzed at an active site in a groove between the enzyme's "thumb" and "fingers." As DNA polymerase moves along the DNA molecule, a doughnut-shaped structure behind it, called the sliding clamp, holds the enzyme in place on the template strand.

The enzyme's product is called the **leading strand,** or **continuous strand,** because it leads into the replication fork and is synthesized continuously. ✔ If you understand leading-strand synthesis, you should be able to list the enzymes involved and predict the consequences if any of them are defective.

How Is the Lagging Strand Synthesized?

Synthesis of the leading strand is straightforward. After an RNA primer is in place, DNA polymerase moves along, adding deoxyribonucleotides to the 3′ end of that strand. The enzyme moves into the replication fork, which "unzips" ahead of it. By comparison, events on the opposite strand are more involved.

Recall that the two strands of the DNA double helix are antiparallel—meaning they lie parallel to one another but oriented in opposite directions. The fact that DNA polymerases can synthesize DNA only in the 5′ → 3′ direction creates a paradox. Only one strand of DNA at the replication fork—the leading strand—can be synthesized in a direction that follows the moving replication fork.

The other strand must be synthesized in a direction that runs *away* from the moving replication fork, as illustrated in **FIGURE 6.9**. The strand of DNA that extends in the direction away from the

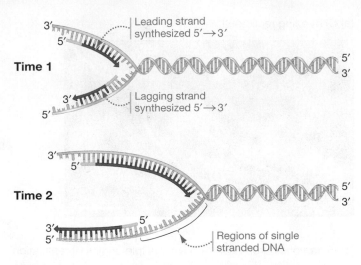

FIGURE 6.9 The Lagging Strand Is Synthesized in a Direction Moving Away from the Replication Fork. This occurs because the DNA strands are antiparallel and DNA polymerase can work only in the 5′ → 3′ direction.

replication fork is called the **lagging strand,** or **discontinuous strand,** because it lags behind the synthesis occurring at the fork. As the replication fork moves, it exposes gaps of single-stranded template DNA (Time 2 in Figure 6.9). How are the growing gaps filled in?

The Discontinuous Replication Hypothesis   The puzzle posed by lagging-strand synthesis was resolved when Reiji Okazaki and colleagues tested a hypothesis called discontinuous replication. This hypothesis held that primase synthesizes new RNA primers for lagging strands as the moving replication fork opens single-stranded regions of DNA, and that DNA polymerase uses these primers to synthesize short lagging-strand DNA fragments that are linked together into a continuous strand. These ideas are illustrated in **FIGURE 6.10**.

Note that Figure 6.10 shows details of how lagging-strand synthesis occurs in *E. coli*. The overall process, however, applies to all groups of organisms—bacteria, archaea, and eukaryotes. The basic reactions of lagging-strand synthesis are universal. The differences lie in the names or specific properties of the key proteins and enzymes.

To explore the discontinuous replication hypothesis, Okazaki's group set out to test a key prediction: Could they find short DNA fragments produced during replication? Their critical experiment was based on the pulse–chase strategy (see Chapter 2). They added a brief "pulse" of radioactive deoxyribonucleotides to *E. coli* cells, followed by a "chase" of nonradioactive deoxyribonucleotides. According to the discontinuous replication model, some of these radioactive deoxyribonucleotides should first appear in short, fragments of DNA.

The Discovery of Okazaki Fragments   As predicted, the researchers succeeded in finding short DNA fragments when they purified DNA from the experimental cells, separated the two strands of DNA, and analyzed the size of the molecules

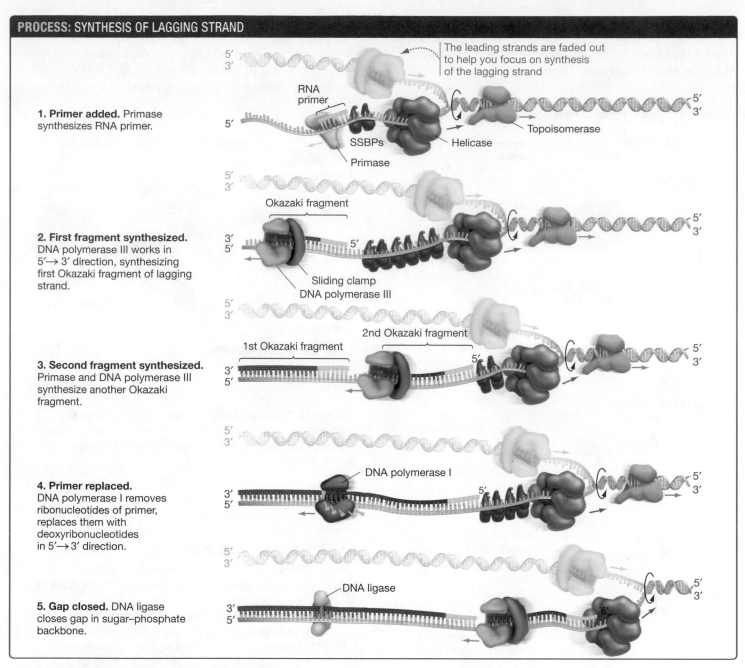

1. Primer added. Primase synthesizes RNA primer.

2. First fragment synthesized. DNA polymerase III works in 5′→3′ direction, synthesizing first Okazaki fragment of lagging strand.

3. Second fragment synthesized. Primase and DNA polymerase III synthesize another Okazaki fragment.

4. Primer replaced. DNA polymerase I removes ribonucleotides of primer, replaces them with deoxyribonucleotides in 5′→3′ direction.

5. Gap closed. DNA ligase closes gap in sugar–phosphate backbone.

The leading strands are faded out to help you focus on synthesis of the lagging strand

RNA primer
SSBPs
Primase
Helicase
Topoisomerase

Okazaki fragment
Sliding clamp
DNA polymerase III

2nd Okazaki fragment
1st Okazaki fragment

DNA polymerase I

DNA ligase

FIGURE 6.10 Lagging-Strand Synthesis.

by centrifugation. A small number of labeled DNA fragments about 1000 base pairs long were present immediately after the pulse. These short DNAs came to be known as **Okazaki fragments** and are shown in steps 2 and 3 of Figure 6.10. These small DNAs became larger during the chase as they were linked together into longer pieces. Subsequent work showed that Okazaki fragments in eukaryotes are even smaller—just 100 to 200 base pairs long.

How are Okazaki fragments connected? First, as step 4 of Figure 6.10 shows, in *E. coli* a specialized DNA polymerase called DNA polymerase I attaches to the 3′ end of an Okazaki fragment. As DNA polymerase I moves along in the 5′ → 3′ direction, it

removes that RNA primer ahead of it and replaces the ribonucleotides with the appropriate deoxyribonucleotides.

Once the RNA primer is removed and replaced by DNA, an enzyme called **DNA ligase** catalyzes the formation of a phosphodiester bond between the adjacent fragments (Figure 6.10, step 5). ✔ **If you understand lagging-strand synthesis, you should be able to draw what the two newly synthesized molecules of DNA at a single replication fork would look like if DNA ligase were defective.**

In eukaryotes, the mechanism for primer removal is different, but the mechanism of synthesizing short Okazaki fragments that are later joined into an unbroken chain of DNA is the same.

Working together, the enzymes that open the replication fork and manage the synthesis of the leading and lagging strands (**TABLE 6.1**) produce faithful copies of DNA before cell division. Although separate enzymes are drawn at different locations around the replication fork in Figures 6.8 and 6.10, in reality, all these enzymes are joined into the **replisome,** a large macromolecular machine. In *E. coli,* the replisome contains two copies of DNA polymerase III that are actively engaged in DNA synthesis. As shown in **FIGURE 6.11**, the lagging strand loops out and around

SUMMARY TABLE 6.1 Proteins Required for DNA Synthesis in Bacteria

Name	Structure	Function
Opening the helix		
Helicase		Catalyzes the breaking of hydrogen bonds between base pairs to open the double helix
Single-strand DNA-binding proteins (SSBPs)		Stabilizes single-stranded DNA
Topoisomerase		Breaks and rejoins the DNA double helix to relieve twisting forces caused by the opening of the helix
Leading strand synthesis		
Primase		Catalyzes the synthesis of the RNA primer
DNA polymerase III		Extends the leading strand
Sliding clamp		Holds DNA polymerase in place during strand extension
Lagging strand synthesis		
Primase		Catalyzes the synthesis of the RNA primer on an Okazaki fragment
DNA polymerase III		Extends an Okazaki fragment
Sliding clamp		Holds DNA polymerase in place during strand extension
DNA polymerase I		Removes the RNA primer and replaces it with DNA
DNA ligase		Catalyzes the joining of Okazaki fragments into a continuous strand

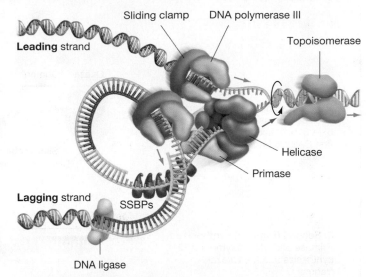

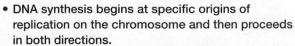

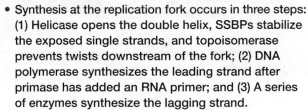

FIGURE 6.11 The Replisome. The enzymes required for DNA synthesis are organized into a macromolecular machine. Note how the lagging strand loops out as the leading strand is being synthesized.

check your understanding

If you understand that . . .

C
Y
U

- DNA synthesis begins at specific origins of replication on the chromosome and then proceeds in both directions.
- Synthesis at the replication fork occurs in three steps: (1) Helicase opens the double helix, SSBPs stabilize the exposed single strands, and topoisomerase prevents twists downstream of the fork; (2) DNA polymerase synthesizes the leading strand after primase has added an RNA primer; and (3) A series of enzymes synthesize the lagging strand.
- Lagging-strand synthesis cannot be continuous, because it moves away from the replication fork. In bacteria, enzymes called primase, DNA polymerase III, DNA polymerase I, and ligase work in sequence to synthesize Okazaki fragments and link them into a continuous whole.

✔ **You should be able to . . .**

1. Explain the function of primase.
2. Explain why DNA polymerase I is used predominantly on the lagging strand.

Answers are available in Appendix A.

the complex, allowing the replisome to move as a single unit as it follows the replication fork. After the DNA polymerase on the lagging strand completes synthesis of an Okazaki fragment, it is released from the DNA and reassembles on the most recently synthesized primer.

6.4 Replicating the Ends of Linear Chromosomes

The circular DNA molecules in bacteria and archaea can be synthesized by the enzymes introduced in Section 6.3, and so can most of the linear DNA molecules found in eukaryotes. But replication at the very ends of linear eukaryotic chromosomes is another story altogether. Replication of chromosome ends requires a specialized DNA replication enzyme that has been the subject of intense research.

The End Replication Problem

The region at the end of a eukaryotic chromosome is called a **telomere** (literally, "end-part"). **FIGURE 6.12** illustrates the problem that arises during the replication of telomeres.

- When the replication fork reaches the end of a linear chromosome, a eukaryotic DNA polymerase synthesizes the leading strand all the way to the end of the parent DNA template (step 1 and step 2, top strand). As a result, leading-strand synthesis results in a double-stranded copy of the DNA molecule.

- On the lagging strand, primase adds an RNA primer close to the tip of the chromosome (see step 2, bottom strand).

- DNA polymerase synthesizes the final Okazaki fragment on the lagging strand (step 3). An enzyme that degrades ribonucleotides removes the primer.

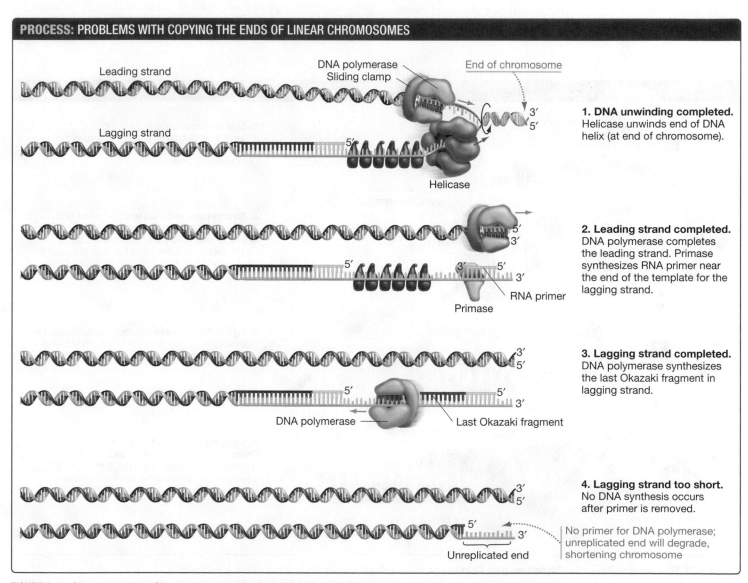

PROCESS: PROBLEMS WITH COPYING THE ENDS OF LINEAR CHROMOSOMES

1. DNA unwinding completed. Helicase unwinds end of DNA helix (at end of chromosome).

2. Leading strand completed. DNA polymerase completes the leading strand. Primase synthesizes RNA primer near the end of the template for the lagging strand.

3. Lagging strand completed. DNA polymerase synthesizes the last Okazaki fragment in lagging strand.

4. Lagging strand too short. No DNA synthesis occurs after primer is removed.

No primer for DNA polymerase; unreplicated end will degrade, shortening chromosome

FIGURE 6.12 Chromosomes Shorten during Normal DNA Replication. An RNA primer is added to the lagging strand near the end of the chromosome. Once the primer is removed, it cannot be replaced with DNA. As a result, the chromosome shortens.

- DNA polymerase is unable to add DNA near the tip of the chromosome, because it cannot synthesize DNA without a primer (step 4). As a result, the single-stranded DNA that is left stays single stranded.

The single-stranded DNA at the end of the lagging strand is eventually degraded, which results in the shortening of the chromosome. If this process were to continue unabated, every chromosome would shorten by about 50 to 100 deoxyribonucleotides each time DNA replication occurred. Over time, linear chromosomes would vanish.

Telomerase Solves the End Replication Problem

How do eukaryotes maintain their chromosomes? One answer emerged after Elizabeth Blackburn, Carol Greider, and Jack Szostak reported two striking discoveries:

1. Telomeres do not contain genes but are made of short stretches of bases that are repeated over and over. In human telomeres, for example, the base sequence TTAGGG is repeated thousands of times.

2. A remarkable enzyme called telomerase that carries its own template is involved in replicating telomeres.

Telomerase is extraordinary because it catalyzes the synthesis of DNA from an RNA template that it contains. Telomerase adds DNA onto the end of a chromosome to prevent it from getting shorter.

FIGURE 6.13 shows one model for how telomerase works to maintain the ends of eukaryotic chromosomes.

Step 1 The unreplicated segment of the telomere at the 3′ end of the template for the lagging strand forms a single-stranded "overhang".

Step 2 Telomerase binds to the overhanging single-stranded DNA and begins DNA synthesis. The template for this reaction is a portion of the RNA held within telomerase.

Step 3 Telomerase synthesizes DNA in the 5′→3′ direction and catalyzes repeated additions of the same short DNA sequence to the end of the growing single strand.

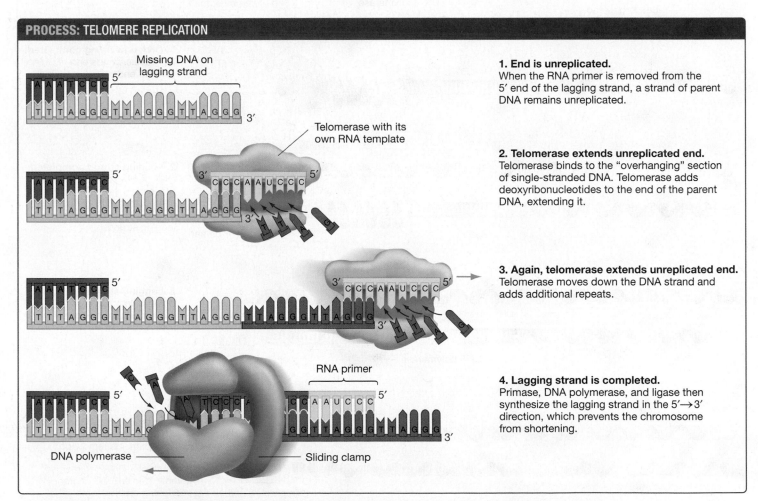

PROCESS: TELOMERE REPLICATION

1. End is unreplicated.
When the RNA primer is removed from the 5′ end of the lagging strand, a strand of parent DNA remains unreplicated.

2. Telomerase extends unreplicated end.
Telomerase binds to the "overhanging" section of single-stranded DNA. Telomerase adds deoxyribonucleotides to the end of the parent DNA, extending it.

3. Again, telomerase extends unreplicated end.
Telomerase moves down the DNA strand and adds additional repeats.

4. Lagging strand is completed.
Primase, DNA polymerase, and ligase then synthesize the lagging strand in the 5′→3′ direction, which prevents the chromosome from shortening.

FIGURE 6.13 Telomerase Prevents Shortening of Telomeres during Replication. By extending the number of repeated sequences in the 5′→3′ direction, telomerase provides room for enzymes to add an RNA primer to the lagging-strand template. Normal DNA replication enzymes can then fill in the missing section of the lagging strand.

✔**QUESTION** Would this telomerase work as well if its RNA template had a different sequence?

Step 4 Once the single-stranded overhang on the parent strand is lengthened, the normal enzymes of DNA synthesis use this strand as a template to synthesize a complementary strand. The result is that the lagging strand becomes slightly longer than it was originally.

Telomerase Regulation

The way telomerase is regulated is just as remarkable as the enzyme itself. Telomerase is active in only a limited number of cell types. In humans, for example, active telomerase is found primarily in the cells that produce gametes. Most **somatic cells,** meaning cells that are not involved in gamete formation, lack telomerase activity. As predicted, the chromosomes of somatic cells gradually shorten with each mitotic division, becoming progressively smaller as an individual ages.

These observations led to the hypothesis that the number of cell divisions possible for a somatic cell would be limited by the initial length of its telomeres. Carol Greider and colleagues tested this hypothesis by obtaining cells with a variety of telomere lengths from donors aged newborn to 90 years old and growing these cells in culture. (For an introduction to cell culture, see **BioSkills 12** in Appendix B.) Results of their study are shown in **FIGURE 6.14**. As predicted, there was a positive relationship between initial telomere length and the number of cell divisions before cells stop dividing—longer initial telomere length allowed a greater number of cell divisions, regardless of the donor's age.

You've probably noticed that the data points in Figure 6.14 do not fall perfectly on a line. This scatter or noise is typical in many studies. In interpreting results like these, researchers must consider what might account for the scatter and use statistical tests (see **BioSkills 4** in Appendix B) to determine how reliable the results are likely to be.

If telomere shortening controls the number of divisions possible for a cell, then a related prediction is that by restoring telomerase in somatic cells, these cells should be freed from growth limitations. As predicted, when researchers added telomerase to human cells growing in culture, the cells continued dividing long past the age when otherwise identical cells stop growing. Most biologists are convinced that telomere shortening has a role in limiting the number of cell divisions for somatic cells.

There is a dark side of telomerase activity, however. Unlike the somatic cells they derive from, most cancer cells have active telomerase. Many cancer biologists have proposed that telomerase activity allows the unlimited divisions of cancer cells. A simple prediction is that by inhibiting telomerase, the progression of cancer can be slowed or stopped. When combined with other approaches, could drugs that knock out telomerase be an effective way to fight cancer? Unfortunately, the complexity of cancer often thwarts such simple predictions. So far, answers to this question are unclear. Research continues.

check your understanding

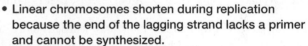

If you understand that . . .

- Linear chromosomes shorten during replication because the end of the lagging strand lacks a primer and cannot be synthesized.
- Shortening is prevented in certain cells—particularly those that produce sperm and egg—because telomerase adds short, repeated DNA sequences to the template strand. Primase can then add an RNA primer to the lagging strand, and DNA polymerase can fill in the missing sections.

✔ **You should be able to . . .**

1. Explain why telomerase is not needed by bacterial cells.

2. Explain why telomerase has to have a built-in template.

Answers are available in Appendix A.

6.5 Repairing Mistakes and DNA Damage

DNA polymerases work fast. In *E. coli*, for example, each replication fork advances about 500 nucleotides per second. But the replication process is also astonishingly accurate. In organisms ranging from *E. coli* to animals, the error rate during DNA replication averages about one mistake per *billion* deoxyribonucleotides.

This level of accuracy is critical. Humans, for example, develop from a fertilized egg that has roughly 12 billion deoxyribonucleotides in its DNA. This DNA is replicated over and over to create the trillions of cells that eventually make up the adult body. If more than one or two mutations occurred during each

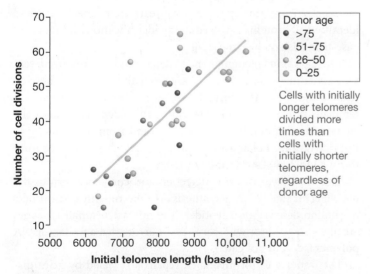

FIGURE 6.14 Telomere Length Predicts the Number of Divisions before Cells Stop Dividing.

DATA: Allsopp, R. C., et al. 1992. *Proceedings of the National Academy of Sciences*, 82: 10114–10118.

cell division cycle as a person developed, genes would be riddled with errors by the time the individual reached maturity. Genes that contain errors are often defective.

Based on these observations, it is no exaggeration to claim that the accurate replication of DNA is a matter of life and death. Natural selection favors individuals with enzymes that copy DNA quickly and accurately.

These observations raise a key question. How can the enzymes of DNA replication be as precise as they are?

Correcting Mistakes in DNA Synthesis

As DNA polymerase marches along a DNA template, hydrogen bonding occurs between incoming deoxyribonucleotides and the deoxyribonucleotides on the template strand. DNA polymerases are selective about the bases they add to a growing strand because (1) the correct base pairings (A-T and G-C) are energetically the most favorable, and (2) these correct pairings have a distinct shape. As a result, DNA polymerase inserts an incorrect deoxyribonucleotide (**FIGURE 6.15a**) only about once in every 100,000 bases added.

An error rate of one in 100,000 seems low, but it is much higher than the rate of one in a billion listed at the start of this section. What happens when DNA polymerase makes a mistake?

DNA Polymerase Proofreads Biologists learned more about how DNA synthesis could be so accurate when they found mutant cells in which DNA synthesis was *in*accurate.

Specifically, researchers found *E. coli* mutants with error rates that were 100 times greater than normal. Recall that a mutant is an individual with a novel trait caused by a mutation (see Chapter 12). In the case of *E. coli* mutants with high error rates

(a) DNA polymerase adds a mismatched base...

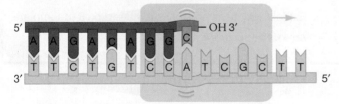

(b) ...but detects the mistake and corrects it.

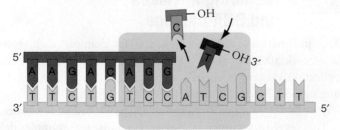

FIGURE 6.15 DNA Polymerase Can Proofread. If a mismatch such as the pairing of A with C occurs **(a)**, DNA polymerase can act as a $3' \rightarrow 5'$ exonuclease, meaning that it can remove bases in that direction **(b)**. The DNA polymerase then adds the correct base.

in DNA replication, biologists found a defect in a portion of the DNA polymerase III enzyme called the ε (epsilon) subunit. Further analyses showed that the ε subunit acts as an exonuclease—meaning an enzyme that removes deoxyribonucleotides from the ends of DNA strands (**FIGURE 6.15b**).

If a newly added deoxyribonucleotide is not correctly paired with a base on the complementary strand, the positioning of the incorrect deoxyribonucleotide provides a poor substrate for DNA polymerase to extend. This is because the geometry of incorrect base pairs differs from that of the correct A-T and G-C pairs. DNA polymerase's active site can detect these shapes and will add a new deoxyribonucleotide only when the previous base pair is correct. In wild-type *E. coli*, the polymerase pauses when it detects the wrong shape, and the exonuclease activity of the ε subunit removes the mismatched deoxyribonucleotide.

These findings led to the conclusion that DNA polymerase III can **proofread.** If the wrong base is added during DNA synthesis, the enzyme pauses, removes the mismatched deoxyribonucleotide that was just added, and then proceeds again with synthesis.

Eukaryotic DNA polymerases have the same type of proofreading ability. Typically, proofreading reduces the overall error rate of DNA synthesis to about one mistake in 10 million bases added. Is this accurate enough? The answer remains no.

Mismatch Repair If—despite its proofreading ability—DNA polymerase leaves a mismatched base behind in the newly synthesized strand, a battery of enzymes springs into action to correct the problem. **Mismatch repair** occurs when mismatched bases are corrected after DNA synthesis is complete.

The proteins responsible for mismatch repair were discovered in the same way proofreading was—by analyzing *E. coli* mutants. In this case, the mutants had normal DNA polymerase III but abnormally high mutation rates.

The first mutation that caused a deficiency in mismatch repair was identified in the late 1960s and was called *mutS*. (The *mut* is short for "mutator.") Twenty years later, researchers had identified 10 proteins involved in the identification and repair of base-pair mismatches in *E. coli*.

These proteins recognize the mismatched base, remove a section containing the incorrect base from the newly synthesized strand, and fill in the correct bases using the older strand as a template. In *E. coli*, chemical marks on the older strand allow the enzymes to distinguish the original strand from the newly synthesized strand. Eukaryotes use a different scheme to recognize the old and new strands of DNA.

This final layer of error detection and correction brings the overall error rate of DNA synthesis down to roughly one mistake per billion deoxyribonucleotides. The mismatch-repair enzymes are like a copy editor who corrects the errors that a writer—DNA polymerase—did not catch.

The importance of mismatch repair is revealed by grim discoveries: Mutations in components of the mismatch repair system are observed in many common human cancers, where they play an important role in cancer development and progression.

Repairing Damaged DNA

Even after DNA is synthesized and proofread and mismatches repaired, the job of ensuring accuracy doesn't end. Genes are under constant assault. DNA is damaged by sunlight, X-rays, and many chemicals like the hydroxyl (OH) radicals produced during aerobic metabolism, aflatoxin B1 found in moldy peanuts and corn, and benzo[α]pyrene in cigarette smoke. If this damage were ignored, mutations would quickly accumulate to lethal levels. To fix problems caused by chemical attack, radiation, or other events, organisms have evolved a wide array of DNA damage-repair systems. As an example, consider the **nucleotide excision repair** system that works on DNA damage caused by ultraviolet light and many different chemicals.

Ultraviolet (UV) light in sunlight—and tanning booths—can cause a covalent bond to form between adjacent pyrimidine bases within the same DNA strand. The thymine-thymine pair illustrated in **FIGURE 6.16** is a common example. This defect, called a thymine dimer, creates a kink in the structure of DNA. The kink stalls standard DNA polymerases, blocking DNA replication. If the damage is not repaired, the cell may die.

Nucleotide excision repair fixes thymine dimers and many other types of damage that distort the DNA helix. In the first step of excision repair, an enzyme recognizes the kink in the DNA helix (step 1 in **FIGURE 6.17**). Once a damaged region is recognized, another enzyme removes a segment of single-stranded DNA containing the defective sequence (step 2). The intact DNA strand provides a template for synthesis of a corrected strand, and the 3′ hydroxyl of the DNA strand next to the gap serves as a primer (step 3). DNA ligase links the newly synthesized DNA to the original undamaged DNA (step 4). As with mismatch repair, multiple enzymes work together and DNA synthesis plays a central role in repair.

What happens when a human DNA repair system is defective?

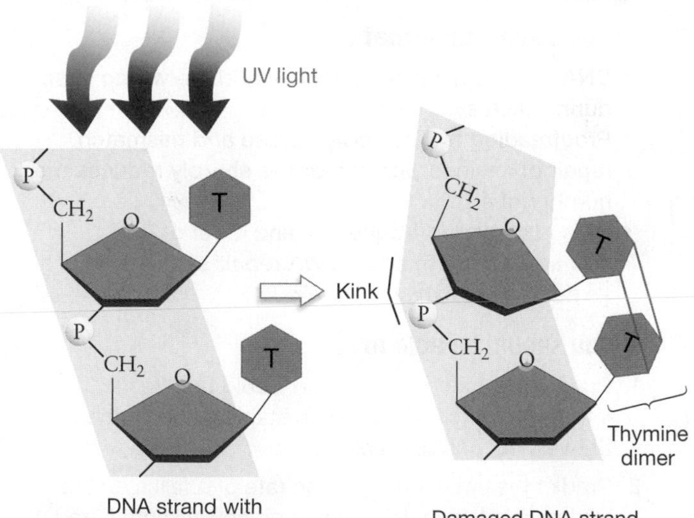

Xeroderma Pigmentosum: A Case Study

Xeroderma pigmentosum (XP) is a rare autosomal recessive disease in humans. Individuals with this condition are extremely sensitive to ultraviolet (UV) light. Their skin develops lesions including rough, scaly patches and irregular dark spots after even slight exposure to sunlight.

In 1968 James Cleaver proposed a connection between XP and DNA nucleotide excision repair. He knew that mutants of *E. coli* had defects in nucleotide excision repair that caused an increased sensitivity to radiation. Cleaver's hypothesis was that people with XP have similar mutations. He proposed that they are extremely sensitive to sunlight because they are unable to repair damage induced by UV light.

Cleaver and other researchers made extensive use of cell cultures (**BioSkills 12**, see Appendix B) to study the hypothesized connection between DNA damage, faulty nucleotide excision repair, and XP. They collected skin cells from people with XP and from people with normal UV light sensitivity. When these cells were grown in culture, the biologists exposed them to increasing amounts of UV radiation and recorded how many survived.

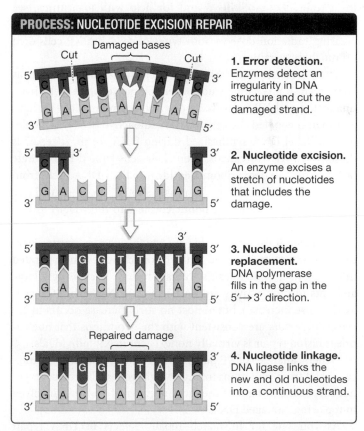

FIGURE 6.16 UV Light Damages DNA. When UV light strikes a section of DNA that has adjacent thymines, the energy can break bonds within each base and lead to the formation of bonds *between* them. The thymine dimer that is produced causes a kink in the DNA.

✔**QUESTION** Why are infrared wavelengths much less likely than UV to damage DNA? (Hint: See Figure 14.4.)

PROCESS: NUCLEOTIDE EXCISION REPAIR

1. Error detection. Enzymes detect an irregularity in DNA structure and cut the damaged strand.

2. Nucleotide excision. An enzyme excises a stretch of nucleotides that includes the damage.

3. Nucleotide replacement. DNA polymerase fills in the gap in the 5′→3′ direction.

4. Nucleotide linkage. DNA ligase links the new and old nucleotides into a continuous strand.

FIGURE 6.17 In Nucleotide Excision Repair, Defective Bases Are Removed and Replaced.

(a) Vulnerability of cells to UV light damage

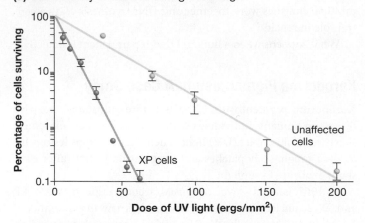

(b) Ability of cells to repair UV light damage

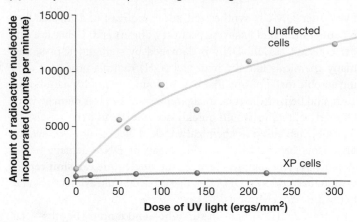

FIGURE 6.18 DNA Damage from UV Light Is Not Repaired Properly in Individuals with XP. (a) When cell cultures from unaffected individuals and XP patients are irradiated with various doses of UV light (expressed here as ergs/mm²), the percentage of cells that survive is strikingly different. **(b)** When cell cultures from unaffected individuals and XP patients are irradiated with various doses of UV light and then provided with a radioactive deoxyribonucleotide, only cells from unaffected individuals incorporate the labeled deoxyribonucleotide into their DNA.

DATA: (a) Cleaver, J. E. 1970. *Int. J. Rad. Biol.* 18: 577–565, Fig 3. (b) Cleaver, J. E. 1972. *J. Invest. Dermatol.* 58: 124–128, Fig 1.

✔ **QUESTION** Why are people who cultivate a sun tan increasing their risk of developing cancer? (Hint: Tanning is a response to UV light.)

FIGURE 6.18a shows the results of one such study by Cleaver. Note that the intensity of the radiation is graphed on the *x*-axis, and the percentage of cells surviving is graphed on the *y*-axis. Note, too, that the *y*-axis is logarithmic. (For help with reading graphs, see **BioSkills 3** and for help with logarithms, see **BioSkills 6**, both in Appendix B.) Cell survival declined with increasing radiation dose in both types of cells, but XP cells died off much more rapidly.

The connection to nucleotide excision repair systems was confirmed in a separate study when Cleaver exposed cells from unaffected and XP individuals to various amounts of UV light and then incubated the cells with a radioactive deoxyribonucleotide to label DNA synthesized during DNA repair. If repair is defective in XP individuals, then their cells should incorporate little radioactive deoxyribonucleotide into their DNA. Cells from unaffected individuals, in contrast, should incorporate large amounts of labeled deoxyribonucleotide into their DNA as it is repaired.

As **FIGURE 6.18b** shows, this is exactly what happens. Here the amount of radioactive deoxyribonucleotides incorporated into DNA is graphed against radiation dose. Increasingly large amounts of radioactivity are found in the DNA of healthy cells as UV dose increases, but almost no such increase occurs in XP cells. These data are consistent with the hypothesis that nucleotide excision repair is virtually nonexistent in XP individuals.

Genetic analyses of XP patients have shown that the condition can result from mutations in any of eight genes. This discovery is not surprising in light of the large number of enzymes involved in repairing damaged DNA.

As you saw for mismatch repair, defects in DNA repair genes are frequently associated with cancer. Individuals with

xeroderma pigmentosum, for example, are 1000 to 2000 times more likely to get skin cancer than are individuals with intact excision repair systems. To explain this pattern, biologists suggest that if DNA damage in the genes involved in the cell cycle goes unrepaired, mutations will result that may allow the cell to grow in an uncontrolled manner. Tumor formation could result. Recall

check your understanding

If you understand that . . .

- DNA polymerases occasionally add the wrong base during DNA synthesis.
- Proofreading by DNA polymerase and mismatch repair of misincorporated bases sharply reduces the number of errors.
- DNA is damaged frequently, and most of this damage can be fixed by DNA repair systems such as nucleotide excision repair.

✔ **You should be able to . . .**

1. Predict how the mutation rate would be affected if there were no differences in stability and shape between all possible base pairs.
2. Predict the effect on mutation rate of a failure in the system for distinguishing old and newly synthesized DNA.
3. State which nucleotide excision repair enzymes are specific for DNA repair and which work in both normal DNA replication and in DNA repair.

Answers are available in Appendix A.

that most cancers develop only after several genes have been damaged (see Chapter 4). If the overall mutation rate in a cell is elevated because of defects in DNA repair, then mutations that trigger cancer become more likely.

At this point, it's clear that genes are made of DNA and that DNA is accurately copied and passed on to offspring. How can information be stored in DNA, and how can this information be used? (These are the topics of the next two chapters.)

If you understand . . .

6.1   What Are Genes Made Of?

- Experiments on viruses that had labeled proteins or DNA showed that DNA is the hereditary material.
- DNA's primary structure consists of a sugar–phosphate backbone and a sequence of nitrogen-containing bases.
- DNA's secondary structure consists of two strands in an antiparallel orientation. The strands twist into a helix and are held together by complementary pairing between bases.

✔ You should be able to interpret an imaginary experiment like the one done by Hershey and Chase that shows that ^{32}P is found only in the pellet and that ^{35}S is found in both the pellet and the solution.

6.2   Testing Early Hypotheses about DNA Synthesis

- By labeling DNA with ^{15}N or ^{14}N, researchers were able to validate the hypothesis that DNA replication is semiconservative.
- In semiconservative replication, each strand of a parent DNA molecule provides a template for the synthesis of a daughter strand, resulting in two complete DNA double helices.

✔ You should be able to write a sequence of double-stranded DNA that is 10 base pairs long, separate the strands, and, without comparing them, write in the bases that are added during DNA replication.

6.3   A Model for DNA Synthesis

- DNA synthesis requires many different enzymes, and it occurs in one direction only.
- DNA synthesis requires both a template and a primer sequence. It takes place at the replication fork where the double helix is opened.
- Synthesis of the leading strand in the $5' \rightarrow 3'$ direction is continuous, but synthesis of the lagging strand is discontinuous because on that strand, the DNA polymerase moves away from the replication fork.

- On the lagging strand, short DNA fragments called Okazaki fragments form and are joined together. Okazaki fragments are primed by a short strand of RNA.

✔ You should be able to draw and label a diagram of a replication bubble that shows (1) the $5' \rightarrow 3'$ polarity of the two parental DNA strands and (2) the leading and lagging daughter strands at each replication fork.

6.4   Replicating the Ends of Linear Chromosomes

- At the ends of linear chromosomes in eukaryotes, the enzyme telomerase adds short, repeated sections of DNA so that the lagging strand can be synthesized without shortening the chromosome.
- Telomerase is active in reproductive cells that eventually undergo meiosis. As a result, gametes contain chromosomes of normal length.
- Chromosomes in cells without telomerase shorten with continued cell division until their telomeres reach a critical length at which cell division no longer occurs.

✔ You should be able to explain the significance of telomerase reactivation in cancer cells.

6.5   Repairing Mistakes and DNA Damage

- DNA replication is remarkably accurate because (1) DNA polymerase selectively adds a deoxyribonucleotide that correctly pairs with the template strand; (2) DNA proofreads each added deoxyribonucleotide; and (3) mismatch repair enzymes remove incorrect bases once synthesis is complete and replace them with the correct base.
- DNA repair occurs after DNA has been damaged by chemicals or radiation.
- Nucleotide excision repair cuts out damaged portions of DNA and replaces them with correct sequences.
- If DNA repair enzymes are defective, mutation rate increases. Because of this, several types of human cancers are associated with defects in the genes responsible for DNA repair.

✔ You should be able to explain the logical connections between failure of repair systems, increases in mutation rate, and high likelihood of cancer developing.

You should be able to . . .

✓ TEST YOUR KNOWLEDGE   *Answers are available in Appendix A*

1. What does it mean to say that strands in a double helix are
   antiparallel?
   a. Their primary sequences consist of a sequence of *complementary*
      bases.
   b. They each have a sugar–phosphate backbone.
   c. They each have a $5' \rightarrow 3'$ directionality.
   d. They have opposite directionality, or polarity.

2. Which of the following is *not* a property of DNA polymerase?
   a. It adds dNTPs only in the $5' \rightarrow 3'$ direction.
   b. It requires a primer to work.
   c. It is associated with a sliding clamp only on the leading strand.
   d. Its exonuclease activity is involved in proofreading.

3. The enzyme that removes twists in DNA ahead of the replication
   fork is _____.

4. What is the function of primase?
   a. synthesis of the short section of double-stranded DNA required
      by DNA polymerase
   b. synthesis of a short RNA, complementary to single-stranded
      DNA
   c. closing the gap at the $3'$ end of DNA after excision repair
   d. removing primers and synthesizing a short section of DNA to
      replace them

5. How are Okazaki fragments synthesized?
   a. using the leading strand template, and synthesizing $5' \rightarrow 3'$
   b. using the leading strand template, and synthesizing $3' \rightarrow 5'$
   c. using the lagging strand template, and synthesizing $5' \rightarrow 3'$
   d. using the lagging strand template, and synthesizing $3' \rightarrow 5'$

6. An enzyme that uses an internal RNA template to synthesize DNA
   is _____.

✓ TEST YOUR UNDERSTANDING   *Answers are available in Appendix A*

7. Researchers design experiments so that only one thing is different
   between the treatments that are being compared. In the Hershey–
   Chase experiment, what was this single difference?

8. What is the relationship between defective DNA repair and
   cancer?

9. Why is the synthesis of the lagging strand of DNA discontinuous?
   How is it possible for the synthesis of the leading strand to be
   continuous?

10. Explain how telomerase prevents linear chromosomes from
    shortening during replication.

11. Predict what would occur in a bacterial mutant that lost the ability
    to chemically mark the template strand of DNA.
    a. The mutation rate would increase.

   b. The ability of DNA polymerase to discriminate between correct
      and incorrect base pairs would decrease.
   c. The energy differences between correct and incorrect base pairs
      would decrease.
   d. The energy differences between correct and incorrect base pairs
      would increase.

12. What aspect of DNA structure makes it possible for the enzymes
    of nucleotide excision repair to recognize many different types of
    DNA damage?
    a. the polarity of each DNA strand
    b. the antiparallel orientation of strands in the double helix
    c. the energy differences between correct and incorrect base pairs
    d. the regularity of DNA's overall structure

13. If you could engineer an activity into DNA polymerase to allow both strands to follow the replication fork, what would this additional activity be?

    a. the ability to begin DNA synthesis without a primer
    b. the ability to proofread in the $5' \rightarrow 3'$ direction
    c. the ability to synthesize DNA in the $3' \rightarrow 5'$ direction
    d. the ability to synthesize DNA without using a template

14. In the late 1950s, Herbert Taylor grew bean root-tip cells in a solution of radioactive thymidine and allowed them to undergo one round of DNA replication. He then transferred the cells to a solution without the radioactive deoxyribonucleotide, allowed them to replicate again, and examined their chromosomes for the presence of radioactivity. His results are shown in the following figure, where red indicates a radioactive chromatid.

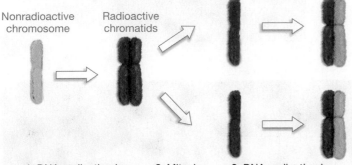

Nonradioactive chromosome   Radioactive chromatids

1. DNA replication in radioactive solution   2. Mitosis   3. DNA replication in nonradioactive solution

    a. Draw diagrams explaining the pattern of radioactivity observed in the sister chromatids after the first and second rounds of replication.
    b. What would the results of Taylor's experiment be if eukaryotes used a conservative mode of DNA replication?

15. The graph that follows shows the survival of four different *E. coli* strains after exposure to increasing doses of ultraviolet light. The wild-type strain is normal, but the other strains have a mutation in either a gene called *uvrA*, a gene called *recA*, or both.

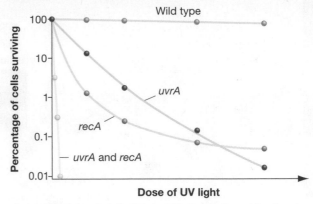

DATA: Howard-Flanders, P., and R. P. Boyce. 1966. *Radiation Research Supplement* 6: 156–184, Fig. 8.

    a. Which strains are most sensitive to UV light? Which strains are least sensitive?
    b. What are the relative contributions of these genes to the repair of UV damage?

16. **QUANTITATIVE** Assuming that each replication fork moves at a rate of 500 base pairs per second, how long would it take to replicate the *E. coli* chromosome (with 4.6 million base pairs) from a single origin of replication?

7 How Genes Work

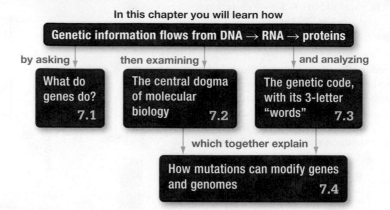

In this chapter you will learn how

Genetic information flows from DNA → RNA → proteins

by asking | then examining | and analyzing

| What do genes do? **7.1** | The central dogma of molecular biology **7.2** | The genetic code, with its 3-letter "words" **7.3** |

which together explain

How mutations can modify genes and genomes 7.4

This image shows a normal human male spectral karyotype—a micrograph of metaphase chromosomes stained to show different homologous chromosome pairs. This chapter explores how DNA sequences in chromosomes are related to phenotypes.

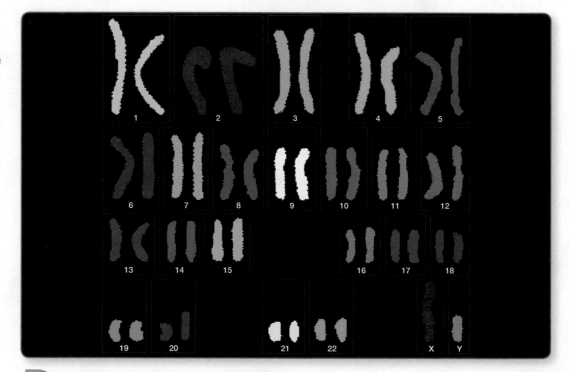

DNA has been called the blueprint of life. If an organism's DNA is like a set of blueprints, then its cells are like construction sites, and the enzymes inside a cell are like construction workers. But how does the DNA inside each cell assemble this team of skilled laborers and specify the materials needed to build and maintain the cell, and remodel it when conditions change?

Mendel provided insights that made the study of these questions possible. He discovered that particular alleles are associated with certain phenotypes and that alleles do not change when transmitted from parent to offspring. Later, the chromosome theory of inheritance established that genes are found in chromosomes, whose movement during meiosis explains Mendel's results.

The science of molecular biology began with the discovery that DNA is the hereditary material and that DNA is a double-helical structure containing sequences of four bases. From these early advances, it was clear that genes are made of DNA and that genes carry the instructions for making and maintaining an individual.

✔ When you see this checkmark, stop and test yourself. Answers are available in Appendix A.

But biologists still didn't know how the information in DNA is translated into action. How does **gene expression**—the process of converting archived information into molecules that actually do things in the cell—occur?

This chapter introduces some of the most pivotal ideas in all of biology—ideas that connect genotypes to phenotypes by revealing how genes work at the molecular level. They also speak to the heart of a key attribute of life: processing genetic information to produce a living organism.

Understanding how genes work triggered a major transition in biological science. Instead of thinking about genes solely in relation to their effects on eye color in fruit flies or on seed shape in garden peas, biologists could begin analyzing the molecular composition of genes and their products. The molecular revolution in biology took flight.

7.1 What Do Genes Do?

Although biologists of the early twentieth century made tremendous progress in understanding how genes are inherited, an explicit hypothesis explaining what genes do did not appear until 1941. That year George Beadle and Edward Tatum published a series of breakthrough experiments on a bread mold called *Neurospora crassa*.

Beadle and Tatum's research was inspired by an idea that was brilliant in its simplicity. As Beadle said: "One ought to be able to discover what genes do by making them defective." The idea was to knock out a gene by damaging it and then infer what the gene does by observing the phenotype of the mutant individual.

Today, alleles that do not function at all are called **knock-out, null,** or **loss-of-function alleles.** Creating knock-out mutant alleles and analyzing their effects is still one of the most common research strategies in studies of gene function. But Beadle and Tatum were the pioneers.

The One-Gene, One-Enzyme Hypothesis

To start their work, Beadle and Tatum exposed a large number of *N. crassa* cells to radiation. As described earlier (Chapter 6), radiation can damage the double-helical structure of DNA—often in a way that makes the affected gene nonfunctional.

Their next step was to examine the mutant cells. Eventually they succeeded in finding *N. crassa* mutants that could not make specific compounds. For example, one of the mutants could not make pyridoxine, also called vitamin B_6, even though normal

individuals can. Further, Beadle and Tatum showed that the inability to synthesize pyridoxine was due to a defect in a single gene, and that the inability to synthesize other molecules was due to defects in other genes.

These results inspired their **one-gene, one-enzyme hypothesis.** Beadle and Tatum proposed that the mutant *N. crassa* could not make pyridoxine because it lacked an enzyme required to synthesize the compound. They further proposed that the lack of the enzyme was due to a genetic defect. Based on analyses of knock-out mutants, the one-gene, one-enzyme hypothesis claimed that each gene contains the information needed to make an enzyme.

An Experimental Test of the Hypothesis

Three years later, Adrian Srb and Norman Horowitz published a rigorous test of the one-gene, one-enzyme hypothesis. These biologists focused on the ability of *N. crassa* to synthesize the amino acid arginine. In the lab, normal cells of this bread mold grow well on a laboratory culture medium that lacks arginine. This is possible because *N. crassa* cells are able to synthesize their own arginine.

Previous work had shown that organisms synthesize arginine in a series of steps called a **metabolic pathway.** As **FIGURE 7.1** shows, compounds called ornithine and citrulline are intermediate products in the metabolic pathway leading to arginine. Specific enzymes are required to synthesize ornithine, convert ornithine to citrulline, and change citrulline to arginine. Srb and Horowitz hypothesized that specific *N. crassa* genes are responsible for producing each of the three enzymes involved.

To test this idea, Srb and Horowitz used radiation to create a large number of mutant cells. However, radiation is equally likely to damage DNA and mutate genes in any part of the organism's genome, and most organisms have thousands or tens of thousands of genes. Of the many mutants the biologists created, how could they find the handful that specifically knocked out a step in the pathway for arginine synthesis?

To find the mutants they were looking for, the researchers performed what is now known as a genetic screen. A **genetic screen** is any technique for picking certain types of mutants out of many randomly generated mutants.

Srb and Horowitz began their screen by raising colonies of irradiated cells on a medium that included arginine. Then they transferred a sample of each colony to a medium that *lacked* arginine. If an individual could grow in the presence of arginine but failed to grow without arginine, they concluded that it couldn't make its own arginine.

Metabolic pathway for arginine synthesis: Precursor → (Enzyme 1) → Ornithine → (Enzyme 2) → Citrulline → (Enzyme 3) → Arginine

FIGURE 7.1 Different Enzymes Catalyze Each Step in the Metabolic Pathway for Arginine.

✔**QUESTION** If a cell lacked enzyme 2 but was placed in growth medium with ornithine, could it grow? Could it grow if it received citrulline instead?

The biologists followed up by confirming that the offspring of these cells also had this defect. Based on these data, they were confident that they had isolated individuals with mutations in one or more of the genes for the enzymes shown in Figure 7.1.

To test the one-gene, one-enzyme hypothesis, the biologists grew each mutant under four different conditions: on normal media without added arginine, and on normal medium supplemented with ornithine, citrulline, or arginine.

As **FIGURE 7.2** shows, the results from these growth experiments were dramatic. Some of the mutant cells were able to grow on some of these media but not on others. More specifically, the mutants fell into three distinct classes, which the researchers called *arg1*, *arg2*, and *arg3*.

As the "Interpretation" section of the figure shows, the data make sense if each type of mutant lacked a different, specific step in a metabolic pathway because of a defect in a particular gene. In short, Srb and Horowitz had documented a correlation between a specific genetic defect and a defect at a specific point in a metabolic pathway. This experiment convinced most investigators that the one-gene, one-enzyme hypothesis was correct.

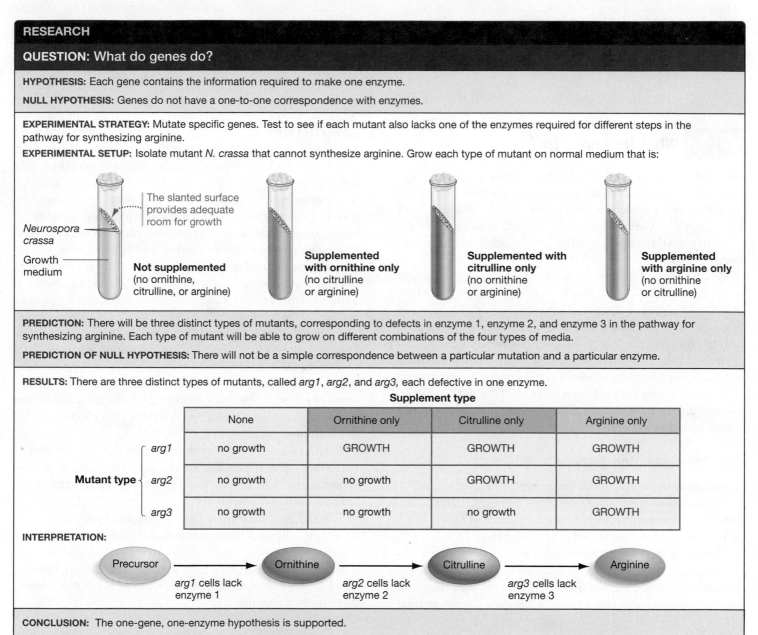

RESEARCH

QUESTION: What do genes do?

HYPOTHESIS: Each gene contains the information required to make one enzyme.

NULL HYPOTHESIS: Genes do not have a one-to-one correspondence with enzymes.

EXPERIMENTAL STRATEGY: Mutate specific genes. Test to see if each mutant also lacks one of the enzymes required for different steps in the pathway for synthesizing arginine.

EXPERIMENTAL SETUP: Isolate mutant *N. crassa* that cannot synthesize arginine. Grow each type of mutant on normal medium that is:

The slanted surface provides adequate room for growth

Neurospora crassa

Growth medium

Not supplemented (no ornithine, citrulline, or arginine)

Supplemented with ornithine only (no citrulline or arginine)

Supplemented with citrulline only (no ornithine or arginine)

Supplemented with arginine only (no ornithine or citrulline)

PREDICTION: There will be three distinct types of mutants, corresponding to defects in enzyme 1, enzyme 2, and enzyme 3 in the pathway for synthesizing arginine. Each type of mutant will be able to grow on different combinations of the four types of media.

PREDICTION OF NULL HYPOTHESIS: There will not be a simple correspondence between a particular mutation and a particular enzyme.

RESULTS: There are three distinct types of mutants, called *arg1*, *arg2*, and *arg3*, each defective in one enzyme.

		Supplement type		
		None	Ornithine only	Citrulline only	Arginine only
Mutant type	*arg1*	no growth	GROWTH	GROWTH	GROWTH
	arg2	no growth	no growth	GROWTH	GROWTH
	arg3	no growth	no growth	no growth	GROWTH

INTERPRETATION:

Precursor → Ornithine → Citrulline → Arginine

arg1 cells lack enzyme 1

arg2 cells lack enzyme 2

arg3 cells lack enzyme 3

CONCLUSION: The one-gene, one-enzyme hypothesis is supported.

FIGURE 7.2 Experimental Support for the One-Gene, One-Enzyme Hypothesis. The association between specific genetic defects in *N. crassa* and specific defects in the metabolic pathway for arginine synthesis provided evidence that supported the one-gene, one-enzyme hypothesis.

SOURCE: Srb, A. M., and N. H. Horowitz. 1944. The ornithine cycle in *Neurospora* and its genetic control. *Journal of Biological Chemistry* 154: 129–139.

✓**QUESTION** Experimental designs must be repeatable so that other investigators can try the experiment themselves to check the results. Name three things that these researchers would need to describe so that others could repeat this experiment.

Follow-up work showed that genes contain the information for all the proteins produced by an organism—not just enzymes. Biologists finally understood what most genes do: They contain the instructions for making proteins.

In many cases, though, a protein is made up of several different polypeptides, each of which is a product of a different gene. Consequently, for greater accuracy, the one-gene, one-enzyme hypothesis is best called the one-gene, one-polypeptide hypothesis.

7.2 The Central Dogma of Molecular Biology

How does a gene specify the production of a protein? As soon as Beadle and Tatum's hypothesis had been supported in *N. crassa* and a variety of other organisms, this question became a central one.

Part of the answer lay in the molecular structure of the gene. Biochemists knew that the primary components of DNA were four nitrogen-containing bases: the pyrimidines thymine (abbreviated T) and cytosine (C), and the purines adenine (A) and guanine (G). They also knew that these bases were connected in a linear sequence by a sugar–phosphate backbone. Watson and Crick's model for the secondary structure of the DNA molecule (see Chapters 5 and 6) revealed that two strands of DNA are wound into a double helix, held together by hydrogen bonds between the complementary base pairs A-T and G-C.

Given DNA's structure, it appeared extremely unlikely that DNA directly catalyzed the reactions that produce proteins. Its shape was too regular to suggest that it could bind a wide variety of substrate molecules and lower the activation energy for chemical reactions. So how, then, did information translate into action?

The Genetic Code Hypothesis

Crick proposed that the sequence of bases in DNA might act as a code. His idea was that DNA was *only* an information-storage molecule. The instructions it contained would have to be read and then translated into proteins.

Crick offered Morse code as an analogy. Morse code is a message-transmission system using dots and dashes to represent the letters of the alphabet, and in that way it can convey all the complex information of human language. Crick proposed that different combinations of bases could specify the 20 amino acids, just as different combinations of dots and dashes specify the 26 letters of the alphabet. A particular stretch of DNA, then, could contain the information needed to produce the amino acid sequence of a particular polypeptide.

In code form, the tremendous quantity of information required to build and operate a cell could be stored compactly. This information could also be copied through complementary base pairing and transmitted efficiently from one generation to the next.

It soon became apparent, however, that the information encoded in the base sequence of DNA is not translated into the

amino acid sequence of proteins directly. Instead, the link between DNA as information repository and proteins as cellular machines is indirect.

RNA as the Intermediary between Genes and Proteins

The first clue that the biological information in DNA must go through an intermediary in order to produce proteins came from knowledge of cell structure. In eukaryotic cells, DNA is enclosed within a membrane-bound organelle called the nucleus (see Chapter 2). But the cells' ribosomes, where protein synthesis takes place, are outside the nucleus, in the cytoplasm.

To make sense of this observation, François Jacob and Jacques Monod suggested that RNA molecules act as a link between genes and the protein-manufacturing centers. Jacob and Monod's hypothesis is illustrated in **FIGURE 7.3**. They predicted that short-lived molecules of RNA, which they called **messenger RNA,** or **mRNA** for short, carry information out of the nucleus from DNA to the site of protein synthesis. Messenger RNA is one of several distinct types of RNA in cells.

Follow-up research confirmed that the messenger RNA hypothesis is correct. One particularly important piece of evidence was the discovery of an enzyme that catalyzes the synthesis of RNA. This protein is called **RNA polymerase** because it polymerizes ribonucleotides into strands of RNA.

RNA polymerase synthesizes RNA molecules according to the information provided by the sequence of bases in a particular stretch of DNA. Unlike DNA polymerase, RNA polymerase

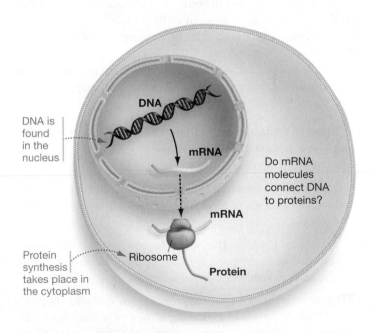

FIGURE 7.3 The Messenger RNA Hypothesis. In cells of eukaryotes such as plants, animals, and fungi, most DNA is found in the nucleus, but proteins are manufactured using ribosomes in the cytoplasm outside the nucleus. Biologists proposed that the information coded in DNA is carried from inside the nucleus out to the ribosomes by messenger RNA (mRNA).

does not require a primer to begin connecting ribonucleotides together to produce a strand of RNA.

To test the mRNA hypothesis, researchers created a reaction mix containing three critical elements: **(1)** the enzyme RNA polymerase; **(2)** ribonucleotides containing the bases adenine (A), uracil (U), guanine (G), and cytosine (C); and **(3)** strands of synthetic DNA that contained deoxyribonucleotides in which the only base was thymine (T).

After allowing the polymerization reaction to proceed, the biologists isolated RNA molecules that contained only the base adenine.

This result supported the hypothesis that RNA polymerase synthesizes RNA according to the rules of complementary base pairing (introduced in Chapter 5), because thymine pairs with adenine. Similar experiments showed that synthetic DNAs containing only cytosine result in the production of RNA molecules containing only guanine.

Dissecting the Central Dogma

Once the mRNA hypothesis was accepted, Francis Crick articulated what became known as the central dogma of molecular biology. The **central dogma** summarizes the flow of information in cells. It simply states that DNA codes for RNA, which codes for proteins:

$$DNA \longrightarrow RNA \longrightarrow proteins$$

Crick's simple statement encapsulates much of the research reviewed in this chapter and the preceding one. DNA is the hereditary material. Genes consist of specific stretches of DNA that code for products used in the cell. The sequence of bases in DNA specifies the sequence of bases in an RNA molecule, which specifies the sequence of amino acids in a protein. In this way, genes ultimately code for proteins.

Proteins are the workers of cells, functioning not only as enzymes but also as motors, structural elements, transporters, and molecular signals.

The Roles of Transcription and Translation   Biologists use specialized vocabulary to summarize the sequence of events captured in the central dogma.

1. DNA is transcribed to RNA by RNA polymerase. **Transcription** is the process of copying hereditary information in DNA to RNA.

2. Messenger RNA is translated to proteins in ribosomes. **Translation** is the process of using the information in nucleic acids to synthesize proteins.

The term transcription is appropriate. In everyday English, transcription simply means making a copy of information. The scientific use is similar because it conveys the idea that DNA acts as a permanent record—an information archive or blueprint. This permanent record is copied, during transcription, to produce the short-lived form called mRNA.

Translation is also an appropriate term. In everyday English, translation refers to converting information from one language

to another. In biology, translation is the transfer of information from one type of molecule to another—from the "language" of nucleic acids to the "language" of proteins. Translation is also referred to simply as protein synthesis.

The following equation summarizes the relationship between transcription and translation as well as the relationships between DNA, RNA, and proteins:

Gene expression occurs via transcription and translation.

Linking Genotypes and Phenotypes   An organism's genotype is determined by the sequence of bases in its DNA, while its phenotype is a product of the proteins it produces.

To appreciate this point, consider that the proteins encoded by genes are what make the "stuff" of the cell and dictate which chemical reactions occur inside. For example, in populations of the oldfield mouse native to southeastern North America, individuals have a gene for a protein called the melanocortin receptor. Melanocortin is a hormone—an important type of molecular signal—that works through the melanocortin receptor to influence how much dark pigment is deposited in fur. An important aspect of a mouse's phenotype—its coat color—is determined in part by the DNA sequence at the gene for this receptor (**FIGURE 7.4a**).

Later work revealed that alleles of a gene differ in their DNA sequence. As a result, the proteins produced by different alleles of the gene may differ in their amino acid sequence. If the primary structures of proteins vary, their functions are likely to vary as well.

To drive this point home, look at the DNA sequence in the portion of the melanocortin receptor gene shown in **FIGURE 7.4b**, and compare it with the sequence in Figure 7.4a. The sequences differ—meaning that they are different alleles. Now look at the protein products of each allele, and note that one of the amino acids in the protein's primary structure differs—one allele specifies an arginine residue; the other specifies a cysteine residue.

At the protein level, the phenotypes associated with these alleles differ. The consequences for the mouse are striking: Melanocortin receptors that have arginine in this location deposit a large amount of pigment, but receptors that have cysteine in this location deposit small amounts of pigment. Whether a mouse is dark or light depends, largely, on a single base change in its DNA sequence. In this case, a tiny difference in genotype produces a large change in phenotype. The central dogma links genotypes to phenotypes.

Exceptions to the Central Dogma   The central dogma provided an important conceptual framework for the burgeoning field of molecular genetics and inspired a series of fundamental questions about how genes and cells work. But important modifications to the central dogma have occurred in the decades since Frances Crick first proposed it:

(a) Genetic information flows from DNA to RNA to proteins.

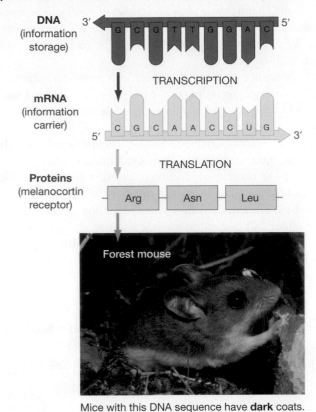

DNA
(information
storage)

3′   G C G T T G G A C   5′

TRANSCRIPTION

mRNA
(information
carrier)

5′   C G C A A C C U G   3′

TRANSLATION

Proteins
(melanocortin
receptor)

| Arg | Asn | Leu |

Forest mouse

Mice with this DNA sequence have **dark** coats.

(b) Differences in genotype may cause differences in phenotype.

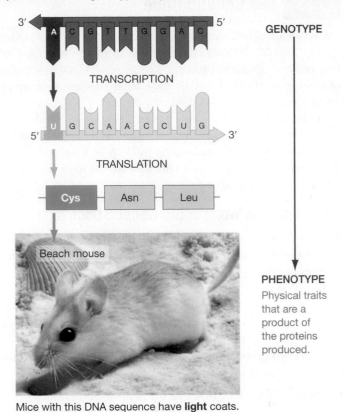

3′   A C G T T G G A C   5′   GENOTYPE

TRANSCRIPTION

5′   U G C A A C C U G   3′

TRANSLATION

| Cys | Asn | Leu |

Beach mouse

Mice with this DNA sequence have **light** coats.

PHENOTYPE
Physical traits
that are a
product of
the proteins
produced.

FIGURE 7.4 The Relationship between Genotype and Phenotype. The central dogma revealed the flow of information within the cell. The DNA sequences given in parts **(a)** and **(b)** are from different alleles (genotypes) that influence coat color (phenotypes) in oldfield mice. Forest-dwelling mice are dark, which camouflages them in their forested habitats. Beach-dwelling mice are light, which camouflages them in their sandy habitat.

- Many genes code for RNA molecules that do not function as mRNAs—they are not translated into proteins.

- In some cases, information flows from RNA back to DNA.

The discovery of a wide array of different RNA types ranks among the most profound advances in the past decade of biological science. Some RNAs form major parts of the ribosome, others help to form mRNA from a much longer precursor RNA (Chapter 8), and yet others regulate which genes are expressed. New types of RNA are still being discovered. For the genes coding for these types of RNA, information flow would be diagrammed as simply DNA → RNA.

In the early 1970s, the discovery of "reverse" information flow created the kind of excitement now being generated by the discovery of so many kinds of RNA. Some viruses, for example, have genes consisting of RNA. When some RNA viruses infect a cell, a specialized viral polymerase called **reverse transcriptase** synthesizes a DNA version of the RNA genes. In these viruses, information flows from RNA to DNA.

The human immunodeficiency virus (HIV), which causes AIDS, is an RNA virus that uses reverse transcriptase. Several of the most commonly prescribed drugs for AIDS patients fight the infection by poisoning the HIV reverse transcriptase. The drugs

prevent viruses from replicating efficiently by disrupting reverse information flow.

The punch line? Crick's hypothesis is a central concept in biology, but cells, viruses, and researchers aren't dogmatic about it.

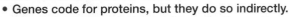

check your understanding

If you understand that . . .

- Genes code for proteins, but they do so indirectly.
- The sequence of bases in DNA is used to produce RNA, including messenger RNA (mRNA), via transcription. The sequence of bases in an RNA molecule is complementary to one of the DNA strands of a gene.
- Messenger RNAs are translated into proteins.
- Differences in DNA sequence can lead to differences in the amino acid sequence of proteins.

✔ **You should be able to . . .**

List the steps that link a change in the base sequence of a gene to a change in the phenotype of an organism.

Answers are available in Appendix A.

7.3 The Genetic Code

Once biologists understood the general pattern of information flow in the cell, the next challenge was to understand the final link between DNA and proteins. Exactly how does the sequence of bases in a strand of mRNA code for the sequence of amino acids in a protein?

If this question could be answered, biologists would have cracked the **genetic code**—the rules that specify the relationship between a sequence of nucleotides in DNA or RNA and the sequence of amino acids in a protein. Researchers from all over the world took up the challenge. A race was on.

How Long Is a Word in the Genetic Code?

The first step in cracking the genetic code was to determine how many bases make up a "word." In a sequence of mRNA, how long is a message that specifies one amino acid?

Based on some simple logic, George Gamow suggested that each code word contains three bases. His reasoning derived from the observation that 20 amino acids are commonly used in cells and from the hypothesis that each amino acid must be specified by a particular sequence of mRNA. **FIGURE 7.5** illustrates Gamow's reasoning:

- There are only four different bases in ribonucleotides (A, U, G, and C), so a one-base code could specify only four different amino acids.

- A two-base code could represent just 4 × 4, or 16, different amino acids.

- A three-base code could specify 4 × 4 × 4, or 64, different amino acids.

A three-base code provides more than enough words to code for all 20 amino acids. A three-base code is known as a **triplet code.**

Gamow's hypothesis suggested that the genetic code could be redundant. That is, more than one triplet of bases might specify the same amino acid. As a result, different three-base sequences in an mRNA—say, AAA and AAG—might code for the same amino acid—say, lysine.

The group of three bases that specifies a particular amino acid is called a **codon.** According to the triplet code hypothesis, many of the 64 codons that are possible might specify the same amino acids.

Work by Francis Crick and Sydney Brenner confirmed that codons are three bases long. Their experiments used chemicals that caused an occasional addition or deletion of a base in DNA. As predicted for a triplet code, a one-base addition or deletion in the base sequence led to a loss of function in the gene being studied. This is because a single addition or deletion mutation throws the sequence of codons, or the **reading frame,** out of register. To understand how a reading frame works, consider the sentence

"The fat cat ate the rat."

The reading frame of this sentence is a three-letter word and a space. If the fourth letter in this sentence—the *f* in *fat*—were deleted, the reading frame would transform the sentence into

"The atc ata tet her at."

This is gibberish.

When the reading frame in a DNA sequence is thrown out of register by the addition or deletion of a base, the composition of each codon changes just like the letters in each word of the example sentence above. The protein produced from the altered DNA sequence has a completely different sequence of amino acids. In terms of its normal function, this protein is gibberish.

Crick and Brenner were also able to produce DNA sequences that had deletions or additions of two base pairs or three base

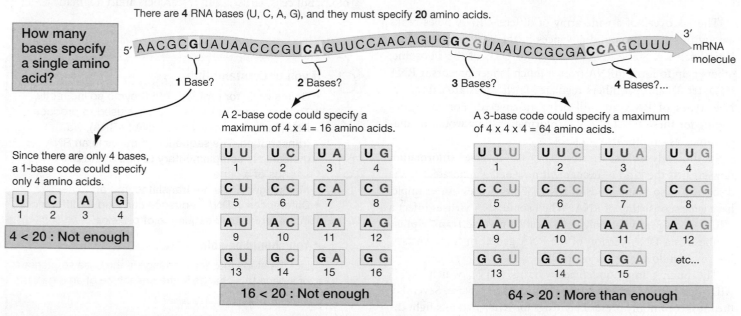

FIGURE 7.5 How Many Bases Form a "Word" in the Genetic Code?

pairs. The only time functional proteins were produced was when three bases were added or removed. In the sentence

"The **f**at ca**t** ate the rat."

the combination of removing one letter from each of the first three words might result in

"Tha tca ate the rat."

Just as the altered sentence still conveys some meaning, genes with three deletion mutations were able to produce a functional protein.

The researchers interpreted these results as strong evidence in favor of the triplet code hypothesis. Most other biologists agreed.

The confirmation of the triplet code launched an effort to determine which amino acid is specified by each of the 64 codons. Ultimately, it was successful.

How Did Researchers Crack the Code?

The initial advance in deciphering the genetic code came in 1961, when Marshall Nirenberg and Heinrich Matthaei developed a method for synthesizing RNAs of known sequence. They began by creating a long polymer of uracil-containing ribonucleotides. These synthetic RNAs were added to an in vitro system for synthesizing proteins. The researchers analyzed the resulting amino acid chain and determined that it was polyphenylalanine—a polymer consisting of the amino acid phenylalanine.

This result provided evidence that the RNA triplet UUU codes for the amino acid phenylalanine. By complementary base pairing, it was clear that the corresponding DNA sequence would be AAA. This initial work was followed by experiments using RNAs consisting of only A or C. RNAs with only AAAAA . . . produced polypeptides composed of only lysine; poly-C RNAs (RNAs consisting of only CCCCC . . .) produced polypeptides composed entirely of proline.

Nirenberg and Philip Leder later devised a system for synthesizing specific codons. With these they performed a series of experiments in which they added each codon to a cell extract containing the 20 different amino acids, ribosomes, and other molecules required for protein synthesis. Recall that ribosomes are macromolecular machines that synthesize proteins (Chapter 2). Then the researchers determined which amino acid became bound to the ribosomes when a particular codon was present. For example, when the codon CAC was in the reaction mix, the amino acid histidine would bind to the ribosomes. This result indicated that CAC codes for histidine.

These ribosome-binding experiments allowed Nirenberg and Leder to determine which of the 64 codons coded for each of the 20 amino acids.

Researchers also discovered that certain codons are punctuation marks signaling "start of message" or "end of message." These codons indicate that protein synthesis should start at a given codon or that the protein chain is complete.

- There is one **start codon** (AUG), which signals that protein synthesis should begin at that point on the mRNA molecule. The start codon specifies the amino acid methionine.
- There are three **stop codons,** also called termination codons (UAA, UAG, and UGA). The stop codons signal that the protein is complete, they do not code for any amino acid, and they end translation.

The complete genetic code is given in **FIGURE 7.6**. Deciphering it was a tremendous achievement, requiring more than five years of work by several teams of researchers.

SECOND BASE

FIRST BASE	U	C	A	G	THIRD BASE
U	UUU, UUC — Phenylalanine (Phe) UUA, UUG — Leucine (Leu)	UCU, UCC, UCA, UCG — Serine (Ser)	UAU, UAC — Tyrosine (Tyr) UAA — **Stop codon** UAG — **Stop codon**	UGU, UGC — Cysteine (Cys) UGA — **Stop codon** UGG — Tryptophan (Trp)	U C A G
C	CUU, CUC, CUA, CUG — Leucine (Leu)	CCU, CCC, CCA, CCG — Proline (Pro)	CAU, CAC — Histidine (His) CAA, CAG — Glutamine (Gln)	CGU, CGC, CGA, CGG — Arginine (Arg)	U C A G
A	AUU, AUC, AUA — Isoleucine (Ile) AUG — Methionine (Met) **Start codon**	ACU, ACC, ACA, ACG — Threonine (Thr)	AAU, AAC — Asparagine (Asn) AAA, AAG — Lysine (Lys)	AGU, AGC — Serine (Ser) AGA, AGG — Arginine (Arg)	U C A G
G	GUU, GUC, GUA, GUG — Valine (Val)	GCU, GCC, GCA, GCG — Alanine (Ala)	GAU, GAC — Aspartic acid (Asp) GAA, GAG — Glutamic acid (Glu)	GGU, GGC, GGA, GGG — Glycine (Gly)	U C A G

FIGURE 7.6 The Genetic Code. To read a codon in mRNA, locate its first base in the red band on the left; then move rightward to the box under the codon's second base in the blue band along the top. Finally, locate the codon's third base in the green band on the right side to learn the amino acid. By convention, codons are always written in the 5′ $\rightarrow$ 3′ direction.

(a) Using the genetic code to predict an amino acid sequence

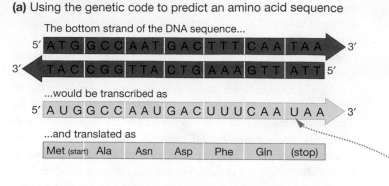

The bottom strand of the DNA sequence...

5′ A T G G C C A A T G A C T T T C A A T A A 3′

3′ T A C C G G T T A C T G A A A G T T A T T 5′

...would be transcribed as

5′ A U G G C C A A U G A C U U U C A A U A A 3′

...and translated as

| Met (start) | Ala | Asn | Asp | Phe | Gln | (stop) |

(b) Your turn—a chance to practice using the genetic code

The bottom strand of the DNA sequence...

5′ A T G C T G G A G G G G G T T A G A C A T 3′

3′ T A C G A C C T C C C C C A A T C T G T A 5′

...would be transcribed as

5′ _____ 3′

...and translated as

| | | | | | | |

Remember that RNA contains U (uracil) instead of T (thymine), and that U forms a complementary base pair with A (adenine)

FIGURE 7.7 Using the Genetic Code.
✔EXERCISE Fill in the mRNA and amino acid sequences in part (b).

Analyzing the Code Once biologists had cracked the genetic code, they realized that it has a series of important properties.

- *The code is redundant.* All amino acids except methionine and tryptophan are coded by more than one codon.

- *The code is unambiguous.* A single codon never codes for more than one amino acid.

- *The code is non-overlapping.* Once the ribosome locks onto the first codon, it then reads each separate codon one after another.

- *The code is nearly universal.* With a few minor exceptions, all codons specify the same amino acids in all organisms.

- *The code is conservative.* When several codons specify the same amino acid, the first two bases in those codons are almost always identical.

The last point is subtle, but important. Here's the key: If a mutation in DNA or an error in transcription or translation affects the third position in a codon, it is less likely to change the amino acid in the final protein. This feature makes individuals less vulnerable to small, random changes or errors in their DNA sequences. Compared with randomly generated codes, the existing genetic code minimizes the phenotypic effects of small changes in DNA sequence and errors during translation. Stated another way, the genetic code does not represent a random assemblage of bases, like letters drawn from a hat. It has been honed by natural selection and is remarkably efficient.

Using the Code Using the genetic code and the central dogma, biologists can:

1. Predict the codons and amino acid sequence encoded by a particular DNA sequence (see **FIGURE 7.7a**).

2. Determine the set of mRNA and DNA sequences that would code for a particular sequence of amino acids.

Why is a *set* of mRNA or DNA sequences predicted from a given amino acid sequence? The answer lies in the code's redundancy. If a polypeptide contains phenylalanine, you don't know if the codon responsible is UUU or UUC.

✔If you understand how to read the genetic code, you should be able to do the following tasks: (1) Identify the codons in Figure 7.4 and decide whether they are translated correctly. (2) Complete the exercise for **FIGURE 7.7b**. (3) Write an mRNA that codes for the amino acid sequence Ala-Asn-Asp-Phe-Gln yet is different from the one given in Figure 7.7a. Indicate the mRNA's 5′ → 3′ polarity. Then write the double-stranded DNA that corresponds to this mRNA. Indicate the 5′ → 3′ polarity of both DNA strands.

Once they understood the central dogma and genetic code, biologists were able to explore and eventually understand the molecular basis of mutation. How do novel traits—such as dwarfing in garden peas and white eye color in fruit flies—come to be?

7.4 How Can Mutation Modify Genes and Chromosomes?

This chapter has explored how the information archived in DNA is put into action in the form of working RNAs and proteins. Now the questions are, what happens if the information in DNA changes? In what ways can this information be changed? What are the consequences for the cell and organism?

A **mutation** is any permanent change in an organism's DNA. It is a modification in a cell's information archive—a change in its genotype. Mutations create new alleles.

Mutations can alter DNA sequences that range in size from a single base pair in DNA to whole sets of chromosomes. Let's look at these different types of mutation and their consequences.

Point Mutation

FIGURE 7.8 shows how a common type of mutation occurs. If a mistake is made during DNA synthesis or DNA repair, a change in the sequence of bases in DNA results. A single-base change such as this is called a **point mutation.**

What happens when point mutations occur in regions of DNA that code for proteins? To answer this question, look back at Figure 7.4 and recall that a change in a single base in DNA is associated with a difference in coat color in populations of oldfield mice. The DNA sequence in Figure 7.4a is found in dark-colored mice that live in forest habitats; the sequence in Figure 7.4b is found in light-colored mice that live in beach habitats.

Because beach-dwelling populations are evolutionarily younger than the nearby forest-dwelling populations, researchers hypothesize the following sequence of events:

1. Forest mice colonized beach habitats.

2. Either before or after the colonization event, a random point mutation occurred in a mouse that altered the melanocortin receptor gene and resulted in some offspring with light coats.

3. Light-colored mice are camouflaged in beach habitats; in sandy environments, they suffer lower predation than dark-colored mice.

4. Over time, the allele created by the point mutation increased in frequency in beach-dwelling populations.

Point mutations that cause these types of changes in the amino acid sequence of proteins are called **missense mutations.** But note that if the same G-to-A change had occurred in the third position of the same DNA codon, instead of the first position, there would have been no change in the protein produced. The mRNA codons CGC and CGU both code for arginine. A point mutation that does not change the amino acid sequence of the gene product is called a **silent mutation.**

Some point mutations disrupt major portions of a protein. Recall that a single addition or deletion mutation throws the sequence of codons out of register and alters the meaning of all subsequent codons. Such mutations are called **frameshift mutations.** Another type of point mutation with a large effect is a **nonsense mutation.** Nonsense mutations occur when a codon that specifies an amino acid is changed by mutation to one that specifies a stop codon. This causes early termination of the polypeptide chain and often results in a non-functional protein.

In terms of the impact on organisms, biologists divide mutations into three categories:

1. **Beneficial** Some mutations increase the fitness of the organism—meaning, its ability to survive and reproduce—in certain environments. The G-to-A mutation is beneficial in beach habitats because it camouflages mice.

2. **Neutral** If a mutation has no effect on fitness, it is termed neutral. Silent mutations are usually neutral.

3. **Deleterious** Because organisms tend to be well adapted to their current habitat, and because mutations are random changes in the genotype, many mutations lower fitness. These mutations are termed harmful or deleterious. The G-to-A mutation would be deleterious in the forest habitat.

Recent studies indicate that the majority of point mutations are slightly deleterious or neutral. **TABLE 7.1** (see page 134) summarizes the types of point mutations that occur in protein-coding sequences of a gene and reviews their consequences for the amino acid sequences of proteins and for fitness.

Point mutations can and do occur in DNA sequences that do not code for proteins. These mutations, however, are not referred to as missense, silent, frameshift, or nonsense mutations

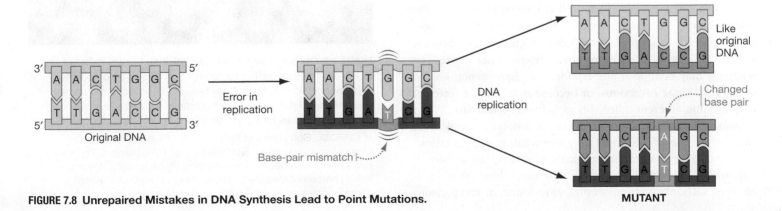

FIGURE 7.8 Unrepaired Mistakes in DNA Synthesis Lead to Point Mutations.

Name	Definition	Example	Consequence
		Original DNA sequence —— TAT TGG CTA GTA CAT	
		Original mRNA transcript —— UAU UGG CUA GUA CAU	
		Tyr—Trp—Leu—Val—His —— Original polypeptide	
Silent	Change in nucleotide sequence that does not change the amino acid specified by a codon	TAC TGG CTA GTA CAT UAC UGG CUA GUA CAU Tyr—Trp—Leu—Val—His	No change in phenotype; neutral with respect to fitness
Missense	Change in nucleotide sequence that changes the amino acid specified by codon	TAT TGT CTA GTA CAT UAU UGU CUA GUA CAU Tyr—Cys—Leu—Val—His	Change in primary structure of protein; may be beneficial, neutral, or deleterious
Nonsense	Change in nucleotide sequence that results in an early stop codon	TAT TGA CTA GTA CAT UAU UGA CUA GUA CAU Tyr—STOP	Leads to mRNA breakdown or a shortened polypeptide; usually deleterious
Frameshift	Addition or deletion of a nucleotide	TAT TCG GCT AGT ACA T UAU UCG GCU AGU ACA U Tyr—Ser—Ala—Ser—Thr	Reading frame is shifted, altering the meaning of all subsequent codons; almost always deleterious

because these terms apply only to mutations that can change the protein-coding potential of a gene. If point mutations alter DNA sequences that are important for *gene expression*, they can have important effects on phenotype even though they do not change the amino acid sequence of a protein.

Chromosome Mutations

Besides documenting various types of point mutations, biologists study larger-scale mutations that change chromosomes. You might recall, for example, that polyploidy is an increase in the number of each type of chromosome, while aneuploidy is the addition or deletion of individual chromosomes (Chapter 11).

Polyploidy, aneuploidy, and other changes in chromosome number result from chance mistakes in moving chromosomes into daughter cells during meiosis or mitosis. Polyploidy and aneuploidy are forms of mutation that don't change DNA sequences, but alter the number of chromosome copies.

In addition to changes in overall chromosome number, the composition of individual chromosomes can change in important ways. For example, chromosome segments can become detached when accidental breaks in chromosomes occur. The segments may be flipped and rejoined—a phenomenon known as a chromosome **inversion**—or become attached to a different chromosome, an event called chromosome **translocation.** When a segment of chromosome is lost, this is a **deletion,** and when additional copies of a segment are present, this is a **duplication.**

Like point mutations, chromosome mutations can be beneficial, neutral, or deleterious. For example, more than 200 different inverted sections of chromosomes were found in comparisons

of the DNA from eight phenotypically normal people. These mutations appear to be neutral. Not all chromosome mutations are so harmless, however. Chromosomes of cancer cells exhibit deleterious chromosome mutations that include aneuploidy, inversions, translocations, deletions, and duplications. **FIGURE 7.9**

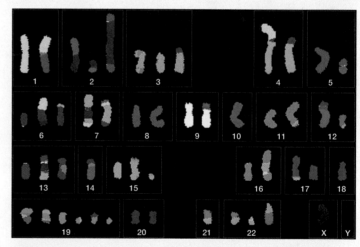

FIGURE 7.9 Chromosome-Level Mutations. A spectral karyotype of a breast cancer cell from a female that shows chromosome rearrangements and aneuploidy typical of cancer. In a normal spectral karyotype, each chromosome is stained a single, solid color, which varies for each chromosome pair.

✓**EXERCISE** Compare this karyotype to the one shown in the chapter-opening image. Remember that females normally have two X chromosomes and males normally have one X chromosome. Which chromosomes show evidence of aneuploidy? Which chromosomes show evidence of rearrangements?

drives this point home by showing the **karyotype**—the complete set of chromosomes in a cell—of a cancerous human cell.

To summarize, point mutations and chromosome mutations are random changes in DNA that can produce new genes, new alleles, and new traits. At the level of individuals, mutations can cause disease or death or lead to increases in fitness. At the level of populations, mutations furnish the heritable variation that Mendel and Morgan analyzed and that makes evolution possible.

If you understand . . .

7.1   What Do Genes Do?

- Experiments with mutants of the bread mold *N. crassa* led to the one-gene, one-enzyme hypothesis.

- The original one-gene, one-enzyme hypothesis has been broadened to account for genes that code for proteins other than enzymes and for genes that have RNA as a final product.

✔ You should be able to use Figure 7.1 to explain what compounds could be added to the medium to allow the growth of a mutant unable to synthesize citrulline because of a mutation in the gene for enzyme 1.

7.2   The Central Dogma of Molecular Biology

- DNA is transcribed to messenger RNA (mRNA) by RNA polymerase, and then mRNA is translated to proteins by ribosomes. In this way, genetic information is converted from DNA to RNA to protein.

- The flow of information from DNA to RNA to protein is called the central dogma of molecular biology.

- Many RNAs do not code for proteins. Instead, these RNAs perform other important functions in the cell.

- Reverse transcriptase reverses information flow by copying RNA into DNA. Some viruses with an RNA genome use this enzyme during their replication.

✔ You should be able to explain how a compound that blocks RNA synthesis will affect protein synthesis.

7.3   The Genetic Code

- Each amino acid in a protein is specified by a codon—a group of three bases in mRNA.

- By synthesizing RNAs of known base composition and then observing the results of translation, researchers were able to decipher the genetic code.

- The genetic code is redundant—meaning that most of the 20 amino acids are specified by more than one codon.

- Certain codons signal where translation starts and stops.

✔ Using the genetic code shown in Figure 7.6, you should be able to write all possible mRNA sequences that would produce the following sequence of amino acids: Met-Trp-Lys-Gln.

7.4   How Can Mutation Modify Genes and Chromosomes?

- Mutations are random, heritable changes in DNA that range from changes in a single base to changes in the structure and number of chromosomes.

- Point mutations in protein-coding regions may have no effect on the protein (silent mutation), may change a single amino acid (missense mutation), may shorten the protein (nonsense mutation), or may shift the reading frame and cause many amino acids to be wrong (frameshift mutation).

- Mutations can have beneficial, neutral, or harmful effects on organisms.

✔ You should be able to explain how redundancy in the genetic code allows for silent mutations and whether a silent mutation is likely to be beneficial, neutral, or harmful.

MasteringBiology

1. **MasteringBiology Assignments**

   Tutorials and Activities Genetic Code; One-Gene One-Enzyme Hypothesis; Overview of Protein Synthesis; Role of the Nucleus and Ribosomes in Protein Synthesis; Triplet Nature of the Genetic Code

   Questions Reading Quizzes, Blue-Thread Questions, Test Bank

2. **eText** Read your book online, search, take notes, highlight text, and more.

3. **The Study Area** Practice Test, Cumulative Test, BioFlix® 3-D Animations, Videos, Activities, Audio Glossary, Word Study Tools, Art

You should be able to . . .

1. What does the one-gene, one-enzyme hypothesis state?
   a. Genes are composed of stretches of DNA.
   b. Genes are made of protein.
   c. Genes code for ribozymes.
   d. A single gene codes for a single protein.

2. Which of the following is an important exception to the central dogma of molecular biology?
   a. Many genes code for RNAs that function directly in the cell.
   b. DNA is the repository of genetic information in all cells.
   c. Messenger RNA is a short-lived "information carrier."
   d. Proteins are responsible for most aspects of the phenotype.

3. DNA's primary structure is made up of just four different bases, and its secondary structure is regular and highly stable. How can a molecule with these characteristics hold all the information required to build and maintain a cell?
   a. The information is first transcribed, then translated.
   b. The messenger RNA produced from DNA has much more complex secondary structures, allowing mRNA to hold much more information.
   c. A protein coded for in DNA has much more complex primary and secondary structures, allowing it to hold much more information.
   d. The information in DNA is in a code form that is based on the sequence of bases.

4. Why did researchers suspect that DNA does not code for proteins directly?

5. Which of the following describes an important experimental strategy in deciphering the genetic code?
   a. comparing the amino acid sequences of proteins with the base sequence of their genes
   b. analyzing the sequence of RNAs produced from known DNA sequences
   c. analyzing mutants that changed the code
   d. examining the polypeptides produced when RNAs of known sequence were translated

6. What is a stop codon?

7. Explain why Morse code is an appropriate analogy for the genetic code.

8. Draw a hypothetical metabolic pathway in *Neurospora crassa* composed of five substrates, five enzymes, and a product called Biological Sciazine. Number the substrates 1–5, and label the enzymes A–E, in order. (For instance, enzyme A catalyzes the reaction between substrates 1 and 2.)
   • Suppose a mutation made the gene for enzyme C nonfunctional. What molecule would accumulate in the affected cells?
   • Suppose a mutant strain can survive if substrate 5 is added to the growth medium but it cannot grow if substrates 1, 2, 3, or 4 are added. Which enzyme in the pathway is affected in this mutant?

9. How did experiments with *Neurospora crassa* mutants support the one-gene, one-enzyme hypothesis?

10. Why does a single-base deletion mutation within a protein-coding sequence usually have a more severe effect than a deletion of three adjacent bases?
    a. because single-base deletions prevent the ribosome from binding to mRNA
    b. because single-base deletions stabilize mRNA
    c. because single-base deletions change the reading frame
    d. because single-base deletions alter the meaning of individual codons

11. When researchers discovered that a combination of three deletion mutations or three addition mutations would restore the function of a gene, most biologists were convinced that the genetic code was read in triplets. Explain the logic behind this conclusion.

12. Explain why all point mutations change the genotype, but why only some point mutations change the phenotype.

13. Recall that DNA and RNA are synthesized only in the $5' \rightarrow 3'$ direction and that DNA and RNA sequences are written in the $5' \rightarrow 3'$ direction, unless otherwise noted. Consider the following DNA sequence:

    5' TTGAAATGCCCGTTTGGAGATCGGGTTACAGCTAGTCAAAG 3'

    3' AACTTTACGGGCAAACCTCTAGCCCAATGTCGATCAGTTTC 5'

    • Identify bases in the bottom strand that can be transcribed into start and stop codons.
    • Write the mRNA sequence that would be transcribed between start and stop codons if the bottom strand served as the template for RNA polymerase.
    • Write the amino acid sequence that would be translated from the mRNA sequence you just wrote.

14. What problems would arise if the genetic code contained only 22 codons—one for each amino acid, a start signal, and a stop signal?

15. Scientists say that a phenomenon is a "black box" if they can describe it and study its effects but don't know the underlying mechanism that causes it. In what sense was genetics—meaning the transmission of heritable traits—a black box before the central dogma of molecular biology was understood?

16. **QUANTITATIVE** One of the possibilities that researchers interested in the genetic code considered was that the code was overlapping, meaning that a single base could be part of up to three codons. How many amino acids would be encoded in the sequence 5' AUGUUACGGAAU 3' by a non-overlapping and maximally overlapping code?
    a. 4 (non-overlapping) and 16 (overlapping)
    b. 4 and 12
    c. 4 and 10
    d. 12 and 4

8 Transcription, RNA Processing, and Translation

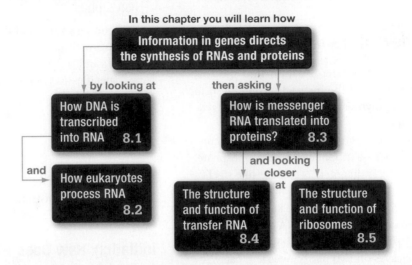

In this chapter you will learn how

Information in genes directs the synthesis of RNAs and proteins

by looking at

then asking

How DNA is transcribed into RNA   8.1

and

How eukaryotes process RNA   8.2

How is messenger RNA translated into proteins?   8.3

and looking closer at

The structure and function of transfer RNA   8.4

The structure and function of ribosomes   8.5

Extensive transcription is occurring along this gene within a frog cell. The horizontal strand in the middle of this micrograph is DNA; the strands that have been colored yellow and red, and that are coming off on either side, are RNA molecules.

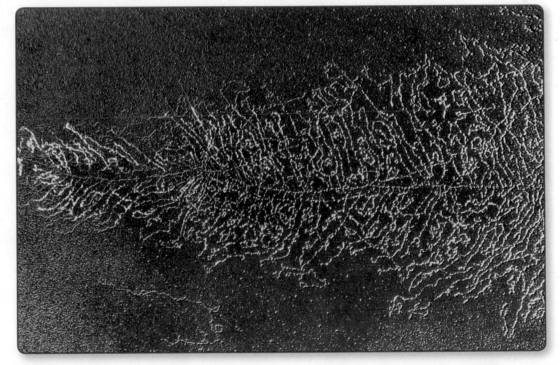

Proteins are the stuff of life. They give shape to our cells, control the chemical reactions that go on inside them, and regulate how materials move into, out of, and through them. Some of these proteins may not be produced at all in some types of cells; others may be present in quantities ranging from millions of copies to fewer than a dozen.

A cell builds the proteins it needs from instructions encoded in its DNA. The central dogma of molecular biology states that the flow of information in cells is from DNA to mRNA to protein (Chapter 7). Once this pattern of information flow had been established, biologists puzzled over how cells actually accomplish the two major steps of the central dogma: transcription and

✔ When you see this checkmark, stop and test yourself. Answers are available in Appendix A.

translation. Specifically, how does RNA polymerase know where to start transcribing a gene, and where to end? And once an RNA message is produced, how is the linear sequence of ribonucleotides translated into the linear sequence of amino acids in a protein?

This chapter delves into the molecular mechanisms of gene expression—the blood and guts of the central dogma. It starts with the monomers that build RNA and ends with a protein.

8.1 An Overview of Transcription

The first step in converting genetic information into proteins is to synthesize an RNA version of the instructions archived in DNA. Enzymes called **RNA polymerases** are responsible for synthesizing mRNA (see Chapter 6).

FIGURE 8.1 shows how the polymerization reaction occurs. Note the incoming monomer—a ribonucleoside triphosphate, or NTP—at the far right of the diagram. NTPs are like dNTPs (introduced in Chapter 6), except that they have a hydroxyl (−OH) group on the 2′ carbon. This makes the sugar in an NTP a ribose instead of the deoxyribose sugar of DNA.

Once an NTP that matches a base on the DNA template is in place, RNA polymerase cleaves off two phosphates and catalyzes the formation of a phosphodiester linkage between the 3′ end of the growing mRNA chain and the new ribonucleoside monophosphate. As this 5′ → 3′ matching-and-catalysis process continues, an RNA that is complementary to the gene is synthesized. This is transcription.

Notice that only one of the two DNA strands is used as a template and transcribed, or "read," by RNA polymerase.

- The strand that is read by the enzyme is the **template strand.**
- The other strand is called the **non-template strand** or **coding strand.** Coding strand is an appropriate name, because, with one exception, its sequence matches the sequence of the RNA that is transcribed from the template strand and codes for a polypeptide.

The coding strand and the RNA don't match exactly, because RNA has uracil (U) rather than the thymine (T) found in the coding strand. Likewise, an adenine (A) in the DNA template strand specifies a U in the complementary RNA strand.

Like DNA polymerases (see Chapter 6), an RNA polymerase performs a template-directed synthesis in the 5′ → 3′ direction. But unlike DNA polymerases, RNA polymerases do not require a primer to begin transcription.

Bacteria have a single RNA polymerase. In contrast, eukaryotes, have at least three distinct types. Let's first take a look at general principles of transcription using bacteria as an example and then examine things that differ in eukaryotes.

Initiation: How Does Transcription Begin in Bacteria?

How does RNA polymerase know where and in which direction to start transcription on the DNA template? The answer to this question defined what biologists call the **initiation** phase of transcription.

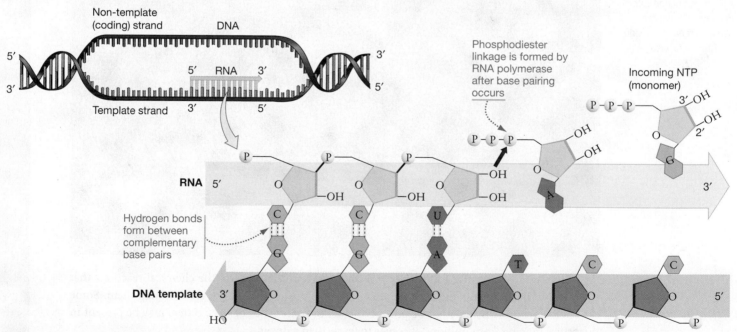

FIGURE 8.1 Transcription Is the Synthesis of RNA from a DNA Template. The reaction catalyzed by RNA polymerase (not shown) results in the formation of a phosphodiester linkage between ribonucleotides. RNA polymerase produces an RNA strand whose sequence is complementary to the bases in the DNA template.

✓**QUESTION** In which direction is RNA synthesized, 5′ → 3′ or 3′ → 5′? In which direction is the DNA template "read"?

Soon after the discovery of bacterial RNA polymerase, researchers found that the enzyme cannot initiate transcription on its own. Instead, a detachable protein subunit called **sigma** must bind to the polymerase before transcription can begin.

Bacterial RNA polymerase and sigma form a **holoenzyme** (literally, "whole enzyme"; **FIGURE 8.2a**). A holoenzyme consists of a **core enzyme** (RNA polymerase, in this case), which contains the active site for catalysis, and other required proteins (such as sigma).

What does sigma do? When researchers mixed the polymerase and DNA together, they found that the core enzyme could bind to any sequence of DNA. When sigma was added to this mixture, the holoenzyme formed and bound only to specific sections of DNA. These binding sites were named **promoters,** because they are sections of DNA that promote the start of transcription.

Most bacteria have alternative sigma proteins that bind to promoters with slightly different DNA base sequences, and may activate a group of genes in response to environmental change. For example, one type of sigma initiates the transcription of genes that help the cell cope with high temperatures. Controlling which sigma proteins are used is one of the ways that bacterial cells regulate which groups of genes are expressed.

The discovery of promoters suggested that sigma was responsible for guiding RNA polymerase to specific locations where transcription should begin. What is the nature of these specific locations? What do promoters look like, and what do they do?

Bacterial Promoters David Pribnow offered an initial answer to these questions in the mid-1970s. When Pribnow analyzed the base sequence of promoters from various bacteria and from viruses that infect bacteria, he found that the promoters were 40–50 base pairs long and had a particular section in common: a series of bases identical or similar to TATAAT. This six-base-pair sequence is now known as the −10 box, because it is centered about 10 bases from the point where bacterial RNA polymerase starts transcription (**FIGURE 8.2b**).

DNA that is located in the direction RNA polymerase moves during transcription is said to be **downstream** from the point of reference; DNA located in the opposite direction is said to be **upstream.** Thus, the −10 box is centered about 10 bases upstream from the transcription start site. The place where transcription begins is called the +1 site.

Soon after the discovery of the −10 box, researchers recognized that the sequence TTGACA also occurred in promoters and was about 35 bases upstream from the +1 site. This second key sequence is called the −35 box. Although all bacterial promoters have a −10 box and a −35 box, the sequences within the promoter but outside these boxes vary.

Events inside the Holoenzyme In bacteria, transcription begins when sigma, as part of the holoenzyme complex, binds to the −35 and −10 boxes. Sigma, and not RNA polymerase, makes the initial contact with DNA of the promoter. Sigma's binding to a promoter determines where and in which direction RNA polymerase will start synthesizing RNA.

Once the holoenzyme is bound to a promoter for a bacterial gene, the DNA helix is opened by RNA polymerase, creating two

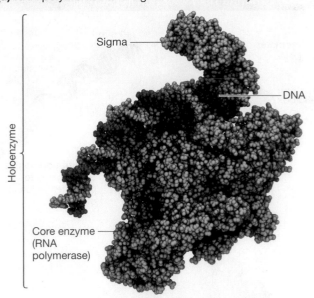

(a) RNA polymerase and sigma form a holoenzyme.

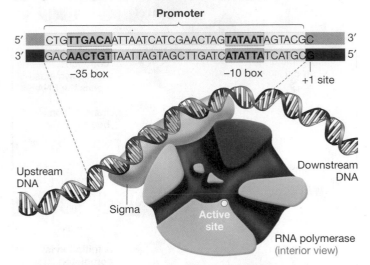

(b) Sigma recognizes and binds to the promoter.

FIGURE 8.2 Sigma Is the Promoter-Recognizing Subunit of Bacterial RNA Polymerase Holoenzyme. (a) A space-filling model of bacterial RNA polymerase holoenzyme. **(b)** A cartoon of bacterial RNA polymerase, showing that sigma binds to the −35 box and −10 box of the promoter.

separated strands of DNA as shown in **FIGURE 8.3** (see page 140), steps 1 and 2. As step 2 shows, the template strand is threaded through a channel that leads to the active site inside RNA polymerase. Ribonucleoside triphosphates (NTPs)—the RNA building blocks—enter a channel in the enzyme and diffuse to the active site.

When an incoming NTP pairs with a complementary base on the template strand of DNA, RNA polymerization begins. The reaction catalyzed by RNA polymerase is exergonic and spontaneous because NTPs have significant potential energy, owing to their three phosphate groups. As step 3 of Figure 8.3 shows, the initiation phase of transcription is complete as RNA polymerase extends the mRNA from the +1 site.

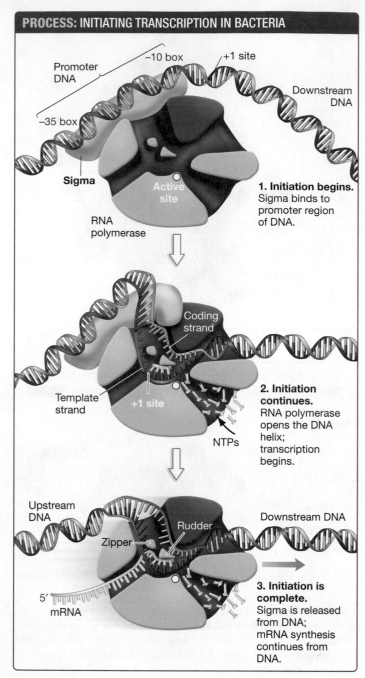

Promoter DNA

−10 box

+1 site

−35 box

Downstream DNA

Sigma

Active site

RNA polymerase

1. Initiation begins. Sigma binds to promoter region of DNA.

Coding strand

Template strand

+1 site

NTPs

2. Initiation continues. RNA polymerase opens the DNA helix; transcription begins.

Upstream DNA

Downstream DNA

Rudder

Zipper

5′ mRNA

3. Initiation is complete. Sigma is released from DNA; mRNA synthesis continues from DNA.

FIGURE 8.3 Sigma Orients the DNA Template inside RNA Polymerase. Sigma binds to the promoter, and RNA polymerase opens the DNA helix and threads the template strand through the active site.

Elongation and Termination

Once RNA polymerase begins moving along the DNA template synthesizing RNA, the **elongation** phase of transcription is under way. RNA polymerase is a macromolecular machine with different parts. In the interior of the enzyme, a group of amino acids forms a rudder to help steer the template and non-template

strands through channels inside the enzyme (see Figure 8.3, step 3). Meanwhile, the enzyme's active site catalyzes the addition of nucleotides to the 3′ end of the growing RNA molecule at the rate of about 50 nucleotides per second. A group of projecting amino acids forms a region called the zipper to help separate the newly synthesized RNA from the DNA template.

During the elongation phase of transcription, all the prominent channels and grooves in the enzyme are filled (Figure 8.3, step 3). Double-stranded DNA goes into and out of one groove, ribonucleoside triphosphates enter another, and the growing RNA strand exits to the rear. The enzyme's structure is critical for its function.

Termination ends transcription. In bacteria, transcription stops when RNA polymerase transcribes a DNA sequence that functions as a transcription-termination signal.

The bases that make up the termination signal in bacteria are transcribed into a stretch of RNA with an important property: As soon as it is synthesized, this portion of the RNA folds back on itself and forms a short double helix that is held together by complementary base pairing (**FIGURE 8.4**). Recall that this type of RNA secondary structure is called a hairpin (Chapter 5). The hairpin structure disrupts the interaction between RNA polymerase and the RNA transcript, resulting in the physical separation of the enzyme and its product.

Transcription in Eukaryotes

Fundamental features of transcription are the same in bacteria and eukaryotes. In fact, these similarities provide compelling evidence for a common ancestor of all cells. There are, however, some differences that are worth noting:

- Eukaryotes have three polymerases—RNA polymerase I, II, and III—that are often referred to as pol I, pol II, and pol III. Each polymerase transcribes only certain types of RNA in eukaryotes. RNA pol II is the only polymerase that transcribes protein-coding genes.

- Promoters in eukaryotic DNA are more diverse than bacterial promoters. Most eukaryotic promoters include a sequence called the **TATA box,** centered about 30 base pairs upstream of the transcription start site, and other important sequences that vary more widely.

- Instead of using a sigma protein, eukaryotic RNA polymerases recognize promoters using a group of proteins called **basal transcription factors.** Basal transcription factors assemble at the promoter, and RNA polymerase follows.

- Termination of eukaryotic protein-coding genes involves a short sequence called the polyadenylation signal or **poly(A) signal.** Soon after the signal is transcribed, the RNA is cut by an enzyme downstream of the poly(A) signal as the polymerase continues to transcribe the DNA template. Eventually RNA polymerase falls off the DNA template and terminates transcription. Bacteria end transcription at a distinct site for each gene, but in eukaryotes, transcription ends variable distances from the poly(A) signal.

PROCESS: ENDING TRANSCRIPTION IN BACTERIA

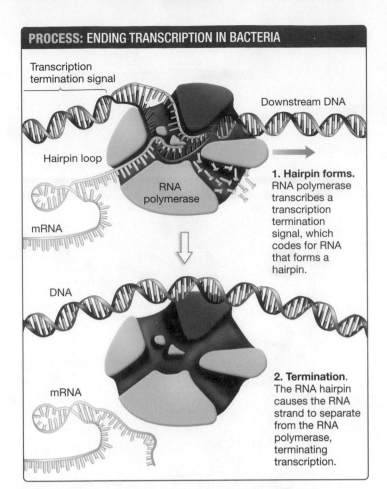

Transcription termination signal

Downstream DNA

Hairpin loop

RNA polymerase

mRNA

1. Hairpin forms. RNA polymerase transcribes a transcription termination signal, which codes for RNA that forms a hairpin.

DNA

mRNA

2. Termination. The RNA hairpin causes the RNA strand to separate from the RNA polymerase, terminating transcription.

FIGURE 8.4 Transcription Terminates When an RNA Hairpin Forms.

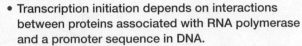
If you understand that . . .

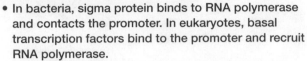

- Transcription initiation depends on interactions between proteins associated with RNA polymerase and a promoter sequence in DNA.
- In bacteria, sigma protein binds to RNA polymerase and contacts the promoter. In eukaryotes, basal transcription factors bind to the promoter and recruit RNA polymerase.
- During transcription elongation, ribonucleoside triphosphates are the substrate for a polymerization reaction catalyzed by RNA polymerase. The enzyme adds ribonucleotides that are complementary to the template strand in DNA.
- Transcription ends in bacteria when a termination signal at the end of the gene is transcribed, leading to the disassociation of RNA polymerase and the DNA template.

✔ You should be able to . . .

1. Predict how a mutation in a bacterial cell that deletes three nucleotides 10 nucleotides upstream from the transcription start site is likely to affect transcription.

2. Explain why ribonucleoside triphosphates, rather than ribonucleoside monophosphates, are the monomers required for RNA synthesis.

Answers are available in Appendix A.

8.2 RNA Processing in Eukaryotes

The molecular machinery required for transcription is much more complex in eukaryotes than in bacteria. But these differences are minor when compared with what happens to the eukaryotic RNA after transcription. In bacteria, when transcription terminates, the result is a mature mRNA that's ready to be translated into a protein. In fact, translation often begins while the mRNA is still being transcribed.

The fate of the transcript in eukaryotes is more complicated. When eukaryotic genes of any type are transcribed, the initial product is termed a **primary transcript.** This RNA must undergo multistep processing before it is functional. For protein-coding genes, the primary transcript is called a **pre-mRNA.**

The processing of primary transcripts has important consequences for gene expression in eukaryotes. Let's delve in to see how and why.

The Startling Discovery of Split Eukaryotic Genes

Eukaryotic genes do not consist of one continuous DNA sequence that codes for a product, as do bacterial genes. Instead, the regions in a eukaryotic gene that code for proteins are intermittently interrupted by stretches of hundreds or even thousands of intervening bases.

Although these intervening bases are part of the gene, they do not code for a product. To make a functional RNA, eukaryotic cells must dispose of certain sequences inside the primary transcript and then combine the separated sections into an integrated whole.

What sort of data would provoke such a startling claim? The first evidence came from work that Phillip Sharp and colleagues carried out in the late 1970s to determine the location of genes within the DNA of a virus that infects mammalian cells. Viruses are often used as tools to provide insights into fundamental processes of the cells they infect.

They began one of their experiments by heating the virus' DNA sufficiently to break the hydrogen bonds between complementary bases. This treatment separated the two strands. The single-stranded DNA was then incubated with the mRNA encoded by the virus. The team's intention was to promote base pairing between the mRNA and the single-stranded DNA.

The researchers expected that the mRNA would form base pairs with the DNA sequence that acted as the template for its synthesis—that the mRNA and DNA would match up exactly.

(a) Micrograph of DNA-RNA hybrid

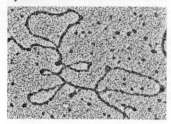

(b) Interpretation of micrograph

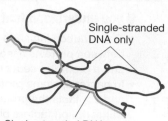

Single-stranded DNA only

Single-stranded DNA base paired with mRNA

FIGURE 8.5 The Discovery of Introns. The loops in the micrograph and drawing represent regions of DNA that are transcribed but are not found in the final mRNA. These regions are introns.

✔ **QUESTION** If the noncoding regions of the gene did not exist, what would the micrograph in part (a) look like?

But when the team examined the DNA–RNA hybrid molecules using an electron microscope, they observed the structure shown in **FIGURE 8.5a**. Instead of matching up exactly, parts of the DNA formed loops.

What was going on? As **FIGURE 8.5b** shows, Sharp's group interpreted these loops as stretches of DNA that are present in the template strand but are *not* in the corresponding mRNA.

Sharp's group and a team headed by Richard Roberts then carried out similar studies on eukaryotic genes. The results were the same as for the viral genes. They went on to propose that there is not a one-to-one correspondence between the nucleotide sequence of a eukaryotic gene and its mRNA. As an analogy, it could be said that eukaryotic genes do not carry messages such as "Biology is my favorite course of all time." Instead, they carry messages that read something like:

BIOLτηεπροτεινχοδινγρεγιονσοφγενεσOGY IS MY
FAVORαρειντερρθπτεθβυνονψοθινγθITE COURSE
OF ανθηαωετοβεσπλιχεθτογετηερ ALL TIME

Here the sections of noncoding sequence are represented with Greek letters. They must be removed from the mRNA before it can carry an intelligible message to the translation machinery.

When it became clear that the genes-in-pieces hypothesis was correct, Walter Gilbert suggested that regions of eukaryotic genes that are part of the final mRNA be referred to as **exons** (because they are *ex*pressed) and the sections of primary transcript not in mRNA be referred to as **introns** (because they are *int*ervening). Introns are sections of genes that are not represented in the final RNA product. Because of introns, eukaryotic genes are much larger than their corresponding mature RNAs. Introns were first discovered in genes that produce mRNA, but researchers later found that genes for other types of RNA also could be split.

RNA Splicing

The transcription of eukaryotic genes by RNA polymerase generates a primary transcript (**FIGURE 8.6a**) that contains both exons and introns. As transcription proceeds, the introns are removed

(a) Introns must be removed from eukaryotic RNA transcripts.

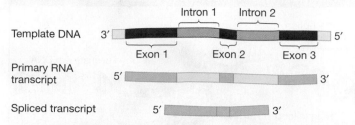

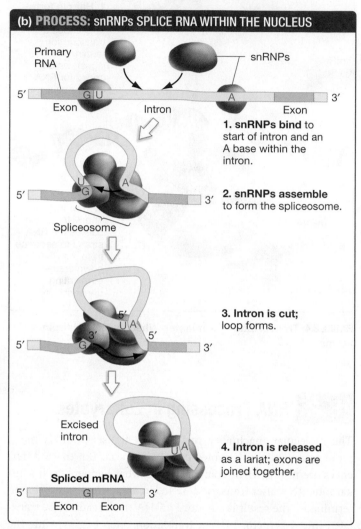

FIGURE 8.6 Introns Are Spliced Out of the Primary Transcript.

from the growing RNA strand by a process known as **splicing**. In this phase of information processing, pieces of the primary transcript are removed and the remaining segments are joined together. Splicing occurs within the nucleus while transcription is still under way and results in an RNA that contains an uninterrupted genetic message.

FIGURE 8.6b provides more detail about how introns are removed from primary transcripts to form mRNA. Splicing of primary transcripts is catalyzed by RNAs called small nuclear RNAs (snRNAs) working with a complex of proteins. These protein-plus-RNA macromolecular machines are known as **small nuclear ribonucleoproteins,** or **snRNPs** (pronounced "snurps").

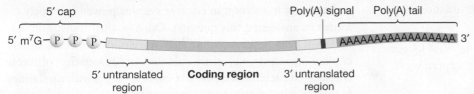

5′ cap   Poly(A) signal   Poly(A) tail

5′ m^7G–P–P–P–   AAAAAAAAAAAAAAAAAAA 3′

        5′ untranslated   **Coding region**   3′ untranslated
          region   region

FIGURE 8.7 In Eukaryotes, a Cap and a Tail Are Added to mRNAs. As part of eukaryotic pre-mRNA processing, a cap consisting of a modified guanine (G) nucleotide (symbolized as m^7G) bonded to three phosphate groups is added to the 5′ end, and a tail made up of a long series of adenine (A) residues is added to the 3′ end after cleavage of the primary transcript.

The snRNAs of the snRNPs recognize RNA sequences critical for splicing. Splicing can be broken into four steps:

1. The process begins when snRNPs bind to the 5′ exon–intron boundary, which is marked by the bases GU, and to a key adenine ribonucleotide (A) near the end the intron.

2. Once the initial snRNPs are in place, other snRNPs arrive to form a multipart complex called a **spliceosome.** The spliceosomes found in human cells contain about 145 different proteins and RNAs, making them the most complex macromolecular machines known.

3. The intron forms a loop plus a single-stranded stem (a lariat) with the adenine at its connecting point.

4. The lariat is cut out, and a phosphodiester linkage links the exons on either side, producing a continuous coding sequence—the mRNA.

Splicing is now complete. In most cases, the excised intron is degraded to ribonucleoside monophosphates.

For many genes, the RNA can be spliced in more than one way. This allows the production of different, related mRNAs and proteins from one gene.

Current data suggest that both the cutting and rejoining reactions that occur during splicing are catalyzed by the snRNA molecules in the spliceosome—meaning that the reactions are catalyzed by a ribozyme. Section 8.5 will demonstrate that ribozymes also play a key role in translation. As the RNA world hypothesis (Chapter 5) predicts, proteins are not the only important catalysts in cells.

What is the origin of introns? One hypothesis is that introns in eukaryotes arose from an ancient type of DNA sequence that is present in many bacteria and archaea. These ancient sequences are related to viruses and, like viruses, can infect cells and insert into their genomes. Remarkably, when this DNA sequence inserts into a gene and is transcribed, the RNA catalyzes its own splicing out of the primary transcript. This is possible in part because these virus-like elements have sequences similar to snRNAs.

The bacterium that was the source of mitochondria likely carried some of these virus-like DNA sequences. When this bacterium was taken up by an ancestral eukaryote, the virus-like sequences are hypothesized to have spread rapidly. Later in evolution, the portion of the sequence that was a precursor to today's snRNA may have separated from the portion of the sequence that was spliced. This spliced sequence is hypothesized to be the ancestor of the modern eukaryotic intron.

Adding Caps and Tails to Transcripts

For pre-mRNAs, intron splicing is accompanied by other important processing steps.

- As soon as the 5′ end of a eukaryotic pre-mRNA emerges from RNA polymerase, enzymes add a structure called the **5′ cap** (**FIGURE 8.7**). The cap consists of a modified guanine (7-methylguanylate) nucleotide with three phosphate groups.

- An enzyme cleaves the 3′ end of the pre-mRNA downstream of the poly(A) signal (introduced in Section 8.1). Another enzyme adds a long row of 100–250 adenine nucleotides that are not encoded on the DNA template strand. This string of adenines is known as the **poly(A) tail.**

With the addition of the cap and tail and completion of splicing, processing of the pre-mRNA is complete. The product is a mature mRNA.

Figure 8.7 also shows that in the mature RNA molecule, the coding sequence for the polypeptide is flanked by sequences that are not destined to be translated. These 5′ and 3′ untranslated regions (or UTRs) help stabilize the mature RNA and regulate its translation. The mRNAs in bacteria also possess 5′ and 3′ UTRs.

Not long after the caps and tails on eukaryotic mRNAs were discovered, evidence began to accumulate that they protect mRNAs from degradation by ribonucleases—enzymes that

check your understanding

If you understand that . . .

- Eukaryotic genes consist of exons, which are parts of the primary transcript that remain in mature RNA, and introns, which are regions of the primary transcript that are removed in forming mature RNA.
- Macromolecular machines, called spliceosomes, splice introns out of pre-mRNAs.
- Enzymes add a 5′ cap and a poly(A) tail to spliced transcripts, producing a mature mRNA that is ready to be translated.

✔ You should be able to . . .

1. Explain why ribonucleoprotein is an appropriate name for the subunits of the spliceosome.
2. Explain the function of the 5′ cap and the poly(A) tail.

Answers are available in Appendix A.

degrade RNA—and enhance the efficiency of translation. For example:

- Experimental mRNAs that have a cap and a tail last longer when they are introduced into cells than do experimental mRNAs that lack a cap or a tail.

- Experimental mRNAs with caps and tails produce more proteins than do experimental mRNAs without caps and tails.

Follow-up work has shown that the 5′ cap and the poly(A) tail are bound by proteins that prevent ribonucleases in the cytoplasm from recognizing and destroying the mRNA. The 5′ cap and the poly(A) tail also are important for initiating translation.

RNA processing is the general term for any of the modifications, such as splicing or poly(A) tail addition, needed to convert a primary transcript into a mature RNA. It is summarized in **TABLE 8.1** along with other important differences in how RNAs are produced in eukaryotes as compared with bacteria.

8.3 An Introduction to Translation

To synthesize a protein, the sequence of bases in a messenger RNA molecule is translated into a sequence of amino acids in a polypeptide. The genetic code specifies the correspondence between each triplet codon in mRNA and the amino acid it codes for (see Chapter 7). But how are the amino acids assembled into a polypeptide according to the information in messenger RNA?

(a) Bacterial ribosomes during translation

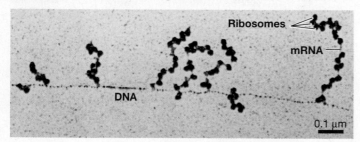

(b) In bacteria, transcription and translation are tightly coupled.

Studies of translation in cell-free systems proved extremely effective in answering this question. Once in vitro translation systems had been developed from human cells, *E. coli*, and a variety of other organisms, biologists could see that the sequence of events is similar in bacteria, archaea, and eukaryotes. As with similarities in transcription across the domains of life, the shared mechanisms of translation argue for a common ancestor of all cells living today.

Ribosomes Are the Site of Protein Synthesis

The first question that biologists answered about translation concerned where it occurs. The answer grew from a simple observation: There is a strong correlation between the number of **ribosomes** in a given type of cell and the rate at which that cell synthesizes proteins. Based on this observation, investigators proposed that ribosomes are the site of protein synthesis.

To test this hypothesis, Roy Britten and collaborators did a pulse–chase experiment similar in design to experiments introduced earlier (Chapter 2). Recall that a pulse–chase experiment labels a population of molecules as they are being produced. The location of the tagged molecules is then followed over time.

In this case, the tagging was done by supplying a pulse of radioactive sulfur atoms that would be incorporated into the amino acids methionine and cysteine, followed by a chase of unlabeled sulfur atoms. If the ribosome hypothesis were correct, the radioactive signal should be associated with ribosomes for a short period of time—when the amino acids are being polymerized into proteins. Later, when translation was complete, all the radioactivity should be found in proteins that are not associated with ribosomes.

This is exactly what the researchers found. Based on these data, biologists concluded that proteins are synthesized at ribosomes and then released.

Translation in Bacteria and Eukaryotes

About a decade after the ribosome hypothesis was confirmed, electron micrographs showed bacterial ribosomes in action (**FIGURE 8.8a**). The images showed that in bacteria, ribosomes

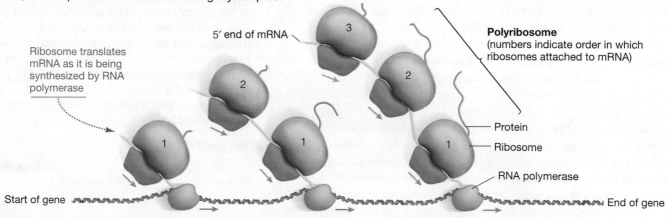

FIGURE 8.8 Transcription and Translation Occur Simultaneously in Bacteria. In bacteria, ribosomes attach to mRNA transcripts and begin translation while RNA polymerase is still transcribing the DNA template strand.

TABLE 8.1 Transcription and RNA Processing in Bacteria and Eukaryotes

Point of Comparison	Bacteria	Eukaryotes
RNA polymerase(s)	One	Three; each produces a different class of RNA
Promoter structure	Typically contains a −35 box and a −10 box	More variable; often includes a TATA box about −30 from the transcription start site
Proteins involved in recognizing promoter	Sigma; different versions of sigma bind to different promoters	Many basal transcription factors
RNA processing	None	Extensive; several processing steps occur in the nucleus before RNA is exported to the cytoplasm: (1) Enzyme-catalyzed addition of 5′ cap on mRNAs, (2) Splicing (intron removal); by spliceosome to produce mRNA, (3) Enzyme-catalyzed addition of 3′ poly(A) tail on mRNAs

attach to mRNAs and begin synthesizing proteins even before transcription is complete. In fact, multiple ribosomes attach to each mRNA, forming a **polyribosome** (**FIGURE 8.8b**). In this way, many copies of a protein can be produced from a single mRNA.

Transcription and translation can occur concurrently in bacteria because there is no nuclear envelope to separate the two processes.

The situation is different in eukaryotes. In these organisms, primary transcripts are processed in the nucleus to produce a mature mRNA, which is then exported to the cytoplasm (**FIGURE 8.9**). This means that in eukaryotes, transcription and translation are separated in time and space. Once mRNAs are outside the nucleus, ribosomes can attach to them and begin translation. As in bacteria, polyribosomes form.

How Does an mRNA Triplet Specify an Amino Acid?

When an mRNA interacts with a ribosome, instructions encoded in nucleic acids are translated into a different chemical language—the amino acid sequences found in proteins. The discovery of the genetic code revealed that triplet codons in mRNA specify particular amino acids in a protein. How does this conversion occur?

One early hypothesis was that mRNA codons and amino acids interact directly. This hypothesis proposed that the bases in a particular codon were complementary in shape or charge to the side group of a particular amino acid (**FIGURE 8.10a**, see page 146). But Francis Crick pointed out that the idea didn't make chemical sense. For example, how could the nucleic acid bases interact with a hydrophobic amino acid side group, which does not form hydrogen bonds?

Crick proposed an alternative hypothesis. As **FIGURE 8.10b** shows, he suggested that some sort of adapter molecule holds amino acids in place while interacting directly and specifically with a codon in mRNA by hydrogen bonding. In essence, Crick predicted the existence of a chemical go-between that produced a physical connection between the two types of molecules. As it turns out, Crick was right.

(a) mRNAs are exported to the cytoplasm.

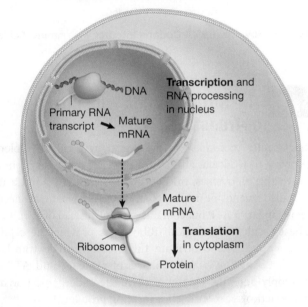

(b) Polypeptides grow from ribosomes translating mRNA.

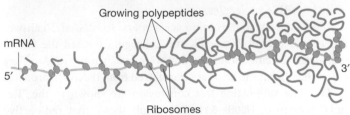

FIGURE 8.9 Transcription and Translation Are Separated in Space and Time in Eukaryotes.

(a) Hypothesis 1: Amino acids interact directly with mRNA codons.

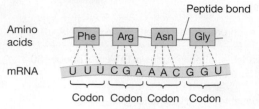

(b) Hypothesis 2: Adapter molecules hold amino acids and interact with mRNA codons.

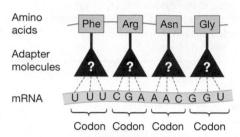

FIGURE 8.10 How Do mRNA Codons Interact with Amino Acids?

8.4 The Structure and Function of Transfer RNA

Crick's adapter molecule was discovered by accident. Biologists were trying to work out an in vitro protein-synthesis system and reasoned that ribosomes, mRNA, amino acids, ATP, and a molecule called guanosine triphosphate, or GTP, would be needed. (GTP is similar to ATP but contains guanine instead of adenine.)

These results were logical: Ribosomes provide the catalytic machinery, mRNAs contribute the message to be translated, amino acids are the building blocks of proteins, and ATP and GTP supply potential energy to drive the endergonic polymerization reactions responsible for forming proteins.

But, in addition, a cellular fraction that contained a previously unknown type of RNA turned out to be indispensable. If this type of RNA is missing, protein synthesis does not occur. What is this mysterious RNA, and why is it essential to translation?

The novel class of RNAs eventually became known as **transfer RNA (tRNA).** The role of tRNA in translation was a mystery until some researchers happened to add a radioactive amino acid—leucine—to an in vitro protein-synthesis system. The treatment was actually done as a control for an unrelated experiment. To the researchers' amazement, some of the radioactive leucine attached to tRNA molecules.

What happens to the amino acids bound to tRNAs? To answer this question, Paul Zamecnik and colleagues tracked the fate of radioactive leucine molecules that were attached to tRNAs. They found that the amino acids are transferred from tRNAs to proteins.

The data supporting this conclusion are shown in the "Results" section of **FIGURE 8.11**. The graph shows that radioactive amino acids are lost from tRNAs and incorporated into polypeptides synthesized by ribosomes. To understand this conclusion:

RESEARCH

QUESTION: What happens to the amino acids attached to tRNAs?

HYPOTHESIS: Aminoacyl tRNAs transfer amino acids to growing polypeptides.

NULL HYPOTHESIS: Aminoacyl tRNAs do not transfer amino acids to growing polypeptides.

EXPERIMENTAL SETUP:

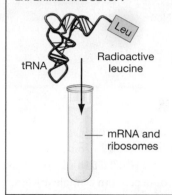

1. Attach radioactive leucine molecules to tRNAs.

2. Add these aminoacyl tRNAs to in vitro translation system. Follow fate of the radioactive amino acids.

PREDICTION: Radioactive amino acids will be found in proteins.

PREDICTION OF NULL HYPOTHESIS: Radioactive amino acids will not be found in proteins.

RESULTS:

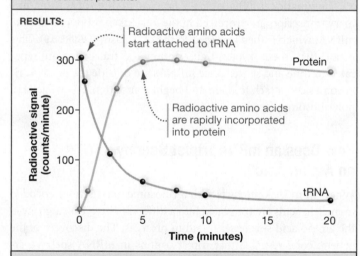

CONCLUSION: Aminoacyl tRNAs transfer amino acids to growing polypeptides.

FIGURE 8.11 Evidence that Amino Acids Are Transferred from tRNAs to Proteins.

SOURCE: Hoagland, M. B., M. L. Stephenson, J. F. Scott, et al. 1958. A soluble ribonucleic acid intermediate in protein synthesis. *Journal of Biological Chemistry* 231: 241–257.

✔ QUESTION What would the graphed results look like if the null hypothesis were correct?

1. Put your finger on the point on the *x*-axis that indicates that one minute has passed since the start of the experiment.

2. Read up until you hit the green line and the gray line. The green line represents data from proteins; the gray line represents data from tRNAs.

3. Check the *y*-axis—which indicates the amount of radioactive leucine present—at each point.

4. It should be clear that early in the experiment, almost all the radioactive leucine is attached to tRNA, not protein.

Next, do the same four steps at the point on the *x*-axis labeled 10 minutes (since the start of the experiment). Your conclusion now should be that late in the experiment, almost all the radioactive leucine is attached to proteins, not tRNA.

These results inspired the use of the word transfer in tRNA's name, because amino acids are transferred from the RNA to a growing polypeptide. The experiment also confirmed that tRNAs act as the interpreter during translation: tRNAs are Crick's adapter molecules.

What Do tRNAs Look Like?

Transfer RNAs serve as chemical go-betweens that allow amino acids to interact with an mRNA template. But precisely how does the connection occur?

This question was answered by research on tRNA's molecular structure. The initial studies established the sequence of nucleotides in various tRNAs, or what is termed their primary structure. Transfer RNA sequences are relatively short, ranging from 75 to 85 nucleotides in length.

When biologists studied the primary sequence closely, they noticed that certain parts of the molecules can form secondary structures. Specifically, some sequences of bases in the tRNA molecule can form hydrogen bonds with complementary base sequences elsewhere in the same molecule. As a result, portions of the molecule form stem-and-loop structures (introduced in Chapter 5). The stems are short stretches of double-stranded RNA; the loops are single stranded.

Two aspects of tRNA's secondary structure proved especially important. A CCA sequence at the 3′ end of each tRNA molecule offered a site for amino acid attachment, while a triplet on the loop at the other end of the structure could serve as an anticodon. An **anticodon** is a set of three ribonucleotides that forms base pairs with the mRNA codon.

Later, X-ray crystallography studies revealed the tertiary structure of tRNAs. Recall that the tertiary structure of a molecule is the three-dimensional arrangement of its atoms (Chapter 9). As **FIGURE 8.12** shows, tRNAs fold into an L-shaped molecule. The anticodon is at one end of the structure; the CCA sequence and attached amino acid are at the other end.

All the tRNAs in a cell have the same general structure, shaped like an upside-down L. They vary at the anticodon and attached amino acid. The tertiary structure of tRNAs is important because it maintains a precise physical distance between the anticodon and amino acid. As it turns out, this separation is important in positioning the amino acid and the anticodon within the ribosome.

✔ If you understand the structure of tRNAs, you should be able to (1) describe where on the L-shaped structure the amino acid attaches; and (2) explain the relationship between the anticodon of a tRNA and a codon in an mRNA.

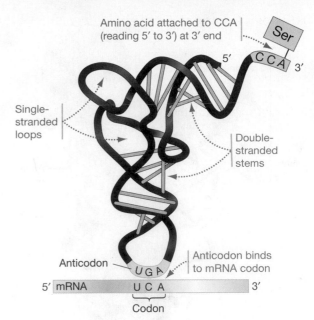

FIGURE 8.12 The Structure of an Aminoacyl Transfer RNA. The anticodon forms complementary base pairs with an mRNA codon.

How Are Amino Acids Attached to tRNAs?

How are amino acids linked to tRNAs? Just as important, what allows the right amino acid for a particular tRNA to be attached?

- An input of energy, in the form of ATP, is required to attach an amino acid to a tRNA.

- Enzymes called **aminoacyl-tRNA synthetases** catalyze the addition of amino acids to tRNAs—what biologists call "charging" a tRNA.

- For each of the 20 major amino acids, there is a different aminoacyl-tRNA synthetase and one or more tRNAs.

Each aminoacyl-tRNA synthetase has a binding site for a particular amino acid and a particular tRNA. Subtle differences in tRNA shape and base sequence allow the enzymes to recognize the correct tRNA for the correct amino acid. The combination of a tRNA molecule covalently linked to an amino acid is called an **aminoacyl tRNA. FIGURE 8.13** (see page 148) shows an aminoacyl-tRNA synthetase bound to a tRNA that has just been charged with an amino acid. Note how tightly the two structures fit together—making it possible for the enzyme and its tRNA and amino acid substrates to interact in a precise way.

How Many tRNAs Are There?

After characterizing all the different types of tRNAs, biologists encountered a paradox. According to the genetic code (Chapter 7), the 20 most common amino acids found in proteins are specified by 61 different mRNA codons. Instead of containing 61 different tRNAs with 61 different anticodons, though, most cells contain only about 40. How can all 61 codons be translated with only two-thirds that number of tRNAs?

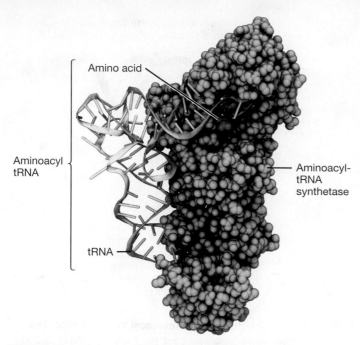

Amino acid

Aminoacyl
tRNA

Aminoacyl-
tRNA
synthetase

tRNA

FIGURE 8.13 Aminoacyl-tRNA Synthetases Couple the Appropriate Amino Acid to the Appropriate tRNA.

To resolve this paradox, Francis Crick proposed what is known as the **wobble hypothesis.** Recall that:

1. Many amino acids are specified by more than one codon.

2. Codons for the same amino acid tend to have the same nucleotides at the first and second positions but a different nucleotide at the third position.

For example, both of the codons CAA and CAG code for the amino acid glutamine. Surprisingly, experimental data have shown that a tRNA with an anticodon of GUU can base-pair with both CAA and CAG in mRNA. The GUU anticodon matches the first two bases (C and A) in both codons, but the U in the anticodon's third position forms a nonstandard base pair with a G in the CAG codon.

Crick proposed that inside the ribosome, certain bases in the third position of tRNA anticodons can bind to bases in the third position of a codon in a manner that does not match Watson–Crick base pairing. If so, this would allow a limited flexibility, or "wobble," in the base pairing.

According to the wobble hypothesis, particular nonstandard base pairs—such as G-U—are acceptable in the third position of a codon and do not change the amino acid that the codon specifies. In this way, wobble in the third position of a codon allows just 40 or so tRNAs to bind to all 61 mRNA codons.

8.5 The Structure and Function of Ribosomes

Recall that protein synthesis occurs when the sequence of bases in an mRNA is translated into a sequence of amino acids in a polypeptide. The translation of each mRNA codon begins when the anticodon of an aminoacyl tRNA binds to the codon. Translation of a codon is complete when a peptide bond forms between the tRNA's amino acid and the growing polypeptide chain.

Both of these events take place inside a ribosome. Biologists have known since the 1930s that ribosomes contain many proteins and **ribosomal RNAs (rRNAs).** Later work showed that ribosomes can be separated into two major substructures, called the large subunit and small subunit. Each ribosome subunit consists of a complex of RNA molecules and proteins. The small subunit holds the mRNA in place during translation; the large subunit is where peptide-bond formation takes place.

FIGURE 8.14 shows two views of how the molecules required for translation fit together. Note that during protein synthesis, three distinct tRNAs are lined up inside the ribosome. All three are bound to their corresponding mRNA codons.

- The tRNA that is on the right in the figure, and colored red, carries an amino acid. This tRNA's position in the ribosome is called the A site—"A" for acceptor or aminoacyl.

- The tRNA that is in the middle (green) holds the growing polypeptide chain and occupies the P site, for peptidyl, inside the ribosome. (Think of "P" for peptide-bond formation.)

- The left-hand (blue) tRNA no longer has an amino acid attached and is about to leave the ribosome. It occupies the ribosome's E site—"E" for exit.

Because all tRNAs have similar secondary and tertiary structure, they all fit equally well in the A, P, and E sites.

The ribosome is a macromolecular machine that synthesizes proteins in a three-step sequence:

1. An aminoacyl tRNA diffuses into the A site; if its anticodon matches a codon in mRNA, it stays in the ribosome.

2. A peptide bond forms between the amino acid held by the aminoacyl tRNA in the A site and the growing polypeptide, which was held by a tRNA in the P site.

3. The ribosome moves down the mRNA by one codon, and all three tRNAs move one position within the ribosome. The tRNA in the E site exits; the tRNA in the P site moves to the E site; and the tRNA in the A site switches to the P site.

The protein that is being synthesized grows by one amino acid each time this three-step sequence repeats. The process occurs up to 20 times per second in bacterial ribosomes and about 2 times per second in eukaryotic ribosomes. Protein synthesis starts at the amino end (N-terminus) of a polypeptide and proceeds to the carboxy end (C-terminus; see Chapter 9).

This introduction to how tRNAs, mRNAs, and ribosomes interact during protein synthesis leaves several key questions unanswered. How do mRNAs and ribosomes get together to start the process? Once protein synthesis is under way, how is peptide-bond formation catalyzed inside the ribosome? And how does protein synthesis conclude when the ribosome reaches the end of the message? Let's consider each question in turn.

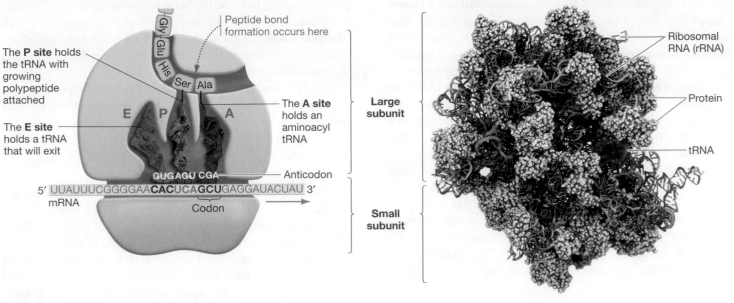

(a) Diagram of ribosome during translation (interior view)

Gly
Glu
His
Ser Ala

Peptide bond formation occurs here

The **P site** holds the tRNA with growing polypeptide attached

The **E site** holds a tRNA that will exit

E P A

The **A site** holds an aminoacyl tRNA

Large subunit

GUGAGU CGA — Anticodon

5′ UUAUUUCGGGGAA**CACUCAGCU**GAGGAUACUAU 3′
mRNA

Codon

Small subunit

(b) Model of ribosome during translation (exterior view)

Ribosomal RNA (rRNA)

Protein

tRNA

FIGURE 8.14 The Structure of the Ribosome. Ribosomes have three distinct tRNA binding sites in their interior.

Initiating Translation

To translate an mRNA properly, a ribosome must begin at a specific point in the message, translate the mRNA up to the message's termination codon, and then stop. Using the same terminology that they apply to transcription, biologists call these three phases of protein synthesis initiation, elongation, and termination, respectively.

One key to understanding translation initiation is to recall that a start codon (usually AUG) is found near the 5′ end of

all mRNAs and that it codes for the amino acid methionine (Chapter 7).

FIGURE 8.15 shows how translation gets under way in bacteria. The process begins when a section of rRNA in a small ribosomal subunit binds to a complementary sequence on an mRNA. The mRNA region is called the **ribosome binding site,** or **Shine–Dalgarno sequence,** after the biologists who discovered it. The site is about six nucleotides upstream from the start codon.

PROCESS: INITIATING TRANSLATION IN BACTERIA

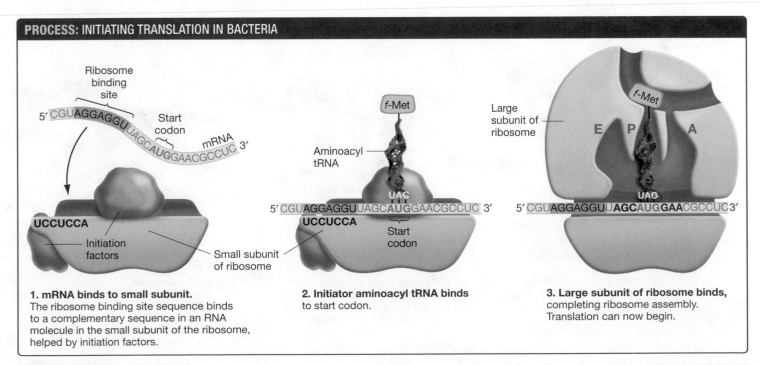

Ribosome binding site

5′ CGU**AGGAGGU**UAGC**AUG**GAACGCCUC 3′

Start codon

mRNA

UCCUCCA

Initiation factors

Small subunit of ribosome

1. mRNA binds to small subunit.
The ribosome binding site sequence binds to a complementary sequence in an RNA molecule in the small subunit of the ribosome, helped by initiation factors.

f-Met

Aminoacyl tRNA

UAC

5′ CGU**AGGAGGU**UAGC**AUG**GAACGCCUC 3′

UCCUCCA

Start codon

2. Initiator aminoacyl tRNA binds to start codon.

Large subunit of ribosome

f-Met

E P A

UAC

5′ CGU**AGGAGGU**U**AGC**AUG**GAA**CGCCUC 3′

3. Large subunit of ribosome binds, completing ribosome assembly. Translation can now begin.

FIGURE 8.15 Initiation of Translation.

The interactions between the small subunit, the message, and the tRNA are mediated by proteins called **initiation factors** (Figure 8.15, step 1). Initiation factors help in preparing the ribosome for translation, including binding the first aminoacyl tRNA to the ribosome. In bacteria this initiator tRNA bears a modified form of methionine called *N*-formylmethionine (abbreviated *f*-met) (Figure 8.15, step 2). In eukaryotes, this initiating tRNA carries a normal methionine. Initiation factors also prevent the small and large subunits of the ribosome from coming together until the initiator tRNA is in place at the AUG start codon, and they help bind the mRNA to the small ribosomal subunit.

Initiation is complete when the large subunit joins the complex (Figure 8.15, step 3). When the ribosome is completely assembled, the tRNA bearing *f*-met occupies the P site.

To summarize, translation initiation is a three-step process in bacteria: (1) The mRNA binds to a small ribosomal subunit, (2) the initiator aminoacyl tRNA bearing *f*-met binds to the start codon, and (3) the large ribosomal subunit binds, completing the complex.

In eukaryotes, the details of initiation are different, but they still involve recognition of a start codon, assembly of the ribosome, assistance from initiation factors, and the positioning of a methionine-carrying tRNA in the P site. The cap and poly(A) tail are also important in assembling the ribosome on the mRNA.

Elongation: Extending the Polypeptide

At the start of elongation, the E and A sites in the ribosome are empty of tRNAs. As a result, an mRNA codon is exposed in the A site. As step 1 in **FIGURE 8.16** illustrates, elongation proceeds when an aminoacyl tRNA binds to the codon in the A site by complementary base pairing between the anticodon and codon.

When both the P site and A site are occupied by tRNAs, the amino acids on the tRNAs are in the ribosome's active site. This is where peptide-bond formation—the essence of protein synthesis—occurs.

Peptide-bond formation is one of the most important reactions that take place in cells because manufacturing proteins is among the most fundamental of all cell processes. Biologists wondered, is it the ribosome's proteins or RNAs that catalyze this reaction?

Is the Ribosome an Enzyme or a Ribozyme?
Because ribosomes contain both protein and RNA, researchers had argued for decades over whether the active site consisted of protein or RNA. The debate was not resolved until the year 2000, when researchers completed three-dimensional models that were detailed enough to reveal the structure of the active site. These models confirmed that the active site consists entirely of ribosomal RNA. Based on these results, biologists are now convinced that protein synthesis is catalyzed by RNA. The ribosome is a ribozyme—not a protein-based enzyme.

The observation that protein synthesis is catalyzed by RNA is important because it supports the RNA-world hypothesis (Chapter 5). Recall that proponents of this hypothesis claim that life began with RNA molecules and that the presence of DNA and proteins in cells evolved later. If the RNA-world hypothesis is correct, then it would make sense that the production of proteins is catalyzed by RNA.

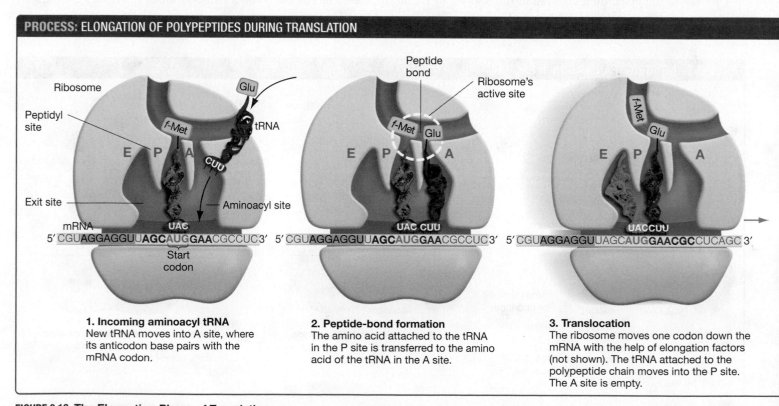

PROCESS: ELONGATION OF POLYPEPTIDES DURING TRANSLATION

1. Incoming aminoacyl tRNA
New tRNA moves into A site, where its anticodon base pairs with the mRNA codon.

2. Peptide-bond formation
The amino acid attached to the tRNA in the P site is transferred to the amino acid of the tRNA in the A site.

3. Translocation
The ribosome moves one codon down the mRNA with the help of elongation factors (not shown). The tRNA attached to the polypeptide chain moves into the P site. The A site is empty.

FIGURE 8.16 The Elongation Phase of Translation.

Moving Down the mRNA What happens after a peptide bond forms? Step 2 in Figure 8.16 shows that when peptide-bond formation is complete, the polypeptide chain is transferred from the tRNA in the P site to the amino acid held by the tRNA in the A site. Step 3 shows the process called **translocation,** which occurs when proteins called **elongation factors** help move the ribosome relative to the mRNA so that translation occurs in the 5′ → 3′ direction. Translocation is an energy-demanding event that requires GTP.

Translocation does several things: It moves the uncharged RNA into the E site; it moves the tRNA containing the growing polypeptide into the P site; and it opens the A site and exposes a new mRNA codon. The empty tRNA that finds itself in the E site is ejected into the cytosol.

The three steps in elongation—(1) arrival of aminoacyl tRNA, (2) peptide-bond formation, and (3) translocation—repeat down the length of the mRNA. Recent three-dimensional models of ribosomes in various stages of translation show that the machine is highly dynamic. The ribosome constantly changes shape as tRNAs come and go and catalysis and translocation occur. The ribosome is a complex and dynamic macromolecular machine.

Terminating Translation

How does protein synthesis end? Recall that the genetic code includes three stop codons: UAA, UAG, and UGA (see Chapter 7). In most cells, no aminoacyl tRNA has an anticodon that binds to these sequences. When the translocating ribosome reaches one of the stop codons, a protein called a **release factor** recognizes the stop codon and fills the A site (**FIGURE 8.17**, see page 152).

Release factors fit tightly into the A site because they have the size and shape of a tRNA coming into the ribosome. However, release factors do not carry an amino acid. When a release factor occupies the A site, the protein's active site catalyzes the hydrolysis of the bond that links the tRNA in the P site to the polypeptide chain. This reaction frees the polypeptide.

The newly synthesized polypeptide and uncharged tRNAs are released from the ribosome, the ribosome separates from the mRNA, and the two ribosomal subunits dissociate. The subunits are ready to attach to the start codon of another message and start translation anew. Termination occurs in very similar ways in bacteria and eukaryotes.

Post-Translational Modifications

Proteins are not fully formed and functional when termination occurs. From earlier chapters, it should be clear that most proteins go through an extensive series of processing steps, collectively called post-translational modification, before they are completely functional. These steps require a wide array of molecules and events and take place in many different locations throughout the cell.

Folding Recall that a protein's function depends on its shape, and that a protein's shape depends on how it folds (see Chapter 9). Although folding can occur spontaneously, it is frequently speeded up by proteins called **molecular chaperones.**

Recent data have shown that in some bacteria, chaperone proteins bind to the ribosome near the "tunnel" where the growing polypeptide emerges from the ribosome. This finding suggests that folding occurs as the polypeptide emerges from the ribosome.

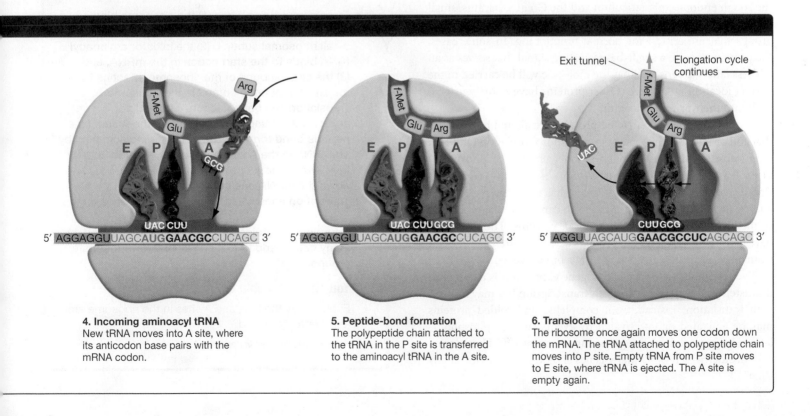

4. Incoming aminoacyl tRNA
New tRNA moves into A site, where its anticodon base pairs with the mRNA codon.

5. Peptide-bond formation
The polypeptide chain attached to the tRNA in the P site is transferred to the aminoacyl tRNA in the A site.

6. Translocation
The ribosome once again moves one codon down the mRNA. The tRNA attached to polypeptide chain moves into P site. Empty tRNA from P site moves to E site, where tRNA is ejected. The A site is empty again.

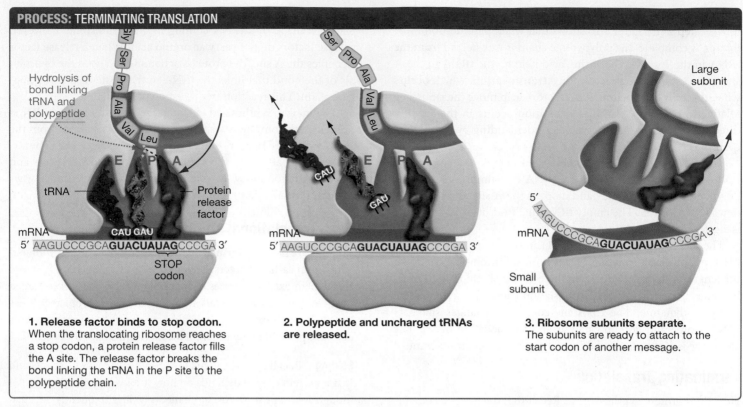

Hydrolysis of bond linking tRNA and polypeptide

tRNA

Protein release factor

mRNA
5′ AAGUCCCGCA**GUACUAUAG**CCCGA 3′

STOP codon

1. Release factor binds to stop codon.
When the translocating ribosome reaches a stop codon, a protein release factor fills the A site. The release factor breaks the bond linking the tRNA in the P site to the polypeptide chain.

mRNA
5′ AAGUCCCGCA**GUACUAUAG**CCCGA 3′

2. Polypeptide and uncharged tRNAs are released.

Large subunit

5′
mRNA

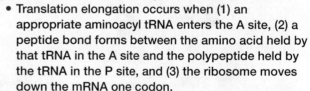

Small subunit

3. Ribosome subunits separate.
The subunits are ready to attach to the start codon of another message.

FIGURE 8.17 Termination of Translation.

Chemical Modifications An earlier chapter pointed out that many eukaryotic proteins are extensively modified after they are synthesized (see Chapter 2). For example, in the organelles called the rough endoplasmic reticulum and the Golgi apparatus, small chemical groups may be added to proteins—often sugar or lipid groups that are critical for normal functioning. In some cases, the proteins receive a sugar-based sorting signal that serves as an address label and ensures that the molecule will be carried to the correct location in the cell. (Other proteins have a sorting signal built into their primary structure.)

In addition, many completed proteins are altered by enzymes that add or remove a phosphate group. Phosphorylation (addition of phosphate) and dephosphorylation (removal of phosphate) of proteins were introduced in previous chapters (Chapter 13). Recall that because a phosphate group has two negative charges, adding or removing a phosphate group can cause major changes in the shape and chemical reactivity of proteins. These changes have a dramatic effect on the protein's activity—often switching it from an inactive state to an active state, or vice versa.

The take-home message is that gene expression is a complex, multistep process that begins with transcription but may not end with translation. Instead, even completed and folded proteins may be activated or deactivated by events such as phosphorylation. In general, how are genes turned on or off? How does a cell "decide" which of its many genes should be expressed at any time?

check your understanding

(C)(Y)(U)

If you understand that . . .

• Translation begins when (1) the ribosome binding site on an mRNA binds to an rRNA sequence in the small ribosomal subunit, (2) the initiator aminoacyl tRNA binds to the start codon in the mRNA, and (3) the large subunit of the ribosome attaches to the small subunit to complete the ribosome.

• Translation elongation occurs when (1) an appropriate aminoacyl tRNA enters the A site, (2) a peptide bond forms between the amino acid held by that tRNA in the A site and the polypeptide held by the tRNA in the P site, and (3) the ribosome moves down the mRNA one codon.

• Translation ends when the ribosome reaches a stop codon.

• Completed proteins are modified by folding and, in many cases, addition of sugar, lipid, or phosphate groups.

✔ **You should be able to . . .**

Explain why the E, P, and A sites in the ribosome are appropriately named.

Answers are available in Appendix A.

If you understand . . .

8.1   An Overview of Transcription

- RNA polymerase catalyzes the production of an RNA molecule whose base sequence is complementary to the base sequence of the DNA template strand.

- RNA polymerase binds DNA with the help of other proteins.

- RNA polymerase begins transcription by binding to promoter sequences in DNA.

- In bacteria, this binding occurs in conjunction with a protein called sigma. Sigma associates with RNA polymerase and then recognizes particular sequences within promoters that are centered 10 bases and 35 bases upstream from the start of the actual genetic message.

- Eukaryotic promoters vary more than bacterial promoters.

- In eukaryotes, transcription begins when a large array of proteins called basal transcription factors bind to a promoter. In response, RNA polymerase binds to the site.

- In both bacteria and eukaryotes, the RNA elongates in a $5' \rightarrow 3'$ direction.

- Transcription in bacteria ends when RNA polymerase encounters a stem-loop structure in the just transcribed RNA; in eukaryotes, transcription terminates after the RNA is cleaved downstream of the poly(A) sequence.

✔ You should be able to predict the consequences of a mutation in bacteria that inserts random nucleotides into the hairpin-coding region near the $3'$ end of a transcribed region.

8.2   RNA Processing in Eukaryotes

- In eukaryotes, the primary (initial) transcript must be processed to produce a mature RNA.

- In primary transcripts, stretches of RNA called introns are spliced out and regions called exons are joined together.

- Complex macromolecular machines called spliceosomes splice introns out of pre-mRNA.

- A "cap" is added to the $5'$ end of pre-mRNAs, and a poly(A) tail is added to their $3'$ end.

- The cap and tail serve as recognition signals for translation and protect the message from degradation by ribonucleases.

- RNA processing occurs in the nucleus.

✔ You should be able to predict whether the protein-coding portion of a gene for an identical protein will be of the same or different lengths in a bacterium and a eukaryote.

8.3   An Introduction to Translation

- Ribosomes translate mRNAs into proteins with the help of adaptor molecules called transfer RNAs.

- In bacteria, an RNA is often transcribed and translated at the same time because there is no nucleus.

- In eukaryotes, transcription and translation of an RNA cannot occur together, because transcription and RNA processing occur in the nucleus and translation occurs in the cytoplasm.

- Experiments with radioactively labeled amino acids showed that transfer RNAs (tRNAs) serve as the chemical bridge between the RNA message and the polypeptide product.

✔ You should be able to explain why it is correct to say that transfer RNAs work as molecular adaptors.

8.4   The Structure and Function of Transfer RNA

- Each transfer RNA carries an amino acid corresponding to the tRNA's three-base-long anticodon.

- tRNAs have an L-shaped, tertiary structure. One leg of the L contains the anticodon, which forms complementary base pairs with the mRNA codon. The other leg holds the amino acid appropriate for that codon.

- Enzymes called aminoacyl-tRNA synthetases link the correct amino acid to the correct tRNA.

- Imprecise pairing—or "wobble pairing"—is allowed in the third position of the codon and anticodon, so only about 40 different tRNAs are required to translate the 61 codons that code for amino acids.

✔ You should be able to predict what would occur if a mutation caused an aminoacyl-tRNA synthetase to recognize two different amino acids.

8.5 The Structure and Function of Ribosomes

- Ribosomes are large macromolecular machines made of many proteins and RNAs.

- In the ribosome, the tRNA anticodon binds to a three-base-long mRNA codon to bring the correct amino acid into the ribosome.

- Peptide-bond formation by the ribosome is catalyzed by a ribozyme (RNA), not an enzyme (protein).

- Protein synthesis occurs in three steps: (1) an incoming aminoacyl tRNA occupies the A site; (2) the growing polypeptide chain is transferred from a peptidyl tRNA in the ribosome's P site to the amino acid bound to the tRNA in the A site, and a peptide bond is formed; and (3) the ribosome is translocated to the next codon on the mRNA, accompanied by ejection of the uncharged RNA from the E site.

- Chaperone proteins help fold newly synthesized proteins into their three-dimensional conformation (tertiary structure).

- Most proteins need to be modified after translation (post-translational modification) to activate them or target them to specific locations.

✔ You should be able to create a concept map (see BioSkills 15 in Appendix B) that describes the relationships among the following concepts and structures: translation, initiation, elongation, termination, growing polypeptide in P site, start codon, ribosome subunits.

 MasteringBiology

1. **MasteringBiology Assignments**

   Tutorials and Activities Chromosomal Mutations; Following the Instructions in DNA; Point Mutations Protein Synthesis (1 of 3): Overview; Protein Synthesis (2 of 3): Transcription and RNA Processing; Protein Synthesis (3 of 3): Translation and Protein Targeting Pathways; RNA Processing; RNA Synthesis; Synthesizing Proteins; Transcription; Translation; Types of RNA

   Questions Reading Quizzes, Blue-Thread Questions, Test Bank

2. **eText** Read your book online, search, take notes, highlight text, and more.

3. **The Study Area** Practice Test, Cumulative Test, BioFlix® 3-D Animations, Videos, Activities, Audio Glossary, Word Study Tools, Art

You should be able to . . .

✔ TEST YOUR KNOWLEDGE *Answers are available in Appendix A*

1. How did the A site of the ribosome get its name?
   a. It is where amino acids are joined to tRNAs, producing aminoacyl tRNAs.
   b. It is where the amino group on the growing polypeptide chain is available for peptide-bond formation.
   c. It is the site occupied by incoming aminoacyl tRNAs.
   d. It is surrounded by α-helices of ribosomal proteins.

2. Where is the start codon located?
   a. at the very start (5′ end) of the mRNA
   b. at the downstream end of the 3′ untranslated region (UTR)
   c. at the downstream end of the 5′ untranslated region (UTR)
   d. at the upstream end of the 3′ untranslated region (UTR)

3. What is the function of a molecular chaperone?

4. What does a bacterial RNA polymerase produce when it transcribes a protein-coding gene?

   a. rRNA
   b. tRNA
   c. mRNA
   d. pre-mRNA

5. Where is an amino acid attached to a tRNA?

6. Compared with mRNAs that have a cap and tail, what do researchers observe when eukaryotic mRNAs that lack a cap and poly(A) tail are translated within a cell?
   a. The primary transcript cannot be processed properly.
   b. Translation occurs inefficiently.
   c. Enzymes on the ribosome add back a cap and poly(A) tail.
   d. tRNAs become resistant to degradation (being broken down).

✔ TEST YOUR UNDERSTANDING *Answers are available in Appendix A*

7. Explain the relationship between eukaryotic promoter sequences, basal transcription factors, and RNA polymerase. Explain the relationship between bacterial promoter sequences, sigma, and RNA polymerase.

8. According to the wobble rules, the correct amino acid can be added to a growing polypeptide chain even if the third base in the mRNA codon is not complementary to the corresponding base in the tRNA anticodon. How do the wobble rules relate to the redundancy of the genetic code?

9. RNases and proteases are enzymes that destroy RNAs and proteins, respectively. Which of the following enzymes when added to a spliceosome is predicted to prevent recognition of pre-mRNA regions critical for splicing?
   a. an RNase specific for tRNAs
   b. an RNase specific for snRNAs
   c. a protease specific for initiation factors
   d. a protease specific for a release factor

10. Describe the sequence of events that occurs during translation as a protein elongates by one amino acid and the ribosome moves down the mRNA. Your answer should specify what is happening in the ribosome's A site, P site, and E site.

11. **QUANTITATIVE** Controlling the rates of transcription and translation is important in bacteria to avoid collisions between ribosomes and RNA polymerases. Calculate the maximum rate of translation by a ribosome in a bacterial cell, provided in units of amino acids per second, so that the ribosome doesn't overtake an RNA polymerase that is transcribing mRNA at a rate of 60 nucleotides per second. How long would it take for this bacterial cell to translate an mRNA containing 1800 codons?

12. In an aminoacyl tRNA, why is the observed distance between the amino acid and the anticodon important?

Answers are available in Appendix A

✔ TEST YOUR PROBLEM-SOLVING SKILLS

13. The 5′ cap and poly(A) tail in eukaryotic mRNAs protect the message from degradation by ribonucleases. But why do ribonucleases exist? What function would an enzyme that destroys messages serve? Answer this question using the example of an mRNA for a hormone that causes human heart rate to increase.

14. The nucleotide shown below is called cordycepin triphosphate.

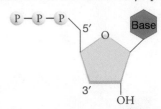

If cordycepin triphosphate is added to a cell-free transcription reaction, the nucleotide is added onto the growing RNA chain but no more nucleotides can be added. The added cordycepin is always found at the 3′ end of an RNA, confirming that synthesis occurs in the 5′ → 3′ direction. Why does cordycepin end transcription?

a. It prevents the association of RNA polymerase and sigma.
b. It irreversibly binds to the active site of RNA polymerase.
c. It cannot be recognized by RNA polymerase.
d. It lacks a 3′ OH.

15. Certain portions of the rRNAs in the large subunit of the ribosome are very similar in all organisms. To make sense of this finding, Carl Woese suggests that the conserved sequences have an important functional role. His logic is that these conserved sequences evolved in a common ancestor of all modern cells and are so important to cell function that any changes in the sequences cause death. In addition to rRNAs, which specific portions of the ribosome would you expect to be identical or nearly identical in all organisms? Explain your logic.

16. Recent structural models show that a poison called α-amanitin inhibits transcription by binding to a site inside eukaryotic RNA polymerase II but not to the active site itself. Based on the model of RNA polymerase in Figure 8.2, predict a place or places where α-amanitin might bind to inhibit transcription.

9 Protein Structure and Function

In this chapter you will learn that

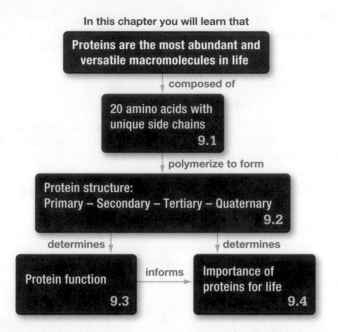

Proteins are the most abundant and versatile macromolecules in life

composed of

20 amino acids with unique side chains 9.1

polymerize to form

Protein structure: Primary – Secondary – Tertiary – Quaternary 9.2

determines ↓   determines ↓

Protein function 9.3 — informs → **Importance of proteins for life** 9.4

A space-filling model of hemoglobin—a protein that is carrying oxygen in your blood right now.

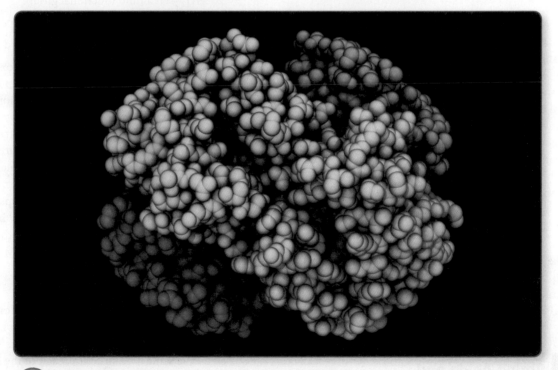

This chapter is part of the Big Picture. See how on pages 68–69.

Chemical reactions in the atmosphere and ocean of ancient Earth are thought to have led to the formation of the first complex carbon-containing compounds. This idea, called chemical evolution, was first proposed by Alexander I. Oparin in 1924. The hypothesis was published again—independently and five years later—by J. B. S. Haldane.

Today, the Oparin–Haldane proposal is considered a formal scientific theory (see Chapter 1). Scientific theories are continuously refined as new information comes to light, and many of Oparin

✔ When you see this checkmark, stop and test yourself. Answers are available in Appendix A.

and Haldane's original ideas have been revised. In its current form, the theory can be broken into four steps.

Step 1 Chemical evolution began with the production of small organic compounds from reactants such as H_2, N_2, NH_3, and CO_2. (Appendix D focuses on this step.)

Step 2 These small, simple organic compounds reacted to form mid-sized molecules, such as amino acids, nucleotides, and sugars. (Amino acids are introduced in this chapter. Nucleotides and sugars are discussed in Chapter 5 and Appendix E, respectively.)

Step 3 Mid-sized, building-block molecules linked to form the types of large molecules found in cells today, including proteins, nucleic acids, and complex carbohydrates. Each of these large molecules is composed of distinctive chemical subunits that join together: Proteins are composed of amino acids, nucleic acids are composed of nucleotides, and complex carbohydrates are composed of sugars.

Step 4 Life became possible when one of these large, complex molecules acquired the ability to replicate itself. By increasing in copy number, this molecule would then emerge from the pool of chemicals. At that point, life had begun—chemical evolution gave way to biological evolution.

What type of molecule was responsible for the origin of life? Answering this question is a recurring theme in this and the next three chapters.

To address this question, researchers first designed experiments to identify the types of molecules that could be produced in the waters of prebiotic Earth (Appendix D). One series of results sparked particular excitement for origin-of-life researchers—the repeated discovery of amino acids among the products of early Earth simulations.

Amino acids have also been found in meteorites and produced in experiments that approximate the environment of interstellar space. Taken together, these observations have led researchers to conclude that amino acids were present and probably abundant during chemical evolution. Since amino acids are the building blocks of proteins, many researchers have therefore asked, Could a protein have been the initial spark of life?

For this question to be valid, proteins would need to possess three of the fundamental attributes of life, namely: information, replication, and evolution. To determine if they do, let's look at the molecules themselves. What are amino acids, and how are they linked to form proteins?

9.1 Amino Acids and Their Polymerization

Modern cells, such as those that make up your body, produce tens of thousands of distinct proteins. Most of these molecules are composed of just 20 different building blocks, called **amino acids.** All 20 of these building blocks have a common structure.

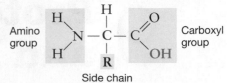

(a) Non-ionized form of amino acid

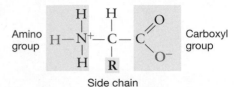

(b) Ionized form of amino acid

FIGURE 9.1 All Amino Acids Have the Same General Structure. The central α-carbon is shown in red.

The Structure of Amino Acids

To understand how amino acids are put together, recall that carbon atoms have a valence of four—they form four covalent bonds (Appendix D). All 20 amino acids thus have a common core structure—with a central carbon atom (referred to as the α-carbon) bonded to the four different atoms or groups of atoms diagrammed in **FIGURE 9.1a**:

1. H—a hydrogen atom
2. NH_2—an amino functional group
3. COOH—a carboxyl functional group
4. a distinctive "R-group" (often referred to as a "side chain")

The combination of amino and carboxyl groups not only inspired the name amino acid, but is key to how these molecules behave. In water at pH 7, the concentration of protons causes the amino group to act as a base. It attracts a proton to form NH_3^+ (**FIGURE 9.1b**). The carboxyl group, in contrast, is acidic because its two oxygen atoms are highly electronegative. They pull electrons away from the hydrogen atom, which means that it is relatively easy for this group to lose a proton to form COO^-.

The charges on these functional groups are important for two reasons: **(1)** They help amino acids stay in solution, where they can interact with one another and with other solutes, and **(2)** they affect the amino acid's chemical reactivity.

The Nature of Side Chains

What about the R-group? The R-groups, or side chains, on amino acids vary from a single hydrogen atom to large structures containing carbon atoms linked into rings. While all amino acids share the same core structure, each of the 20 R-groups is unique. The properties of amino acids vary because their R-groups vary.

FIGURE 9.2 highlights the R-groups on the 20 most common amino acids found in cells.[1] As you examine these side chains,

---

[1]There are actually 22 amino acids found in proteins that occur in organisms, but two are very rare.

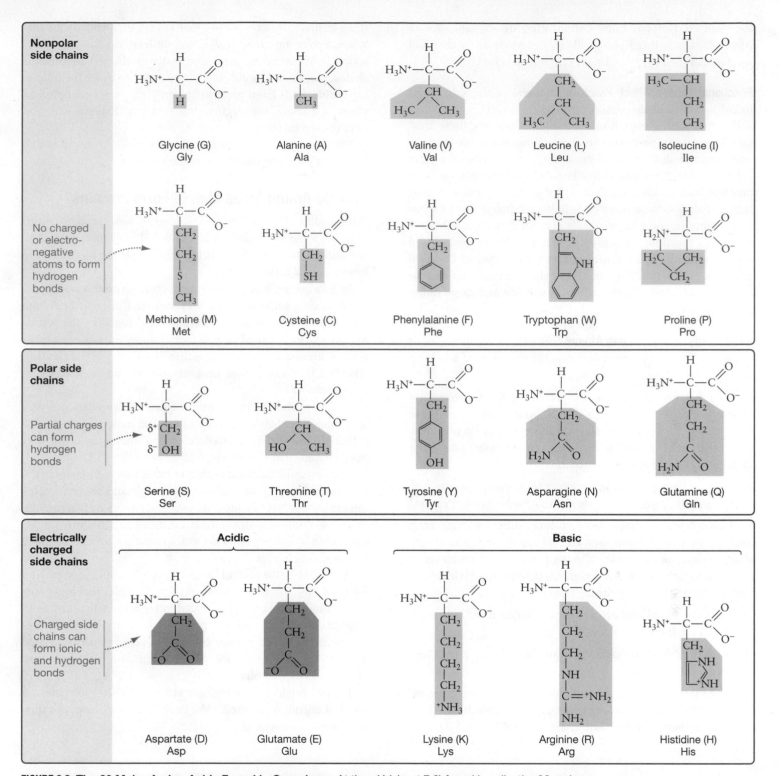

FIGURE 9.2 The 20 Major Amino Acids Found in Organisms. At the pH (about 7.0) found in cells, the 20 major amino acids found in organisms have the structural formulas shown here. The side chains are highlighted, and standard single-letter and three-letter abbreviations for each amino acid are given. For clarity, the carbon atoms in the ring structures of phenylalanine, tyrosine, tryptophan, and histidine are not shown; each bend in a ring is the site of a carbon atom. The hydrogen atoms in these structures are also not shown. A double line inside a ring indicates a double bond.

✔**EXERCISE** Explain why the green R-groups are nonpolar and why the pink R-groups are polar, based on the relative electronegativities of O, N, C, and H (see Appendix D). Note that sulfur (S) has an electronegativity almost equal to that of carbon and slightly higher than that of hydrogen, making cysteine's side chain mildly hydrophobic.

ask yourself two questions (while referring to Table 2.3 of Appendix D): Is this R-group likely to participate in chemical reactions? Will it help this amino acid stay in solution?

Functional Groups Affect Reactivity Several of the side chains found in amino acids contain carboxyl, sulfhydryl, hydroxyl, or amino functional groups. Under the right conditions, these functional groups can participate in chemical reactions. For example, amino acids with a sulfhydryl group (SH) in their side chains can form disulfide (S—S) bonds that help link different parts of large proteins. Such bonds naturally form between the proteins in your hair; curly hair contains many cross-links and straight hair far fewer.

In contrast, some amino acids contain side chains that are devoid of functional groups—consisting solely of carbon and hydrogen atoms. These R-groups rarely participate in chemical reactions. As a result, the influence of these amino acids on protein function depends primarily on their size and shape rather than reactivity.

The Polarity of Side Chains Affects Solubility The nature of its R-group affects the polarity, and thus the solubility, of an amino acid in water.

- Nonpolar side chains lack charged or highly electronegative atoms capable of forming hydrogen bonds with water. These R-groups are **hydrophobic,** meaning that they do not interact with water. Instead of dissolving, hydrophobic side chains tend to coalesce in aqueous solution.

- Polar or charged side chains interact readily with water and are **hydrophilic.** Hydrophilic side chains dissolve in water easily.

Amino acid side chains distinguish the different amino acids and can be grouped into four general types: acidic, basic, uncharged polar, and nonpolar. If given a structural formula for an amino acid, as in Figure 9.2, you can determine which type of amino acid it is by asking three questions:

1. Does the side chain have a negative charge? If so, it has lost a proton, so it must be acidic.

2. Does the side chain have a positive charge? If so, it has taken on a proton, so it must be basic.

3. If the side chain is uncharged, does it have an oxygen atom? If so, the highly electronegative oxygen will result in a polar covalent bond and thus is uncharged polar.

If the answers to all three questions are no, then you are looking at a nonpolar amino acid. ✔ If you understand how the interaction between amino acids and water is affected by the side chains, you should be able to use Figure 9.2 to order the following amino acids from most hydrophilic to most hydrophobic: valine, aspartate, asparagine, and tyrosine. Explain why you have chosen this order.

Now that you have seen the diversity of structures in amino acids, let's put them together to make a protein.

How Do Amino Acids Link to Form Proteins?

Amino acids are linked to one another to form proteins. Similarly, the molecular building blocks called nucleotides attach to one another to form nucleic acids, and simple sugars connect to form complex carbohydrates.

In general, a molecular subunit such as an amino acid, a nucleotide, or a sugar is called a **monomer** ("one-part"). When a large number of monomers are bonded together, the resulting structure is called a **polymer** ("many-parts"). The process of linking monomers together is called **polymerization** (**FIGURE 9.3**). Thus, amino acid monomers can polymerize to form proteins.

Biologists also use the word **macromolecule** to denote a very large molecule that is made up of smaller molecules joined together. Proteins are macromolecules—polymers—that consist of linked amino acid monomers.

The theory of chemical evolution states that monomers in the prebiotic soup polymerized to form larger and more complex molecules, such as the proteins and other types of macromolecules found in organisms. This is a difficult step, because monomers such as amino acids do not spontaneously self-assemble into macromolecules such as proteins.

According to the second law of thermodynamics (reviewed in Appendix D), this fact is not surprising. Complex and highly organized molecules are not expected to form spontaneously from simpler constituents, because polymerization organizes the molecules involved into a more complex, ordered structure. Stated another way, polymerization decreases the disorder, or entropy, of the molecules involved.

For monomers to link together and form macromolecules, an input of energy is required. How could this have happened during chemical evolution?

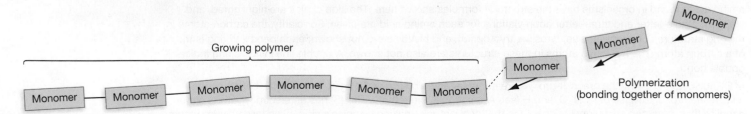

FIGURE 9.3 Monomers Are the Building Blocks of Polymers.

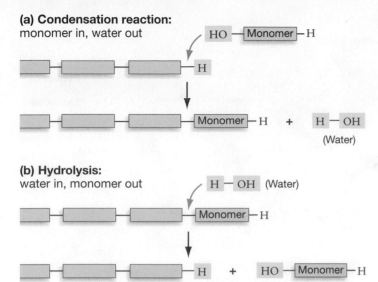

(a) Condensation reaction:
monomer in, water out

(b) Hydrolysis:
water in, monomer out

FIGURE 9.4 Polymers Can Be Extended or Broken Apart.

Could Polymerization Occur in the Energy-Rich Environment of Early Earth?

Monomers polymerize through **condensation reactions,** also known as **dehydration reactions.** These reactions are aptly named because the newly formed bond results in the loss of a water molecule (**FIGURE 9.4a**). The reverse reaction, called **hydrolysis,** breaks polymers apart by adding a water molecule (**FIGURE 9.4b**). The water molecule reacts with the bond linking the monomers, separating one monomer from the polymer chain.

In a solution such as the prebiotic soup, condensation and hydrolysis represent the forward and reverse reactions of a chemical equilibrium:

$$\text{Monomer 1} + \text{Monomer 2} \underset{\text{hydrolysis}}{\overset{\text{condensation}}{\rightleftharpoons}} \text{Monomer 1} - \text{Monomer 2}$$

Hydrolysis dominates because it increases entropy and is favorable energetically.

This means that, in the prebiotic soup, polymerization would occur only if there were a very high concentration of amino acids to push the reaction toward condensation. Since the equilibrium favors free monomers over polymers even under concentrated conditions, a polymer is unlikely to have grown much beyond a short chain.

According to recent experiments, though, there are several ways that amino acids could have polymerized early in chemical evolution.

- Researchers evaluating the surface metabolism model of chemical evolution have been able to generate stable polymers by mixing free amino acids with a source of chemical energy and tiny mineral particles. Apparently, growing macromolecules are protected from hydrolysis if they cling, or adsorb, to a mineral surface. One such experiment produced polymers that were 55 amino acids long.

- In conditions that simulate the hot, metal-rich environments of undersea volcanoes, researchers have observed not only amino acid formation but also their polymerization.

- Amino acids have also joined into polymers in experiments in cooler water if a carbon- and sulfur-containing gas—one that is commonly ejected from undersea volcanoes—is present.

The current consensus is that several mechanisms could have led to polymerization reactions between amino acids, early in chemical evolution. What kind of bond is responsible for linking these monomers?

The Peptide Bond As **FIGURE 9.5** shows, amino acids polymerize when a bond forms between the carboxyl group of one amino acid and the amino group of another. The $C-N$ covalent bond that results from this condensation reaction is called a **peptide bond.** When a water molecule is removed in the condensation reaction, the carboxyl group is converted to a carbonyl functional group ($C=O$) in the resulting polymer, and the amino group is reduced to an $N-H$.

Peptide bonds are unusually stable compared to linkages in other types of macromolecules. This is because a pair of valence electrons on the nitrogen is partially shared in the $C-N$ bond (see Figure 9.5). The degree of electron sharing is great enough that peptide bonds actually have some of the characteristics of a double bond. For example, the peptide bond is planar, limiting the movement of the atoms participating in the peptide bond.

When amino acids are linked by peptide bonds into a chain, the amino acids are referred to as residues to distinguish them from free monomers.

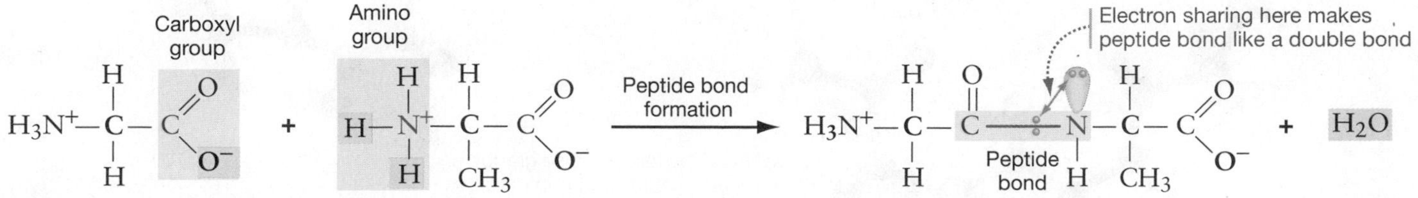

FIGURE 9.5 Peptide Bonds Form When the Carboxyl Group of One Amino Acid Reacts with the Amino Group of a Second Amino Acid.

(a) Peptide chain

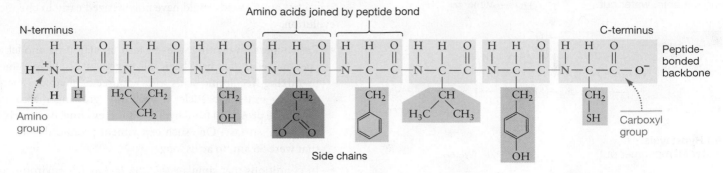

(b) Numbering system

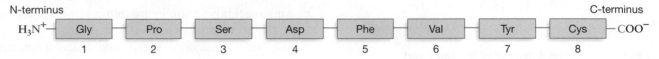

FIGURE 9.6 Amino Acids Polymerize to Form Chains.

FIGURE 9.6a shows how the chain of peptide bonds in a short polymer gives the molecule a structural framework, or a "backbone." There are three key points to note about the peptide-bonded backbone:

1. **R-group orientation** The side chains present in each residue extend out from the backbone, making it possible for them to interact with each other and with water.

2. **Directionality** There is an amino group (NH_3^+) on one end of the backbone and a carboxyl group (COO^-) on the other. The end of the sequence that has the free amino group is called the N-terminus, or amino-terminus, and the end with the free carboxyl group is called the C-terminus, or carboxy-terminus. By convention, biologists always write amino acid sequences

from the N-terminus to the C-terminus (**FIGURE 9.6b**), because the N-terminus is the start of the chain when proteins are synthesized in cells.

3. **Flexibility** Although the peptide bond itself cannot rotate because of its double-bond nature, the single bonds on either side of the peptide bond can rotate. As a result, the structure as a whole is flexible (**FIGURE 9.7**).

When fewer than 50 amino acids are linked together in this way, the resulting polymer is called an **oligopeptide** ("few peptides") or simply a **peptide.** Polymers that contain 50 or more amino acids are called **polypeptides** ("many peptides").

The term **protein** is often used to describe any chain of amino acid residues, but formally protein refers to the complete, often

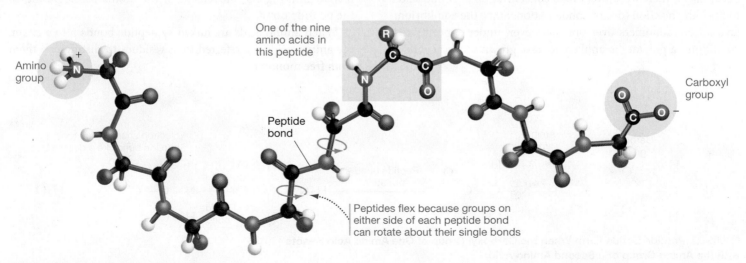

FIGURE 9.7 Peptide Chains Are Flexible.

functional form of the molecule. In Section 9.2, you'll see that some proteins consist of a single polypeptide while others are functional only when multiple polypeptides are bonded to one another.

Proteins are the stuff of life. Let's take a look at how they are put together and then see what they do.

check your understanding

If you understand that . . .

- Amino acids are small molecules with a central carbon atom bonded to a carboxyl group, an amino group, a hydrogen atom, and a side chain called an R-group.
- Each amino acid has distinctive chemical properties because each has a unique R-group.
- Proteins are polymers made up of amino acids.
- When the carboxyl group of one amino acid reacts with the amino group of another amino acid, a strong covalent bond called a peptide bond forms. Small chains are called oligopeptides; large chains are called polypeptides, or proteins.

✔ **You should be able to . . .**

Draw the structural formulas of two glycine residues (glycine's R-group is an H) linked by a peptide bond, and label the amino- and carboxy-terminus.

Answers are available in Appendix A.

9.2 What Do Proteins Look Like?

The unparalleled diversity of proteins—in size, shape, and other aspects of structure—is important because function follows from structure. Proteins can serve diverse functions in cells because they are diverse in size and shape as well as in the chemical properties of their amino acid residues.

FIGURE 9.8 illustrates some of the variety in the sizes and shapes observed in proteins. In the case of the TATA box–binding protein in **FIGURE 9.8a** and the porin protein in **FIGURE 9.8b**, the shape of the molecule has a clear correlation with its function. The TATA box–binding protein has a groove where DNA molecules fit; porin has a hole that forms a pore. The groove in the TATA box–binding protein interacts with specific regions of a DNA molecule, while porin fits in cell membranes and allows certain hydrophilic molecules to pass through. Proteins that provide structural support for cells or tissues, such as the collagen triple helix in **FIGURE 9.8d**, often form long, cable-like fibers.

But many of the proteins found in cells do not have shapes that are noticeably correlated with their functions. For example, the trypsin protein in **FIGURE 9.8c** has an overall globular shape that tells little about its function, which is to bind and cleave peptide bonds of other proteins.

How can biologists make sense of this diversity of protein size and shape? Initially, the amount of variation seems overwhelming. Fortunately, it is not. No matter how large or complex a protein may be, its underlying structure can be broken down into just four basic levels of organization.

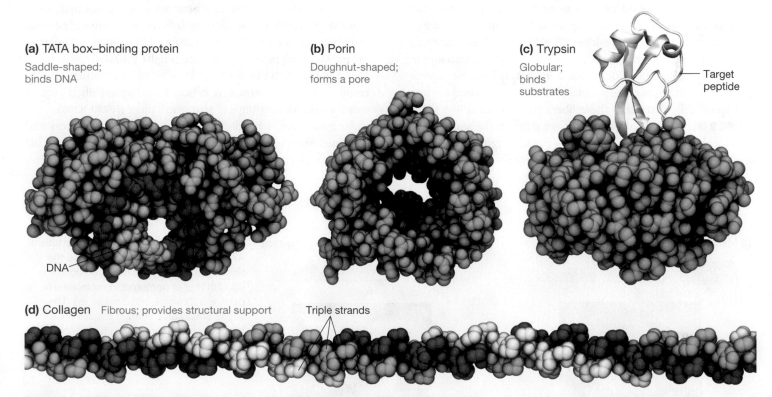

(a) TATA box–binding protein
Saddle-shaped; binds DNA

DNA

(b) Porin
Doughnut-shaped; forms a pore

(c) Trypsin
Globular; binds substrates

Target peptide

(d) Collagen   Fibrous; provides structural support   Triple strands

FIGURE 9.8 In Overall Shape, Proteins Are the Most Diverse Class of Molecules Known.

Primary Structure

Each protein has a unique sequence of amino acids. That simple conclusion was the culmination of 12 years of study by Frederick Sanger and co-workers during the 1940s and 1950s. Sanger's group worked out the first techniques for determining the amino acid sequence of insulin, a hormone that helps regulate sugar concentrations in the blood of humans and other mammals. When other proteins were analyzed, it rapidly became clear that each protein has a definite and distinct amino acid sequence.

Biochemists call the unique sequence of amino acids in a protein the **primary structure** of that protein. The sequence of amino acid residues in Figure 9.6, for example, defines the peptide's primary structure.

With 20 types of amino acids available and length ranging from two amino acid residues to tens of thousands, the number of primary structures that are possible is practically limitless. There may, in fact, be 20^n different combinations of amino acid residues for a polymer with a given length of n. For example, a peptide that is just 10 amino acids long has 20^{10} possible sequences. This is over 10,000 billion.

Why is the order and type of residues in the primary structure of a protein important? Recall that the R-groups present on each amino acid affect its chemical reactivity and solubility. It's therefore reasonable to predict that the R-groups present in a polypeptide will affect that molecule's properties and function.

This prediction is correct. In some cases, even a single change in the sequence of amino acids can cause radical changes in the way the protein as a whole behaves.

As an example, consider hemoglobin, an oxygen-binding protein in human red blood cells. In some individuals, hemoglobin has a valine instead of a glutamate at the 6th position of a strand containing 146 amino acid residues (**FIGURE 9.9a**). Valine's side chain is radically different from the R-group in glutamate. The change in R-group produces hemoglobin molecules that stick to one another and form fibers when oxygen concentrations in the blood are low. Red blood cells that carry these fibers adopt a sickle-like shape (**FIGURE 9.9b**). Sickled red blood cells get stuck in the small blood vessels called capillaries and starve downstream cells of oxygen. A debilitating illness called sickle-cell disease results.

A protein's primary structure is fundamental to its function. Primary structure is also fundamental to the higher levels of protein structure: secondary, tertiary, and quaternary.

Secondary Structure

Even though variation in the amino acid sequence of a protein is virtually limitless, it is only the tip of the iceberg in terms of generating structural diversity.

The next level of organization in proteins—**secondary structure**—is created in part by hydrogen bonding between components of the peptide-bonded backbone. Secondary structures are distinctively shaped sections of proteins that are stabilized largely by hydrogen bonding that occurs between the oxygen on the C=O group of one amino acid residue and the hydrogen on the N—H groups of another (**FIGURE 9.10a**). The oxygen atom in the C=O group has a partial negative charge due to its high electronegativity, while the hydrogen atom in the N—H group has a partial positive charge because it is bonded to nitrogen, which has high electronegativity.

Note a key point: Hydrogen bonding between sections of the same backbone is possible only when a polypeptide bends in a way that puts C=O and N—H groups close together. In most proteins, these polar groups are aligned and form hydrogen bonds with one another when the backbone bends to form one of two possible structures (**FIGURE 9.10b**):

1. an α-**helix** (alpha-helix), in which the polypeptide's backbone is coiled; or

2. a β-**pleated sheet** (beta-pleated sheet), in which segments of a peptide chain bend 180° and then fold in the same plane.

In both structures, the distance between residues that hydrogen-bond to one another is small. In an α-helix, for example, H-bonds form between residues that are just four linear positions apart in the polypeptide's primary sequence (Figure 9.10a).

When biologists use illustrations called ribbon diagrams to represent the shape of a protein, α-helices are shown as coils; β-pleated sheets are shown by groups of arrows in a plane (**FIGURE 9.10c**).

In most cases, secondary structure consists of α-helices and β-pleated sheets. Which one forms, if either, depends on the molecule's primary structure—specifically, the geometry and

---

(a) Normal amino acid sequence

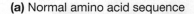

Pro	**Glu**	Glu
5	6	7

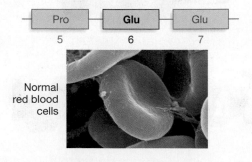

Normal red blood cells

(b) Single change in amino acid sequence

Pro	**Val**	Glu
5	6	7

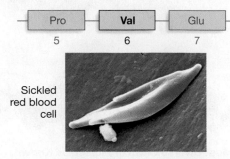

Sickled red blood cell

FIGURE 9.9 Changes in Primary Structure Affect Protein Function. Compare the primary structure of normal hemoglobin **(a)** with that of hemoglobin molecules in people with sickle-cell disease **(b)**. The single amino acid change causes red blood cells to change from their normal disc shape in (a) to a sickled shape in (b) when oxygen concentrations are low.

properties of the amino acids in the sequence. Certain amino acids are more likely to be involved in α-helices than in β-pleated sheets, and vice versa, due to the specific geometry of their side chains. Proline, for example, may be present in β-pleated sheets,

(a) Hydrogen bonds can form between nearby amino and carbonyl groups on the same polypeptide chain.

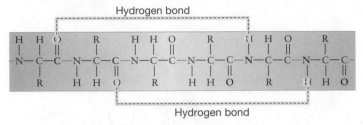

Hydrogen bond

Hydrogen bond

(b) Secondary structures of proteins result.

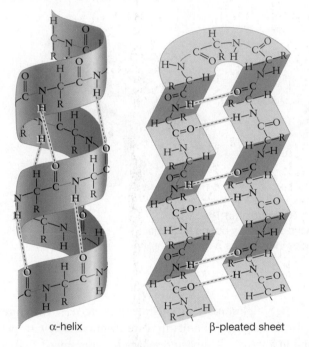

α-helix   β-pleated sheet

(c) Ribbon diagrams of secondary structure

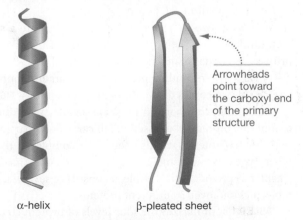

Arrowheads point toward the carboxyl end of the primary structure

α-helix   β-pleated sheet

FIGURE 9.10 Secondary Structures of Proteins. A polypeptide chain can coil or fold in on itself when hydrogen bonds form between N−H and C=O groups on its peptide-bonded backbone.

but it will terminate α-helices due to its unusual side chain. The bond formed between proline's R-group and the nitrogen of the core amino group introduces kinks in the backbone that do not conform to the shape of the helix.

Although each of the hydrogen bonds in an α-helix or a β-pleated sheet is weak relative to a covalent bond, the large number of hydrogen bonds in these structures makes them highly stable. As a result, they increase the stability of the molecule as a whole and help define its shape. In terms of overall shape and stability, though, the tertiary structure of a protein is even more important.

Tertiary Structure

Most of the overall shape, or **tertiary structure,** of a polypeptide results from interactions between R-groups or between R-groups and the backbone. In contrast to the secondary structures, where hydrogen bonds link backbone components together, these side chains can be involved in a wide variety of bonds and interactions. In addition, the amino acid residues that interact with one another are often far apart in the linear sequence. Because each contact between R-groups causes the peptide-bonded backbone to bend and fold, each contributes to the distinctive three-dimensional shape of a polypeptide.

Five types of interactions involving side chains are particularly important:

1. *Hydrogen bonding* Hydrogen bonds form between polar R-groups and opposite partial charges either in the peptide backbone or other R-groups.

2. *Hydrophobic interactions* In an aqueous solution, water molecules interact with the hydrophilic polar side chains of a polypeptide and force the hydrophobic nonpolar side chains to coalesce into globular masses. When these nonpolar R-groups come together, the surrounding water molecules form more hydrogen bonds with each other, increasing the stability of their own interactions.

3. *van der Waals interactions* Once hydrophobic side chains are close to one another, their association is further stabilized by electrical attractions known as **van der Waals interactions.** These weak attractions occur because the constant motion of electrons gives molecules a tiny asymmetry in charge that changes with time. If nonpolar molecules get extremely close to each other, the minute partial charge on one molecule induces an opposite partial charge in the nearby molecule and causes an attraction. Although the interaction is very weak relative to covalent bonds or even hydrogen bonds, a large number of van der Waals attractions can significantly increase the stability of the structure.

4. *Covalent bonding* Covalent bonds can form between the side chains of two cysteines through a reaction between the sulfhydryl groups. These **disulfide ("two-sulfur") bonds** are frequently referred to as bridges, because they create strong links between distinct regions of the same polypeptide or two separate polypeptides.

(a) Interactions that determine the tertiary structure of proteins

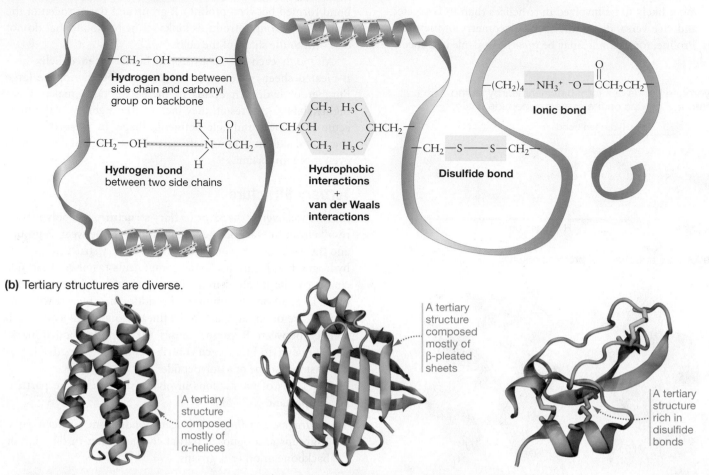

(b) Tertiary structures are diverse.

A tertiary structure composed mostly of α-helices

A tertiary structure composed mostly of β-pleated sheets

A tertiary structure rich in disulfide bonds

FIGURE 9.11 Tertiary Structure of Proteins Results from Interactions Involving R-Groups. (a) The overall shape of a single polypeptide is called its tertiary structure. This level of structure is created by bonds and other interactions that cause it to fold. **(b)** The tertiary structure of these proteins includes interactions between α-helices and β-pleated sheets.

5. *Ionic bonding* Ionic bonds form between groups that have full and opposing charges, such as the ionized acidic and basic side chains highlighted on the right in **FIGURE 9.11a**.

In addition, the overall shape of many proteins depends in part on the presence of secondary structures like α-helices and β-pleated sheets. Thus, tertiary structure depends on both primary and secondary structures.

With so many interactions possible between side chains and peptide-bonded backbones, it's not surprising that polypeptides vary in shape from rod-like filaments to ball-like masses. (See **FIGURE 9.11b**, and look again at Figure 9.8.)

Quaternary Structure

The first three levels of protein structure involve individual polypeptides. But some proteins contain multiple polypeptides that interact to form a single structure. The combination of polypeptides, referred to as subunits, gives a protein **quaternary structure.** The individual polypeptides are held together by the same types of bonds and interactions found in the tertiary level of structure.

In the simplest case, a protein with quaternary structure can consist of just two subunits that are identical. The Cro protein found in a virus called bacteriophage λ (pronounced *LAMB-da*) is an example (**FIGURE 9.12a**). Proteins with two polypeptide subunits are called dimers ("two-parts").

More than two polypeptides can be linked into a single protein, however, and the polypeptides involved may be distinct in primary, secondary, and tertiary structure. For example hemoglobin, an oxygen-binding protein, is a tetramer ("four-parts"). It consists of two copies of two different polypeptides (**FIGURE 9.12b**).

In addition, cells contain **macromolecular machines:** groups of multiple proteins that assemble to carry out a particular function. Some proteins are also found in complexes that include other types of macromolecules. The ribosome (introduced in Chapter 2) provides an example; it consists of several nucleic acid molecules and over 50 different proteins.

TABLE 9.1 summarizes the four levels of protein structure, using hemoglobin as an example. The key thing to note is that protein structure is hierarchical. Quaternary structure is based on tertiary structure, which is based in part on secondary

(a) Cro protein, a dimer

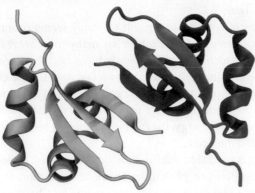

(b) Hemoglobin, a tetramer

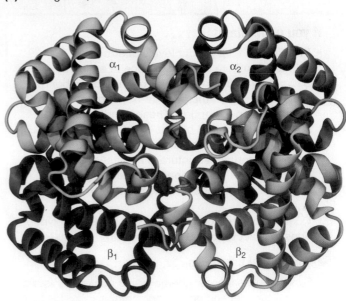

FIGURE 9.12 Quaternary Structures of Proteins Are Created by Multiple Polypeptides. These diagrams represent primary sequences as ribbons. **(a)** The Cro protein is a dimer—it consists of two polypeptide subunits, colored light and dark green. The subunits are identical in this case. **(b)** Hemoglobin is a tetramer—it consists of four polypeptide subunits. The α subunits (light and dark green) are identical; so are the β subunits (light and dark blue).

structure. All three of the higher-level structures are based on primary structure.

The summary table and preceding discussion convey three important messages:

1. The combination of primary, secondary, tertiary, and quaternary levels of structure is responsible for the fantastic diversity of sizes and shapes observed in proteins.

2. Protein folding is directed by the sequence of amino acids present in the primary structure.

3. Most elements of protein structure are based on folding of polypeptide chains.

Does protein folding occur spontaneously? What happens to the function of a protein if normal folding is disrupted? Let's use these questions as a guide to dig deeper into how proteins fold.

SUMMARY TABLE 9.1 Protein Structure

Level	Description	Stabilized by	Example: Hemoglobin
Primary	The sequence of amino acids in a polypeptide	Peptide bonds	Gly — Ser — Asp — Cys
Secondary	Formation of α-helices and β-pleated sheets in a polypeptide	Hydrogen bonding between groups along the peptide-bonded backbone; thus, depends on primary structure	One α-helix
Tertiary	Overall three-dimensional shape of a polypeptide (includes contribution from secondary structures)	Bonds and other interactions between R-groups, or between R-groups and the peptide-bonded backbone; thus, depends on primary structure	One of hemoglobin's subunits
Quaternary	Shape produced by combinations of polypeptides (thus, combinations of tertiary structures)	Bonds and other interactions between R-groups, and between peptide backbones of different polypeptides; thus, depends on primary structure	Hemoglobin consists of four polypeptide subunits

If you understand that . . .

- Proteins have up to four levels of structure.
- Primary structure is the sequence of amino acids.
- Secondary structure results from hydrogen bonds between atoms in the peptide-bonded backbone of the same polypeptide. These bonds produce structures such as α-helices and β-pleated sheets.
- Tertiary structure is the overall shape of a polypeptide. Most tertiary structure is a consequence of bonds or other interactions between R-groups or between R-groups and the peptide-bonded backbone.
- Quaternary structure occurs when multiple polypeptides interact to form a single protein.

✔ **You should be able to . . .**

1. Explain how secondary, tertiary, and quaternary levels of structure depend on primary structure.

2. **QUANTITATIVE** Calculate the number of different primary sequences that could be generated by randomly assembling amino acids into peptides that are five residues long.

Answers are available in Appendix A.

9.3 Folding and Function

If you were able to synthesize one of the polypeptides in hemoglobin from individual amino acids, and you then placed the resulting chain in an aqueous solution, it would spontaneously fold into the shape of the tertiary structure shown in Table 9.1.

In terms of entropy, this result probably seems counterintuitive. Because an unfolded protein has many more ways to move about, it has much higher entropy than the folded version. Folding *does* tend to be spontaneous, however, because the chemical bonds, hydrophobic interactions, and van der Waals forces that occur release enough energy to overcome the decrease in entropy. In terms of energy, the folded molecule is more stable than the unfolded molecule.

Folding is crucial to the function of a completed protein. This relationship between protein structure and function was hammered home in a set of classic experiments by Christian Anfinsen and colleagues during the 1950s.

Normal Folding Is Crucial to Function

Anfinsen studied a protein called ribonuclease that is found in many organisms. Ribonuclease is an enzyme that cleaves ribonucleic acid polymers. Anfinsen found that ribonuclease could be unfolded, or **denatured**, by treating it with compounds that break hydrogen bonds and disulfide bonds. The denatured ribonuclease was unable to function normally—it could no longer break apart nucleic acids (**FIGURE 9.13**).

When the denaturing agents were removed, however, the molecule refolded and began to function normally again. These experiments confirmed that ribonuclease folds spontaneously and that folding is essential for normal function.

More recent work has shown that in cells, folding is often facilitated by specific proteins called **molecular chaperones.** Many molecular chaperones belong to a family of molecules called the heat-shock proteins. Heat-shock proteins are produced in large quantities after cells experience high temperatures or other

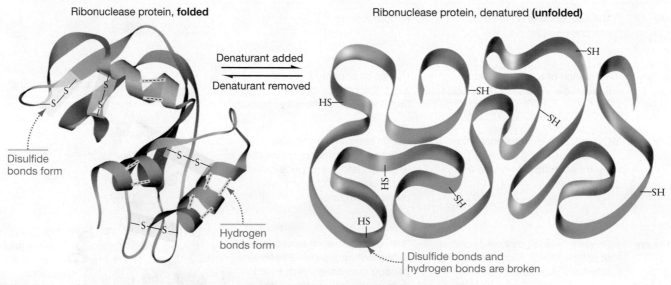

FIGURE 9.13 Protein Structure Determines Function. (left) Ribonuclease is functional when properly folded via hydrogen and disulfide bonds. **(right)** When the disulfide and various noncovalent bonds are broken, ribonuclease is no longer able to function. The double arrow indicates that this process is reversible.

treatments that make other proteins lose their tertiary structure. Heat-shock proteins recognize denatured proteins by binding to hydrophobic patches that would not normally be exposed in properly folded proteins. This interaction blocks inappropriate interactions with other molecules and allows the proteins to refold.

So what is the "normal shape" of a protein? Is only one shape possible for each protein, or could there be several different folded shapes with only one serving as the functional form?

Protein Shape Is Flexible

Although each protein has a characteristic folded shape that is necessary for its function, most proteins are flexible and dynamic, not rigid and static. As it turns out, many polypeptides are unable to fold into their active shape on their own. Over half of the proteins that have been analyzed to date have been found to contain disordered regions lacking any apparent structure. These proteins exist in an assortment of shapes. Only when they interact with particular ions or molecules, or are chemically modified, will they adopt the shape, or conformation, that allows them to perform their function in the cell.

Protein Folding Is Often Regulated Since the function of a protein is dependent on its shape, controlling when or where it is folded will regulate the protein's activity.

For example, proteins involved in cell signaling are often regulated by controlling their shape. The inactive form of calmodulin—a protein that helps maintain normal blood pressure—has a disordered shape. When the concentration of calcium ions increases in the cell, calmodulin binds these ions, folds into an ordered, active conformation, and sends a signal to increase the diameter of blood vessels. **FIGURE 9.14** illustrates the major shape change that is induced in calmodulin when it binds to calcium.

Misfolding Can Be "Infectious" In 1982, Stanley Prusiner published what may be the most surprising result to emerge from research on protein folding: Certain proteins can be folded into infectious, disease-causing agents. These proteins are called **prions** (pronounced *PREE-ons*), or proteinaceous infectious particles.

Infectious prions are alternate forms of normal proteins that are present in healthy individuals. The infectious and normal forms do not necessarily differ in amino acid sequence, but their *shapes* are radically different. The infectious form propagates by inducing conformational changes in normal proteins that cause them to adopt the alternate, infectious shape.

FIGURE 9.15 illustrates the differences in shape observed between the normal and infectious forms of the prion responsible for "mad cow disease" in cattle. The molecule in Figure 9.15a is called the prion protein (PrP) and is a normal component of mammalian cells. The improperly folded version of this protein, like the one in Figure 9.15b, represents the infectious form of the prion.

Prions cause a family of diseases known as the spongiform encephalopathies—literally, "sponge-brain-illnesses." Sheep, cows, goats, and humans afflicted with these diseases undergo massive degeneration of the brain. Although some spongiform encephalopathies

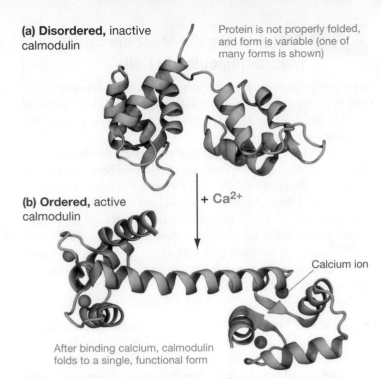

(a) Disordered, inactive calmodulin

Protein is not properly folded, and form is variable (one of many forms is shown)

(b) Ordered, active calmodulin

+ Ca²⁺

Calcium ion

After binding calcium, calmodulin folds to a single, functional form

FIGURE 9.14 Calmodulin Requires Calcium to Fold Properly. Many proteins, like calmodulin, do not complete their folding until after interacting with ions or other molecules. Once calmodulin binds to calcium, it assumes its functional shape.

can be inherited, in many cases the disease is transmitted when individuals eat tissues containing the infectious form of PrP. All the prion illnesses are fatal.

Prions are a particularly dramatic example of how a protein's function depends on its shape as well as how the final shape of a protein depends on folding.

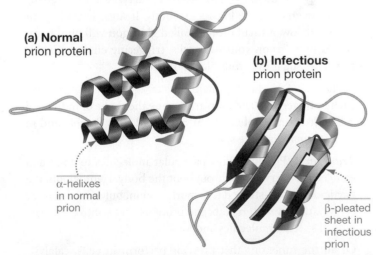

(a) Normal prion protein

(b) Infectious prion protein

α-helixes in normal prion

β-pleated sheet in infectious prion

FIGURE 9.15 Prion Infectivity Is Linked to Structure. Ribbon model of **(a)** a normal, noninfectious prion protein; and **(b)** the infectious form that causes mad cow disease in cattle. Secondary structure is represented by coils (α-helices) and arrows (β-pleated sheets).

9.4 Proteins Are the Most Versatile Macromolecules in Cells

As a group, proteins perform more types of cell functions than any other type of molecule does. It makes sense to hypothesize that life began with proteins, simply because proteins are so vital to the life of today's cells.

Consider the red blood cells that are moving through your arteries right now. Each of these cells contains about 300 million copies of hemoglobin. Hemoglobin carries oxygen from your lungs to cells throughout the body. But every red blood cell also has thousands of copies of a protein called carbonic anhydrase, which is important for moving carbon dioxide from cells back to the lungs, where it can be breathed out. Other proteins form the cell's internal "skeleton" or reside on the cell's membrane to interact with neighboring cells.

Proteins are crucial to most tasks required for cells to exist:

- **Catalysis** Many proteins are specialized to **catalyze,** or speed up, chemical reactions. A protein that functions as a catalyst is called an **enzyme.** The carbonic anhydrase molecules in red blood cells are catalysts. So is the protein called salivary amylase, found in your mouth. Salivary amylase helps begin the digestion of starch and other complex carbohydrates into simple sugars. Most chemical reactions that make life possible depend on enzymes.

- **Defense** Proteins called antibodies and complement proteins attack and destroy viruses and bacteria that cause disease.

- **Movement** Motor proteins and contractile proteins are responsible for moving the cell itself, or for moving large molecules and other types of cargo inside the cell. As you turn this page, for example, specialized proteins called actin and myosin will slide past one another to flex or extend muscle cells in your fingers and arm.

- **Signaling** Proteins are involved in carrying and receiving signals from cell to cell inside the body. If sugar levels in your blood are low, a small protein called glucagon will bind to receptor proteins on your liver cells, triggering enzymes inside to release sugar into your bloodstream.

- **Structure** Structural proteins make up body components such as fingernails and hair, and define the shape of individual cells. Structural proteins keep red blood cells flexible and in their normal disc-like shape.

- **Transport** Proteins allow particular molecules to enter and exit cells or carry them throughout the body. Hemoglobin is a particularly well-studied transport protein, but virtually every cell is studded with membrane proteins that control the passage of specific molecules and ions.

Of all the functions that proteins perform in cells, catalysis may be the most important. The reason is speed. Life, at its most basic level, consists of chemical reactions. But most don't occur fast enough to support life unless a catalyst is present. Enzymes are the most effective catalysts on Earth. Why is this so?

Why Are Enzymes Good Catalysts?

Part of the reason enzymes are such effective catalysts is that they bring reactant molecules—called **substrates**—together in a precise orientation so the atoms involved in the reaction can interact.

The initial hypothesis for how enzymes work was proposed by Emil Fischer in 1894. According to Fischer's "lock-and-key" model, enzymes are analogous to a lock and the keys are substrates that fit into the lock and then react.

Several important ideas in this model have stood the test of time. For example, Fischer was correct in proposing that enzymes bring substrates together in a precise orientation that makes reactions more likely. His model also accurately explained why most enzymes catalyze one specific reaction effectively. Enzyme specificity is a product of the geometry and types of functional groups in the sites where substrates bind.

As researchers began to test Fischer's model, the location where substrates bind and react became known as the enzyme's **active site.** The active site is where catalysis actually occurs.

When techniques for solving the three-dimensional structure of enzymes became available, the active sites were identified as clefts or cavities within the globular shapes. The digestive enzyme trypsin, which is at work in your body now, is a good example. As **FIGURE 9.16** shows, the active site in trypsin is a small notch that contains three key amino acid residues with functional groups that catalyze the cleavage of peptide bonds in other proteins. No other class of macromolecule can match proteins for their catalytic potential. The variety of reactive functional groups present in amino acids is much better suited for this activity than those found in nucleotides or sugars.

The role of enzymes in catalyzing reactions is discussed in more detail in the next unit (see Chapter 8). There you will see that Fischer's model had to be modified as research on enzyme action progressed.

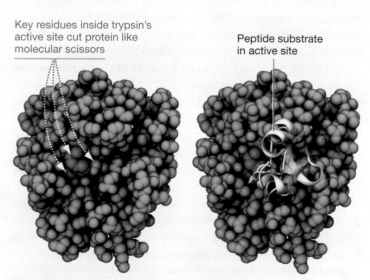

Key residues inside trypsin's active site cut protein like molecular scissors

Peptide substrate in active site

FIGURE 9.16 Substrates Bind to a Specific Location in an Enzyme Called the Active Site. The active site in trypsin, as in many enzymes, is a cleft that contains key amino acid residues that bind substrates and catalyze a reaction.

Was the First Living Entity a Protein Catalyst?

Several observations in the preceding sections could argue that a protein was the first molecule capable of replication. Experimental studies have shown that amino acids were likely abundant during chemical evolution, and that they could have polymerized to form small proteins. In addition, proteins are the most efficient catalysts known.

To date, however, attempts to simulate the origin of life with proteins have not been successful. The only experimental glimpse of a protein's potential to replicate involved an enzyme that could link two oligopeptides together to form a functional duplicate of itself. However, this result required a high concentration of preformed, specific oligopeptides that would not have been present during chemical evolution.

Although it is too early to arrive at definitive conclusions, most origin-of-life researchers are increasingly skeptical that life began with a protein. Their reasoning is that to make a copy of something, a mold or template is required. Proteins cannot furnish this information. Nucleic acids, in contrast, *can*. How they do so is the subject of the next chapter.

CHAPTER 9 REVIEW

If you understand . . .

9.1 Amino Acids and Their Polymerization

- Amino acids have a central carbon bonded to an amino group, a hydrogen atom, a carboxyl group, and an R-group.
- The structure of the R-group affects the chemical reactivity and solubility of the amino acid.
- In proteins, amino acids are joined by a peptide bond between the carboxyl group of one amino acid and the amino group of another amino acid.

✔ You should be able to explain how you could use the structural formula of an amino acid to determine if it is acidic, basic, uncharged polar, or nonpolar.

9.2 What Do Proteins Look Like?

- A protein's primary structure, or sequence of amino acids, is responsible for most of its chemical properties.
- Interactions that take place between C=O and N−H groups in the same peptide-bonded backbone create secondary structures, which are stabilized primarily by hydrogen bonding.
- Tertiary structure results from interactions between R-groups—or R-groups and the peptide-bonded backbone—that stabilize a folded protein into a characteristic overall shape.
- In many cases, a complete protein consists of several different polypeptides, bonded together. The combination of polypeptides represents the protein's quaternary structure.

✔ You should be able to predict where nonpolar amino acid residues would be found in a globular protein, such as the trypsin molecule shown in Figure 9.8c.

9.3 Folding and Function

- Protein folding is a spontaneous process.
- A protein's normal folded shape is essential to its function.
- Many proteins must first bind to other molecules or ions before they can adopt their active conformation.
- Improperly folded proteins can be detrimental to life, and certain proteins even cause deadly infectious diseases.

✔ You should be able to identify one way in which the process of folding in calmodulin and infectious prions is similar.

9.4 Proteins Are the Most Versatile Macromolecules in Cells

- In organisms, proteins function in catalysis, defense, movement, signaling, structural support, and transport of materials.
- Proteins can have diverse functions in cells because they have such diverse structures and chemical properties.
- Catalysis takes place at the enzyme's active site, which has unique chemical properties and a distinctive size and shape.

✔ You should be able to provide the characteristics of proteins that make them especially useful for the following cellular activities: catalysis, defense, and signaling.

You should be able to . . .

✓ TEST YOUR KNOWLEDGE   *Answers are available in Appendix A*

1. What two functional groups are present on every amino acid?
   a. a carbonyl (C=O) group and a carboxyl group
   b. an N–H group and a carbonyl group
   c. an amino group and a hydroxyl group
   d. an amino group and a carboxyl group

2. Twenty different amino acids are found in the proteins of cells. What distinguishes these molecules?

3. By convention, biologists write the sequence of amino acids in a polypeptide in which direction?
   a. carboxy- to amino-terminus
   b. amino- to carboxy-terminus
   c. polar residues to nonpolar residues
   d. charged residues to uncharged residues

4. In a polypeptide, what bonds are responsible for the secondary structure called an α-helix?
   a. peptide bonds
   b. hydrogen bonds that form between the core C=O and N−H groups on different residues
   c. hydrogen bonds and other interactions between side chains
   d. disulfide bonds that form between cysteine residues

5. Where is the information stored that directs different polypeptides to fold into different shapes?

6. What is an active site?
   a. the position in an enzyme where substrates bind
   b. the place where a molecule or ion binds to a protein to induce a shape change
   c. the portion of a motor protein that is involved in moving cargo in a cell
   d. the site on an antibody where it binds to bacterial cells or viruses

✓ TEST YOUR UNDERSTANDING   *Answers are available in Appendix A*

7. Explain how water participates in the development of the interactions that glue nonpolar amino acids together in the interior of globular proteins.

8. If amino acids were mixed together in a solution, resembling the prebiotic soup, would they spontaneously polymerize into polypeptides? Why or why not?

9. Provide an example of how a specific shape of a protein is correlated with its function.

10. A major theme in this chapter is that the structure of molecules correlates with their function. Use this theme to explain why proteins can perform so many different functions in organisms and why enzymes are such effective catalysts.

11. Why are proteins not considered to be a good candidate for the first living molecule?
    a. Their catalytic capability is insufficient.
    b. Their amino acid monomers were likely not present during chemical evolution.
    c. They cannot serve as a template for replication.
    d. They could not have polymerized on their own from amino acids during chemical evolution.

12. If proteins folded only into rigid, inflexible structures, how might this affect the cell's ability to regulate protein function?

✓ TEST YOUR PROBLEM-SOLVING SKILLS   *Answers are available in Appendix A*

13. Based on what you know of the peptide bonds that link together amino acid residues, why would proline's side chain reduce the flexibility of the backbone?

14. Make a concept map (see **BioSkills 15** in Appendix B) that relates the four levels of protein structure and shows how they can contribute to the formation of an active site. Your map should include the following boxed terms: Primary structure, Secondary structure, Tertiary structure, Quaternary structure, Active site, Amino acid sequence, R-groups, Helices and sheets, 3-D shape.

15. Proteins that interact with DNA often interact with the phosphates that are part of this molecule. Which of the following types of amino acids would you predict to be present in the DNA binding sites of these proteins?
    a. acidic amino acids
    b. basic amino acids
    c. uncharged polar amino acids
    d. nonpolar amino acids

16. Some prion-associated diseases are inherited, such as fatal familial insomnia. What is likely to be different between the infectious forms of these inherited prions compared to those that arise via transmission from one animal to another?

CHAPTER 10

Energy and Enzymes: An Introduction to Metabolic Pathways

10 Energy and Enzymes: An Introduction to Metabolic Pathways

In this chapter you will learn how

Enzymes use energy to drive the chemistry of life

looking at energy, asking

> **What happens to energy in chemical reactions?** 10.1

> **Can chemical energy drive nonspontaneous reactions?** 10.2

looking at enzymes, asking

> **How do enzymes help speed chemical reaction rates?** 10.3

> **What factors affect enzyme function?** 10.4

> **How do enzymes work together in metabolic pathways?** 10.5

When table sugar is heated in the presence of oxygen, it undergoes the uncontrolled oxidation reaction known as burning. The heat energy in the flame is released as electrons are transferred from sugar to oxygen. Cells use the energy released from this type of reaction to drive the energy-demanding processes required for life.

This chapter is part of the Big Picture. See how on pages 284–285.

Cells are dynamic. Vesicles move cargo from the Golgi apparatus to the plasma membrane and other destinations, enzymes catalyze the synthesis of a complex array of macromolecules, and millions of proteins transport ions and molecules across cellular membranes. These activities change constantly in response to signals from other cells or the environment.

What drives all this action? The answer is twofold—energy and enzymes. Because staying alive takes work, there is no life without energy. Life, at its most basic level, consists of chemical reactions catalyzed by enzymes. By using enzymes to direct which reactions occur and which do not, life possesses the distinguishing feature of creating order from a naturally disordered environment.

✔ When you see this checkmark, stop and test yourself. Answers are available in Appendix A.

This chapter is about how enzymes work to help cells acquire and use energy. It is also your introduction to metabolic pathways—the ordered series of chemical reactions that build up or break down a particular molecule.

Let's begin by reviewing some fundamental concepts about energy and how it is used in cells.

10.1 What Happens to Energy in Chemical Reactions?

When biologists consider energy in chemical reactions, they often use the term **free energy** to describe the amount of energy that is available to do work. Recall that two types of energy exist: kinetic energy or potential energy (Appendix D). **Kinetic energy** is energy of motion. There are several different forms of kinetic energy—at the molecular level, the energy of motion is called thermal energy. **Potential energy** is energy that is associated with position or configuration. In molecules, this is referred to as chemical energy and is stored in the position of electrons.

Chemical Reactions Involve Energy Transformations

The existence of two types of energy does not mean that energy is locked into either the kinetic or the potential type. Energy is often transformed from one type to the other. To drive this point home, consider a water molecule sitting at the top of a waterfall, as in **FIGURE 10.1**.

Step 1 The molecule has potential energy (E_p) because of its position.

Step 2 As the molecule passes over the waterfall, its potential energy is converted to the kinetic energy (E_k) of motion.

Step 3 When the molecule reaches the rocks below, it undergoes a change in potential energy because it has changed position. The difference in potential energy is transformed into an equal amount of kinetic energy that is manifested in a variety of forms: mechanical energy, which tends to break up the rocks; heat (thermal energy), which raises the temperature of the rocks and the water itself; and sound.

The amount of potential energy in an electron is based on its position relative to other electrons and the protons in the nuclei of nearby atoms (see **FIGURE 10.2a** on page 176). If an electron is close to negative charges on other electrons and far from the positive charges in nuclei, it has high potential energy. In general, the potential energy of a molecule is a function of the way its electrons are configured or positioned.

An electron in an outer electron shell is analogous to the water molecule at the top of a waterfall (**FIGURE 10.2b**). If the electron falls to a lower shell, its potential energy is converted to the kinetic energy of motion. After the electron occupies the lower electron shell, it undergoes a change in potential energy. As panel 3 in Figure 10.1b shows, the change in potential energy is transformed

PROCESS: ENERGY TRANSFORMATION IN A WATERFALL

1. Potential energy
A water molecule sitting at the top of a waterfall has a defined amount of potential energy, E_p.

2. Kinetic energy
As the molecule falls, some of this stored energy is converted to kinetic energy (the energy of motion), E_k.

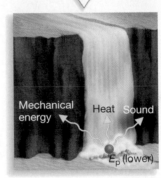

3. Other forms of kinetic energy
When the molecule strikes the rocks below, its energy of motion is converted to thermal, mechanical, and sound energy. The molecule's potential energy is now much lower. The change in potential energy has been transformed into an equal amount of other forms of kinetic energy.

Conclusion: Energy is neither created nor destroyed; it simply changes form.

FIGURE 10.1 Energy Transformations. During an energy transformation, the total amount of energy in the system remains constant.

into an equal amount of kinetic energy—usually thermal energy, but sometimes light.

These examples illustrate the **first law of thermodynamics,** which states that energy is conserved. Energy cannot be created or destroyed, but only transferred and transformed.

The total energy in a molecule is referred to as its **enthalpy** (represented by H). Enthalpy includes the potential energy of the molecule, often referred to as heat content, plus the effect of the molecule on its surroundings in terms of pressure and volume.

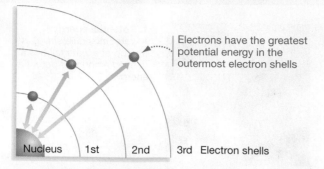

(a) The potential energy of an electron is related to its position.

Electrons have the greatest potential energy in the outermost electron shells

Nucleus   1st   2nd   3rd   Electron shells

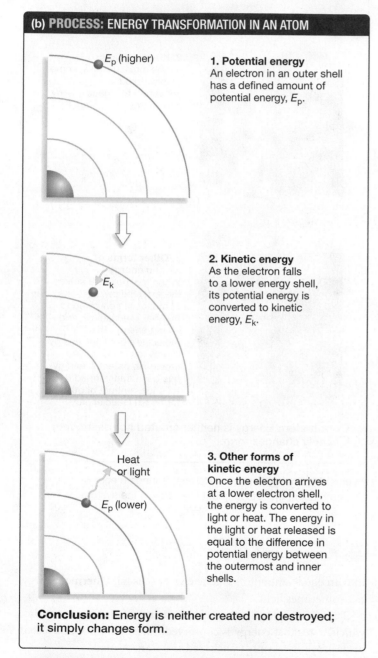

(b) PROCESS: ENERGY TRANSFORMATION IN AN ATOM

E_p (higher)

1. Potential energy
An electron in an outer shell has a defined amount of potential energy, E_p.

E_k

2. Kinetic energy
As the electron falls to a lower energy shell, its potential energy is converted to kinetic energy, E_k.

Heat or light

E_p (lower)

3. Other forms of kinetic energy
Once the electron arrives at a lower electron shell, the energy is converted to light or heat. The energy in the light or heat released is equal to the difference in potential energy between the outermost and inner shells.

Conclusion: Energy is neither created nor destroyed; it simply changes form.

FIGURE 10.2 Chemical energy transformations Potential energy energy stored in atoms or molecules may be transformed into kinetic energy by changes in electron position.

The contributions of heat, pressure, and volume to the enthalpy of a molecule are best understood by observing the changes in enthalpy in a chemical reaction. For example, let's examine the reaction responsible for the explosive bursts of scalding hot liquid a bombardier beetle can produce when provoked, as seen in **FIGURE 10.3**:

$$2\ H_2O_2(aq) \longrightarrow 2\ H_2O(l) + O_2(g)$$

In this reaction, hydrogen peroxide (H_2O_2) is broken down into water and O_2 gas, which expands to over 500 times the original volume of the H_2O_2. Heat given off from the reaction also increases the temperature of the liquid dramatically. These massive increases in temperature and volume generate the pressure that propels the boiling liquid out of an opening at the tip of the beetle's abdomen.

Changes in enthalpy in chemical reactions can be measured and are represented by ΔH. (The uppercase Greek letter delta, Δ, is often used in chemical and mathematical notation to represent change.) The value of ΔH is primarily based on the difference in heat content, since—apart from the reaction in the bombardier beetle—most biological reactions do not result in substantial changes in pressure and volume. When a reaction releases heat energy (products have less potential energy than the reactants), it is **exothermic** and the ΔH is negative. If heat energy is taken up during the reaction, generating products that have higher potential energy than the reactants, the reaction is **endothermic** and ΔH is positive.

Another factor that changes during a chemical reaction is the amount of disorder or **entropy** (symbolized by ΔS). When the products of a chemical reaction become less ordered than the reactant molecules were, entropy increases and ΔS is positive. The **second law of thermodynamics,** in fact, states that total entropy always increases in an isolated system. Keep in mind that the isolated system in this case is the universe, which includes the surroundings as well as the products of the reaction.

To determine whether a chemical reaction is spontaneous, it's necessary to assess the combined contributions of changes in heat and disorder. Chemists do this with a quantity called the **Gibbs free-energy change,** symbolized by ΔG.

$$\Delta G = \Delta H - T\Delta S$$

Here, T stands for temperature measured on the Kelvin scale (see **BioSkills 1**, in Appendix B). Water freezes at 273.15 K and boils at 373.15 K.

In words, the free-energy change in a reaction is equal to the change in enthalpy minus the change in entropy multiplied by the temperature. The $T\Delta S$ term simply means that entropy becomes more important in determining free-energy change as the temperature of the molecules increases. Thermal energy increases the amount of disorder in the system, so the faster molecules are moving, the more important entropy becomes in determining the overall free-energy change.

Chemical reactions are spontaneous when ΔG is less than zero. Such reactions are said to be **exergonic.** Reactions are

FIGURE 10.3 Reactions May Be Explosive due to Changes in Enthalpy. When provoked, the bombardier beetle mixes reactants with enzymes in a special chamber near the tip of its abdomen. The enzyme-catalyzed reaction releases heat energy and oxygen gas. The result is the projection of boiling hot liquid at a predator.

nonspontaneous when ΔG is greater than zero. Such reactions are termed **endergonic.** When ΔG is equal to zero, reactions are at equilibrium. ✔ If you understand these concepts, you should be able to explain (1) why the same reaction can be nonspontaneous at low temperature but spontaneous at high temperature, and (2) why some exothermic reactions are nonspontaneous.

Free energy changes when the potential energy and/or entropy of substances change. Spontaneous chemical reactions run in the direction that lowers the free energy of the system. Exergonic reactions are spontaneous and release energy; endergonic reactions are nonspontaneous and require an input of energy to proceed.

Temperature and Concentration Affect Reaction Rates

Even if a chemical reaction occurs spontaneously, it may not happen quickly. The reactions that convert iron to rust or sugar molecules to carbon dioxide and water are spontaneous, but at room temperature they occur very slowly, if at all.

For most reactions to proceed, one or more chemical bonds have to break and others have to form. For this to happen, the substances involved must collide in a specific orientation that brings the electrons involved near each other. (See Appendix D to review the forces involved in bond formation.)

The number of collisions occurring between the substances in a mixture depends on their temperature and concentration:

- When the concentration of reactants is high, more collisions should occur and reactions should proceed more quickly.

- When their temperature is high, reactants should move faster and collide more frequently.

Higher concentrations and higher temperatures should speed up chemical reactions. To test this hypothesis, students at Parkland College in Champaign, Illinois, performed the experiments shown in **FIGURE 10.4** (see page 178). Pay special attention to the two graphs in the "Results" section:

- *Temperature versus reaction rate* The graph on the left is based on experiments where the concentration of the reactants was the same, but the temperature varied. Each data point represents one experiment. Notice that the points represent a trend that rises from left to right—meaning, in this case, that the reaction rate speeded up when the temperature of the reaction mixture was higher.

- *Concentration versus reaction rate* The graph on the right is based on experiments where the temperature was constant, but the concentration of reactants varied. Each bar represents the average reaction rate over many replicates of each treatment, or set of concentrations. The thin lines at the top of each bar indicate the standard error of the mean—a measure of variability (see **BioSkills 4** in Appendix B). The take-home message of this graph is that reaction rates are higher when reactant concentrations are higher.

The reactions shown in Figure 10.4 were exergonic, meaning that the products had lower free energy than the reactants, so no input of energy was required. But, what drives nonspontaneous, endergonic reactions? Let's take a closer look.

10.2 Nonspontaneous Reactions May Be Driven Using Chemical Energy

By definition, endergonic reactions require an input of energy to proceed. Recall that radiation from the Sun and electricity from lightning could have driven nonspontaneous reactions during

QUESTION: Do chemical reaction rates increase with increased temperature and concentration?

RATE INCREASE HYPOTHESIS: Chemical reaction rates increase with increased temperature. They also increase with increased concentration of reactants.

NULL HYPOTHESIS: Chemical reaction rates are not affected by increases in temperature or concentration of reactants.

EXPERIMENTAL SETUP:

Experimental reaction: $3 HSO_3^- (aq) + IO_3^- (aq) \rightleftharpoons 3 HSO_4^- (aq) + I^- (aq)$

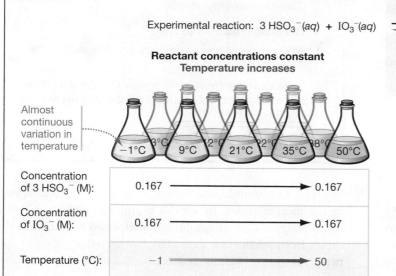

Reactant concentrations constant
Temperature increases

Almost continuous variation in temperature

−1°C 3°C 9°C 12°C 21°C 32°C 35°C 38°C 50°C

Concentration of 3 HSO₃⁻ (M):	0.167 ⟶ 0.167	
Concentration of IO₃⁻ (M):	0.167 ⟶ 0.167	
Temperature (°C):	−1 ⟶ 50	

Reactant concentrations vary
Temperature constant

Treatment 1 Treatment 2 Treatment 3

Many replicates at each concentration

0.167	0.167	0.333
0.167	0.333	0.333
23	23	23

PREDICTION: Reaction rate, measured as 1/(time for reaction to go to completion), will increase with increased concentrations of reactants and increased temperature of reaction mix.

PREDICTION OF NULL HYPOTHESIS: There will be no difference in reaction rates among treatments in each setup.

RESULTS:

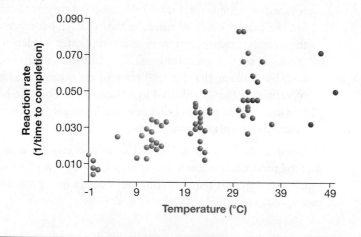

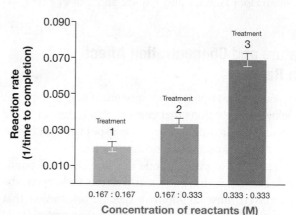

CONCLUSION: Chemical reaction rates increase with increased temperature or concentration.

FIGURE 10.4 Testing the Hypothesis that Reaction Rates Are Sensitive to Changes in Temperature and Concentration.

✔**QUESTION** Use **BioSkills 4** in Appendix B to explain why no error bars are used for the points shown on the graph on the left side of the "Results" section.

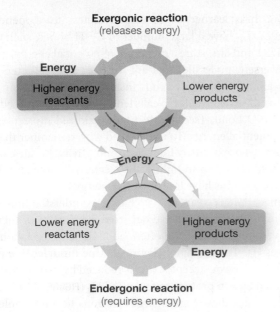

Exergonic reaction
(releases energy)

Energy

Higher energy reactants → Lower energy products

Energy

Lower energy reactants → Higher energy products

Energy

Endergonic reaction
(requires energy)

FIGURE 10.5 **Energetic Coupling Allows Endergonic Reactions to Proceed Using the Energy Released from Exergonic Reactions.**

chemical evolution (Appendix D). What source of energy drives these reactions inside cells?

Exergonic reactions release free energy. **FIGURE 10.5** shows how **energetic coupling** between exergonic and endergonic reactions allows chemical energy released from one reaction to drive another. In cells, this process generally occurs in one of two ways, either through the transfer of high-energy electrons or the transfer of a phosphate group.

Redox Reactions Transfer Energy via Electrons

Chemical reactions that involve the loss or gain of one or more electrons are called **reduction–oxidation reactions,** or **redox reactions.** When an atom or molecule loses one or more electrons, it is oxidized. This makes sense if you notice that the term

oxidized sounds as if oxygen has done something to an atom or molecule. Recall that oxygen is highly electronegative and often pulls electrons from other atoms (Appendix D). On the other hand, when an atom or molecule gains one or more electrons, it is reduced. To keep these terms straight, students often use the mnemonic "OIL RIG"—**Oxidation** *Is* *Loss* of electrons; **Reduction** *Is* *Gain* of electrons.

Oxidation events are always paired with a reduction; if one atom loses an electron, another has to gain it, and vice versa. Since electron position is related to energy levels, redox reactions represent the energetic coupling of two half-reactions, one exergonic and one endergonic. Oxidation is the exergonic half-reaction, and reduction is the endergonic half-reaction. Some of the energy that is lost by the oxidized molecule is used to increase potential energy of the reduced molecule. In cases where more free energy is released by the oxidation step than is necessary for the reduction step, the overall reaction is exergonic.

The gain or loss of an electron can be relative, however. During a redox reaction, an electron can be transferred completely from one atom to another, or an electron can simply shift its position in a covalent bond.

An Example of Redox in Action   To see how redox reactions work, consider the spontaneous reaction that occurs when reduced carbons in glucose ($C_6H_{12}O_6$) are oxidized as the sugar is burned in the presence of oxygen (O_2) (**FIGURE 10.6**). The orange dots in the illustration represent the positions of the electrons involved in covalent bonds.

Now compare the position of the electrons in the first reactant, glucose, with their position in the first product, carbon dioxide. Notice that many of the electrons have moved farther from the carbon nucleus in carbon dioxide. This means that carbon has been oxidized: it has "lost" electrons. The change occurred because the carbon and hydrogen atoms in glucose share electrons equally, while the carbon and oxygen atoms in CO_2 don't. In CO_2, the high electronegativity of the oxygen atoms pulled electrons away from the carbon atom.

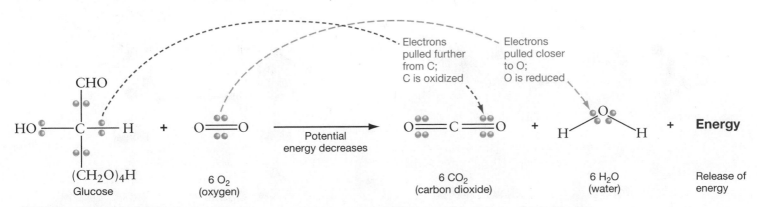

FIGURE 10.6 **Redox Reactions Involve the Gain or Loss of One or More Electrons.** This diagram shows how the position of electrons changes when glucose reacts with oxygen. The carbons of glucose are oxidized while the oxygen atoms of O_2 are reduced.

Energy and Enzymes: An Introduction to Metabolic Pathways

Now compare the position of the electrons in the reactant O_2 molecules with their position in the product water molecules. In water, the electrons have moved closer to the oxygen nuclei than they were in the O_2 molecules, meaning that the oxygen atoms have been reduced. Oxygen has "gained" electrons. Thus, when glucose burns, carbon atoms are oxidized while oxygen atoms are reduced.

These shifts in electron position change the amount of chemical energy in the reactants and products. When glucose reacts with oxygen, electrons are held much tighter in the product molecules than in the reactant molecules. This means their potential energy has decreased. The entropy of the products is also much higher than that of the reactants, as indicated by the increase in the number of molecules. As a result, this reaction is exergonic. It releases energy in the form of heat and light.

Another Approach to Understanding Redox During the redox reactions that occur in cells, electrons (e^-) may also be transferred from an atom in one molecule, called the **electron donor**, to an atom in a different molecule, the **electron acceptor**. When this occurs, the electron may be accompanied by a proton (H^+), which would result in the addition of a neutral hydrogen (H) atom to the electron acceptor.

Molecules that obtain hydrogens via redox reactions tend to gain potential energy because the electrons in C−H bonds are equally shared and hence relatively far from the positive charges on the C and H nuclei. This observation should sound familiar, from what you have learned about carbohydrates (see Appendix E). Molecules that have a large number of C−H bonds, such as carbohydrates and fats, store a great deal of potential energy.

Conversely, molecules that are oxidized in cells often lose a proton along with an electron. Instead of having many C−H bonds, oxidized molecules in cells tend to have an increased number of C−O bonds (see Figure 10.6). Oxidized molecules tend to lose potential energy. To understand why, remember that oxygen atoms have extremely high electronegativity. Because oxygen atoms hold electrons so tightly, the electrons involved in bonds with oxygen atoms have low potential energy.

In many redox reactions in biology, understanding where oxidation and reduction have occurred is a matter of following hydrogen atoms—reduction often "adds Hs" and oxidation often "removes Hs." For example, **flavin adenine dinucleotide (FAD)** is a cellular electron acceptor that is reduced by two electrons accompanied by two protons to form $FADH_2$ (**FIGURE 10.7a**). $FADH_2$ readily donates these high-energy electrons to other molecules. As a result, it is called an **electron carrier** and is said to have "reducing power."

Another common electron carrier is **nicotinamide adenine dinucleotide (NAD^+)**, which is reduced to form **NADH**. Like FAD, two electrons reduce NAD^+. These two carriers differ, however, in the number of hydrogen atoms transferred. NAD^+ acquires only one of the two hydrogens and releases the second into the environment as H^+ (**FIGURE 10.7b**).

(a) Flavin adenine dinucleotide

$$AH_2 + FAD \longrightarrow A + FADH_2$$

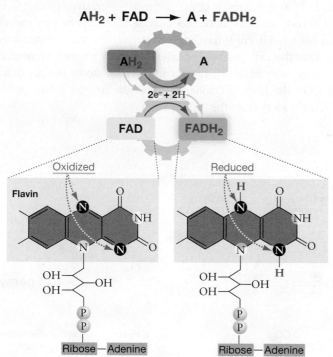

(b) Nicotinamide adenine dinucleotide

$$BH_2 + NAD^+ \longrightarrow B + NADH + H^+$$

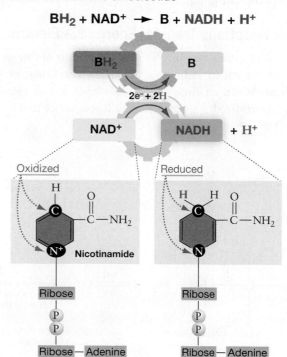

FIGURE 10.7 Redox Reactions May Transfer Protons Along with Electrons. The potential energy of NAD^+ and FAD is increased by redox reactions that transfer high-energy electrons, which may or may not be accompanied by protons. The products $FADH_2$ and NADH are important electron carriers.

The two examples in Figure 10.6 illustrate an important point—all redox reactions involve the transfer of electrons, but they do not always involve the transfer of hydrogens. Redox reactions are central in biology—they transfer energy via electrons. The energy released from certain key redox reactions (see Chapters 13 and 14) is used to drive the endergonic formation of the nucleotide ATP from ADP and P_i. How is the energy stored in ATP used by the cell?

ATP Transfers Energy via Phosphate Groups

Adenosine triphosphate (ATP) (introduced in Chapter 4) makes things happen in cells because it has a great deal of potential energy. As **FIGURE 10.8a** shows, four negative charges are confined to a small area in the three phosphate groups in ATP. In part because these negative charges repel each other, the potential energy of the electrons in the phosphate groups is extraordinarily high.

ATP Hydrolysis Releases Free Energy When ATP reacts with water during a hydrolysis reaction, the bond between ATP's outermost phosphate group and its neighbor is broken, resulting in the formation of ADP and inorganic phosphate, P_i, which has the formula $H_2PO_4^-$ (**FIGURE 10.8b**). This reaction is highly exergonic. Under standard conditions of temperature and pressure in the laboratory, a total of 7.3 kilocalories of energy per mole of ATP (or 7.3 kcal/mol), is released during the reaction. A **kilocalorie (kcal)** of energy raises 1 kilogram (kg) of water 1°C.

ATP hydrolysis is exergonic because the entropy of the product molecules is higher than that of the reactants, and because there is a large drop in potential energy when ATP breaks down into ADP and P_i. The change in potential energy occurs in part because the electrons from ATP's phosphate groups are now spread across two molecules instead of being clustered on one molecule—meaning that there is now less electrical repulsion.

In addition, the destabilizing effect of the negative charges is reduced in ADP and P_i since these products interact with the partial positive charges on surrounding water molecules more efficiently than the clustered negative charges on ATP did.

How Does ATP Drive Endergonic Reactions? In the time it takes to read this sentence, millions of endergonic reactions have occurred in your cells. This chemical activity is possible, in part, because cells are able to use the energy released from the exergonic hydrolysis of ATP.

If the reaction diagrammed in Figure 10.8b occurred in a test tube, the energy released would be lost as heat. But cells don't lose that 7.3 kcal/mole as heat. Instead, they use it to make things happen. Specifically, the energy that is released when ATP is hydrolyzed may be used to transfer the cleaved phosphate to a target molecule, called a **substrate.**

The addition of a phosphate group to a substrate is called **phosphorylation.** When ATP is used as the phosphate donor, phosphorylation is exergonic because the electrons in ADP and the phosphate added to the substrate have much less potential energy than they did in ATP.

To see how this process works, consider an endergonic reaction between two reactant molecules—compound A and compound B—that results in a product AB needed by your cells. For this reaction to proceed, an input of energy is required.

When a phosphate group from ATP is added to one or both of the reactant molecules, the potential energy of the reactant is increased. This phosphorylated intermediate is referred to as an activated substrate. This is the critical point: Activated substrates have high enough potential energy that the reaction between compound A and, for example, the activated form of compound B is now exergonic. The two compounds then go on to react and form the product molecule AB.

(a) ATP stores a large amount of potential energy.

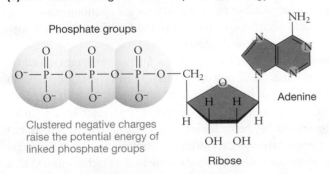

Phosphate groups

Adenine

Ribose

Clustered negative charges raise the potential energy of linked phosphate groups

FIGURE 10.8 Adenosine Triphosphate (ATP) Has High Potential Energy. (a) ATP's high potential energy results, in part, from the four negative charges clustered in its three phosphate groups. The negative charges repel each other, raising the potential energy of the electrons. **(b)** When ATP is hydrolyzed to ADP and inorganic phosphate, a large free-energy change occurs.

(b) Energy is released when ATP is hydrolyzed.

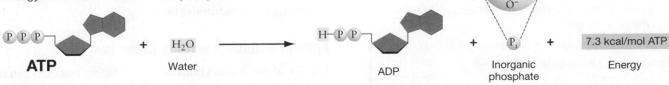

ATP   + H_2O ⟶   ADP   + P_i +   7.3 kcal/mol ATP

Water   Inorganic phosphate   Energy

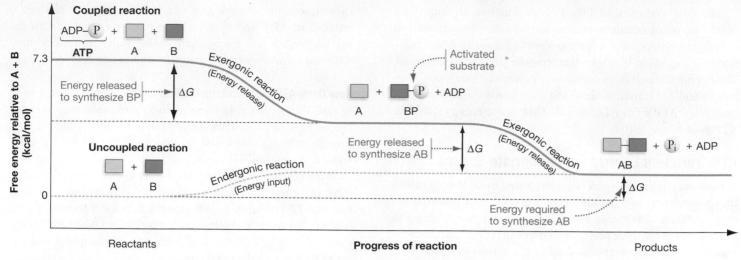

FIGURE 10.9 Exergonic Phosphorylation Reactions Are Coupled to Endergonic Reactions. In cells, many reactions only occur if one reactant is activated by phosphorylation. The phosphorylated reactant molecule has high enough free energy that the subsequent reaction is exergonic. In this graph, the free energy being tracked on the *y*-axis represents A, B, and the 7.3 kcal/mol that is released when ATP is hydrolyzed. For simplicity, the free energy in ADP and P_i is not shown. ΔG represents the change in free energy between the reactants and products for each indicated step.

✔ **EXERCISE** Label the ΔG in the uncoupled reaction and the two steps of the coupled reaction to indicate if the change is representing a positive (> 0) or negative (< 0) value.

FIGURE 10.9 graphs how phosphorylation can couple exergonic and endergonic reactions. Note that the reaction between A and B to produce the product AB is endergonic—the ΔG is positive. But after the exergonic transfer of a phosphate group from ATP to B occurs, the free energy of the reactants A and BP is high enough to make the reaction that forms AB exergonic. When reactant molecules in an endergonic reaction are phosphorylated, the free energy released during phosphorylation is coupled to the endergonic reaction to make the combined overall reaction exergonic.

✔ If you understand the principles of energetic coupling, you should be able to compare and contrast how energy is transferred via redox reactions and ATP hydrolysis.

It is hard to overstate the importance of energetic coupling: Without it, life is impossible. If the cells in your body could no longer drive endergonic reactions by coupling them to exergonic reactions, you would die within minutes.

Now the question is, What role do enzymes play in these reactions?

10.3 How Enzymes Work

Regardless of whether reactions in cells are spontaneous or not, none would occur at the speed required for life without the support of enzymes. How do they do it?

Recall that the initial hypothesis for how enzymes speed up reactions—the "lock-and-key" model—was first proposed in 1894 by Emil Fischer (introduced in Chapter 9). In this model, the substrates would fit into enzymes and react in a manner analogous to a key being inserted into a lock. In other words, enzymes are **catalysts**—they bring substrates together in a precise orientation that makes reactions more likely. Fischer's model also explained why many enzymes are specific for a single reaction—specificity is a product of the geometry and chemical properties of the sites where substrates bind.

Enzymes Help Reactions Clear Two Hurdles

Recall that two hurdles must be cleared before reactions can take place: Reactants need to **(1)** collide in a precise orientation and

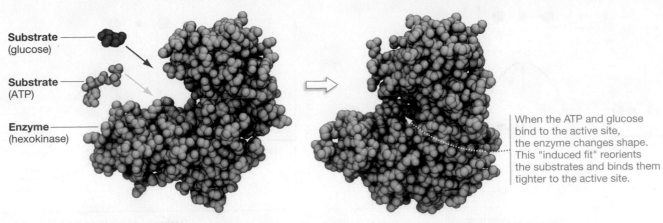

Substrate (glucose)

Substrate (ATP)

Enzyme (hexokinase)

When the ATP and glucose bind to the active site, the enzyme changes shape. This "induced fit" reorients the substrates and binds them tighter to the active site.

FIGURE 10.10 Reactant Molecules Bind to Specific Locations in an Enzyme. The reactant molecules, shown in red and yellow, fit into a precise location, called the active site, in the green enzyme. In this enzyme and in many others, the binding event causes the protein to change shape.

(2) have enough kinetic energy to overcome repulsion between electrons that come into contact as a bond forms (Appendix D). To appreciate how enzymes work, let's consider each hurdle in turn.

Enzymes Bring Substrates Together

Part of the reason enzymes are such effective catalysts is that they bring substrate molecules together in a substrate binding site known as the enzyme's **active site** (Chapter 9). In this way, enzymes help substrates collide in a precise orientation so that the electrons involved in the reaction can interact.

Enzymes generally are very large relative to substrates and roughly globular. The active site is in a cleft or cavity within the globular shape. A good example can be seen in the enzyme glucokinase, which catalyzes the phosphorylation of the sugar glucose. (Many enzymes have names that hint at the identity of the substrate and end with *-ase*.) As the left side of **FIGURE 10.10** shows, the active site in glucokinase is a small notch in an otherwise large, crescent-shaped enzyme.

In Fischer's original lock-and-key model, enzymes were conceived of as being rigid—almost literally as rigid as a lock. As research on enzyme action progressed, however, Fischer's model had to be modified. Perhaps the most important realization was that enzymes are not rigid and static, but flexible and dynamic. In fact, many enzymes undergo a significant change in shape, or conformation, when reactant molecules bind to the active site. You can see this conformational change, called an **induced fit,** in the glucokinase molecule on the right side of Figure 10.10. Once glucokinase binds its substrates—ATP and glucose—the enzyme rocks forward over the active site to bring the two substrates together.

In addition, recent research has clarified the nature of Fischer's key. When one or more substrate molecules enter the active site, they are held in place through hydrogen bonding or other weak interactions with amino acids in the active site. Once the substrate is bound, one or more R-groups in the active site come into play. The degree of interaction between the substrate and enzyme increases and reaches a maximum when a temporary,

unstable, intermediate condition called the **transition state** is formed. When Fischer's key is in its lock, it represents the transition state of the substrate.

There is more to achieving this transition state than simply an enzyme binding to its substrates, however. Even if the reaction is spontaneous, a certain amount of kinetic energy is required to strain the chemical bonds in substrates so they can achieve this transition state—called the **activation energy.** How do enzymes help clear the activation energy hurdle?

Enzymes Lower the Activation Energy

Reactions happen when reactants have enough kinetic energy to reach the transition state. The kinetic energy of molecules, in turn, is a function of their temperature. (This is why reactions tend to proceed faster at higher temperatures.)

FIGURE 10.11 (see page 184) graphs the changes in free energy that take place during the course of a chemical reaction. As you read along the x-axis from left to right, note that a dramatic rise in free energy occurs when the reactants combine to form the transition state—followed by a dramatic drop in free energy when products form. The free energy of the transition state is high because the bonds that existed in the substrates are destabilized—it is the transition point between breaking old bonds and forming new ones.

The ΔG label on the graph indicates the overall change in free energy in the reaction—that is, the energy of the products minus the energy of the reactants. In this particular case, the products have lower free energy than the reactants, meaning that the reaction is exergonic. But because the activation energy for this reaction, symbolized by E_a, is high, the reaction would proceed slowly—even at high temperature.

This is an important point: The more unstable the transition state, the higher the activation energy and the less likely a reaction is to proceed quickly.

Reaction rates, then, depend on both the kinetic energy of the reactants and the activation energy of the particular reaction—meaning the free energy of the transition state. If the kinetic

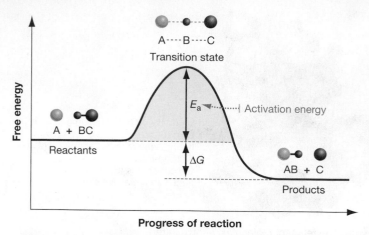

FIGURE 10.11 **Changes in Free Energy during a Chemical Reaction.** The energy profile shows changes in free energy that occur over the course of a hypothetical reaction between a molecule A and a molecule containing parts B and C. The overall reaction would be written as A + BC → AB + C. E_a is the activation energy of the reaction.

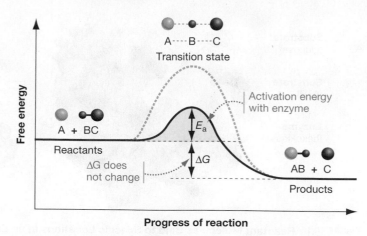

FIGURE 10.12 **A Catalyst Changes the Activation Energy of a Reaction.** The energy profile for the same reaction diagrammed in Figure 10.11, but now with a catalyst present. Even though the energy barrier to the reaction, E_a, is much lower, ΔG does not change.

✔ **QUESTION** Can a catalyst make a nonspontaneous reaction occur spontaneously? Explain why or why not.

energy of the participating molecules is high, such as at high temperatures, then molecular collisions are more likely to overcome the activation energy barrier. At this point, the transition state is formed and the reaction takes place.

Enzymes don't change the temperature of a solution, though. How do they fit in?

Interactions with amino acid R-groups at the enzyme active site stabilize the transition state and thus lower the activation energy required for the reaction to proceed. At the atomic level, R-groups that line the active site may form short-lived covalent bonds that assist with the transfer of atoms or groups of atoms from one reactant to another. More commonly, the presence of acidic or basic R-groups allows the reactants to lose or gain a proton more readily.

FIGURE 10.12 diagrams how enzymes lower the activation energy for a reaction by lowering the free energy of the transition state. Note that the presence of an enzyme does not affect the overall

energy change, ΔG, or change the energy of the reactants or the products. An enzyme changes only the free energy of the transition state.

Most enzymes are specific in their activity—they catalyze just a single reaction by lowering the activation energy that is required—and many are astonishingly efficient. Most of the important reactions in biology would not occur at all, or else proceed at imperceptible rates, without a catalyst. It's not unusual for enzymes to speed up reactions by a factor of a million; some enzymes make reactions go many *trillions* of times faster than they would without a catalyst.

It's also important to note that an enzyme is not consumed in a chemical reaction, even though it participates in the reaction. The composition of an enzyme is exactly the same after the reaction as it was before.

Enzyme catalysis can be analyzed as a three-step process. **FIGURE 10.13** summarizes this model:

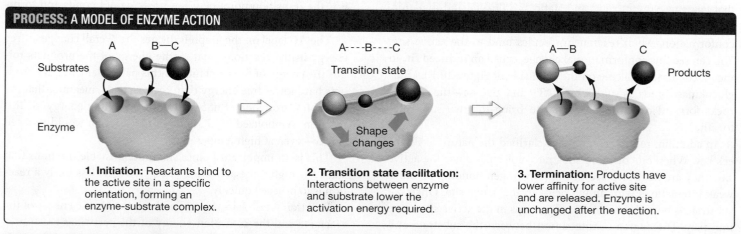

PROCESS: A MODEL OF ENZYME ACTION

1. **Initiation:** Reactants bind to the active site in a specific orientation, forming an enzyme-substrate complex.

2. **Transition state facilitation:** Interactions between enzyme and substrate lower the activation energy required.

3. **Termination:** Products have lower affinity for active site and are released. Enzyme is unchanged after the reaction.

FIGURE 10.13 **Enzyme Action Can Be Analyzed as a Three-Step Process.**

1. **Initiation** Instead of reactants occasionally colliding in a random fashion, enzymes orient reactants precisely as they bind at specific locations within the active site.

2. **Transition state facilitation** Inside a catalyst's active site, reactant molecules are more likely to reach their transition state. In some cases the transition state is stabilized by a change in the enzyme's shape. Interactions between the substrate and R-groups in the enzyme's active site lower the activation energy required for the reaction. Thus, the catalyzed reaction proceeds much more rapidly than the uncatalyzed reaction.

3. **Termination** The reaction products have less affinity for the active site than the transition state does. Binding ends, the enzyme returns to its original conformation, and the products are released.

✔ If you understand the basic principles of enzyme catalysis, you should be able to complete the following sentences: (1) Enzymes speed reaction rates by _____ and lowering activation energy. (2) Activation energies drop because enzymes destabilize bonds in the substrates, forming the _____. (3) Enzyme specificity is a function of the active site's shape and the chemical properties of the _____ at the active site. (4) In enzymes, as in many molecules, function follows from _____.

What Limits the Rate of Catalysis?

For several decades after Fischer's model was published, most research on enzymes focused on rates of enzyme action, or what biologists call enzyme kinetics. Researchers observed that, when the amount of product produced per second—indicating the speed of the reaction—is plotted as a function of substrate concentration, a graph like that shown in **FIGURE 10.14** results.

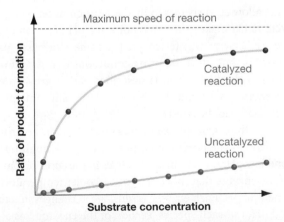

FIGURE 10.14 Enzyme-Catalyzed Reactions Can Be Saturated. At high substrate concentration, enzyme-catalyzed reactions reach a maximum rate. Uncatalyzed reactions slowly increase as substrate concentration increases.

✔**EXERCISE** Label the parts of the *catalyzed reaction curve* that represent where (1) the reaction rate is most sensitive to changes in substrate concentration and (2) most or all of the active sites present are occupied.

In this graph, each data point represents an experiment where reaction rate was measured when substrates were at various concentrations. The two lines represent two series of experiments: one with the reactions catalyzed by an enzyme and the other uncatalyzed. As you read the curve for the catalyzed reaction from left to right, note that it has three basic sections:

1. When substrate concentrations are low, the speed of an enzyme-catalyzed reaction increases in a steep, linear fashion.

2. At intermediate substrate concentrations, the increase in speed begins to slow.

3. At high substrate concentration, the reaction rate plateaus at a maximum speed.

This pattern is in striking contrast to the situation for the uncatalyzed reactions, where the reaction speed is far slower, but tends to show a continuing linear increase with substrate concentration. The "saturation kinetics" of enzyme-catalyzed reactions were taken as strong evidence that the enzyme–substrate complex proposed by Fischer actually exists. The idea was that, at some point, active sites cannot accept substrates any faster, no matter how large the concentration of substrates gets. Stated another way, reaction rates level off because all available enzyme molecules are being used.

Do Enzymes Work Alone?

The answer to this question, in many cases, is no. Atoms or molecules that are not part of an enzyme's primary structure are often required for an enzyme to function normally. These enzyme "helpers" can be divided into three different types:

1. **Cofactors:** Inorganic ions, such as the metal ions Zn^{2+} (zinc), Mg^{2+} (magnesium), and Fe^{2+} (iron), which reversibly interact with enzymes. Cofactors that now participate in key reactions in virtually all living cells are thought to have been involved in catalysis early on in chemical evolution (see Appendix D).

2. **Coenzymes:** Organic molecules that reversibly interact with enzymes, such as the electron carriers NADH or $FADH_2$.

3. **Prosthetic groups:** Non-amino acid atoms or molecules that are permanently attached to proteins, such as the molecule retinal. Retinal is involved in converting light energy into chemical energy.

In many cases, these enzyme helpers are part of the active site and play a key role in stabilizing the transition state. Their presence is therefore essential for the catalytic activity of many enzymes.

To appreciate why this is important, consider that many of the vitamins in your diet are required for the production of coenzymes. Vitamin deficiencies result in coenzyme deficiencies. Lack of coenzymes, in turn, disrupts normal enzyme function and causes disease. For example, thiamine (vitamin B_1) is required for the production of a coenzyme called thiamine pyrophosphate, which is required by three different enzymes. Lack of thiamine in the diet dramatically reduces the activity of these enzymes and causes an array of nervous system and heart disorders collectively known as beriberi.

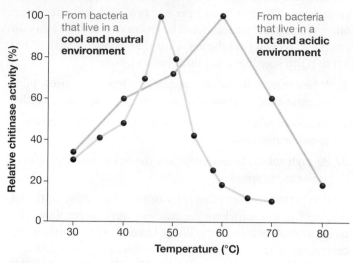

(a) Enzymes from different organisms may function best at different temperatures.

From bacteria that live in a **cool and neutral environment**

From bacteria that live in a **hot and acidic environment**

Relative chitinase activity (%)

Temperature (°C)

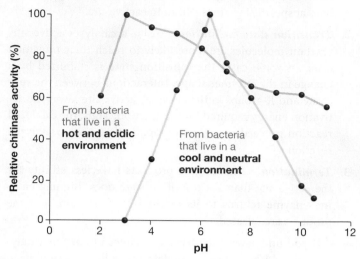

(b) Enzymes from different organisms may function best at different pHs.

From bacteria that live in a **hot and acidic environment**

From bacteria that live in a **cool and neutral environment**

Relative chitinase activity (%)

pH

FIGURE 10.15 Enzymes Have an Optimal Temperature and pH. The activity of enzymes is sensitive to changes in temperature **(a)** and pH **(b)**.

DATA: Nawani, N., B. P. Kapadnis, A. D. Das, et al. 2002. *Journal of Applied Microbiology* 93: 865–975. Also Nawani, N., and B. P. Kapadnis. 2001. *Journal of Applied Microbiology* 90: 803–808.

10.4 What Factors Affect Enzyme Function?

Given that an enzyme's structure is critical to its function, it's not surprising that an enzyme's activity is sensitive to conditions that alter protein shape. Recall that protein structure is dependent on the sequence of amino acids and a variety of chemical bonds and interactions that fold the polypeptide into its functional form (Chapter 9).

In particular, the activity of an enzyme often changes drastically as a function of temperature, pH, interactions with other molecules, and modifications of its primary structure. Let's take a look at how enzyme function is affected by, and sometimes even regulated by, each of these factors.

Enzymes Are Optimized for Particular Environments

Temperature affects the folding and movement of an enzyme as well as the kinetic energy of its substrates. The concentration of protons in a solution, as measured by pH, also affects enzyme structure and function. pH affects the charge on carboxyl and amino groups in residue side chains, and also the active site's ability to participate in reactions that involve the transfer of protons or electrons.

Do data support these assertions? **FIGURE 10.15a** shows how the activity of an enzyme, plotted on the *y*-axis, changes as a function of temperature, plotted on the *x*-axis. These data were collected for an enzyme called chitinase, which is used by bacteria to digest cell walls of fungi. In this graph, each data point represents the enzyme's relative activity—meaning the rate of the enzyme-catalyzed reaction, scaled relative to the highest rate observed—in

experiments conducted under conditions that differed only in temperature. Results are shown for two types of bacteria.

Note that, in both bacterial species, the enzyme has a distinct optimum or peak—a temperature at which it functions best. One of the bacterial species lives in the cool soil under palm trees, where the temperature is about 25°C, while the other lives in hot springs, where temperatures can be close to 100°C. The temperature optimum for the enzyme reflects these environments.

The two types of bacteria have different versions of the enzyme that differ in primary structure. Natural selection (introduced in Chapter 1) has favored a structure in each species that is best suited for its distinct environment. The two versions are adaptations that allow each species to thrive at different temperatures.

FIGURE 10.15b makes the same point for pH. The effect of pH on enzyme activity was tested on the same chitinases used in Figure 10.15a, but this time using conditions that varied only in pH. The soil-dwelling bacteria described earlier grow in a neutral pH environment, but the species that lives in hot springs is also exposed to acidic conditions.

Note that the organism that thrives in a hot, acidic environment has a version of the enzyme that performs best at high temperatures and low pH; the organism that lives in the cool soil has a version of the enzyme that functions best at cooler temperatures and nearly neutral pH. Each enzyme is sensitive to changes in temperature and pH, but each species' version of the enzyme has a structure that allows it to function best in its particular environment.

To summarize, the rate of an enzyme-catalyzed reaction depends not only on substrate concentration and the enzyme's intrinsic affinity for the substrate but also on temperature and pH (among other factors). Temperature affects the movement of the substrates and enzyme; pH affects the enzyme's shape and reactivity.

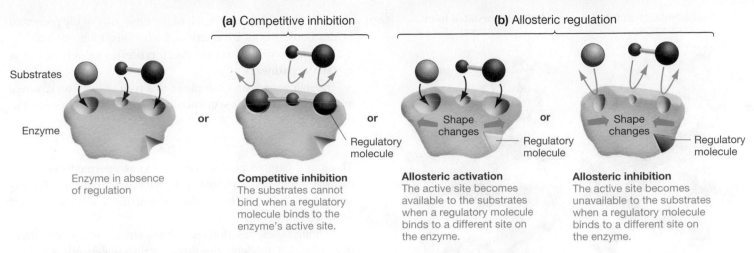

(a) Competitive inhibition

(b) Allosteric regulation

Substrates

Enzyme

Enzyme in absence
of regulation

or

Competitive inhibition
The substrates cannot
bind when a regulatory
molecule binds to the
enzyme's active site.

Regulatory
molecule

or

Shape
changes

Allosteric activation
The active site becomes
available to the substrates
when a regulatory molecule
binds to a different site on
the enzyme.

Regulatory
molecule

or

Shape
changes

Allosteric inhibition
The active site becomes
unavailable to the substrates
when a regulatory molecule
binds to a different site on
the enzyme.

Regulatory
molecule

FIGURE 10.16 An Enzyme's Activity Is Precisely Regulated. Enzymes are turned on or off when specific regulatory
molecules bind to them.

Most Enzymes Are Regulated

Controlling when and where enzymes will function is vital to
the work of a cell. While temperature and pH affect the activity of enzymes, they are not often used as a means of regulating
enzyme function. Instead, other molecules, in some cases other
enzymes, regulate most of the cell's enzymatic activity. These regulatory molecules often change the enzyme's structure in some
way, and their activity either activates or inactivates the enzyme.

Regulating Enzymes via Noncovalent Modifications   Many molecules that regulate enzyme activity bind non-covalently to the
enzyme to either activate or inactivate it. Since the interaction
does not alter the enzyme's primary structure, it is often referred
to as a "reversible" modification.

Reversible modifications affect enzyme function in one of two
ways:

1. The regulatory molecule is similar in size and shape to the
   enzyme's natural substrate and inhibits catalysis by binding
   to the enzyme's active site. This event is called **competitive
   inhibition** because the molecule involved competes with the
   substrate for access to the enzyme's active site (**FIGURE 10.16a**).

2. The regulatory molecule binds at a location other than the
   active site and changes the shape of the enzyme. This type
   of regulation is called **allosteric** ("different-structure") **regulation** because the binding event changes the shape of the
   enzyme in a way that makes the active site available or unavailable (**FIGURE 10.16b**).

Both strategies depend on the concentration of the regulatory molecule—the more regulatory molecule present, the more
likely it will be to bind to the enzyme and affect its activity. The
amount of regulatory molecule is often tightly controlled and, as
you'll see in Section 10.5, the regulatory molecules themselves
often manage the enzymes that produce them.

Regulating Enzymes via Covalent Modifications   In some cases,
the function of an enzyme is altered by a chemical change in its

primary structure. This change may be reversible or irreversible,
depending on the type of modification.

Irreversible changes often result from the cleavage of peptide
bonds that make up the primary structure of the enzyme. The
enzyme trypsin, for example, is not functional until a small section of the protein is removed by a specific protease.

The most common modification of enzymes is the addition
of one or more phosphate groups, similar to what was described
for activated substrates in Section 10.2. In this case, however, the
enzyme is phosphorylated instead of the substrate molecule. The
transfer of a phosphate from ATP to the enzyme may be catalyzed by the enzyme itself or by a different enzyme.

When phosphorylation adds a negative charge to one or more
amino acid residues in a protein, the electrons in that part of
the protein change configuration. The enzyme's conformation

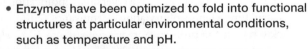
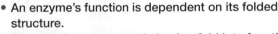
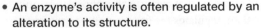

check your understanding

If you understand that . . .

C
Y
U

- An enzyme's function is dependent on its folded
  structure.
- Enzymes have been optimized to fold into functional
  structures at particular environmental conditions,
  such as temperature and pH.
- An enzyme's activity is often regulated by an
  alteration to its structure.

✔ You should be able to . . .

1. Explain why the relative activity appears to drop off in
   Figure 10.15b, when it has been shown that reaction rates
   tend to increase at higher temperatures (Figure 10.4).

2. Predict how the shape change that occurs when an
   enzyme is phosphorylated would affect its catalytic
   activity.

Answers are available in Appendix A.

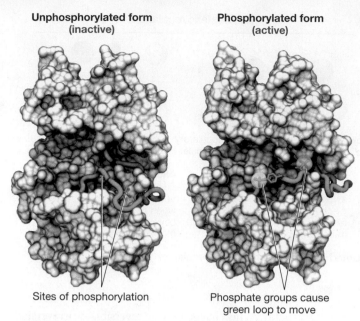

Unphosphorylated form
(inactive)

Phosphorylated form
(active)

Sites of phosphorylation

Phosphate groups cause
green loop to move

FIGURE 10.17 Phosphorylation Changes the Shape and Activity of Proteins. When proteins are phosphorylated, they often change shape in a way that alters their activity. The figure shows the subtle structural change that occurs when mitogen-activated protein kinase (MAPK) is activated by adding two phosphate groups (yellow) to the enzyme.

usually changes as well, which may activate or inactivate its function. Note that although a substrate or an enzyme may be "activated" via phosphorylation, this activation does not represent the same effect. When a substrate is activated, its potential energy has increased, and this energy is used to convert an endergonic reaction to one that is exergonic. When an enzyme is activated, its catalytic function has been turned on—any change in the potential energy of the enzyme is not directly used in driving the reaction.

To see how phosphorylation affects the shape and activity of an enzyme, let's look at an enzyme called mitogen-activated protein kinase (MAPK), which is involved in cell signaling. As shown in **FIGURE 10.17**, phosphorylation of amino acid residues in a particular loop of the primary sequence causes a shape change, which functions like a switch to activate the enzyme.

Phosphorylation of an enzyme is a reversible modification to the protein's structure. Dephosphorylation—removal of phosphates—can quickly return the protein to its previous shape. The relative abundance of enzymes that catalyze phosphorylation and dephosphorylation, then, regulates the function of the protein.

10.5 Enzymes Can Work Together in Metabolic Pathways

The eukaryotic cell has been compared to an industrial complex, where distinct organelles are functionally integrated into a cooperative network with a common goal—life (see Chapter 2). Similarly, enzymes often work together in a manner resembling an assembly line in a factory. Each of the molecules of life presented in this book is built by a series of reactions, each catalyzed by a different enzyme. These multistep processes are referred to as **metabolic pathways.**

The following is an example of this type of teamwork, where an initial substrate A is sequentially modified by enzymes 1–3 to produce product D:

$$A \xrightarrow{enzyme\ 1} B \xrightarrow{enzyme\ 2} C \xrightarrow{enzyme\ 3} D$$

The B and C molecules are referred to as intermediates in the pathway—they serve as both a product and a reactant. For example, molecule B is the product of reaction 1 and the reactant for reaction 2.

Although these reactions have been written in a single direction, from left to right, the directionality is dependent on the relative concentrations of the reactants and products. At equilibrium, however, the concentration of the product for each reaction will be higher than the concentration of its respective reactant. Since D is the overall product for this pathway, it will have the highest concentration at equilibrium.

Metabolic Pathways Are Regulated

Since enzymes catalyze the reactions in metabolic pathways, the mechanisms that regulate enzyme function introduced in Section 10.4 also apply to the individual steps in a pathway. For example, to understand how blocking an individual reaction can affect an entire pathway, go back to the three-step model presented earlier and inactivate enzyme 2 by crossing it out. ✔ If you understand the assembly-line behavior of enzymes in a metabolic pathway, you should be able to predict how inactivating enzyme 2 would affect the concentration of molecules A, B, C, and D relative to what they would be if the pathway were fully functional.

When an enzyme in a pathway is inhibited by the product of the reaction sequence, **feedback inhibition** occurs. This is a convenient way for pathways to shut themselves down when their activity is no longer needed. As the concentration of the product molecule becomes abundant, it "feeds back" to stop the reaction sequence (**FIGURE 10.18**). By inhibiting a step early in the pathway, the amount of the initial substrate is not depleted unnecessarily, allowing it to be stored or used for other reactions.

Metabolic Pathways Evolve

While many enzymes are extraordinarily specific, some can catalyze a range of reactions and are able to interact with a family of related substrates. Research suggests that this flexibility allowed new enzymes to evolve and that enzymes specialized for catalyzing key reactions provided cells with a selective advantage. Could the same flexibility also help explain the evolution of the stepwise series of reactions seen in metabolic pathways?

In 1945, Norman Horowitz proposed a simple, stepwise process that could have directed pathway evolution. In Horowitz's model, enzymes first would have evolved to make the building blocks of life from readily available substrates, such as small organic compounds (see Appendix D).

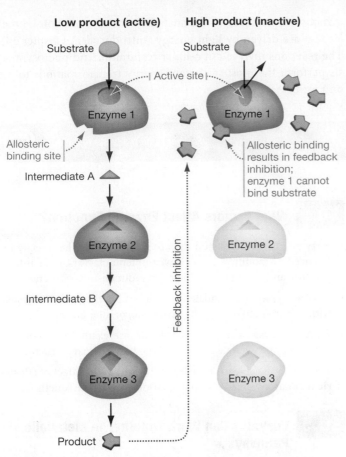

Low product (active)

Substrate

|Active site|

Allosteric binding site

Enzyme 1

Intermediate A

Enzyme 2

Intermediate B

Enzyme 3

Product

High product (inactive)

Substrate

Enzyme 1

Allosteric binding results in feedback inhibition; enzyme 1 cannot bind substrate

Feedback inhibition

Enzyme 2

Enzyme 3

FIGURE 10.18 Feedback Inhibition May Regulate Metabolic Pathways. Feedback inhibition occurs when the product of a metabolic pathway inhibits an enzyme that functions early in the pathway.

If an original substrate were depleted, natural selection would next favor the evolution of a new enzyme to make more of it from other existing molecules. By evolving a new reaction step to produce the original substrate—now serving as an intermediate in a two-step pathway—the original enzyme would have been able to continue its work. **FIGURE 10.19** illustrates this model—referred to as retro-evolution—in which repetition of this backward process produces a multistep metabolic pathway.

Researchers also speculate that as early pathways emerged, early enzymes may have been recruited to new pathways, where they evolved new catalytic activities that performed new tasks. This hypothesis is called patchwork evolution, since the new reaction series would consist of enzymes brought together from different pathways.

Evidence of patchwork evolution has been observed in modern organisms, where new metabolic activities have emerged in response to human-made chemicals. For example, a novel pathway has recently evolved in one species of bacterium to break down the pesticide pentachlorophenol, for use as a source of energy and carbon building blocks. Pentachlorophenol was first introduced into the environment in the 1930s as a timber preservative. The new pathway uses enzymes from two preexisting pathways, which had evolved the ability to work together. The metabolic activity of microbes is now being scrutinized and engineered to clean up a variety of human-made pollutants—giving rise to a new technology called **bioremediation.**

Regardless of how they evolved, metabolic pathways are now vital to the function of all cells. Those that break down molecules for sources of energy and carbon building blocks are called **catabolic pathways;** those that use energy and carbon building blocks to synthesize molecules are called **anabolic pathways.**

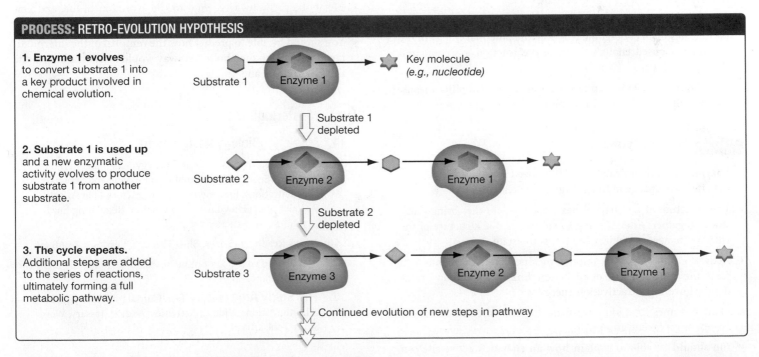

PROCESS: RETRO-EVOLUTION HYPOTHESIS

1. Enzyme 1 evolves to convert substrate 1 into a key product involved in chemical evolution.

Substrate 1 — Enzyme 1 → Key molecule (e.g., nucleotide)

Substrate 1 depleted

2. Substrate 1 is used up and a new enzymatic activity evolves to produce substrate 1 from another substrate.

Substrate 2 — Enzyme 2 → Enzyme 1 →

Substrate 2 depleted

3. The cycle repeats. Additional steps are added to the series of reactions, ultimately forming a full metabolic pathway.

Substrate 3 — Enzyme 3 → Enzyme 2 → Enzyme 1 →

Continued evolution of new steps in pathway

FIGURE 10.19 A Hypothetical Model for Metabolic Pathway Evolution.

You are being kept alive by key catabolic and anabolic pathways. The catabolic pathways of cellular respiration (introduced in Chapter 13) harvest high-energy electrons from reduced carbons (from foods such as starch and sugar) and pass them through redox reactions to generate ATP. These reduced carbons are produced by the anabolic pathways of photosynthesis that are driven by light energy (introduced in Chapter 14). The reactions involved in cellular respiration and photosynthesis perform the most important energy transformations to life on Earth.

If you understand . . .

10.1 What Happens to Energy in Chemical Reactions?

- Spontaneous reactions do not require an input of energy to occur.
- The Gibbs free energy change, ΔG, summarizes the combined effects of changes in enthalpy and entropy during a chemical reaction.
- Spontaneous reactions have a negative ΔG and are said to be exergonic; nonspontaneous reactions have a positive ΔG and are said to be endergonic.

✔ You should be able to explain why changes in enthalpy and entropy are used to determine whether a reaction is spontaneous.

10.2 Nonspontaneous Reactions May Be Driven Using Chemical Energy

- Redox reactions transfer energy by coupling exergonic oxidation reactions to endergonic reduction reactions.
- High-energy C−H bonds may be formed during the reduction step of a redox reaction when an H^+ is combined with a transferred electron.
- The hydrolysis of ATP is an exergonic reaction and may be used to drive a variety of cellular processes.
- When a phosphate group from ATP is added to a substrate that participates in an endergonic reaction, the potential energy of the substrate is raised enough to make the reaction exergonic and thus spontaneous.

✔ You should be able to explain what energetic coupling means, and why life would not exist without it.

10.3 How Enzymes Work

- Enzymes are protein catalysts. They speed reaction rates but do not affect the change in free energy of the reaction.
- The structure of an enzyme has an active site that brings substrates together. After binding to substrates, the structure of the enzyme changes to stabilize the transition state.
- Activation energy is the amount of kinetic energy required to reach the transition state of a reaction. Enzymes speed up a reaction by lowering the activation energy.
- Many enzymes function only with the help of cofactors, coenzymes, or prosthetic groups.

✔ You should be able to explain how an enzyme's active site can reduce the activation energy of a reaction.

10.4 What Factors Affect Enzyme Function?

- Enzymes are proteins, and thus their activity can be directly influenced by modifications or environmental factors, such as temperature and pH, that alter their three-dimensional structure.
- Most enzymes are regulated by molecules that either compete with substrates to occupy the active site, or alter enzyme shape.
- Protein cleavage and phosphorylation are examples of how enzymes may be regulated by modifying their primary structure.

✔ You should be able to compare and contrast the effect of allosteric regulation versus phosphorylation on enzyme function.

10.5 Enzymes Can Work Together in Metabolic Pathways

- In cells, enzymes often work together in metabolic pathways that sequentially modify a substrate to make a product.
- A pathway may be regulated by controlling the activity of one enzyme, often the first in the series of reactions. Feedback inhibition results from the accumulation of a product that binds to an enzyme in the pathway and inactivates it.
- Metabolic pathways were vital to the evolution of life, and new pathways continue to evolve in cells.

✔ You should be able to predict how the removal of the intermediate in a two-step metabolic pathway would affect the enzymatic rates of the first and last.

MB MasteringBiology

1. **MasteringBiology Assignments**

   Tutorials and Activities ATP and Energy; Chemical Reactions and ATP; Energy Transformations; Enzyme and Substrate Concentrations; Enzyme Inhibition; Factors That Affect Reaction Rate; How Enzymes Function; Regulating Enzyme Action; Redox Reactions

   Questions Reading Quizzes, Blue-Thread Questions, Test Bank

2. **eText** Read your book online, search, take notes, highlight text, and more.

3. **The Study Area** Practice Test, Cumulative Test, BioFlix® 3-D Animations, Videos, Activities, Audio Glossary, Word Study Tools, Art

You should be able to . . .

1. The first law of thermodynamics states which of the following?
   a. Energy exists in two forms: kinetic and potential.
   b. Reactions will take place only if energy is released.
   c. Energy is conserved: it cannot be created or destroyed.
   d. Disorder always increases in the universe.

2. If a reaction is exergonic, then which of these statements is true?
   a. The products have lower free energy than the reactants.
   b. Energy must be added for the reaction to proceed.
   c. The products have lower entropy (are more ordered) than the reactants.
   d. The reaction occurs extremely quickly.

3. What is a transition state?
   a. the complex formed as covalent bonds are being broken and re-formed during a reaction
   b. the place where an allosteric regulatory molecule binds to an enzyme

c. an interaction between reactants with high kinetic energy, due to high temperature
d. the shape adopted by an enzyme that has an inhibitory molecule bound at its active site

4. What often happens to an enzyme after it binds to its substrate? Is this a permanent change?

5. How does pH affect enzyme-catalyzed reactions?
   a. Protons serve as substrates for most reactions.
   b. Energy stored in protons is used to drive endergonic reactions.
   c. Proton concentration increases the kinetic energy of the reactants, allowing them to reach their transition state.
   d. The concentration of protons affects the folded structure of the enzyme.

6. When does feedback inhibition occur?

7. Explain the lock-and-key model of enzyme activity. What was incorrect about this model?

8. If you were to expose glucose to oxygen on your lab bench, why would you not expect to see it burn as shown in Figure 10.6?
   a. The reaction is endergonic and requires an input of energy.
   b. The reaction is not spontaneous unless an enzyme is added to the substrates.
   c. The sugar must first be phosphorylated to increase its potential energy.
   d. Energy is required for the sugar and oxygen to reach their transition state.

9. Explain why substrate phosphorylation using ATP is an exergonic reaction. How does the phosphorylation of reactants result in driving reactions that would normally be endergonic?

10. **QUANTITATIVE** In Figure 10.9, the energetic coupling of ATP hydrolysis and an endergonic reaction are shown. If the hydrolysis of ATP releases 7.3 kcal of free energy, use the graph in this figure to estimate what you would expect the ΔG values to be for the uncoupled reaction and the two steps in the coupled reaction.

11. Compare and contrast competitive inhibition and allosteric regulation.

12. Using what you have learned about changes in free energy, would you predict the ΔG value of catabolic reactions to be positive or negative? What about anabolic reactions? Justify your answers using the terms enthalpy and entropy.

13. Draw a redox reaction that occurs between compounds AH_2 and B^+ to form A, BH, and H^+. On the drawing, connect the reactant and product forms of each compound and state if it is the reduction or oxidation step and how many electrons are transferred. If this represents an exergonic reaction, identify which of the five substances would have the highest-energy electrons.

14. Researchers can analyze the atomic structure of enzymes during catalysis. In one recent study, investigators found that the transition state included the formation of a free radical (see Appendix D) and that a coenzyme bound to the active site donated an electron to help stabilize the free radical. How would the reaction rate and the stability of the transition state change if the coenzyme were not available?

15. Recently, researchers were able to measure movement that occurred in a single amino acid in an enzyme as reactions were taking place in its active site. The amino acid that moved was

located in the active site, and the rate of movement correlated closely with the rate at which the reaction was taking place. Discuss the significance of these findings, using the information in Figures 10.10 and 10.13.

16. You have discovered an enzyme that appears to function only when a particular sugar accumulates. Which of the following scenarios would you predict to be responsible for activating this enzyme?
   a. The sugar cleaves the enzyme so it is now in an active conformation.
   b. The sugar binds to the enzyme and changes the conformation of the active site.
   c. The sugar binds to the active site and competes with the normal substrate.
   d. The sugar phosphorylates the enzyme, triggering a conformational change.

11 Meiosis

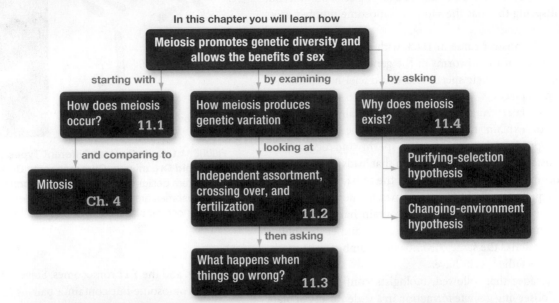

In this chapter you will learn how

Meiosis promotes genetic diversity and allows the benefits of sex

starting with

How does meiosis occur? 11.1

and comparing to

Mitosis Ch. 4

by examining

How meiosis produces genetic variation

looking at

Independent assortment, crossing over, and fertilization 11.2

then asking

What happens when things go wrong? 11.3

by asking

Why does meiosis exist? 11.4

Purifying-selection hypothesis

Changing-environment hypothesis

Scanning electron micrograph (with color added) showing human sperm attempting to enter a human egg. This chapter introduces the type of nuclear division called meiosis, which in animals occurs before the formation of sperm and eggs.

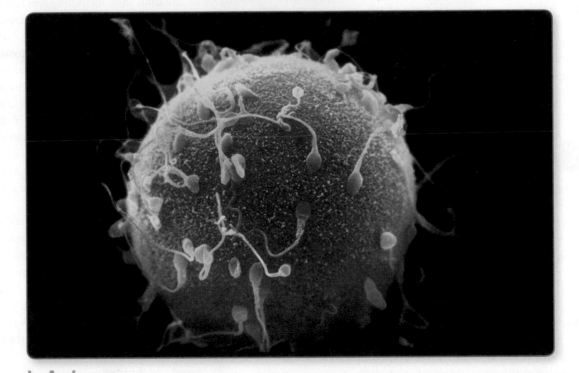

Why sex?

Simple questions—such as why sexual reproduction exists—are sometimes the best. This chapter asks what sexual reproduction is and why some organisms employ it. The focus here is on how organisms reproduce, or replicate—one of the five fundamental attributes of life introduced in Chapter 1.

For centuries people have known that during sexual reproduction, a male reproductive cell—a **sperm**—and a female reproductive cell—an **egg**—unite to form a new individual. The process of uniting sperm and egg is called **fertilization.** The first biologists to observe fertilization studied the large, translucent eggs of sea urchins. Owing to the semitransparency of the sea urchin egg cell, researchers were able to see the nuclei of a sperm and an egg fuse.

✔ When you see this checkmark, stop and test yourself. Answers are available in Appendix A.

When these observations were published in 1876, they raised an important question, because biologists had already established that the number of chromosomes is constant from cell to cell within a multicellular organism. The question is, How can the chromosomes from a sperm cell and an egg cell combine, but form an offspring that has the same chromosome number as its mother and its father?

A hint at the answer came in 1883, with the observation that cells in the body of roundworms of the genus *Ascaris* have four chromosomes, while their sperm and egg nuclei have only two chromosomes apiece.

Four years later, August Weismann formally proposed a hypothesis to explain the riddle: During the formation of **gametes**—reproductive cells such as sperm and eggs—there must be a distinctive type of cell division that leads to a reduction in chromosome number. Specifically, if the sperm and egg contribute an equal number of chromosomes to the fertilized egg, Weismann reasoned, they must each contain half of the usual number of chromosomes. Then, when sperm and egg combine, the resulting cell has the same chromosome number as its mother's cells and its father's cells have.

In the decades that followed, biologists confirmed this hypothesis by observing gamete formation in a wide variety of plant and animal species. Eventually this form of cell division came to be called meiosis (literally, "lessening-act").

Meiosis is nuclear division that leads to a halving of chromosome number and ultimately to the production of sperm and egg. To a biologist, asking "Why sex?" is equivalent to asking "Why meiosis?" Let's delve in by first looking at how meiosis happens.

11.1 How Does Meiosis Occur?

To understand meiosis, it is critical to grasp some key ideas about chromosomes. For example, when cell biologists began to study the cell divisions that lead to gamete formation, they made an important observation: Each organism has a characteristic number of chromosomes.

Consider the drawings in **FIGURE 11.1**, based on a paper published by Nettie Maria Stevens in 1908. They show the chromosomes of the fruit fly *Drosophila melanogaster*, or *Drosophila* for short. This model organism has been a focus of biological research for more than 100 years (see **BioSkills 13** in Appendix B). Stevens was studying the cell divisions leading up to the formation of egg and sperm. In total, she found eight chromosomes in *Drosophila* cells. Your cells have 46 chromosomes, and some ferns have over 1000.

Chromosomes Come in Distinct Sizes and Shapes

Stevens found that each *Drosophila* cell has eight chromosomes, but just five distinct types, distinguished by their size and shape. Three of these chromosomes always occurred in pairs and are labeled chromosomes 2–4 in Figure 11.1. In males, Stevens observed an unpaired set of chromosomes, which came to be known

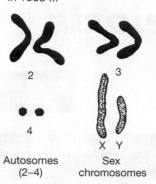 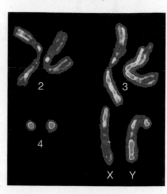

Drosophila chromosomes drawn by Nettie Stevens in 1908 ...

... and photographed through a modern microscope.

Autosomes (2–4)   Sex chromosomes

FIGURE 11.1 Cells Contain Different Types of Chromosomes, and in Diploid Organisms, Chromosomes Come in Pairs. Numbers and letters designate the types of *Drosophila* chromosomes. These chromosomes are from the cell of a male, so there is an X and a Y chromosome plus three homologous pairs of autosomes.

as the X and the Y chromosomes. Stevens found that females lack a Y chromosome but contain a pair of X chromosomes. This is the same situation in some other insects and in mammals. The X and Y chromosomes are called **sex chromosomes** and are associated with an individual's sex. Non-sex chromosomes, such as chromosomes 2–4 in *Drosophila*, are **autosomes.**

Chromosomes that are the same size and shape are called **homologous** ("same-proportion") **chromosomes,** or **homologs,** and the pair is called a homologous pair. Later work showed that homologous chromosomes are similar in content as well as in size and shape. Homologous chromosomes carry the same genes. A **gene** is a section of DNA that influences some hereditary trait in an individual. For example, each copy of chromosome 2 found in *Drosophila* carries genes that influence eye color, wing size and shape, and bristle size.

The versions of a gene found on homologous chromosomes may differ, however. Biologists use the term **allele** to denote different versions of the same gene. For example, the allele for an eye-color gene on one homolog of chromosome 2 may be associated with red eyes, the normal color in *Drosophila*, whereas the allele of the same eye-color gene on the other homolog may be associated with purple eyes (**FIGURE 11.2**); the particular alleles of the bristle-size gene will influence whether the fly's bristles are long or short, and so on.

Homologous chromosomes carry the same genes, but each homolog may contain different alleles.

The Concept of Ploidy

At this point in her study, Stevens had determined the *Drosophila* **karyotype**—meaning the number and types of chromosomes present. As karyotyping studies became more common, cell biologists realized that, like *Drosophila*, the vast majority of plants and animals have more than one of each type of chromosome.

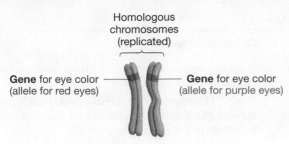

Gene for eye color
(allele for red eyes)

Gene for eye color
(allele for purple eyes)

Homologous
chromosomes
(replicated)

Drosophila autosome 2

FIGURE 11.2 Homologous Chromosomes May Contain Different Alleles of the Same Gene. The homologs of *Drosophila* chromosome 2 are shown; the location of only one of many genes is indicated.

Insects, humans, oak trees, and other organisms that have two versions of each type of chromosome are called **diploid** ("double-form"). Diploid organisms have two alleles of each gene. One allele is carried on each of the homologous pairs of chromosomes. Although a diploid individual can carry only two different alleles of a gene, there can be many different alleles in a population.

Organisms whose cells contain just one of each type of chromosome—for example, bacteria, archaea, and many algae and fungi—are called **haploid** ("single-form"). Haploid organisms have only one copy of each chromosome and just one allele of each gene.

Biologists use a compact notation to indicate the number of chromosomes and chromosome sets in a particular organism or type of cell:

- By convention, the letter n stands for the number of distinct types of chromosomes in a given cell and is called the **haploid number.** If sex chromosomes are present, they are counted as a single type in the haploid number. In humans, n is 23.

- To indicate the number of complete chromosome sets observed, a number is placed before the n. Thus, a cell can be n, or $2n$, or $3n$, and so on.

The combination of the number of sets and n is termed the cell's **ploidy.** Diploid cells or species are designated $2n$, because two chromosomes of each type are present—one from each parent. A **maternal chromosome** comes from the mother, and a **paternal chromosome** comes from the father.

Humans are diploid; $2n$ is 46. Haploid cells or species are labeled simply n, because they have just one set of chromosomes—no homologs are present. In haploid cells, the number 1 in front of n is implied and is not written out.

To summarize, the haploid number n indicates the number of distinct types of chromosomes present. In contrast, a cell's ploidy (n, $2n$, $3n$, etc.) indicates the number of each type of chromosome present. Stating a cell's ploidy is the same as stating the number of haploid chromosome sets present. ✔ If you understand how these terms relate, you should be able to state the haploid number, ploidy, and total number of chromosomes present in a male *Drosophila*.

Later work revealed that it is common for species in some lineages—particularly certain land plants, such as ferns—to contain more than two of each type of chromosome. Instead of having two homologous chromosomes per cell, **polyploid** ("many-form") species have three or more of each type of chromosome in each cell.

Depending on the number of homologs present, polyploid species are called triploid ($3n$), tetraploid ($4n$), hexaploid ($6n$), octoploid ($8n$), and so on.

Stevens and other early cell biologists did more than just describe the karyotypes observed in their study organisms. Through careful examination, they were able to track how chromosome numbers change during meiosis. These studies confirmed Weismann's hypothesis that a special type of cell division occurs during gamete formation.

An Overview of Meiosis

Cells replicate each of their chromosomes before undergoing meiosis. At the start of meiosis, chromosomes are in the same state they are in before mitosis.

Recall that an unreplicated eukaryotic chromosome consists of a single, long DNA double helix organized around proteins called histones (see Chapter 4). When chromosome replication is complete, each chromosome will consist of two identical **sister chromatids.** Sister chromatids contain identical copies of the DNA double helix present in the unreplicated chromosome and therefore the same genetic information. They remain physically joined along their entire length during much of meiosis (**FIGURE 11.3**).

To understand meiosis, it is critical to understand the relationship between chromosomes and sister chromatids. The trick is to recognize that unreplicated and replicated chromosomes are both considered *single* chromosomes—even though the replicated chromosome contains *two* sister chromatids. This makes sense if you consider that a chromosome carries a particular set of genetic information in its DNA and that the amount of *unique* information is the same whether there is one copy of it present or two.

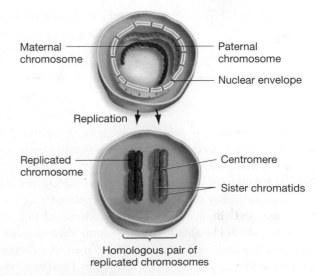

Maternal
chromosome

Paternal
chromosome

Nuclear envelope

Replication

Replicated
chromosome

Centromere

Sister chromatids

Homologous pair of
replicated chromosomes

FIGURE 11.3 Each Chromosome Replicates before Undergoing Meiosis.

Term	Definition	Example or Comment
Chromosome	Structure made up of DNA and proteins; carries the cell's hereditary information (genes)	Eukaryotes have linear chromosomes; most bacteria and archaea have just one, circular, chromosome
• **Sex chromosome**	Chromosome associated with an individual's sex	X and Y chromosomes of humans (males are XY, females XX); Z and W chromosomes of birds and butterflies (males are ZZ, females ZW)
• **Autosome**	A non-sex chromosome	Chromosomes 1–22 in humans
Unreplicated chromosome	A chromosome that consists of one double-helical molecule of DNA packaged with proteins	
Replicated chromosome	A chromosome that has been copied; consists of two identical chromatids, each containing one double-helical DNA molecule	Centromere
Sister chromatids	The two identical chromatid copies in a replicated chromosome	Sister chromatids
Homologous chromosomes (homologs)	In a diploid organism, chromosomes that are similar in size, shape, and gene content	You have a chromosome 22 from each parent — Homologous chromosomes
Non-sister chromatids	Chromatids belonging to homologous chromosomes	Non-sister chromatids
Bivalent (or tetrad)	Homologous replicated chromosomes that are joined together during prophase I and metaphase I of meiosis	Bivalent
Haploid number	The number of different types of chromosomes in a cell; symbolized n	Humans have 23 different types of chromosomes ($n = 23$)
Diploid number	The number of chromosomes present in a diploid cell (see below); symbolized $2n$	In humans all cells except gametes are diploid and contain 46 chromosomes ($2n = 46$)
Ploidy	The number of each type of chromosome present	The number of haploid chromosome sets present
• **Haploid**	Having one of each type of chromosome (n)	Bacteria and archaea are haploid, as are many algae; plant and animal gametes are haploid
• **Diploid**	Having two of each type of chromosome ($2n$)	Most familiar plants and animals are diploid
• **Polyploid**	Having more than two of each type of chromosome; cells may be triploid ($3n$), tetraploid ($4n$), hexaploid ($6n$), and so on	Seedless bananas are triploid; many ferns are tetraploid; bread wheat is hexaploid

Note that an unreplicated chromosome is never called a chromatid; you can refer to chromatids only as the structures in a replicated chromosome.

TABLE 11.1 summarizes the vocabulary that biologists use to describe chromosomes and illustrates the relationship between chromosomes and chromatids. ✔ If you understand this relationship, you should be able to draw the same chromosome in the unreplicated and replicated state, label the sister chromatids, indicate the number of DNA molecules present in each structure, and explain why both structures represent a single chromosome.

Meiosis Comprises Two Cell Divisions Meiosis consists of two cell divisions, called **meiosis I** and **meiosis II**. As **FIGURE 11.4** shows, the two divisions occur consecutively but differ sharply.

During meiosis I, the homologs in each chromosome pair separate from each other. One homolog goes to one daughter cell; the other homolog goes to the other daughter cell. It is a matter of chance which daughter cell receives which homolog.

At the end of meiosis I, each of the two daughter cells has one of each type of chromosome instead of two, and thus half as many chromosomes as the parent cell had. Put another way: During meiosis I, the diploid ($2n$) parent cell produces two haploid (n)

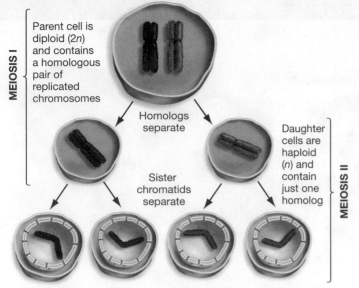

Parent cell is diploid (2*n*) and contains a homologous pair of replicated chromosomes

MEIOSIS I

Homologs separate

Daughter cells are haploid (*n*) and contain just one homolog

Sister chromatids separate

MEIOSIS II

Four daughter cells contain one chromosome each (*n*). In animals, these cells become gametes.

FIGURE 11.4 The Major Events in Meiosis. Before undergoing meiosis, chromosomes are replicated so there are two chromatids per chromosome. Meiosis reduces chromosome number by half. In diploid organisms, the products of meiosis are haploid. Maternal chromosomes are shown in red; paternal chromosomes, blue. Note that in this cell, 2*n* = 2.

daughter cells. Notice, however, that each chromosome still consists of two sister chromatids—meaning that chromosomes are still replicated at the end of meiosis I.

During meiosis II, sister chromatids from each chromosome separate. One sister chromatid (now called a daughter chromosome) goes to one daughter cell; the other sister chromatid goes to the other daughter cell as a daughter chromosome. Remember that the cell that started meiosis II had one of each type of chromosome, but each chromosome was still replicated (meaning still consisting of two sister chromatids). The cells produced by meiosis II also have one of each type of chromosome, but now the daughter chromosomes are no longer replicated.

To reiterate, sister chromatids separate into daughter chromosomes during meiosis II. This is just what happens during mitosis. Meiosis II is actually equivalent to mitosis occurring in a haploid cell. In meiosis I, on the other hand, sister chromatids stay together. This sets meiosis I apart from both mitosis and meiosis II.

As in mitosis, chromosome movements during meiosis I and II are coordinated by microtubules of the **spindle apparatus** that attach to **kinetochores** located at the **centromere** of each chromosome. Recall that the centromere is a region on the chromosome; kinetochores are structures in that region (see Chapter 4). Chromosome movement is driven by fraying of the ends of microtubules at each kinetochore, just as it is in mitosis (see Figure 4.7).

Meiosis I is a Reduction Division A host of early cell biologists worked out this sequence of events through careful observation of cells with the light microscope. Based on these studies, they came to a key realization: The outcome of meiosis I is a reduction

in chromosome number. For this reason, meiosis I is known as a reduction division. Reduction is another important way in which meiosis I differs from meiosis II and mitosis.

In most plants and animals, the original cell entering meiosis is diploid and the four final daughter cells are haploid. In animals, the haploid daughter cells, each containing one of each homologous chromosome, eventually go on to form egg cells or sperm cells via a process called **gametogenesis** ("gamete-origin").

When two haploid gametes fuse during fertilization, a full complement of chromosomes is restored (**FIGURE 11.5**). The cell that results from fertilization is diploid and is called a **zygote.** In this way, each diploid individual receives a haploid chromosome set from its mother and a haploid set from its father.

FIGURE 11.6 puts these events into the context of an animal's **life cycle**—the sequence of events that occurs over the life span of an individual, from fertilization to the production of offspring. As you study the figure, note how ploidy changes as the result of

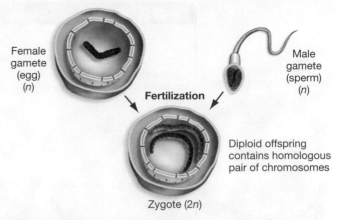

Female gamete (egg) (*n*)

Male gamete (sperm) (*n*)

Fertilization

Diploid offspring contains homologous pair of chromosomes

Zygote (2*n*)

FIGURE 11.5 Fertilization Restores a Full Complement of Chromosomes.

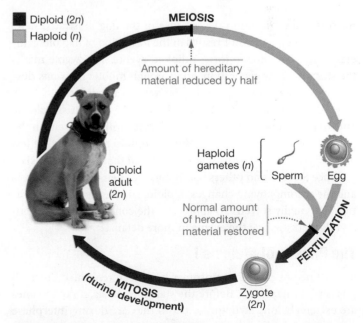

■ Diploid (2*n*)
■ Haploid (*n*)

MEIOSIS

Amount of hereditary material reduced by half

Haploid gametes (*n*)
Sperm   Egg

Diploid adult (2*n*)

Normal amount of hereditary material restored

FERTILIZATION

MITOSIS (during development)

Zygote (2*n*)

FIGURE 11.6 Ploidy Changes during the Life Cycle of a Dog. Most of the dog life cycle involves diploid cells.

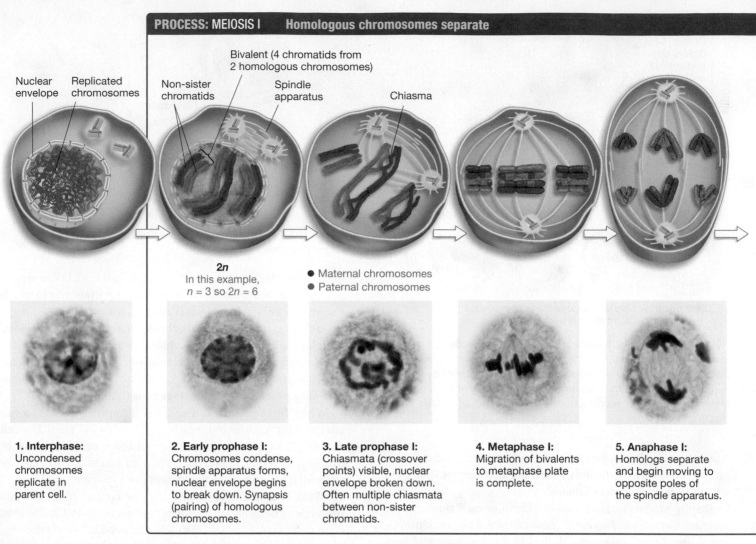

FIGURE 11.7 The Phases of Meiosis. The micrographs of each phase are from a species of salamander.

meiosis and fertilization. In the case of the dog illustrated here, meiosis in a diploid adult results in the formation of haploid gametes, which combine to form a diploid zygote. The zygote marks the start of a new generation, and through mitotic divisions during development, the zygote goes on to form an adult dog.

✔ **If you understand the events of meiosis, you should be able to predict how many DNA molecules will be present in the gametes of the fruit fly *Drosophila*, a diploid organism that has eight replicated chromosomes in each cell that enters meiosis.**

Once Stevens and others had published their work on meiosis and the accompanying changes in ploidy, the mystery of fertilization was finally solved. To appreciate the consequences of meiosis fully, let's analyze the events in more detail.

The Phases of Meiosis I

Meiosis begins after chromosomes have been replicated during S phase (see Chapter 4). Before the start of meiosis, chromosomes are extremely long structures, just as they are during interphase of the normal cell cycle. The major steps that occur once meiosis begins are shown in **FIGURE 11.7**.

Early Prophase I   During early prophase I, the nuclear envelope begins to break down, chromosomes condense and the spindle apparatus begins to form. Then a crucial event occurs: Homologous chromosome pairs come together. The end result of this process is called **synapsis** and is illustrated in step 2 of Figure 11.7. Synapsis is possible because regions of homologous chromosomes that are similar at the molecular level come together. In most organisms, synapsis requires breaking and then connecting together DNA of the two homologs at one or more spots along their length.

The structure that results from synapsis is called a **bivalent** (*bi* means "two" in Latin) or **tetrad** (*tetra* means "four" in Greek). A bivalent consists of paired homologous chromosomes, with each homolog consisting of two sister chromatids. Chromatids from different homologs are referred to as **non-sister chromatids.** In the figure, the red-colored chromatids are non-sister chromatids with respect to the blue-colored chromatids.

Late Prophase I   During late prophase I, the nuclear envelope breaks down and microtubules of the spindle apparatus attach to

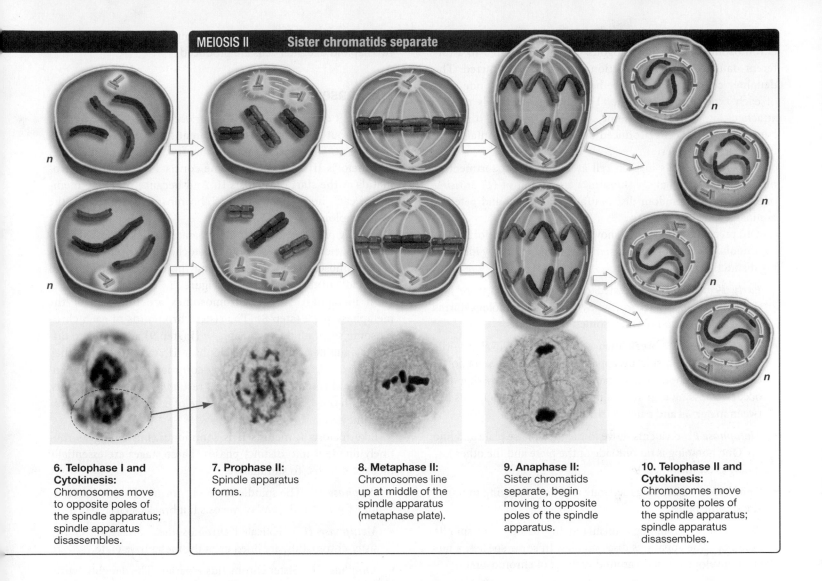

6. Telophase I and Cytokinesis: Chromosomes move to opposite poles of the spindle apparatus; spindle apparatus disassembles.

7. Prophase II: Spindle apparatus forms.

8. Metaphase II: Chromosomes line up at middle of the spindle apparatus (metaphase plate).

9. Anaphase II: Sister chromatids separate, begin moving to opposite poles of the spindle apparatus.

10. Telophase II and Cytokinesis: Chromosomes move to opposite poles of the spindle apparatus; spindle apparatus disassembles.

kinetochores. Non-sister chromatids begin to separate at many points along their length. They stay joined at certain locations, however, each of which forms an X-shaped structure called a **chiasma** (plural: **chiasmata**). (In the Greek alphabet, the letter X is called "chi.") Normally, at least one chiasma forms in every pair of homologous chromosomes; often there are several chiasmata. The chiasmata mark sites where DNA was broken and rejoined between homologs early in prophase I.

As step 3 of Figure 11.7 shows, the chromatids that meet to form a chiasma are non-sister chromatids. At each chiasma there is an exchange of parts of chromosomes between paternal and maternal homologs. These reciprocal exchanges between different homologs create non-sister chromatids that have both paternal and maternal segments. This process of chromosome exchange is called **crossing over.**

In step 4 of Figure 11.7, the result of crossing over is illustrated by chromosomes with a combination of red and blue segments. When crossing over occurs, the chromosomes that result have a mixture of maternal and paternal alleles. Crossing over is a major way that meiosis creates genetic diversity.

Metaphase I   The next major stage in meiosis I is metaphase I. This is when kinetochore microtubules move the pairs of homologous chromosomes (bivalents) to a region called the **metaphase plate** in the middle of the spindle apparatus (step 4). The metaphase plate is not a physical structure but an imaginary plane dividing the spindle apparatus.

Here are two key points about chromosome movement: Each bivalent moves to the metaphase plate independently of the other bivalents, and the alignment on one side or the other of the metaphase plate is random for maternal and paternal homologs from each chromosome. This movement explains the most basic principles of genetics (see Chapter 12).

Anaphase and Telophase I   Sister chromatids of each chromosome remain together. During anaphase I, the homologous chromosomes in each bivalent separate and begin moving to opposite poles of the spindle apparatus (step 5). Meiosis I concludes with telophase I, when the homologs finish moving to opposite sides of the spindle (step 6). When meiosis I is complete, **cytokinesis** (division of cytoplasm) occurs and two haploid daughter cells form.

Meiosis I: A Recap The end result of meiosis I is that one chromosome of each homologous pair is distributed to a different daughter cell. A reduction division has occurred: The daughter cells of meiosis I are haploid, having only one copy of each type of chromosome. The sister chromatids remain attached in each chromosome, however, meaning that the haploid daughter cells produced by meiosis I still contain replicated chromosomes.

The chromosomes in each cell are a random assortment of maternal and paternal chromosomes as a result of (1) crossing over and (2) the random distribution of maternal and paternal homologs during metaphase.

The preceding discussion shows that although meiosis I is a continuous process, biologists summarize the events by identifying distinct phases:

- *Early Prophase I* Replicated chromosomes condense and the spindle apparatus forms. Synapsis of homologs forms pairs of homologous chromosomes, or bivalents.

- *Late Prophase I* Breakdown of the nuclear envelope. Microtubules of the spindle apparatus attach to kinetochores. Chiasmata become visible, marking sites where crossing over occurs. Crossing over results in an exchange of segments between maternal and paternal chromosomes.

- *Metaphase I* Bivalents move to the metaphase plate and line up. One homolog is on one side of the plate and the other homolog is on the other.

- *Anaphase I* Homologs separate and begin moving to opposite spindle poles.

- *Telophase I* Homologs finish moving to opposite spindle poles. Spindle apparatus disassembles. In some species, a nuclear envelope re-forms around each set of chromosomes.

Throughout, chromosome movement takes place as microtubules that are attached to the kinetochore dynamically assemble and disassemble. When meiosis I is complete, the cell divides and two haploid daughter cells are produced.

The Phases of Meiosis II

Recall that chromosome replication occurred before meiosis I. Throughout meiosis I, sister chromatids remained attached. Because no chromosome replication occurs between meiosis I and meiosis II, each chromosome consists of two sister chromatids at the start of meiosis II. And because only one member of each homologous pair of chromosomes is present, the cell is haploid.

During prophase II, a spindle apparatus forms in both daughter cells. Microtubules attach to kinetochores on each side of every chromosome and begin moving the chromosomes toward the middle of each cell (step 7 of Figure 11.7).

In metaphase II, the chromosomes are lined up at the metaphase plate (step 8). The sister chromatids of each chromosome separate during anaphase II (step 9) and move to different daughter cells during telophase II (step 10). Once they are separated, each chromatid is considered an independent daughter chromosome. Meiosis II results in four haploid cells, each with one daughter chromosome of each type in the chromosome set.

Like meiosis I, meiosis II is continuous, but biologists routinely divide it into distinct phases. These stages are essentially those of mitosis. To summarize,

- *Prophase II* The spindle apparatus forms. If a nuclear envelope formed at the end of meiosis I, it breaks apart.

- *Metaphase II* Replicated chromosomes, consisting of two sister chromatids, are lined up at the metaphase plate.

- *Anaphase II* Sister chromatids separate. The daughter chromosomes that result begin moving to opposite poles of the spindle apparatus.

SUMMARY TABLE 11.2 **Key Differences between Mitosis and Meiosis**

Feature	Mitosis	Meiosis
Number of cell divisions	One	Two
Number of chromosomes in daughter cells compared with parent cell	Same	Half
Synapsis of homologs	No	Yes
Number of crossing-over events	None	One or more per pair of homologous chromosomes
Makeup of chromosomes in daughter cells	Identical	Different—various combinations of maternal and paternal chromosomes, paternal and maternal segments mixed within chromosomes
Role in organism life cycle	Asexual reproduction in some eukaryotes; cell division for growth	Halving of chromosome number in cells that will produce gametes

- *Telophase II* Chromosomes finish moving to opposite poles of the spindle apparatus. A nuclear envelope forms around each haploid set of chromosomes.

When meiosis II is complete, each cell divides to form two daughter cells. Because meiosis II occurs in both daughter cells of meiosis I, the process results in a total of four daughter cells from each original, parent cell. To describe meiosis in a nutshell, one diploid cell with replicated chromosomes gives rise to four haploid cells with unreplicated chromosomes.

TABLE 11.2 and **FIGURE 11.8** provide a comparison of mitosis and meiosis. A key difference between the two processes is that homologous chromosomes pair early in meiosis but do not pair at all during mitosis. Because homologs pair through synapsis in prophase of meiosis I, they can migrate to the metaphase plate together and then separate during anaphase of meiosis I, resulting in a reduction division. ✔ If you understand this key distinction between meiosis and mitosis, you should be able to describe the consequences for meiosis if homologs do not pair.

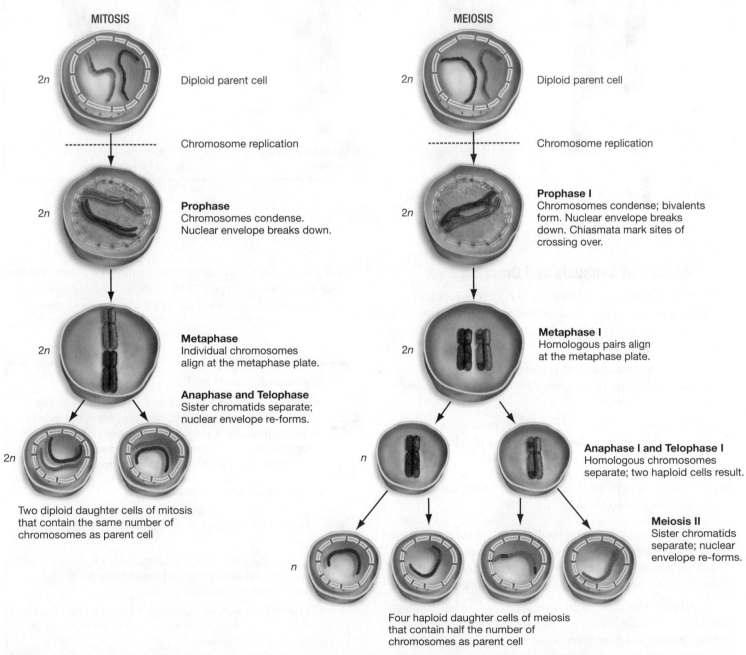

MITOSIS

2n — Diploid parent cell

------- Chromosome replication

2n — **Prophase** Chromosomes condense. Nuclear envelope breaks down.

2n — **Metaphase** Individual chromosomes align at the metaphase plate.

Anaphase and Telophase Sister chromatids separate; nuclear envelope re-forms.

2n — Two diploid daughter cells of mitosis that contain the same number of chromosomes as parent cell

MEIOSIS

2n — Diploid parent cell

------- Chromosome replication

2n — **Prophase I** Chromosomes condense; bivalents form. Nuclear envelope breaks down. Chiasmata mark sites of crossing over.

2n — **Metaphase I** Homologous pairs align at the metaphase plate.

n — **Anaphase I and Telophase I** Homologous chromosomes separate; two haploid cells result.

Meiosis II Sister chromatids separate; nuclear envelope re-forms.

n — Four haploid daughter cells of meiosis that contain half the number of chromosomes as parent cell

FIGURE 11.8 A Comparison of Mitosis and Meiosis. Mitosis produces two daughter cells with chromosomal complements identical to the parent cell. Meiosis produces four haploid cells with chromosomal complements unlike one another and unlike the diploid parent cell.

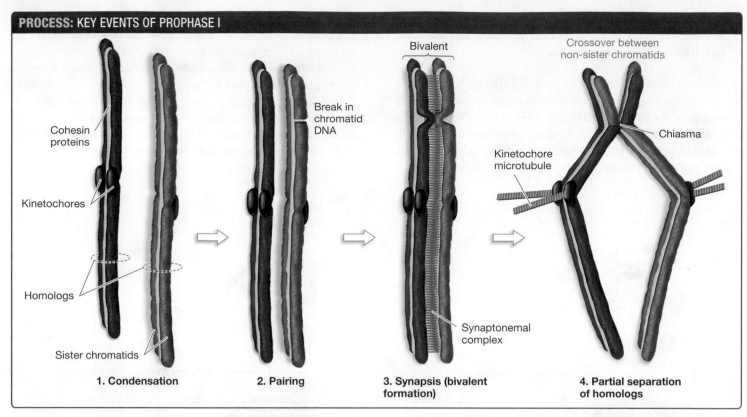

FIGURE 11.9 A Closer Look at Key Events in Prophase of Meiosis I.

A Closer Look at Synapsis and Crossing Over

The pairing of homologs and crossing over in prophase I are important events unique to meiosis. **FIGURE 11.9** takes a closer look at how chromosomes come together and exchange parts during meiosis I.

Step 1 Sister chromatids are held together along their full length by proteins known as cohesins. At the entry to prophase I, chromosomes begin to condense.

Step 2 Homologs pair. In many organisms, pairing begins when a break is made in the DNA of one chromatid. This break initiates a crossover between non-sister chromatids.

Step 3 A network of proteins forms the **synaptonemal complex,** which holds the two homologs tightly together.

Step 4 The synaptonemal complex disassembles in late prophase I. The two homologs partially separate and are held together only at chiasmata. Attachments at chiasmata are eventually broken to restore individual, unconnected chromosomes.

At a chiasma the non-sister chromatids from each homolog have been physically broken at the same point and *attached to each other*. As a result, corresponding segments of maternal and paternal chromosomes are exchanged.

Crossing over can occur at many locations along the length of paired homologs, and it routinely occurs at least once between each pair of non-sister chromatids. In humans, each chromosome undergoes an average of 1½ crossovers during meiosis.

Why does meiosis exist at all? What are its consequences?

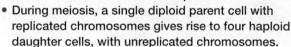

 If you understand that . . .

- Meiosis is called a reduction division because the total number of chromosomes present is cut in half.
- During meiosis, a single diploid parent cell with replicated chromosomes gives rise to four haploid daughter cells, with unreplicated chromosomes.

✔ You should be able to . . .

1. Demonstrate the phases of meiosis I illustrated in Figure 11.7 by using pipe cleaners or pieces of cooked spaghetti.

2. Identify the event that makes meiosis a reduction division, unlike mitosis, and explain why it is responsible for reduction division.

3. Explain how meiosis generates cells with one of every kind of chromosome rather than random mixtures of different chromosomes.

Answers are available in Appendix A.

11.2 Meiosis Promotes Genetic Variation

The cell biologists who worked out the details of meiosis in the late 1800s and early 1900s realized that the process solved the riddle of fertilization. Weismann's hypothesis—that a reduction division precedes gamete formation in animals—was confirmed.

By now, having come to appreciate that meiosis is an intricate, tightly regulated process, you shouldn't be surprised to learn that it involves dozens, if not hundreds, of different proteins. Given this complexity, it is logical to hypothesize that meiosis accomplishes something extremely important: Thanks to the independent shuffling of maternal and paternal chromosomes and crossing over during meiosis I, the chromosomes in one gamete are different from the chromosomes in another gamete and different from the chromosomes in parental cells. Subsequently, fertilization brings haploid sets of chromosomes from a mother and father together to form a diploid offspring. The chromosome complement of this offspring is unlike that of either parent. It is a random combination of genetic material from each parent.

This change in chromosomal complement is crucial. The critical factor here is that changes in chromosome sets occur only during sexual reproduction—*not* during asexual reproduction.

- **Asexual reproduction** is any mechanism of producing offspring that does not involve the production and fusion of gametes. Asexual reproduction in eukaryotes is based on mitosis. The chromosomes in cells produced by mitosis are identical to the chromosomes in the parental cell.

- **Sexual reproduction** is the production of offspring through the production and fusion of gametes. Sexual reproduction results in offspring that have chromosome complements unlike those of their siblings or their parents.

Why is this difference important?

Chromosomes and Heredity

The changes in chromosomes produced by meiosis and fertilization are significant because chromosomes contain the cell's hereditary material. Stated another way, chromosomes contain the instructions for specifying particular traits. These inherited traits range from eye color and height in humans to the number or shape of the bristles on a fruit fly's leg to the color or shape of the seeds found in pea plants.

In the early 1900s, biologists began using the term gene to refer to the inherited instructions for a particular trait. Recall that the term allele refers to a particular version of a gene and that homologous chromosomes may carry different alleles.

Chromosomes are the repositories of genes, and identical copies of chromosomes are distributed to daughter cells during mitosis. Thus, cells that are produced by mitosis are genetically identical to the parent cell, and offspring produced during asexual reproduction are genetically identical to one another as well as to their parent. Offspring produced by asexual reproduction

are **clones**—or exact copies—of their parent. A familiar example of asexual reproduction is growing a new plant from a cutting.

In contrast, the offspring produced by sexual reproduction are genetically different from one another and unlike either their mother or their father.

Let's begin by analyzing two aspects of meiosis that create variation among chromosomes: (1) separation and distribution of homologous chromosomes and (2) crossing over. We'll then look at how these processes interact with fertilization to produce genetically variable offspring.

The Role of Independent Assortment

Each somatic cell in your body contains 23 homologous pairs of chromosomes and 46 chromosomes in total. Half of these chromosomes came from your mother, and half came from your father. Each chromosome contains genes, and genes influence particular traits. For example, one gene that affects your eye color might be located on one chromosome, while one of the genes that affects your hair color might be located on a different chromosome (**FIGURE 11.10a**).

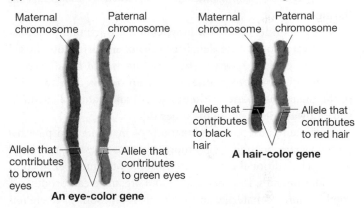

(a) Example: Individual with different alleles of two genes

Maternal chromosome   Paternal chromosome   Maternal chromosome   Paternal chromosome

Allele that contributes to brown eyes   Allele that contributes to green eyes

An eye-color gene

Allele that contributes to black hair   Allele that contributes to red hair

A hair-color gene

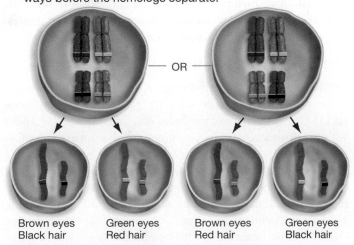

(b) During meiosis I, bivalents can line up two different ways before the homologs separate.

— OR —

Brown eyes Black hair   Green eyes Red hair   Brown eyes Red hair   Green eyes Black hair

FIGURE 11.10 Independent Assortment of Homologous Chromosomes Results in Varied Combinations of Genes.

Suppose that the chromosomes you inherited from your mother contain alleles associated with brown eyes and black hair, but the chromosomes you inherited from your father include alleles associated with green eyes and red hair. (This is a simplification for the purpose of explanation. In reality, several genes with various alleles interact in complex ways to produce human eye color and hair color.)

Will any particular gamete you produce contain the genetic instructions inherited from your mother or the instructions inherited from your father? To answer this question, study the diagram of meiosis in **FIGURE 11.10b**. It shows that when pairs of homologous chromosomes line up during meiosis I and the homologs separate, a variety of combinations of maternal and paternal chromosomes can result. Each daughter cell gets a random assortment of maternal and paternal chromosomes.

This phenomenon is known as the principle of independent assortment. In the example given here, meiosis results in gametes with alleles for brown eyes and black hair, the traits from your mother, and green eyes and red hair, the traits from your father. But two additional combinations also occur: brown eyes and red hair, or green eyes and black hair. The appearance of new combinations of alleles is called **genetic recombination.** Four different combinations of paternal and maternal chromosomes are possible when two chromosomes are distributed to daughter cells during meiosis I.

✔ **If you understand how independent assortment produces genetic variation in the daughter cells of meiosis, you should be able to explain how genetic variation would be affected if maternal chromosomes always lined up together on one side of the metaphase plate during meiosis I and paternal chromosomes always lined up on the other side.**

How many different combinations of maternal and paternal homologs are possible when more chromosomes are involved? With each additional pair of chromosomes, the number of combinations doubles. In general, a diploid organism can produce 2^n combinations of maternal and paternal chromosomes, where n is the haploid chromosome number. This means that you ($n = 23$) can produce 2^{23}, or about 8.4 million, gametes that differ in their combination of maternal and paternal chromosome sets. The random assortment of whole chromosomes generates an impressive amount of genetic variation among gametes.

The Role of Crossing Over

Recall from Section 11.1 that segments of paternal and maternal chromatids exchange when crossing over occurs during meiosis I. Thus, crossing over produces new combinations of alleles within a chromosome—combinations that did not exist in either parent. This phenomenon is known as recombination. Crossing over is an important source of genetic recombination.

Genetic recombination is important because it dramatically increases the genetic variability of gametes produced by meiosis. The independent assortment of homologous chromosomes during meiosis generates varied combinations of chromosomes in gametes; genetic recombination due to crossing over varies the combinations of alleles along each chromosome that is involved

in a crossover. With crossing over, the number of genetically different gametes that you can produce is much more than the 8.4 million—it is virtually limitless.

How Does Fertilization Affect Genetic Variation?

Crossing over and the independent assortment of maternal and paternal chromosomes ensure that each gamete is genetically unique. Even if two gametes produced by the same individual fuse to form a diploid offspring—in which case **self-fertilization,** or "selfing," is taking place—the offspring are very likely to be genetically different from the parent (**FIGURE 11.11**). Selfing is common in many plant species, and it also occurs in animal species in which single individuals—called hermaphrodites—contain both male and female sex organs.

Self-fertilization, however, is rare or nonexistent in many sexually reproducing species. Instead, gametes from different individuals combine to form offspring. This process is called **outcrossing.** Outcrossing increases the genetic diversity of offspring even further because it combines chromosomes from different individuals. These chromosomes are likely to contain different alleles.

How many genetically distinct offspring can be produced when outcrossing occurs? Let's answer this question using humans as an example. Recall that a single human can produce about 8.4 million different gametes by independent assortment alone. When a sperm and egg come together at fertilization, the number of possible genetic combinations that can result is equal to the product of the numbers of different gametes produced by each parent. (To understand this logic, see **BioSkills 5** in Appendix B.) In humans this means that two parents can potentially produce 8.4 million × 8.4 million = 70.6×10^{12} genetically distinct offspring, even without crossing over. This number is far greater than the total number of people who have ever lived.

check your understanding

If you understand that . . .

- The daughter cells produced by meiosis are genetically different from the parent cell because (1) maternal and paternal homologs align randomly at metaphase of meiosis I and (2) crossing over leads to recombination within chromosomes.

✔ **You should be able to . . .**

1. Draw a diploid parent cell with $2n = 6$ (three types of chromosomes) and then sketch the genetically distinct types of daughter cells that may result by independent assortment of these chromosomes at meiosis.

2. Discuss how crossing over would influence the genetic diversity of these gametes.

3. Compare and contrast the degree of genetic variation that results from asexual reproduction, selfing, and outcrossing.

Answers are available in Appendix A.

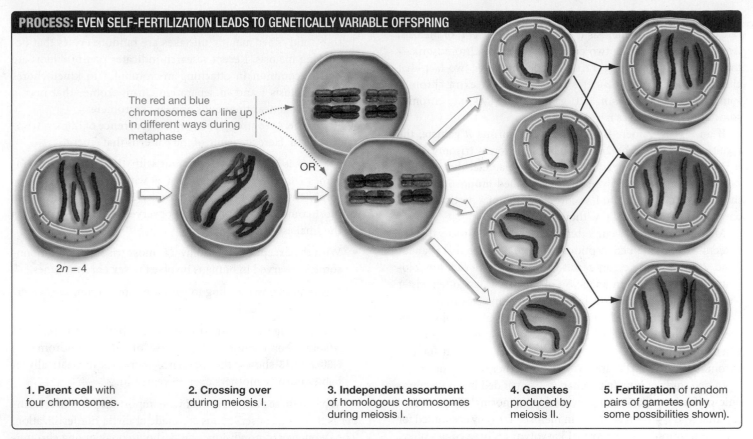

The red and blue chromosomes can line up in different ways during metaphase

OR

2*n* = 4

1. **Parent cell** with four chromosomes.

2. **Crossing over** during meiosis I.

3. **Independent assortment** of homologous chromosomes during meiosis I.

4. **Gametes** produced by meiosis II.

5. **Fertilization** of random pairs of gametes (only some possibilities shown).

FIGURE 11.11 Crossing Over, Independent Assortment, and the Random Pairing of Gametes during Fertilization Increase Genetic Variation, Even in Offspring Produced by Self-Fertilization.

✔**EXERCISE** In step 5, only a few of the many types of offspring that could be produced are shown. Sketch two additional types that are different from those shown.

In any complicated process such as meiosis, things can and do go wrong. What happens if there is a mistake, and the chromosomes are not properly distributed?

11.3 What Happens When Things Go Wrong in Meiosis?

Errors in meiosis are surprisingly common. If this were like a spelling mistake, it might be only an annoyance. But in humans, a conservative estimate is that 25 percent of conceptions are spontaneously terminated because of problems in meiosis. What are the consequences for offspring if gametes contain an abnormal set of chromosomes?

In 1866 Langdon Down described a distinctive set of co-occurring conditions observed in some people. The syndrome was characterized by mental retardation, a high risk for heart problems and leukemia, and a degenerative brain disorder similar to Alzheimer's disease. **Down syndrome,** as the disorder came to be called, is observed in about 0.15 percent of live births (1 infant in every 666).

For over 80 years the cause of the syndrome was unknown. Then, in the late 1950s, a study of the chromosome sets of nine Down syndrome children suggested that the condition is associated with the presence of an extra copy of chromosome 21. This situation is called **trisomy** ("three-bodies")—in this case, trisomy-21—because each cell has three copies of the chromosome. The explanation proposed for the trisomy was that a mistake had occurred during meiosis in either the mother or the father.

How Do Mistakes Occur?

For a gamete to get one complete set of chromosomes, two steps in meiosis must be perfectly executed.

1. The chromosomes in each homologous pair must separate from each other during the first meiotic division, so that only one homolog ends up in each daughter cell.

2. Sister chromatids must separate from each other and move to opposite poles of the dividing cell during meiosis II.

If both homologs in meiosis I or both sister chromatids in meiosis II move to the same pole of the parent cell, the products of meiosis will be abnormal. This sort of meiotic error is referred to as **nondisjunction,** because the homologs or sister chromatids fail to separate, or disjoin.

FIGURE 11.12 shows what happens when homologs do not separate correctly during meiosis I. Notice that at the end of meiosis, two daughter cells have two copies of the same chromosome—the smaller one in Figure 11.12—while the other two lack that chromosome entirely. Gametes that contain an extra chromosome are symbolized as $n + 1$; gametes that lack one chromosome are symbolized as $n - 1$.

If an $n + 1$ gamete is fertilized by a normal n gamete, the resulting zygote will be $2n + 1$. This situation is trisomy. If the $n - 1$ gamete is fertilized by a normal n gamete, the resulting zygote will be $2n - 1$. This situation is called **monosomy**. Cells that have too many or too few chromosomes of a particular type are said to be **aneuploid** ("without-form").

Meiotic mistakes occur often. Researchers estimate that 25 percent of all human conceptions produce a zygote that is aneuploid. Most of these errors result from the failure of a homologous pair to separate in anaphase of meiosis I; less often, sister chromatids stay together during anaphase of meiosis II.

The consequences of meiotic mistakes are almost always severe. Trisomy-21 is unusual in allowing development to proceed when there are three copies of chromosome 21. Even for this chromosome, live births are not seen when there is only one copy.

In one study of human pregnancies that ended in early embryonic or fetal death, 38 percent involved abnormal chromosome sets that resulted from mistakes in meiosis. Trisomy accounted for about one-third of the abnormal karyotypes. Three copies of every chromosome ($3n$), a condition called triploidy, was also common. Monosomy and abnormally sized or shaped chromosomes were also seen. Mistakes in meiosis are common and are the leading cause of spontaneous abortion (miscarriage) in humans.

Why Do Mistakes Occur?

Trisomy and other meiotic mistakes are random errors that occur during meiosis. Recent research indicates that problems are especially common in attaching microtubules to kinetochores early in meiosis I and in separating chromosomes that have a single chiasma near their ends or near centromeres.

Researchers see strong patterns in occurrence of human trisomies at birth. Here are some of the patterns that emerge:

- Trisomy is much more common with the smaller chromosomes (numbers 13–22) than it is with the larger chromosomes (numbers 1–12), and trisomy-21 is far and away the most common type of trisomy observed. Chromosome 21 is the smallest human autosome.

- With the exception of trisomy-21, most trisomies and monosomies observed in humans involve the sex chromosomes.

- Errors in meiosis leading to eggs are more common than errors in meiosis leading to sperm.

- Maternal age is an important factor in the occurrence of trisomy. For example, in the case of Down syndrome, as **FIGURE 11.13** shows, the incidence increases dramatically in babies born to mothers over 35 years old.

Why do these patterns occur? One important point to remember is that these observations are made at birth, not fertilization. The frequency of nondisjunction is about equal among chromosomes, but aneuploidy tends to be lethal to embryos if it involves chromosomes that contain a large number of genes. Trisomy-21 is common most likely because it involves a small chromosome with a correspondingly small number of genes.

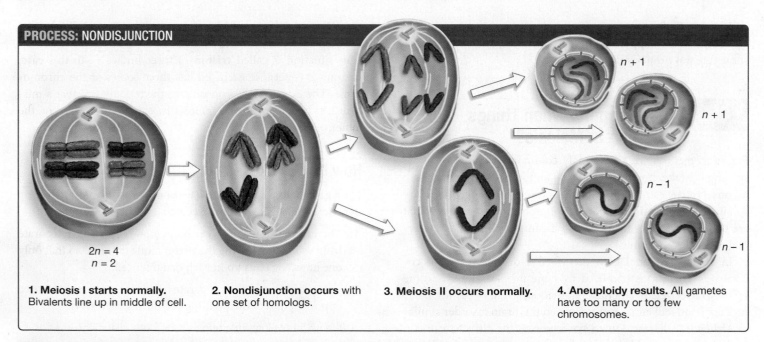

PROCESS: NONDISJUNCTION

$2n = 4$
$n = 2$

$n + 1$

$n + 1$

$n - 1$

$n - 1$

1. Meiosis I starts normally. Bivalents line up in middle of cell.

2. Nondisjunction occurs with one set of homologs.

3. Meiosis II occurs normally.

4. Aneuploidy results. All gametes have too many or too few chromosomes.

FIGURE 11.12 Nondisjunction Leads to Gametes with Abnormal Chromosome Numbers. If homologous chromosomes fail to separate during meiosis I, the gametes that result will have an extra chromosome or will lack a chromosome. Nondisjunction can also occur during meiosis II if sister chromatids fail to separate.

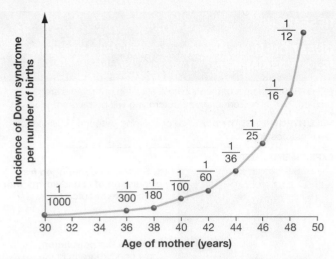

FIGURE 11.13 The Frequency of Down Syndrome Increases as a Function of a Mother's Age.

DATA: National Down Syndrome Society. 2012. www.ndss.org/index.php?option=com_content&view=article&id=61&Itemid=78

There are more questions than answers. Why are there more errors in women than men? Why is there such a strong correlation between maternal age and frequency of trisomy-21?

In part, the answers lie with an unusual feature of human egg development (oogenesis). Diploid precursors to eggs enter meiosis I before birth and arrest in prophase I until ovulation. For some eggs, this is 40 years or more later. Spindle apparatus function and the ability to separate chromosomes properly appear to decline after this long wait. Much remains to be discovered, but one thing is clear: Successful meiosis is critical to the health of offspring.

11.4 Why Does Meiosis Exist?

Why sex and meiosis? Although it seems obvious that sex and meiosis are needed universally for reproduction, that's not the case. Meiosis and sexual reproduction occur in only a small fraction of the lineages on the tree of life. Bacteria and archaea normally undergo only asexual reproduction; most algae, all fungi, and some animals and land plants reproduce asexually as well as sexually. Asexual reproduction is even observed in some vertebrates. Several species of guppy in the genus *Poeciliopsis*, for example, reproduce exclusively by mitosis.

Although sexual reproduction plays a central role in the life of most familiar organisms—including us—until recently, scientists had no clear idea of why it occurs. In fact, on the basis of theory, biologists had good reason to think that sexual reproduction should *not* exist.

The Paradox of Sex

In 1978 John Maynard Smith pointed out that the existence of sexual reproduction presents a paradox. Maynard Smith developed a mathematical model showing that because asexually reproducing individuals do not have to produce male offspring, their progeny on average can produce twice as many offspring as individuals that reproduce sexually. **FIGURE 11.14** diagrams this result by showing the number of females (♀), males (♂), and asexually reproducing organisms (**O**) produced over several generations by asexual versus sexual reproduction.

In this example, each asexually reproducing individual and each sexually reproducing couple produces four offspring over the course of their lifetimes. Note that in the sexual population, it takes two individuals—one male and one female—to produce

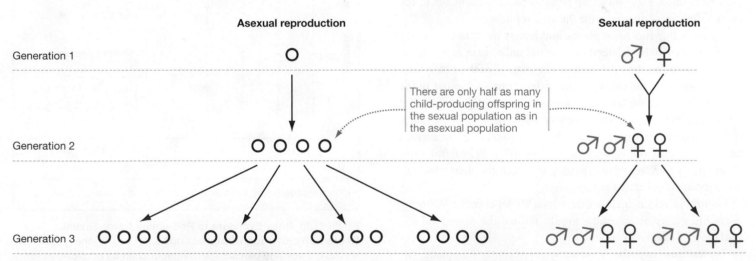

FIGURE 11.14 Asexual Reproduction Produces More Offspring. Each female (♀), male (♂), and asexual (**O**) symbol represents an individual. This hypothetical example assumes that (1) every asexual individual or sexually reproducing couple produces four offspring over the course of a lifetime, (2) sexually reproducing individuals produce half males and half females, and (3) all offspring survive to breed.

✔**QUANTITATIVE** How many asexually produced offspring would be present in generation 4? How many sexually produced offspring?

four offspring. Two out of every four children that each female produces sexually are males who cannot have children of their own. As a result, after one generation (generation 2 in Figure 11.14) the sexual population has just half as many child-producing individuals as the asexual population. Maynard Smith referred to this as the "two-fold cost of males." Asexual reproduction is much more efficient than sexual reproduction because no males are produced.

Based on this analysis, what will happen when asexual and sexual individuals exist in the same population and compete with one another? If all other things are equal, individuals that reproduce asexually should increase in frequency in the population while individuals that reproduce sexually should decline in frequency. In fact, Maynard Smith's model predicts that sexual reproduction is so inefficient that it should be completely eliminated.

To resolve this paradox, biologists began examining the assumption "If all other things are equal." Stated another way, biologists began looking for ways that meiosis and outcrossing could lead to the production of offspring that reproduce more than asexually produced individuals do. After decades of debate and analysis, two solid hypotheses to explain the paradox of sex are beginning to emerge.

The Purifying Selection Hypothesis

The first clue to unraveling the paradox of sex is a simple observation: If a gene is damaged or altered in a way that causes it to function poorly, it will be inherited by *all* of that individual's offspring when asexual reproduction occurs. Suppose the altered gene arose in generation 1 of Figure 11.14. If this gene is important, its alteration might cause the four asexual females present in generation 2 to produce fewer than four offspring apiece—perhaps because the members of generation 2 die young. If so, then generation 3 will not have twice as many individuals in the asexual lineage compared with the sexual lineage.

An allele that functions poorly and lowers the fitness of an individual is said to be deleterious. Asexual individuals are doomed to transmitting all their deleterious alleles to all of their offspring.

Suppose, however, that the same deleterious allele arose in the sexually reproducing female in generation 1 of Figure 11.14. If the female also has a normal copy of the gene, and if she mates with a male that has normal copies of the gene, then on average half her offspring will lack the deleterious allele. Sexual individuals are likely to have some offspring that lack the deleterious alleles that are present in a parent.

Natural selection against deleterious alleles is called purifying selection. Purifying selection should reduce the numerical advantage of asexual reproduction.

To test this hypothesis, researchers recently compared the same genes in two closely related species of *Daphnia*, a tiny crustacean that is a common inhabitant of ponds and lakes. One of these species reproduces asexually and the other reproduces sexually. As predicted, the researchers found that individuals in the asexual species contained many more deleterious alleles than individuals in the sexual species. Results like these have convinced

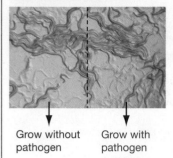
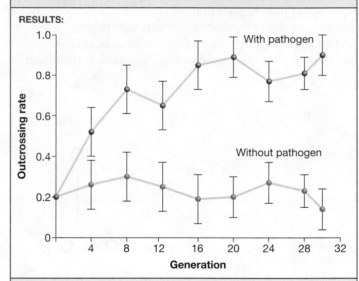
FIGURE 11.15 Does Exposure to Pathogens Favor Sexual Reproduction through Outcrossing? Each point in the graph shows the average percentage of reproduction by outcrossing for five populations. The bars indicate the degree of variation in the data (see **BioSkills 4** in Appendix B for a description of error bars).

Morran, L. T., et al. 2011. Running with the red queen: Host-parasite coevolution selects for biparental sex. *Science* 333: 216–218.

✔**QUESTION** What would you predict if a non-evolving pathogen were used?

biologists that purifying selection is an important factor promoting the success of sexual reproduction.

The Changing-Environment Hypothesis

The second hypothesis to explain sexual reproduction also focuses on the benefits of producing genetically diverse offspring. Here's the key idea: Offspring that are genetic clones of their parents are unlikely to thrive if the environment changes.

What type of environmental change might favor genetically diverse offspring? The leading hypothesis points to pressure put on hosts by rapidly changing pathogens and parasites—bacteria, viruses, fungi, and other entities that cause disease. In your own lifetime, for example, several new disease-causing agents have emerged that afflict humans. These include the SARS virus, HIV, and new strains of the tuberculosis bacterium. Hundreds of genes help defend you against these types of invaders. Certain alleles help you fight off particular strains of disease-causing bacteria, eukaryotes, or viruses. In this evolutionary arms race, pathogens and parasites constantly evolve new ways to infect the most common types of host.

What happens if all the offspring produced by an individual are genetically identical? If a new strain of disease-causing agent evolves, then all the asexually produced offspring are likely to be susceptible to that new strain. But if the offspring are genetically varied, then it is likely that at least some offspring will have combinations of alleles that enable them to fight off the new strain of pathogen or parasite and produce offspring of their own.

Recall from Section 11.2 that over multiple generations, outcrossing—mating between two different individuals—increases the amount of genetic diversity relative to self-fertilization. A logical question to ask is: Does exposure to evolving pathogens favor outcrossing in sexually reproducing organisms? To address this question, Levi Morran, Curtis Lively, and colleagues carried out a pivotal study on a tiny (only about 1 mm long) roundworm named *Caenorhabditis elegans*.

C. elegans is an important model organism (see **BioSkills 13** in Appendix B) that was chosen for this study because it leads an unusual sex life. There are no females, only males and hermaphrodites. Because hermaphrodites have both male and female sex organs, this means that *C. elegans* can reproduce either by self-fertilization or by outcrossing with males. The proportion of roundworms that reproduce by self-fertilization versus outcrossing can vary in different strains or in different environments over time. So, the research team was able to test whether the rate of outcrossing increased in response to intense selection by a pathogen.

The setup of Morran, Lively, and colleagues' experiment is shown in **FIGURE 11.15**. The team began with a population of roundworms that had not been exposed to the pathogen and that reproduced predominantly by self-fertilization. The researchers then split the starting population into different groups. Half the groups were grown in the presence of a pathogen—a deadly bacterium—and the other half were grown without it. Once ingested by a roundworm, the bacterial pathogen could kill a susceptible individual within 24 hours.

At each generation, bacteria were collected from the carcasses of roundworms killed in the previous generation. Companion experiments showed that the pathogen evolved to become even more infectious over the course of the study.

The results are shown at the bottom of Figure 11.15. The rate of outcrossing stayed low over 32 generations in populations that did not encounter the pathogen. In contrast, populations that were exposed to the evolving pathogen showed a rapid increase in the rate of outcrossing.

At the end of the experiment, the roundworms in the pathogen-exposed population were significantly more resistant to the evolved pathogen than their ancestors. In other words, the roundworms in the predominantly outcrossing population had evolved along with the pathogen. In striking contrast, when a parallel experiment was done with a strain of roundworms that could reproduce only by self-fertilization, those populations were unable to evolve resistance to the pathogen. In fact, they became extinct.

These results and many others support the changing-environment hypothesis. Although the paradox of sex remains an active area of research, more biologists are becoming convinced that sexual reproduction is helpful for two reasons: (1) Offspring are not doomed to inherit harmful alleles, and (2) the production of genetically varied offspring means that at least some may be able to resist rapidly evolving pathogens and parasites.

CHAPTER 11   REVIEW

For media, go to MasteringBiology

If you understand . . .

11.1 How Does Meiosis Occur?

- Meiosis is a nuclear division resulting in cells that have only one of each type of chromosome and half as many chromosomes as the parent cell. In animals it leads to the formation of eggs and sperm.

- In diploid (2n) organisms, individuals have two versions of each type of chromosome. The two versions are called homologs. One homolog is inherited from the mother and one from the father. Haploid organisms (n) have just one of each type of chromosome.

- Each chromosome is replicated before meiosis begins. At the start of meiosis I, each chromosome consists of a pair of sister chromatids.

- Homologous pairs of chromosomes synapse early in meiosis I, forming a bivalent—two closely paired homologous chromosomes. Non-sister chromatids undergo crossing over.

- When crossing over is complete, the pair of homologous chromosomes is moved to the metaphase plate.

- At the end of meiosis I, the homologous chromosomes are separated and distributed to two daughter cells. The daughter cells are haploid, because each receives one of each type of chromosome.

- During meiosis II, sister chromatids separate and are distributed to two daughter cells.

- From one diploid cell with replicated chromosomes, meiosis produces four haploid daughter cells with unreplicated chromosomes.

✔ You should be able to diagram a diploid cell with a homologous pair of chromosomes and show when in meiosis this cell produces haploid daughter cells. Be sure to show all chromatids.

11.2 Meiosis Promotes Genetic Variation

- Each cell produced by meiosis receives a different combination of chromosomes. Because genes are located on chromosomes, each cell produced by meiosis receives a different complement of genes. The resulting offspring are genetically distinct from one another and from their parents.

- When meiosis and outcrossing occur, the chromosome complements of offspring differ from one another and from their parents for three reasons:

1. Gametes receive a random assortment of maternal and paternal chromosomes when homologs separate in meiosis I. This is independent assortment.
2. Because of crossing over, each chromosome contains a random assortment of paternal and maternal alleles.
3. Outcrossing results in a combination of chromosome sets from different individuals.

✔ You should be able to draw a diploid cell with four chromosomes entering meiosis and illustrate (a) how different combinations of chromosomes can result from independent assortment; and (b) focusing on a single homologous pair, show how many recombinant chromosomes (chromosomes with mixtures of maternal and paternal segments) are produced when crossing over occurs once along this homologous pair.

11.3 What Happens When Things Go Wrong in Meiosis?

- If mistakes occur during meiosis, the resulting egg and sperm cells may contain the wrong number of chromosomes. It is rare for offspring with an incorrect number of chromosomes to develop normally.

- Mistakes during meiosis lead to gametes and offspring with an abnormal number of chromosomes. Children with Down syndrome, for example, have an extra copy of chromosome 21.

- The leading hypothesis to explain meiotic mistakes is that they are accidental failures of homologous chromosomes or sister chromatids to separate properly during meiosis.

✔ Using pipe cleaners or spaghetti to model a homologous pair of chromosomes, you should be able to demonstrate (a) what happens if one pair of homologous chromosomes fails to separate at anaphase of meiosis I and (b) what happens if sister chromatids of one chromosome fail to separate at anaphase of meiosis II but later separate in a daughter cell.

11.4 Why Does Meiosis Exist?

- Asexual reproduction is much more efficient than sexual reproduction because all individuals produced asexually are capable of bearing progeny. With sexual reproduction, half the offspring (the males) are unable to bear progeny.

- The leading hypotheses to explain the existence of meiosis and sexual reproduction are that:

1. parents can produce offspring that lack harmful alleles; and
2. genetically diverse offspring are likely to include some that are better able to resist evolving pathogens and parasites.

✔ You should be able to predict whether, in species that alternate between asexual and sexual reproduction, sexual reproduction occurs during times when environmental conditions are stable or times when conditions change rapidly.

(MB) **MasteringBiology**

1. **MasteringBiology Assignments**

   Tutorials and Activities Asexual and Sexual Life Cycles; Genetic Variation from Sexual Recombination; Meiosis; Meiosis (1 of 3): Genes, Chromosomes, and Sexual Reproduction; Meiosis (2 of 3): The Mechanism; Meiosis (3 of 3): Determinants of Heredity and Genetic Variation; Meiosis Animation; Mistakes in Meiosis; Origins of Genetic Variation

   Questions Reading Quizzes, Blue-Thread Questions, Test Bank

2. **eText** Read your book online, search, take notes, highlight text, and more.

3. **The Study Area** Practice Test, Cumulative Test, BioFlix® 3-D Animations, Videos, Activities, Audio Glossary, Word Study Tools, Art

You should be able to . . .

1. In the roundworm *Ascaris*, eggs and sperm have two chromosomes, but all other cells have four. Observations such as this inspired which important hypothesis?
   a. Before gamete formation, a special type of cell division leads to a quartering of chromosome number.
   b. Before gamete formation, a special type of cell division leads to a halving of chromosome number.
   c. After gamete formation, half the chromosomes are destroyed.
   d. After gamete formation, either the maternal or the paternal set of chromosomes disintegrates.

2. What are homologous chromosomes?
   a. chromosomes that are similar in their size, shape, and gene content
   b. similar chromosomes that are found in different individuals of the same species
   c. the two "threads" in a replicated chromosome (they are identical copies)
   d. the products of crossing over, which contain a combination of segments from maternal chromosomes and segments from paternal chromosomes

3. What is a bivalent?
   a. the X that forms when chromatids from homologous chromosomes cross over
   b. a group of four chromatids produced when homologs synapse
   c. the four points where homologous chromosomes touch as they synapse
   d. the group of four genetically identical daughter cells produced by mitosis

4. What is an outcome of genetic recombination?
   a. the synapsing of homologs during prophase of meiosis I
   b. the new combination of maternal and paternal chromosome segments that results when homologs cross over
   c. the new combinations of chromosome segments that result when self-fertilization occurs
   d. the combination of a haploid phase *and* a diploid phase in a life cycle

5. What proportion of chromosomes in a human skin cell are paternal chromosomes?

6. Meiosis II is similar to _____.

7. Explain the relationship between homologous chromosomes and the relationship between sister chromatids.

8. Lay four pens and four pencils on a tabletop, and imagine that they represent replicated chromosomes in a diploid cell where $n = 2$. Explain the phases of meiosis II by moving the pens and pencils around. (If you don't have enough pens and pencils, use strips of paper or fabric.)

9. Meiosis is called a reduction division, but all the reduction occurs during meiosis I—no reduction occurs during meiosis II. Explain why meiosis I is a reduction division but meiosis II is not.

10. Dogs have 78 chromosomes in their diploid cells. If a diploid dog cell enters meiosis, how many chromosomes and chromatids will be present in each daughter cell at the end of meiosis I?

   a. 39 chromosomes and 39 chromatids
   b. 39 chromosomes and 78 chromatids
   c. 78 chromosomes and 78 chromatids
   d. 78 chromosomes and 156 chromatids

11. Triploid ($3n$) watermelons are produced by crossing a tetraploid ($4n$) strain with a diploid ($2n$) plant. Briefly explain why this mating produces a triploid individual. Why can mitosis proceed normally in triploid cells, but meiosis cannot?

12. Some plant breeders are concerned about the susceptibility of asexually cultivated plants, such as seedless bananas, to new strains of disease-causing bacteria, viruses, or fungi. Briefly explain their concern by discussing the differences in the genetic "outcomes" of asexual and sexual reproduction.

13. The gibbon has 44 chromosomes per diploid set, and the siamang has 50 chromosomes per diploid set. In the 1970s a chance mating between a male gibbon and a female siamang produced an offspring. Predict how many chromosomes were observed in the somatic cells of the offspring. Do you predict that this individual would be able to form viable gametes? Why or why not?

14. Meiosis results in a reassortment of maternal and paternal chromosomes. If $n = 3$ for a given organism, there are eight different combinations of paternal and maternal chromosomes. If no crossing over occurs, what is the probability that a gamete will receive *only* paternal chromosomes?
   a. 0; b. 1/16; c. 1/8; d. 1/3

15. Some researchers hypothesize that older women are less responsive to triggers of spontaneous abortion than younger women. How could the data shown in Figure 11.13, which graphs

a mother's age versus the incidence of Down syndrome, be used to support this hypothesis?

16. A species of rotifer, a small freshwater invertebrate, abandoned sexual reproduction millions of years ago. A remarkable feature of the rotifer's life cycle is its ability to withstand extreme drying. When the rotifer's watery environment dries out, so does the rotifer, and it can be blown in the wind to a new environment. Once blown to water, the rotifer rehydrates and resumes an active life. A major pathogen of these rotifers is a species of fungus. Some scientists hypothesize that fungus-infected rotifers rid themselves of the pathogen when they dry.
   a. Design an experimental study to test this hypothesis.
   b. Provide an explanation for how these asexually reproducing rotifers are able to evade pathogens even though they are genetically identical.

12 Mendel and the Gene

In this chapter you will learn how

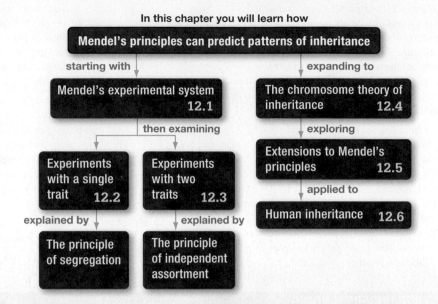

Mendel's principles can predict patterns of inheritance

starting with → Mendel's experimental system **12.1**

then examining →

Experiments with a single trait **12.2**

Experiments with two traits **12.3**

explained by → The principle of segregation

explained by → The principle of independent assortment

expanding to → The chromosome theory of inheritance **12.4**

exploring → Extensions to Mendel's principles **12.5**

applied to → Human inheritance **12.6**

Experiments on garden peas and sweet peas (shown here) helped launch the science of genetics.

The science of biology is built on a series of great ideas. Two of these—the cell theory and the theory of evolution—were introduced in Chapter 1. The cell theory describes the basic structure of organisms; the theory of evolution by natural selection clarifies why species change through time. Life is cellular; populations evolve. These are two of the five fundamental attributes of life.

This chapter introduces a third great idea in biology: the chromosome theory of inheritance. The chromosome theory explained how genetic information is transmitted from one generation to the next. It shed light on a third fundamental attribute of life: Organisms process information.

✔ When you see this checkmark, stop and test yourself. Answers are available in Appendix A.

An Austrian monk named Gregor Mendel laid the groundwork for the theory in 1865, when he announced that he had worked out the rules of inheritance through a series of experiments on garden peas. Another key insight emerged during the final decades of the nineteenth century, when biologists described the details of meiosis (see Chapter 11).

The chromosome theory of inheritance, formulated in 1902 by Walter Sutton and Theodor Boveri, linked these two insights. This theory contends that meiosis causes the patterns of inheritance that Mendel observed. It also asserts that the hereditary factors called genes are located on chromosomes.

The chromosome theory launched the study of **genetics,** the branch of biology that focuses on the inheritance of traits. Let's start at the beginning: What are the rules of inheritance that Mendel discovered?

12.1 Mendel's Experimental System

When biological science began to emerge as an important discipline, questions about **heredity**—meaning inheritance, or the transmission of traits from parents to offspring—were primarily the concern of animal breeders and horticulturists. A **trait** is any characteristic of an individual, ranging from height to the primary structure of a particular membrane protein.

In the city where Gregor Mendel lived, there was particular interest in how selective breeding could result in hardier and more productive varieties of sheep, fruit trees, and vines; and an agricultural society had been formed there to promote research into making selective breeding more efficient. Mendel was an active member of this society, and the monastery he belonged to was also devoted to scientific teaching and research.

What Questions Was Mendel Trying to Answer?

Mendel set out to address the most fundamental of all issues concerning heredity: What are the basic patterns in the transmission of traits from parents to offspring?

At the time, two hypotheses had been formulated to answer this question:

1. *Blending inheritance* claimed that the traits observed in a mother and father blend together to form the traits observed in their offspring. As a result, an offspring's traits are intermediate between the mother's and father's traits.

2. *Inheritance of acquired characters* claimed that traits present in parents are modified, through use, and passed on to their offspring in the modified form.

Each of these hypotheses made predictions. Blending inheritance contended that when black sheep and white sheep mate, their hereditary determinants will blend to form a new hereditary determinant for gray wool. Therefore, their offspring should be gray. Inheritance of acquired characters predicts that if giraffes extend their necks by straining to reach leaves high in the tops of trees, they subsequently produce longer-necked offspring.

These hypotheses were being promoted by the greatest scientists of Mendel's time. Are they correct?

The Garden Pea Served as the First Model Organism in Genetics

After investigating and discarding several candidate species to study, Mendel chose the garden pea, *Pisum sativum*. His reasons were practical: Peas are inexpensive and easy to grow from seed, have a relatively short generation time, and produce reasonably large numbers of seeds. These features made it possible for him to continue experiments over several generations and collect data from large numbers of individuals.

Peas served as a **model organism:** a species that is used for research because it is practical and because conclusions drawn from studying it turn out to apply to many other species as well. **BioSkills 13** in Appendix B introduces some of the important model organisms used in biological science today.

Two additional features of the pea made it possible for Mendel to design his experiments: Individuals were available that differed in easily recognizable traits, such as flower color or seed shape, and he could control which parents were involved in a mating.

How Did Mendel Control Matings? **FIGURE 12.1a** shows the male and female reproductive organs of a garden pea flower. Sperm cells are produced in pollen grains, which are small sacs that

(a) Self-pollination

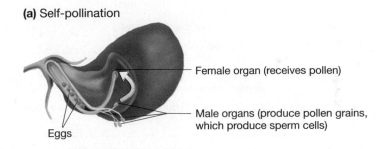

Female organ (receives pollen)

Male organs (produce pollen grains, which produce sperm cells)

Eggs

(b) Cross-pollination

Collect pollen from one individual and transfer it ...

... to the female organs of an individual whose male organs have been removed.

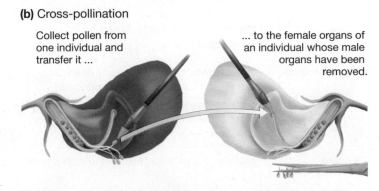

FIGURE 12.1 Peas Can Be Self-Pollinated or Cross-Pollinated.
(a) Under normal conditions, garden peas pollinate themselves.
(b) Mendel developed a method of controlling the matings of his model organism.

mature in the male reproductive structure of the plant. Eggs are produced in the female reproductive structure.

Under normal conditions, garden peas **self-fertilize:** a flower's pollen falls on the female reproductive organ of that same flower. As **FIGURE 12.1b** shows, however, Mendel could prevent self-fertilization by removing the male reproductive organs from a flower before any pollen formed. Later he could transfer pollen from another pea plant to the target flower's female reproductive organ with a brush. This type of mating is referred to as a cross-fertilization, or simply a **cross.** Using this technique, Mendel could control the matings of his model organism.

What Traits Did Mendel Study? Mendel conducted his experiments on varieties of peas that differed in seven traits: seed shape, seed color, pod shape, pod color, flower color, flower and pod position, and stem length. Biologists refer to the observable traits of an individual, such as the shape of a pea seed or the eye color of a person, as its **phenotype** (literally, "show-type"). Phenotype is just one term in the rich vocabulary of genetics. You can review many of these terms in **TABLE 12.1**. In the first pea populations that Mendel studied, two distinct phenotypes existed for each of the seven traits.

Mendel began his work by obtaining individuals from what breeders called pure lines or true-breeding lines. A **pure line** consists of individuals that produce offspring identical to themselves when they are self-pollinated or crossed to another member of the pure-line population. For example, earlier breeders had developed pure lines for wrinkled seeds and round seeds. During two years of trial experiments, Mendel confirmed that individuals that germinated from his wrinkled seeds produced only wrinkled-seeded offspring when they were mated to themselves or to another pure-line individual that germinated from a wrinkled seed, and he confirmed that the same was true for round seeds.

Why is this important? Remember that Mendel wanted to find out how traits are transmitted from parents to offspring. Once he had confirmed that he was working with pure lines, he could compare the results of crosses within a pure line with crosses between individuals from different pure lines.

SUMMARY TABLE 12.1 **Vocabulary Used in Mendelian Genetics**

Term	Definition	Example or Comment
Gene	A hereditary factor that influences a particular trait.	This definition will become more precise in later chapters.
Allele	A particular form of a gene.	The two alleles in a diploid may be the same or different.
Genotype	A listing of the alleles in an individual.	In diploids, the genotype lists two alleles of each gene; in haploids, the genotype lists one allele of each gene.
Phenotype	An individual's observable traits.	Can be observed at levels from molecules to the whole organism; influenced, not dictated, by the genotype.
Homozygous	Having two of the same allele.	Refers to a particular gene.
Heterozygous	Having two different alleles.	Refers to a particular gene.
Dominant allele	An allele that produces its phenotype in heterozygous and homozygous form.	Dominance does not imply high frequency or high fitness.
Recessive allele	An allele that produces its phenotype only in homozygous form.	Phenotype "recedes" or disappears in heterozygous individuals.
Pure line	Individuals of the same phenotype that, when crossed, always produce offspring with the same phenotype.	Pure-line individuals are homozygous for the gene in question.
Hybrid	Offspring from crosses between homozygous parents with different genotypes.	Hybrids are heterozygous.
Reciprocal cross	A cross in which the phenotypes of the male and female are reversed compared with a prior cross.	If reciprocal crosses give identical results, the sex of the parent does not influence transmission of the trait.
Testcross	A cross between a homozygous recessive individual and an individual with the dominant phenotype but an unknown genotype.	Usually used to determine whether a parent with a dominant phenotype is homozygous or heterozygous.
X-linked	Referring to a gene located on the X chromosome.	X-linked genes and traits show different patterns of inheritance in males and females.
Y-linked	Referring to a gene located on the Y chromosome.	In humans, Y-linked genes determine male-specific development.
Autosomal	Referring to a gene located on any non-sex chromosome (an autosome) or a trait determined by an autosomal gene.	Mendel studied only autosomal genes and traits.

Suppose that Mendel arranged matings between a pure-line individual with round seeds and a pure-line individual with wrinkled seeds. He knew that one parent carried a hereditary determinant for round seeds, while the other carried a hereditary determinant for wrinkled seeds. But each offspring from this mating would contain both types of hereditary determinants. They would be **hybrids**—offspring from matings between true-breeding parents that differ in one or more traits.

Would these hybrid offspring have wrinkled seeds, round seeds, or a blended combination of wrinkled and round? What would the seed shape in subsequent generations be when hybrid individuals self-pollinated or were crossed with members of the pure lines?

12.2 Mendel's Experiments with a Single Trait

Mendel's first set of experiments consisted of crossing pure lines that differed in just one trait. This is an important research strategy in biological science: Start with a simple situation. Once you understand what's going on, you can consider more complex questions, such as, What happens in crosses between individuals that differ in two traits?

Mendel began his single-trait crosses by crossing individuals from round-seeded and wrinkled-seeded pure lines. The adults used in an initial experimental cross are the **parental generation.** Their progeny (that is, offspring) are the **F₁ generation.** F_1 stands for "first filial"; the Latin roots *filius* and *filia* mean "son" and "daughter," respectively. Subsequent generations are called the F_2 generation, F_3 generation, and so on.

The Monohybrid Cross

In his first set of crosses, Mendel took pollen from round-seeded plants and placed it on the female reproductive organs of plants from the wrinkled-seeded line. As **FIGURE 12.2a** shows, all the seeds produced by progeny from this cross were round.

This was a remarkable result, for two reasons:

1. The traits did not blend together to form an intermediate phenotype. Instead, the round-seeded form appeared intact. This result was in stark contrast to the predictions of the blending-inheritance hypothesis shown in **FIGURE 12.2b.**

2. The genetic determinant for wrinkled seeds seemed to have disappeared. Where did it go?

Dominant and Recessive Traits To figure out what was going on, Mendel did something that turned out to be brilliant: He planted the F_1 seeds and allowed the individuals to self-pollinate when they matured.

Remember that he knew that each of these individuals had inherited a genetic determinant for round seeds and a genetic determinant for wrinkled seeds. A mating like this—between parents that each carry two different genetic determinants for the same trait—is called a **monohybrid cross.**

When he collected the seeds that were produced by many plants in the resulting F_2 generation, he observed that 5474 were round and 1850 were wrinkled (see Figure 12.2a). This observation was astonishing. The wrinkled seed shape had reappeared in the F_2 generation after disappearing completely in the F_1 generation. No one had observed the phenomenon before, simply because it had been customary for biologists to stop their breeding experiments with F_1 offspring.

Mendel invented some important terms to describe this result.

- He designated wrinkled shape as a **recessive** trait relative to the round-seed trait. This was an appropriate term because none of the F_1 individuals had wrinkled seeds—meaning the wrinkled-seed phenotype appeared to recede or temporarily become latent or hidden.

- He referred to round seeds as **dominant** to the wrinkled-seed trait. This term was apt because the round-seed phenotype appeared to dominate over the wrinkled-seed determinant when both were present.

It's important to note, though, that in genetics the term dominant has nothing to do with its everyday English usage as powerful

(a) Results of Mendel's single-trait (monohybrid) cross

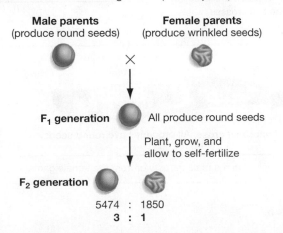

Male parents
(produce round seeds)

Female parents
(produce wrinkled seeds)

×

F₁ generation — All produce round seeds

Plant, grow, and allow to self-fertilize

F₂ generation

5474 : 1850
3 : 1

(b) Prediction of blending-inheritance hypothesis

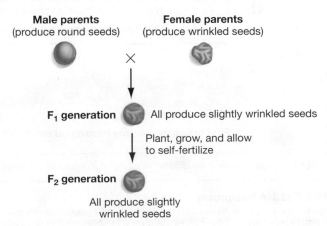

Male parents
(produce round seeds)

Female parents
(produce wrinkled seeds)

×

F₁ generation — All produce slightly wrinkled seeds

Plant, grow, and allow to self-fertilize

F₂ generation

All produce slightly wrinkled seeds

FIGURE 12.2 A Monohybrid Cross. The results of Mendel's crosses involving a single trait **(a)** contrasted strongly with the predictions of the blending-inheritance hypothesis **(b).**

or superior. Subsequent research has shown that individuals with the dominant phenotype do not necessarily have higher fitness than individuals with the recessive phenotype. Nor are genetic determinants associated with a dominant phenotype necessarily more common than recessive ones. For example, a fatal illness—a type of brain degeneration called Huntington's disease—is caused by a rare, dominant genetic determinant. In genetics, the terms dominant and recessive identify *only* which phenotype is observed in individuals carrying two different genetic determinants for a given trait.

Mendel also noticed that the round and wrinkled seeds of the F_2 generation were present in a ratio of 2.96:1, or essentially 3:1. The 3:1 ratio means that for every four individuals, on average three had the dominant phenotype and one had the recessive phenotype. The results can also be stated in terms of frequencies or proportions: In this case, about ¾ of the F_2 seeds were round and ¼ were wrinkled.

A Reciprocal Cross Mendel wanted to test the hypothesis that it mattered which parent and gamete type had a particular genetic determinant—that gender influenced the inheritance of seed shape. To do this, he performed a second set of crosses between two pure-breeding lines—this time with pollen taken from an individual from a pure line of wrinkled-seeded peas (**FIGURE 12.3**).

These experiments completed a **reciprocal cross**—a set of matings where the mother's phenotype in the initial cross is the father's phenotype in a subsequent cross, and the father's phenotype in the initial cross is the mother's phenotype in a subsequent cross.

In this case the results of the reciprocal crosses were identical: All the F_1 progeny had round seeds, just as in the initial cross. The reciprocal cross established that it does not matter whether the genetic determinants for seed shape are located in the male or female parent.

Do Mendel's Results Hold for Other Traits? Before he tried to interpret this pattern, it was important for Mendel to establish that the results were not restricted to inheritance of seed shape. So he repeated the experiments with each of the six other traits listed earlier. As **TABLE 12.2** shows, in each case, he obtained similar results:

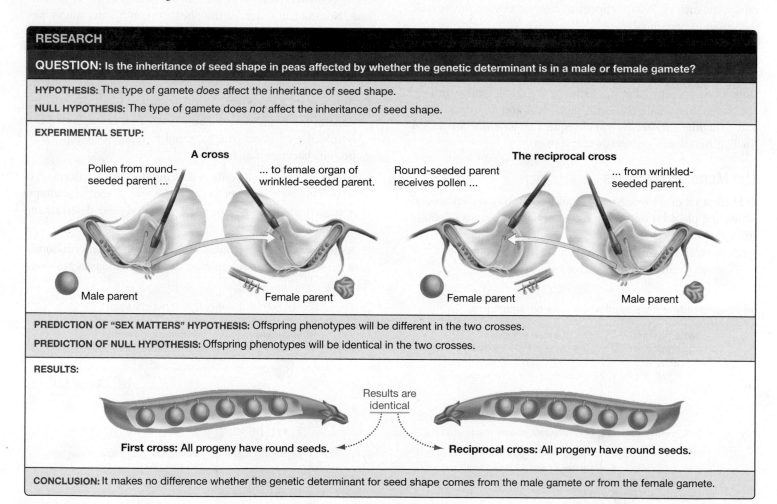

RESEARCH

QUESTION: Is the inheritance of seed shape in peas affected by whether the genetic determinant is in a male or female gamete?

HYPOTHESIS: The type of gamete *does* affect the inheritance of seed shape.

NULL HYPOTHESIS: The type of gamete does *not* affect the inheritance of seed shape.

EXPERIMENTAL SETUP:

A cross

Pollen from round-seeded parent ...

... to female organ of wrinkled-seeded parent.

Male parent   Female parent

The reciprocal cross

Round-seeded parent receives pollen ...

... from wrinkled-seeded parent.

Female parent   Male parent

PREDICTION OF "SEX MATTERS" HYPOTHESIS: Offspring phenotypes will be different in the two crosses.

PREDICTION OF NULL HYPOTHESIS: Offspring phenotypes will be identical in the two crosses.

RESULTS:

Results are identical

First cross: All progeny have round seeds.   **Reciprocal cross:** All progeny have round seeds.

CONCLUSION: It makes no difference whether the genetic determinant for seed shape comes from the male gamete or from the female gamete.

FIGURE 12.3 A Reciprocal Cross.

SOURCE: Mendel, G. 1866. Versuche über Pflanzen-hybriden. *Verhandlungen des naturforschenden Vereines in Brünn.* 4: 3–47. English translation available from ESP: Electronic Scholarly Publishing (www.esp.org).

✔**QUESTION** Some people think that experiments are failures if the hypothesis being tested is not supported. What does it mean to say that an experiment failed? Was this experiment a failure?

TABLE 12.2 **F₂ Results from Mendel's Monohybrid Reciprocal Cross Experiments***

Trait	Dominant Phenotype	Recessive Phenotype	Ratio
Seed shape	5474 round	1850 wrinkled	2.96 : 1
Seed color	6022 yellow	2001 green	3.01 : 1
Pod shape	882 inflated	299 constricted	2.95 : 1
Pod color	428 green	152 yellow	2.82 : 1
Flower color	705 purple	224 white	3.15 : 1
Flower and pod position	651 axial	207 terminal	____ : __
Stem length	787 tall	____ dwarf	2.96 : 1

*Mendel pooled the results from the reciprocal crosses for each trait because the results were the same whether the dominant trait originated from the male parent or the female parent.
DATA: Mendel, G. 1866. *Verhandlungen des naturforschenden Vereines in Brünn*. 4: 3–47.

✔**EXERCISE** Two entries in the last rows are left blank. Fill in these entries with the correct values calculated from the available data.

- The F₁ progeny showed only the dominant trait and did not exhibit an intermediate phenotype.
- Reciprocal crosses produced the same results.
- The ratio of F₂ generation individuals with dominant and recessive phenotypes was about 3 to 1.

How could these patterns be explained? Mendel answered this question with a series of propositions about the nature and behavior of the hereditary determinants. These hypotheses are considered some of the most brilliant insights in the history of biological science.

Particulate Inheritance

Mendel's results were clearly inconsistent with either the hypothesis of blending inheritance or the hypothesis of acquired characters. To explain the patterns that he observed, Mendel proposed a competing hypothesis called **particulate inheritance.** He maintained that the hereditary determinants for traits do not blend together or become modified through use. In fact, hereditary determinants maintain their integrity from generation to generation. Instead of blending together, they act as discrete entities or particles.

Mendel's hypothesis was the only way to explain the observation that phenotypes disappeared in one generation and reappeared intact in the next. It also represented a fundamental break with ideas that had prevailed for hundreds of years.

Genes, Alleles, and Genotypes   Today, geneticists use the word **gene** to indicate the hereditary determinant for a trait. For example, the hereditary factor that determines whether the seeds of garden peas are round or wrinkled is referred to as the gene for seed shape.

Mendel also proposed that each individual can have two versions of any gene. Today different versions of the same gene are called **alleles.** Different alleles are responsible for the variation in the traits that Mendel studied. In the case of the gene for seed shape, one allele of this gene is responsible for the round form of the seed while another allele is responsible for the wrinkled form.

The alleles found in a particular individual are called the **genotype.** An individual's genotype has a profound effect on the phenotype—the observable physical traits.

The hypothesis that pea plants have two copies of each gene—either two of the same allele or two different alleles—was important because it gave Mendel a framework for explaining dominance and recessiveness. He proposed that some alleles are dominant and others are recessive. Recall that dominance and recessiveness determine which phenotype appears in an individual when two different alleles are present. In garden peas, the allele for round seeds is dominant; the allele for wrinkled seeds is recessive. Therefore, so long as one allele for round seeds is present, seeds are round. When both alleles present are for wrinkled seeds (thus no allele for round seeds is present), seeds are wrinkled.

These hypotheses explain why the wrinkled-seed phenotype disappeared in the F₁ generation. But why did wrinkled seeds reappear in the F₂, and why was there a 3 : 1 ratio of round and wrinkled seeds in the F₂ generation?

The Principle of Segregation   To explain the reappearance of the recessive phenotype and the characteristic 3 : 1 ratio of phenotypes in F₂ individuals, Mendel reasoned that the two members of each gene pair must segregate—that is, separate—into different gamete cells during the formation of eggs and sperm. As a result, each gamete contains one allele of each gene. This idea is called the **principle of segregation.**

To show how this principle works, Mendel used a letter to indicate the gene for a particular trait. For example, he used uppercase R to symbolize a dominant allele for seed shape and lowercase r to symbolize a recessive allele for seed shape. (Notice that the symbols for genes are always italicized.)

Using this notation, Mendel described the genotype of the individuals in the round-seed pure line as RR (having two of the dominant allele). The genotype of the wrinkled-seed pure line is rr (two of the recessive allele). Because RR and rr individuals have two copies of the same allele, they are said to be **homozygous** for the seed-shape gene (*homo* is the Greek root for "same," while *zygo* means "yoked"). Crosses of individuals from the same pure line always produce offspring with the same phenotype because they are homozygous—no other allele is present.

FIGURE 12.4a uses a diagram called a Punnett square to show what happened to these alleles when Mendel crossed the RR and rr pure lines. R. C. Punnett invented this straightforward technique for predicting the genotypes and phenotypes of different crosses years after Mendel published his work. According to Mendel's hypothesis, RR parents produce eggs and sperm that all carry the R allele, while rr parents produce gametes with the r allele only. When two gametes—one from each parent—come together at fertilization, they create offspring with the Rr genotype. Such individuals, with two different alleles for the same gene, are said to be **heterozygous** (*hetero* is the Greek root for "different"). Heterozygous individuals, or heterozygotes, show that the R allele is dominant because only the round phenotype is expressed even though the wrinkled allele is present.

Why do the two phenotypes appear in a 3:1 ratio in the F_2 generation? Mendel proposed that during gamete formation in the F_1 heterozygotes, the paired Rr alleles separate into different gamete cells. As a result, and as shown in the Punnett square of **FIGURE 12.4b**, half the gametes should carry the R allele and half should carry the r allele. A given sperm has an equal chance of fertilizing either an R-bearing egg or an r-bearing egg.

Predicting Offspring Genotypes and Phenotypes with a Punnett Square

The box you've just studied in Figure 12.4b is an example of a simple Punnett square. To produce a Punnett square, follow these steps:

1. Write each of the *unique* gamete genotypes produced by one parent in a horizontal row along the top of the diagram.

2. Write each of the *unique* gamete genotypes produced by the other parent in a vertical column down the left side of the diagram.

3. Create a table under the horizontal row of gametes and to the right of the vertical column of gametes.

4. Fill in the table with the entries for the parental gamete genotypes that are written at the top and at the left side. This step represents fertilization and produces the offspring genotypes.

(a) A cross between two **homozygotes**

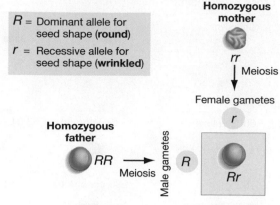

Offspring genotypes: All Rr (heterozygous)

Offspring phenotypes: All round seeds

(b) A cross between two **heterozygotes**

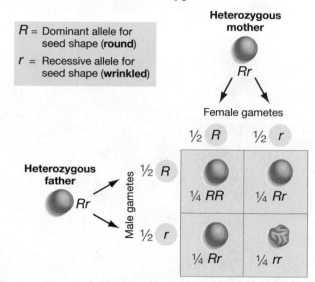

Offspring genotypes: ¼ RR : ½ Rr : ¼ rr

Offspring phenotypes: ¾ round : ¼ wrinkled

FIGURE 12.4 Mendel Analyzed the F_1 and F_2 Offspring of a Cross between Pure Lines. Notice that when you construct a Punnett square, you only need to list each unique type of gamete once at the head of a row or column. For example, even though the RR alleles segregate in the male parent of part (a), you have to list just one R gamete to represent the male's contribution, not two.

✓**QUESTION** In constructing a Punnett square, does it matter whether the male or female gametes go on the left or across the top? Why or why not?

5. Tally the proportions or ratios of each offspring genotype and phenotype.

✓ If you understand these concepts, you should be able to state how filling in the top and side of the Punnett square is related to the principle of segregation and predict the phenotype and genotype ratios for a cross between Rr and rr peas.

SUMMARY TABLE 12.3 Mendel's Model to Explain the Results of a Cross between Pure Lines*

Mendel's Claims	Comments
1. Peas have two copies of each gene and thus may have two different alleles of the gene.	This also turns out to be true for many other organisms.
2. Genes are particles of inheritance that do not blend together.	Genes maintain their integrity from generation to generation.
3. Each gamete contains one copy of each gene (one allele).	This is because of the principle of segregation—the members of each gene pair segregate during the formation of gametes.
4. Males and females contribute equally to the genotype of their offspring.	When gametes fuse, offspring acquire a total of two of each gene—one from each parent.
5. Some alleles are dominant to other alleles.	When a dominant and a recessive allele for the same gene are found in the same individual (a heterozygote), that individual has the dominant phenotype.

*Mendel did not use these modern terms. He expressed these ideas in different words.

check your understanding

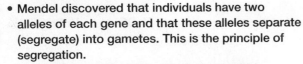
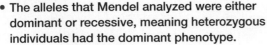

If you understand that . . .

- Mendel discovered that individuals have two alleles of each gene and that these alleles separate (segregate) into gametes. This is the principle of segregation.
- The alleles that Mendel analyzed were either dominant or recessive, meaning heterozygous individuals had the dominant phenotype.

✔ You should be able to . . .

Use the genetic problems at the end of this chapter to practice the following skills:

1. Starting with parents of known genotypes, create and analyze Punnett squares of crosses involving a single trait to predict the genotypes and phenotypes that will occur in their F_1 and F_2 offspring; then use the Punnett square to determine the expected frequency of each genotype and phenotype. (Do Problem 13 in Test Your Problem-Solving Skills.)

2. Given the outcome of a cross, infer the genotypes and phenotypes of the parents. (Do Problem 15 in Test Your Problem-Solving Skills.)

Answers are available in Appendix A.

As an example of the concluding step in analyzing a cross, the Punnett square in Figure 12.4b predicts that ¼ of the F_2 offspring will be RR, ½ will be Rr, and ¼ will be rr. Because the R allele is dominant to the r allele, ¾ of the offspring should be round-seeded (the sum of the RR and the Rr offspring) and ¼ should be wrinkled-seeded (the rr offspring). These results are what Mendel found in his experiments with peas. In the simplest and most elegant fashion possible, Mendel's interpretation explains the 3 : 1 ratio of round to wrinkled seeds observed in the F_2 offspring and the mysterious reappearance of the wrinkled seeds.

The term genetic model refers to a set of hypotheses that explains how a particular trait is inherited. **TABLE 12.3** summarizes Mendel's model for explaining the basic patterns in the transmission of traits from parents to offspring; these hypotheses are sometimes referred to as Mendel's rules. They represent a radical break from the ideas of blending inheritance and the inheritance of acquired characters that had dominated scientific thinking about heredity.

12.3 Mendel's Experiments with Two Traits

Working with one trait at a time allowed Mendel to establish that blending inheritance does not occur. It also allowed him to infer that each pea plant had two copies of each gene and to recognize the principle of segregation.

Mendel's next step extended these results. The important question now was whether the principle of segregation holds true if individuals differ with respect to two traits, instead of just one. Do different genes segregate together, or independently?

The Dihybrid Cross

Mendel crossed a pure-line parent that produced round, yellow seeds with a pure-line parent that produced wrinkled, green seeds. According to his model, the F_1 offspring of this cross should be heterozygous for both genes. A mating between two such individuals—both heterozygous for two traits—is called a **dihybrid cross.**

Mendel's earlier experiments had established that the allele for yellow seeds was dominant to the allele for green seeds; these alleles were designated Y for yellow and y for green. As **FIGURE 12.5** (see page 220) indicates, two distinct possibilities existed for how the alleles of these two different genes—the gene for seed shape and the gene for seed color—would be transmitted to offspring.

- The first possibility was that the allele for seed shape and the allele for seed color originally present in each parent would separate from each other and be transmitted independently. This hypothesis is called independent assortment because the two alleles would be sorted into gametes independently of each other (Figure 12.5a).

- The second possibility was that the allele for seed shape and the allele for seed color originally present in each parent

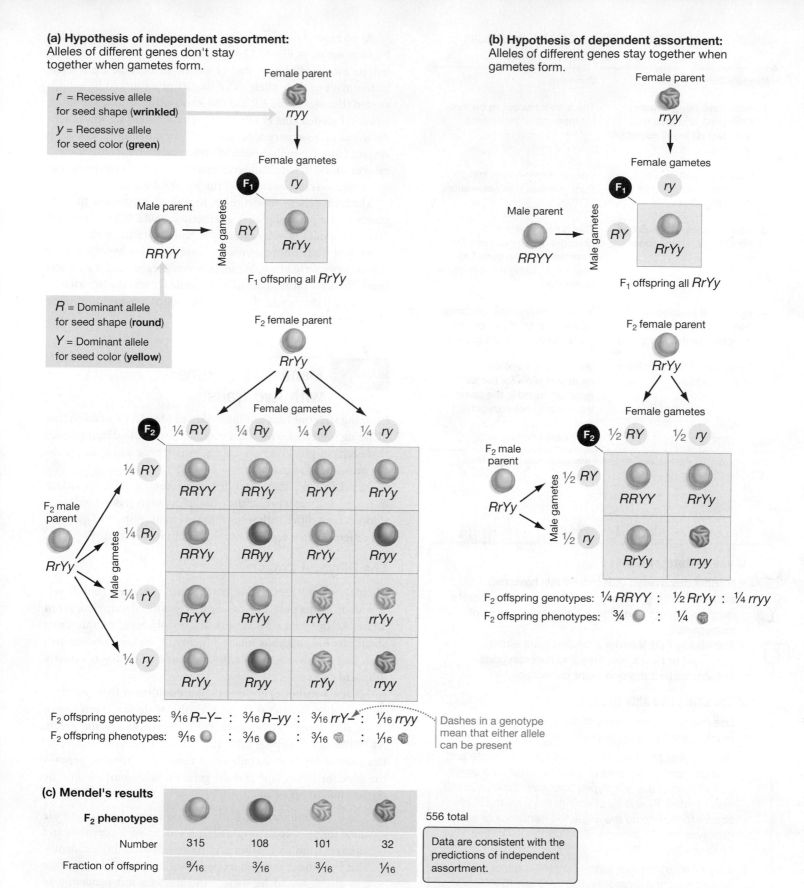

(a) Hypothesis of independent assortment:
Alleles of different genes don't stay together when gametes form.

r = Recessive allele for seed shape (**wrinkled**)

y = Recessive allele for seed color (**green**)

R = Dominant allele for seed shape (**round**)

Y = Dominant allele for seed color (**yellow**)

Female parent

$rryy$

Female gametes

ry

Male parent

$RRYY$

Male gametes

RY

F_1

$RrYy$

F_1 offspring all $RrYy$

F_2 female parent

$RrYy$

Female gametes

F_2 ¼ RY ¼ Ry ¼ rY ¼ ry

F_2 male parent

$RrYy$

Male gametes

¼ RY | $RRYY$ | $RRYy$ | $RrYY$ | $RrYy$
¼ Ry | $RRYy$ | $RRyy$ | $RrYy$ | $Rryy$
¼ rY | $RrYY$ | $RrYy$ | $rrYY$ | $rrYy$
¼ ry | $RrYy$ | $Rryy$ | $rrYy$ | $rryy$

F_2 offspring genotypes: 9/16 $R-Y-$: 3/16 $R-yy$: 3/16 $rrY-$: 1/16 $rryy$

F_2 offspring phenotypes: 9/16   : 3/16   : 3/16   : 1/16

Dashes in a genotype mean that either allele can be present

(b) Hypothesis of dependent assortment:
Alleles of different genes stay together when gametes form.

Female parent

$rryy$

Female gametes

ry

Male parent

$RRYY$

Male gametes

RY

F_1

$RrYy$

F_1 offspring all $RrYy$

F_2 female parent

$RrYy$

Female gametes

F_2 ½ RY ½ ry

F_2 male parent

$RrYy$

Male gametes

½ RY | $RRYY$ | $RrYy$
½ ry | $RrYy$ | $rryy$

F_2 offspring genotypes: ¼ $RRYY$: ½ $RrYy$: ¼ $rryy$

F_2 offspring phenotypes: ¾   : ¼

(c) Mendel's results

F_2 phenotypes					556 total
Number	315	108	101	32	Data are consistent with the predictions of independent assortment.
Fraction of offspring	9/16	3/16	3/16	1/16	

FIGURE 12.5 Mendel Analyzed the F₁ and F₂ Offspring of a Cross between Pure Lines for Two Traits. Each of two hypotheses predicted a different pattern for the outcome when alleles of different genes are transmitted to offspring: **(a)** The alleles could be sorted into gametes independently of each other, or **(b)** particular alleles could always be transmitted together. **(c)** Mendel's results supported independent assortment.

would be transmitted to gametes together. This hypothesis can be called dependent assortment because the transmission of one allele would depend on the transmission of another (Figure 12.5b).

As Figure 12.5 shows, the F_1 offspring of Mendel's mating are expected to have the dominant round and yellow phenotypes whether the different genes are transmitted together or independently. When Mendel did the cross and observed the F_1 individuals, this is exactly what he found. All the F_1 offspring had round, yellow seeds.

The two hypotheses make radically different predictions, however, about what will be observed when the F_1 individuals are allowed to self-fertilize and produce an F_2 generation. If the alleles of different genes assort independently to form gametes, then each heterozygous parent should produce four different gamete genotypes, as shown in Figure 12.5a. A 4-row-by-4-column Punnett square results, and it predicts that there should be 9 different offspring genotypes and 4 phenotypes. Further, the yellow-round, green-round, yellow-wrinkled, and green-wrinkled phenotypes should be present in frequencies of $\frac{9}{16}$, $\frac{3}{16}$, $\frac{3}{16}$, and $\frac{1}{16}$, respectively. This is a ratio of $9:3:3:1$.

On the other hand, if the alleles from each parent stay together, then the prediction is for only three possible offspring genotypes and a $3:1$ ratio of two phenotypes—yellow-round or green-wrinkled—in the F_2, as Figure 12.5b shows.

When Mendel examined the phenotypes of the F_2 offspring, he found that they conformed to the predictions of the hypothesis of independent assortment. Four phenotypes were present in proportions that closely approximated the predicted ratio of $9:3:3:1$ (Figure 12.5c). On the basis of these data, Mendel accepted the hypothesis that alleles of different genes are transmitted independently of one another. This result became known as the **principle of independent assortment.**

✔ If you understand the principle of independent assortment, it should make sense to you that an individual with the genotype *AaBb* produces gametes with the genotypes *AB, Ab, aB,* and *ab*. You should be able to predict the genotypes of the gametes produced by individuals with the genotypes *AABb, PpRr,* and *AaPpRr*.

Using a Testcross to Confirm Predictions

Mendel did experiments with combinations of traits other than seed shape and color and obtained results similar to those in Figure 12.5c. Each paired set of traits produced a $9:3:3:1$ ratio of progeny phenotypes in the F_2 generation. He even did a limited set of crosses examining three traits at a time. Although all these data were consistent with the principle of independent assortment, his most powerful support for the hypothesis came from a different type of experiment.

In designing this study, Mendel's goal was to test the prediction that an *RrYy* plant produces four different types of gametes in equal proportions. To accomplish this, Mendel invented a technique called a testcross. A **testcross** uses a parent that

contributes only recessive alleles to its offspring and helps to determine the unknown genotype of the second parent.

Testcrosses are useful because the genetic contribution of the homozygous recessive parent is known. As a result, a testcross allows experimenters to test the genetic contribution of the other parent. If the other parent has the dominant phenotype but an unknown genotype, the results of the testcross allow researchers to infer whether that parent is homozygous or heterozygous for the dominant allele.

In this case, Mendel performed a cross between a parent that was homozygous for the recessive green and wrinkled phenotypes (*rryy*) and a parent that had an unknown genotype but was known from its yellow- and round-seeded phenotype to possess the dominant *R* and *Y* alleles. Two (of four) possible genotypes for this yellow- and round-seeded parent are *RrYy* and *RRYY*. The types and proportions of offspring that could result from a testcross involving *RrYy* or *RRYY* pea plants can be predicted with the Punnett square shown in **FIGURE 12.6** (see page 222). If the principle of independent assortment is valid, the testcross should produce four types of offspring in equal proportions if the tested parent is *RrYy*, and only one type of offspring if the tested parent is *RRYY*.

What were the actual proportions observed? Mendel did a testcross using the F_1 offspring of a pure line yellow-, round-seeded parent and a green-, wrinkled-seeded parent. These F_1 offspring were expected to have an *RrYy* genotype as shown in Figure 12.5a. When he examined the seeds produced by the testcross, Mendel found that among the 110 progeny, 31 were round

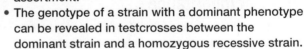
check your understanding

If you understand that . . .

C Y U

- Mendel found that alleles of different genes are transmitted to gametes independently of one another. This is the principle of independent assortment.
- The genotype of a strain with a dominant phenotype can be revealed in testcrosses between the dominant strain and a homozygous recessive strain.

✔ **You should be able to . . .**

Use the genetics problems at the end of this chapter to practice the following skills:

1. Starting with parents of known genotypes for two different traits, create and analyze Punnett squares to predict the genotypes and phenotypes that will occur in their F_1 and F_2 offspring and then calculate the expected frequency of each genotype and phenotype. (Do Problem 14 in Test Your Problem-Solving Skills.)

2. Given the outcome of a cross, infer the genotypes and phenotypes of the parents. (Do Problem 16 in Test Your Problem-Solving Skills.)

Answers are available in Appendix A.

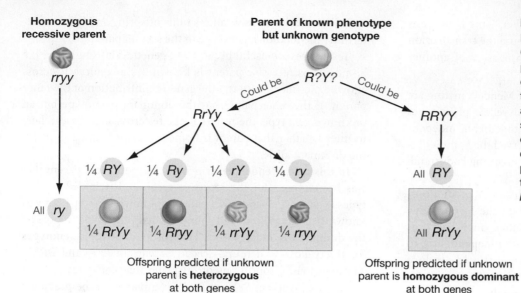

Offspring predicted if unknown
parent is **heterozygous**
at both genes

Offspring predicted if unknown
parent is **homozygous dominant**
at both genes

FIGURE 12.6 The Predictions Made by the Principle of Independent Assortment Can Be Evaluated in a Testcross. If the principle of independent assortment is correct, and *RrYy* parents produce four types of gametes in equal proportions, then a mating between *RrYy* and *rryy* parents should produce four types of offspring in equal proportions, as shown on the left. Test crosses can also reveal the genotype of a parent with dominant phenotypes, as seen in the example of different results obtained from *RrYy* and *RRYY* parental genotypes.

and yellow, 26 were round and green, 27 were wrinkled and yellow, and 26 were wrinkled and green. This is almost exactly ¼ of each type, which matched the predicted proportions for offspring of an *RrYy* parent. The testcross had confirmed the principle of independent assortment.

Mendel's work provided a powerful conceptual framework for thinking about transmission genetics—the patterns that occur as alleles pass from one generation to the next. This framework was based on (1) the segregation of discrete, paired genes into separate gametes, and (2) the independent assortment of genes that affect different traits.

The experiments you've just reviewed were brilliant in design, execution, and interpretation. Unfortunately, they were ignored for 34 years.

12.4 The Chromosome Theory of Inheritance

Historians of science debate why Mendel's work was overlooked for so long. It is probably true that his use of ratios and proportions were difficult for biologists of that time to understand and absorb. It may also be true that the theory of blending inheritance was so well entrenched that his results were dismissed as peculiar or unbelievable.

Whatever the reason, Mendel's work was not appreciated until 1900, when three biologists, working with a variety of plants and animals, independently "discovered" Mendel's work and reached the same main conclusions.

The rediscovery of Mendel's work more than three decades after its publication ignited the young field of genetics. Mendel's experiments had established the basic patterns of inheritance, but what process is responsible for these patterns? Two biologists, working independently, came up with the answer. Walter Sutton and Theodor Boveri each realized that meiosis could account for

Mendel's rules. When this hypothesis was published in 1902, research in genetics exploded.

Meiosis Explains Mendel's Principles

What Sutton and Boveri grasped is that meiosis explains the principle of segregation and the principle of independent assortment. The cell at the top of **FIGURE 12.7** illustrates Sutton and Boveri's central insight: Mendel's hereditary determinants, or genes, are located on chromosomes. In this example, the gene for seed shape is shown at a particular position along a certain chromosome. This location is known as a **locus** ("place"; plural, **loci**).

The paternal and maternal chromosomes shown in Figure 12.7 happen to possess different alleles at the seed shape gene locus: One allele specifies round seeds (*R*) and the other specifies wrinkled seeds (*r*).

The subsequent steps in Figure 12.7 show how these alleles segregate into different daughter cells during meiosis I, when homologous chromosomes separate. The physical separation of alleles during anaphase of meiosis I is responsible for Mendel's principle of segregation.

FIGURE 12.8 follows the segregation of two different gene pairs—in this case, for seed shape and seed color—as meiosis proceeds. If the alleles for different genes are located on different chromosomes, they assort independently of one another at meiosis I. This is the physical basis of Mendel's principle of independent assortment. Over many meiotic divisions, four types of gametes will be produced in equal proportions.

Sutton and Boveri formalized these observations in the **chromosome theory of inheritance**. Like other theories in biology, the chromosome theory describes a predictable pattern—a set of observations about the natural world—and a process that explains the pattern. The chromosome theory states that Mendel's rules can be explained by the independent alignment and separation of homologous chromosomes at meiosis I.

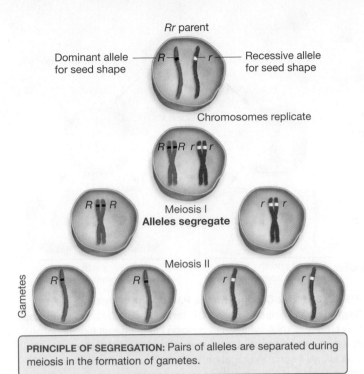

Chromosomes replicate

Meiosis I
Alleles segregate

Meiosis II

Gametes

PRINCIPLE OF SEGREGATION: Pairs of alleles are separated during meiosis in the formation of gametes.

FIGURE 12.7 Meiosis Explains the Principle of Segregation. The two members of a parent's gene pair segregate into different gametes because homologous chromosomes separate during meiosis I.

When Sutton and Boveri published their ideas, however, the hypothesis that genes are located on chromosomes was untested. What experiments confirmed that chromosomes contain genes?

Testing the Chromosome Theory

During the first decade of the twentieth century, an unassuming insect rose to prominence as a model organism for testing the chromosome theory of inheritance. This organism—the fruit fly *Drosophila melanogaster*—has been at the center of genetic studies ever since (see **BioSkills 13** in Appendix B).

Drosophila melanogaster has all the attributes of a useful model organism for studies in genetics: small size, ease of rearing in the lab, a short generation time (about 10 days), and abundant offspring (up to a few hundred per mating). The elaborate external anatomy of this insect also makes it possible to identify interesting phenotypic variation among individuals (**FIGURE 12.9a**; see page 224).

Drosophila was adopted as a model organism by Thomas Hunt Morgan and his students. But because *Drosophila* is not a domesticated species like the garden pea, common phenotypic variants such as Mendel's round and wrinkled seeds were not available to Morgan. Instead, he had access only to flies with the most common phenotype for each trait, phenotypes referred to as **wild type.** Consequently, an early goal of Morgan's research

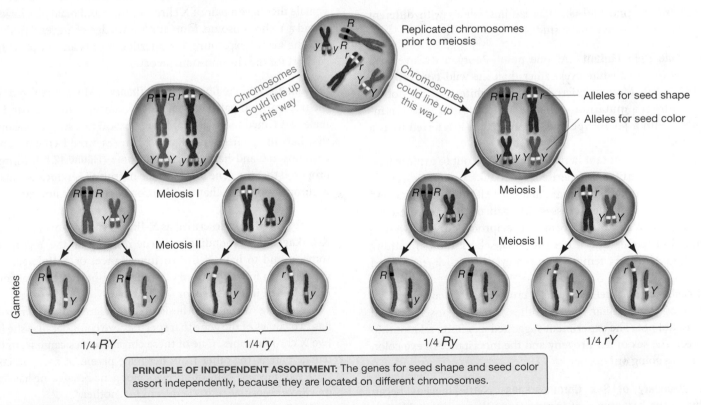

PRINCIPLE OF INDEPENDENT ASSORTMENT: The genes for seed shape and seed color assort independently, because they are located on different chromosomes.

FIGURE 12.8 Meiosis Is Responsible for the Principle of Independent Assortment. The genes for different traits assort independently because nonhomologous chromosomes assort independently during meiosis.

(a) The fruit fly *Drosophila melanogaster*

1 mm

(b) Eye color is a variable trait.

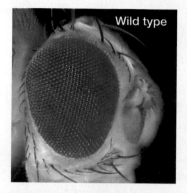

Wild type

Mutant

FIGURE 12.9 The Fruit Fly *Drosophila melanogaster* Is an Important Model Organism in Genetics.

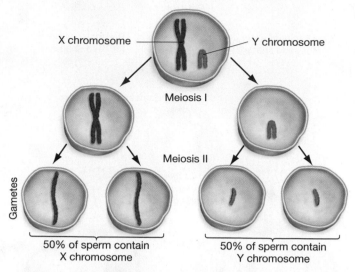

X chromosome

Y chromosome

Meiosis I

Meiosis II

Gametes

50% of sperm contain
X chromosome

50% of sperm contain
Y chromosome

FIGURE 12.10 Sex Chromosomes Pair during Meiosis I, Then Segregate in Males to Form X-Bearing and Y-Bearing Gametes. Sex chromosomes synapse at meiosis I in male fruit flies because of a small, gene-free region shared by the X and Y chromosomes. This allows normal segregation, so half the sperm cells bear an X chromosome and half have a Y chromosome.

was simply to find and characterize individuals with different phenotypes to use in genetic studies.

The White-Eyed Mutant At one point, Morgan discovered a male fly that had white eyes rather than the wild-type red eyes (**FIGURE 12.9b**). Morgan inferred that the white-eyed phenotype resulted from a **mutation**—a heritable change in a gene. An individual with a phenotype due to a mutation is referred to as a **mutant.**

With his first mutant in hand, Morgan set out to explore how the eye-color trait was inherited. He mated a red-eyed female fly with the mutant white-eyed male fly. All the F₁ progeny had red eyes. By continued crosses, Morgan obtained white-eyed female flies. When he performed a reciprocal cross between a white-eyed female and a red-eyed male, he found something puzzling: All the F₁ females had red eyes, but all F₁ males had white eyes.

Recall that Mendel's reciprocal crosses had always given results that were similar to each other. But Morgan's reciprocal crosses did not. The experiment suggested a definite relationship between the sex of the progeny and the inheritance of eye color. What was going on?

The Discovery of Sex Chromosomes Nettie Stevens began studying the karyotypes of insects about the time that Morgan began his work with *Drosophila*. First, in the beetle *Tenebrio*

molitor, and later in other insects, including *Drosophila*, she noticed a striking difference in the chromosome complements of males and females.

Recall that Stevens and others discovered that there were sex chromosomes (the X and the Y) and autosomes (see Chapter 11). Female flies have a pair of X chromosomes and male flies have an X and a Y chromosome. Morgan's knowledge of Stevens' findings was the key to explaining his puzzling results and in providing support for the chromosome theory.

Sex Linkage and the Chromosome Theory Morgan realized that the transmission pattern of the X chromosome in males and females explained the results of his reciprocal crosses. He reasoned that half the gametes produced by males would contain an X chromosome and half a Y chromosome (**FIGURE 12.10**). Morgan proposed that the gene for eye color in fruit flies is located on the X chromosome and that the Y chromosome does not carry this gene.

This situation is described as **X-linked inheritance,** or simply **X-linkage.** Correspondingly, a gene residing on the Y chromosome is said to have **Y-linked inheritance,** or **Y-linkage.** The general term for inheritance of genes on either sex chromosome is **sex-linked inheritance,** or **sex-linkage.**

According to the hypothesis of X-linkage, a female fruit fly has two copies of the gene that specifies eye color because she has two X chromosomes. One of these chromosomes came from her female parent, the other from her male parent. A male, in contrast, has only one copy of the eye-color gene because he has only one X chromosome, inherited from his mother.

The Punnett squares in **FIGURE 12.11** show that Morgan's experimental results can be explained if the gene for eye color is located

(a) One half of reciprocal cross

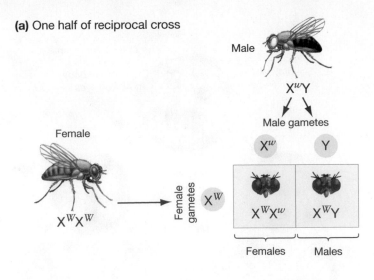

Male

X^wY

Male gametes

X^w Y

Female

X^WX^W

Female gametes

X^W

X^WX^w	X^WY

Females   Males

(b) Other half of reciprocal cross

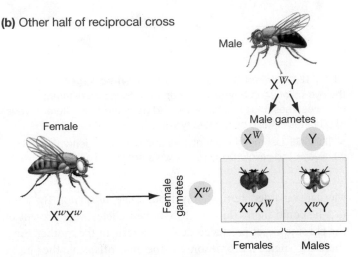

Male

X^WY

Male gametes

X^W Y

Female

X^wX^w

Female gametes

X^w

X^wX^W	X^wY

Females   Males

FIGURE 12.11 Reciprocal Crosses Confirm that Eye Color in *Drosophila* Is an X-Linked Trait. When Morgan crossed red-eyed females with white-eyed males **(a)** and then crossed white-eyed females with red-eyed males **(b)**, he observed strikingly different results.

on the X chromosome, and if the allele for red color is dominant to the allele for white color. In this figure, the allele for red eyes is denoted X^W while the allele for white eyes is denoted X^w. The Y chromosome present in males is simply designated by Y. Using this notation,[1] the genotypes used in the experiment are written as X^WX^W for red-eyed females; X^wY for white-eyed males; X^wX^w for white-eyed females; and X^WY for red-eyed males.

Notice how the symbol for *Drosophila* alleles represents the mutant phenotype. Instead of showing alleles for the eye color gene with an *R* for wild-type red eyes and an *r* for mutant white eyes, the alleles are shown with a *W* (red eyes) or a *w* (white eyes).

---

[1]Scientific papers on fruit fly genetics use a different notation. The wild-type allele is designated with a superscript +, and no X is used for X-linked traits. The red-eye allele, for example, is denoted w^+; the white-eye allele *w*. The notation used here is simplified and conforms to conventions used in human genetics.

By applying the principles of segregation and random fertilization, you should see that the results predicted by the hypothesis of X-linkage match the observed results.

When reciprocal crosses give different results, such as those illustrated in Figure 12.11, it is likely that the gene in question is located on a sex chromosome—it is sex-linked. Recall that non-sex chromosomes are called autosomes (see Chapter 11). Genes on non-sex chromosomes are said to show **autosomal inheritance.**

Morgan's discovery of X-linked inheritance carried an even more fundamental message. In *Drosophila*, the gene for white eye color is clearly correlated with inheritance of the X chromosome. This correlation was important evidence in support of the hypothesis that chromosomes contain genes. The discovery of X-linked inheritance convinced most biologists that the chromosome theory of inheritance was correct.

check your understanding

C Y U

If you understand that . . .

- Meiosis is the process responsible for Mendel's principle of segregation. It occurs because alleles on homologous chromosomes separate at anaphase of meiosis I.
- Meiosis is the process responsible for Mendel's principle of independent assortment. Alleles of different genes go to gametes independently because pairs of homologous chromosomes line up randomly at metaphase of meiosis I.

✔ You should be able to . . .

1. Draw the chromosomes involved in a cross between *Pp* and *Pp* peas, and use your diagram to explain the segregation of alleles.
2. Draw the chromosomes involved in a cross between *YyRr* and *YyRr* peas, and use your diagram to explain the independent assortment of alleles.

Answers are available in Appendix A.

12.5 Extending Mendel's Rules

Biologists point out that Mendel analyzed the simplest possible genetic system. The traits that he was studying were not sex-linked. Moreover, they were influenced by just two alleles of each gene, and each allele was completely dominant or recessive.

With this well-chosen model system, Mendel was able to discover the most fundamental rules of inheritance. Mendel probably would have failed, as so many others had done before him, had he been trying to analyze more complex patterns of inheritance.

Once Mendel's work was rediscovered, researchers began to analyze traits and alleles whose inheritance was more complicated.

If experimental crosses produced F_2 progeny that did not conform to the expected 3:1 or 9:3:3:1 ratios, researchers had a strong hint that something interesting was going on. The discovery of sex-linkage is a prominent example. How can other traits that don't appear to follow Mendel's rules contribute to a more complete understanding of heredity?

Linkage: What Happens When Genes Are Located on the Same Chromosome?

Once the chromosome theory had been tested and supported, biologists began to reevaluate Mendel's principle of independent assortment. It seemed unlikely that genes on the same chromosome would assort independently.

Linkage is the tendency of particular alleles of different genes to be inherited together. Linkage is seen when genes are on the same chromosome. Notice that the terms linkage and sex-linkage have different meanings. If genes are linked, it means that they are located on the same chromosome. If a gene is sex-linked, it means that it is located on a sex chromosome but says nothing about its location relative to other genes.

The first examples of linked genes were those on the X chromosome of fruit flies. After Morgan established that the *white-eye* gene was located on *Drosophila's* X chromosome, he and colleagues established that one of the several genes that affects body color is also located on the X. Red eyes and gray body are the wild-type phenotypes; white eyes and a yellow body occur as rare mutant phenotypes. The alleles for red eyes (X^W) and gray body (X^Y) are dominant to the alleles for white eyes (X^w) and yellow body (X^y). (Be sure not to confuse the notation for the Y chromosome in males, Y, with the gray body allele, X^Y.)

Linked Genes Do Not Assort Independently Because linked genes are located on the same chromosome, it is logical to predict that they should always be transmitted together during gamete formation. Stated another way, linked genes should violate the principle of independent assortment.

Recall from Section 12.4 that genes on different chromosomes show independent assortment because different chromosomes assort independently during meiosis I. How will the X-linked body-color and eye-color genes be inherited? **FIGURE 12.12** shows a cell of a female fruit fly with one X chromosome carrying the white eye and gray body alleles, written X^{wY}, and the homologous X chromosome carrying the red eye and yellow body alleles, written X^{Wy}. This female would be expected to generate just two classes of gametes in equal numbers during meiosis, instead of the four classes that are predicted under the principle of independent assortment. Is this what actually occurs?

The Role of Crossing Over To determine whether linked traits always stay linked, Morgan performed crosses like the one described in the "Experimental Setup" section of **FIGURE 12.13**. In this case, $X^{wY}X^{Wy}$ females mated with $X^{wY}Y$ males.

The "Results" table in Figure 12.13 summarizes the phenotypes and genotypes observed in this experimental cross.

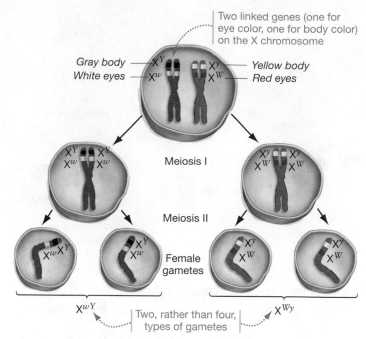

FIGURE 12.12 Linked Genes Are Often Inherited Together. If the eye-color and body-color genes were found on different chromosomes, then this female would generate four different types of gametes instead of just two types as shown here.

✔**EXERCISE** List the four genotypes that would be generated if the white-eye and yellow-body genes were not linked.

Morgan recorded results only from male offspring. By doing this he could figure out which X-linked alleles were present on the chromosomes produced during meiosis in the mother. Since there is a single X chromosome in the male offspring, the phenotype associated with any X-linked allele, dominant or recessive, is expressed:

- Most of these males carried an X chromosome with one of the two combinations of alleles found in the chromosomes of their mothers: X^{wY} or X^{Wy}.

- A small percentage of males had novel combinations of phenotypes and genotypes: X^{wy} and X^{WY}. Morgan referred to these individuals as **recombinant** because the combination of alleles on their X chromosome was different from the combinations of alleles present in their mother.

Morgan concluded that alleles on the same chromosome don't always stay together. To explain the recombinant phenotypes, Morgan proposed that gametes with new combinations of alleles were generated when crossing over occurred during prophase of meiosis I in the females.

Recall that crossing over involves a physical exchange of segments of non-sister chromatids between homologous chromosomes (see Chapter 11). Crossing over typically occurs at least once in every synapsed pair of homologous chromosomes, and usually multiple times. (Male fruit flies are an exception to this rule. For unknown reasons, no crossing over occurs in male fruit flies.)

QUESTION: Will genes undergo independent assortment if they are on the same chromosome?

LINKAGE HYPOTHESIS: Linked genes will violate the principle of independent assortment.

NULL HYPOTHESIS: Linked genes will adhere to the principle of independent assortment.

EXPERIMENTAL SETUP:

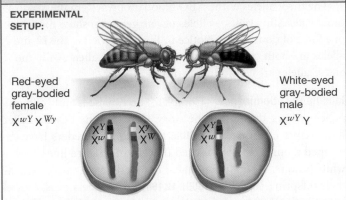

Red-eyed gray-bodied female $X^{wY}X^{Wy}$

White-eyed gray-bodied male $X^{wY}Y$

PREDICTION: Because these two genes are X-linked, male offspring will have only one copy of each gene, from their mother; the two possible male offspring genotypes are $X^{wY}Y$ and $X^{Wy}Y$

PREDICTION OF NULL HYPOTHESIS: Four male genotypes are possible ($X^{wY}Y : X^{Wy}Y : X^{wy}Y : X^{WY}Y$) and will occur with equal frequency.

RESULTS:

Male offspring

	Phenotype	Genotype	Number	
	🪰	$X^{wY}Y$	4292	Four male genotypes were observed (rather than two), but not the equal frequencies predicted by independent assortment
	🪰	$X^{Wy}Y$	4605	
Recombinant genotypes	🪰	$X^{wy}Y$	86	
	🪰	$X^{WY}Y$	44	

CONCLUSION: Neither hypothesis is fully supported. Independent assortment does not apply to linked genes—linked genes segregate together except when crossing over and genetic recombination have occurred.

FIGURE 12.13 Linked Genes Are Inherited Together Unless Recombination Occurs.

SOURCE: Morgan, T. H. 1911. An attempt to analyze the constitution of the chromosomes on the basis of sex-limited inheritance in *Drosophila. Journal of Experimental Zoology* 11: 365–414.

✔**QUESTION** Why didn't Morgan observe equal numbers of white-eyed, yellow-bodied males and red-eyed, gray-bodied males?

As **FIGURE 12.14** shows, a crossover between the eye-color and body-color genes in the $X^{wY}X^{Wy}$ females can explain the recombinant gametes. Male progeny produced from fertilization with these gametes are predicted to have either yellow bodies and white eyes or gray bodies and red eyes. This is what Morgan observed.

Notice, however, that the results of Figure 12.14 don't fit either the model of independent assortment or complete linkage. Independent assortment predicts a 1:1:1:1 ratio of all four

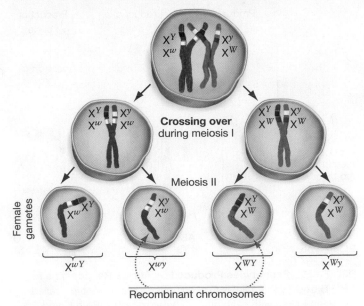

Crossing over during meiosis I

Meiosis II

Female gametes

X^{wY} X^{wy} X^{WY} X^{Wy}

Recombinant chromosomes

FIGURE 12.14 Genetic Recombination Results from Crossing Over. To explain the results in Figure 12.13, Morgan proposed that crossing over occurred between the body color (*y*) and eye color (*w*) genes in a small percentage of meiotic divisions in the female parent. The recombinant chromosomes that resulted would produce the recombinant phenotypes observed in the male offspring.

combinations of phenotypes, while complete linkage would give only the two phenotypes associated with the nonrecombinant or parental chromosomes. Instead, most flies have parental phenotypes and a smaller number have recombinant phenotypes.

As **Quantitative Methods 12.1** (see page 230) explains, the percentage of recombinant offspring that occur in crosses like the one diagrammed in Figure 12.14 can be used to estimate the relative distance between genes. The reasoning is that the farther genes are apart on the same chromosome, the more likely it is that a crossover will occur someplace between these genes. Data on the frequency of crossing over between many genes on the same chromosome can be used to create a **genetic map**—a diagram showing the relative positions of genes along a particular chromosome.

Knowing a gene's locus relative to others can be very useful. An important example is genes involved in human genetic diseases. Most of these genes have been identified on the basis of mapping their location relative to other known genes.

The take-home message of Morgan's experiments is simple: Linked genes are inherited together unless crossing over occurs between them. When crossing over takes place, genetic recombination occurs. Linkage is an important exception to Mendel's rules.

How Many Alleles Can a Gene Have?

Mendel worked with genes that each had two alleles. In most populations, however, it's not unusual to find dozens of alleles of a single gene. The existence of more than two alleles of the same gene is known as **multiple allelism.** When you consider that

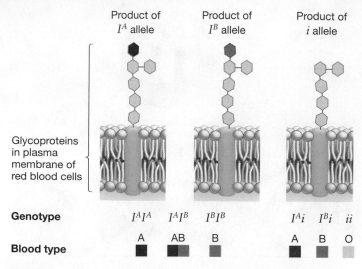

Product of I^A allele   Product of I^B allele   Product of i allele

Glycoproteins
in plasma
membrane of
red blood cells

Genotype I^AI^A I^AI^B I^BI^B I^Ai I^Bi ii

Blood type   A   AB   B   A   B   O

FIGURE 12.15 Phenotypes Produced by Alleles Responsible for ABO Blood Types. Alleles I^A and I^B produce a phenotype called AB when paired with each other in heterozygotes. Both I^A and I^B produce a dominant phenotype when paired with allele i. The different colored hexagons on the products of the I^A and I^B alleles represent related but distinct sugars.

genes are made of DNA sequences that can change over time, the idea of multiple alleles isn't surprising.

The ABO blood group types in humans are coded for by a gene with three common alleles. The gene is known as I, and it has I^A, I^B, and i alleles. As the number of alleles for a gene increases, the number of possible genotypes rises sharply. When more than two distinct phenotypes are present in a population owing to multiple allelism, the trait is **polymorphic** ("many-formed"). ABO blood type is a polymorphic trait.

Each I gene allele controls the production of a different polysaccharide attached to a glycoprotein (see Appendix E) found in the plasma membrane of red blood cells. The I^A and I^B alleles code for different forms of an enzyme that adds a different sugar to the end of a core polysaccharide. The i allele codes for a nonfunctional form of this enzyme, so no sugar is added to the core polysaccharide. ABO blood group types are important in blood transfusions. Some mismatches of blood type between a donor and recipient are tolerated, but others can cause fatal reactions.

The type of polysaccharide associated with each allele is shown in **FIGURE 12.15** along with all possible genotypes and phenotypes. As you can see, there are six possible genotypes for the three alleles of the I gene. The I^A allele codes for the type A polysaccharide, and the I^B allele codes for the type B polysaccharide. What happens in a person with both alleles?

Are Alleles Always Dominant or Recessive?

The terms dominant and recessive describe which phenotype is observed when two different alleles of a gene occur in a heterozygous individual. In all traits that Mendel studied, only the phenotype associated with one allele—the "dominant" one—appeared in heterozygotes. However, not all combinations of alleles work this way.

Codominance Many alleles show a relationship that is called **codominance.** The type AB blood group shown in Figure 12.15 is an example of codominance. In this case, an AB heterozygote expresses both the A and the B polysaccharides together on the surface of red blood cells. This is the essence of codominance—the simultaneous expression of the phenotype associated with each allele in a heterozygote. An AB individual expresses both the A and the B phenotypes.

The three alleles of the ABO blood group system illustrate another interesting point—alleles of one gene can show more than one form of dominance. Notice in Figure 12.15 that the I^A and I^B alleles are both completely dominant to the i allele while the I^A and I^B alleles are codominant with each other.

Incomplete Dominance Complete dominance and codominance are not the end of the story. Consider the flowers called four-o'clocks, pictured in **FIGURE 12.16a**. Plant breeders have developed a pure line that has red flowers and a pure line that has white flowers. When individuals from these strains are mated, all their offspring are pink (**FIGURE 12.16b**). In Mendel's peas, crosses between dominant and recessive parents produced only offspring with the dominant phenotype. Why the difference?

Biologists answered this question by allowing the pink flowered F_1 plants to self-fertilize and examining the phenotypes of F_2 four-o'clocks. Of the F_2 plants, ¼ have red flowers, ½ have pink flowers, and ¼ have white flowers. This 1:2:1 ratio of phenotypes exactly matches the 1:2:1 ratio of genotypes that is produced when flower color is controlled by one gene with two alleles.

To convince yourself that this explanation is sound, study the genetic model shown in Figure 12.16b. According to the diagram, the pattern of inheritance of flower color genotypes in four-o'clocks and peas is identical, but the four-o'clock alleles show a different form of dominance known as **incomplete dominance.**

When incomplete dominance occurs, heterozygotes have a phenotype that is between the two different homozygous parents. In the case of four-o'clocks, neither red nor white alleles dominate. Instead, the heterozygous F_1 progeny show a phenotype in between the two parental strains.

By this point, it should be clear that the answer to the question of whether alleles are always dominant or recessive is a resounding no. Instead, there are three possible dominance relationships between different alleles: complete, incomplete, and codominance.

Does Each Gene Affect Just One Trait?

Mendel's results led him to hypothesize that one gene influences one trait. The gene for seed color in garden peas, for example, did not appear to affect other aspects of the individual's phenotype. In reality, however, many genes influence more than one trait.

A gene that influences many traits is said to be **pleiotropic** ("more-turning"). For example, mutations in one gene, *FBN1*, cause Marfan syndrome in humans. In this case the mutant

(a) Flower color is variable in four-o'clocks.

(b) Incomplete dominance in flower color

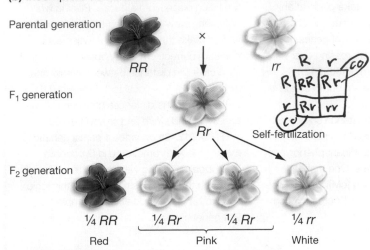

FIGURE 12.16 When Incomplete Dominance Occurs, Heterozygotes Have Intermediate Phenotypes. The cross in part (b) is explained by hypothesizing that a single gene influences flower color and that alleles *R* and *r* exhibit incomplete dominance.

FBN1 allele is dominant to the wild-type allele. What is the phenotype of an individual with a mutant *FBN1* allele?

People with a mutant *FBN1* allele are tall, have disproportionately long limbs and fingers and an abnormally shaped chest, and often have severe heart problems. Therefore, the gene associated with Marfan syndrome influences many traits and is pleiotropic. On the basis of this set of phenotypes, many medical scientists believe Abraham Lincoln had Marfan syndrome.

Is There More to Phenotype than Genotype?

After analyzing the results of Mendel's experiments, it would be tempting to conclude that *R* alleles dictate that seeds are round and *T* alleles dictate that individual plants are tall—that there is a strict correspondence between alleles and phenotypes.

It's important to recognize, though, that when Mendel analyzed height in his experiments, he ensured that each plant received a similar amount of sunlight and grew in similar soil. This was critical because even individuals with alleles for tallness will be stunted if they are deprived of nutrients, sunlight, or water—so much so that they look similar to individuals with alleles for dwarfing. Mendel also worked with pure lines that had been inbred for many generations. This breeding method reduces the genetic variation in each line.

For Mendel to analyze the hereditary determinants of height, he had to control the environmental determinants of height. Let's consider how the environment and alleles at other gene loci affect phenotype.

The Environment Affects Phenotypes The phenotypes produced by most genes are strongly affected by the individual's environment. Consequently, an individual's phenotype is often as much a product of the environment as it is a product of the genotype. Environmental influences include temperature, sunlight, nutrient availability, competition, and even a mother's hormone levels during development of an embryo. To capture this point, biologists refer to the combined effect of genes and environment as gene-by-environment interaction.

Gene-by-environment interactions have a profound effect on how physicians treat people with the genetic disease phenylketonuria (PKU). These individuals are homozygous for a recessive allele of an enzyme-coding gene. The enzyme helps convert the amino acid phenylalanine to the amino acid tyrosine. In PKU, this enzyme is absent and, as a result, phenylalanine and a related molecule, phenylpyruvic acid, accumulate. These compounds interfere with the development of the nervous system and produce severe mental retardation.

But are people without the ability to metabolize phenylalanine genetically fated to mental retardation?

In many countries, newborns are routinely tested for the defect. If identified at birth, individuals with PKU can be placed on a low-phenylalanine diet. The change in environment—reduced phenylalanine in the diet—has a dramatic influence on phenotype. Treated individuals develop normally. PKU is a genetic disease, but by controlling the environment, it is neither inevitable nor invariant.

Interactions Between Genes Affect Phenotypes In Mendel's pea plants, there was a one-to-one correspondence between genes and traits. The pea seeds he analyzed were round or wrinkled regardless of the types of alleles present at other loci. Only one gene influenced each trait.

In many cases, however, different genes work together to control a single trait. Consider a classic experiment published in 1905 on comb shape in chickens. William Bateson and R. C. Punnett crossed parents from pure lines with comb shapes called rose and pea and found that the F₁ offspring had a new phenotype, called walnut combs, a new phenotype not seen in either parent. When these individuals bred, their offspring had walnut, rose,

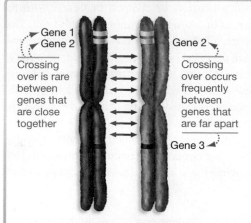

FIGURE 12.17 The Physical Distance between Genes Determines the Frequency of Crossing Over. The arrows show that crossing over is possible at any point between the genes, but the chance of a crossover between a pair of genes increases when the distance between the genes is large.

Gene 1
Gene 2
Crossing over is rare between genes that are close together

Gene 2
Crossing over occurs frequently between genes that are far apart
Gene 3

In experiments like the one diagrammed in Figure 12.13, researchers calculate the recombination frequency as the number of offspring with recombinant phenotypes divided by the total number of offspring. With crosses involving the X-linked traits of white eyes and yellow bodies, 1.4 percent of offspring have recombinant phenotypes and genotypes.

But in crosses with different pairs of X-linked traits, the fraction of recombinant offspring varies, and this variation provides information on the relative distance separating linked genes. For example, in crosses of fruit flies with X-linked genes for white eyes and another mutant phenotype called singed bristles, recombinant phenotypes are seen 19.6 percent of the time.

To explain these observations, Alfred Sturtevant, an undergraduate student working with Morgan, proposed that the physical distance between genes determines how frequently crossing over occurs between them. His idea was that crossing over occurs at random and can take place at any location along a chromosome. The shorter the distance between a pair of genes, the lower the probability that crossing over will take place between them (**FIGURE 12.17**). Using this reasoning, he set out to create a genetic map.

To define the unit of distance on his genetic map, Sturtevant used the percentage of offspring that have recombinant phenotypes with respect to two genes. One map unit (later called 1 centiMorgan [cM]) is the physical distance that produces 1 percent recombinant offspring.

The eye-color and bristle-shape genes of fruit flies are 19.6 cM apart on the X chromosome, because recombination between these genes results in 19.6 percent recombinant offspring, on average. The genes for yellow body and white eye color, in contrast, are just 1.4 cM apart.

Where is the *yellow-body* gene relative to the *singed-bristles* gene? Twenty-one percent of the offspring were recombinant for these traits, meaning that the *yellow-body* and *singed-bristles* genes are 21.0 cM apart. Sturtevant inferred that the gene for white eyes must be located *between* the genes for yellow body and singed bristles, as shown in **FIGURE 12.18a**.

Mapping genes relative to one another is like fitting pieces into a puzzle: Placing *white* between *yellow* and *singed bristles* is the only way to make the distances between each pair sum correctly. The key observation is that 21.0 cM—the distance between *yellow* and *singed bristles*—is equal to 1.4 cM + 19.6 cM, or the sum of the distances between *yellow* and *white* and *white* and *singed bristles*.

FIGURE 12.18b provides a partial genetic map of the X chromosome in *Drosophila melanogaster,* along with the data used to establish the map positions. Using this logic and similar data, Sturtevant assembled the first genetic map.

(a) Mapping genetic distance

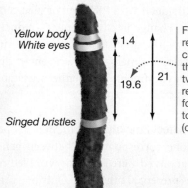

Yellow body
White eyes
1.4
19.6
21
Singed bristles

Frequency of recombinant offspring correlates directly with the distance between two genes; 19.6% recombinant offspring, for example, translates to 19.6 map units (centiMorgans, cM).

(b) Constructing a genetic map

% Frequency of crossing over between some genes on the X chromosome of fruit flies		
	Miniature Wings	Ruby Eyes
Yellow body	36.1	7.5
White eyes	34.7	6.1
Singed bristles	15.1	13.5
Miniature wings	—	28.6

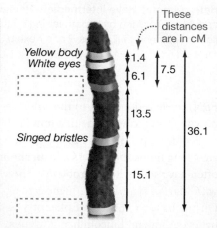

These distances are in cM

Yellow body
White eyes
1.4
6.1
7.5
13.5
36.1
Singed bristles
15.1

FIGURE 12.18 The Locations of Genes Can Be Mapped by Analyzing the Frequency of Recombination. (a) The *yellow body* gene is on the end of the fruit fly X chromosome. To explain the recombination frequencies observed in experimental crosses, the *yellow body, white eyes,* and *singed bristles* genes must be in the locations shown here. **(b)** A partial genetic map of the X chromosome in fruit flies.

✔**EXERCISE** In part (b), label the orange and blue genes. (Which is *ruby* and which is *miniature wings?*)

pea, and a fourth phenotype called single combs in a 9:3:3:1 ratio (**FIGURE 12.19a**).

The genetic model in **FIGURE 12.19b** shows how the interaction between two different genes that control one trait (comb shape) can account for the results. If comb morphology results from interactions between two genes (symbolized R and P), if a dominant and a recessive allele exist for each gene, and if the four comb phenotypes are associated with the genotypes indicated at the bottom of the figure, then a cross between *RRpp* and *rrPP* parents would give the results that Bateson and Punnett observed.

When gene-by-gene interactions occur, one trait is influenced by the alleles of two or more different genes. If a chicken has an *R* allele, its phenotype depends on the allele present at the *P* gene.

Gene-by-gene interaction is very common and has important implications in human genetics. Imagine that two people have the same genotype at one locus that increases risk for a heart disease. If there is gene-by-gene interaction, then the risk of developing heart disease also depends on the genotype at other loci. Even if they experience identical environments, these two people may have very different overall risks from genetic factors alone.

Can Mendel's Principles Explain Traits That Don't Fall into Distinct Categories?

Mendel worked with **discrete traits**—traits that are clearly different from each other. In garden peas, seed color is either yellow or green—no intermediate phenotypes exist. But many traits in peas and other organisms don't fall into discrete categories. In humans, for example, height, weight, and skin color vary continuously. People are not limited to being either 160 cm tall or 180 cm tall—countless other heights are possible.

For height and many other characteristics, individuals differ by degree. These types of continuously varying traits that don't fall into discrete categories are called **quantitative traits.** Like discrete traits, quantitative traits are greatly influenced by the environment. The effects of nutrition on human height, intelligence, and disease resistance, for example, have been well documented.

Many quantitative traits share a common characteristic: When the frequencies of different trait values observed in a population are plotted on a histogram, or frequency distribution (see **BioSkills 3** in Appendix B), they often form a bell-shaped curve, or normal distribution (**FIGURE 12.20**).

In 1909 Herman Nilsson-Ehle had an important insight: If many genes each contribute a small amount to the value of a quantitative trait, then a normal distribution results for the population as a whole.

(a) Crosses between chickens with different comb phenotypes give odd results.

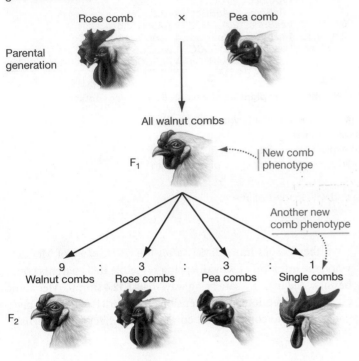

(b) A genetic model based on gene-by-gene interactions can explain the results.

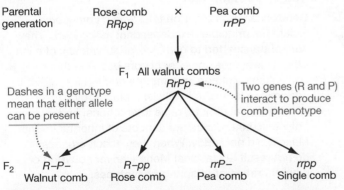

FIGURE 12.19 Genes at Different Loci Can Interact to Influence a Trait. (a) This cross is notable because new phenotypes show up in the F₁ and the F₂ generation. **(b)** To explain the results, researchers hypothesized that comb shape depends on two genes that interact. The phenotype associated with any one allele of one gene depends on the alleles at a second gene.

✓**EXERCISE** What is different about the 9:3:3:1 ratio in the F₂ of this cross compared with the ratio observed in a standard dihybrid cross?

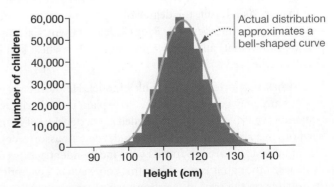

FIGURE 12.20 Quantitative Traits Have a Normal Distribution.
A histogram showing the heights of first-grade schoolchildren in Guatemala in 2001.

DATA: Pan American Health Organization/WHO. 2004. *Epidemiological Bulletin* 25: 9-13, Graph 1.

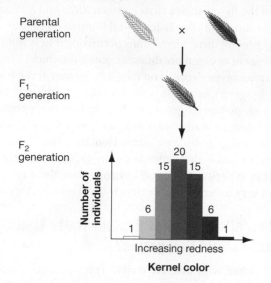

(a) Wheat kernel color is a quantitative trait.

Parental generation   ×

F₁ generation

F₂ generation

Number of individuals

1   6   15   20   15   6   1

Increasing redness →

Kernel color

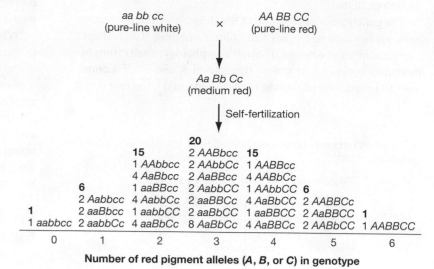

(b) Hypothesis to explain inheritance of kernel color

aa bb cc (pure-line white)   ×   *AA BB CC* (pure-line red)

Aa Bb Cc (medium red)

Self-fertilization

		20				
	15	2 *AABbcc*	**15**			
	1 *AAbbcc*	2 *AAbbCc*	1 *AABBcc*			
	4 *AaBbcc*	2 *AaBBcc*	4 *AABbCc*			
	6	1 *aaBBcc*	2 *AabbCC*	1 *AAbbCC*	**6**	
	2 *Aabbcc*	4 *AabbCc*	2 *aaBBCc*	4 *AaBbCC*	2 *AABBCc*	
1	2 *aaBbcc*	1 *aabbCC*	2 *aaBbCC*	1 *aaBBCC*	2 *AaBBCC*	**1**
1 *aabbcc*	2 *aabbCc*	4 *aaBbCc*	8 *AaBbCc*	4 *AaBBCc*	2 *AABbCC*	1 *AABBCC*
0	1	2	3	4	5	6

Number of red pigment alleles (*A*, *B*, or *C*) in genotype

FIGURE 12.21 Quantitative Traits Result from the Action of Many Genes. (a) When wheat plants with white kernels were crossed with wheat plants with red kernels, the F₂ offspring showed a range of kernel colors. The frequency of these phenotypes approximates a normal distribution. **(b)** This model can explain the results of part (a). The bold numbers above each genotype match the numbers shown in part (a) and indicate the relative number of plants with each phenotype.

✔**QUESTION** Why are there fewer very dark or very light wheat kernels compared with kernels of intermediate coloration?

Nilsson-Ehle established this finding using strains of wheat that differed in kernel color. **FIGURE 12.21a** includes a histogram showing the distribution of F₂ phenotypes from a cross he performed between pure lines of white wheat and dark-red wheat. Notice that the frequency of colors in F₂ progeny approximates a bell-shaped curve. To explain these results, Nilsson-Ehle proposed the hypotheses illustrated in **FIGURE 12.21b**:

- The parental strains differ with respect to three genes that control kernel color: *AABBCC* produces dark-red kernels, and *aabbcc* produces white kernels.

- The three genes assort independently.

- The *a, b,* and *c* alleles do not contribute to pigment production, but the *A, B,* and *C* alleles contribute to pigment production in an equal and additive way. This is a form of incomplete dominance. As a result, the degree of red pigmentation is determined by the number of *A, B,* or *C* alleles present. Each uppercase (dominant) allele that is present makes a wheat kernel slightly darker red.

Later work supported Nilsson-Ehle's model. He did not have to propose any new genetic principles to explain the inheritance of a quantitative trait. All that was needed was extension of Mendel's hypotheses about segregation and independent assortment.

Quantitative traits are produced by the independent actions of many genes, although it is now clear that some genes have much greater effects on the trait in question than other genes do. As a result, the transmission of quantitative traits is said to result from polygenic ("many-genes") inheritance. In **polygenic inheritance,** each gene adds a small amount to the value of the phenotype.

In the decades immediately after the rediscovery of Mendel's work, the question of why offspring resemble their parents could be answered in more satisfying ways. **TABLE 12.4** summarizes some of the key exceptions and extensions to Mendel's rules and gives you a chance to compare and contrast their effects on patterns of inheritance.

check your understanding

If you understand that . . .

- Genes near each other on the same chromosome violate the principle of independent assortment. They are not transmitted to gametes independently of each other unless crossing over occurs between them.

- Sex linkage, linkage, incomplete dominance, codominance, multiple allelism, pleiotropy, environmental effects, gene interactions, and polygenic inheritance are aspects of inheritance that Mendel did not study. When they occur, crosses do not result in classical Mendelian monohybrid or dihybrid ratios of offspring phenotypes.

✔ You should be able to . . .

Explain why the following crosses don't produce a 3:1 phenotype ratio in F₂ offspring:

1. Rose-comb × pea-comb chickens
2. Red-kernel × white-kernel wheat plants

Answers are available in Appendix A.

Type of Inheritance	Definition	Consequences or Comments
Sex linkage	Genes located on sex chromosomes.	Patterns of inheritance in males and females differ.
Linkage	Two genes found on same chromosome.	Linked genes violate principle of independent assortment.
Incomplete dominance	Heterozygotes have intermediate phenotype.	Polymorphism—heterozygotes have unique phenotype.
Codominance	Heterozygotes have phenotype of both alleles.	Polymorphism is possible—heterozygotes have unique phenotype.
Multiple allelism	In a population, more than two alleles present at a locus.	Polymorphism is possible.
Polymorphism	In a population, more than two phenotypes associated with a single gene are present.	Can result from actions of multiple alleles, incomplete dominance, and codominance.
Pleiotropy	A single gene affects many traits.	This is common.
Gene-by-gene interaction	In discrete traits, the phenotype associated with an allele depends on which alleles are present at another gene.	One allele can be associated with different phenotypes.
Gene-by-environment interaction	Phenotype influenced by environment experienced by individual.	Same genotypes can be associated with different phenotypes.
Polygenic inheritance of quantitative traits	Many genes are involved in specifying traits that exhibit continuous variation.	Unlike alleles that determine discrete traits, each allele adds a small amount to phenotype.

12.6 Applying Mendel's Rules to Human Inheritance

When researchers set out to study how a particular gene is transmitted in wheat or fruit flies or garden peas, they begin by making a series of controlled experimental crosses. For obvious reasons, this strategy is not possible with humans. But suppose you are concerned about an illness that runs in your family and go to a genetic counselor to find out how likely your children are to have the disease. To advise you, the counselor needs to know how the trait is transmitted, including whether the gene involved is autosomal or sex-linked and what type of dominance is associated with the disease allele.

To understand the transmission of human traits, investigators have to analyze human genotypes and phenotypes that already exist. A **mode of transmission** describes a trait as autosomal or sex-linked and gives the type of dominance of the allele. To learn the mode of transmission, scientists construct a **pedigree,** or family tree, of affected and unaffected individuals. By analyzing pedigrees, biomedical researchers have been able to discover how more than 2000 human genetic diseases are inherited.

A pedigree records the genetic relationships between the individuals in a family along with each person's sex and phenotype with respect to the trait in question. If the trait is governed by a single gene, then analyzing the pedigree may reveal whether a given phenotype is due to a dominant or recessive allele and whether the gene responsible is located on a sex chromosome or

on an autosome. Let's look at a series of specific case histories to see how this work is done.

Identifying Human Alleles as Recessive or Dominant

To analyze the inheritance of a discrete trait, biologists begin by assuming that a single autosomal gene is responsible and that the alleles present in the population have a simple dominant–recessive relationship.

This is the simplest possible situation. If the pattern of inheritance fits this model, then the assumptions—of inheritance by a single autosomal gene and simple dominance—are supported. Let's first analyze the pattern of inheritance that is typical of autosomal recessive traits and then examine patterns that emerge in pedigrees for autosomal dominant traits.

Patterns of Inheritance: Autosomal Recessive Traits If a phenotype is due to an autosomal recessive allele, then

- Individuals with the trait must be homozygous.

- If the parents of an affected individual do not have the trait, then the parents are heterozygous for the trait.

Heterozygous individuals who carry a recessive allele for an inherited disease are referred to as **carriers** of the disease. These individuals carry the allele and may transmit it even though they do not exhibit signs of the disease. When two carriers mate,

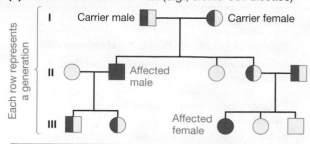

(a) Autosomal recessive trait (e.g., sickle-cell disease)

Carrier male ▉ Carrier female ◐

Affected male ■

Affected female ●

CHARACTERISTICS:
- Males and females are equally likely to be affected
- Affected offspring often have unaffected parents
- Unaffected parents of affected offspring are heterozygous (carriers)
- Affected offspring are homozygous
- If both parents are heterozygous, about ¼ of the offspring will be affected
- Trait often skips generations

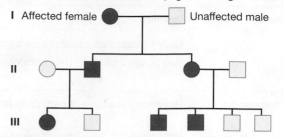

(b) Autosomal dominant trait (e.g., Huntington's disease)

Affected female ● Unaffected male ☐

CHARACTERISTICS:
- Males and females are equally likely to be affected
- Affected offspring have at least one affected parent
- Affected offspring are heterozygous if only one parent is affected
- Unaffected offspring are homozygous recessive
- If one parent is heterozygous, about ½ of the offspring will be affected
- Trait does not skip generations

FIGURE 12.22 Pedigrees of Families with Autosomal Recessive and Autosomal Dominant Traits. Pedigrees use standard symbols: squares = males, circles = females; unfilled symbols = unaffected individuals (those without the trait), filled symbols = affected individuals, half-filled symbols = heterozygotes for a recessive trait (carriers); horizontal lines connect parents, vertical lines connect parents to children.

about ¼ of their offspring are expected to express the recessive phenotype.

FIGURE 12.22a is a pedigree from a family in which an autosomal recessive trait, such as sickle-cell disease, occurs. The key feature to notice in this pedigree is that both boys and girls can exhibit the trait even though their parents do not. This is the pattern you would expect when the parents of an individual with the trait are heterozygous. It is also logical to observe that when an affected (homozygous) individual has children, those children do not necessarily have the trait. This pattern is predicted if affected people marry individuals who are homozygous for the dominant allele. This is likely to occur if the recessive allele is rare in the population.

In general, a recessive phenotype should show up in offspring only when both parents have that recessive allele and pass it on to their offspring. By definition, a recessive allele produces a given phenotype only when the individual is homozygous for that allele.

Patterns of Inheritance: Autosomal Dominant Traits When a trait is autosomal dominant, individuals who are homozygous or heterozygous for it must have the dominant phenotype. Even if one parent is heterozygous and the other is homozygous recessive, on average half their children should show the dominant phenotype. And unless a new mutation has occurred in a gamete, any child with the trait must have a parent with this trait. The latter observation is in strong contrast to the pattern seen in autosomal recessive traits.

FIGURE 12.22b shows the inheritance of the degenerative brain disorder called Huntington's disease (see Section 12.2). This pedigree has two features that indicate Huntington's disease is passed to the next generation through an autosomal dominant allele.

First, if a child shows the trait, then one of its parents shows the trait as well. Second, if families have a large number of children, the trait usually shows up in every generation—owing to the high probability of heterozygous parents having affected children.

Identifying Human Traits as Autosomal or Sex-Linked

When it is not possible to arrange reciprocal crosses, can data in a pedigree indicate whether a trait is autosomal or sex-linked? The answer is based on a simple premise. If a trait appears about equally often in males and females, then it is likely to be autosomal. But if males express the trait in question more often than females, then the allele responsible is likely to be recessive and found on the X chromosome.

X-linked Recessive Traits X-linked recessive traits are relatively common. They include the form of red–green color blindness that affects about 10 percent of males and the devastating blood clotting disorder hemophilia. A pedigree for red–green color blindness is shown in **FIGURE 12.23a**.

A key characteristic of X-linked recessive traits is that males express the trait more often than females. This is because males have only one copy of the X chromosome. Therefore, any X-linked allele will be expressed in a male.

Because human females have two X chromosomes, they have two copies of each X-linked gene and a recessive allele will not be expressed in heterozygotes. In the pedigree of Figure 12.23a the fact that only males are affected gives an immediate clue that this is an X-linked recessive trait.

Further, the appearance of an X-linked recessive trait usually skips a generation in the pedigree. Notice how on the right-hand

(a) X-linked recessive trait (e.g., red–green color blindness)

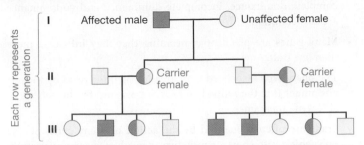

CHARACTERISTICS:
- Males are affected more frequently than females
- Trait is never passed from father to son
- Affected sons are usually born to carrier mothers
- About ½ of the sons of a carrier mother will be affected
- All daughters of affected males and unaffected non-carrier females are carriers
- Trait often skips generations

(b) X-linked dominant trait (e.g., hypophosphatemia)

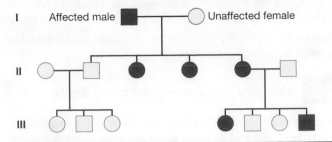

CHARACTERISTICS:
- Males and females are equally likely to be affected
- All daughters of an affected father are affected, but no sons
- Affected sons always have affected mothers
- About ½ of the offspring of an affected mother will be affected
- Affected daughters can have an affected mother or father
- Trait does not skip generations

FIGURE 12.23 Pedigrees of Families with X-linked Recessive (a) and X-linked Dominant (b) Traits.

✔**QUESTION** What genotype in a mother and a father would be predicted to produce a 1:1 ratio of normal : color-blind offspring? What would the ratio of color-blind male : female be from this mating?

side of the pedigree the trait appears in generations I and III but not in generation II. This pattern occurs because an affected male passes his only X chromosome on to his daughters. But because his daughters almost always receive a wild-type allele from their mother, the daughters don't show the trait. They will pass the defective allele on to about half their sons, however.

Most X-linked traits are recessive. There are only a few rare examples of X-linked dominant traits.

X-linked Dominant Traits One example of an X-linked dominant trait is a bone disorder known as hypophosphatemia, or vitamin D–resistant rickets. What can be predicted about the inheritance of an X-linked dominant trait? As the pedigree in **FIGURE 12.23b** shows, the most telling feature is that an affected male will pass the trait to all his daughters and none of his sons.

This is because daughters receive their father's only X chromosome. In contrast, a heterozygous female will pass the trait to half her daughters and half her sons. This occurs because there is an equal chance that a heterozygous mother will pass on an X chromosome with either the dominant or the recessive trait.

What about Y-linked traits? Although the patterns for Y-linked inheritance can easily be predicted, the reality is that very few genes occur on the Y chromosome. These genes are involved with male-specific sexual development. Except for maleness, there are no known human Y-linked traits.

Within a few decades of the rediscovery of Mendel's work, the burning question in genetics was no longer the nature of inheritance but the nature of the gene. What are genes made of, and how are they copied so that parents pass their alleles on to their offspring? These are the questions turned to in Chapter 6.

CHAPTER 12 REVIEW

For media, go to MasteringBiology

If you understand . . .

12.1 Mendel's Experimental System

- When Mendel began his work, there were two leading hypotheses of inheritance: blending inheritance and the inheritance of acquired characteristics.
- Mendel chose pea plants as a model organism and began his work with pure lines that he crossed to produce hybrids.
- Mendel sought to discover rules of heredity that explained how phenotypes were transmitted from parent to offspring.

✔ You should be able explain why pure lines are homozygous.

12.2 Mendel's Experiments with a Single Trait

- From analysis of the trait expressed in hybrids, Mendel concluded that one trait was dominant and the other recessive.
- From the results of monohybrid crosses, Mendel concluded that inheritance is particulate—genes do not blend together.
- The traits that Mendel studied are specified by paired hereditary determinants (genes) that separate from each other during gamete formation.

- Analysis of monohybrid crosses led to the principle of segregation: Before the formation of gametes, the alleles of each gene separate so that each egg or sperm cell receives only one of them.

✓ You should be able to predict the gamete genotypes generated by a parent with the genotype *Bb*.

12.3 Mendel's Experiments with Two Traits

- Analysis of dihybrid crosses led to the principle of independent assortment: alleles of different genes are transmitted to egg cells and sperm cells independently of each other.

- Testcrosses allow an investigator to determine whether an individual of dominant phenotype is homozygous or heterozygous.

✓ You should be able to predict the gamete genotypes generated by a parent with the genotype *BbRr*.

12.4 The Chromosome Theory of Inheritance

- The chromosome theory states that chromosomes contain genes and that Mendel's rules can be explained by the segregation and independent assortment of homologous chromosomes at meiosis I.

- The chromosome theory was supported by the discovery of sex linkage. Crosses with X-linked traits supported the theory's contention that genes are found on chromosomes.

- X-linked traits give different results in reciprocal crosses.

✓ You should be able to use a Punnett square to show why reciprocal crosses involving an X-linked recessive gene give different results.

12.5 Extending Mendel's Rules

- There are important exceptions and extensions to the basic patterns of inheritance that Mendel discovered.

- All genes follow the principle of segregation, but genes close together on the same chromosome do not follow the principle of independent assortment.

- Crossing over between homologous chromosomes creates new combinations of alleles along each homolog.

- The frequency of crossing over can be used to create genetic maps that show the position and spacing of genes along chromosomes.

- Many genes have more than two alleles; this is multiple allelism. When more than two phenotypes are due to multiple allelism, the trait is polymorphic.

- Not all heterozygotes show a dominant phenotype. In addition to complete dominance, incomplete dominance and codominance are also common.

- Many genes are pleiotropic, meaning that they influence more than one trait.

- The phenotype associated with an allele is influenced by the environment that the individual experiences, and by the actions of alleles of other genes.

- Traits are often influenced by the action of many genes. These polygenic traits show quantitative instead of discrete variation. The frequency of different phenotypes is distributed normally (a plot produces a "bell curve" or normal distribution).

✓ You should be able to explain why crossing over is said to break up linkage between alleles.

12.6 Applying Mendel's Rules to Human Inheritance

- Pedigrees map out the transmission of human traits.

- Applying Mendel's rules to pedigrees can reveal the mode of transmission—whether a trait is dominant or recessive, autosomal or X-linked.

✓ You should be able to draw a pedigree that shows two sons and two daughters produced by a red–green color-blind father and a homozygous mother with normal color vision and explain why all the daughters are expected to be carriers of color blindness and none of the sons are expected to be color-blind.

(MB) MasteringBiology

1. **MasteringBiology Assignments**

Tutorials and Activities Determining Genotype: Pea Pod Color; What Is the Inheritance Pattern of Sex-Linked Traits? Gregor's Garden; Incomplete Dominance; Inheritance of Fur Color in Mice; Linked Genes and Crossing Over; Linked Genes and Linkage Mapping; Mendel's Experiments; Mendel's Law of Independent Assortment; Mendel's Law of Segregation; Pedigree Analysis: Dominant and Recessive Autosomal Conditions; Pedigree Analysis: Galactosemia, Sex Linkage, Sex-Linked Genes

Questions Reading Quizzes, Blue-Thread Questions, Test Bank

2. **eText** Read your book online, search, take notes, highlight text, and more.

3. **The Study Area** Practice Test, Cumulative Test, BioFlix® 3-D Animations, Videos, Activities, Audio Glossary, Word Study Tools, Art

You should be able to . . .

1. In studies of how traits are inherited, what makes certain species candidates for model organisms?
   a. They are the first organisms to be used in a particular type of experiment, so they are a historical "model" of what researchers expect to find.
   b. They are easy to study because a great deal is already known about them.
   c. They are the best or most fit of their type.
   d. They are easy to maintain, have a short life cycle, produce many offspring, and yield data that are relevant to many other organisms.

2. Why is the allele for wrinkled seed shape in garden peas considered recessive?
   a. It "recedes" in the F_2 generation when homozygous parents are crossed.
   b. The trait associated with the allele is not expressed in heterozygotes.
   c. Individuals with the allele have lower fitness than that of individuals with the dominant allele.
   d. The allele is less common than the dominant allele. (The wrinkled allele is a rare mutant.)

3. The alleles found in haploid organisms cannot be dominant or recessive. Why?
   a. Dominance and recessiveness describe which allele is expressed in phenotype when different alleles occur in the same individual.
   b. Because only one allele is present, alleles in haploid organisms are always dominant.
   c. Alleles in haploid individuals are transmitted like mitochondrial DNA or chloroplast DNA.
   d. Most haploid individuals are bacteria, and bacterial genetics is completely different from eukaryotic genetics.

4. Why can you infer that individuals that are "pure line" are homozygous for the gene in question?
   a. Because they are highly inbred.
   b. Because only two alleles are present at each gene in the populations to which these individuals belong.
   c. Because in a pure line, phenotypes are not affected by environmental conditions or gene interactions.
   d. Because no other phenotype is ever observed in a pure-line population, this implies that only one allele is present.

5. The genes for the traits that Mendel worked with are either located on different chromosomes or so far apart on the same chromosome that crossing over almost always occurs between them. How did this circumstance help Mendel recognize the principle of independent assortment?
   a. Otherwise, his dihybrid crosses would not have produced a $9:3:3:1$ ratio of F_2 phenotypes.
   b. The occurrence of individuals with unexpected phenotypes led him to the discovery of recombination.
   c. It led him to the realization that the behavior of chromosomes during meiosis explained his results.
   d. It meant that the alleles involved were either dominant or recessive, which gave $3:1$ ratios in the F_1 generation.

6. What is meant by the claim that Mendel worked with the simplest possible genetic system?
   a. Discrete traits, two alleles, simple dominance and recessiveness, no sex chromosomes, and unlinked genes are the simplest situation known.
   b. The ability to self-fertilize or cross-pollinate made it simple for Mendel to set up controlled crosses.
   c. Mendel was aware of meiosis and the chromosome theory of inheritance, so it was easy to reach the conclusions he did.
   d. Mendel's experimental designs and his rules of inheritance are actually neither complex nor sophisticated.

7. Mendel's rules do not correctly predict patterns of inheritance for tightly linked genes or the inheritance of alleles that show incomplete dominance. Does this mean that his hypotheses are incorrect?
   a. Yes, because they are relevant to only a small number of organisms and traits.
   b. Yes, because not all data support his hypotheses.
   c. No, because he was not aware of meiosis or the chromosome theory of inheritance.
   d. No, it just means that his hypotheses are limited to certain conditions.

8. The artificial sweetener NutraSweet consists of a phenylalanine molecule linked to aspartic acid. The labels of diet sodas that contain NutraSweet include a warning to people with PKU. Why?
   a. NutraSweet stimulates the same taste receptors that natural sugars do.
   b. People with PKU have to avoid phenylalanine in their diet.
   c. In people with PKU, phenylalanine reacts with aspartic acid to form a toxic compound.
   d. People with PKU cannot lead normal lives, even if their environment is carefully controlled.

9. When Sutton and Boveri published the chromosome theory of inheritance, research on meiosis had not yet established that paternal and maternal homologs of different chromosomes assort independently. Then, in 1913, Elinor Carothers published a paper about a grasshopper species with an unusual karyotype: One chromosome had no homolog (meaning no pairing partner at meiosis I); another chromosome had homologs that could be distinguished under the light microscope. If chromosomes assort independently, how often should Carothers have observed each of the four products of meiosis shown in the following figure?

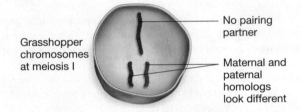

Grasshopper chromosomes at meiosis I — No pairing partner — Maternal and paternal homologs look different

Four types of gametes possible (each meiotic division can produce only two of the four)

   a. Only the gametes with one of each type of chromosome would occur.
   b. The four types of gametes should be observed to occur at equal frequencies.
   c. The chromosome with no pairing partner would disintegrate, so only gametes with one copy of the other chromosome would be observed.
   d. Gametes with one of each type of chromosome would occur twice as often as gametes with just one chromosome.

10. Which of the following is the strongest evidence that a trait might be influenced by polygenic inheritance?
    a. F_1 offspring of parents with different phenotypes have an intermediate phenotype.
    b. F_1 offspring of parents with different phenotypes have the dominant phenotype.
    c. The trait shows qualitative (discrete) variation.
    d. The trait shows quantitative variation.

The best way to test and extend your knowledge of transmission genetics is to work problems. Most genetics problems are set up as follows: You are given some information about the genotypes or phenotypes of one or both parents, along with data on the phenotypes of F_1 or F_2 offspring. Your task is to generate a set of hypotheses—a genetic model—to explain the results. Your hypotheses should address each of the following questions:

- Is the trait under study discrete or quantitative?
- Is the phenotype a product of one gene or many genes?
- For each gene involved, how many alleles are present—one, two, or many?
- Do the alleles involved show complete dominance, incomplete dominance, or codominance?
- Are the genes involved sex-linked or autosomal?
- If more than one gene is involved, are they linked or unlinked? If they are linked, does crossing over occur frequently?

It's also helpful to ask yourself whether gene interactions or pleiotropy might be occurring and whether it is safe to assume that the experimental design carefully controlled for effects of variation in other genes and in the environment.

In working the problem, be sure to start with the simplest possible explanation. For example, if you are dealing with a discrete trait, you might hypothesize that the cross involves a single autosomal gene with two alleles that show complete dominance. Your next step is to infer what the parental genotypes would be (according to your hypothesis), if they are not already given, and then do a Punnett square to predict what the offspring phenotypes and their frequencies should be based on your hypothesis. Next, check whether these predictions match the observed results given in the problem. If the

answer is yes, you have a valid solution. But if the answer is no, you need to go back and change one of your hypotheses, redo the Punnett square, and check to see if the predictions and observations match. Keep repeating these steps until you have a model that fits the data.

11. **Example Problem** *Plectritis congesta* plants produce fruits that either have or do not have prominent structures called wings. The alleles involved are W^+ = winged fruit; W^- = wingless fruit. Researchers collected an array of individuals from the field and performed a series of crosses. The results are given in the following table. Complete the table by writing down the genotype of the parent or parents involved in each cross.

Parental Phenotype(s)	Number of Offspring with Winged Fruits	Number of Offspring with Wingless Fruits	Parental Genotype(s)
Wingless (self-fertilized)	0	80	
Winged (self-fertilized)	90	30	
Winged × wingless	46	0	
Winged × winged	44	0	

A worked solution is available in Appendix A.

12. **Example Problem** Two black female mice are crossed with a brown male. In several litters, female I produced 9 blacks and 7 browns; female II produced 57 blacks. What deductions can you make concerning the inheritance of black and brown coat color in mice? What are the genotypes of the parents in this case?

A worked solution is available in Appendix A.

13. In peas, purple flowers are dominant to white. If a purple-flowered, heterozygous plant were crossed with a white-flowered plant, what is the expected ratio of genotypes and phenotypes among the F_1 offspring? If two of the purple-flowered F_1 offspring were randomly selected and crossed, what is the expected ratio of genotypes and phenotypes among the F_2 offspring?

14. In garden peas, yellow seeds (Y) are dominant to green seeds (y), and inflated pods (I) are dominant to constricted pods (i). Suppose you have crossed $YYII$ parents with $yyii$ parents.
   - Draw the F_1 Punnett square and predict the expected F_1 phenotype(s).
   - List the genotype(s) of gametes produced by F_1 individuals.
   - Draw the F_2 Punnett square. Based on this Punnett square, predict the expected phenotype(s) in the F_2 generation and the expected frequency of each phenotype.

15. The smooth feathers on the back of the neck in pigeons can be reversed by a mutation to produce a "crested" appearance in which feathers form a distinctive spike at the back of the head. A pigeon breeder examined offspring produced by a single pair of non-crested birds and recorded the following: 22 non-crested and 7 crested. She then made a series of crosses using offspring from the first cross. When she crossed two of the crested birds, all 20 of the offspring were crested. When she crossed a non-crested bird with a crested bird, 7 offspring were non-crested and 6 were crested.

   - For these three crosses, provide genotypes for parents and offspring that are consistent with these results.
   - Which allele is dominant?

16. A plant with orange, spotted flowers was grown in the greenhouse from a seed collected in the wild. The plant was self-pollinated and gave rise to the following progeny: 88 orange with spots, 34 yellow with spots, 32 orange with no spots, and 8 yellow with no spots. What can you conclude about the dominance relationships of the alleles responsible for the spotted and unspotted phenotypes? For the orange and yellow phenotypes? What can you conclude about the genotype of the original plant that had orange, spotted flowers?

17. As a genetic counselor, you routinely advise couples about the possibility of genetic disease in their offspring based on their family histories. This morning you met with an engaged couple, both of whom are phenotypically normal. The man, however, has a brother who died of Duchenne-type muscular dystrophy, an X-linked condition that results in death before the age of 20. The allele responsible for this disease is recessive. His prospective bride, whose family has no history of the disease, is worried that the couple's sons or daughters might be afflicted.
   - How would you advise this couple?
   - The sister of this man is planning to marry his fiancée's brother. How would you advise this second couple?

18. Suppose you are heterozygous for two genes that are located on different chromosomes. You carry alleles *A* and *a* for one gene and alleles *B* and *b* for the other. Draw a diagram illustrating what happens to these genes and alleles when meiosis occurs in your reproductive tissues. Label the stages of meiosis, the homologous chromosomes, sister chromatids, nonhomologous chromosomes, genes, and alleles. Be sure to list all the genetically different gametes that could form and indicate how frequently each type should be observed. On the diagram, identify the events responsible for the principle of segregation and the principle of independent assortment.

19. Review the text's description of ABO blood types. Suppose a woman with blood type O married a man with blood type AB. What phenotypes and genotypes would you expect to observe in their offspring, and in what proportions? Answer the same question for a heterozygous mother with blood type A and a heterozygous father with blood type B.

20. An alien friend named Tukan has two sets of eyes, one set forward-looking and one set backward-looking, and smooth skin. His mate, Valco, lacks eyes but has skin covered with tiny hooks that attract all sorts of debris. Tukan and Valco have thrived on earth and have had four children, all with no eyes and smooth skin. Typical of their ways, the children interbred and produced 32 children of their own.
    - Under the models of inheritance proposed by Mendel, identify which alleles are dominant and which are recessive.
    - Provide gene symbols that would reflect the dominant–recessive allelic relationships.
    - Of the 32 children, how many would you expect to have two sets of eyes and smooth skin?

21. Phenylketonuria (PKU) is a genetic disease caused by homozygosity for a recessive mutation in the enzyme that converts the amino acid phenylalanine to tyrosine. In the absence of this enzyme, phenylalanine and some of its derivatives accumulate in the body and cause mental retardation. If individuals are identified soon enough after birth, they can be treated by a low-phenylalanine diet for the early years of their lives. As adults, though, homozygous recessive individuals are allowed to adopt a diet with normal amounts of phenylalanine. Not long after such treatments were initiated, a troubling phenomenon was observed. A high number of children born to treated mothers were mentally retarded even though the children were heterozygous for the PKU gene. Children born of treated PKU males suffered no ill effects.
    - Can you offer an explanation as to why genetically heterozygous children of treated PKU mothers might be prone to mental retardation?
    - Propose a solution to reduce the likelihood of mental retardation in children of treated PKU mothers.

22. The blending-inheritance hypothesis proposed that the genetic material from parents is unavoidably and irreversibly mixed in the offspring. As a result, offspring and later descendants should always appear intermediate in phenotype to their forebears. Mendel, in contrast, proposed that genes are discrete and that their integrity is maintained in the offspring and in subsequent generations. Suppose the year is 1890. You are a horse breeder and have just read Mendel's paper. You don't believe his results,

however, because you often work with cremello (very light-colored) and chestnut (reddish-brown) horses. You know that if you cross a cremello individual from a pure-breeding line with a chestnut individual from a pure-breeding line, the offspring will be palomino—meaning they have an intermediate (golden-yellow) body color. What additional crosses would you do to test whether Mendel's model is valid in the case of genes for horse color? List the crosses and the offspring genotypes and phenotypes you'd expect to obtain. Explain why these experimental crosses would provide a test of Mendel's model.

23. Two mothers give birth to sons at the same time in a busy hospital. The son of couple 1 is afflicted with hemophilia A, which is a recessive X-linked disease. Neither parent has the disease. Couple 2 has a normal son even though the father has hemophilia A. The two couples sue the hospital in court, claiming that a careless staff member swapped their babies at birth. You appear in court as an expert witness. What do you tell the jury? Make a diagram that you can submit to the jury.

24. You have crossed two *Drosophila melanogaster* individuals that have long wings and red eyes—the wild-type phenotype. In the progeny, the mutant phenotypes called curved wings and lozenge eyes appear as follows:

Females	Males
600 long wings, red eyes	300 long wings, red eyes
200 curved wings, red eyes	100 curved wings, red eyes
	300 long wings, lozenge eyes
	100 curved wings, lozenge eyes

   - According to these data, is the curved-wing allele autosomal recessive, autosomal dominant, sex-linked recessive, or sex-linked dominant?
   - Is the lozenge-eyed allele autosomal recessive, autosomal dominant, sex-linked recessive, or sex-linked dominant?
   - What is the genotype of the female parent?
   - What is the genotype of the male parent?

25. In parakeets, two autosomal genes that are located on different chromosomes control the production of feather pigment. Gene *B* codes for an enzyme that is required for the synthesis of a blue pigment, and gene *Y* codes for an enzyme required for the synthesis of a yellow pigment. Recessive mutations that result in no production of the affected pigment are known for both genes. Suppose that a bird breeder has two green parakeets and mates them. The offspring are green, blue, yellow, and albino (unpigmented).
   - Based on this observation, what are the genotypes of the green parents? What is the genotype of each type of offspring? What fraction of the total progeny should exhibit each type of color?
   - Suppose that the parents were the progeny of a cross between two true-breeding strains. What two types of crosses between true-breeding strains could have produced the green parents? Indicate the genotypes and phenotypes for each cross.

26. Recall that hemophilia is an X-linked recessive disease. If a woman with hemophilia had children with a man without hemophilia, what is the chance that their first child will have the disease? What is the chance that their first child will be a carrier?

13 Cellular Respiration and Fermentation

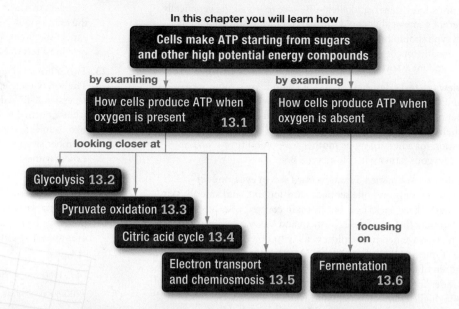

In this chapter you will learn how

Cells make ATP starting from sugars and other high potential energy compounds

by examining

How cells produce ATP when oxygen is present **13.1**

by examining

How cells produce ATP when oxygen is absent

looking closer at

Glycolysis **13.2**

Pyruvate oxidation **13.3**

Citric acid cycle **13.4**

Electron transport and chemiosmosis **13.5**

focusing on

Fermentation **13.6**

This hydroelectric dam on the Duero river between Spain and Portugal uses pumps to move water from the lower reservoir to the upper reservoir. During periods of high energy demand, the potential energy stored by this activity is used to generate electricity. A similar process is used by cells to produce ATP during cellular respiration.

This chapter is part of the Big Picture. See how on pages 284–285.

ife requires energy. From the very start, chemical evolution was driven by energy from chemicals, radiation, heat, or other sources (see Appendix D). Harnessing energy and controlling its flow has been the single most important step in the evolution of life.

What fuels life in cells? The answer is the nucleotide adenosine triphosphate (ATP). ATP has high potential energy and allows cells to overcome life's energy barriers (see Chapter 10).

This chapter investigates how cells make ATP, starting with an introduction to the metabolic pathways that harvest energy from high-energy molecules like **glucose**—the most common source of chemical energy used by organisms. The four central pathways of cellular respiration will be

✔ When you see this checkmark, stop and test yourself. Answers are available in Appendix A.

presented with emphasis on how the oxidation of glucose leads to ATP production. Fermentation will also be introduced as an alternative pathway used to make ATP when key reactions in cellular respiration are either shut down or not available.

As cells process sugar, the energy that is released is used to transfer a phosphate group to adenosine diphosphate (ADP), generating ATP. (You can see the Big Picture of how the production of glucose in photosynthesis is related to its catabolism in cellular respiration on pages 284–285.)

13.1 An Overview of Cellular Respiration

In general, a cell contains only enough ATP to last from 30 seconds to a few minutes. Because it has such high potential energy, ATP is unstable and is not stored. Like many other cellular processes, the production and use of ATP is fast. Most cells are making ATP all the time.

Most of the glucose that is used to make ATP is produced by plants and other photosynthetic species. These organisms use the energy in sunlight to reduce carbon dioxide (CO_2) to glucose and other carbohydrates. While they are alive, photosynthetic species use the glucose that they produce to make ATP for themselves. When photosynthetic species decompose or are eaten, they provide glucose to animals, fungi, and many bacteria and archaea.

All organisms use glucose in the synthesis of complex carbohydrates, fats, and other energy-rich compounds. Storage carbohydrates, such as starch and glycogen, act like savings accounts for chemical energy. ATP, in contrast, is like cash. To withdraw chemical energy from the accounts to get cash, storage carbohydrates are first hydrolyzed into their glucose monomers. The glucose is then used to produce ATP through one of two general processes: cellular respiration or fermentation (**FIGURE 13.1**). The primary difference between these two processes lies in the degree to which glucose is oxidized.

What Happens When Glucose Is Oxidized?

When glucose undergoes the uncontrolled oxidation reaction called burning, some of the potential energy stored in its chemical bonds is converted to kinetic energy in the form of heat:

$$\underset{\text{glucose}}{C_6H_{12}O_2} + \underset{\text{oxygen}}{6\ O_2} \longrightarrow \underset{\text{carbon dioxide}}{6\ CO_2} + \underset{\text{water}}{6\ H_2O} + \text{Heat}$$

More specifically, a total of about 685 kilocalories (kcal) of heat is released when one mole of glucose is oxidized. To put this in perspective, if you burned this amount of glucose, it would give off enough heat to bring almost 2.5 gallons of room-temperature water to a boil.

Glucose does not burn in cells, however. Instead, the glucose in cells is oxidized through a long series of carefully controlled redox reactions. These reactions are occurring, millions of

Energy conversion
Photosynthesis
$CO_2 + H_2O + $ sunlight

$O_2 + (CH_2O)_n$

Glucose

Energy storage
Starch, glycogen, fats
(synthesized from glucose)

Energy use

Cellular Respiration	Fermentation
Glucose + O_2 + ADP + P_i	Glucose + ADP + P_i
$CO_2 + H_2O +$ **ATP**	Small organic molecules + **ATP**

FIGURE 13.1 Glucose Is the Hub of Energy Processing in Cells. Glucose is a product of photosynthesis. Both plants and animals store glucose and oxidize it to provide chemical energy in the form of ATP.

times per minute, in your cells right now. Instead of releasing all of this energy as heat, much of it is being used to make the ATP you need to read, think, move, and stay alive. In cells, the change in free energy (Chapter 10) that occurs during the oxidation of glucose is used to synthesize ATP from ADP and P_i.

So how does fermentation differ from cellular respiration? Respiration, like burning, results in the complete oxidation of glucose into CO_2 and water. Fermentation, on the other hand, does not fully oxidize glucose. Instead, small, reduced organic molecules are produced as waste. As a result, cellular respiration releases more energy from glucose than fermentation.

The complete oxidation of glucose via cellular respiration can be thought of as a four-step process used to convert the chemical energy in glucose to chemical energy in ATP. Each of the four steps consists of a series of chemical reactions, and each step has a distinctive starting molecule and a characteristic set of products.

1. *Glycolysis* During **glycolysis,** one 6-carbon molecule of glucose is broken into two molecules of the three-carbon compound pyruvate. During this process, ATP is produced from ADP, and nicotinamide adenine dinucleotide (NAD^+) is reduced to form NADH.

2. *Pyruvate processing* Pyruvate is processed to release one molecule of CO_2, and the remaining two carbons are used to form the compound acetyl CoA. The oxidation of pyruvate results in more NAD^+ being reduced to NADH.

3. *Citric acid cycle* Acetyl CoA is oxidized to two molecules of CO_2. During this sequence of reactions, more ATP and NADH are produced, and flavin adenine dinucleotide (FAD) is reduced to form $FADH_2$.

4. *Electron transport and oxidative phosphorylation* Electrons from NADH and $FADH_2$ move through a series of proteins called an electron transport chain (ETC). The energy released in this chain of redox reactions is used to create a proton gradient across a membrane; the ensuing flow of protons back across the membrane is used to make ATP. Because this mode of ATP production links the phosphorylation of ADP with the oxidation of NADH and $FADH_2$, it is called **oxidative phosphorylation.**

FIGURE 13.2 summarizes the four steps in cellular respiration. Formally, **cellular respiration** is defined as any suite of reactions that uses electrons harvested from high-energy molecules to produce ATP via an electron transport chain.

The enzymes, products, and intermediates involved in cellular respiration and fermentation do not exist in isolation. Instead, they are part of a huge and dynamic inventory of chemicals inside the cell.

This complexity can be boiled down to a simple essence, however. Two of the most fundamental requirements of a cell are energy and carbon. They need a source of high-energy electrons for generating chemical energy in the form of ATP, and a source of carbon-containing molecules that can be used to synthesize DNA, RNA, proteins, fatty acids, and other molecules. Let's take a closer look at the central role cellular respiration plays in metabolic pathways as a whole.

Cellular Respiration Plays a Central Role in Metabolism

Recall that sets of reactions that break down molecules are called catabolic pathways (Chapter 10). These reactions often harvest stored chemical energy to produce ATP. On the other hand, sets of reactions that synthesize larger molecules from smaller components are called anabolic pathways. Anabolic reactions often use energy in the form of ATP.

How does the process of cellular respiration interact with other catabolic and anabolic pathways? Let's first consider how

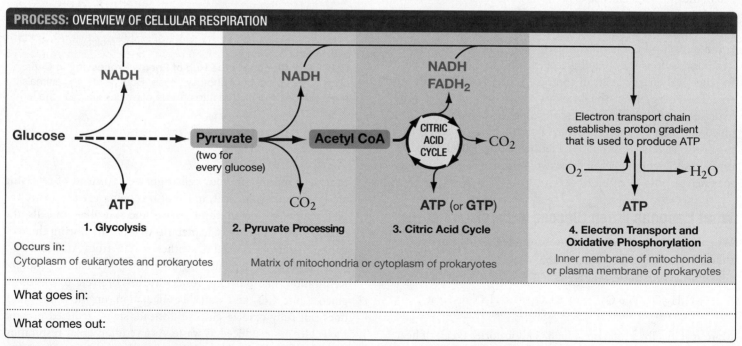

FIGURE 13.2 Cellular Respiration Oxidizes Glucose to Make ATP. Cells produce ATP from glucose via a series of processes: (1) glycolysis, (2) pyruvate processing, (3) the citric acid cycle, and (4) electron transport and oxidative phosphorylation. Each component produces high-energy molecules in the form of nucleotides (ATP or GTP) or electron carriers (NADH or $FADH_2$). Because the four components are connected, glucose oxidation is an integrated metabolic pathway. The first three steps oxidize glucose to produce NADH and $FADH_2$, which then feed the electron transport chain.

✔**EXERCISE** Fill in the chart along the bottom.

eukaryotes extract energy from molecules other than glucose and then examine how intermediates produced in glycolysis and the citric acid cycle are used as building blocks to synthesize cell components.

Catabolic Pathways Break Down a Variety of Molecules
Most organisms ingest, absorb, or synthesize many different carbohydrates. These molecules range from sucrose, maltose, and other simple sugars to large polymers such as glycogen and starch (see Appendix E).

Recall that both glycogen and starch are polymers of glucose, but differ in the way their long chains of glucose branch. Using enzyme-catalyzed reactions, cells can produce glucose from glycogen, starch, and most simple sugars. Glucose and fructose can then be processed in glycolysis.

Carbohydrates are not the only important source of carbon compounds used in catabolic pathways, however. Fats are highly reduced macromolecules consisting of glycerol bonded to chains of fatty acids (see Chapter 3). In cells, enzymes routinely break down fats to release the glycerol and convert the fatty acids into acetyl CoA molecules. Glycerol can be further processed and enter glycolysis. Acetyl CoA enters the citric acid cycle.

Proteins can also be catabolized, meaning that they can be broken down and used to produce ATP. Once they are hydrolyzed to their constituent amino acids, enzyme-catalyzed reactions remove the amino ($-NH_2$) groups. The amino groups are excreted in urine as waste. The carbon compounds that remain are converted to pyruvate, acetyl CoA, and other intermediates in glycolysis and the citric acid cycle.

The top half of **FIGURE 13.3** summarizes the catabolic pathways of carbohydrates, fats, and proteins and shows how their breakdown products feed an array of steps in glucose oxidation and cellular respiration. When all three types of molecules are available in the cell to generate ATP, carbohydrates are used up first, then fats, and finally proteins.

Catabolic Intermediates Are Used in Anabolic Pathways
Where do cells get the precursor molecules required to synthesize amino acids, RNA, DNA, phospholipids, and other cell components? Not surprisingly, the answer often involves intermediates in carbohydrate metabolism. For example,

- In humans, about half the required amino acids can be synthesized from molecules siphoned from the citric acid cycle.
- Acetyl CoA is the starting point for anabolic pathways that result in the synthesis of fatty acids. Fatty acids can then be used to build phospholipid membranes or fats.
- Intermediates in glycolysis can be oxidized to start the synthesis of the sugars in ribonucleotides and deoxyribonucleotides. Nucleotides, in turn, are building blocks used in RNA and DNA synthesis.
- If ATP is abundant, pyruvate and lactate (from fermentation) can be used in the synthesis of glucose. Excess glucose may be converted to glycogen or starch and stored.

The bottom half of Figure 13.3 summarizes how intermediates in carbohydrate metabolism are drawn off to synthesize macromolecules. The take-home message is that the same molecule can serve many different functions in the cell. As a result, catabolic and anabolic pathways are closely intertwined.

Metabolism comprises thousands of different chemical reactions, yet the amounts and identities of molecules inside cells are relatively constant. By regulating key reactions involved in catabolic and anabolic pathways, the cell is able to maintain its internal environment even under different environmental conditions—a process referred to as **homeostasis**. Cellular respiration and

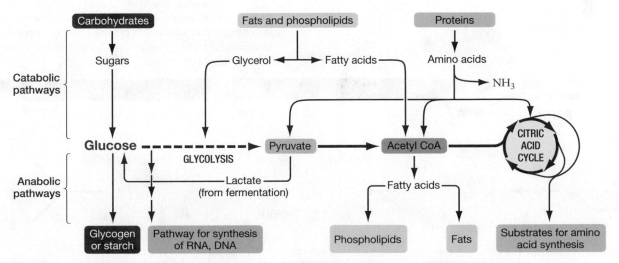

FIGURE 13.3 Cellular Respiration Interacts with Other Catabolic and Anabolic Pathways. A variety of high-energy compounds from carbohydrates, fats, or proteins can be broken down in catabolic reactions and used by cellular respiration for ATP production. Several of the intermediates in carbohydrate metabolism act as precursor molecules in anabolic reactions leading to the synthesis of glycogen or starch, RNA, DNA, fatty acids, and amino acids.

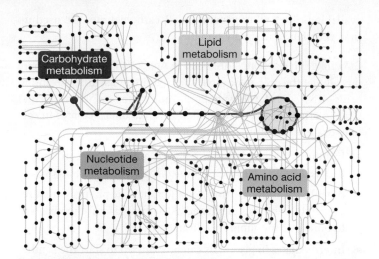

FIGURE 13.4 Pathways of Cellular Respiration Play a Central Role in the Metabolic Activity of Cells. A representation of a few of the thousands of chemical reactions that occur in cells. The dots represent molecules, and the lines represent enzyme-catalyzed reactions. At the center of all this, the first three steps of cellular respiration are emphasized by bold dots and thick lines. For reference, glucose, pyruvate, and acetyl CoA are represented by the distinctive colors used in Figure 13.3.

fermentation pathways may be crucial to the life of a cell, but they also have to be seen as central parts of a whole (**FIGURE 13.4**).

Once you've filled in the chart at the bottom of Figure 13.2, you'll be ready to analyze each of the four steps of cellular respiration in detail. As you delve in, keep asking yourself the same key questions: What goes in and what comes out? What happens to the potential energy that is released? Where does each step occur, and how is it regulated? Then take a look in the mirror. All these processes are occurring right now, in virtually all your cells.

13.2 Glycolysis: Processing Glucose to Pyruvate

Because the enzymes responsible for glycolysis have been observed in nearly every bacterium, archaean, and eukaryote, it is logical to infer that the ancestor of all organisms living today made ATP by glycolysis. It's ironic, then, that the process was discovered by accident.

In the 1890s Hans and Edward Buchner were working out techniques for breaking open baker's yeast cells and extracting the contents for commercial and medicinal use. (Yeast extracts are still added to some foods as a flavor enhancer or nutritional supplement.) In one set of experiments, the Buchners added sucrose to their extracts. At the time, sucrose was commonly used as a preservative—a substance used to preserve food from decay.

Instead of preserving the yeast extracts, though, the sucrose was quickly broken down and fermented, and alcohol appeared as a by-product. This was a key finding: It showed that metabolic pathways like fermentation could be studied in vitro—outside the organism. Until then, researchers thought that metabolism could take place only in intact organisms.

When researchers studied how the sugar was being processed, they found that the reactions could go on much longer than normal if inorganic phosphate were added to the mixture. This result implied that some of the compounds involved were being phosphorylated. Soon after, a molecule called fructose bisphosphate was isolated. (The prefix *bis–* means that the phosphate groups are attached to the fructose molecule at two different locations.) Subsequent work showed that all but the starting

FIGURE 13.5 Glycolysis Pathway. This sequence of 10 reactions oxidizes glucose to pyruvate. Each reaction is catalyzed by a different enzyme to produce two net ATP (4 ATP are produced, but 2 are invested), two molecules of NADH, and two molecules of pyruvate. In step 4, fructose-1,6-bisphosphate is divided into two products that both proceed through steps 6–10. The amounts for "What goes in" and "What goes out" are the combined totals for both molecules.

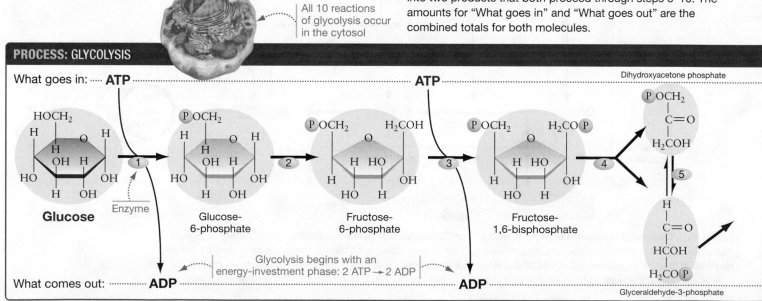

and ending molecules in glycolysis—glucose and pyruvate—are phosphorylated.

In 1905 researchers found that the processing of sugar by yeast extracts stopped if they boiled the reaction mix. Because it was known that enzymes could be inactivated by heat, their discovery suggested that enzymes were involved in at least some of the processing steps. Years later, investigators realized that each step in glycolysis is catalyzed by a different enzyme. Eventually, each of the reactions and enzymes involved was worked out.

Glycolysis Is a Sequence of 10 Reactions

In both eukaryotes and prokaryotes, all 10 reactions of glycolysis occur in the cytosol (**FIGURE 13.5**). Note three key points about this reaction sequence:

1. Glycolysis starts by *using* ATP, not producing it. In the initial step, glucose is phosphorylated to form glucose-6-phosphate. After the second reaction rearranges the sugar to form fructose-6-phosphate, the third reaction adds a second phosphate group, forming the fructose-1,6-bisphosphate observed by early researchers. Thus, two ATP molecules are used up before any ATP is produced.

2. Once the energy-investment phase of glycolysis is complete, the subsequent reactions represent an energy-payoff phase. The sixth reaction in the sequence results in the reduction of two molecules of NAD^+; the seventh produces two molecules of ATP. This is where the energy "debt"—of two molecules of ATP invested early in glycolysis—is paid off. The final reaction in the sequence produces another two ATPs. For each molecule of glucose processed, the net yield is two molecules of NADH, two of ATP, and two of pyruvate.

3. In reactions 7 and 10 of Figure 13.5, an enzyme catalyzes the transfer of a phosphate group from a phosphorylated substrate to ADP, forming ATP. Enzyme-catalyzed reactions that result in

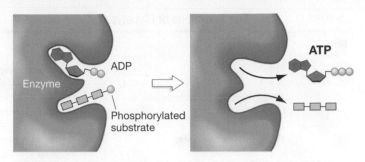

FIGURE 13.6 Substrate-Level Phosphorylation Involves an Enzyme and a Phosphorylated Substrate. Substrate-level phosphorylation occurs when an enzyme catalyzes the transfer of a phosphate group from a phosphorylated substrate to ADP, forming ATP.

ATP production are termed **substrate-level phosphorylation** (**FIGURE 13.6**). The key idea to note here is that the energy to produce the ATP comes from the phosphorylated substrate—not from a proton gradient, as it does when ATP is produced by oxidative phosphorylation.

The discovery and elucidation of the glycolytic pathway ranks as one of the great achievements in the history of biochemistry. For more detail concerning the enzymes that catalyze each step, see **TABLE 13.1** (on page 246). While the catabolism of glucose can occur via other pathways, this set of reactions is among the most ancient and fundamental of all life processes.

How Is Glycolysis Regulated?

An important advance in understanding how glycolysis is regulated occurred when biologists observed that high levels of ATP inhibit a key glycolytic enzyme called phosphofructokinase. **Phosphofructokinase** catalyzes reaction 3 in Figure 13.5—the synthesis of fructose-1,6-bisphosphate from fructose-6-phosphate. This is a crucial step in the sequence.

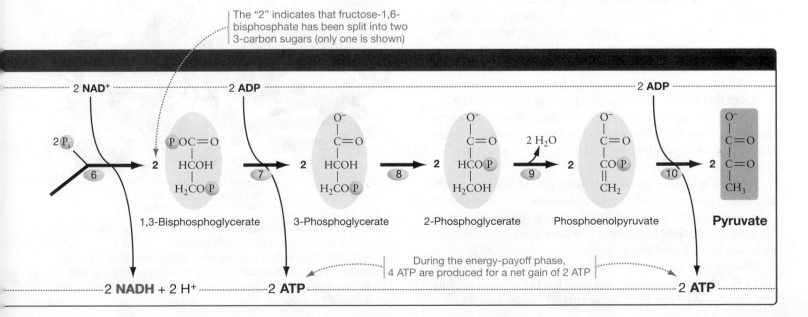

The "2" indicates that fructose-1,6-bisphosphate has been split into two 3-carbon sugars (only one is shown)

During the energy-payoff phase, 4 ATP are produced for a net gain of 2 ATP

1,3-Bisphosphoglycerate   3-Phosphoglycerate   2-Phosphoglycerate   Phosphoenolpyruvate   **Pyruvate**

2 NAD$^+$ 2 ADP   2 ADP

2 P$_i$

2 **NADH** + 2 H$^+$ 2 **ATP**   2 **ATP**

Step	Enzyme	Reaction
1	Hexokinase	Transfers a phosphate from **ATP** to glucose, increasing its potential energy.
2	Phosphoglucose isomerase	Converts glucose-6-phosphate to fructose-6-phosphate; referred to as an isomer of glucose-6-phosphate.
3	Phosphofructokinase	Transfers a phosphate from **ATP** to the opposite end of fructose-6-phosphate, increasing its potential energy.
4	Fructose-bis-phosphate aldolase	Cleaves fructose-1,6-bisphosphate into two different 3-carbon sugars.
5	Triose phosphate isomerase	Converts dihydroxyacetone phosphate (DAP) to glyceraldehyde-3-phosphate (G3P). Although the reaction is fully reversible, the DAP-to-G3P reaction is favored because G3P is immediately used as a substrate for step 6.
6	Glyceraldehyde-3-phosphate dehydrogenase	A two-step reaction that first oxidizes G3P using the **NAD** coenzyme to produce **NADH**. Energy from this reaction is used to attach a P_i to the oxidized product to form 1,3-bisphosphoglycerate.
7	Phosphoglycerate kinase	Transfers a phosphate from 1,3-bisphosphoglycerate to **ADP** to make 3-phosphoglycerate and **ATP**.
8	Phosphoglycerate mutase	Rearranges the phosphate in 3-phosphoglycerate to make 2-phosphoglycerate.
9	Enolase	Removes a water molecule from 2-phosphoglycerate to form a C=C double bond and produce phosphoenolpyruvate.
10	Pyruvate kinase	Transfers a phosphate from phosphoenolpyruvate to **ADP** to make pyruvate and **ATP**.

After reactions 1 and 2 occur, an array of enzymes can reverse the process and regenerate glucose for use in other pathways. Before step 3, then, the sequence is not committed to glycolysis. But once fructose-1,6-bisphosphate is synthesized, there is no point in stopping the process. Based on these observations, it makes sense that the pathway is regulated at step 3. How do cells do it?

As shown in Figure 13.5, ATP serves as a substrate for the addition of a phosphate to fructose-6-phosphate. In the vast majority of cases, increasing the concentration of a substrate would *speed* the rate of a chemical reaction, but in this case, it inhibits it. Why would ATP—a substrate that is required for the reaction—also serve as an inhibitor of the reaction? The answer lies in the fact that ATP is also the end product of the overall catabolic pathway.

Recall that when an enzyme in a pathway is inhibited by the product of the reaction sequence, feedback inhibition occurs (see Chapter 10). When the product molecule is abundant, it can inhibit its own production by interfering with the reaction sequence used to create it.

Feedback inhibition increases efficiency. Cells that are able to stop glycolytic reactions when ATP is abundant can conserve their stores of glucose for times when ATP is scarce. As a result, natural selection should favor individuals who have phosphofructokinase molecules that are inhibited by high concentrations of ATP.

How do high levels of the substrate inhibit the enzyme? As **FIGURE 13.7** shows, phosphofructokinase has two distinct binding sites for ATP. ATP can bind at the enzyme's active site, where it

is used to phosphorylate fructose-6-phosphate, or at a regulatory site, where it turns off the enzyme's activity.

The key to feedback inhibition lies in the ability of the two sites to bind to ATP. When concentrations are low, ATP binds

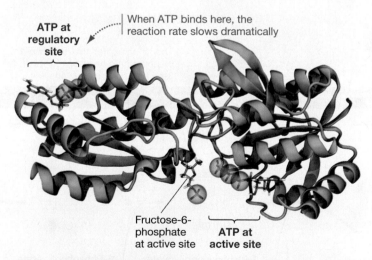

ATP at regulatory site

When ATP binds here, the reaction rate slows dramatically

Fructose-6-phosphate at active site

ATP at active site

FIGURE 13.7 Phosphofructokinase Has Two Binding Sites for ATP. A model of one of the four identical subunits of phosphofructokinase. In the active site, ATP is used as a substrate to transfer one of its phosphate groups to fructose-6-phosphate. In the regulatory site, ATP binding inhibits the reaction by changing the shape of the enzyme.

only to the active site, which has a greater affinity for ATP than does the regulatory site. As ATP concentrations increase, however, it also binds at the regulatory site on phosphofructokinase. When ATP binds at this second location, the enzyme's conformation changes in a way that dramatically lowers the reaction rate at the active site. In phosphofructokinase, ATP acts as an allosteric regulator (see Chapter 10). ✔ **If you understand the principle behind the difference in affinity between the two ATP binding sites, you should be able to predict the consequences if the regulatory site had higher affinity for ATP than the active site did.**

To summarize, glycolysis starts with one 6-carbon glucose molecule and ends with two 3-carbon pyruvate molecules. The reactions occur in the cytoplasm, and the energy that is released is used to produce a net total of two ATP and two NADH. Now the question is, what happens to the pyruvate?

13.3 Processing Pyruvate to Acetyl CoA

In eukaryotes, the pyruvate produced by glycolysis is transported from the cytosol to mitochondria. Mitochondria are organelles found in virtually all eukaryotes (see Chapter 2).

As shown in **FIGURE 13.8**, mitochondria have two membranes, called the inner membrane and outer membrane. The interior of the organelle is filled with layers of sac-like structures called **cristae.** Short tubes connect the cristae to the main part of the inner membrane. The region inside the inner membrane but outside the cristae is the **mitochondrial matrix.**

Pyruvate moves across the mitochondrion's outer membrane through small pores, but how it is transported across the inner membrane is still unclear. Current research suggests that either pyruvate is transported directly into the matrix using an unknown

transporter, or it is converted first into lactate, transported across the membrane, and then converted back into pyruvate.

Inside the mitochondrion, pyruvate reacts with a compound called **coenzyme A (CoA).** Coenzyme A is sometimes abbreviated as CoA-SH to call attention to its key sulfhydryl functional group. In this and many other reactions, CoA acts as a coenzyme by accepting and then transferring an acetyl group ($-COCH_3$) to a substrate (the A stands for acetylation). Pyruvate reacts with CoA, through a series of steps, to produce **acetyl CoA.**

The reaction sequence occurs inside an enormous and intricate enzyme complex called **pyruvate dehydrogenase.** In eukaryotes, pyruvate dehydrogenase is located in the mitochondrial matrix. In bacteria and archaea, pyruvate dehydrogenase is located in the cytosol.

As pyruvate is being processed, one of the carbons in the pyruvate is oxidized to CO_2 and NAD^+ is reduced to NADH. The remaining two-carbon acetyl unit is transferred to CoA (**FIGURE 13.9**).

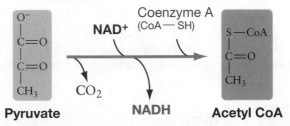

FIGURE 13.9 Pyruvate Is Oxidized to Acetyl CoA. The reaction shown here is catalyzed by pyruvate dehydrogenase.

✔**EXERCISE** Above the reaction arrow, list three molecules whose presence speeds up the reaction. Label them "Positive control." Below the reaction arrow, list three molecules whose presence slows down the reaction. Label them "Negative control by feedback inhibition."

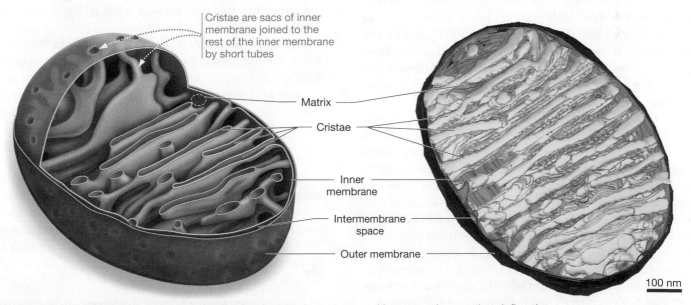

Cristae are sacs of inner membrane joined to the rest of the inner membrane by short tubes

Matrix

Cristae

Inner membrane

Intermembrane space

Outer membrane

100 nm

FIGURE 13.8 The Structure of the Mitochondrion. Mitochondria have outer and inner membranes that define the intermembrane space and matrix. Pyruvate processing occurs within the mitochondrial matrix. Recent research using cryo-electron tomography (the colorized micrograph on the right) shows the inner membrane is connected by short tubes to sac-like cristae.

Acetyl CoA is the final product of the pyruvate-processing step in glucose oxidation. Pyruvate, NAD^+, and CoA go in; CO_2, NADH, and acetyl CoA come out.

When supplies of ATP are abundant, however, the process shuts down. Pyruvate processing stops when the pyruvate dehydrogenase complex becomes phosphorylated and changes shape. The rate of phosphorylation increases when other products—specifically acetyl CoA and NADH—are at high concentration.

These regulatory changes are more examples of feedback inhibition. Reaction products feed back to stop or slow down the pathway.

On the contrary, high concentrations of NAD^+, CoA, or adenosine monophosphate (AMP)—which indicates low ATP supplies—*speed up* the reactions catalyzed by the pyruvate dehydrogenase complex.

Pyruvate processing is under both positive and negative control. Large supplies of products inhibit the enzyme complex; large supplies of reactants and low supplies of products stimulate it.

To summarize, pyruvate processing starts with the three-carbon pyruvate molecule and ends with one carbon released as CO_2 and the remaining two carbons in the form of acetyl CoA. The reactions occur in the mitochondrial matrix, and the potential energy that is released is used to produce one NADH for each pyruvate that is processed. Now the question is, what happens to the acetyl CoA?

13.4 The Citric Acid Cycle: Oxidizing Acetyl CoA to CO_2

While researchers were working out the sequence of reactions in glycolysis, biologists in other laboratories were focusing on redox reactions that oxidize small organic acids called **carboxylic acids**. Note that carboxylic acids all have carboxyl functional groups (R-COOH), hence the name.

A key finding emerged from their studies: Redox reactions that involve carboxylic acids such as citrate, malate, and succinate produce carbon dioxide. Recall from Section 13.1 that carbon dioxide is the endpoint of glucose oxidation via cellular respiration. Thus, it was logical for researchers to propose that the oxidation of small carboxylic acids could be an important component of glucose catabolism.

Early researchers identified eight small carboxylic acids that are rapidly oxidized in sequence, from least to most oxidized. What they found next was puzzling. When they added one of the eight carboxylic acids to cells, the rate of glucose oxidation increased, suggesting that the reactions are somehow connected to pathways involved in glucose catabolism. But, the added molecules did not appear to be used up. Instead, virtually all the carboxylic acids added were recovered later. How is this possible?

Hans Krebs solved the mystery when he proposed that the reaction sequence occurs in a cycle instead of a linear pathway. Krebs had another crucial insight when he suggested that the reaction sequence was directly tied to the processing of pyruvate—the endpoint of the glycolytic pathway.

To test these hypotheses, Krebs and a colleague set out to determine if adding pyruvate could link the two ends of the sequence of eight carboxylic acids. If pyruvate is the key link in forming a cycle, it would need to be involved in the conversion of oxaloacetate, the most oxidized of the eight carboxylic acids, to citrate, the most reduced carboxylic acid. When Krebs added pyruvate, the series of redox reactions occurred. The conclusion? The sequence of eight carboxylic acids is indeed arranged in a cycle (**FIGURE 13.10**).

Many biologists now refer to the cycle as the **citric acid cycle** because it starts with citrate, which is the salt of citric acid after the protons are released. The citric acid cycle is also known as the tricarboxylic acid (TCA) cycle, because citrate has three carboxyl groups, and also as the Krebs cycle, after its discoverer.

When radioactive isotopes of carbon became available in the early 1940s, researchers showed that carbon atoms cycle through the reactions just as Krebs had proposed. For more detail concerning the enzymes that catalyze each step, see **TABLE 13.2** (on page 250). In each cycle, the energy released by the oxidation of one molecule of acetyl CoA is used to produce three molecules of NADH, one of $FADH_2$, and one of **guanosine triphosphate (GTP)**, or ATP, through substrate-level phosphorylation. Whether GTP or ATP is produced depends on the type of cell being considered.[1] For example, GTP appears to be produced in the liver cells of mammals, while ATP is produced in muscle cells.

In bacteria and archaea, the enzymes responsible for the citric acid cycle are located in the cytosol. In eukaryotes, most of the enzymes responsible for the citric acid cycle are located in the mitochondrial matrix. Because glycolysis produces two molecules of pyruvate, the cycle turns twice for each molecule of glucose processed in cellular respiration.

How Is the Citric Acid Cycle Regulated?

By now, it shouldn't surprise you to learn that the citric acid cycle is carefully regulated. The citric acid cycle can be turned off at multiple points, via several different mechanisms of feedback inhibition. Reaction rates are high when ATP is scarce; reaction rates are low when ATP is abundant.

FIGURE 13.11 highlights the major control points. Notice that in step 1, the enzyme that combines acetyl CoA and oxaloacetate to form citrate is shut down when ATP binds to it. This is another example of feedback inhibition, which also regulates enzymes at two additional points in the cycle. In step 3, NADH interferes with the reaction by binding to the enzyme's active site. This is an example of competitive inhibition (see Chapter 10). In step 4, ATP binds to the enzyme at an allosteric regulatory site.

To summarize, the citric acid cycle starts with the two-carbon acetyl molecule in the form of acetyl CoA and ends with the release of two CO_2. The reactions occur in the mitochondrial matrix, and the potential energy that is released is used to produce three NADH, one $FADH_2$, and one ATP or GTP for each acetyl oxidized. But a major question remains.

---

[1]Traditionally it was thought that the citric acid cycle produced GTP, which was later converted to ATP in the same cell. Recent work suggests that ATP is produced directly in some cell types, while GTP is produced in other cells. See C. O. Lambeth, Reconsideration of the significance of substrate-level phosphorylation in the citric acid cycle. *Biochemistry and Molecular Biology Education* 34 (2006): 21–213.

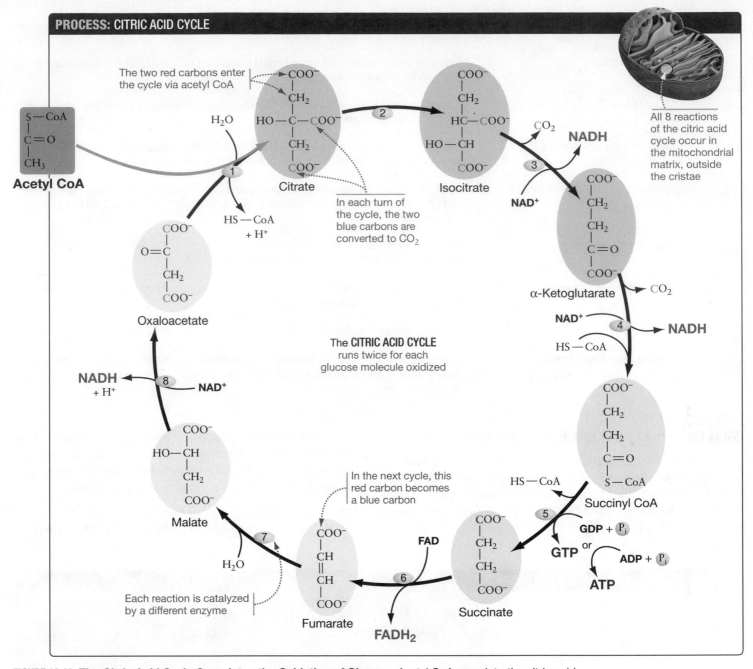

The two red carbons enter the cycle via acetyl CoA

H_2O

In each turn of the cycle, the two blue carbons are converted to CO_2

All 8 reactions of the citric acid cycle occur in the mitochondrial matrix, outside the cristae

Acetyl CoA

$HS — CoA + H^+$

Citrate

CO_2

NADH

Isocitrate

NAD^+

α-Ketoglutarate

CO_2

NAD^+

NADH

$HS — CoA$

Oxaloacetate

The **CITRIC ACID CYCLE** runs twice for each glucose molecule oxidized

NADH + H^+

NAD^+

Succinyl CoA

$HS — CoA$

Malate

In the next cycle, this red carbon becomes a blue carbon

FAD

$GDP + P_i$

GTP or

ATP

$ADP + P_i$

H_2O

Each reaction is catalyzed by a different enzyme

Fumarate

FADH₂

Succinate

FIGURE 13.10 The Citric Acid Cycle Completes the Oxidation of Glucose. Acetyl CoA goes into the citric acid cycle, and carbon dioxide, NADH, $FADH_2$, and GTP or ATP come out. GTP or ATP is produced by substrate-level phosphorylation. If you follow individual carbon atoms around the cycle several times, you'll come to an important conclusion: each of the carbons in the cycle is eventually a "blue carbon" that is released as CO_2.

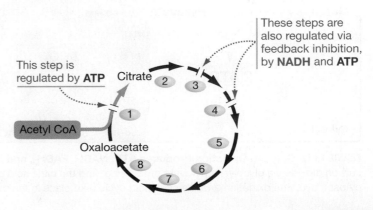

These steps are also regulated via feedback inhibition, by **NADH** and **ATP**

This step is regulated by **ATP**

Citrate

Acetyl CoA

Oxaloacetate

FIGURE 13.11 The Citric Acid Cycle Is Regulated by Feedback Inhibition. The citric acid cycle slows down when ATP and NADH are plentiful. ATP acts as an allosteric regulator, while NADH acts as a competitive inhibitor.

Step	Enzyme	Reaction
1	Citrate synthase	Transfers the 2-carbon acetyl group from acetyl CoA to the 4-carbon oxaloacetate to produce the 6-carbon citrate.
2	Aconitase	Converts citrate to isocitrate by the removal of one water molecule and the addition of another water molecule.
3	Isocitrate dehydrogenase	Oxidizes isocitrate using the **NAD**⁺ coenzyme to produce **NADH** and release one CO_2, resulting in the formation of the 5-carbon molecule α-ketoglutarate.
4	α-Ketoglutarate dehydrogenase	Oxidizes α-ketoglutarate using the **NAD**⁺ coenzyme to produce **NADH** and release one CO_2. The remaining 4-carbon molecule is added to coenzyme A (CoA) to form succinyl CoA.
5	Succinyl-CoA synthetase	CoA is removed, converting succinyl CoA to succinate. The energy released is used to transfer P_i to GDP to form **GTP**, or to ADP to form **ATP**.
6	Succinate dehydrogenase	Oxidizes succinate by transferring two hydrogens to the coenzyme **FAD** to produce **FADH₂**, resulting in the formation of fumarate.
7	Fumarase	Converts fumarate to malate by the addition of one water molecule.
8	Malate dehydrogenase	Oxidizes malate by using the **NAD**⁺ coenzyme to produce **NADH**, resulting in the regeneration of the oxaloacetate that will be used in step 1 of the cycle.

What Happens to the NADH and FADH₂?

FIGURE 13.12 reviews the relationships of glycolysis, pyruvate processing, and the citric acid cycle and identifies where each process takes place in eukaryotic cells. As the carbons in glucose are oxidized in these steps, the relative changes in free energy are shown in **FIGURE 13.13**.

As you study these figures, note that for each molecule of glucose that is fully oxidized to 6 carbon dioxide molecules, the cell produces 10 molecules of NADH, 2 of FADH₂, and 4 of ATP. The overall reaction for glycolysis and the citric acid cycle can be written as

$$C_6H_{12}O_2 + 10 \text{ NAD}^+ + 2 \text{ FAD} + 4 \text{ ADP} + 4 \text{ P}_i \longrightarrow$$
$$6 \text{ CO}_2 + 10 \text{ NADH} + 2 \text{ FADH}_2 + 4 \text{ ATP}$$

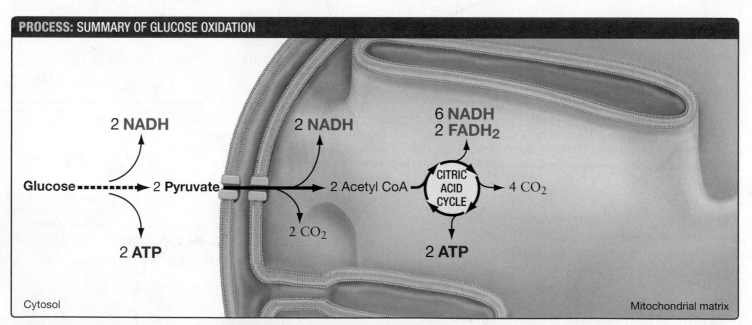

PROCESS: SUMMARY OF GLUCOSE OXIDATION

FIGURE 13.12 Glucose Oxidation Produces ATP, NADH, FADH₂, and CO₂. Glucose is completely oxidized to carbon dioxide via glycolysis, pyruvate processing, and the citric acid cycle. In eukaryotes, glycolysis occurs in the cytosol; pyruvate oxidation and the citric acid cycle take place in the mitochondrial matrix.

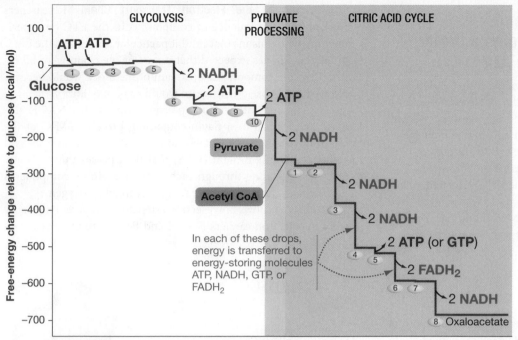

FIGURE 13.13 Free Energy Changes as Glucose Is Oxidized. If you read the vertical axis of this graph carefully, it should convince you that about 685 kcal/mol of free energy is released from the oxidation of glucose. Much of the energy is harnessed in the form of ATP, NADH, and $FADH_2$. The numbered green ovals identify the reaction steps in glycolysis and the citric acid cycle (see Tables 13.1 and 13.2).

DATA: Li, X., R. K. Dash, R. K. Pradhan, et al. 2010. *Journal of Physical Chemistry B.* 114: 16068–16082.

✔ QUANTITATIVE Based on the data in this graph, which of the three high-energy molecules produced during glucose oxidation would you expect to carry the highest amount of chemical energy? Justify your answer.

The ATP molecules are produced by substrate-level phosphorylation and can be used to drive endergonic reactions. The CO_2 molecules are a gas that is disposed of as waste—you exhale it; plants release it or use it as a reactant in photosynthesis.

What happens to the NADH and $FADH_2$ produced by glycolysis, pyruvate processing, and the citric acid cycle? Recall that the overall reaction for glucose oxidation is

$$C_6H_{12}O_6 + 6\,O_2 \longrightarrow 6\,CO_2 + 6\,H_2O + \text{Energy}$$

These three steps account for the glucose, the CO_2, and—because ATP is produced—some of the chemical energy that results from the overall reaction. But the O_2 and the H_2O are still unaccounted for. As it turns out, so is much of the chemical energy. The reaction that has yet to occur is

$$NADH + FADH_2 + O_2 + ADP + P_i \longrightarrow$$
$$NAD^+ + FAD + 2\,H_2O + ATP$$

In the above reaction, the electrons from NADH and $FADH_2$ are transferred to oxygen. NADH and $FADH_2$ are oxidized to NAD^+ and FAD, and oxygen is reduced to form water.

In effect, glycolysis, pyruvate processing, and the citric acid cycle transfer electrons from glucose to NAD^+ and FAD to form NADH and $FADH_2$. When oxygen accepts electrons from these reduced molecules, water is produced.

At this point, all the components of the overall reaction for glucose oxidation are accounted for, except for the energy. What happens to the energy that is released as electrons are transferred from NADH and $FADH_2$ to the highly electronegative oxygen atoms?

Specifically, how is the transfer of electrons linked to the production of ATP? In the 1960s—decades after the details of glycolysis and the citric acid cycle had been worked out—a startling answer to these questions emerged.

check your understanding

C Y U

If you understand that . . .

- During glycolysis, glucose is oxidized to pyruvate, in the cytosol.
- During pyruvate processing, pyruvate is oxidized to acetyl CoA, in the mitochondrial matrix.
- In the citric acid cycle, the acetyl from acetyl CoA is oxidized to carbon dioxide (CO_2), in the mitochondrial matrix.
- Glycolysis, pyruvate processing, and the citric acid cycle are all regulated processes. The cell produces ATP only when ATP is needed.

✔ You should be able to . . .

Model the following components of cellular respiration by pretending that a large piece of paper is a cell. Draw a large mitochondrion inside it. Cut out small circles of paper and label them glucose, pyruvate, acetyl CoA, CO_2, ADP → ATP, NAD^+ → NADH, and FAD → $FADH_2$. Cut out small squares of paper and label them as glycolytic reactions, citric acid cycle reactions, and pyruvate dehydrogenase complex.

1. Put each of the squares in the appropriate location in the cell.
2. Add the circles and draw arrows to connect the appropriate molecules and reactions.
3. Using 12 paper triangles for pairs of electrons, show how electrons from glucose are transferred to NADH or $FADH_2$ (one pair should go to each NADH or $FADH_2$ formed) as glucose is oxidized to CO_2.
4. Label points where regulation occurs.

Answers are available in Appendix A.

13.5 Electron Transport and Chemiosmosis: Building a Proton Gradient to Produce ATP

The answer to one fundamental question about the oxidation of NADH and $FADH_2$ turned out to be relatively straightforward. By isolating different parts of mitochondria, researchers determined that NADH is oxidized by components in the inner membrane of the mitochondria, including the cristae. In prokaryotes, the oxidation of NADH occurs in the plasma membrane.

Biologists made a key discovery when they isolated membrane components—they were found to cycle between oxidized and reduced states after the addition of NADH and $FADH_2$. The membrane-associated molecules were hypothesized to be the key to processing NADH and $FADH_2$. What are these molecules, and how do they work?

The Electron Transport Chain

Collectively, the molecules responsible for the oxidation of NADH and $FADH_2$ are designated the **electron transport chain (ETC).** As electrons are passed from one molecule to another in the chain, the energy released by the redox reactions is used to move protons across the inner membrane of mitochondria.

Several points are fundamental to understanding how the ETC works:

- Most of the molecules are proteins that contain distinctive cofactors and prosthetic groups where the redox events take place (see Chapter 10). They include iron–sulfur complexes, ring-containing structures called flavins, or iron-containing heme groups called cytochromes. Each of these groups is readily reduced or oxidized.

- The inner membrane of the mitochondrion also contains a molecule called **ubiquinone,** which is not a protein. Ubiquinone got its name because it is nearly ubiquitous in organisms and belongs to a family of compounds called quinones. Also called **coenzyme Q** or simply Q, ubiquinone is lipid soluble and moves efficiently throughout the hydrophobic interior of the inner mitochondrial membrane.

- The molecules involved in processing NADH and $FADH_2$ differ in electronegativity, or their tendency to hold electrons. Some of the molecules pick up a proton with each electron, forming hydrogen atoms, while others obtain only electrons.

Because Q and the ETC proteins can cycle between a reduced state and an oxidized state, and because they differ in electronegativity, investigators realized that it should be possible to arrange them into a logical sequence. The idea was that electrons would pass from a molecule with lower electronegativity to one with higher electronegativity, via a redox reaction.

As electrons moved through the chain, they would be held more and more tightly. A small amount of energy would be released in each reaction, and the potential energy in each successive bond would lessen.

Organization of the Electron Transport Chain
Researchers worked out the sequence of compounds in the ETC by experimenting with poisons that inhibit particular proteins in the inner membrane. It was expected that if part of the chain were inhibited, then the components upstream of the block would become reduced, but those downstream would remain oxidized.

Experiments with various poisons showed that NADH donates an electron to a flavin-containing protein (FMN) at the top of the chain, while $FADH_2$ donates electrons to an iron- and sulfur-containing protein (Fe·S) that then passes them directly to Q. After passing through each of the remaining components in the chain, the electrons are finally accepted by oxygen.

FIGURE 13.14 shows how electrons step down in potential energy from the electron carriers NADH and $FADH_2$ to O_2. The x-axis

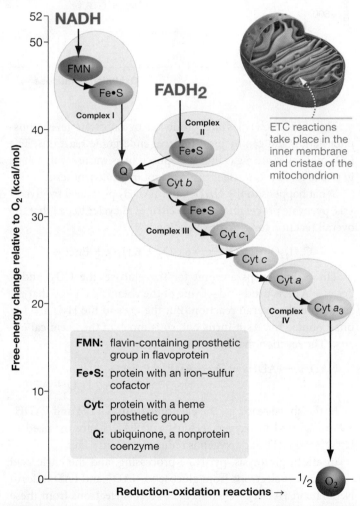

ETC reactions take place in the inner membrane and cristae of the mitochondrion

FMN: flavin-containing prosthetic group in flavoprotein

Fe•S: protein with an iron–sulfur cofactor

Cyt: protein with a heme prosthetic group

Q: ubiquinone, a nonprotein coenzyme

Reduction-oxidation reactions →

FIGURE 13.14 A Series of Reduction–Oxidation Reactions Occur in an Electron Transport Chain. Electrons step down in potential energy from the electron carriers NADH and $FADH_2$ through an electron transport chain to a final electron acceptor. When oxygen is the final electron acceptor, water is formed. The overall free-energy change of 52 kcal/mol (from NADH to oxygen) is broken into small steps.

DATA: Wilson D. F., M. Erecinska, and P. L. Dutton. 1974. *Annual Review of Biophysics and Bioengineering* 3: 203–230. Also Sled, V. D., N. I. Rudnitzky, Y. Hatefi, et al. 1994. *Biochemistry* 33: 10069–10075.

plots the sequence of redox reactions in the ETC; the *y*-axis plots the free-energy changes that occur.

The components of the electron transport chain are organized into four large complexes of proteins, often referred to as simply complexes I–IV. Q and the protein **cytochrome *c*** act as shuttles that transfer electrons between these complexes. Once the electrons at the bottom of the ETC are accepted by oxygen to form water, the oxidation of glucose is complete. Details on the names of the complexes and their role in the electron transport chain are provided in **TABLE 13.3** (on page 254).

Under controlled conditions in the laboratory, the total potential energy difference from NADH to oxygen is a whopping 53 kilocalories/mole (kcal/mol). Oxidation of the 10 molecules of NADH produced from each glucose accounts for almost 80 percent of the total energy released from the sugar. What does the ETC do with all this energy?

Role of the Electron Transport Chain Throughout the 1950s most biologists working on cellular respiration assumed that electron transport chains include enzymes that catalyze substrate-level phosphorylation. Recall that when substrate-level

phosphorylation occurs, a phosphate group is transferred from a phosphorylated substrate to ADP, forming ATP. Despite intense efforts, however, no one was able to find an enzyme among the components of the ETC that would catalyze the phosphorylation of ADP to produce ATP.

What researchers did find, however, is that the movement of electrons through the ETC actively transports protons from the matrix, across the inner membrane, and into the intermembrane space (see **FIGURE 13.15**). The exact route and mechanism used to pump protons is still being worked out. In some cases, it is not clear how the redox reactions taking place inside each complex result in the movement of protons.

The best-understood interaction between electron transport and proton transport takes place in complex III. Research has shown that when Q accepts electrons from complex I or complex II, it picks up protons from the matrix side of the inner membrane. The reduced form of Q then diffuses through the inner

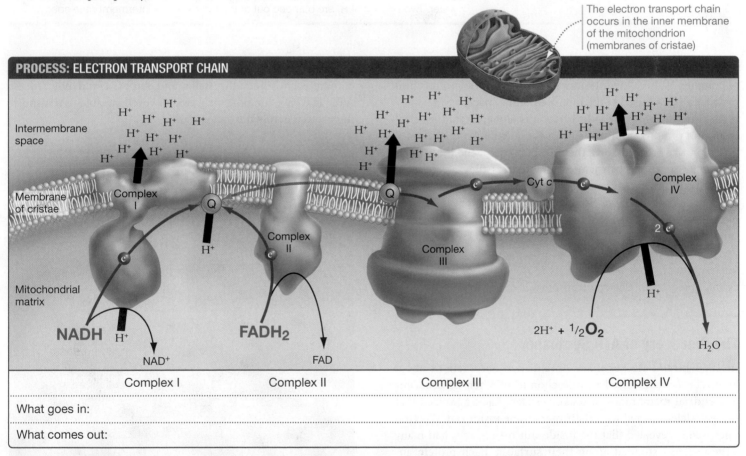

The electron transport chain occurs in the inner membrane of the mitochondrion (membranes of cristae)

FIGURE 13.15 How Does the Electron Transport Chain Work? The individual components of the electron transport chain diagrammed in Figure 13.14 are found in the inner membrane of mitochondria. Electrons are carried from one complex to another by Q and by cytochrome *c*; Q also shuttles protons across the membrane. The orange arrow indicates Q moving back and forth. Complexes I and IV use the potential energy released by the redox reactions to pump protons from the mitochondrial matrix to the intermembrane space.

✔**EXERCISE** Add an arrow across the membrane and label it "Proton gradient." In the boxes at the bottom, list "What goes in" and "What comes out" for each complex.

ETC Component	Descriptive Name	Reaction
Complex I	NADH dehydrogenase	Oxidizes **NADH** and transfers the two electrons through proteins containing FMN prosthetic groups and Fe·S cofactors to reduce an oxidized form of ubiquinone (Q). Four **H·** are pumped out of the matrix to the intermembrane space.
Complex II	Succinate dehydrogenase	Oxidizes **FADH₂** and transfers the two electrons through proteins containing Fe·S cofactors to reduce an oxidized form of Q. This complex is also used in step 6 of the citric acid cycle.
Q	Ubiquinone	Reduced by complexes I and II and moves throughout the hydrophobic interior of the ETC membrane, where it is oxidized by complex III.
Complex III	Cytochrome *c* reductase	Oxidizes Q and transfers one electron at a time through proteins containing heme prosthetic groups and Fe·S cofactors to reduce an oxidized form of cytochrome *c* (cyt *c*). A total of four **H·** for each pair of electrons is transported from the matrix to the intermembrane space.
Cyt *c*	Cytochrome *c*	Reduced by accepting a single electron from complex III and moves along the surface of ETC membrane, where it is oxidized by complex IV.
Complex IV	Cytochrome *c* oxidase	Oxidizes cyt *c* and transfers each electron through proteins containing heme prosthetic groups to reduce oxygen gas (O_2), which picks up two **H·** from the matrix to produce water. Two additional **H·** are pumped out of the matrix to the intermembrane space.

membrane, where its electrons are used to reduce a component of complex III near the intermembrane space. The protons held by Q are then released to the intermembrane space.

In this way, through redox reactions alone, Q shuttles electrons and protons from one side of the membrane to the other. The electrons proceed down the transport chain, and the protons contribute to an electrochemical gradient as they are released into the intermembrane space.

Once the nature of the electron transport chain became clear, biologists understood the fate of the electrons and the energy carried by NADH and FADH₂. Much of the chemical energy that was originally present in glucose is now accounted for in the proton electrochemical gradient. This is satisfying, except for one crucial question: If electron transport does not make ATP, what does?

The Discovery of ATP Synthase

In 1960 Efraim Racker made several key observations about how ATP is synthesized in mitochondria. When he used mitochondrial membranes to make vesicles, Racker noticed that some vesicles formed with their membrane inside out. Electron microscopy revealed that the inside-out membranes had many large proteins studded along their surfaces. Each protein appeared to have a base in the membrane, from which a lollipop-shaped stalk and a knob project (**FIGURE 13.16**). If the solution was vibrated or treated with a compound called urea, the stalks and knobs fell off.

Racker seized on this technique to isolate the stalks and knobs and do experiments with them. For example, he found that isolated stalks and knobs could hydrolyze ATP, forming ADP and

inorganic phosphate. The vesicles that contained just the base component, without the stalks and knobs, could not process ATP. The base components were, however, capable of transporting protons across the membrane.

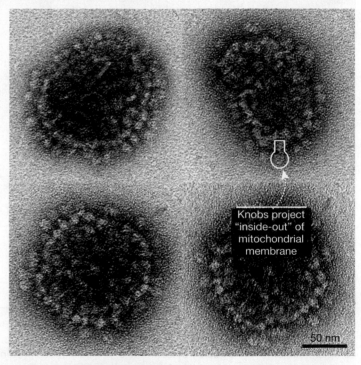

Knobs project "inside-out" of mitochondrial membrane

50 nm

FIGURE 13.16 The Discovery of ATP Synthase. When patches of mitochondrial membrane turn inside out and form vesicles, the lollipop-shaped stalk-and-knob structures of ATP synthase proteins face outward. Normally, the stalk and knob face inward, toward the mitochondrial matrix.

Based on these observations, Racker proposed that the stalk-and-knob component of the protein was an enzyme that both hydrolyzes and synthesizes ATP. To test his idea, Racker added the stalk-and-knob components back to vesicles that had been stripped of them and confirmed that the vesicles regained the ability to synthesize ATP. The entire complex is known as **ATP synthase.** Follow-up work also confirmed his hypothesis that the membrane-bound base component of ATP synthase is a proton channel. Is there a connection between proton transport and ATP synthesis?

The Chemiosmosis Hypothesis

In 1961 Peter Mitchell broke with the prevailing ideas that electron transport produces ATP via substrate phosphorylation. Instead, he proposed something completely new—an indirect connection between electron transport and ATP production. Mitchell's novel hypothesis? The real job of the electron transport chain is to pump protons across the inner membrane of mitochondria from the matrix to the intermembrane space. After a proton gradient is established, an enzyme in the inner membrane, like Racker's ATP synthase, would synthesize ATP from ADP and P_i.

Mitchell introduced the term **chemiosmosis** to describe the use of a proton gradient to drive energy-requiring processes, like the production of ATP. Here, osmosis refers to the force generated from the proton gradient rather than the transport of water. Although proponents of a direct link between electron transport and substrate-level phosphorylation objected vigorously to Mitchell's idea, several key experiments supported it.

FIGURE 13.17 illustrates how the existence of a key element in Mitchell's hypothesis was confirmed: A proton gradient alone can be used to synthesize ATP via ATP synthase. The researchers made vesicles from artificial membranes that contained Racker's ATP synthase isolated from mitochondria. Along with this enzyme, they inserted bacteriorhodopsin, a well-studied membrane protein that acts as a light-activated proton pump.

When light strikes bacteriorhodopsin, it absorbs some of the light energy and changes conformation in a way that pumps protons from the interior of a membrane to the exterior. As a result, the experimental vesicles established a strong electrochemical gradient favoring proton movement to the interior. When the vesicles were illuminated to initiate proton pumping, ATP began to be produced from ADP and P_i inside the vesicles.

Mitchell's prediction was correct: In this situation, ATP production depended solely on the existence of a **proton-motive force,** which is based on a proton electrochemical gradient. It could occur in the *absence* of an electron transport chain. This result, along with many others, has provided strong support for the hypothesis of chemiosmosis. Most of the ATP produced by cellular respiration is made by a flow of protons.

✔ If you understand chemiosmosis, you should be able to explain why ATP production during cellular respiration is characterized as indirect. More specifically, you should be able to explain the relationship between glucose oxidation, the proton gradient, and ATP synthase.

RESEARCH

QUESTION: How are the electron transport chain and ATP production linked?

CHEMIOSMOTIC HYPOTHESIS: The linkage is indirect. The ETC creates a proton-motive force that drives ATP synthesis by the mitochondrial ATP synthase.

ALTERNATIVE HYPOTHESIS: The linkage is direct. The ETC is associated with enzymes that perform substrate-level phosphorylation.

EXPERIMENTAL SETUP:

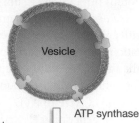

1. **Produce vesicles from artificial membranes;** add ATP synthase, an enzyme found in mitochondria.

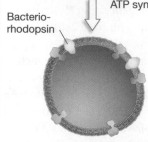

2. **Add bacteriorhodopsin,** a protein that acts as a light-activated proton pump.

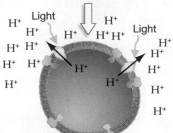

3. **Illuminate vesicle** so that bacteriorhodopsin pumps protons out of vesicle, creating a proton gradient.

PREDICTION OF CHEMIOSMOTIC HYPOTHESIS: ATP will be produced within the vesicle.

PREDICTION OF ALTERNATIVE HYPOTHESIS: No ATP will be produced.

RESULTS:

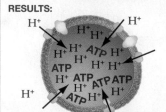

ATP is produced within the vesicle, in the absence of the electron transport chain.

CONCLUSION: The linkage between electron transport and ATP synthesis is indirect; the movement of protons drives the synthesis of ATP.

FIGURE 13.17 Evidence for the Chemiosmotic Hypothesis.

Racker, E., and W. Stoeckenius. 1974. Reconstitution of purple membrane vesicles catalyzing light-driven proton uptake and adenosine triphosphate formation. *Journal of Biological Chemistry*. 249: 662–663.

✔**QUESTION** If bacteriorhodopsin were not available, what could the researchers have done with the ATP synthase vesicles to test their hypothesis?

Electron transport chains and ATP synthases are used by organisms throughout the tree of life. They are humming away in your cells now. Let's look in more detail at how they function.

The Proton-Motive Force Couples Electron Transport to ATP Synthesis As FIGURE 13.18 shows, the structure of ATP synthase is now well understood. The ATP synthase "knob" component is called the F_1 unit; the membrane-bound, proton-transporting base component is the F_0 unit. The F_1 and F_0 units are connected by a shaft, as well as by a stator, which holds the two units in place.

The F_0 unit serves as a rotor, whose turning is conveyed to the F_1 unit via the shaft. A flow of protons through the F_0 unit causes the rotor and shaft to spin. By attaching long actin filaments to the shaft and examining them with a videomicroscope, researchers have been able to see the rotation, which can reach speeds of 350 revolutions per second. As the shaft spins within the F_1 unit, it is thought to change the conformation of the F_1 subunits in a way that catalyzes the phosphorylation of ADP to ATP.

Chemiosmosis is like the process of generating electricity in a hydroelectric dam (like the one pictured on page 240). The ETC is analogous to a series of gigantic pumps that force water up and behind the dam. The inner mitochondrial membrane functions as the dam, with ATP synthase spinning and generating electricity inside as water passes through—like a turbine. In a mitochondrion, protons are pumped instead of water. When protons move through ATP synthase, the protein spins and generates ATP.

It has been determined that the ETC transports enough protons to produce approximately three ATP for each NADH and two for each $FADH_2$, depending on the type of ATP synthase used. These yields, however, are not observed in cells, since the proton-motive force is also used to drive other processes, such as the import of phosphates into the mitochondrial matrix.

Unlike the turbines in a hydroelectric dam, however, ATP synthase can reverse its direction and hydrolyze ATP to build a proton gradient. If the proton gradient dissipates, the direction of the spin is reversed and ATP is hydrolyzed to pump protons from the matrix to the intermembrane space. Understanding how these reactions occur is currently the focus of intense research. ATP synthase makes most of the ATP that keeps you alive.

The Proton-Motive Force and Chemical Evolution How was energy first transformed into a usable form during the evolution of life? Since chemiosmosis is responsible for most of the ATP produced by cells throughout the tree of life, it is likely to have arisen early in evolution. But how could a complex electron transport chain evolve to produce the proton-motive force without a proton-motive force to supply the energy?

This apparent conundrum left many of the chemical evolution theorists perplexed until a key discovery was made deep in the ocean along the Mid-Atlantic Ridge—the Lost City hydrothermal vents (see Appendix D). Researchers propose that the alkaline fluid (low proton concentration) released from these vents in the acidic oceans (high proton concentration) of early Earth may have provided such a gradient.

While there is still considerable debate concerning the role hydrothermal vents may have played in chemical evolution, their discovery has generated much excitement. By harnessing the natural electrochemical gradient deep in the early oceans, the proton-motive force of life may have evolved to mimic the environment of its origin.

Organisms Use a Diversity of Electron Acceptors

FIGURE 13.19 summarizes glucose oxidation and cellular respiration by tracing the fate of the carbon atoms and electrons in glucose. Notice that electrons from glucose are transferred to NADH and $FADH_2$, passed through the electron transport chain, and accepted by oxygen. Proton pumping during electron transport creates the proton-motive force that drives ATP synthesis.

The diagram also indicates the approximate yield of ATP from each component of the process. Recent research shows that about 29 ATP molecules are produced from each molecule of glucose.[2] Of these, 25 ATP molecules are produced by ATP synthase. The fundamental message here? The vast majority of the "payoff" from the oxidation of glucose occurs via oxidative phosphorylation.

Aerobic Versus Anaerobic Respiration During cellular respiration, oxygen is the electron acceptor used by all eukaryotes and

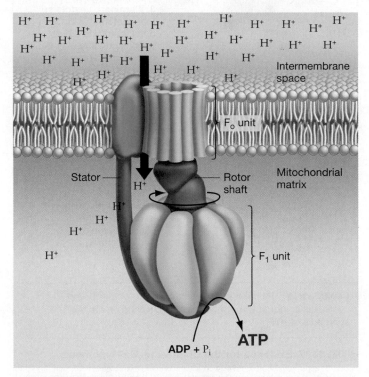

FIGURE 13.18 ATP Synthase Is a Motor. ATP synthase has two major components, designated F_0 and F_1, connected by a shaft. The F_0 unit spins as protons pass through. The shaft transmits the rotation to the F_1 unit, causing it to make ATP from ADP and P_i.

[2]Traditionally, biologists thought that 36 ATP would be synthesized for every molecule of glucose oxidized in eukaryotic cells. More recent work has shown that actual yield is only about 29 ATP [see M. Brand, Approximate yield of ATP from glucose, designed by Donald Nicholson. *Biochemistry and Molecular Biology Education* 31 (2003): 2–4]. Also, it's important to note that yield varies with conditions in the cell.

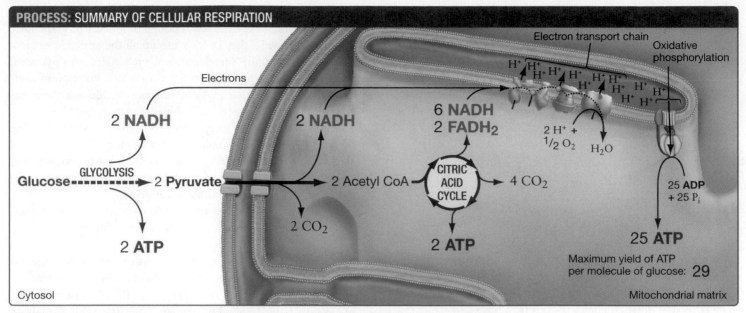

Electron transport chain

Oxidative phosphorylation

Electrons

2 **NADH**

2 **NADH**

6 **NADH**
2 **FADH₂**

$2 H^+ + \frac{1}{2} O_2$ H_2O

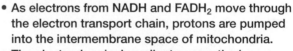

GLYCOLYSIS

Glucose - - - - - - - - → 2 **Pyruvate** → 2 Acetyl CoA → CITRIC ACID CYCLE → $4 CO_2$

$2 CO_2$

25 **ADP** + 25 P_i

2 **ATP**

2 **ATP**

25 **ATP**

Maximum yield of ATP per molecule of glucose: 29

Cytosol

Mitochondrial matrix

FIGURE 13.19 ATP Yield during Cellular Respiration. The actual yield of ATP per glucose (29 ATP) is lower than the theoretical calculation (38 ATP) because of energy required for the import of NADH from the cytoplasm and the use of the proton-motive force to actively transport P_i into the mitochondrial matrix.

a wide diversity of bacteria and archaea. Species that depend on oxygen as an electron acceptor for the ETC use **aerobic** respiration and are called aerobic organisms. (The Latin root *aero* means "air.")

It is important to recognize, though, that cellular respiration can occur without oxygen. Many thousands of bacterial and archaeal species rely on electron acceptors other than oxygen, and electron donors other than glucose. For example, nitrate (NO_3^-) and sulfate (SO_4^{2-}) are particularly common electron acceptors in species that live in oxygen-poor environments. In addition, many bacteria and archaea use H_2, H_2S, CH_4, or other inorganic compounds as electron donors—not glucose.

Cells that depend on electron acceptors other than oxygen are said to use **anaerobic** ("no air") respiration. Even though the starting and ending points of cellular respiration differ, aerobic and anaerobic cells still use electron transport chains to create a proton-motive force that drives the synthesis of ATP. In bacteria and archaea, the ETC and ATP synthase are located in the plasma membrane.

Aerobic Respiration Is Most Efficient   Even though an array of compounds can serve as the final electron acceptor in cellular respiration, oxygen is the most efficient. Because oxygen holds electrons so tightly, the potential energy of electrons in a bond between an oxygen atom and a non-oxygenic atom, such as hydrogen, is low. As a result, there is a large difference between the potential energy of electrons in NADH and the potential energy of electrons bonded to an oxygen atom, such as found in water (see Figure 13.14). The large differential in potential energy means that the electron transport chain can generate a large proton-motive force.

Cells that do not use oxygen as an electron acceptor cannot generate such a large potential energy difference. As a result, they make less ATP from each glucose molecule than cells that use aerobic respiration. This finding is important: It means that anaerobic organisms tend to grow much more slowly than aerobic organisms. If cells that use anaerobic respiration compete with cells using aerobic respiration, those that use oxygen as an electron acceptor almost always grow faster and reproduce more.

What happens when oxygen or other electron acceptors get used up? When there is no terminal electron acceptor, the electrons in

check your understanding

C Y U

If you understand that . . .

• As electrons from NADH and FADH₂ move through the electron transport chain, protons are pumped into the intermembrane space of mitochondria.

• The electrochemical gradient across the inner mitochondrial membrane drives protons through ATP synthase, resulting in the production of ATP from ADP.

✓ **You should be able to . . .**

Add paper squares labeled ETC and ATP synthase and a paper circle labeled ½ O_2 → H_2O to the model you made in Section 13.4. Explain the steps in electron transport and chemiosmosis using paper triangles to represent electron pairs and dimes to represent protons.

Answers are available in Appendix A.

each of the complexes of the electron transport chain have no place to go and the electron transport chain stops. Without an oxidized complex I, NADH remains reduced. The concentration of NAD^+ drops rapidly as cells continue to convert NAD^+ to NADH.

This situation is life threatening. When there is no longer any NAD^+ to drive glycolysis, pyruvate processing, and the citric acid cycle, then no ATP can be produced. If NAD^+ cannot be regenerated somehow, the cell will die. How do cells cope?

13.6 Fermentation

Fermentation is a metabolic pathway that regenerates NAD^+ by oxidizing stockpiles of NADH. The electrons removed from NADH are transferred to pyruvate, or a molecule derived from pyruvate, instead of an electron transport chain (**FIGURE 13.20**).

In respiring cells, fermentation serves as an emergency back-up that allows glycolysis to continue producing ATP even when the ETC is shut down. It allows the cell to survive and even grow in the absence of electron transport chains.

In many cases, the cell cannot use the molecule that is formed when pyruvate (or another electron acceptor) accepts electrons from NADH. This by-product may even be toxic and excreted from the cell as waste even though it has not been fully oxidized.

Many Different Fermentation Pathways Exist When you run up a long flight of stairs, your muscles begin metabolizing glucose so fast that the supply of oxygen is rapidly used up by their mitochondria. When oxygen is absent, the electron transport chains shut down and NADH cannot donate its electrons there. The pyruvate produced by glycolysis then begins to accept electrons from NADH, and fermentation takes place. This process, called **lactic acid fermentation,** regenerates NAD^+ by forming a product molecule called lactate: a deprotonated form of lactic acid (**FIGURE 13.21a**). Your body reacts by making you breathe faster and increasing your heart rate. By getting more oxygen to your muscle cells, the electron transport chain is revived.

FIGURE 13.21b illustrates a different fermentation pathway, **alcohol fermentation,** which occurs in the fungus *Saccharomyces*

cerevisiae—baker's and brewer's yeast. When yeast cells are placed in an environment such as bread dough or a bottle of grape juice and begin growing, they quickly use up all the available oxygen. Instead of depositing the electrons from NADH into pyruvate, yeast first convert pyruvate to the two-carbon compound acetaldehyde. This reaction gives off carbon dioxide, which causes bread to rise and produces the bubbles in champagne and beer.

Acetaldehyde then accepts electrons from NADH, forming the NAD^+ required to keep glycolysis going. The addition of electrons to acetaldehyde forms ethanol as a waste product. The yeast cells excrete ethanol as waste. In essence, the active ingredient in alcoholic beverages is like yeast urine.

Cells that employ other types of fermentation are used commercially in the production of soy sauce, tofu, yogurt, cheese, vinegar, and other products.

Bacteria and archaea that exist exclusively through fermentation are present in phenomenal numbers in the oxygen-free environment of your small intestine and in the first compartment of a cow's stomach, called the rumen. The rumen is a specialized digestive organ that contains over 10^{10} (10 billion) bacterial and archaeal cells per *milliliter* of fluid. The fermentations that occur in these cells produce an array of fatty acids. Cattle don't actually live off grass directly—they eat it to feed their bacteria and archaea and then use the fermentation by-products from these organisms as a source of energy.

Fermentation as an Alternative to Cellular Respiration Even though fermentation is a widespread type of metabolism, it is extremely inefficient compared with aerobic cellular respiration. Fermentation produces just 2 molecules of ATP for each molecule of glucose metabolized, while cellular respiration produces about 29—almost 15 times more energy per glucose molecule than fermentation. The reason for the disparity is that oxygen has much higher electronegativity than electron acceptors such as pyruvate and acetaldehyde. As a result, the potential energy drop between the start and end of fermentation is a tiny fraction of the potential energy change that occurs during cellular respiration.

Based on these observations, it is not surprising that organisms capable of both processes almost never use fermentation

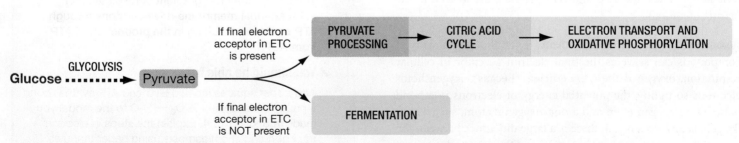

FIGURE 13.20 Cellular Respiration and Fermentation Are Alternative Pathways for Producing Energy. When oxygen or another electron acceptor used by the ETC is present in a cell, the pyruvate produced by glycolysis enters the citric acid cycle and the electron transport system is active. But if no electron acceptor is available to keep the ETC running, the pyruvate undergoes reactions known as fermentation.

(a) Lactic acid fermentation occurs in humans.

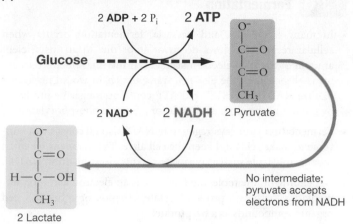

2 Lactate

(b) Alcohol fermentation occurs in yeast.

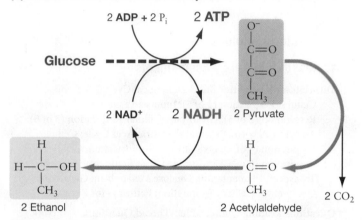

2 Ethanol   2 Acetylaldehyde

FIGURE 13.21 Fermentation Regenerates NAD⁺ So That Glycolysis Can Continue. These are just two examples of the many types of fermentation that occur among bacteria, archaea, and eukaryotes.

when an appropriate electron acceptor is available for cellular respiration. In organisms that usually use oxygen as an electron acceptor, fermentation is an alternative mode of ATP production when oxygen supplies temporarily run out.

Organisms that can switch between fermentation and cellular respiration that uses oxygen as an electron acceptor are called **facultative anaerobes.** The adjective facultative reflects the ability to use cellular respiration when oxygen is present and fermentation when it is absent (anaerobic). Many of your cells can function as facultative anaerobes to a certain extent; however, you cannot survive for long without oxygen. To make this point clear, try holding your breath—it should take only a minute for you to realize how important electron transport is to your cells.

check your understanding

C Y U

If you understand that . . .

• Fermentation occurs in the absence of an electron acceptor at the end of an ETC. It consists of reactions that oxidize NADH to regenerate the NAD⁺ required for glycolysis.

✔ **You should be able to . . .**

Explain why organisms that have an ETC as well as fermentation pathways seldom ferment pyruvate if an electron acceptor at the end of the ETC is readily available.

Answers are available in Appendix A.

CHAPTER 13 REVIEW

For media, go to MasteringBiology **MB**

If you understand . . .

13.1 An Overview of Cellular Respiration

• Cellular respiration is based on redox reactions that transfer electrons from a compound with high free energy, such as glucose, to a molecule with lower free energy, such as oxygen, through an electron transport chain.

• In eukaryotes, cellular respiration consists of four steps: glycolysis, pyruvate processing, the citric acid cycle, and electron transport coupled to oxidative phosphorylation.

• Glycolysis, pyruvate processing, and the citric acid cycle are central to the metabolism of most cells. Other catabolic pathways feed into them, and the intermediates of the central pathways are used in the synthesis of many key molecules.

✔ You should be able to explain why many different molecules—including lipids, amino acids, and CO_2—are radiolabeled when cells are fed glucose with ^{14}C radioactive carbons.

13.2 Glycolysis: Processing Glucose to Pyruvate

• The glycolytic pathway is a 10-step reaction sequence in which glucose is broken down into two molecules of pyruvate. It takes place in the cytosol, where ATP and NADH are produced.

• Glycolysis slows when ATP binds to phosphofructokinase.

✔ **QUANTITATIVE** You should be able to draw a graph predicting how the rate of ATP production in glycolysis changes as a function of ATP concentration. (Write "ATP concentration" on the *x*-axis and "ATP production" on the *y*-axis.)

13.3 Processing Pyruvate to Acetyl CoA

- During pyruvate processing, a series of reactions convert pyruvate to acetyl CoA. NADH is produced and CO_2 is released.

- The pyruvate dehydrogenase complex is inhibited when it is phosphorylated by ATP. It speeds up in the presence of substrates like NAD and ADP.

✔ You should be able to explain why it is not surprising that pyruvate dehydrogenase consists of a large, multi-enzyme complex.

13.4 The Citric Acid Cycle: Oxidizing Acetyl CoA to CO_2

- The citric acid cycle is an eight-step reaction cycle that begins with acetyl CoA. $FADH_2$, NADH, and GTP or ATP are produced; CO_2 is released. By the end of the citric acid cycle, glucose is completely oxidized to CO_2.

- Certain enzymes in the citric acid cycle are inhibited when NADH or ATP binds to them.

✔ You should be able to describe what would happen to NADH levels in a cell in the first few seconds after a drug has poisoned the enzyme that combines acetyl CoA and oxaloacetate to form citrate.

13.5 Electron Transport and Chemiosmosis: Building a Proton Gradient to Produce ATP

- NADH and $FADH_2$ donate electrons to an electron transport chain that resides in the inner membrane of mitochondria and the plasma membrane of many bacteria. The series of redox reactions in these chains gradually steps the electrons down in potential energy until they are transferred to a final electron acceptor (often O_2).

- The energy released from redox reactions in the electron transport chain is used to move protons across the inner mitochondrial membrane, creating an electrochemical gradient. ATP synthase uses the energy stored in this gradient to produce ATP via chemiosmosis—a process called oxidative phosphorylation.

✔ You should be able to predict the effect of a drug that inhibits ATP synthase on the pH in the mitochondrial matrix.

13.6 Fermentation

- In many eukaryotes and bacteria, fermentation occurs when cellular respiration slows down or stops due to an insufficient amount of the final electron acceptor. If the final electron acceptor is absent, then the electron transport chain would no longer oxidize NADH to NAD^+ and ATP could no longer be produced by glycolysis, the citric acid cycle, or oxidative phosphorylation.

- Fermentation pathways regenerate NAD^+, so glycolysis can continue to make ATP and keep the cell alive. This happens when an organic molecule such as pyruvate accepts electrons from NADH.

- Depending on the molecule that acts as an electron acceptor, fermentation pathways produce lactate, ethanol, or other reduced organic compounds as a by-product.

✔ You should be able to explain why you would expect organisms that produce ATP only via fermentation to grow much more slowly than organisms that produce ATP via cellular respiration.

You should be able to . . .

✔ TEST YOUR KNOWLEDGE
Answers are available in Appendix A

1. Make a flowchart indicating the relationships among the four steps of cellular respiration. Which steps are responsible for glucose oxidation? Which produce the most ATP?

2. Where does the citric acid cycle occur in eukaryotes?
   a. in the cytosol
   b. in the matrix of mitochondria
   c. in the inner membrane of mitochondria
   d. in the intermembrane space of mitochondria

3. What does the chemiosmotic hypothesis claim?
   a. Substrate-level phosphorylation occurs in the electron transport chain.
   b. Substrate-level phosphorylation occurs in glycolysis and the citric acid cycle.
   c. The electron transport chain is located in the inner membrane of mitochondria.
   d. Electron transport chains generate ATP indirectly, by the creation of a proton-motive force.

4. After glucose is fully oxidized by glycolysis, pyruvate processing, and the citric acid cycle, where is most of the energy stored?

5. What is the function of the reactions in a fermentation pathway?
   a. to generate NADH from NAD^+, so electrons can be donated to the electron transport chain
   b. to synthesize pyruvate from lactate
   c. to generate NAD^+ from NADH, so glycolysis can continue
   d. to synthesize electron acceptors, so that cellular respiration can continue

6. Which of the following would cause cells to switch from cellular respiration to fermentation?
   a. The final electron acceptor in the ETC is not available.
   b. The proton-motive force runs down.
   c. NADH and $FADH_2$ supplies are low.
   d. Pyruvate is not available.

TEST YOUR UNDERSTANDING   *Answers are available in Appendix A*

7. Describe the relationship between carbohydrate metabolism, the catabolism of proteins and fats, and anabolic pathways.

8. Compare and contrast substrate-level phosphorylation and oxidative phosphorylation.

9. Why does aerobic respiration produce much more ATP than anaerobic respiration?

10. If you were to expose cells that are undergoing cellular respiration to a radioactive oxygen isotope in the form of O_2, which of the following molecules would you expect to be radiolabeled?
    a. pyruvate
    b. water
    c. NADH
    d. CO_2

11. In step 3 of the citric acid cycle, the enzyme isocitrate dehydrogenase is regulated by NADH. Compare and contrast the regulation of this enzyme with what you have learned about phosphofructokinase in glycolysis.

12. Explain the relationship between electron transport and oxidative phosphorylation. What does ATP synthase look like, and how does it work?

TEST YOUR PROBLEM-SOLVING SKILLS   *Answers are available in Appendix A*

13. Cyanide ($C \equiv N^-$) blocks complex IV of the electron transport chain. Suggest a hypothesis for what happens to the ETC when complex IV stops working. Your hypothesis should explain why cyanide poisoning in humans is fatal.

14. The presence of many sac-like cristae results in a large amount of membrane inside mitochondria. Suppose that some mitochondria had few cristae. How would their output of ATP compare with that of mitochondria with many cristae? Justify your answer.

15. QUANTITATIVE Early estimates suggested that the oxidation of glucose via aerobic respiration would produce 38 ATP. Based on

what you know of the theoretical yields of ATP from each step, show how this total was determined. Why do biologists now think this amount of ATP/glucose is not achieved in cells?

16. Suppose a drug were added to mitochondria that allowed protons to freely pass through the inner membrane. Which of the following mitochondrial activities would most likely be inhibited?
    a. the citric acid cycle
    b. oxidative phosphorylation
    c. substrate-level phosphorylation
    d. the electron transport chain

14 Photosynthesis

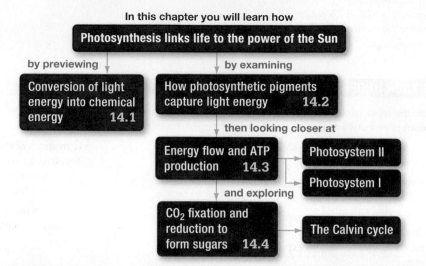

In this chapter you will learn how

Photosynthesis links life to the power of the Sun

by previewing

Conversion of light energy into chemical energy 14.1

by examining

How photosynthetic pigments capture light energy 14.2

then looking closer at

Energy flow and ATP production 14.3

→ Photosystem II

→ Photosystem I

and exploring

CO$_2$ fixation and reduction to form sugars 14.4

→ The Calvin cycle

A close-up of moss cells filled with chloroplasts, where photosynthesis converts the energy in sunlight to chemical energy in the bonds of sugar. The sugar produced by photosynthetic organisms fuels cellular respiration and growth. Photosynthetic organisms, in turn, are consumed by other organisms, including you. Directly or indirectly, most organisms on Earth get their energy from photosynthesis.

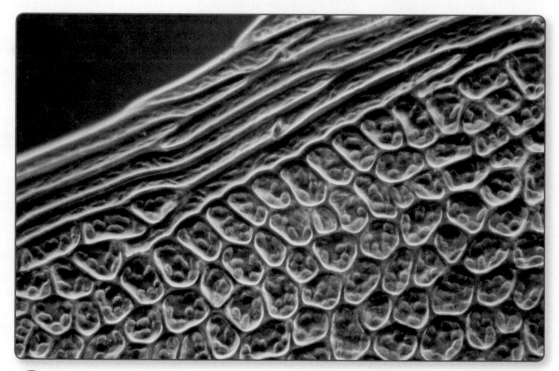

This chapter is part of the Big Picture. See how on pages 284–285.

Some 3 billion years ago, a novel combination of light-absorbing molecules and enzymes gave a bacterial cell the capacity to convert light energy into chemical energy in the C−C and C−H bonds of sugar. The origin of **photosynthesis**—the use of sunlight to manufacture carbohydrate—ranks as one of the great events in the history of life.

The vast majority of organisms alive today rely on photosynthesis, either directly or indirectly, to stay alive. Maples, mosses, and other photosynthetic organisms are termed **autotrophs** (literally, "self-feeders") because they make all their own food from ions and simple molecules. Humans, houseflies, and other non-photosynthetic organisms are called **heterotrophs** ("different-feeders") because they have to obtain the sugars and many of the other macromolecules they need from other organisms.

✔ When you see this checkmark, stop and test yourself. Answers are available in Appendix A.

Because there could be no heterotrophs without autotrophs, photosynthesis is fundamental to almost all life. Glycolysis may qualify as the most ancient set of energy-related chemical reactions from an evolutionary viewpoint, but ecologically—meaning, in terms of how organisms interact with one another—photosynthesis is easily the most important.

How does photosynthesis work? Let's begin with an overview and then delve into a step-by-step analysis of some of the most remarkable chemistry on Earth.

14.1 Photosynthesis Harnesses Sunlight to Make Carbohydrate

Research on photosynthesis began early in the history of biological science. In the 1770s, Joseph Priestley performed a series of experiments showing that the green parts of plants would "restore air" that had been consumed by animals or fire. This work led to the discovery of oxygen (O_2) and the finding that plants produce it in the presence of sunlight, carbon dioxide (CO_2), and water (H_2O).

By the 1840s, enough was known about the process for biologists to propose that photosynthesis allows plants to convert the electromagnetic energy of sunlight into chemical energy in the $C-C$ and $C-H$ bonds of carbohydrates. When glucose is the carbohydrate that is eventually produced, the overall reaction—the sum of many independent reactions—can be simplified and written as

$$6\ CO_2 + 6\ H_2S + \text{light energy} \longrightarrow C_6H_{12}O_6 + 6\ O_2$$
$$\text{glucose}$$

Now read the reaction again, and note the contrast with cellular respiration. Photosynthesis is an endergonic suite of redox reactions that produce sugars from carbon dioxide and light energy. Cellular respiration is an exergonic suite of redox reactions that produces carbon dioxide and ATP from sugars.

FIGURE 14.1 provides an incomplete electron-sharing diagram for the reaction shown above. ✔ If you understand the fundamental principles of reduction–oxidation (see Chapter 10), you should be able to complete Figure 14.1 (following the instructions in the caption exercise) and then use the data from the figure to explain why the reaction is endergonic.

So how does photosynthesis produce O_2 and glucose? Early investigators assumed that CO_2 and H_2O react directly to produce the CH_2O found in carbohydrates and release O_2 as a byproduct. This idea, however, turned out to be incorrect. Instead, CO_2 and H_2O participate in entirely different reactions, and the oxygen atoms in O_2 come from water. How was this discovered?

Photosynthesis: Two Linked Sets of Reactions

Starting in the 1930s, two independent lines of research on photosynthesis converged, leading to a major advance in biologists' understanding of how oxygen gas and carbohydrates are produced.

The first research program, led by Cornelius van Niel, focused on photosynthesis in organisms called purple sulfur bacteria. Van Niel and his group found that these cells are autotrophs that manufacture their own carbohydrates from CO_2, sunlight, and hydrogen sulfide (H_2S).

Van Niel also showed that these cells did not produce oxygen as a by-product of photosynthesis. Instead, elemental sulfur (S) accumulated in their medium. In these organisms, the overall reaction for photosynthesis was

$$CO_2 + 2\ H_2S + \text{light energy} \longrightarrow (CH_2O)_n + H_2O + 2\ S$$

Van Niel's work was crucial for two reasons:

1. It showed that H_2S, the equivalent of H_2O in the plant reactions, and CO_2 do *not* combine directly during photosynthesis.

2. It showed that the oxygen atoms in CO_2 are *not* released as oxygen gas (O_2). The purple sulfur bacteria produced no oxygen, even though carbon dioxide participated in the reaction—just as it did in plants.

Based on these findings, biologists hypothesized that the oxygen atoms released during plant photosynthesis must come from H_2O. The hypothesis was confirmed when heavy isotopes

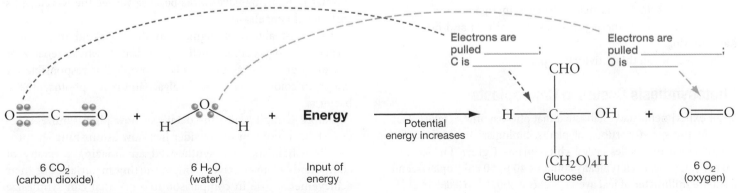

FIGURE 14.1 Electron Transfer during the Reduction of Glucose.

✔**EXERCISE** Fill in the electron positions for each bond in the reaction products, and complete the labels explaining which product is reduced and which is oxidized.

of oxygen—^{18}O in contrast to the normal isotope, ^{16}O—became available to researchers. They observed the ^{18}O in oxygen gas only when algae or plants were exposed to ^{18}O-labeled H_2O, not the ^{18}O-labeled CO_2.

In addition, the reactions responsible for producing oxygen gas occurred only in the presence of sunlight, but did not require the presence of CO_2. These data suggested that there were two distinct sets of reactions: one that uses light to produce O_2 from H_2O and one that converts CO_2 into sugars.

A second major line of research supported the idea of two sets of reactions. Between 1945 and 1955, a team led by Melvin Calvin began introducing radioactively labeled carbon dioxide ($^{14}CO_2$) to algae and identifying the molecules that subsequently became labeled with the radioisotope. These experiments allowed researchers to identify the sequence of reactions involved in reducing CO_2 to sugars.

Because Calvin played an important role in this research, the reactions that reduce carbon dioxide and produce sugar came to be known as the **Calvin cycle.** Later research showed that the Calvin cycle can function only if the light-capturing reactions are occurring.

To summarize: Early research showed that photosynthesis consists of two linked sets of reactions. One set is triggered by light; the other set—the Calvin cycle—requires the products of the light-capturing reactions. The light-capturing reactions produce oxygen from water; the Calvin cycle produces sugar from carbon dioxide.

The two reactions are linked by electrons that are released when water is split to form oxygen gas. During the light-capturing reactions, these electrons are promoted to a high-energy state by light and then transferred through a series of redox reactions to a phosphorylated version of NAD^+, called **$NADP^+$ (nicotinamide adenine dinucleotide phosphate).** This reaction forms **NADPH,** which functions as a reducing agent similar to the NADH produced in cellular respiration. Some of the energy released from these redox reactions is also used to produce ATP (**FIGURE 14.2**).

During the Calvin cycle, the electrons in NADPH and the potential energy in ATP are used to reduce CO_2 to carbohydrate. The resulting sugars are used in cellular respiration to produce ATP for the cell. Plants oxidize sugars in their mitochondria and consume O_2 in the process, just as animals and other eukaryotes do.

Where does all this activity take place?

Photosynthesis Occurs in Chloroplasts

Once experiments had established that photosynthesis takes place only in the green portions of plants, biologists focused on the bright green organelles called **chloroplasts** ("green-formed elements"). One leaf cell typically contains 40 to 50 chloroplasts, and a square millimeter of leaf averages about 500,000 (**FIGURE 14.3**).

When membranes derived from chloroplasts were found to release oxygen after exposure to sunlight, the hypothesis that chloroplasts are the site of photosynthesis became widely accepted.

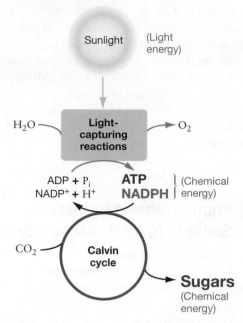

FIGURE 14.2 Photosynthesis Has Two Linked Components. In the light-capturing reactions of photosynthesis, light energy is transformed to chemical energy in the form of ATP and NADPH. During the Calvin cycle, the ATP and NADPH produced in the light-capturing reactions are used to reduce carbon dioxide to carbohydrate.

As Figure 14.3 shows, a chloroplast is enclosed by an outer membrane and an inner membrane (see Chapter 2). The interior is dominated by flattened, sac-like structures called **thylakoids,** which often occur in interconnected stacks called **grana** (singular: **granum**). The space inside a thylakoid is its **lumen.** (Recall that lumen is a general term for the interior of any sac-like structure. Your stomach and intestines have a lumen.) The fluid-filled space between the thylakoids and the inner membrane is the **stroma.**

When researchers analyzed the chemical composition of thylakoid membranes, they found huge quantities of pigments. **Pigments** are molecules that absorb only certain wavelengths of light—other wavelengths are either reflected or transmitted (pass through). Pigments have colors because we see the wavelengths that they do *not* absorb.

The most abundant pigment in the thylakoid membranes turned out to be chlorophyll ("green-leaf"), which reflects or transmits green light. As a result, chlorophyll is responsible for the green color of plants, some algae, and many photosynthetic bacteria.

Before plunging into the details of how photosynthesis occurs, take a moment to consider just how astonishing the process is. Chemists have synthesized an amazing diversity of compounds from relatively simple starting materials, but their achievements pale in comparison to a cell that can synthesize sugar from just carbon dioxide, water, and sunlight. If photosynthesis is not *the* most sophisticated chemistry on Earth, it is certainly a contender.

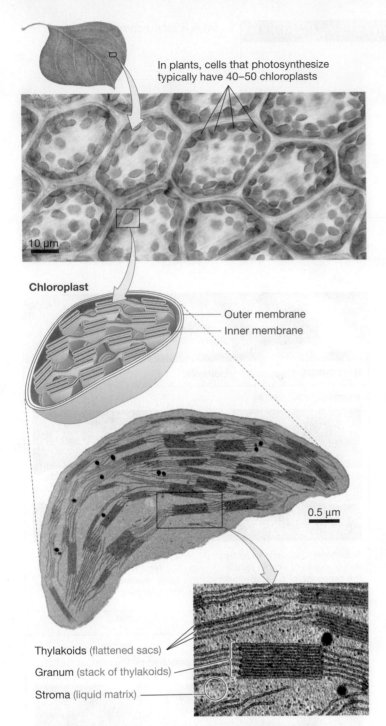

In plants, cells that photosynthesize typically have 40–50 chloroplasts

10 μm

Chloroplast

Outer membrane
Inner membrane

0.5 μm

Thylakoids (flattened sacs)
Granum (stack of thylakoids)
Stroma (liquid matrix)

FIGURE 14.3 Photosynthesis Takes Place in Chloroplasts.

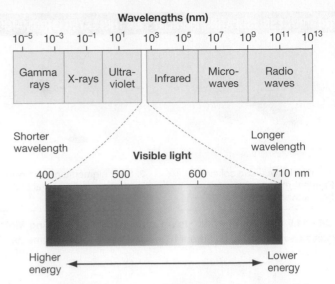

Wavelengths (nm)

10^{-5} 10^{-3} 10^{-1} 10^{1} 10^{3} 10^{5} 10^{7} 10^{9} 10^{11} 10^{13}

Gamma rays	X-rays	Ultra-violet	Infrared	Micro-waves	Radio waves

Shorter wavelength

Longer wavelength

Visible light

400   500   600   710 nm

Higher energy

Lower energy

FIGURE 14.4 The Electromagnetic Spectrum. Electromagnetic energy radiates through space in the form of waves. Humans can see radiation at wavelengths between about 400 nanometers (nm) to 710 nm. The shorter the wavelength of electromagnetic radiation, the higher its energy.

sunlight into chemical energy in the C—C and C—H bonds of sugar.

Physicists describe light's behavior as both wavelike and particle-like. Like water waves or airwaves, electromagnetic radiation is characterized by its **wavelength**—the distance between two successive wave crests (or wave troughs). The wavelength determines the type of electromagnetic radiation.

FIGURE 14.4 illustrates the range of wavelengths of electromagnetic radiation—the **electromagnetic spectrum.** The electromagnetic radiation that humans can see, the **visible light,** ranges in wavelength from about 400 to about 710 nanometers (nm, or 10^{-9} m). Shorter wavelengths of electromagnetic radiation contain more energy than longer wavelengths do. Thus, there is more energy in blue light than in red light.

To emphasize the particle-like nature of light, physicists point out that it exists in discrete packets called **photons.** Each photon of light has a characteristic wavelength and energy level. Pigment molecules absorb the energy of some of these photons. How?

Photosynthetic Pigments Absorb Light

When a photon strikes an object, the photon may be absorbed, transmitted, or reflected. A pigment molecule absorbs photons of particular wavelengths. Sunlight includes white light, which consists of all wavelengths in the visible portion of the electromagnetic spectrum at once.

If a pigment absorbs all the visible wavelengths, the pigment appears black because no visible wavelength of light is reflected back to your eye. If a pigment absorbs many or most of the wavelengths in the blue and green parts of the spectrum but transmits or reflects longer wavelengths, it appears red.

What wavelengths do various plant pigments absorb? In one approach to answering this question, researchers grind up leaves

14.2 How Do Pigments Capture Light Energy?

The light-capturing reactions of photosynthesis begin with the simple act of sunlight striking chlorophyll. To understand the consequences of this event, it's helpful to review the nature of light.

Light is a type of electromagnetic radiation, a form of energy. Photosynthesis converts electromagnetic energy in the form of

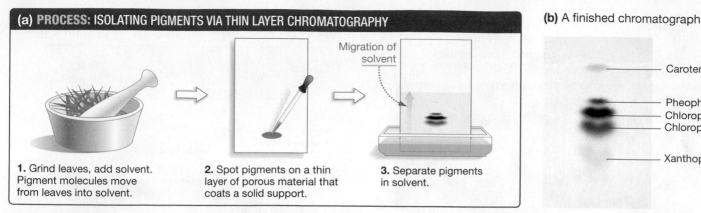

(a) PROCESS: ISOLATING PIGMENTS VIA THIN LAYER CHROMATOGRAPHY

1. Grind leaves, add solvent. Pigment molecules move from leaves into solvent.

Migration of solvent

2. Spot pigments on a thin layer of porous material that coats a solid support.

3. Separate pigments in solvent.

(b) A finished chromatograph

Carotene

Pheophytin
Chlorophyll *a*
Chlorophyll *b*

Xanthophyll

FIGURE 14.5 Chromatography Is a Technique for Separating Molecules. Different species of photosynthetic organisms may contain different types and quantities of pigments. This example shows grass leaves.

in a liquid that acts as a solvent to extract pigment molecules from the leaf mixture. A technique called thin layer chromatography separates the pigments in the extract (**FIGURE 14.5a**).

To begin, spots of raw leaf extract are placed near the bottom of a stiff support that is coated with a thin layer of silica gel, cellulose, or similar porous material. The coated support is then placed in a solvent solution. As the solvent wicks upward through the coating, it carries the pigment molecules in the mixture with it. Because the pigment molecules vary in size, solubility, or both, they are carried at different rates.

FIGURE 14.5b shows a chromatograph from a grass-leaf extract. Notice that this leaf contains an array of pigments. To find out which wavelengths are absorbed by each of these molecules, researchers cut out a single region (color band) of the porous material, extract the pigment, and use an instrument to record the wavelengths absorbed.

Different Pigments Absorb Different Wavelengths of Light Research based on the techniques shown in Figure 14.5 has confirmed that there are two major pigment classes in plant leaves: chlorophylls and carotenoids.

1. **Chlorophylls,** designated chlorophyll *a* and chlorophyll *b*, absorb strongly in the blue and red regions of the visible spectrum. The presence of chlorophylls makes plants look green because they reflect green light, which they do not absorb.

2. **Carotenoids** absorb in the blue and green parts of the visible spectrum. Thus, carotenoids appear yellow, orange, or red. The carotenoids found in plants belong to two classes, called carotenes and xanthophylls.

FIGURE 14.6 Certain Wavelengths of Light Are Used to Drive Photosynthesis.

SOURCE: Engelmann, T. W. 1882. Oxygen excretion from plant cells in a microspectrum. *Botanische Zeitung* 40: 419–426.

✔**EXERCISE** Draw what you expect the results of this experiment would look like if the pigments that drive photosynthesis in the algae were to absorb most strongly at 500 nm and 560 nm.

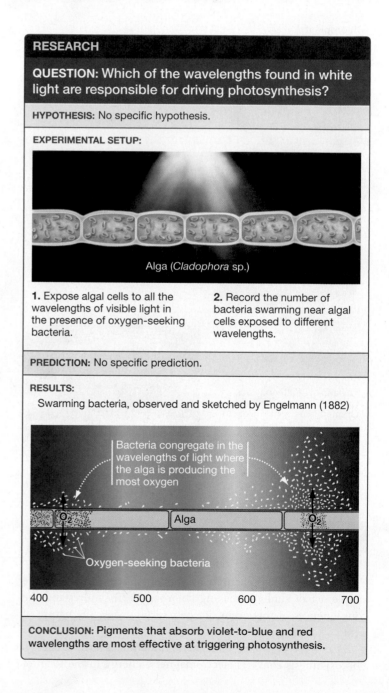

RESEARCH

QUESTION: Which of the wavelengths found in white light are responsible for driving photosynthesis?

HYPOTHESIS: No specific hypothesis.

EXPERIMENTAL SETUP:

Alga (*Cladophora* sp.)

1. Expose algal cells to all the wavelengths of visible light in the presence of oxygen-seeking bacteria.

2. Record the number of bacteria swarming near algal cells exposed to different wavelengths.

PREDICTION: No specific prediction.

RESULTS:

Swarming bacteria, observed and sketched by Engelmann (1882)

Bacteria congregate in the wavelengths of light where the alga is producing the most oxygen

O₂   Alga   O₂

Oxygen-seeking bacteria

400   500   600   700

CONCLUSION: Pigments that absorb violet-to-blue and red wavelengths are most effective at triggering photosynthesis.

Which of these wavelengths drive photosynthesis?

In 1882, T. W. Engelmann answered this question by laying a filamentous alga across a microscope slide that was illuminated with a spectrum of colors generated by passing light through a prism to separate the wavelengths (**FIGURE 14.6**). The idea was that the algal cells would begin performing photosynthesis in response to the various wavelengths of light and produce oxygen as a by-product. To determine exactly where oxygen was being produced, Engelmann added bacterial cells from a species that is attracted to oxygen.

As the drawing in the "Results" section of Figure 14.6 shows, most of the bacteria congregated in the violet-to-blue and red regions of the slide. Because wavelengths in these parts of the spectrum were associated with high oxygen concentrations, Engelmann concluded that they defined the **action spectrum** for photosynthesis—the wavelengths that drive the light-capturing reactions. Engelmann's data indicate that violet-to-blue and red photons are the most effective at driving photosynthesis. Because the chlorophylls absorb these wavelengths, this early experiment showed that chlorophylls are the main photosynthetic pigments.

Using thin layer chromatography, and more advanced techniques to evaluate photosynthetic activity, biologists have produced data like those shown in **FIGURE 14.7**. This graph shows the action spectrum and the absorption spectra for three different pigments found in chloroplasts. An **absorption spectrum** measures how the wavelength of photons influences the amount of light absorbed by a pigment. In the combined graph, peaks indicate wavelengths where absorbance or photosynthetic activity is high; troughs indicate wavelengths where absorbance or photosynthetic activity is low.

Which Part of a Pigment Absorbs Light?

As **FIGURE 14.8a** shows, chlorophyll *a* and chlorophyll *b* are similar in structure. Both have two fundamental parts: a long isoprenoid "tail" (introduced in Chapter 3) and a "head" consisting of a large ring structure

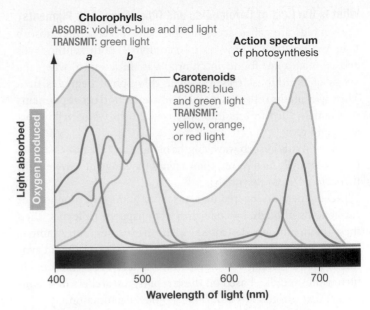

FIGURE 14.7 There Is a Strong Correlation between the Absorption Spectra of Pigments and the Action Spectrum for Photosynthesis.

DATA: Singhal, G. S., et al. 1999. *Concepts in Photobiology: Photosynthesis and Photomorphogenesis*. Dordrecht: Kluwer Academic; co-published with Narosa Publishing House (New Delhi), 11–51.

with a magnesium atom in the middle. The tail interacts with proteins embedded in the thylakoid membrane; the head is where light is absorbed.

The structure of β-carotene, shown in **FIGURE 14.8b**, has an isoprenoid chain connecting two rings that are responsible for absorbing light. This pigment is what gives carrots their orange color. A xanthophyll called zeaxanthin, which gives corn kernels their bright yellow color, is nearly identical to β-carotene, except that the ring structures on either end of the molecule contain a hydroxyl ($-OH$) group.

Researchers had shown that chlorophylls are the main photosynthetic pigments, but carotenoids also absorb light. What do they do? Before analyzing what happens when chlorophyll pigments absorb light, let's first look at the function of the carotenoids.

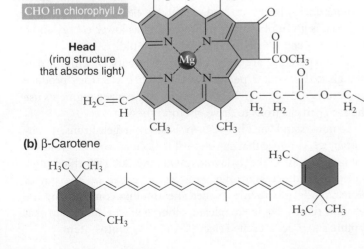

(a) Chlorophylls *a* and *b*

(b) β-Carotene

FIGURE 14.8 Photosynthetic Pigments Contain Ring Structures. **(a)** Although chlorophylls *a* and *b* are very similar structurally, they have the distinct absorption spectra shown in Figure 14.7. **(b)** Carotene is an orange pigment found in carrot roots and other plant tissues.

What Is the Role of Carotenoids and Other Accessory Pigments?

Carotenoids are called accessory pigments because they absorb light and pass the energy on to chlorophyll. Both xanthophylls and carotenes are found in chloroplasts. In autumn, when the leaves of deciduous trees die, their chlorophyll degrades first. The wavelengths reflected by the carotenoids and other pigments that remain turn forests into spectacular displays of yellow, orange, and red.

Carotenoids absorb wavelengths of light that are not absorbed by chlorophyll. As a result, they extend the range of wavelengths that can drive photosynthesis.

Researchers discovered an even more important function for carotenoids, though, by analyzing what happens to leaves when these pigments are destroyed. Many herbicides, for example, work by inhibiting enzymes that are involved in carotenoid synthesis. Plants lacking carotenoids rapidly lose their chlorophyll, turn white, and die. Based on these results, researchers have concluded that carotenoids also serve a protective function.

To understand why carotenoids are protective, recall that photons—especially the high-energy, short-wavelength photons in the ultraviolet part of the electromagnetic spectrum—contain enough energy to knock electrons out of atoms and create free radicals (see Appendix D). Free radicals, in turn, trigger reactions that can disrupt and degrade molecules.

Carotenoids "quench" free radicals by accepting or stabilizing unpaired electrons. As a result, they protect chlorophyll molecules from harm. When carotenoids are absent, chlorophyll molecules are destroyed and photosynthesis stops. Starvation and death follow.

When Light Is Absorbed, Electrons Enter an Excited State

Just what is absorption? What happens when a photon of a particular wavelength—say, red light with a wavelength of 680 nm—strikes a chlorophyll molecule?

When a photon strikes a chlorophyll molecule, the photon's energy can be transferred to an electron in the chlorophyll molecule's head region. In response, the electron is "excited," or raised to a higher energy state.

The excited electron states that are possible in a particular pigment are discrete—meaning, incremental rather than continuous—and can be represented as lines on an energy scale. These discrete energy levels are a property of the electron configurations in a particular pigment.

FIGURE 14.9 shows the ground state, or unexcited state, as 0 and the higher energy states as 1 and 2. If the difference between the possible energy states is the same as the energy in the photon, the photon can be absorbed and an electron excited to a higher energy state.

In chlorophyll, for example, the energy difference between the ground state and state 1 is equal to the energy in a red photon, while the energy difference between state 0 and state 2 is equal to the energy in a blue photon. Thus, chlorophyll can readily absorb red photons and blue photons.

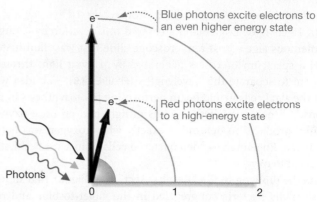

FIGURE 14.9 Electrons Are Promoted to High-Energy States When Photons Strike Chlorophyll. The unexcited, or ground state, is labeled 0, and the discrete energy states are labeled 1 and 2. The wavelength of light that will excite electrons to these energy states is a property of chlorophyll's structure.

✔ **QUESTION** Suppose a pigment had a discrete energy state that corresponded to the energy in green light. Where would you draw this energy state on this diagram?

Chlorophyll does not absorb green light well, because there is no discrete step—no difference in possible energy states for its electrons—that corresponds to the amount of energy in a green photon.

Wavelengths in the ultraviolet part of the spectrum have so much energy that they may actually eject electrons from a pigment molecule and create a free radical. In contrast, wavelengths in the infrared regions have so little energy that in most cases they merely increase the movement of atoms in the pigment, generating heat—meaning molecular movement—rather than exciting electrons.

But if a pigment absorbs a photon with the right amount of energy, energy in the form of electromagnetic radiation is transferred to that electron. The electron now has high potential energy. What happens next?

If the excited electron simply falls back to its ground state, the absorbed energy is released as heat or a combination of heat and electromagnetic radiation (light). When the electron energy produces light, it is called **fluorescence.** Because some of the original photon's energy is transformed to heat, the electromagnetic radiation that is given off during fluorescence has lower energy and a longer wavelength than the original photon did.

When photons are absorbed by pigments in chloroplasts though, only about 2 percent of the excited electrons produce fluorescence. The other 98 percent of the energized pigments use their excited electrons to drive photosynthesis.

To understand what happens to these excited electrons, it's important to recognize that chlorophyll molecules work in groups—not individually. In the thylakoid membrane, 200–300 chlorophyll molecules and accessory pigments are organized by an array of proteins to form structures called the **antenna complex** and the **reaction center.** These complexes, along with the molecules that capture and process excited electrons, form a **photosystem.**

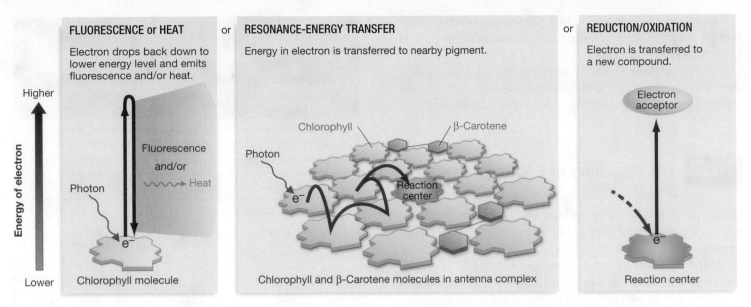

| FLUORESCENCE or HEAT | or | RESONANCE-ENERGY TRANSFER | or | REDUCTION/OXIDATION |

FLUORESCENCE or HEAT

Electron drops back down to lower energy level and emits fluorescence and/or heat.

RESONANCE-ENERGY TRANSFER

Energy in electron is transferred to nearby pigment.

REDUCTION/OXIDATION

Electron is transferred to a new compound.

FIGURE 14.10 Four Fates for Excited Electrons in Photosynthetic Pigments. When sunlight promotes electrons in pigments to a high-energy state, four things can happen: They can fluoresce, release heat, pass energy to a nearby pigment via resonance, or transfer the electron to an electron acceptor.

The Antenna Complex When a red or blue photon strikes a pigment molecule in the antenna complex, the energy is absorbed and an electron is excited in response. This energy—but not the electron itself—is passed to a nearby chlorophyll molecule, where another electron is excited in response. This phenomenon is known as resonance energy transfer.

Resonance energy transfer is possible only between pigments that are able to absorb different wavelengths of photons—from those absorbing higher-energy photons to those absorbing lower-energy photons. The organization of the antenna complex makes it possible for this resonance energy to be efficiently moved between pigments, as the potential energy drops at each step.

Once the energy is transferred, the original excited electron falls back to its ground state. In this way, energy is transferred inside the antenna complex in a manner that may be likened to the transfer of excitement between fans at a sports event during the "wave." But unlike the stadium wave, most of this resonance energy is directed to a particular location in a photosystem, called the reaction center.

The Reaction Center When a chlorophyll molecule is excited in the **reaction center,** its excited electron is transferred to an electron acceptor. When the acceptor becomes reduced, the energy transformation event that started with the absorption of light becomes permanent: Electromagnetic energy is transformed to chemical energy. The redox reaction that occurs in the reaction center results in the production of chemical energy from sunlight.

Note that in the absence of light, the electron acceptor does not accept electrons. It remains in an oxidized state because the redox reaction that transfers an electron to the electron acceptor is endergonic. But when light excites electrons in chlorophyll to a high-energy state, the reaction becomes exergonic. In this way, the energy in light transforms an endergonic reaction to an exergonic one.

FIGURE 14.10 summarizes the four possible fates of electrons in chlorophyll that are excited by photons. The energy released from these electrons can

1. be emitted in the form of light via fluorescence, or

2. be given off as heat alone, or

3. excite an electron in a nearby pigment and induce resonance, or

4. be transferred to an electron acceptor in a redox reaction.

check your understanding

If you understand that . . .

• Pigments absorb specific wavelengths of light.

• When a chlorophyll molecule in the antenna complex of a chloroplast membrane absorbs red or blue light, one of its electrons is promoted to a high-energy state.

• In the antenna complex, high-energy electrons transmit their energy between chlorophyll molecules toward the reaction center.

• When energy is transferred to a chlorophyll molecule in the reaction center, the excited electron reduces an electron acceptor. In this way, light energy is transformed to chemical energy.

✔ **You should be able to . . .**

Predict how the pigments of the antenna complex would be organized, with regard to the wavelength of photons absorbed, to allow the directional transport of energy from the outer pigments to the reaction center.

Answers are available in Appendix A.

Fluorescence is typical of isolated pigments, resonance energy transfer occurs in antenna complex pigments, and redox occurs in reaction center pigments.

Now the question is, what happens to the high-energy electrons that are transferred to the electron acceptor in the reaction center? Specifically, how are they used to manufacture sugar?

14.3 The Discovery of Photosystems I and II

During the 1950s, the fate of the high-energy electrons in photosystems was the central issue facing biologists interested in photosynthesis. A key breakthrough began with simple experiments by Robert Emerson on how green algae responded to various wavelengths of light. The algal cells being studied responded to wavelengths in the red and far-red regions of the visible spectrum.

Emerson found that if the algal cells were illuminated with either red or far-red wavelengths of light, the photosynthetic response was moderate. But if cells were exposed to a combination of both wavelengths, the rate of photosynthesis increased more than the sum of the rates produced by each wavelength independently. This phenomenon was called the enhancement effect, and is not limited to algal cells. In follow-up work by other researchers, it was also observed in isolated chloroplasts from plants (**FIGURE 14.11**). Why the enhancement effect occurred was a complete mystery at the time.

A solution to this puzzle was proposed by Robin Hill and Faye Bendall, who hypothesized that this enhancement effect resulted from two distinct types of reaction centers, each absorbing different wavelengths of light. According to the two-photosystem hypothesis, the enhancement effect occurs because photosynthesis is much more efficient when both photosystems operate together.

Subsequent work has shown that the two-photosystem hypothesis is correct for cyanobacteria ("blue-green bacteria") and the chloroplasts of eukaryotes, such as algae and plants. These two photosystems differ in structure and function, but work together in the light-capturing reactions.

To figure out how the two photosystems work, investigators focused on species of photosynthetic bacteria that possess one or the other of the two photosystems, but not both. Once each type of photosystem was understood in isolation, researchers explored how they work in combination. Let's do the same—first let's analyze **photosystem II,** then **photosystem I** (so named because it was discovered first), and then how the two interact.

How Does Photosystem II Work?

To study photosystem II, researchers focused on purple photosynthetic bacteria, including the purple sulfur bacteria that were studied by van Niel (see Section 14.1). These cells have a single photosystem that has many of the same components observed in photosystem II of cyanobacteria and the chloroplasts of algae and plants. (For simplicity, the eukaryotic chloroplast will serve as the model system for the remainder of the chapter.)

RESEARCH

QUESTION: Red and far-red light each stimulate a moderate rate of photosynthesis. How does a combination of both wavelengths affect the rate of photosynthesis?

HYPOTHESIS: When red and far-red light are combined, the rate of photosynthesis will be the sum of the single wavelength rates.

NULL HYPOTHESIS: When red and far-red light are combined, the rate of photosynthesis will be no more than the highest single wavelength rate.

EXPERIMENTAL SETUP:

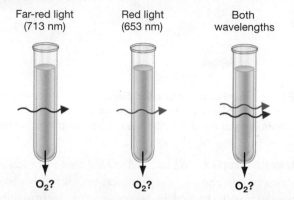

1. Expose algal cells to far-red light and then red light. Record oxygen produced as a measure of rate of photosynthesis.

2. Expose same cells to a combination of both lights.

PREDICTION: When the two wavelengths are combined, the amount of oxygen produced will be the sum of the single wavelength tests.

PREDICTION OF NULL HYPOTHESIS: When the two wavelengths are combined, the amount of oxygen produced will be no more than the single wavelength test that yielded the highest amount of oxygen.

RESULTS:

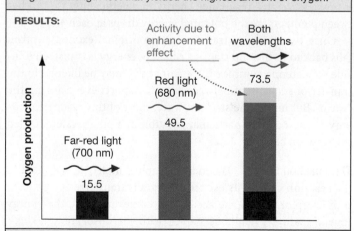

CONCLUSION: Neither hypothesis is correct. The combination of both wavelengths yielded more oxygen than the sum of the single tests. A new hypothesis is required to explain this enhancement effect.

FIGURE 14.11 The "Enhancement Effect" of Two Different Wavelengths in Isolated Chloroplasts.

SOURCE: Govindjee, R., Govindjee, and G. Hoch. 1964. Emerson enhancement effect in chloroplast reactions. *Plant Physiology* 39: 10–14.

✔ **QUESTION** Was it important for the researchers to keep the density of chloroplasts fairly constant in each treatment? Explain why or why not.

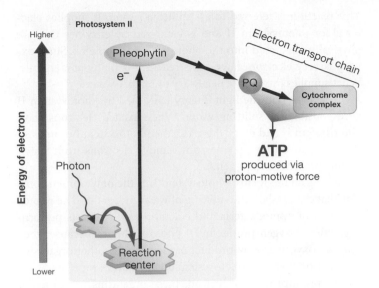

FIGURE 14.12 Photosystem II Feeds High-Energy Electrons to an Electron Transport Chain. When an excited electron leaves the chlorophyll in the reaction center of photosystem II, the electron is accepted by pheophytin, transferred to plastoquinone (PQ), and then stepped down in energy along an electron transport chain.

Converting Light Energy into Chemical Energy

In photosystem II, the action begins when the antenna complex transmits resonance energy to the reaction center, where the electron acceptor pheophytin comes into play (**FIGURE 14.12**). Structurally,

pheophytin is identical to chlorophyll except that pheophytin lacks a magnesium atom in its head region. Functionally, the two molecules are extremely different.

Instead of acting as a pigment that energizes an electron when it absorbs a photon, pheophytin accepts high-energy electrons from the excited reaction center chlorophylls. The reduction of pheophytin (and the accompanying oxidation of the reaction center chlorophyll pigment) is a key step in the transformation of light energy into chemical energy.

Electrons that reduce pheophytin are passed through additional carriers to an electron transport chain (ETC) in the thylakoid membrane. In both structure and function, this ETC is similar to components in the mitochondrial ETC (see Chapter 13).

- Structurally, the ETC associated with photosystem II and the ETC in the mitochondrion both contain quinones and cytochromes.

- Functionally, the redox reactions that occur in both ETCs result in protons being actively transported from one side of an internal membrane to the other. The resulting proton electrochemical gradient forms a proton-motive force that drives ATP production via ATP synthase. Photosystem II triggers chemiosmosis and ATP synthesis in the chloroplast.

FIGURE 14.13 explains how the electron transport chain associated with photosystem II works in more detail. Start by focusing on the molecule called **plastoquinone (PQ)**—a quinone similar to ubiquinone in the ETC of cellular respiration. Recall that

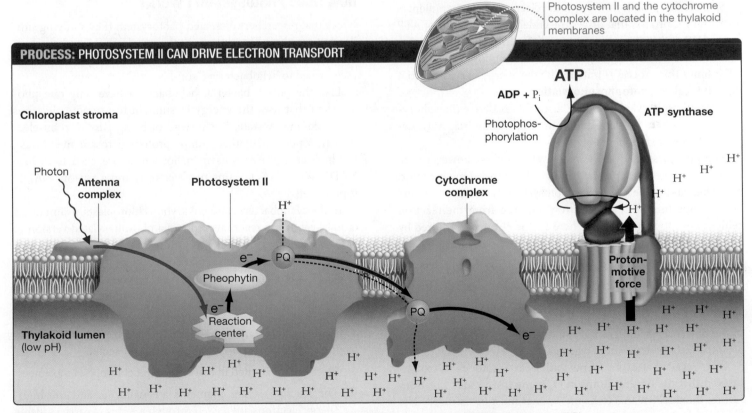

FIGURE 14.13 Electron Transport between Photosystem II and the Cytochrome Complex. Plastoquinone (PQ) carries electrons from photosystem II along with protons from the stroma. The cytochrome complex oxidizes plastoquinone, releasing the protons in the thylakoid lumen that drive ATP synthesis.

quinones are small hydrophobic molecules that can transport electrons between molecules (see Chapter 13). Because plastoquinone is lipid soluble and not anchored to the thylakoid membrane, it is free to move from one side of the thylakoid membrane to the other.

When plastoquinone receives electrons from photosystem II, it carries them across the membrane to the lumen side of the thylakoid and delivers them to more electronegative molecules in the cytochrome complex. In this way, plastoquinone shuttles electrons from photosystem II to the cytochrome complex much like ubiquinone shuttled electrons between complexes I or II and complex III in mitochondria. The potential energy released by these reactions allows protons to be picked up from the stroma and dropped off in the lumen side of the thylakoid membrane.

The protons transported by plastoquinone result in a large concentration of protons in the thylakoid lumen. When photosystem II is active, the pH of the thylakoid interior reaches 5 while the pH of the stroma hovers around 8. Because the pH scale is logarithmic, the difference of 3 units means that the concentration of H^+ is $10 \times 10 \times 10 = 1000$ times higher in the lumen than in the stroma. In addition, the stroma becomes negatively charged relative to the thylakoid lumen.

The net effect of electron transport, then, is to set up a large proton electrochemical gradient, resulting in a proton-motive force that drives H^+ out of the thylakoid lumen and into the stroma. Based on what you know of cellular respiration, it should come as no surprise that this proton-motive force drives the production of ATP.

Specifically, proton flow down the electrochemical gradient is an exergonic process that drives the endergonic synthesis of ATP from ADP and P_i. The stream of protons through ATP synthase causes conformational changes that drive the phosphorylation of ADP. Since this process is initiated by the energy harvested from light, it is called **photophosphorylation.**

Photophosphorylation is similar to the oxidative phosphorylation that occurs in plant and animal mitochondria. Both depend on chemiosmosis.

The photosystem II story is not yet complete, however. The electrons from PQ are passed through the cytochrome complex, but what about the oxidized photosystem II reaction center? To continue this ETC, the electron removed from the reaction center needs to be replaced. Where do the electrons required by photosystem II come from?

Photosystem II Obtains Electrons by Oxidizing Water
Think back to the overall reaction for photosynthesis:

$$6\,CO_2 + 6\,H_2O + \text{light energy} \longrightarrow C_6H_{12}O_6 + 6\,O_2$$

In the presence of sunlight, carbon dioxide and water are used to produce carbohydrate and oxygen gas.

Now recall that experiments with heavy isotopes of oxygen showed that the oxygen atoms in O_2 come from water, not from carbon dioxide. For this to happen, water must be oxidized. The oxygen-generating reaction can be written as

$$2\,H_2O \longrightarrow 4\,H^+ + 4\,e^- + O_2$$

This reaction is referred to as "splitting" water. It supplies electrons for photosystem II and is catalyzed by enzymes that are physically integrated into the photosystem II complex. Since oxygen is very electronegative, this reaction is highly endergonic. What supplies the energy necessary to oxidize water?

As it turns out, the light energy harvested by photosystem II is responsible for splitting water. When excited electrons leave photosystem II and enter the ETC, the photosystem becomes so electronegative that enzymes can remove electrons from water, leaving protons and oxygen.

Among all life-forms, photosystem II is the only protein complex that can catalyze the splitting of water molecules. The photosystem II of cyanobacteria and eukaryotic chloroplasts perform **oxygenic** ("oxygen-producing") photosynthesis, because they generate oxygen as a by-product of the process. Other organisms that have only a single photosystem do not oxidize water, and thus do not produce O_2 gas. Instead, these organisms use different electron donors, such as H_2S in the purple sulfur bacteria, to perform **anoxygenic** ("no oxygen-producing") photosynthesis.

✔ If you understand photosystem II, you should be able to make an energy flowchart that includes the antenna complex, ATP synthase, pheophytin, light, the proton gradient, an ETC, and a reaction center and then add notes explaining where the enzyme complex that splits water fits in.

What happens next in green algae and land plants? The answer lies in photosystem I. Let's take a closer look.

How Does Photosystem I Work?

Recall that researchers dissected photosystem II by studying similar, but simpler, photosystems in the purple photosynthetic bacteria. To understand the structure and function of photosystem I, they turned to heliobacteria ("sun-bacteria").

Like the purple bacteria, heliobacteria have only one photosystem that uses the energy in sunlight to promote electrons to a high-energy state. But instead of being passed to an electron transport chain that pumps protons across a membrane, the high-energy electrons in heliobacteria are used to reduce NAD^+. When NAD^+ gains two electrons and a proton, NADH is produced.

In the cyanobacteria and eukaryotic chloroplasts, a similar set of light-capturing reactions reduces a phosphorylated version of NAD^+, symbolized $NADP^+$, to yield NADPH. Both NADH and NADPH function as electron carriers.

FIGURE 14.14 explains how photosystem I works in chloroplasts—put your finger on the "2 photons" arrows and trace the steps that follow.

1. Pigments in the antenna complex absorb photons and pass the energy to the photosystem I reaction center.

2. Electrons are excited in reaction center chlorophyll molecules.

3. The reaction center pigments are oxidized, and the high-energy electrons are passed through a series of carriers inside the photosystem, then to a molecule called **ferredoxin,** and then to the enzyme called $NADP^+$ reductase.

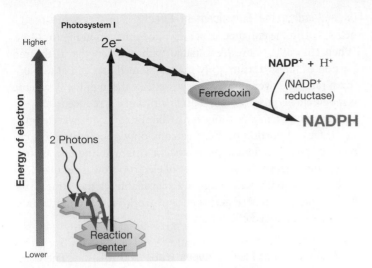

FIGURE 14.14 Photosystem I Produces NADPH. When excited electrons leave the chlorophyll molecule in the reaction center of photosystem I, they pass through a series of iron- and sulfur-containing proteins until they are accepted by ferredoxin. In an enzyme-catalyzed reaction, the reduced form of ferredoxin reacts with $NADP^+$ to produce NADPH.

4. $NADP^+$ reductase transfers two electrons and a proton to $NADP^+$. This reaction forms NADPH.

Photosystem I and $NADP^+$ reductase are anchored in the thylakoid membrane; ferredoxin is in the stroma, but it is closely associated with the thylakoid membrane.

To summarize: Electrons from photosystem I are used to produce NADPH, which is a reducing agent similar in function to the NADH and $FADH_2$ produced by the citric acid cycle. Electrons from photosystem II, in contrast, are used to produce a proton-motive force that drives the synthesis of ATP.

In combination, then, photosystems II and I produce chemical energy stored in ATP and NADPH. But there are still gaps in the flow of electrons through these two photosystems. Where do the electrons from photosystem II end up? How does the oxidized reaction center of photosystem I obtain electrons so NADPH will continue to be made?

The Z Scheme: Photosystems II and I Work Together

FIGURE 14.15 illustrates the **Z-scheme** model for how photosystems II and I interact. The name was inspired by the changes occurring in electron potential energy as plotted on a vertical axis, which takes on the shape of a Z that has fallen over.

To drive home how energy flows through the light-capturing reactions, trace the route of electrons through Figure 14.15 with your finger. Start on the lower left. The process starts when photons excite electrons in the chlorophyll molecules of photosystem II's antenna complex. When the energy in the excited electrons is transferred to the reaction center, a special pair of chlorophyll molecules, called P680, passes excited electrons to pheophytin. These are the same reaction center pigments described previously, and the name represents the wavelength of photons absorbed (680 nm).

When pheophytin is reduced, it transfers the high-energy electron to an electron transport chain. There the electron is gradually stepped down in potential energy through redox reactions among a series of quinones and cytochromes. Using the energy released by the redox reactions, plastoquinone (PQ) carries protons across the thylakoid membrane, from the stroma to the lumen. ATP synthase uses the resulting proton-motive force to phosphorylate ADP, creating ATP.

When electrons reach the end of the cytochrome complex, they are passed to a small diffusible protein called **plastocyanin**

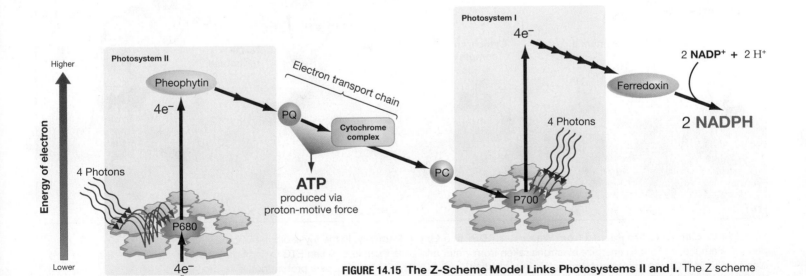

FIGURE 14.15 The Z-Scheme Model Links Photosystems II and I. The Z scheme proposes that electrons from water are first energized by photosystem II to generate ATP and then energized again by photosystem I to reduce $NADP^+$ to NADPH.

(symbolized as PC in Figure 14.15). The reduced plastocyanin diffuses through the lumen of the thylakoid, and donates the electron to an oxidized reaction center pigment in photosystem I.

Stop tracing for a moment, and consider the following:

- Plastocyanin is critical—it forms a physical link between photosystem II and photosystem I.

- A single plastocyanin molecule can shuttle over 1000 electrons per second between the cytochrome complex and photosystem I.

- The flow of electrons between photosystems, by means of plastocyanin, is important because it replaces electrons that are carried away from the pair of pigments in the photosystem I reaction center. This pair of specialized chlorophyll molecules is called P700 (absorbs 700-nm photons).

Now keep going. The electrons that flow from photosystem II to P700, via plastocyanin, are eventually transferred to the protein ferredoxin, which passes electrons to an enzyme that catalyzes the reduction of NADP$^+$ to NADPH.

Finally, direct your attention back to the lower-left portion of the figure. Note that the electrons that initially left photosystem II are replaced by electrons that are stripped away from water, producing oxygen gas as a by-product.

✔ If you understand the Z-scheme model, you should be able to describe (1) the role of plastocyanin in linking the two photosystems, and (2) the point where the electrons that flow through the system have their highest potential energy.

Understanding the Enhancement Effect The Z-scheme model helps explain the enhancement effect documented in Figure 14.11. When chloroplasts are illuminated with wavelengths in the red portion of the spectrum, only photosystem II can run at a maximum rate. The overall rate of electron flow through the Z scheme is moderate because photosystem I's efficiency is reduced.

Similarly, when chloroplasts are illuminated with wavelengths in the far-red portion of the spectrum, only photosystem I is capable of peak efficiency; photosystem II is working at a below-maximum rate, so the overall rate of electron flow is reduced.

But when both wavelengths are available at the same time, both photosystems are activated and work at a maximum rate, leading to enhanced efficiency.

Noncyclic Electron Flow between Water and NADP$^+$ The complete path that electrons follow from photosystem II to photosystem I and how it is oriented in the thylakoid membrane is shown in **FIGURE 14.16**. Note that electrons pass from water to NADP$^+$ through a chain of redox reactions in a linear fashion, referred to as **noncyclic electron flow.**

Compare the movement of electrons and protons in Figure 14.16 with what you have learned about electron transport chains in mitochondria (see Figure 13.15). In both these organelles, the energy released from redox reactions is used to build a proton gradient for ATP production. At the end of the chains, electrons are donated to terminal electron acceptors.

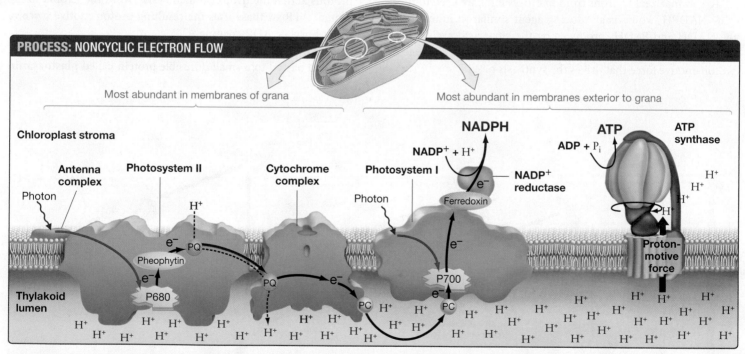

FIGURE 14.16 Electrons Are Passed from Water to NADP$^+$ in a Linear Pathway. In the thylakoid membrane, photosystem II uses light to energize electrons taken from water and pass them through an ETC including plastoquinone (PQ), the cytochrome complex, and plastocyanin (PC). The ETC produces a proton motive force that is used to make ATP. Photosystem I energizes electrons from PC and passes them on to ferredoxin to reduce NADP$^+$ to NADPH.

Chloroplasts and mitochondria differ, however, in how electron potential energy changes between the primary electron donor and the terminal electron acceptor. In the mitochondrial ETC, electron potential energy starts high and then steadily drops as the electrons are transferred to the terminal electron acceptor, which has the lowest potential energy. In chloroplasts, the reduced terminal electron acceptor (NADPH) has higher potential energy than the electron donor (H_2O) (see Figure 14.15).

Cyclic Electron Flow Recycles Electrons and Drives Photophosphorylation

Recent evidence indicates that an alternative electron path, called **cyclic electron flow,** also occurs in green algae and plants (**FIGURE 14.17**). In these organisms, ATP is produced via cyclic as well as noncyclic photophosphorylation.

During cyclic electron flow, photosystem I transfers electrons back to the electron transport chain associated with photosystem II, generating ATP through photophosphorylation instead of reducing $NADP^+$. This "extra" ATP is used for the chemical reactions that reduce carbon dioxide (CO_2) and produce sugars. Cyclic electron flow coexists with the noncyclic electron flow and produces additional ATP.

Where Are Photosystems II and I Located?

Although both photosystems reside in the thylakoid membrane, their distribution is far from random. Photosystem II and the cytochrome complex are much more abundant in the interior, stacked membranes of grana, while photosystem I and ATP synthase are much more common in the exterior, unstacked membranes.

This organization seems appropriate for ATP synthase. As shown in Figure 14.16, this enzyme complex is oriented with its bulky head toward the stroma, so avoiding the tightly stacked grana makes sense. In addition, ATP synthase and the $NADP^+$ reductase that is associated with photosystem I require substrates that are found in the stroma, such as ADP, P_i, and $NADP^+$. These substrates would not be as readily available if the enzymes were buried in the membrane folds of the grana.

The benefit of physically separating the two photosystems is the focus of intense research and debate. Unlike ATP synthase, the functions of photosystems I and II are tightly integrated, requiring electrons to be transported between them in noncyclic electron flow. Compared to other electron transport chains, the distance between where plastocyanin is reduced—the cytochrome complex—and where it is oxidized—the photosystem I reaction center—is huge. This separation between the photosystems is currently thought to be involved in regulating the switch between noncyclic and cyclic electron flow.

Oxygenic Photosynthesis and the Evolution of Earth

Although oxygen is a by-product of photosynthesis, the impact of producing this molecule on the environment of early Earth cannot be overstated. Photosynthesis produces the oxygen that is keeping you alive right now. Biologists rank the evolution of Earth's oxygen-rich atmosphere as one of the most important events in the history of life. Why?

According to the geologic record, oxygen levels in the atmosphere and oceans began to rise only about 2 billion years ago, as organisms that performed oxygenic photosynthesis increased in abundance. O_2 was, in fact, almost nonexistent on Earth before enzymes evolved that could catalyze the oxidation of water. Since ozone is formed from O_2 gas, this protective layer would have arisen in our atmosphere only after the evolution of oxygenic photosynthesis. Without the ozone layer, Earth's surface would have been bombarded continually by the searing intensity of ultraviolet radiation—making the evolution of life on land nearly impossible.

As oxygen became more abundant, bacterial cells that evolved the ability to use it as an electron acceptor via cellular respiration began to dominate. O_2 is so electronegative that it creates a huge potential energy drop for the electron transport chains involved in cellular respiration. As a result, organisms that use O_2 as an electron acceptor in cellular respiration can produce much more ATP than can organisms that use other electron acceptors (see Chapter 13). In addition, this accumulation of oxygen was a disaster for anaerobic organisms because O_2 is such a powerful oxidant it is toxic to them.

Determining exactly how photosystem II splits water and generates oxygen may be the greatest challenge currently facing researchers interested in photosynthesis. This issue has important practical applications: If human chemists could replicate the reaction, it might be possible to produce huge volumes of O_2 and hydrogen gas (H_2) from water. The resulting H_2 could provide a clean, inexpensive fuel for vehicles.

Despite the importance of oxygen in the evolution and maintenance of life, in terms of photosynthesis, it is simply waste. The useful products of the light-capturing reactions are ATP and NADPH, which are required to reduce carbon dioxide to sugar. Your life, and the life of most organisms, also depends on this process. How does it happen?

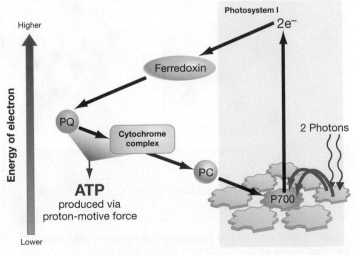

FIGURE 14.17 Cyclic Electron Flow Leads to ATP Production. Cyclic electron flow is an alternative to the Z scheme. Instead of being donated to $NADP^+$, electrons are returned to plastoquinone (PQ) and cycle between photosystem I and the ETC, resulting in the production of additional ATP via photophosphorylation.

If you understand that . . .

- Photosystem II contributes high-energy electrons to an electron transport chain that pumps protons, creating a proton-motive force that drives ATP synthase.
- Photosystem I uses high-energy electrons to make NADPH and can produce additional ATP by building a proton-motive force via cyclic electron flow.

✔ **You should be able to . . .**

Compare and contrast the flow of electrons in mitochondria and chloroplasts. What are the primary electron donors and terminal electron acceptors, and how do they differ in terms of energy?

Answers are available in Appendix A.

14.4 How Is Carbon Dioxide Reduced to Produce Sugars?

The reactions analyzed in Section 14.3 are triggered by light. This is logical, because their entire function is focused on transforming electromagnetic energy in the form of sunlight into chemical energy in the phosphate bonds of ATP and the electrons of NADPH. The reactions that produce sugar from carbon dioxide, in contrast, are not triggered directly by light. Instead, they depend on the ATP and NADPH produced by the light-capturing reactions of photosynthesis.

The Calvin Cycle Fixes Carbon

Carbon fixation is the addition of carbon dioxide to an organic compound. The word fix is appropriate because the process converts or fixes CO_2 gas to a biologically useful form. Once carbon atoms are fixed, they can be used as sources of energy and as building blocks to construct the molecules found in cells.

Carbon fixation is a redox reaction—the carbon atom in CO_2 is reduced. Research on how this happens in chloroplasts gained momentum just after World War II, when radioactive isotopes of carbon became available for research purposes.

Melvin Calvin's group made great strides early in this effort by tracking the incorporation of $^{14}CO_2$ into molecules during photosynthesis (**FIGURE 14.18**). After injecting $^{14}CO_2$ into a culture of algae that were undergoing photosynthesis, they stopped the reaction after different periods of time by killing the cells in hot alcohol. This treatment immediately denatured the enzymes involved in the reactions, effectively halting any further change in the radiolabeled intermediates.

The molecules labeled with the ^{14}C in this extract were separated by chromatography and detected using X-ray film. If radioactively labeled molecules were present in the chromatograph,

---

RESEARCH

QUESTION: What intermediates are produced as carbon dioxide is reduced to sugar?

HYPOTHESIS: No specific hypothesis.

EXPERIMENTAL SETUP:

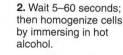

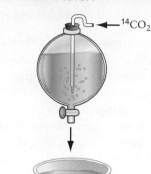

1. Add $^{14}CO_2$ to actively photosynthesizing algae.

2. Wait 5–60 seconds; then homogenize cells by immersing in hot alcohol.

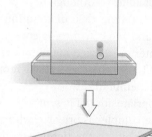

3. Separate molecules via chromatography.

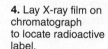

4. Lay X-ray film on chromatograph to locate radioactive label.

PREDICTION: No specific prediction.

RESULTS:

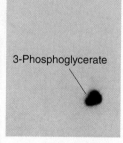

3-Phosphoglycerate

Compounds produced after 5 seconds

Compounds produced after 60 seconds

CONCLUSION: 3-Phosphoglycerate is the first intermediate product. Other intermediates appear later.

FIGURE 14.18 Experiments Revealed the Reaction Pathway Leading to Reduction of CO_2.

SOURCE: Benson, A. A., J. A. Bassham, M. Calvin, et al. 1950. The path of carbon in photosynthesis. V. Paper chromatography and radioautography of the products. *Journal of the American Chemistry Society* 72: 1710–1718.

✔ **QUESTION** Why wasn't this experiment based on a specific hypothesis and set of predictions?

the energy they emitted would expose the film and create a dark spot. The labeled compounds could then be isolated and identified.

By varying the amount of time the algae were exposed to labeled $^{14}CO_2$, Calvin and co-workers pieced together the sequence in which various intermediates formed. For example, when the team analyzed cells almost immediately after adding the $^{14}CO_2$, they found that the ^{14}C was predominantly in a three-carbon compound called 3-phosphoglycerate (3PGA). This result suggested that 3PGA was the initial product of carbon reduction. Stated another way, it appeared that carbon dioxide reacted with some unknown molecule to produce 3PGA.

This was an intriguing result, because 3-phosphoglycerate is also one of the 10 intermediates in glycolysis. The Calvin cycle manufactures carbohydrate; glycolysis breaks it down. Because the two processes are related in this way, it was logical that at least some intermediates in glycolysis and the Calvin cycle are the same.

RuBP Is the Initial Reactant with CO_2 Which compound reacts with CO_2 to produce 3-phosphoglycerate? This was the key, initial step. Calvin's group searched in vain for a two-carbon compound that might serve as the initial carbon dioxide acceptor and yield 3PGA.

Then, while Calvin was running errands one day, it occurred to him that the molecule reacting with carbon dioxide might contain five carbons, not two. Adding CO_2 to a five-carbon molecule would produce a six-carbon compound, which could then split in half to form 2 three-carbon molecules.

Experiments to test this hypothesis confirmed that the five-carbon compound **ribulose bisphosphate (RuBP)** is the initial reactant.

The Calvin Cycle Is a Three-Step Process The complete Calvin cycle, as it came to be called, has three phases (**FIGURE 14.19**):

1. *Fixation phase* The Calvin cycle begins when CO_2 reacts with RuBP. This phase fixes carbon and produces two molecules of 3PGA.

2. *Reduction phase* The 3PGA is phosphorylated by ATP and then reduced by electrons from NADPH. The product is the phosphorylated three-carbon sugar **glyceraldehyde-3-phosphate (G3P)**. Some of the G3P that is synthesized is drawn off to manufacture glucose and fructose.

3. *Regeneration phase* The rest of the G3P keeps the cycle going by serving as the substrate for the third phase in the cycle: reactions that use additional ATP in the regeneration of RuBP.

All three phases take place in the stroma of chloroplasts. One turn of the Calvin cycle fixes one molecule of CO_2. Three turns of the cycle fix three molecules of CO_2, yielding one molecule of G3P and fully regenerated RuBP (Figure 14.19).

The discovery of the Calvin cycle clarified how the ATP and NADPH produced by light-capturing reactions allow cells to reduce CO_2 gas to carbohydrate $(CH_2O)_n$. Because sugars store a great deal of potential energy, producing them takes a great deal of chemical energy. In the Calvin cycle, each mole of CO_2 requires the energy from 3 moles of ATP and 2 moles of

(a) The Calvin cycle has three phases.

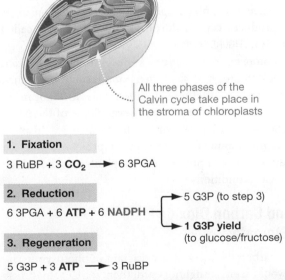

All three phases of the Calvin cycle take place in the stroma of chloroplasts

1. Fixation

3 RuBP + 3 CO_2 ⟶ 6 3PGA

2. Reduction

6 3PGA + 6 **ATP** + 6 **NADPH** ⟶ 5 G3P (to step 3)
⟶ 1 G3P yield (to glucose/fructose)

3. Regeneration

5 G3P + 3 **ATP** ⟶ 3 RuBP

(b) The reaction occurs in a cycle.

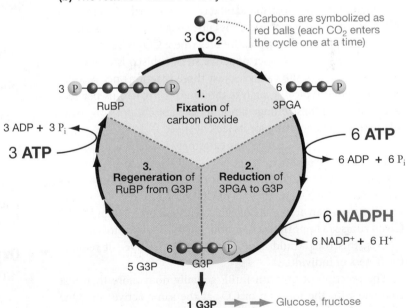

FIGURE 14.19 Carbon Dioxide Is Reduced in the Calvin Cycle. The number of reactants and products resulting from three turns of the cycle are shown. Of the six G3Ps that are generated during the reduction phase, one is used in the synthesis of glucose or fructose and the other five are used to regenerate RuBP. The 3 RuBPs that are regenerated participate in fixation reactions for additional turns of the cycle.

NADPH to fix it and reduce it to sugar. ✔ **QUANTITATIVE** If you understand the Calvin cycle, you should be able to provide the *minimum number* of RuBP, ATP, and NADPH molecules that would be required to run through six complete cycles. Explain why you would not need six RuBP molecules to fix and reduce six CO_2.

The conversion of CO_2 gas into carbohydrate is, without doubt, worthy of this energy investment. Plants use sugars to fuel cellular respiration and build leaves and other structures. Millions of non-photosynthetic organisms—from fungi to mammals—also depend on this reaction to provide the sugars they need for cellular respiration.

Ecologically, the addition of CO_2 to RuBP may be the most important chemical reaction on Earth. The enzyme that catalyzes it is fundamental to life. How does this protein work?

The Discovery of Rubisco

Most reactions involved in reducing CO_2 also occur during glycolysis or other metabolic pathways. The initial CO_2 fixation phase of the Calvin cycle, however, is one of only two reactions that are entirely unique to the Calvin cycle.

To find the enzyme that fixes CO_2 to RuBP, Arthur Weissbach and colleagues ground up spinach leaves, purified a large series of proteins from the resulting cell extracts, and tested each protein to see if it could catalyze this step. Eventually they isolated the catalyst, which happens to be the most abundant enzyme in leaf tissue. The researchers' data suggested that it constituted almost 50 percent of the total protein in spinach leaves.

The CO_2-fixing enzyme, ribulose-1,5-bisphosphate carboxylase/oxygenase (commonly referred to as **rubisco**), is found in all photosynthetic organisms that use the Calvin cycle to fix carbon and is thought to be the most abundant enzyme on Earth. As shown in **FIGURE 14.20a**, the rubisco enzyme is cube-shaped and consists of 16 polypeptides that form eight active sites where CO_2 is fixed.

Despite its large number of active sites, rubisco is a slow enzyme. Each active site catalyzes just three reactions per second; other enzymes typically catalyze thousands of reactions per second. Plants synthesize huge amounts of rubisco, possibly as an adaptation compensating for its lack of speed.

Besides being slow, rubisco is extremely inefficient because it will catalyze the addition of either O_2 or CO_2 to RuBP. This is a key point: Oxygen and carbon dioxide compete at the enzyme's active sites, which slows the rate of CO_2 reduction.

Why would an active site of rubisco accept both O_2 and CO_2? Given rubisco's importance in producing food for photosynthetic species, this trait would appear to be **maladaptive**—it reduces the fitness of individuals.

The reaction of O_2 with RuBP actually does more than just compete with the reaction of CO_2 at the same active site. One of the molecules produced from the addition of oxygen to RuBP is processed in reactions that consume ATP and release CO_2 in order to regenerate 3PGA. Part of this pathway occurs in chloroplasts, and part occurs in peroxisomes and mitochondria. The

(a) Rubisco has 16 subunits and a total of 8 active sites.

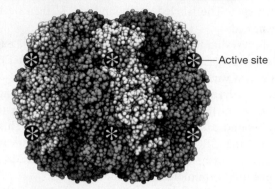

Active site

(b) Rubisco's active sites can interact with CO_2 or O_2.

Reaction with carbon dioxide during photosynthesis:

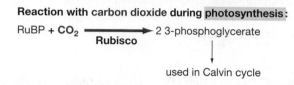

RuBP + **CO_2** $\xrightarrow{\text{Rubisco}}$ 2 3-phosphoglycerate

used in Calvin cycle

Reaction with oxygen during photorespiration:

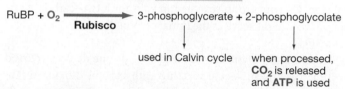

RuBP + **O_2** $\xrightarrow{\text{Rubisco}}$ 3-phosphoglycerate + 2-phosphoglycolate

used in Calvin cycle

when processed, **CO_2** is released and **ATP** is used

FIGURE 14.20 Rubisco Is a Large Enzyme Complex That Can React with CO_2 or O_2. (a) The cube shape of rubisco consists of multiple polypeptides that form eight catalytic active sites. **(b)** In addition to fixing CO_2 in photosynthesis, rubisco catalyzes a competing reaction with O_2 with a very different outcome.

reaction sequence resembles respiration, because it consumes oxygen and produces carbon dioxide. As a result, it is called **photorespiration** (**FIGURE 14.20b**).

Because photorespiration consumes energy and releases fixed CO_2, it "undoes" photosynthesis. When photorespiration occurs, the overall rate of photosynthesis declines. This does not mean that there is no benefit to the plant, however. Some of the products from photorespiration are known to be involved in plant signaling and development. In addition, a protective role for photorespiration has been proposed when plants are under high light and low CO_2 conditions.

Oxygen and Carbon Dioxide Pass through Stomata

Atmospheric carbon dioxide is a key reactant in photosynthesizing cells. It would seem straightforward, then, for CO_2 to diffuse directly into plants along a concentration gradient. But the situation is not this simple, because plants are covered with a waxy coating called a cuticle. This lipid layer prevents water from evaporating out of tissues, but it also prevents the transport of gases like CO_2 and O_2.

How does CO_2 get into photosynthesizing tissues? The surface of a leaf is dotted with openings bordered by two distinctively shaped cells called **guard cells** (**FIGURE 14.21a**). The opening between these paired cells is called a pore, and the entire structure is a **stoma** (plural: **stomata**).

An open stoma allows CO_2 from the atmosphere to diffuse into air-filled spaces inside the leaf and excess O_2 to diffuse out (**FIGURE 14.21b**). Eventually the CO_2 diffuses along a concentration gradient into the chloroplasts of photosynthesizing cells. A strong concentration gradient favoring entry of CO_2 is maintained by the Calvin cycle, which constantly uses up the CO_2 in chloroplasts.

Stomata are normally open during the day, when photosynthesis is occurring, and closed at night. But if the daytime is extremely hot and dry, leaf cells may lose a great deal of water to evaporation through their stomata. When this occurs, they must either close the openings and halt photosynthesis or risk death from dehydration.

(a) Leaf surfaces contain stomata.

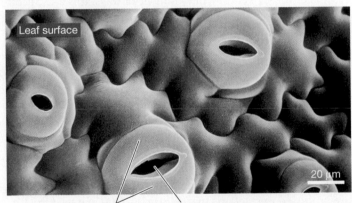

Guard cells + Pore = **Stoma**

(b) Carbon dioxide diffuses into leaves through stomata.

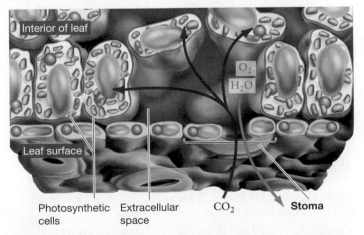

Photosynthetic cells   Extracellular space CO_2 **Stoma**

FIGURE 14.21 Leaf Cells Obtain Carbon Dioxide through Stomata.

When conditions are hot and dry, then, stomata must close and CO_2 and O_2 transport stops—meaning that photosynthesis slows and photorespiration increases. How do plants that live in hot, dry environments prevent dehydration while keeping CO_2 supplies high enough to avoid photorespiration?

Mechanisms for Increasing CO_2 Concentration

The oxygenation reaction that triggers photorespiration is favored when oxygen concentrations are high and CO_2 concentrations are low. But even with the stomata open, the atmosphere is 21 percent oxygen and only 0.03 percent carbon dioxide. How can photosynthesizing cells raise CO_2 concentrations to make photosynthesis more efficient? An answer emerged in a surprising experimental result.

The C_4 Pathway   After the Calvin cycle had been worked out in algae, researchers in a variety of labs used the same radioactive carbon dioxide tracking approach to investigate how carbon fixation occurs in other species. Hugo Kortschak and colleagues and Y. S. Karpilov and associates exposed leaves of sugarcane and maize (corn) to $^{14}CO_2$ and sunlight; then they isolated and identified the intermediates.

Both research teams expected to find the first of the radioactive carbon atoms in 3-phosphoglycerate—the normal product of carbon fixation by rubisco. Instead, they found that in their species, the radioactive carbon atom ended up in four-carbon compounds such as malate and aspartate.

Instead of creating a three-carbon molecule as in the Calvin cycle, it appeared that these species were able to fix CO_2 to produce four-carbon molecules. This newly identified set of reactions became known as the C_4 **pathway** to distinguish it from Calvin's CO_2 fixation via what is now termed the C_3 **pathway** (**FIGURE 14.22**).

Researchers who followed up on the initial reports found that the C_4 pathway does not replace the Calvin cycle, but serves as an additional fixation step. C_4 plants can actually fix carbon dioxide using both pathways—to a three-carbon compound by an enzyme called **PEP carboxylase** (C_4) and to RuBP by rubisco (C_3). They also showed that the two pathways are found in distinct cell types within the same leaf. PEP carboxylase is common in **mesophyll cells** near the surface of leaves, while rubisco is found in **bundle-sheath cells** that surround the vascular tissue in the

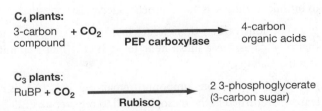

FIGURE 14.22 Initial Carbon Fixation in C_4 Plants Is Different from That in C_3 Plants.

(a) C$_4$ plant

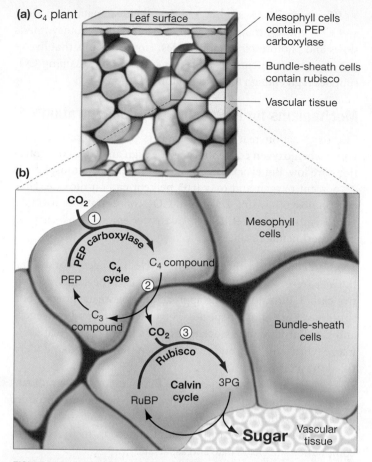

Leaf surface

Mesophyll cells contain PEP carboxylase

Bundle-sheath cells contain rubisco

Vascular tissue

(b)

CO$_2$

① PEP carboxylase

PEP · C$_4$ cycle · C$_4$ compound

②

C$_3$ compound

CO$_2$ ③

Rubisco

Mesophyll cells

Bundle-sheath cells

Calvin cycle · 3PG

RuBP

Sugar Vascular tissue

FIGURE 14.23 In C$_4$ Plants, Carbon Fixation and the Calvin Cycle Occur in Different Cell Types. (a) The carbon-fixing enzyme PEP carboxylase is located in mesophyll cells, while rubisco is in bundle-sheath cells. **(b)** CO$_2$ is fixed to the three-carbon compound PEP by PEP carboxylase, forming a four-carbon organic acid. A CO$_2$ molecule from the four-carbon sugar then feeds the Calvin cycle.

interior of the leaf (**FIGURE 14.23a**). Vascular tissue conducts water and nutrients in plants.

Based on the observations about C$_4$ plants, Hal Hatch and Roger Slack proposed a four-step model to explain how CO$_2$ that is fixed to a four-carbon sugar feeds the Calvin cycle (**FIGURE 14.23b**):

Step 1 PEP carboxylase fixes CO$_2$ to a three-carbon molecule (phosphoenolpyruvate, or PEP) in mesophyll cells.

Step 2 The four-carbon organic acids that result are transported to bundle-sheath cells via channels called plasmodesmata.

Step 3 The four-carbon organic acids release a CO$_2$ molecule that rubisco uses as a substrate to form 3PGA. This step initiates the Calvin cycle.

Step 4 The three-carbon compound remaining after CO$_2$ is released is returned to the mesophyll cell to regenerate PEP.

In effect, then, the C$_4$ pathway acts as a CO$_2$ concentrator. The reactions that take place in mesophyll cells require energy in the

form of ATP, but they increase CO$_2$ concentrations in cells where rubisco is active. Because it increases the ratio of carbon dioxide to oxygen in photosynthesizing cells, less O$_2$ binds to rubisco's active sites. As a result, the C$_4$ pathway improves the efficiency of the Calvin cycle.

The C$_4$ pathway is an adaptation that keeps CO$_2$ concentrations in leaves high, but it comes at a cost. For each glucose molecule generated via photosynthesis, C$_4$ plants expend 30 ATP molecules compared to the 18 ATP molecules required by C$_3$ plants. This energy expenditure, however, is justified by the increased efficiency of photosynthesis in conditions where stomata are mostly closed to prevent dehydration. The affinity for CO$_2$ by PEP carboxylase is also much higher than that of rubisco, which means that stomata can be open for shorter periods in C$_4$ plants.

This strategy is not the only mechanism that plants use to continue growth in hot, dry climates, however. Some environments are so arid that even C$_4$ plants are unable to avoid dehydration. Nevertheless, certain plants use the C$_4$ pathway in a unique way that allows them to thrive in these deserts. How do they do it?

CAM Plants Researchers studying a group of flowering plants called the Crassulaceae discovered a second mechanism for limiting the effects of dehydration and photorespiration. This photosynthetic pathway, **crassulacean acid metabolism**, or **CAM**, resembles the C$_4$ pathway in a number of ways. It is a CO$_2$ concentrator that acts as an additional, preparatory step to the Calvin cycle. It also generates an organic acid with four carbons in its first CO$_2$ fixation step. But unlike the C$_4$ pathway, CAM occurs at a different time than the Calvin cycle does—not in a different place.

CAM occurs in cacti and other species that routinely keep their stomata closed on hot, dry days. At night, when conditions are cooler and more humid, CAM plants open their stomata and take in huge quantities of CO$_2$. The CO$_2$ is temporarily fixed to organic acids and stored in the central vacuoles of photosynthetic cells. During the day, when stomata are closed, these acids are processed in reactions that release the CO$_2$ and feed the Calvin cycle (**FIGURE 14.24**).

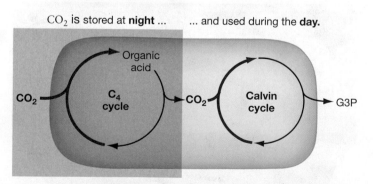

CO$_2$ is stored at **night** ... ... and used during the **day**.

CO$_2$ → C$_4$ cycle → Organic acid → CO$_2$ → Calvin cycle → G3P

FIGURE 14.24 In CAM Plants, Carbon Fixation Occurs at Night and the Calvin Cycle Occurs during the Day.

✔ **QUESTION** At what part of the day would there be the highest concentration of four-carbon acids in the vacuoles of CAM plants?

The C_4 and CAM pathways function as CO_2 pumps. They minimize photorespiration when stomata are closed and CO_2 cannot diffuse in directly from the atmosphere. Both are found in species that live in hot, dry environments.

But while C_4 plants stockpile CO_2 by fixing and storing organic acids in cells *where* rubisco is not active, CAM plants store CO_2 *when* rubisco is inactive. In C_4 plants, the reactions catalyzed by PEP carboxylase and rubisco are separated in space; in CAM plants, the reactions are separated in time.

How Is Photosynthesis Regulated?

Like cellular respiration, photosynthesis is regulated. Although the mechanisms responsible for turning photosynthesis on or off are still under investigation, several patterns have emerged:

- The presence of light triggers the production of proteins required for photosynthesis.

- When sugar supplies are high, the production of proteins required for photosynthesis is inhibited, but the production of proteins required to process and store sugars is stimulated.

- Rubisco is activated by regulatory molecules that are produced when light is available, but inhibited in conditions of low CO_2 availability—when photorespiration is favored.

The central message here is that the rate of photosynthesis is finely tuned to use resources efficiently in response to changes in environmental conditions.

What Happens to the Sugar That Is Produced by Photosynthesis?

The products of the Calvin cycle enter one of several reaction pathways. The most important of these reaction sequences produces the monosaccharides glucose and fructose from G3P, a process called **gluconeogenesis.** This glucose is often combined with fructose to form the disaccharide ("two-sugar") **sucrose.**

When photosynthesis is taking place slowly, almost all the glucose that is produced is used to make sucrose. Sucrose is water soluble and readily transported to other parts of the plant. If sucrose is delivered to rapidly growing parts of the plant, it is broken down to fuel cellular respiration and growth.

An alternative pathway occurs when photosynthesis is proceeding rapidly and sucrose is abundant. Under these conditions, the glucose molecules are polymerized to form **starch** in the leaves and in storage cells in the roots. Starch production occurs inside the chloroplast; sucrose synthesis takes place in the cytosol.

In photosynthesizing cells, starch acts as a temporary sugar-storage product. At night, the starch that is stored in leaf cells is broken down and used to manufacture sucrose molecules. The sucrose is then broken down via cellular respiration or transported to other parts of the plant. In this way, chloroplasts provide sugars for cells throughout the plant by day and by night.

If a mouse eats the starch that is stored in the leaves or roots of a plant, however, the chemical energy in the reduced carbons of starch fuels the mouse's growth and reproduction. If an owl eats the mouse, the chemical energy in the mouse's tissues fuels the predator's growth and reproduction. (You can see the Big Picture of how energy is processed via photosynthesis and cellular respiration on pages 284–285.)

In this way, virtually all cell activity can be traced back to the sun's energy that was originally captured by photosynthesis. Photosynthesis is the staff of life.

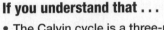

check your understanding

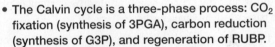

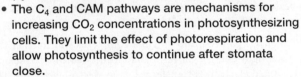

If you understand that . . .

- The Calvin cycle is a three-phase process: CO_2 fixation (synthesis of 3PGA), carbon reduction (synthesis of G3P), and regeneration of RUBP.
- The C_4 and CAM pathways are mechanisms for increasing CO_2 concentrations in photosynthesizing cells. They limit the effect of photorespiration and allow photosynthesis to continue after stomata close.
- In photosynthesizing cells, G3P is used to make sucrose or stored as starch. Sucrose is transported to all plant cells and used to drive cellular respiration.

✔ You should be able to . . .

1. Describe how CO_2 is delivered to rubisco (a) via organic acids in mesophyll cells, (b) via organic acids stored in vacuoles, and (c) directly.

2. Predict the relative concentration of starch in leaves at the start of the day versus the end of the day.

Answers are available in Appendix A.

If you understand . . .

14.1 Photosynthesis Harnesses Sunlight to Make Carbohydrate

- The light-capturing reactions occur in internal membranes of the chloroplast that are organized into structures called thylakoids in stacks known as grana.

- The Calvin cycle takes place in a fluid portion of the chloroplast called the stroma.

- The CO_2-reduction reactions of photosynthesis depend on the products of the light-capturing reactions.

✔ You should be able to explain why it is not entirely accurate to adopt the common phrase "light-independent reactions" when referring to the Calvin cycle.

14.2 How Do Pigments Capture Light Energy?

- Pigment molecules capture light energy by exciting electrons after a photon is absorbed. Each pigment absorbs particular photons on the basis of their wavelengths.

- After a pigment molecule absorbs a photon, the energy may be released as fluorescence, resonance energy that excites a neighboring pigment, or the reduction of an electron acceptor.

- Pigments organized into antenna complexes will transfer the absorbed light energy via resonance to the reaction center, where an excited electron is transferred to an electron acceptor. The reduction of this electron acceptor completes the transformation of light energy into chemical energy.

✔ You should be able to explain why extracted chlorophyll molecules produce more fluorescence compared to the same number of chlorophyll molecules that remain in chloroplasts.

14.3 The Discovery of Photosystems I and II

- In photosystem II, high-energy electrons are accepted by pheophytin and passed along an electron transport chain, releasing energy that moves protons across the thylakoid membrane. The resulting proton-motive force drives the synthesis of ATP by ATP synthase. Photosystem II takes electrons from water, releasing oxygen and protons.

- In photosystem I, high-energy electrons are passed to ferredoxin. In an enzyme-catalyzed reaction, the reduced form of ferredoxin passes electrons to $NADP^+$, forming NADPH.

- The Z scheme connects photosystems II and I. Plastocyanin carries electrons from the end of photosystem II's ETC to photosystem I. They are promoted to a high-energy state in photosystem I's reaction center, and subsequently used to reduce $NADP^+$.

- Electrons from photosystem I may occasionally be passed back to photosystem II's ETC instead of being used to reduce $NADP^+$. A cyclic flow of electrons between the two photosystems boosts ATP supplies.

✔ You should be able to explain why measuring the rate of oxygen production in chloroplasts is appropriate for estimating the rate of photosynthesis.

14.4 How Is Carbon Dioxide Reduced to Produce Sugars?

- The Calvin cycle starts when CO_2 is attached to a five-carbon compound called ribulose bisphosphate (RuBP) in a reaction catalyzed by the enzyme rubisco.

- The six-carbon compound that results immediately splits in half to form two molecules of 3-phosphoglycerate (3PGA), which is then phosphorylated by ATP and reduced by NADPH to produce a sugar called glyceraldehyde-3-phosphate (G3P).

- Some G3P is used to synthesize glucose and fructose, which combine to form sucrose; the rest are phosphorylated by more ATP in a series of reactions that regenerate RuBP so the cycle can continue.

- Rubisco catalyzes the addition of oxygen as well as carbon dioxide to RuBP. The reaction with oxygen leads to a loss of fixed CO_2 and ATP and is called photorespiration.

- C_4 plants and CAM plants fix CO_2 to organic acids, before it is transferred to rubisco. As a result, they can increase CO_2 levels in their tissues, reducing the effect of photorespiration and allowing photosynthesis to continue when stomata close.

✔ QUANTITATIVE You should be able to connect the light-capturing reactions and Calvin cycle by estimating the number of photons required to produce one glucose molecule from CO_2. How would photorespiration affect the number of photons required per glucose?

(MB) MasteringBiology

1. **MasteringBiology Assignments**

   Tutorials and Activities Calvin Cycle; Chemiosmosis; Energy Flow in Plants; Experimental Inquiry: Which Wavelengths of Light Drive Photosynthesis?; Light Energy and Pigments; Light Reactions; Overview of Photosynthesis; Photosynthesis: Inputs, Outputs, and Chloroplast Structure; Photosynthesis: The Light Reactions; Photosynthesis in Dry Climates; Sites of Photosynthesis

   Questions Reading Quizzes, Blue-Thread Questions, Test Bank

2. **eText** Read your book online, search, take notes, highlight text, and more.

3. **The Study Area** Practice Test, Cumulative Test, BioFlix® 3-D Animations, Videos, Activities, Audio Glossary, Word Study Tools, Art

You should be able to . . .

1. In antenna complexes, how is energy transferred among the pigment molecules?
   a. photophosphorylation
   b. redox reactions
   c. fluorescence
   d. resonance

2. Why is chlorophyll green?
   a. It absorbs all wavelengths in the visible spectrum.
   b. It absorbs wavelengths only in the red portions of the spectrum (680 nm, 700 nm).
   c. It absorbs wavelengths in only the blue and red parts of the visible spectrum.
   d. It absorbs wavelengths only in the blue part of the visible spectrum.

3. What do the light-capturing reactions of photosynthesis produce?
   a. G3P
   b. RuBP
   c. ATP and NADPH
   d. sucrose or starch

4. Why do the absorption spectrum for chlorophyll and the action spectrum for photosynthesis coincide?
   a. Photosystems I and II are activated by different wavelengths of light.
   b. Wavelengths of light that are absorbed by chlorophyll trigger the light-capturing reactions.
   c. Energy from wavelengths absorbed by carotenoids is passed on to chlorophyll.
   d. The rate of photosynthesis depends on the amount of light received.

5. At what point in the light-capturing reactions is the electromagnetic energy of light converted into chemical energy? Where does this occur?

6. In noncyclic electron flow, photosystems I and II function as an integrated unit. What connects the two photosystems?

7. Explain how electrons from water can be used to produce both ATP and NADPH.

8. In addition to their protective function, carotenoids absorb certain wavelengths of light and pass the energy to other pigments via resonance. Based on this function, where would you expect carotenoids to be located in the chloroplast?
   a. the reaction centers of photosystems I and II
   b. the inner membrane of chloroplasts
   c. the antenna complex
   d. the stroma

9. Describe the three phases of the Calvin cycle and how the products of the light-capturing reactions participate in this process.

10. What conditions favor photorespiration? What are its consequences for the plant?

11. Compare and contrast how C_4 plants and CAM plants separate the acquisition of CO_2 from the production of sugar in the Calvin cycle.

12. Why do plants need both chloroplasts and mitochondria? How do their roles differ in the cell?

13. Predict how the following conditions would affect the production of O_2, ATP, and NADPH and state whether noncyclic or cyclic electron flow would occur in each: (1) Only blue photons hit a chloroplast; (2) blue and red photons hit a chloroplast, but no $NADP^+$ is available; (3) blue and red photons hit a chloroplast, but a proton channel has been introduced into the thylakoid membrane, so it is fully permeable to protons.

14. Some biologists claim that photorespiration is an evolutionary "holdover," because rubisco evolved over a billion years ago when O_2 levels were extremely low and CO_2 concentrations relatively high. Do you agree with this hypothesis? Why or why not?

15. An investigator exposes chloroplasts to 700-nm photons and observes low O_2 production, but high ATP production. Which of the following best explains this observation?

   a. The electrons from water are directly transferred to $NADP^+$, which is used to generate ATP.
   b. Photosystem II is not splitting water, and the ATP is being produced by cycling electrons via photosystem I.
   c. The O_2 is being converted to water as a terminal electron acceptor in the production of ATP.
   d. Electron transport has stopped and ATP is being produced by the Calvin cycle.

16. Consider plants that occupy the top, middle, or ground layer of a forest, and algae that live near the surface of the ocean or in deeper water. Would you expect the same photosynthetic pigments to be found in species that live in these different habitats? Why or why not? How would you test your hypothesis?

The Big Picture

It takes energy to stay alive. Use this concept map to study how the information on energy and energetics presented in this book fits together.

As you read the map, remember that chemical energy is potential energy. Potential energy is based on the position of matter in space, and chemical energy is all about the position of electrons in covalent bonds. When hydrogen gas reacts explosively with oxygen, all that's happening is that electrons are moving from high-energy positions to lower-energy positions.

In essence, organisms transform energy from the Sun into chemical energy in the C–C and C–H bonds of glucose, and then into chemical energy in the P–P bonds of ATP.

The potential energy in ATP allows cells to do work: pump ions, synthesize molecules, move cargo, and send and receive signals.

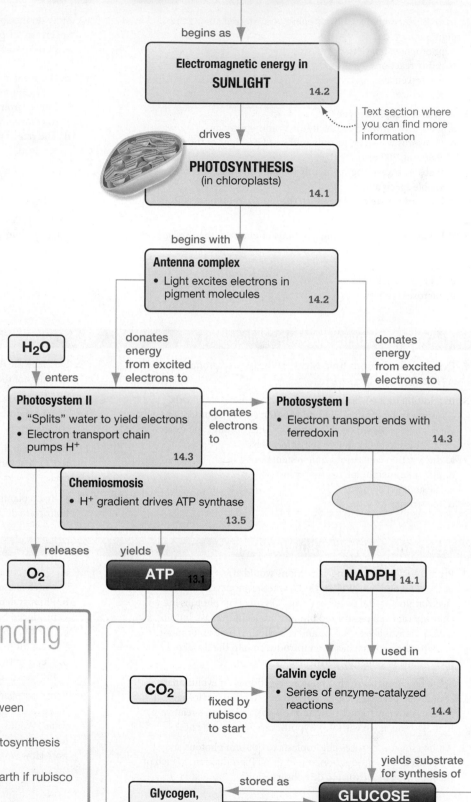

ENERGY FOR LIFE

begins as

Electromagnetic energy in SUNLIGHT 14.2

Text section where you can find more information

drives

PHOTOSYNTHESIS (in chloroplasts) 14.1

begins with

Antenna complex
- Light excites electrons in pigment molecules 14.2

H_2O

enters

donates energy from excited electrons to

donates energy from excited electrons to

Photosystem II
- "Splits" water to yield electrons
- Electron transport chain pumps H^+ 14.3

donates electrons to

Photosystem I
- Electron transport ends with ferredoxin 14.3

Chemiosmosis
- H^+ gradient drives ATP synthase 13.5

releases

yields

O_2

ATP 13.1

NADPH 14.1

used in

CO_2

fixed by rubisco to start

Calvin cycle
- Series of enzyme-catalyzed reactions 14.4

yields substrate for synthesis of

Glycogen, starch

stored as

broken down to yield

GLUCOSE

check your understanding

C
Y
U

If you understand the big picture . . .
✔ You should be able to . . .

1. Explain how H_2O and O_2 are cycled between photosynthesis and cellular respiration.

2. Explain how CO_2 is cycled between photosynthesis and cellular respiration.

3. Describe what might happen to life on Earth if rubisco were suddenly unable to fix CO_2.

4. Fill in the blue ovals with appropriate linking verbs or phrases.

Answers are available in Appendix A.

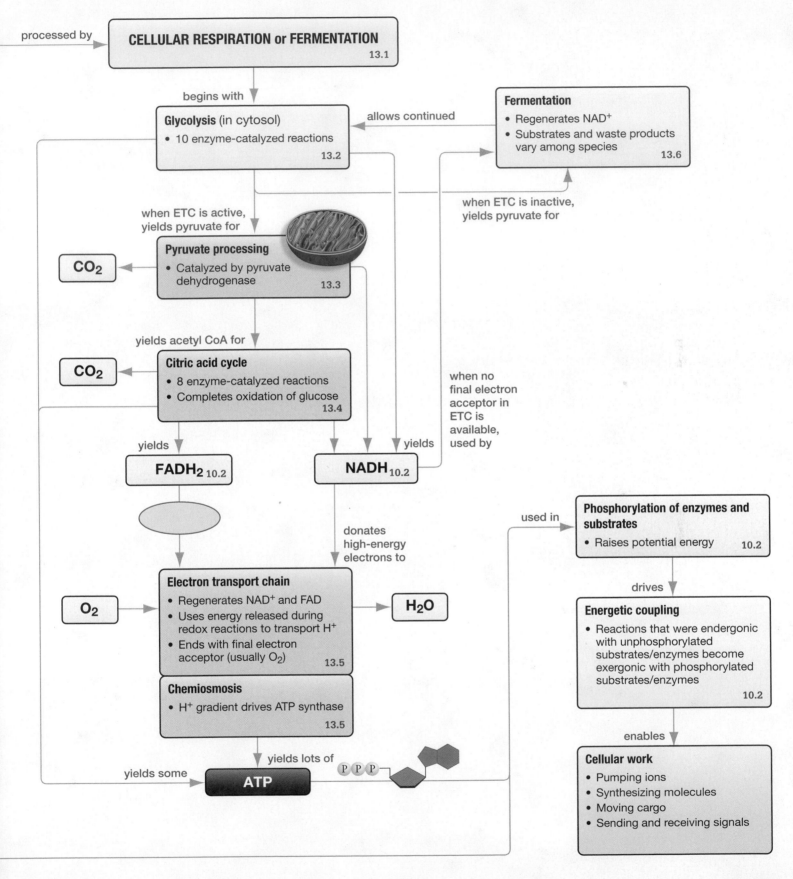

CELLULAR RESPIRATION or FERMENTATION
13.1

processed by →

begins with

Glycolysis (in cytosol)
• 10 enzyme-catalyzed reactions
13.2

← allows continued

Fermentation
• Regenerates NAD^+
• Substrates and waste products vary among species
13.6

when ETC is active, yields pyruvate for

when ETC is inactive, yields pyruvate for

Pyruvate processing
• Catalyzed by pyruvate dehydrogenase
13.3

CO_2 ←

yields acetyl CoA for

CO_2 ←

Citric acid cycle
• 8 enzyme-catalyzed reactions
• Completes oxidation of glucose
13.4

when no final electron acceptor in ETC is available, used by

yields

yields

FADH$_2$ 10.2

NADH 10.2

donates high-energy electrons to

Phosphorylation of enzymes and substrates
• Raises potential energy
10.2

used in

drives

O_2 →

Electron transport chain
• Regenerates NAD^+ and FAD
• Uses energy released during redox reactions to transport H^+
• Ends with final electron acceptor (usually O_2)
13.5

H_2O

Energetic coupling
• Reactions that were endergonic with unphosphorylated substrates/enzymes become exergonic with phosphorylated substrates/enzymes
10.2

Chemiosmosis
• H^+ gradient drives ATP synthase
13.5

enables

yields lots of

yields some →

ATP

P P P

Cellular work
• Pumping ions
• Synthesizing molecules
• Moving cargo
• Sending and receiving signals

APPENDIX A Answers

CHAPTER 1

IN-TEXT QUESTIONS AND EXERCISES

p. 4 Fig. 1.2 analyze If Pasteur had done any of the things listed, he would have had more than one variable in his experiment. This would allow critics to claim that he got different results because of the differences in broth types, heating, or flask types—not the difference in exposure to preexisting cells. The results would not be definitive.

p. 6 apply The average kernel protein content would decline, from 11 percent to a much lower value over time.

p. 6 CYU apply The data points would all be about 11 percent, indicating no change in average kernel protein content over time.

p. 7 Fig. 1.4 apply Molds and other fungi are more closely related to green algae because they differ from plants at two positions (5 and 8 from left) but differ from green algae at only one position (8).

p. 8 Fig. 1.6 apply The eukaryotic cell is roughly 10 times the size of the prokaryotic cell.

p. 9 CYU evaluate From the sequence data provided, species A and B differ only in one ribonucleotide of the rRNA sequence (position 10 from left). Species C differs from species A and B in four ribonucleotides (positions 1, 2, 9, and 10). A correctly drawn phylogenetic tree would indicate that species A and B appear to be closely related, and species C is more distantly related. See **FIGURE A1.1**.

p. 13 (1) analyze You could conclude that the ants weren't navigating normally, because they had been caught and released and transferred to a new channel. **(2)** analyze You could conclude that the ants can't navigate normally on their manipulated legs.

p. 13 CYU The key here is to test predation rates during the hottest part of the day (when desert ants actually feed) versus other parts of the day. The experiment would best be done in the field, where natural predators are present. One approach would be to capture a large number of ants, divide the group in two, and measure predation rates (number of ants killed per hour) when they are placed in normal habitat during the hottest part of the day versus an hour before (or after). **(1)** analyze The control group here is the normal condition—ants out during the hottest part of the day. If you didn't include a control, a critic could argue that predation did or did not occur because of your experimental setup or manipulation, not because of differences in temperature. **(2)** analyze You would need to make sure that there is no difference in body size, walking speed, how they were captured and maintained, or other traits that might make the ants in the two groups more or less susceptible to predators. They should also be put out in the same habitat, so the presence of predators is the same in the two treatments.

p. 13 Fig. 1.10 analyze The interpretation of the experiment would not likely change, but your confidence in the conclusions drawn would be reduced if you used just one ant.

IF YOU UNDERSTAND . . .

1.1. understand Dead cells cannot regulate the passage of materials between exterior and interior spaces, replicate, use energy, or process information. **1.2** understand Observations on thousands of diverse species supported the claim that all organisms consist of cells. The hypothesis that all cells come from preexisting cells was supported when Pasteur showed that new cells do not arise and grow in a boiled liquid unless they are introduced from the air. **1.3** understand If seeds with higher protein content leave the most offspring, then individuals with low protein in their seeds will become rare over time. **1.4** understand A newly discovered species can be classified as a member of the Bacteria if the sequence of its rRNA contains some features found only in Bacteria. The same logic applies to classifying a new species in the Archaea or Eukarya. **1.5** understand (1) A hypothesis is an explanation of how the world works; a prediction is an outcome you should observe if the hypothesis is correct. (2) Experiments are convincing because they measure predictions from two opposing hypotheses. Both predicted actions cannot occur, so one hypothesis will be supported while the other will not.

YOU SHOULD BE ABLE TO . . .

✔ Test Your Knowledge

1. remember d **2.** understand d **3.** remember populations **4.** understand b **5.** understand An individual's ability to survive and reproduce **6.** understand c

✔ Test Your Understanding

7. evaluate That the entity they discovered replicates, processes information, acquires and uses energy, is cellular, and that its populations evolve. **8.** understand a **9.** understand Over time, traits that increased the fitness of individuals in this habitat became increasingly frequent in the population. **10.** understand Individuals with certain traits are selected, in the sense that they produce the most offspring. **11.** analyze Yes. If evolution is defined as "change in the characteristics of a population over time," then those organisms that are most closely related should have experienced less change over time. On a phylogenetic tree, species with substantially similar rRNA sequences would be diagrammed with a closer common ancestor—one that had the sequences they inherited—than the ancestors shared between species with dissimilar rRNA sequences. **12.** understand A null hypothesis specifies what a researcher should observe when the hypothesis being tested isn't correct.

✔ Test Your Problem-Solving Skills

13. analyze A scientific theory is not a guess—it is an idea whose validity can be tested with data. Both the cell theory and the theory of evolution have been validated by large bodies of observational and experimental data. **14.** apply If all eukaryotes living today have a nucleus, then it is logical to conclude that the nucleus arose in a common ancestor of all eukaryotes, indicated by the arrow you should have added to the figure. See **FIGURE A1.2**. If it had arisen in a common ancestor of Bacteria or Archaea, then species in those groups would have had to lose the trait—an unlikely event. **15.** evaluate The data set was so large and diverse that it was no longer reasonable to argue that noncellular lifeforms would be discovered. **16.** apply b

BIG PICTURE Doing Biology

p. 16 CYU (1) understand Biologists design and carry out a study, either observational or experimental, to test their ideas. As part of this process, they state their ideas as a hypothesis and null hypothesis and make predictions. They analyze and interpret the data they have gathered, and determine whether the data support their ideas. If not, they revisit their ideas and come up with an alternative hypothesis and design another study to test these new predictions. **(2)** understand There are many possible examples. Consider, for example, the experiment on navigation in foraging desert ants (Chapter 1). In addition to testing how the ants use information on stride length and number to calculate how far they are from the nest (multicellular organism and population levels), researchers also could test how the "pedometer" works at the level of cells and molecules. **(3)** analyze A hypothesis is a testable statement to explain a specific phenomenon or a set of observations. The word theory refers to proposed explanations for very broad patterns in nature that are supported by a wide body of evidence. A theory serves as a framework for the development of new hypotheses. **(4)** analyze The next step is to relate your findings to existing theories and the current scientific literature, and then to communicate your findings to colleagues through informal conversations, presentations at scientific meetings, and eventually publication in peer-reviewed journals.

CHAPTER 2

IN-TEXT QUESTIONS AND EXERCISES

p. 22 CYU remember (1) The nucleoid compacts the chromosome to fit inside the cell via supercoiling while still keeping it accessible for replication and transmission of information. (2) Photosynthetic membranes increase food production by providing a large surface area to hold the pigments and enzymes required for photosynthesis. (3) Flagella propel cells through liquid, often toward a food source. (4) The layer of thick, strong material stiffens the cell wall and provides protection from mechanical damage.

p. 26 Fig. 2.12 create Storing the toxins in vacuoles prevents the toxins from damaging the plant's own organelles and cells.

p. 28 CYU (1) understand Both organelles contain specific sets of enzymes. Lysosomal enzymes digest macromolecules in the acidic lumen of this organelle, releasing

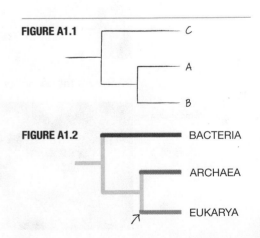

FIGURE A1.1

C

A

B

FIGURE A1.2

BACTERIA

ARCHAEA

EUKARYA

monomers that can be recycled into new macromol-ecules. Peroxisomes contain catalase and other enzymes that process fatty acids and toxins via oxidation reactions. **(2)** `understand` From top to bottom: administrative/information hub, protein factory, large molecule manufacturing and shipping (protein synthesis and folding center, lipid factory, protein finishing and shipping line, waste processing and recycling center), warehouse, fatty-acid processing and detox center, power station, food-manufacturing facility, support beams, perimeter fencing with secured gates, and leave blank.

p. 30 Fig. 2.16 `remember` See **FIGURE A2.1**.

p. 33 `analyze` (1) Nucleotides are small enough that they would diffuse through the nuclear pore complex along their gradients—a passive process that would not require energy. (2) Large proteins must be escorted through the nuclear pore complex, which is directional and requires energy, since the protein is concentrated inside the nucleus.

p. 33 Fig. 2.18 `apply` "Prediction": The labeled tail region fragments or the labeled core region fragments of the nucleoplasmin protein will be found in the cell nucleus. "Prediction of null hypothesis": Either both the fragments (no required signal) or neither of them (whole protein signal) will be found in the nucleus of the cell. "Conclusion": The send-to-nucleus signal is in the tail region of the nucleoplasmin protein.

p. 35 `apply` During the chase period, proteins appear to have first entered the Golgi after 7 minutes and then started to move into secretory granules after 37 minutes. This means that in this experiment, it took approximately 30 minutes for the fastest-moving proteins to pass through the Golgi.

p. 38 `apply` In receptor-mediated endocytosis, the conversion of a late endosome to a lysosome is dependent on receiving acid hydrolases from the Golgi. If this receptor is not present, then the enzymes will not be sent and the late endosome will not mature into a lysosome to digest the endocytosed products.

p. 38 CYU (1) `apply` Proteins that enter the nucleus are fully synthesized and have an NLS that interacts with another protein to get it into the organelle. The NLS is not removed. Proteins that enter the ER have a signal sequence that interacts with the SRP during translation. The ribosome is moved to the ER and synthesis continues, moving the protein into the ER. The signal is removed once it enters the organelle. **(2)** `apply` The protein would be in the lysosome. The ER signal would direct the protein into the ER before it is completely synthesized. The M-6-P tag will direct the protein from the Golgi to the late endosome to the lysosome. Thus the complete protein is never free in the cytosol, where the NLS could direct it into the nucleus.

p. 44 CYU `analyze` Actin filaments are made up of two strands of actin monomers, microtubules are made up of tubulin protein dimers that form a tube, and intermediate filaments are made up of a number of different protein subunits. Actin filaments and microtubules exhibit polarity (or directionality), and new subunits are constantly being added or subtracted at either end (but added faster to the plus end). All three elements provide structural support, but only actin filaments and microtubules serve as tracks for motors involved in movement and cell division.

p. 44 Fig. 2.30 `apply` The microtubule doublets of the axoneme would slide past each other completely, but the axoneme would not bend.

IF YOU UNDERSTAND . . .

2.1 `understand` (1) Cells will be unable to synthesize new proteins and will die. (2) In many environments, cells will be unable to resist the osmotic pressure of water entering the cytoplasm and will burst. (3) The cell shape will be different, and cells will not be able to divide. **2.2** `understand` (1) The cell will be unable to produce a sufficient amount of ATP and will die. (2) Reactive molecules, like hydrogen peroxide, will damage the cell, and it will likely die. (3) Nothing will happen, since plants do not have centrioles. **2.3** `analyze` The liver cell would be expected to have more peroxisomes and less rough endoplasmic reticulum than the salivary cells would. **2.4** `create` The addition or removal of phosphates would change the folded structure of the protein, exposing the NLS for nuclear transport. **2.5** `create` As a group, proteins have complex and highly diverse shapes and chemical properties that allow them to recognize a great number of different zip codes in a very specific manner. **2.6** `apply` The Golgi is positioned near the microtubule organizing center, which has microtubules running from the minus end out to the plus end (near the plasma membrane). Kinesin would be used to move these vesicles as it walks toward the plus end.

YOU SHOULD BE ABLE TO . . .

✔ Test Your Knowledge

1. `understand` b **2.** `remember` They have their own small, circular chromosomes; they produce their own ribosomes; and they divide in a manner that is similar to bacterial fission, independent of cellular division. **3.** `remember` c **4.** `remember` b **5.** `remember` a **6.** `understand` The phosphate links to the motor protein and causes it to change shape, which results in the protein moving along the filament.

✔ Test Your Understanding

7. `analyze` All cells are bound by a plasma membrane, are filled with cytoplasm, carry their genetic information (DNA) in chromosomes, and contain ribosomes

FIGURE A2.1

(a) Animal pancreatic cell: Exports digestive enzymes.

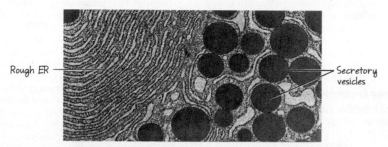

Rough ER

Secretory vesicles

(b) Animal testis cell: Exports lipid-soluble signals.

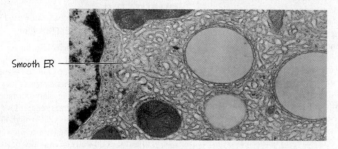

Smooth ER

(c) Plant leaf cell: Manufactures ATP and sugar.

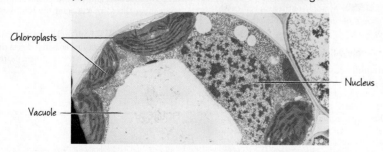

Chloroplasts

Nucleus

Vacuole

(d) Brown fat cells: Burn fat to generate heat in lieu of ATP.

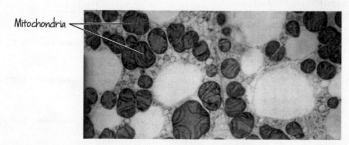

Mitochondria

(the sites of protein synthesis). Some prokaryotes have organelles not found in plants or animals, such as a magnetite-containing structure. Plant cells have chloroplasts, vacuoles, and a cell wall. Animal cells contain lysosomes and lack a cell wall. **8.** analyze a; the endoplasmic reticulum is responsible for synthesizing the membrane proteins required for the transport of solutes across the plasma membrane. **9.** create The NLS will be used to actively import the protein into the nucleus, leaving very little of the protein in the cytoplasm. Diffusion alone would not drive all the protein into the nucleus. **10.** create Ribosome in cytoplasm (signal is synthesized) → Ribosome at rough ER (protein is completed, folded, and glycosylated) → Transport vesicle → Golgi apparatus (protein is processed; has molecular zip code indicating destination) → Transport vesicle → Plasma membrane → Extracellular space. **11.** create This occurs in microfilaments and microtubules because they have ends that differ structurally and functionally—they have different filament growth rates. Intermediate filaments have identical ends, so there is no difference in the rate of assembly between the two ends. **12.** understand Polarized cytoskeletal filaments (microtubules or microfilaments) are present between the organelles. End-directed motor proteins use ATP to move these transport vesicles between them.

✔ Test Your Problem-Solving Skills

13. understand b; fimbriae are involved in bacterial attachment to surfaces and other cells, which would be important in the ability to grow on teeth. **14.** create The proteins must receive a molecular zip code that binds to a receptor on the surface of peroxisomes. They could diffuse randomly to peroxisomes or be transported in a directed way by motor proteins. **15.** create The tails cleaved from nucleoplasmin could be attached to the gold particles that were excluded from crossing the pore complex owing to their size. If these modified particles entered the nucleus, then the tail is not limited to the nucleoplasmin transport alone. **16.** apply The proteins would likely be found in the cytoplasm (e.g., actin and myosin) or imported into the mitochondria. Since there is a high energy demand, you would predict that there are many active mitochondria.

CHAPTER 3

IN-TEXT QUESTIONS AND EXERCISES

p. 51 understand Fatty acids are amphipathic because their hydrocarbon tails are hydrophobic but their carboxyl functional groups are hydrophilic.
p. 51 Fig. 3.4 apply At the polar hydroxyl group in cholesterol and the polar head group in phospholipids.
p. 52 CYU (1) analyze Fats consist of three fatty acids linked to glycerol; steroids have a distinctive four-ring structure with variable side groups attached; phospholipids have a hydrophilic, phosphate-containing "head" region and a hydrocarbon tail. **(2)** understand In cholesterol, the hydrocarbon steroid rings and isoprenoid chain are hydrophobic; the hydroxyl group is hydrophilic. In phospholipids, the phosphate-containing head group is hydrophilic; the hydrocarbon chains are hydrophobic.
p. 53 apply Amino acids have amino and carboxyl groups that are ionized in water and nucleotides have negatively charged phosphates. Due to their charge and larger size, both would be placed below the small ions at the bottom of the scale (permeability$<10^{-12}$ cm/sec).
p. 54 CYU create See **TABLE A3.1**.
p. 55 Fig. 3.10 apply Increasing the number of phospholipids with polyunsaturated tails would increase permeability of the liposomes. Starting from the left, the first line (no cholesterol) would represent liposomes with 50% polyunsaturated phospholipids, the second line would be 20% polyunsaturated phospholipids, and the third line would contain only saturated phospholipids.

p. 56 apply If there is a difference in temperature, then there would be a difference in thermal motion. The solute concentration on the side with a higher temperature would decrease because the solute particles would be moving faster and hence be more likely to move to the cooler side of the membrane, where they would slow down.
p. 57 Fig. 3.13 apply Higher, because less water would have to move to the right side to achieve equilibrium.
p. 58 CYU create See **FIGURE A3.1**.
p. 60 Fig. 3.18 create Repeat the procedure using a lipid bilayer that is free of membrane proteins, such as synthetic liposomes constructed from only phospholipids. If proteins were responsible for the pits and mounds, then this control would not show these structures.
p. 61 apply Your arrow should point out of the cell. There is no concentration gradient for chloride, but the outside has a net positive charge, which favors outward movement of negative ions.
p. 61 Fig. 3.21 analyze No—the 10 replicates where no current was recorded probably represent instances where the CFTR protein was damaged and not functioning properly. (In general, no experimental method works "perfectly.")
p. 65 CYU understand Passive transport does not require an input of energy—it happens as a result of energy already present in existing concentration or electrical gradients. Active transport is active in the sense of requiring an input of energy from, for example, ATP. In cotransport, a second ion or molecule is transported against its concentration gradient along with (i.e., "co") an ion that is transported along its concentration gradient.
p. 65 Fig. 3.26 understand *Diffusion:* description as given; no proteins involved. *Facilitated diffusion:* Passive movement of ions or molecules that cannot cross a phospholipid bilayer readily along a concentration gradient; facilitated by channel or carrier proteins. *Active transport:* Active movement of ions or molecules that build a gradient; facilitated by pump proteins powered by an energy source such as ATP.

IF YOU UNDERSTAND . . .

3.1. analyze Adding H_2 increases the saturation of the oil by converting C=C bonds into C−C bonds with added hydrogens. Lipids with more C−H bonds tend to be solid at room temperature. **3.2** understand Highly permeable and fluid bilayers possess short, unsaturated hydrocarbon tails while those that are highly impermeable and less fluid contain long, saturated hydrocarbon tails. **3.3** apply (1) The solute will diffuse until both sides are at equal concentrations. (2) Water will diffuse toward the side with the higher solute concentration. **3.4** apply See **FIGURE A3.2**.

YOU SHOULD BE ABLE TO . . .

✔ Test Your Knowledge

1. understand c **2.** remember a **3.** understand b **4.** understand d
5. understand For osmosis to occur, a concentration

TABLE A3.1

Factor	Effect on permeability	Reason
Temperature	Decreases as temperature decreases.	Lower temperature slows movement of hydrocarbon tails, allowing more interactions (membrane is more dense).
Cholesterol	Decreases as cholesterol content increases.	Cholesterol molecules fill in the spaces between the hydrocarbon tails, making the membrane more tightly packed.
Length of hydrocarbon tails	Decreases as length of hydrocarbon tails increases.	Longer hydrocarbon tails have more interactions (membrane is more dense).
Saturation of hydrocarbon tails	Decreases as degree of saturation increases.	Saturated fatty acids have straight hydrocarbon tails that pack together tightly, leaving few gaps.

FIGURE A3.1

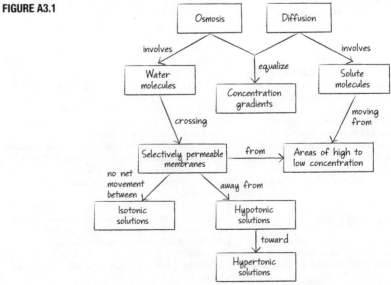

FIGURE A3.2

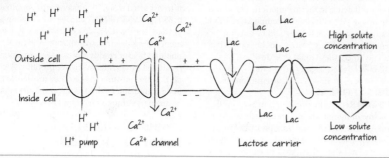

gradient and membrane that allows water to pass, but not the solute, must be present. **6.** analyze Channel proteins form pores in the membrane and carrier proteins undergo conformational changes to shuttle molecules or ions across the membrane.

✔ Test Your Understanding

7. apply b **8.** analyze No, because they have no polar end to interact with water. Instead, these lipids would float on the surface of water, or collect in droplets suspended in water, reducing their interaction with water to a minimum. **9.** understand Hydrophilic, phosphate-containing head groups interact with water; hydrophobic hydrocarbon tails associate with each other. A bilayer is more stable than are independent phospholipids in solution. **10.** apply Ethanol's polar hydroxyl group reduces the speed at which it can cross a membrane, but its small size and lack of charge would allow it to slowly cross membranes—between the rates of water and glucose transport. **11.** understand Only nonpolar, hydrophobic amino acid residues would be found in the portion of the protein that crosses the membrane. In the interior of the bilayer, these residues would be hidden from the water solvent and interact with the nonpolar lipid tails. **12.** apply Chloride ions from sodium chloride will move from the left side to the right through the CFTR. Water will initially move from the right side to the left by osmosis, but as chloride ions move to the right, water will follow. Na^+ and K^+ ions will not move across the membrane.

✔ Test Your Problem-Solving Skills

13. apply c **14.** create Flip-flops should be rare, because they require a polar head group to pass through the hydrophobic portion of the lipid bilayer. To test this prediction, you could monitor the number of dyed phospholipids that transfer from one side of the membrane to the other in a given period of time. **15.** apply Organisms that live in very cold environments are likely to have highly unsaturated phospholipids. The kinks in unsaturated hydrocarbon tails keep membranes fluid and permeable, even at low temperature. Organisms that live in very hot environments would likely have phospholipids with saturated tails, to prevent membranes from becoming too fluid and permeable. **16.** analyze Adding a methyl group makes a drug more hydrophobic and thus more likely to pass through a lipid bilayer. Adding a charged group makes it hydrophilic and reduces its ability to pass through the lipid bilayer. These modifications would help target the drug to either the inside or outside of cells, respectively.

BIG PICTURE Chemistry of Life

p. 68 CYU (1) understand Oxygen is much more electronegative than hydrogen, so within water, the electrons are unequally shared in the O−H covalent bonds. The

resulting partial negative charge around the oxygen and partial positive charges around the hydrogen atoms allow for hydrogen bonds to form among water molecules. **(2)** analyze Unlike other macromolecules, nucleic acids can serve as templates for their own replication. RNA is generally single-stranded and can adopt many different three-dimensional structures. The flexibility in structure, combined with the presence of reactive hydroxyl groups, contribute to the formation of active sites that catalyze chemical reactions. One or more of these catalytic RNA molecules may have evolved the ability to self-replicate. DNA is not likely to have catalyzed its own replication, as it is most often double-stranded, with no clear tertiary structure, and it lacks the reactive hydroxyl groups. **(3)** remember In the amino acid, the nitrogen in the amino (NH_3^+) group and the carbon in the carboxyl (COO^-) group should be circled. In the nucleotide, the oxygen in the hydroxyl (OH) group and the phosphorus in the phosphate (PO_4^{2-}) group on the nucleotide should be circled. **(4)** understand A line representing a protein should be drawn such that it completely crosses the lipid bilayer at least once. The protein could be involved in a variety of different roles, including transport of substances across the membrane in the form of a channel, carrier, or pump.

CHAPTER 4

IN-TEXT QUESTIONS AND EXERCISES

p. 75 understand **(1)** Genes are segments of chromosomes that code for RNAs and proteins. **(2)** Chromosomes are made of chromatin. **(3)** Sister chromatids are identical copies of the same chromosome, joined together.
p. 76 Fig. 4.5 apply **(1)** prophase cells would have 4 chromosomes with $2x$ DNA. **(2)** Anaphase cells would have 8 chromosomes and $2x$ DNA. **(3)** Each daughter cell will have 4 chromosomes with x DNA.
p. 78 apply See **TABLE A4.1**.
p. 79 Fig. 4.6 apply The chromosome and black bar would move at the same rate toward the spindle pole.
p. 81 CYU (1) apply See **FIGURE A4.1**. **(2)** apply Loss of the motors would result in two problems: (1) It would reduce the ability of chromosomes to attach to microtubules via their kinetochores; (2) cytokinesis would be inhibited since the Golgi-derived vesicles would not be moved to the center of the spindle to build the cell plate.
p. 82 Fig. 4.10 create Inject cytoplasm from an M-phase frog egg into a somatic cell that is in interphase. If the somatic cell starts mitosis, then the meiotic factor is not limited to gametes.
p. 82 Fig. 4.11 analyze In effect, MPF turns itself off after it is activated. If this didn't happen, the cell might undergo mitosis again before the cell has replicated its DNA.
p. 83 understand MPF activates proteins that get mitosis under way. MPF consists of a cyclin and a Cdk, and it is turned on by phosphorylation at the activating site and

dephosphorylation at the inhibitory site. Enzymes that degrade cyclin reduce MPF levels.
p. 84 CYU (1) remember $G_1 \rightarrow S \rightarrow G_2 \rightarrow M$. Checkpoints occur at the end of G_1 and G_2 and during M phase. **(2)** understand Cdk levels are fairly constant throughout the cycle, but cyclin increases during interphase and peaks in M phase. This accumulation of cyclin is a prerequisite for MPF activity, which turns on at the end of G_2, initiating M phase, and declines at the end of M phase.

IF YOU UNDERSTAND . . .

4.1 understand The G_1 and G_2 phases give the cell time to replicate organelles and grow before division as well as perform the normal functions required to stay alive. Chromosomes replicate during S phase and are separated from one another during M phase. Cytokinesis also occurs during M phase, when the parent cell divides into two daughter cells. **4.2** understand In cells that do not dissolve the nuclear envelope, the spindle must be constructed inside the nucleus to attach to the chromosomes and separate them. **4.3** apply Cells would prematurely enter M phase, shortening the length of G_2 and resulting in the daughter cells' being smaller than normal. **4.4** analyze The absence of growth factors in normal cells would cause them to arrest in the G_1 phase—eventually all the cells in the culture would be in G_1. The cancerous cells are not likely to be dependent on these growth factors, so the cells would not arrest and would continue through the cell cycle.

YOU SHOULD BE ABLE TO . . .

✔ Test Your Knowledge

1. remember b **2.** remember d **3.** remember d **4.** remember c
5. understand Daughter chromosomes were observed to move toward the pole faster than do the marked regions of fluorescently labeled kinetochore microtubules.
6. remember The cycle would arrest in M phase, and cytokinesis would not occur.

✔ Test Your Understanding

7. apply For daughter cells to have identical complements of chromosomes, all the chromosomes must be replicated during the S phase, the spindle apparatus must connect with the kinetochores of each sister chromatid in prometaphase, and the sister chromatids of each replicated chromosome must be partitioned in anaphase and fully separated into daughter cells by cytokinesis. **8.** create One possible concept map is shown in **FIGURE A4.2. 9.** understand Microinjection experiments suggested that something in the cytoplasm of M-phase cells activated the transition from interphase to M phase. The control for this experiment was to inject cytoplasm from a G_2-arrested oocyte into another G_2-arrested oocyte. **10.** apply Protein kinases phosphorylate proteins. Phosphorylation changes a protein's shape, altering its function (activating or inactivating it). As a result, protein kinases regulate the function of proteins. **11.** understand Cyclin concentrations change during the cell cycle. At high concentration, cyclins bind to a specific cyclin-dependent kinase (or Cdk), forming a dimer. This dimer becomes active MPF by changing its shape through the phosphorylation (activating site) and dephosphorylation (inhibitory site) of Cdk. **12.** analyze b.

✔ Test Your Problem-Solving Skills

13. analyze a; adding up each phase allows you to determine that the cell cycle is 8.5 hours long. After 9 hours, the radiolabeled cells would have passed through a full cycle and be in either S phase or G_2—none would have entered M phase. **14.** apply The embryo passes through multiple rounds of the cell cycle, but cytokinesis does not occur during M phases. **15.** apply Early detection of cancers leads to a greater likelihood of survival. The

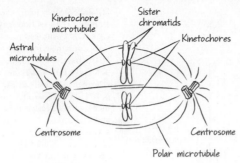

FIGURE A4.1

FIGURE A4.2

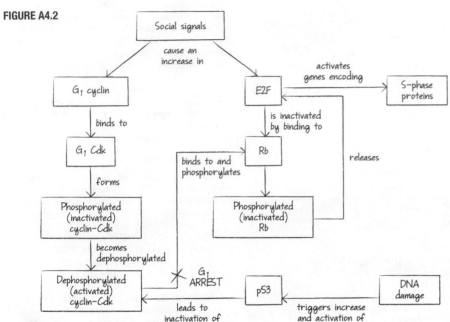

TABLE A4.1

	Prophase	Prometaphase	Metaphase	Anaphase	Telophase
Spindle apparatus	Starts to form	Contacts and moves chromosomes	Anchors poles to membrane and produces tension at kinetochores	Pulls chromatids apart	Defines site of cytokinesis
Nuclear envelope	Present	Disintegrates	Nonexistent	Nonexistent	Re-forms
Chromosomes	Condense	Attach to microtubules	Held at metaphase plate	Sister chromatids separate into daughter chromosomes	Collect at opposite poles

widespread implementation of breast and prostate exams allows for the identification and removal of benign tumors before they become malignant. **16.** analyze Cancer requires many defects. Older cells have had more time to accumulate defects. Individuals with a genetic predisposition to cancer start out with some cancer-related defects, but this does not mean that the additional defects required for cancer to occur will develop.

CHAPTER 5

IN-TEXT QUESTIONS AND EXERCISES

p. 91 understand See **FIGURE A5.1**.
p. 92 Fig. 5.3 understand 5'-UAGC-'3
p. 93 CYU understand See **FIGURE A5.2**.
p. 95 understand If the two strands were parallel, the G-C pairing would align N−H groups together and C=O

groups together, which would not allow hydrogen bonds to form.
p. 96 Fig. 5.8 analyze It is not spontaneous—energy must be added (as heat) for the reaction to occur.
p. 97 CYU remember See **FIGURE A5.3**.

FIGURE A5.1

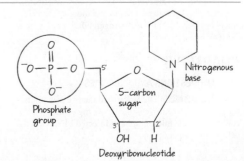

Ribonucleotide

Deoxyribonucleotide

IF YOU UNDERSTAND . . .

5.1. understand Cells activate nucleotides by linking additional phosphates to an existing 5' phosphate. Activation increases the chemical energy in the nucleotides enough to offset the decrease in entropy that will result from the polymerization reaction. **5.2** understand C-G pairs involve three hydrogen bonds, so they are more stable than A-T pairs with just two hydrogen bonds. **5.3** analyze A single-stranded RNA molecule has unpaired bases that can pair with other bases on the same RNA strand, thereby folding the molecule into stem-and-loop configurations. These secondary structures can further fold on themselves, giving the molecule a tertiary structure. Because DNA molecules are double stranded, with no unpaired bases, further internal folding is not possible. **5.4** understand Examples would include (1) the production of nucleotides, and (2) polymerization of RNA. It is thought that nucleotides were scarce during chemical evolution, so their catalyzed synthesis by a ribozyme would have been advantageous. Catalysis by an RNA replicase would have dramatically increased the reproductive rate of RNA molecules.

YOU SHOULD BE ABLE TO . . .

✔ **Test Your Knowledge**

1. remember c **2.** remember c **3.** remember a **4.** remember d **5.** remember
One end has a free phosphate group on the 5' carbon; the other end has a free hydroxyl group bonded to the 3' carbon. **6.** understand DNA is a more stable molecule than RNA because it lacks a hydroxyl group on the 2' carbon and is therefore more resistant to cleavage, and because the two sugar-phosphate backbones are held together by many hydrogen bonds between nitrogenous bases.

✔ **Test Your Understanding**

7. apply In DNA, the secondary structure requires that every guanine pairs with a cytosine and every thymine pairs with an adenine, resulting in consistent ratios between the nucleotides. Chargaff's rules do not apply to RNA, since it is single-stranded and the pairing is not consistent throughout the molecules. **8.** apply a; if 30 percent is adenine, then 30 percent would be thymine, since they are base-paired together. This means that 40 percent consists of G-C base pairs, which would be equally divided between the two bases. **9.** apply The DNA sequence of the new strand would be 5'-ATCGATATC-3'. The RNA sequence would be the same, except each T would be replaced by a U. **10.** understand DNA has limited catalytic ability because it (1) lacks functional groups that can participate in catalysis and (2) has a regular structure that is not conducive to forming shapes required for catalysis. RNA molecules can catalyze some reactions because they (1) have exposed hydroxyl functional groups and (2) can fold into shapes that that can function in catalysis. **11.** apply No. Catalytic activity in ribozymes depends on the tertiary structure generated from single-stranded molecules. Double-stranded nucleic acids do not form tertiary structures. **12.** understand An RNA replicase would undergo replication and be able to evolve. It would

FIGURE A5.2

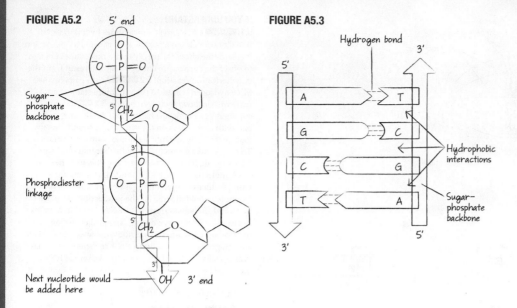

FIGURE A5.3

FIGURE A5.4

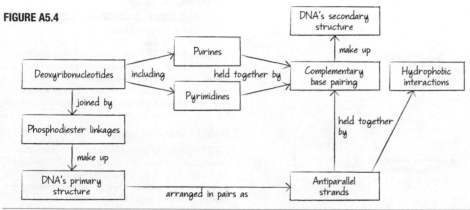

process information in the sense of copying itself, and it would use energy to drive polymerization reactions. It would not be bound by a membrane and considered a cell, however, and it would not be able to acquire energy. It would best be considered as an intermediate step between nonlife and true life (as outlined in Chapter 1).

✔ Test Your Problem-Solving Skills

13. `create` See **FIGURE A5.4 14.** `apply` Yes—if the complementary bases lined up over the entire length of the two strands, they would twist into a double helix analogous to a DNA molecule. The same types of hydrogen bonds and hydrophobic interactions would occur as observed in the "stem" portion of hairpins in single-stranded RNA. **15.** `apply` In a triple helix, the bases are unlikely to align properly for hydrogen bonding to occur, so hydrophobic interactions would probably be more important. **16.** `apply` b; the high temperature would make it more likely that the secondary and tertiary structures would be denatured in the ribozymes. To overcome this effect, you would expect the hairpins to possess more G-C pairs, since they consist of three hydrogen bonds compared to the two found in A-T pairs.

CHAPTER 6

IN-TEXT QUESTIONS AND EXERCISES

p. 106 Fig. 6.2 `analyze` The lack of radioactive protein in the pellet (after centrifugation) is strong evidence; they could also make micrographs of infected bacterial cells before and after agitation.

p. 107 Fig. 6.3 `apply` 5′-TAG-3′.
p. 108 Fig. 6.5 `apply` The same two bands should appear, but the upper band (DNA containing only ^{14}N) should get bigger and darker and the lower band (hybrid DNA) should get smaller and lighter in color since each succeeding generation has relatively less heavy DNA.
p. 110 `apply` See **FIGURE A6.1.** The new strands grow in opposite directions, each in the 5′ → 3′ direction.
p. 112 `apply` Helicase, topoisomerase, single-strand DNA-binding proteins, primase, and DNA polymerase are all required for leading-strand synthesis. If any one of these proteins is nonfunctional, DNA replication will not occur.
p. 113 `apply` See **FIGURE A6.2.** If DNA ligase were defective, then the leading strand would be continuous, and the lagging strand would have gaps in it where the Okazaki fragments had not been joined.
p. 114 CYU (1) `understand` DNA polymerase adds nucleotides only to the free 3′ −OH on a strand. Primase synthesizes a short RNA sequence that provides the free 3′ end necessary for DNA polymerase to start working. **(2)** `understand` The need to begin DNA synthesis many times on the lagging strand requires many new primers. Since DNA polymerase I is needed to remove primers, it is required predominantly on the primer-rich lagging strand.
p. 116 Fig. 6.13 `apply` As long as the RNA template could bind to the "overhanging" section of single-stranded DNA, any sequence could produce a longer strand. For example, 5′-CCCAUUCCC-3′ would work just as well.
p. 117 CYU (1) `understand` This is because telomerase is needed only to replicate one end of a linear DNA and bacterial DNAs lack ends because they are circular.

(2) `understand` Since telomerase works by extending one strand of DNA without any external template and because DNA synthesis requires a template, telomerase must contain an internal template to allow it to extend a DNA chain.
p. 119 Fig. 6.16 `analyze` They are lower in energy and not absorbed effectively by the DNA bases.
p. 120 CYU (1) `apply` The mutation rate would be predicted to rise because differences in base-pair stability and shape make it possible for DNA polymerase to distinguish correct from incorrect base pairs during DNA replication. **(2)** `apply` The mutation rate should increase because without a way to distinguish which strand to use as a template for repair, about half of mismatches on average would be repaired using the incorrect strand as a template. **(3)** `remember` The enzyme that removes the dimer and surrounding DNA is specific to nucleotide excision repair. DNA polymerase and DNA ligase work in both nucleotide excision repair and normal DNA synthesis.
p. 120 Fig. 6.18 `apply` Exposure to UV radiation can cause formation of thymine dimers. If thymine dimers are not repaired, they represent mutations. If such mutations occur in genes controlling the cell cycle, cells can grow abnormally, resulting in cancers.

IF YOU UNDERSTAND . . .

6.1 `apply` These results would not allow distinguishing whether DNA or protein was the genetic material.
6.2 `understand` The bases added during DNA replication are shown in red type.

Original DNA:	CAATTACGGA
	GTTAATGCCT
Replicated DNA:	CAATTACGGA
	GTTAATGCCT
	CAATTACGGA
	GTTAATGCCT

6.3 `understand` See **FIGURE A6.3. 6.4** `understand` Because cancer cells divide nearly without limit, it's important for these cells to have active telomerase so that chromosomes don't shorten to the point where cell division becomes impossible. **6.5** `understand` If errors in DNA aren't corrected, they represent mutations. When DNA repair systems fail, the mutation rate increases. As the mutation rate increases, the chance that one or more cell-cycle genes will be mutated increases. Mutations in these genes often result in uncontrolled cell division, ultimately leading to cancer.

YOU SHOULD BE ABLE TO . . .

✔ Test Your Knowledge

1. `remember` d **2.** `understand` a **3.** `remember` topoisomerase **4.** `remember` b **5.** `remember` c **6.** `remember` telomerase

✔ Test Your Understanding

7. `remember` Labeling DNA or labeling proteins. **8.** `understand` DNA is constantly damaged, and many pathways have evolved to repair this onslaught of damage. If a DNA repair pathway is inactivated by mutation, damage is inefficiently repaired. Consequently mutation rates increase, and the increased number of mutations increases the probability that cancer-causing mutations will occur.
9. `understand` On the lagging strand, DNA polymerase moves away from the replication fork. When helicase unwinds a new section of DNA, primase must build a new primer on the template for the lagging strand (closer to the fork) and another polymerase molecule must begin synthesis at this point. This makes the lagging-strand synthesis discontinuous. On the leading strand, DNA polymerase moves in the same direction as helicase, so synthesis can continue, without interruption, from a single primer (at the origin of replication).
10. `understand` Telomerase binds to the overhang at the end of a chromosome. Once bound, it begins catalyzing the

FIGURE A6.1

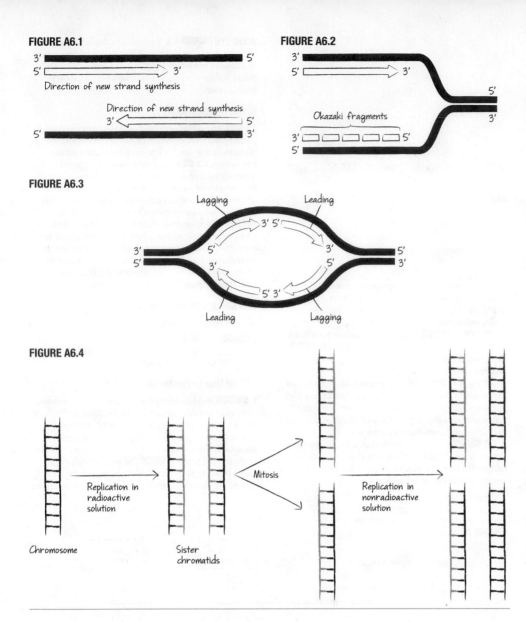

FIGURE A6.2

FIGURE A6.3

FIGURE A6.4

p. 126 Fig. 7.2 **p. 126 Fig. 7.2** create Many possibilities: strain of fungi used, exact method for creating mutants and harvesting spores to grow, exact growing conditions (temperature, light, recipe for growth medium—including concentrations of supplements), objective criteria for determining growth or no growth.

p. 129 CYU remember Change in DNA sequence, change in sequence of transcribed mRNA, potential change in amino acid sequence of protein, likely altered protein function (if amino acid sequence was altered), likely change in phenotype.

p. 132 analyze (1) The codons in Figure 16.4 are translated correctly. (2) See **FIGURE A7.1**. (3) There are many possibilities (just pick alternative codons for one or more of the amino acids); one is an mRNA sequence (running 5′ → 3′): 5′ GCG-AAC-GAU-UUC-CAG 3′. To get the corresponding DNA sequence, write this sequence but substitute Ts for Us: 5′ GCG-AAC-GAT-TTC-CAG 3′. Now write the complementary bases, which will be in the 3′ → 5′ direction: 3′ CGC-TTG-CTA-AAG-GTC 5′. When this second strand is transcribed by RNA polymerase, it will produce the mRNA given with the proper 5′ → 3′ orientation.

p. 132 CYU (1) apply Note the 3′ → 5′ polarity of the DNA sequences in the accompanying table, and in the subsequent answer. This means that the complementary mRNA codon will read 5′ → 3′. U (rather than T) is the base transcribed from A.

DNA	mRNA Codon	Amino Acid
ATA	UAU	Tyrosine
ATG	UAC	Tyrosine
ATT	UAA	Stop
GCA	UGC	Cysteine

(2) understand The ATA → ATG mutation would have no effect on the protein. The ATA → ATT mutation introduces a stop codon, so the resulting polypeptide would be shortened. This would result in synthesis of a mutant protein much shorter than the original protein. The ATA → GCA mutation might have a profound effect on the protein's conformation because cysteine's structure is different from tyrosine's.

p. 132 Fig. 7.7 apply See **FIGURE A7.1**.

p. 134 Fig. 7.9 analyze Chromosomes 2, 3, 6, 10, 13, 14, 15, 18, 19, 21, 22, and the X chromosome show aneuploidy. Virtually every chromosome has structural rearrangements, and translocations are the most obvious. These are seen when two or more different colors occur on the same chromosome.

IF YOU UNDERSTAND . . .

7.1 understand Ornithine, citrulline or arginine could be added to allow growth. As Figure 7.1 shows, these compounds are made after the steps catalyzed by the enzymes 1, 2, and 3 that are needed to produce arginine.
7.2 understand An inhibitor of RNA synthesis will eventually prevent the synthesis of new proteins because newly synthesized mRNA is needed for translation. **7.3** apply AUG UGG AAA/AAG CAA/CAG **7.4** understand Since redundancy is having more than one codon specify a particular amino acid, redundancy makes it possible for there to be a point mutation without altering the amino acid. This is a silent mutation. A silent mutation is likely to be neutral because there is no change in amino acid sequence.

YOU SHOULD BE ABLE TO . . .
✔ **Test Your Knowledge**

1. remember d **2.** understand a **3.** understand d **4.** remember Because there is no chemical complementarity between nucleotides and amino acids; and because in eukaryotes, DNA

addition of deoxyribonucleotides to the overhang in the 5′ → 3′ direction, lengthening the overhang. This allows primase, DNA polymerase, and ligase to catalyze the addition of deoxyribonucleotides to the lagging strand in the 5′ → 3′ direction, restoring the lagging strand to its original length. **11.** apply a (Because the ability to distinguish which strand contains the incorrect base would be lost). **12.** analyze d (The regularity of DNA's structure allows enzymes to recognize any type of damage that distorts this regular structure.)

✔ **Test Your Problem-Solving Skills**

13. analyze c (If DNA polymerase could synthesize DNA 3′ → 5′ as well as the normal 5′ → 3′, then both newly synthesized DNA strands could be extended to follow the replication fork.) **14.** apply (a) In **FIGURE A6.4**, the gray lines represent DNA strands containing radioactivity. (b) After one round of replication in radioactive solution, one double-stranded DNA would be radioactive in both strands and the other would not be radioactive in either strand. After another round of DNA synthesis, this time in nonradioactive solution, one of the four DNA molecules would be radioactive in both strands and the other three DNA molecules would contain no

radioactivity in any strand. **15.** analyze (a) The double mutant of both *uvrA* and *recA* is most sensitive to UV light; the single mutants are in between; and the wild type is least sensitive. (b) The *recA* gene contributes more to UV repair through most of the UV dose levels. But at very high UV doses, the *uvrA* gene is somewhat more important than the *recA* gene. **16.** apply About 4600 seconds or 77 minutes. This answer comes from knowing that replication proceeds bidirectionally, so replication from each fork is predicted to replicate half the chromosome. This is 4.6 million base pairs/2 = 2.3 million base pairs. At 500 base pairs per second, this requires 2.3 million base pairs/500 base pairs per second = 4600 seconds. To obtain the time in minutes, divide 4600 seconds by 60 seconds per minute.

CHAPTER 7

IN-TEXT QUESTIONS AND EXERCISES

p. 125 Fig. 7.1 apply No, it could not make citrulline from ornithine without enzyme 2. Yes, it would no longer need enzyme 2 to make citrulline.

FIGURE A7.1

mRNA sequence:
5' AUG-CUG-GAG-GGG-GUU-AGA-CAU 3'

Amino acid sequence:
Met–Leu–Glu–Gly–Val–Arg–His

FIGURE A7.2

Bottom DNA strand:
3' AACTT-TAC(start)-GGG-CAA-ACC-TCT-AGC-CCA-ATG-TCG-ATC(stop)-AGTTTC 5'

mRNA sequence:
5' AUG-CCC-GUU-UGG-AGA-UCG-GGU-UAC-AGC-UAG 3'

Amino acid sequence:
Met–Pro–Val–Trp–Arg–Ser–Gly–Tyr–Ser

---

is in the nucleus but translation occurs in the cytoplasm. **5.** understand d **6.** remember A codon that signals the end of translation.

✔ **Test Your Understanding**

7. understand Because the Morse code and genetic code both use simple elements (dots and dashes; 4 different bases) in different orders to encode complex information (words; amino acid sequences).
8.

Substrate 1 $\xrightarrow{A}$ Substrate 2 $\xrightarrow{B}$ Substrate 3 $\xrightarrow{C}$
Substrate 4 $\xrightarrow{D}$ Substrate 5 $\xrightarrow{E}$ Biological Sciazine

apply Substrate 3 would accumulate. Hypothesis: The individuals have a mutation in the gene for enzyme D.
9. understand They supported an important prediction of the hypothesis: Losing a gene (via mutation) resulted in loss of an enzyme. **10.** understand c **11.** understand In a triplet code, addition or deletion of 1–2 bases disrupts the reading frame "downstream" of the mutation site(s), resulting in a dysfunctional protein. But addition or deletion of 3 bases restores the reading frame—the normal sequence is disrupted only between the first and third mutation. The resulting protein is altered but may still be able to function normally. Only a triplet code would show these patterns. **12.** understand A point mutation changes the nucleotide sequence of an existing allele, creating a new one, so it always changes the genotype. But because the genetic code is redundant, and because point mutations can occur in DNA sequences that do not code for amino acids, these point mutations do not change the protein product and therefore do not change the phenotype.

✔ **Test Your Problem-Solving Skills**

13. apply See **FIGURE A7.2**. **14.** analyze Every copying error would result in a mutation that would change the amino acid sequence of the protein and would likely affect its function. **15.** analyze Before the central dogma was understood, DNA was known to be the hereditary material, but no one knew how particular sequences of bases resulted in the production of RNA and protein products. The central dogma clarified how genotypes produce phenotypes. **16.** analyze c

CHAPTER 8

IN-TEXT QUESTIONS AND EXERCISES

p. 138 Fig. 8.1 remember RNA is synthesized in the 5' → 3' direction; the DNA template is "read" 3' → 5'.
p. 141 CYU (1) apply Transcription would be reduced or absent because the missing nucleotides are in the −10 region, one of the two critical parts of the promoter.
(2) understand NTPs are required because the three

phosphate groups raise the monomer's potential energy enough to make the polymerization reaction exergonic.
p. 142 Fig. 8.5 apply There would be no loops—the molecules would match up exactly.
p. 143 CYU (1) understand The subunits contain both RNA (the *ribonucleo–* in the name) and proteins. **(2)** understand The cap and tail protect mRNAs from degradation and facilitate translation.
p. 146 Fig. 8.11 analyze If the amino acids stayed attached to the tRNAs, the gray line in the graph would stay high and the green line low. If the amino acids were transferred to some other cell component, the gray line would decline but the green line would be low.
p. 147 understand (1) The amino acid attaches on the top right of the L-shaped structure. (2) The anticodon is antiparallel in orientation to the mRNA codon, and it contains the complementary bases.

p. 152 CYU understand E is for exit—the site where uncharged tRNAs are ejected; P is for peptidyl (or peptide bond)—the site where peptide bond formation takes place; A is for aminoacyl—the site where aminoacyl tRNAs enter.

IF YOU UNDERSTAND . . .

8.1 apply Transcription would continue past the normal point because the insertion of nucleotides would disrupt the structure of the RNA hairpin that functions as a terminator. **8.2** apply The protein-coding segment of the gene is predicted to be longer in eukaryotes because of the presence of introns. **8.3** understand The tRNAs act as adaptors because they couple the information contained in the nucleotides of mRNA to that contained in the amino acid sequence of proteins. **8.4** apply An incorrect amino acid would appear often in proteins. This is because the altered synthetase would sometimes add the correct amino acid for a particular tRNA and at other times add the incorrect amino acid. **8.5** create One possible concept map is shown in **FIGURE A8.1**.

YOU SHOULD BE ABLE TO . . .

✔ **Test Your Knowledge**

1. understand c **2.** remember c **3.** understand To speed the correct folding of newly synthesized proteins **4.** remember d **5.** remember At the 3' end **6.** apply b

✔ **Test Your Understanding**

7. understand Basal transcription factors bind to promoter sequences in eukaryotic DNA and facilitate the binding of RNA polymerase. As part of the RNA polymerase holoenzyme, sigma binds to a promoter sequence in bacterial DNA and to allow RNA polymerase to initiate at the start of genes. **8.** analyze The wobble rules allow a single tRNA to pair with more than one type of mRNA codon. This is distinct from redundancy, in which more

---

FIGURE A8.1

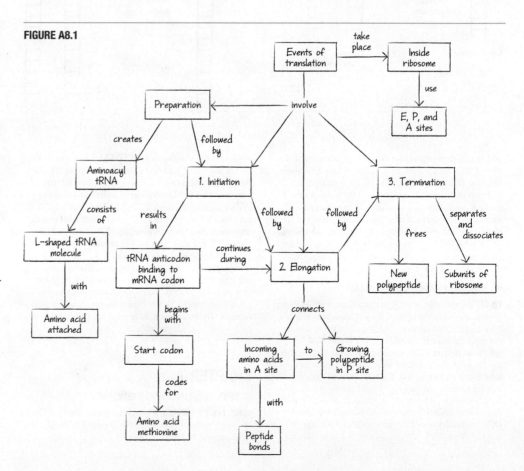

than one codon can specify a single amino acid. If the wobble rules did not exist, there would need to be one tRNA for each amino-acid-specifying codon in the redundant genetic code. **9.** apply b **10.** apply After a peptide bond forms between the polypeptide and the amino acid held by the tRNA in the A site, the ribosome moves down the mRNA. As it does, an uncharged tRNA leaves the E site. The now-uncharged tRNA that was in the P site enters the E site; the tRNA holding the polypeptide chain moves from the A site to the P site, and a new aminoacyl tRNA enters the A site. **11.** apply The ribosome's active site is made up of RNA, not protein. **12.** understand The separation allows the aminoacyl tRNA to place the amino acid into the ribosome's active site while reaching to the distant codon on the mRNA.

✔ Test Your Problem-Solving Skills

13. create Ribonucleases degrade mRNAs that are no longer needed by the cell. If an mRNA for a hormone that increased heart rate were never degraded, the hormone would be produced continuously and heart rate would stay elevated—a dangerous situation. **14.** apply d **15.** analyze The regions most crucial to the ribosome's function should be the most highly conserved: the active site, the E, P, and A sites, and the site where mRNAs initially bind. **16.** analyze The most likely locations are one of the grooves or channels where RNA, DNA, and ribonucleotides move through the enzyme—plugging one of them would prevent transcription.

CHAPTER 9

IN-TEXT QUESTIONS AND EXERCISES

p. 159 Fig. 9.2 understand The green R-groups contain mostly C and H, which have roughly equal electro-

negativities. Electrons are evenly shared in C—H bonds and C—S bonds, so the groups are nonpolar. Cysteine has a sulfur that is slightly more electronegative than hydrogen, so it will be less nonpolar than the other green groups. All of the pink R-groups have a highly electronegative oxygen atom with a partial negative charge, making them polar.
p. 160 apply From most hydrophilic to most hydrophobic: (1) aspartate, (2) asparagine, (3) tyrosine, (4) valine. The most hydrophilic amino acids will have side chains with full charges (ionized), like aspartate, followed by those with the largest number of highly electronegative atoms, like oxygen or nitrogen. Highly electronegative atoms produce polar covalent bonds with carbon or hydrogen. The most hydrophobic will not have oxygen or nitrogen in their side chains, but instead will have the largest number of C—H bonds, which are nonpolar covalent.
p. 163 CYU understand See **FIGURE A9.1**.
p. 168 CYU (1) understand Secondary, tertiary, and quaternary structure all depend on bonds and other interactions between amino acids that are linked in a chain in a specific order (primary structure). **(2)** There would be 20^5 different peptides, or 3.2×10^6 different primary sequences.
p. 171 CYU apply Amino acid changes would be expected to be in the active site or in regions that affect the folded structure of this site. Either of these changes could result in a different active site that either binds a new substrate or catalyzes a different reaction.

IF YOU UNDERSTAND . . .

9.1. understand Look at the R-group of the amino acid. If there is a positive charge, then it is basic. If there is a negative charge, then it is acidic. If there is not a charge, but there is an oxygen atom, then it is polar uncharged. If there is no charge or oxygen, then it is nonpolar.

9.2 apply Nonpolar amino acid residues would be found in the interior of a globular protein, grouped with other nonpolar residues due to hydrophobic interactions.
9.3 analyze Both calmodulin and infectious prions require some form of induction to achieve their active conformations. Calcium ions are required for calmodulin to fold into its functional structure while prions are induced to change their shape by other, improperly folded prion proteins. **9.4** analyze *Catalysis:* Proteins are made of amino acids, which have many reactive functional groups, and can fold into different shapes that allow the formation of active sites. *Defense:* Similar to catalysis, the chemical properties and capacity for different shapes allows proteins to be made that can attach to virtually any type of invading virus or cell. *Signaling:* The flexibility in protein structure allows protein activities to be quickly turned on or off based on binding to signal molecules or ions.

YOU SHOULD BE ABLE TO . . .

✔ Test Your Knowledge

1. remember d **2.** remember The atoms and functional groups found in the side chains. **3.** remember b **4.** remember b **5.** understand The order and type of amino acids (i.e., the primary structure) contains the information that directs folding. **6.** understand a

✔ Test Your Understanding

7. understand Because the nonpolar amino acid residues are not able to interact with the water solvent, they are crowded together in the interior of a protein and surrounded by a network of hydrogen-bonded water molecules. This crowding leads to the development of van der Waals interactions that help glue the nonpolar side chains together. **8.** understand No, polymerization is a nonspontaneous reaction because the product molecules have lower entropy than the free form of the reactants and there would be nothing to prevent hydrolysis from reversing the reaction. **9.** understand Many possible correct answers, including (1) the presence of an active site in an enzyme that is precisely shaped to fit a substrate or substrates in the correct orientation for a reaction to occur; (2) the doughnut shape of porin that allows certain substances to pass through it; (3) the cable shape of collagen to provide structural support for cells and tissues. **10.** create Proteins are highly variable in overall shape and chemical properties due to variation in the composition of R-groups and the array of secondary through quaternary structures that are possible. This variation allows them to fulfill many different roles in the cell. Diversity in the shape and reactivity of active sites also makes them effective catalysts. **11.** understand c **12.** create In many proteins, especially those involved in cell signaling, their structure is affected by binding to other molecules or ions. Since the shape of the protein is directly involved in its function, the protein's activity is regulated by controlling how it is folded. If proteins were inflexible, this type of control could not occur.

✔ Test Your Problem-Solving Skills

13. analyze The side chain of proline is a cyclic structure that is covalently bonded to the nitrogen in the core amino group. This restricts the movement of the side chain relative to the core nitrogen, which further restricts the backbone when the nitrogen participates in a peptide bond with a neighboring amino acid. **14.** create See **FIGURE A9.2 15.** apply b. Phosphates have a negative charge, so they are most likely to form ionic bonds with the positively-charged side chains of basic amino acid residues. **16.** apply The inherited forms likely have some alteration in the primary structure such that the infectious form is spontaneously generated at a higher rate than normal. The amino acid sequence in these prions would likely differ from those transmitted between animals.

FIGURE A9.1

FIGURE A9.2

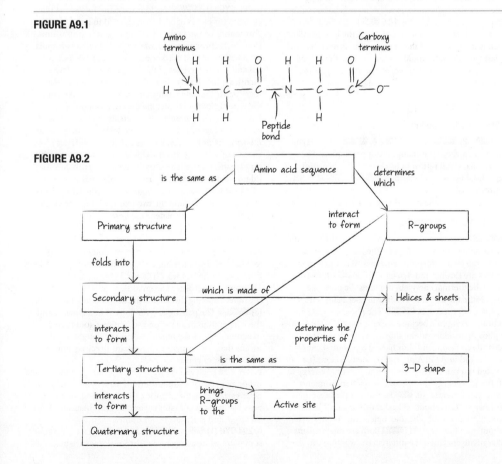

CHAPTER 10

IN-TEXT QUESTIONS AND ANSWERS

p. 177 `apply` (1) If ΔS is positive (products have more disorder than reactants), then according to the free energy equation, ΔG is more likely to be negative as temperature (T) increases even if ΔH is positive. The increased temperature represents added heat energy that may be used to drive an endothermic reaction to completion, making the reaction spontaneous. (2) Exothermic reactions may be nonspontaneous if they result in a decrease in entropy—meaning that the products are more ordered than the reactants (ΔS is negative).

p. 177 CYU (1) `understand` Gibbs equation: $\Delta G = \Delta H - T \Delta S$. ΔG symbolizes the change in the Gibbs free energy. ΔH represents the difference in enthalpy (heat, pressure, and volume) between the products and the reactants. T represents the temperature (in degrees Kelvin) at which the reaction is taking place. ΔS symbolizes the change in entropy (amount of disorder). **(2)** `understand` When ΔH is negative—meaning that the reactants have lower enthalpy than the products—and when ΔS is positive, meaning that the products have higher entropy (are more disordered) than the reactants.

p. 178 Fig. 10.4 `understand` Each point represents the data from a single test, not an average of many experiments, so it is not possible to calculate the standard error of the average.

p. 182 `analyze` Redox reactions transfer energy between molecules or atoms via electrons. When oxidized molecules are reduced, their potential energy increases. ATP hydrolysis is often coupled with the phosphorylation of another molecule. This phosphorylation increases the potential energy of the molecule.

p. 182 CYU (1) `understand` Electrons in C−H bonds are not held as tightly as electrons in C−O bonds, so they have higher potential energy. **(2)** `understand` In part, because its three phosphate groups have four negative charges in close proximity. The electrons repulse each other, raising their potential energy.

p. 182 Fig. 10.9 `understand` The ΔG in the uncoupled reaction would be positive (>0), and each of the steps in the coupled reaction would have a negative (<0) ΔG.

p. 185 `remember` (1) binding substrates, (2) transition state, (3) R-groups, (4) structure

p. 184 Fig. 10.12 `understand` No—a catalyst affects only the activation energy, not the overall change in free energy.

p. 185 Fig. 10.14 `analyze` See **FIGURE A10.1**.

p. 187 CYU (1) `create` The rate of the reaction is based primarily on the activity of the enzyme. Once the temperature reaches a level that causes unfolding and inactivation of the enzyme, the rate decreases to the uncatalyzed rate. **(2)** `apply` The shape change would most likely alter the shape of the active site. If phosphorylation activates catalytic activity, the change to the active site would allow substrates to bind and be brought to their transition state. If phosphorylation inhibits catalytic activity, the shape change to the active site would likely prevent substrates from binding or no longer orient them correctly for the reaction to occur.

p. 188 `apply` The concentration of A and B would be higher than in the fully functional pathway since they are not depleted to produce C. If D is not being depleted by other reactions, then equilibrium would be established between C and D, resulting in lower concentrations of both.

IF YOU UNDERSTAND . . .

10.1 `understand` Reactions are spontaneous when the free energy in the products is lower than that of the reactants (ΔG is negative). Enthalpy and entropy are measures used to determine free-energy changes. Enthalpy measures the potential energy of the molecules, and entropy measures the disorder. For exergonic, spontaneous reactions, disorder normally increases and the potential energy stored in the products normally decreases relative

FIGURE A10.1

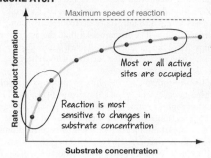

to the reactants. **10.2** `understand` Energetic coupling transfers free energy released from exergonic reactions to drive endergonic reactions. Since endergonic reactions are required for sustaining life, without energetic coupling, life would not exist. **10.3** `understand` Amino acid R-groups lining the active site interact with the substrates, orienting them in a way that stabilizes the transition state, thereby lowering the activation energy needed for the reaction to proceed. **10.4** `analyze` Allosteric regulation and phosphorylation cause changes in the conformation of the enzyme that affects its catalytic function. Allosteric regulation involves non-covalent bonding, while phosphorylation is a covalent modification of the enzyme's primary structure. **10.5** `apply` In the first step of the pathway, the rate would increase as the intermediate, which is the product of the first reaction, is removed. In the last step, the rate would decrease due to the loss of the intermediate, which serves as the substrate for the last reaction.

FIGURE A10.2

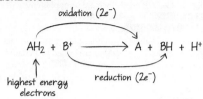

YOU SHOULD BE ABLE TO . . .

✔ Test Your Knowledge

1. `remember` c **2.** `remember` a **3.** `remember` a **4.** `remember` The enzyme changes shape, but the change is not permanent. The enzyme shape will return to its original conformation after releasing the products. **5.** `remember` d **6.** `remember` When the product of a pathway feeds back to interact with an enzyme early in the same pathway to inhibit its function.

✔ Test Your Understanding

7. `understand` The shape of reactant molecules (the key) fits into the active site of an enzyme (the lock). Fischer's original model assumed that enzymes were rigid; in fact, enzymes are flexible and dynamic. **8.** `understand` d. Energy, such as the thermal energy in fire, must be provided to overcome the activation energy barrier before the reaction can proceed. **9.** `understand` The phosphorylation reaction is exergonic because the electrons in ADP and the phosphate added to the substrate experience less electrical repulsion, and thus have less potential energy, than they did in ATP. A phosphorylated reactant (i.e., an activated intermediate) gains enough potential energy to shift the free energy change for the reaction from endergonic to exergonic. **10.** `apply` For the coupled reaction, step 1 has a ΔG of about −3 kcal/mol and step 2 has a ΔG of about −3 kcal/mol. The uncoupled reaction has a ΔG of about +1.3 kcal/mol. **11.** `analyze` Both are mechanisms that regulate enzymes; the difference is whether the

regulatory molecule binds at the active site (competitive inhibition) or away from the active site (allosteric regulation). **12.** `apply` Catabolic reactions will often have a negative ΔG based on a decrease in enthalpy and increase in entropy. Anabolic reactions are the opposite—a positive ΔG that is based on an increase in enthalpy and decrease in entropy.

✔ Test Your Problem-Solving Skills

13. `create` See **FIGURE A10.2**. **14.** `apply` Without the co-enzyme, the free-radical-containing transition state would not be stabilized and the reaction rate would drop dramatically. **15.** `analyze` The data suggest that the enzyme and substrate form a transition state that requires a change in the shape of the active site, and that each movement corresponds to one reaction. **16.** `apply` b. The sugar likely functions as an allosteric regulator to activate the enzyme.

CHAPTER 11

IN-TEXT QUESTIONS AND EXERCISES

p. 195 `apply` $n = 4$; the organism is diploid with $2n = 8$.

p. 196 `remember` See **FIGURE A11.1**. Because the two sister chromatids are identical and attached, it is sensible to consider them as parts of a single chromosome.

p. 198 `apply` There will be four DNA molecules in each gamete because the 8 replicated chromosomes in a diploid cell are reduced to 4 replicated chromosomes per cell at the end of meiosis I. In meiosis II, the sister chromatids of each replicated chromosome are separated. Each cell now contains 4 unreplicated chromosomes, each with a single molecule of DNA.

p. 201 `apply` Crossing over would not occur and the daughter cells produced by meiosis would be diploid, not haploid. There would be no reduction division.

p. 202 CYU (1) `understand` Use four long and four short pipe cleaners (or pieces of cooked spaghetti) to represent the chromatids of two replicated homologous chromosomes (four total chromosomes). Mark two long and two short ones with a colored marker pen to distinguish maternal and paternal copies of these chromosomes. Twist identical pipe cleaners (e.g., the two long colored ones) together to simulate replicated chromosomes. Arrange the pipe cleaners to depict the different phases of meiosis I as follows: *Early prophase I:* Align sister chromatids of each homologous pair to form two tetrads. *Late prophase I:* Form one or more crossovers between non-sister chromatids in each tetrad. (This is hard to simulate with pipe cleaners—you'll have to imagine that each chromatid now contains both maternal and paternal segments.) *Metaphase I:* Line up homologous pairs (the two pairs of short pipe cleaners and the two pairs of long pipe cleaners) at the metaphase plate. *Anaphase I:* Separate homologs. Each homolog still consists of sister chromatids joined at the centromere. *Telophase I and cytokinesis:* Move homologs apart to depict formation of two haploid cells, each containing a single replicated copy of two different chromosomes. **(2)** `understand` During anaphase I, homologs (not sister chromatids, as in mitosis) are separated, making the cell products of meiosis I haploid. **(3)** `understand` The pairing of homologs in metaphase I and their separation in anaphase I so that one goes to one daughter cell and the other to the other daughter cell means that each daughter cell obtains precisely one copy of each type of chromosome.

p. 204 `apply` Each gamete would inherit either all maternal or all paternal chromosomes. This would limit genetic variation in the offspring by precluding the many possible gametes containing various combinations of maternal and paternal chromosomes.

p. 204 CYU (1) `apply` See **FIGURE A11.2**. Maternal chromosomes are white and paternal chromosomes are black.

Daughter cells with other possible combinations of chromosomes than shown could result from meiosis of this parent cell. **(2)** understand Crossing over would increase the genetic diversity of these gametes by creating many different combinations of maternal and paternal alleles along each of the chromosomes. **(3)** analyze Asexual reproduction generates no appreciable genetic diversity. Self-fertilization is preceded by meiosis so it generates gametes, through crossing over and independent assortment, that have combinations of alleles not present in the parent. Outcrossing generates the most genetic diversity among offspring because it produces new combinations of alleles from two different individuals.
p. 205 Fig. 11.11 apply See **FIGURE A11.3**.
p. 207 Fig. 11.14 apply Asexually: 64 (16 individuals from generation three produce 4 offspring per individual). Sexually: 16 (8 individuals from generation three form 4 couples; each couple produces 4 offspring).
p. 208 Fig. 11.15 apply The rate of outcrossing is predicted to rise initially, as the pathogen selects for resistant roundworms, and then to fall as the roundworms in the population gain resistance and take advantage of the increased numbers of offspring offered by having more hermaphrodites that can reproduce by self-fertilization.

IF YOU UNDERSTAND . . .

11.1 remember See the right panel of Figure 11.7 and note how the cells transition from diploid to haploid in meiosis I. Also note that each chromosome contains two sister chromatids before and after meiosis I.
11.2 understand (a) See Figure 11.10 and note how the two different ways of aligning two homologous pairs of chromosomes at metaphase I of meiosis can create four different combinations of maternal and paternal chromosomes in daughter cells. (b) See Figure 11.11. Note that for each homologous pair with one crossover, two chromatids are recombinant and two are unaltered. Since each chromatid will produce a chromosome at

the end of meiosis II, your drawing should show that two out of four of these chromosomes are recombinant.
11.3 apply (a) Your model should show events similar to those of Figure 11.12. (b) Your model should show two cells with one of each type of chromosome (n), one cell with an extra copy of one chromosome ($n + 1$), and one gamete without any copies of one chromosome ($n - 1$).
11.4 remember Sexual reproduction will likely occur during times when conditions are changing rapidly, because genetically diverse offspring may have an advantage in the new conditions.

YOU SHOULD BE ABLE TO . . .

✔ Test Your Knowledge

1. remember b **2.** remember a **3.** remember b **4.** understand b
5. remember 1/2 **6.** remember mitosis.

✔ Test Your Understanding

7. remember Homologous chromosomes are similar in size, shape, and gene content, and originate from different parents. Sister chromatids are exact copies of a chromosome that are generated when chromosomes are replicated (S phase of the cell cycle). **8.** understand Refer to Figure 11.7 as a guide for this exercise. The four pens represent the chromatids in one replicated homologous pair; the four pencils, the chromatids in a different homologous pair. To simulate meiosis II, make two "haploid cells"—each with a pair of pens and a pair of pencils representing two replicated chromosomes (one of each type in this species). Line them up in the middle of the cell; then separate the two pens and the two pencils in each cell such that one pen and one pencil go to each of four daughter cells. **9.** understand Meiosis I is a reduction division because homologs separate—daughter cells have just one of each type of chromosome instead of two. Meiosis II is not a reduction division because sister chromatids separate— daughter cells have unreplicated chromosomes instead of replicated chromosomes, but still just one of each type. **10.** apply b. **11.** apply Tetraploids

produce diploid gametes, which combine with a haploid gamete from a diploid individual to form a triploid offspring. Mitosis proceeds normally in triploid cells because mitosis doesn't require forming pairs of chromosomes. But during meiosis in a triploid, homologous chromosomes can't pair up correctly. The third set of chromosomes does not have a homologous partner to pair with. **12.** understand Asexually produced individuals are genetically identical, so if one is susceptible to a new disease, all are. Sexually produced individuals are genetically unique, so if a new disease strain evolves, at least some plants are likely to be resistant.

✔ Test Your Problem-Solving Skills

13. apply The gibbon would have 22 chromosomes in each gamete, and the siamang would have 25. Each somatic cell of the offspring would have 47 chromosomes. The offspring should be sterile because it has some chromosomes that would not form homologous pairs at prophase I of meiosis. **14.** apply c **15.** apply Aneuploidy is the major cause of spontaneous abortion. If spontaneous abortion is rare in older women, it would result in a higher incidence of aneuploid conditions such as Down syndrome in older women, as recorded in the Figure 11.13. **16. (a)** create Such a study might be done in the laboratory, controlling conditions in identical dishes. A population of rotifers infected with fungus could be established in each dish. One dish of rotifers would be kept moist; the other dishes of rotifers would be allowed to dry out. After various periods of time, water would be added to each dish and then the rotifers would be observed to see if fungal infections reappeared. **(b)** create Wind disperses the rotifer to new and often pathogen-free environments. In this case, the ticket to a sex-free existence is not genetic diversity but the evolution of an alternative means of evading pathogens made possible by fungus-infected rotifers ridding themselves of the pathogen when they dry.

CHAPTER 12

IN-TEXT QUESTIONS AND EXERCISES

p. 216 Fig. 12.3 evaluate An experiment is a failure if you didn't learn anything from it. That is not the case here.
p. 217 Table 12.2 analyze Row 6: 3.14 : 1; Row 7: 266.
p. 218 apply Filling in the top and side of a Punnett square requires writing out the types and ratios of gametes. For a cross involving one gene (monohybrid cross), this amounts to applying the principle of segregation as one allele is segregated from another. The phenotype ratios are 1 : 1 round : wrinkled; the genotype ratios are 1 : 1 Rr : rr.
p. 218 Fig. 12.4 understand No—the outcome (the expected offspring genotypes that the Punnett square generates) will be the same.
p. 219 CYU (1) apply See answer to Problem 13 in Test Your Problem-Solving Skills, below. **(2)** apply See answer to Problem 15 in Test Your Problem-Solving Skills.
p. 221 apply $AABb \rightarrow AB$ and Ab. $PpRr \rightarrow PR, Pr, pR$, and pr. $AaPpRr \rightarrow APR, APr, ApR, Apr, aPR, apR, apr$, and aPr.
p. 221 CYU (1) apply See answer to Problem 14 in Test Your Problem-Solving Skills. **(2)** apply See answer to Problem 16 in Test Your Problem-Solving Skills.
p. 225 CYU (1) understand See **FIGURE A12.1**. Segregation of alleles occurs when homologs that carry those alleles are separated during anaphase I. One allele ends up in each daughter cell. **(2)** understand See **FIGURE A12.2**. Independent assortment occurs because homologous pairs line up randomly at the metaphase plate during metaphase I. The figure shows two alternative arrangements of homologs in metaphase I. As a result, it is equally possible for a gamete to receive the following four combinations of alleles: YR, Yr, yR, yr.
p. 226 Fig. 12.12 apply XWY, XWy, XwY, Xwy.

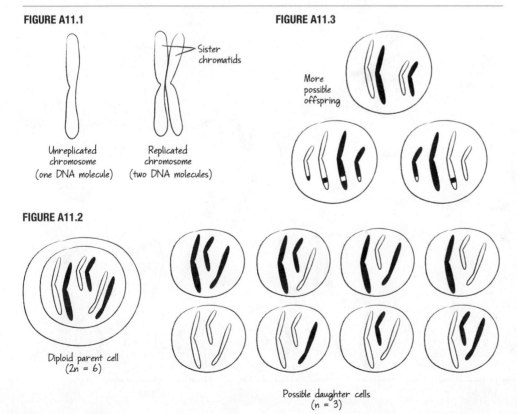

FIGURE A11.1

Sister chromatids

Unreplicated chromosome (one DNA molecule)

Replicated chromosome (two DNA molecules)

FIGURE A11.2

Diploid parent cell (2n = 6)

Possible daughter cells (n = 3)

FIGURE A11.3

More possible offspring

p. 227 Fig. 12.13 analyze Random chance (or perhaps red-eyed, gray-bodied males don't survive well).

p. 229 Fig. 12.16 analyze The gene colored orange is *ruby*; the gene colored blue is *miniature wings*.

p. 231 Fig. 12.19 understand In this case of gene-by-gene interaction, the 9:3:3:1 ratio comes from four different forms of one trait (comb shape), whereas in a standard dihybrid cross, the four different phenotypes come from two different phenotypes for each of two genes.

p. 232 CYU (1) apply The comb phenotype results from interactions between alleles at two different genes, not a single gene. Matings between rose- and pea-comb chickens produce F₂ offspring that may have a new combination of alleles and thus new phenotypes. **(2)** apply Kernel color in wheat is influenced by alleles at many different genes, not a single gene. F₂ offspring have a normal distribution of phenotypes, not a 3:1 ratio.

p. 232 Fig. 12.21 understand Because there are many different genotypes that can produce intermediate coloration and fewer that can produce the extremes of coloration.

p. 235 Fig. 12.23 apply A heterozygous female and a color-blind male. 1 color-blind male:1 color-blind female.

IF YOU UNDERSTAND . . .

12.1 understand Because crosses within a pure line never produce individuals with a different phenotype, this indicates that there must be only one allele in pure-line individuals. **12.2** apply B and b. **12.3** apply BR, Br, bR, and br, in equal proportions. The B and b alleles are located on different but homologous chromosomes, which separate into different daughter cells during meiosis I. The $BbRr$ notation indicates that the B and R genes are on different chromosomes. As a result, the chromosomes line up independently of each other in metaphase of meiosis I. The B allele is equally likely to go to a daughter cell with R as with r; likewise, the b allele is equally likely to go to a daughter cell with R as with r. **12.4** apply There are many ways to show this. If eye color in *Drosophila* is chosen as an example, then a pair of Punnett squares like those in Figure 12.11 illustrate how reciprocal crosses involving an X-linked recessive gene give different results.

12.5 understand Linkage refers to the physical connection of two alleles on the same chromosome. Crossing over breaks this linkage between particular alleles as segments of maternal and paternal homologs are exchanged.

12.6 apply See **FIGURE A12.3** for the pedigree. Note that the birth order of daughters and sons is arbitrary; other birth orders are equally valid. A Punnett square will show that all the sons are predicted to be X⁺Y and all the daughters X⁺Xᶜ, where X⁺ shows the dominant, X-linked allele for normal color vision and Xᶜ shows the X-linked recessive color blindness allele.

YOU SHOULD BE ABLE TO . . .

✔ Test Your Understanding

1. understand d **2.** understand b **3.** understand a **4.** understand d
5. understand a **6.** understand a **7.** evaluate d **8.** remember b **9.** apply b
10. understand d

FIGURE A12.1

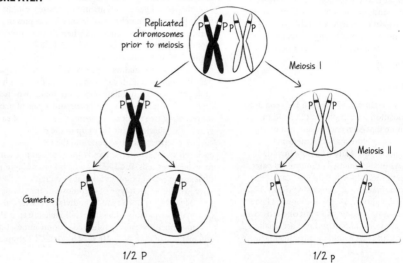

FIGURE A12.2

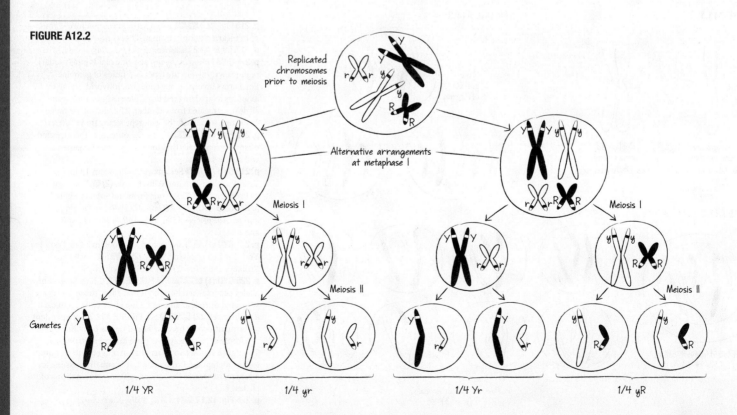

FIGURE A12.3

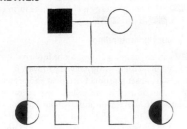

cross in the chart. If W^+ is dominant, then a wingless parent must be W^-W^-. When you do the Punnett square to predict offspring genotypes from selfing, you find that all the offspring will produce wingless fruits, consistent with the data. In the third cross, all the offspring make winged fruits even though one of the parents produces wingless fruits and thus is W^-W^-. This would happen only if the winged parent is W^+W^+. (If this reasoning isn't immediately clear to you, work the Punnett square.) In the fourth cross, you could get offspring that all make winged fruits if the parents were W^+W^+ and W^+W^+, or if the parents were W^+W^+ and W^+W^-. Either answer is correct. Again, you can write out the Punnett squares to see that this statement is correct.

12. apply Example Solution Here you are given parental and offspring phenotypes and are asked to infer the parental genotypes. As a starting point, assume that the coat colors are due to the simplest genetic system possible: one autosomal gene with two alleles, where one allele is dominant and the other recessive. Because female II produces only black offspring, it's logical to suppose that black is dominant to brown. Let's use B for black and b for brown. Then the male parent is bb. To produce offspring with a 1:1 ratio of black:brown, female I must be Bb. But to produce all black offspring, female II must be BB. This model explains the data, so you can accept it as correct.

13. apply 3/4; 1/256 (see BioSkills 5 in Appendix B); 1/2 (the probabilities of transmitting the alleles or having sons does not change over time). **14. apply** Your answer to the first three parts should conform to the F_1 and F_2 crosses diagrammed in Figure 12.5b, except that different alleles and traits are being analyzed. The recombinant gametes would be Yi and yI. Yes—there would be some individuals with yellow seeds and constricted pods and with green seeds and inflated pods. **15. apply** Cross 1: non-crested (Cc) × non-crested (Cc) = 22 non-crested ($C\_$); 7 crested (cc). Cross 2: crested (cc) × crested (cc) = 20 crested (cc). Cross 3: non-crested (Cc) × crested (cc) = 7 non-crested (Cc); 6 crested (cc). Non-crested (C) is the dominant allele. **16. apply** This is a dihybrid cross that yields progeny phenotypes in a 9:3:3:1 ratio. Let O stand for the allele for orange petals and o the allele for yellow petals; let S stand for the allele for spotted petals and s the allele for unspotted petals. Start with the hypothesis that O is dominant to o, that S is dominant to s, that the two genes are found on different chromosomes so they assort independently, and that the parent individual's genotype is $OoSs$. If you do a Punnett square for the $OoSs × OoSs$ mating, you'll find that progeny phenotypes should be in the observed 9:3:3:1 proportions. **17. analyze** Let D stand for the normal allele and d for the allele responsible for Duchenne-type muscular dystrophy. The woman's family has no history of the disease, so her genotype is almost certainly DD. The man is not afflicted, so he must be DY. (The trait is X-linked, so he has only one allele; the "Y" stands for the Y chromosome.) Their children are not at risk. The man's sister could be a carrier, however—meaning she has the genotype Dd. If so, then half of the second couple's male children are likely

to be affected. **18. understand** Your stages of meiosis should look like a simplified version of Figure 11.7, except with $2n = 4$ instead of $2n = 6$. The A and a alleles could be on the red and blue versions of the longest chromosome, and the B and b alleles could be on the red and blue versions of the smallest chromosomes, similar to the way the hair- and eye-color genes are shown in Figure 11.10. The places you draw them are the locations of the A and B genes, but each chromosome has only one allele. Each pair of red and blue chromosomes is a homologous pair. Sister chromatids bear the same allele (e.g., both sister chromatids of the long blue chromosomes might bear the a allele). Chromatids from the longest and shortest chromosomes are not homologous. To identify the events that result in the principles of segregation and independent assortment, see Figures 12.7 and 12.8 and substitute A, a, and B, b for R, r and Y, y. **19. apply** Half their offspring should have the genotype $i I^A$ and the type A blood phenotype. The other half of their offspring should have the genotype $i I^B$ and the type B blood phenotype. Second case: the genotype and phenotype ratios would be 1:1:1:1 $I^A I^B$ (type AB) : $I^A i$ (type A) : $I^B i$ (type B) : ii (type O). **20. apply** Because the children of Tukan and Valco had no eyes and smooth skin, you can conclude that the allele for eyelessness is dominant to eyes and the allele for smooth skin is dominant to hooked skin. E = eyeless, e = two eye sets, S = smooth skin, s = hooked skin. Tukan is $eeSS$; Valco is $EEss$. The children are all $EeSs$. Grandchildren with eyes and smooth skin are eeS-. Assuming that the genes are on different chromosomes, one-fourth of the children's gametes are ee and three-fourths are S-. So 1/4 ee × 3/4 S- × 32 = 6 children would be expected to have two sets of eyes and smooth skin. **21. create** Although the mothers were treated as children by a reduction of dietary phenylalanine, they would have accumulated phenylalanine and its derivatives once they went off the low-phenylalanine diet as young adults. Children born of such mothers were therefore exposed to high levels of phenylalanine during pregnancy. For this reason, a low-phenylalanine diet is recommended for such mothers throughout the pregnancy. **22. apply** According to Mendel's model, palomino individuals should be heterozygous at the locus for coat color. If you mated palomino individuals, you would expect to see a combination of chestnut, palomino, and cremello offspring. If blending inheritance occurred, however, all the offspring should be palomino. **23. apply** Because this is an X-linked trait, the father who has hemophilia could not have passed the trait on to his son. Thus, the mother in couple 1 must be a carrier and must have passed the recessive allele on to her son, who is XY and affected. To educate a jury about the situation, you should draw what happens to the X and Y during meiosis and then make a drawing showing the chromosomes in couple 1 and couple 2, with a Punnett square showing how these chromosomes are passed to the affected and unaffected children. **24. apply** The curved-wing allele is autosomal recessive; the lozenge-eyed allele is sex-linked (specifically, X-linked) recessive. Let L be the allele for long wings and l be the allele for curved wings; let X^R be the allele for red eyes and X^r the allele for lozenge eyes. The female parent is LlX^RX^r; the male parent is LlX^RY. **25. apply** Albinism indicates the absence of pigment, so let b stand for an allele that gives the absence of blue and y for an allele that gives the absence of yellow pigment. If blue and yellow pigment blend to give green, then both green parents are $BbYy$. The green phenotype is found in $BBYY$, $BBYy$, $BbYY$, and $BbYy$. The blue phenotype is found in $BByy$ or $Bbyy$ offspring. The yellow phenotype is observed in $bbYY$ or $bbYy$ offspring. Albino offspring are $bbyy$. The phenotypes of the offspring should be in the ratio 9:3:3:1 as green:blue:yellow:albino. Two types of crosses yield $BbYy$ F_1 offspring: $BByy × bbYY$ (blue × yellow) and $BBYY × bbyy$ (green × albino). **26. apply** The chance that their first child will have hemophilia is 1/2.

This is because all sons will have the disease and there is a 1/2 chance of having a firstborn son. The chance of having a carrier as their first child is also 1/2. This is because all daughters and none of the sons will be carriers and there is a 1/2 chance of having a firstborn daughter. (Recall that males cannot carry an X-linked recessive trait—with only one X chromosome, males either have the trait or not.) **27. apply** Autosomal dominant.

CHAPTER 13

IN-TEXT QUESTIONS AND EXERCISES

p. 242 Fig. 13.2 remember *Glycolysis:* "What goes in" = glucose, NAD^+, ADP, inorganic phosphate; "What comes out" = pyruvate, NADH, ATP. *Pyruvate processing:* "What goes in" = pyruvate, NAD^+; "What comes out" = NADH, CO_2, acetyl CoA. *Citric acid cycle:* "What goes in" = acetyl CoA, NAD^+, FAD, GDP or ADP, inorganic phosphate; "What comes out" = NADH, $FADH_2$, ATP or GTP, CO_2. *Electron transport and oxidative phosphorylation:* "What goes in" = NADH, $FADH_2$, O_2, ADP, inorganic phosphate; "What comes out" = ATP, H_2O, NAD^+, FAD.

p. 247 apply If the regulatory site had a higher affinity for ATP than the active site, then ATP would always be bound at the regulatory site, and glycolysis would always proceed at a very slow rate.

p. 247 Fig. 13.9 remember "Positive control": AMP, NAD^+, CoA (reaction substrates). "Negative control by feedback inhibition": acetyl CoA, NADH, ATP (reaction products).

p. 251 CYU remember (1) and (2) are combined with the answer to p. 171 CYU (3) Start with 12 triangles on glucose. (These triangles represent the 12 pairs of electrons that will be moved to electron carriers during redox reactions throughout glycolysis and the citric acid cycle.) Move two triangles to the NADH circle generated by glycolysis and the other 10 triangles to the pyruvate circle. Then move these 10 triangles through the pyruvate dehydrogenase square, placing two of them in the NADH circle next to pyruvate dehydrogenase. Add the remaining eight triangles in the acetyl CoA circle. Next move the eight triangles in the acetyl CoA circle through the citric acid cycle, placing six of them in the NADH circle and two in the $FADH_2$ circle generated during the citric acid cycle. (4) These boxes are marked with stars in the diagram.

p. 251 Fig. 13.13 apply NADH would be expected to have the highest amount of chemical energy since its production is correlated with the largest drop in free energy in the graph.

p. 253 Fig. 13.15 understand The proton gradient arrow should start above in the inner membrane space and point down across the membrane into the mitochondrial matrix. *Complex I:* "What goes in" = NADH; "What comes out" = NAD^+, e^-, transported H^+. *Complex II:* "What goes in" = $FADH_2$; "What comes out" = FAD, e^-, H^+. *Complex III:* "What goes in" = e^-, H^+; "What comes out" = e^-, transported H^+. *Complex IV:* "What goes in" = e^-, H^+, O_2; "What comes out" = H_2O, transported H^+.

p. 255 explain "Indirect" is accurate because most of the energy released during glucose oxidation is not used to produce ATP directly. Instead, this energy is stored in reduced electron carriers that are used by the ETC to generate a proton gradient across a membrane. These protons then diffuse down their concentration gradient across the inner membrane through ATP synthase, which drives ATP synthesis.

p. 255 Fig. 13.17 create They could have placed the vesicles in an acidic solution that has a pH below that of the solution in the vesicle. This would set up a proton gradient across the membrane to test for ATP synthesis.

p. 257 CYU understand See **FIGURE A13.1**. To illustrate the chemiosmotic mechanism, take the triangles (electrons) piled on the NADH and $FADH_2$ circles and move them through the ETC. While moving these triangles, also move dimes from the mitochondrial matrix to the intermembrane space. As the triangles exit the ETC, add them to the oxygen to water circle. Once all the dimes have been pumped to the intermembrane space, move them through ATP synthase back into the mitochondrial matrix to fuel the formation of ATP. **p. 259 CYU** understand Electron acceptors such as oxygen have a much higher electronegativity than pyruvate. Donating an electron to O_2 causes a greater drop in potential energy, making it possible to generate much more ATP per molecule of glucose.

IF YOU UNDERSTAND . . .

13.1 understand The radioactive carbons in glucose can be fully oxidized by the central pathways to generate CO_2, which would be radiolabeled. Other molecules, like lipids and amino acids, would also be expected to be radiolabeled since they are made using intermediates from the central pathways in other anabolic pathways. **13.2** apply See **FIGURE A13.2**. **13.3** understand Pyruvate dehydrogenase accomplishes three different tasks that would be expected to require multiple enzymes and active sites: CO_2 release, NADH production, and linking of an acetyl group to CoA. **13.4** apply NADH would decrease if a drug poisoned the acetyl CoA and oxaloacetate-to-citrate enzyme, since the citric acid cycle would no longer be able to produce NADH in the steps following this reaction in the pathway. **13.5** apply The ATP synthase allows protons to reenter the mitochondrial matrix after they have been pumped out by the ETC. By blocking ATP synthase, you would expect the pH of the matrix to increase (decreased proton concentration). **13.6** understand Organisms that produce ATP by fermentation would be expected to grow more slowly than those that produce ATP via cellular respiration simply because fermentation produces fewer ATP molecules per glucose molecule than cellular respiration does.

YOU SHOULD BE ABLE TO . . .

✔ Test Your Knowledge

1. understand Glycolysis → Pyruvate processing → citric acid cycle → ETC and chemiosmosis. The first three steps are responsible for glucose oxidation; the final step produces the most ATP. **2.** remember b **3.** understand d **4.** understand Most of the energy is stored in the form of NADH. **5.** remember c **6.** remember a

✔ Test Your Understanding

7. understand Stored carbohydrates can be broken down into glucose that enters the glycolytic pathway. If carbohydrates are absent, products from fat and protein catabolism can be used to fuel cellular respiration or fermentation. If ATP is plentiful, anabolic reactions use intermediates from the glycolytic pathway and the citric acid cycle to synthesize carbohydrates, fats, and proteins. **8.** analyze Both processes produce ATP from ADP and P_i, but substrate-level phosphorylation occurs when enzymes remove a "high-energy" phosphate from a substrate and directly transfer it to ADP, while oxidative phosphorylation occurs when electrons move through an ETC and produce a proton-motive force that drives ATP synthase. **9.** understand Aerobic respiration is much more productive because oxygen has extremely high electronegativity compared with other electron acceptors, resulting in a greater release of energy during electron transport and more proton pumping. **10.** apply b **11.** analyze Both phosphofructokinase and isocitrate dehydrogenase are regulated by feedback inhibition, where the product of the reaction or series of reactions inhibits the enzyme activity. They differ in that phosphofructokinase is regulated by allosteric inhibition while isocitrate dehydrogenase is controlled by competitive inhibition. **12.** understand Oxidative phosphorylation is possible via a proton gradient that is established by redox reactions in the ETC. ATP synthase consists of a membrane-associated F_o unit and a F_1 unit joined by a rotor shaft. When protons flow through the F_o unit, it spins the rotor shaft within the fixed F_1 unit. This spinning shaft causes structural changes in the F_1 that drives the synthesis of ATP from ADP and P_i.

✔ Test Your Problem-Solving Skills

13. create When complex IV is blocked, electrons can no longer be transferred to oxygen, the final acceptor, and cellular respiration stops. Fermentation could keep glycolysis going, but it is inefficient and unlikely to fuel a cell's energy needs over the long term. Cells that lack the enzymes required for fermentation would die first. **14.** apply Because mitochondria with few cristae would have fewer electron transport chains and ATP synthase molecules, they would produce much less ATP than mitochondria with numerous cristae. **15.** apply For each glucose molecule, two ATP are produced in glycolysis and two ATP are produced in the citric acid cycle via substrate-level phosphorylation. A total of 10 NADH and 2 FADH$_2$ molecules are produced from glycolysis, pyruvate oxidation, and the citric acid cycle. If each NADH were to yield 3 ATP, and each FADH$_2$ were to

FIGURE A13.1

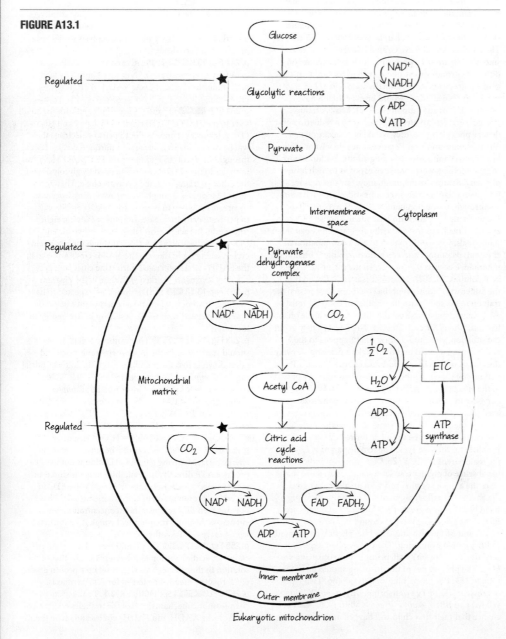

Eukaryotic mitochondrion

FIGURE A13.2

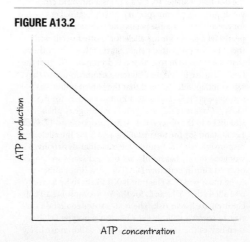

FIGURE A14.1

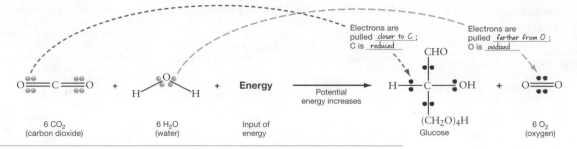

Electrons are pulled _closer to C_ ; C is _reduced_

Electrons are pulled _farther from O_ ; O is _oxidized_

Potential energy increases

6 CO_2 (carbon dioxide)   +   6 H_2O (water)   +   Energy   →   Glucose ($CH_2O)_4H$ +   6 O_2 (oxygen)

Input of energy

---

yield 2 ATP, then a total of 34 ATP would be produced via oxidative phosphorylation. Adding these totals would result in 38 ATP. A cell will not produce this much ATP, because the proton-motive force is used in other transport steps and because of other issues that may reduce the overall efficiency. **16.** apply b

CHAPTER 14

IN-TEXT QUESTIONS AND EXERCISES

p. 263 understand See **FIGURE A14.1**. This reaction is endergonic because there are more high-energy chemical bonds in the products compared with the reactants, and there is a decrease in entropy.

p. 263 Fig. 14.1 apply See **FIGURE A14.1**.

p. 266 Fig. 14.6 apply See **FIGURE A14.2**.

p. 268 Fig. 14.9 apply The energy state corresponding to a photon of green light would be located between the energy states corresponding to red and blue photons.

p. 269 CYU apply The outer pigments would be more likely to absorb blue photons (short wavelength, high energy), and interior pigments would absorb red photons (long wavelength, low energy). This establishes a pathway to direct photon energy toward the reaction center since resonance energy is transferred from higher to lower energy levels.

p. 270 Fig. 14.11 understand Yes—otherwise, changes in the production of oxygen could be due to differences in the number of chloroplasts, not differences in the rate of photosynthesis.

p. 272 analyze Light → Antenna complex → Reaction center → Pheophytin → ETC → Proton gradient → ATP synthase. Electrons from water are donated to the reaction center to replace those that were transferred to pheophytin.

p. 274 remember (1) Plastocyanin transfers electrons that move through the cytochrome complex in the ETC to the reaction center of photosystem (PS) I. (2) After they are excited by a photon and donated to the initial electron acceptor.

p. 276 CYU analyze In mitochondria, high-energy electrons are donated by NADH or $FADH_2$ (primary donors) and passed through an ETC to generate a proton-motive force. The low-energy electrons at the end of the chain are accepted by O_2 (terminal acceptor) to form water. In chloroplasts, low-energy electrons are donated by H_2O (primary donor), energized by photons or resonance energy, and passed through an ETC to generate a proton-motive force. These electrons are then excited a second time by photons or resonance energy, and the high-energy electrons are accepted by NADP$^+$ (terminal acceptor) to form NADPH.

p. 276 Fig. 14.18 understand The researchers didn't have any basis on which to predict these intermediates. They needed to perform the experiment to identify them.

p. 278 apply Each complete cycle requires 3 ATP and 2 NADPH molecules. To complete 6 runs through the cycle, a total of 18 ATP and 12 NADPH molecules are needed. By following the number of carbons, it is apparent that only three RuBP molecules are required, since they are fully regenerated every 3 cycles: 3 RuBP (15 carbons) fix and reduce 3 CO_2 to generate 6 G3P (18 carbons), yielding 1 G3P (3 carbons); the other 5 are used to regenerate 3 RuBP (15 carbons). The regeneration of RuBP means that only three would be required for continued runs through the Calvin cycle.

p. 280 Fig. 14.24 apply The morning would have the highest concentration of organic acids in the vacuoles of CAM plants, since these acids are made during the night and used up during the day.

p. 281 CYU (1) understand (a) C_4 plants use PEP carboxylase to fix CO_2 into organic acids in mesophyll cells. These organic acids are then transported into bundle-sheath cells, where they release carbon dioxide to rubisco. (b) CAM plants take in CO_2 at night and have enzymes that fix it into organic acids stored in the central vacuoles of photosynthesizing cells. During the day, the organic acids are processed to release CO_2 to rubisco. (c) By diffusion through a plant's stomata when they are open. **(2)** apply The concentration of starch would be highest at the end of the day and lowest at the start of the day. Starch is made and stored in the chloroplasts of leaves during periods of high photosynthetic activity during the day. At night, it is broken down to make sucrose, which is transported throughout the plant to drive cellular respiration. (Cellular respiration also occurs during the day, but the impact is minimized due to the photosynthetic production of sugar.)

IF YOU UNDERSTAND . . .

14.1 understand The Calvin cycle depends on the ATP and NADPH produced by the light-capturing reactions, so it is not independent of light. **14.2** understand Most of the energy captured by pigments in chloroplasts is converted into chemical energy by reducing electron acceptors in ETCs. When pigments are extracted, the antenna complexes, reaction centers, and ETCs have been disassembled, so the energy is given off as fluorescence and heat. **14.3** understand Oxygen is produced by a critical step in photosynthesis: splitting water to provide electrons to PS II. If oxygen production increases, it means that more electrons are moving through the photosystems. **14.4** apply Each CO_2 that is fixed and reduced by the Calvin cycle requires 2 NADPH, which means that 12 NADPH molecules are required for a 6-carbon glucose. Each NADPH is made when two high-energy electrons reduce NADP$^+$. Each of these high-energy electrons originates from H_2O only after being excited by 2 photons (one in PS II and one in PS I). This means that 48 photons are required to produce 24 high-energy electrons to reduce 12 NADP$^+$ molecules for the fixation and reduction of 6 CO_2 to make glucose. Photorespiration would increase the number of photons required, since some of the CO_2 that is fixed would be released.

FIGURE A14.2

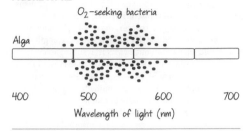

O_2-seeking bacteria

Alga

400   500   600   700

Wavelength of light (nm)

YOU SHOULD BE ABLE TO . . .

✓ Test Your Knowledge

1. remember d **2.** understand c **3.** remember c **4.** understand b **5.** remember The conversion of light energy to chemical energy occurs when electrons are transferred from excited pigments to an electron carrier in the photosystems. **6.** remember The electron transport chain that accepts electrons from PS II. Plastocyanin is the molecule that transfers electrons from this chain to the PS I reaction center.

✓ Test Your Understanding

7. understand The electrons taken from water in PS II are excited twice by either photons or resonance energy. When excited in PS II, the electrons are transferred to PQ and used to build a proton-motive force that makes ATP. After reaching PS I, they are excited a second time and will either be used to reduce NADP$^+$ to make NADPH (noncyclic) or be transported back to PQ to produce more ATP (cyclic). **8.** analyze c **9.** understand The fixation phase is when CO_2 is fixed to RuBP by rubisco to form 3-phosphoglycerate. The reduction phase uses ATP to phosphorylate the carbons and NADPH to reduce them with high-energy electrons to form G3P. The regeneration phase uses more ATP to convert some of the G3P to RuBP to continue the cycle. **10.** understand Photorespiration occurs when levels of CO_2 are low and O_2 are high. Less sugar is produced because (1) CO_2 doesn't participate in the initial reaction catalyzed by rubisco and (2) when rubisco catalyzes the reaction with O_2 instead, one of the products is eventually broken down to CO_2 in a process that uses ATP. **11.** understand In both C_4 and CAM plants, atmospheric CO_2 is brought in through stomata and first captured by fixing it to a 3-carbon molecule by PEP carboxylase. The C_4 pathway and CAM differ in the timing of this first fixation step—it occurs during the day in C_4 plants and during the night in CAM plants. They also differ in the location of the Calvin cycle with respect to this first fixation step. In C_4 plants, the two processes occur in different cells, while in CAM plants they occur in the same cell, but at different times (Calvin cycle during the day). **12.** analyze Photosynthesis in chloroplasts produces sugar, which is used as a source of carbon for building organic molecules and energy for cellular respiration. Mitochondria harvest the energy stored in sugar to produce ATP, which is used to drive many cellular activities.

✔ **Test Your Problem-Solving Skills**

13. `apply` (1) O_2, ATP, and NADPH would be formed by noncyclic electron flow. (2) No O_2 or NADPH would be formed, but ATP may be made by cyclic electron flow. (3) Initially, O_2 and NADPH would be formed by noncyclic electron flow, but no ATP would be made. Without ATP, the Calvin cycle would halt and, once all the NADP$^+$ is used up, noncyclic electron flow would switch to cyclic electron flow. **14.** `evaluate` Because rubisco evolved in a high CO_2, low O_2 environment, which would minimize the impact of photorespiration, the hypothesis is credible. But once O_2 levels increased, any change in rubisco that minimized photorespiration would give individuals a huge advantage over organisms with "old" forms of rubisco. There has been plenty of time for such changes to occur, making the "holdover" hypothesis less credible. **15.** `analyze` b; the wavelength of light could excite PS I, but not PS II, resulting in cyclic electron flow since no electrons could be harvested from water by PS II. **16.** `create` No—they are unlikely to have the same complement of photosynthetic pigments. Different wavelengths of light are available in various layers of a forest and water depths. It is logical to predict that plants and algae have pigments that absorb the available wavelengths efficiently. One way to test this hypothesis would be to isolate pigments from species in different locations and test the absorbance spectra of each.

BIG PICTURE Energy

p. 198 CYU (1) `understand` Photosynthesis uses H_2O as a substrate and releases O_2 as a by-product; cellular respiration uses O_2 as a substrate and releases H_2O as a by-product. **(2)** `understand` Photosynthesis uses CO_2 as a substrate; cellular respiration releases CO_2 as a by-product. **(3)** `analyze` CO_2 fixation would essentially stop; CO_2 would continue to be released by cellular respiration. CO_2 levels in the atmosphere would increase rapidly, and production of new plant tissue would cease—meaning that most animals would quickly starve to death. **(4)** `analyze` ATP "is used by" the Calvin cycle; photosystem I "yields" NADPH.

APPENDIX D

IN-TEXT QUESTIONS AND EXERCISES

p. D:3 Fig. 2.3 `apply` There are 15 electrons in phosphorus, so there must be 15 protons, which is the atomic number. Since the mass number is 31, then the number of neutrons is 16.

p. D:6 `understand` *Water:* arrows pointing from hydrogens to oxygen atom; *ammonia:* arrows pointing from hydrogens to nitrogen atom; *methane:* double arrows between carbons and hydrogens; *carbon dioxide:* arrows pointing from carbon to oxygens; *molecular nitrogen:* double arrows between nitrogens.

p. D:6 Fig. 2.7 `understand` Oxygen and nitrogen have high electronegativities. They hold shared electrons more tightly than C, H, and many other atoms, resulting in polar bonds.

p. D:7 CYU `evaluate` See **FIGURE A2.1**.

p. D:8 (1) `evaluate` δ^+H—O$^{\delta-}$—H$^{\delta+}$ **(2)** `apply` If water were linear, the partial negative charge on oxygen would have partial positive charges on either side. Compared to the actual, bent molecule, the partial negative charge would be much less exposed and less able to participate in hydrogen bonding.

p. D:9 Fig. 2.14 `understand` Oils are nonpolar. They have long chains of carbon atoms bonded to hydrogen atoms, which share electrons evenly because their electronegativities are similar. When an oil and water are mixed, the polar water molecules interact with each other via hydrogen bonding rather than with the nonpolar oil molecules, which interact with themselves instead.

p. D:11 Table 2.2 `understand` "Cause" (Row 1): electrostatic attractions between partial charges on water and opposite charges on ions; hydrogen bonds; water and other polar molecules. "Biological Consequences" (Row 2): ice to float; freezing solid. "Cause" (Row 4): lots of heat energy; break hydrogen bonds and change water to a gas.

p. D:12 `apply` The proton concentration would be 3.2×10^{-9} M.

p. D:12 Fig. 2.17 `apply` The concentration of protons would decrease because milk is more basic (pH 6.5) than black coffee (pH 5).

p. D:13 `apply` The bicarbonate concentration would increase. The protons (H$^+$) released from carbonic acid would react with the hydroxide ions (OH$^-$) dissociated from NaOH to form H_2O, leaving fewer protons free to react with bicarbonate to reform carbonic acid.

p. D:15 CYU (1) `apply` The reaction would be spontaneous based on the change in potential energy; the reactants have higher chemical energy than the products. The entropy, however, is not increased based on the number of molecules, although heat given off from the reaction still results in increased entropy. **(2)** `understand` The electrons are shifted farther from the nuclei of the carbon and hydrogen atoms and closer to the nuclei of the more electronegative oxygen atoms.

p. D:15 Fig. 2.19 `remember` See **FIGURE A2.2**.

p. D:16 Fig. 2.21 `analyze` The water-filled flask is the ocean; the gas-filled flask is the atmosphere; the condensed water droplets are rain; the electrical sparks are lightning.

p. D:20 Table 2.3 `understand` All the functional groups in Table 2.3, except the sulfhydryl group (—SH), are highly polar. The sulfhydryl group is only very slightly polar.

IF YOU UNDERSTAND . . .

2.1. `understand` The bonds in methane and ammonia are all covalent, but differ in polarity: Methane has nonpolar covalent bonds while ammonia has polar covalent bonds. Sodium chloride does not have covalent bonds; instead, ionic bonds hold the ionized sodium and chloride together. **2.2** `understand` Assuming neutral pH, amino and hydroxyl groups would interact with the partial negative charge on water's oxygen, because they both carry a positive charge (partial for the hydrogen in the hydroxyl). The carboxyl group would interact with the partial positive charges on water's hydrogens, since it would carry a negative charge after losing the proton from its hydroxyl. **2.3** `understand` Like solar radiation, the energy in electricity generates free radicals that would promote the reaction. **2.4** `understand` "Top-down" approach: The reaction responsible for synthesizing acetic acid is observed in cells and can serve as an intermediate for the formation of a more complex molecule (acetyl CoA) that is used by cells throughout the tree of life. "Bottom-up" approach: This reaction can also occur under conditions that mimic the early Earth environment in deep-sea vents. **2.5** `apply` The hydroxyls would increase the solubility of octane by introducing polar covalent bonds, which would make the molecule more hydrophilic. The high electronegativity of oxygen would decrease the potential energy of the modified molecule.

YOU SHOULD BE ABLE TO . . .

✔ **Test Your Knowledge**

1. `understand` b **2.** `remember` a **3.** `remember` c **4.** `remember` d **5.** `remember` Potential energy and entropy. **6.** `remember` The prebiotic soup model and the surface metabolism model.

✔ **Test Your Understanding**

7. `apply` c. Acetic acid has more highly electronegative oxygen atoms than the other molecules. When bonded to carbon or hydrogen, each oxygen will result in a polar covalent bond. **8.** `apply` Relative electronegativities would be F > O > H > Na. One bond would form with sodium, and it would be ionic. **9.** `understand` When oxygen is covalently bonded to hydrogen, the difference in electronegativities between the atoms causes the electrons to spend more time near the oxygen. In contrast, the atoms in H_2 and O_2 have the same electronegativities, so they equally share electrons in their covalent bonds. **10.** `apply` See **FIGURE A2.3**. **11.** `apply` The dissociation reaction of carbonic acid lowers the pH of the solution by releasing extra H$^+$ into the solution. If additional CO_2 is added, the sequence of reactions would be driven to the right, which would make the ocean more acidic. **12.** `understand` The carbon framework determines the overall shape of an organic molecule. The functional groups attached to the carbons determine the molecule's chemical behavior, because these groups are likely to interact with other molecules.

✔ **Test Your Problem-Solving Skills**

13. `analyze` b. **14.** `analyze` No, they don't conflict. Shells that are farther from the protons (positive charges) in the nucleus house electrons that have greater potential energy than shells closer to the nucleus. **15.** `analyze` One

---

FIGURE A2.2

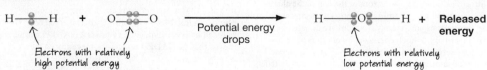

FIGURE A2.1

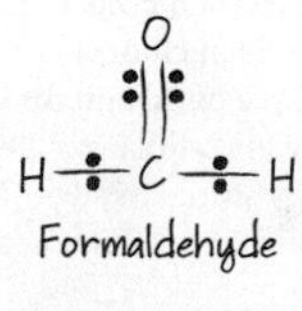

O

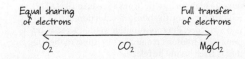

Formaldehyde

FIGURE A2.3

Equal sharing of electrons ———— Full transfer of electrons

O_2 CO_2 $MgCl_2$

FIGURE A2.4

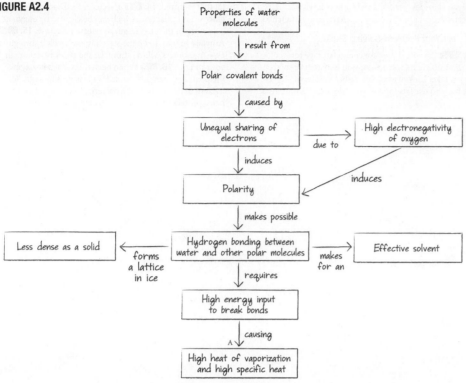

Properties of water molecules

↓ result from

Polar covalent bonds

↓ caused by

Unequal sharing of electrons — due to → High electronegativity of oxygen

↓ induces   ↘ induces

Polarity

↓ makes possible

Less dense as a solid ← forms a lattice in ice — Hydrogen bonding between water and other polar molecules → makes for an → Effective solvent

↓ requires

High energy input to break bonds

A ↓ causing

High heat of vaporization and high specific heat

---

possible concept map relating the structure of water to its properties is shown below (see **FIGURE A2.4**). **16.** create In hot weather, water absorbs large amounts of heat due to its high specific heat and high heat of vaporization. In cold weather, water releases the large amount of heat that it has absorbed.

APPENDIX E

IN-TEXT QUESTIONS AND EXERCISES

p. E:2 Fig. 5.2 understand See the structure of mannose in **FIGURE A5.1**.

p. E:4 CYU apply See **FIGURE A5.2**.

p. E:7 CYU remember They could differ in (1) location of linkages (e.g., 1,4 or 1,6); (2) types of linkages (e.g., α or β); (3) the sequence of the monomers (e.g., two galactose and then two glucose, versus alternating galactose and glucose); and/or (4) whether the four monomers are linked in a line or whether they branch.

p. E:8 Fig. 5.6 apply The percentage of inhibition would not change for the intact glycoprotein bar. The purified carbohydrate bar would be at zero inhibition, and the glycoprotein with digested carbohydrate bar would be similar to the intact glycoprotein bar.

p. E:9 Fig. 5.7 understand All of the C−C and C−H bonds should be circled.

p. E:10 CYU (1) understand *Aspect 1:* The β-1,4-glycosidic linkages in these molecules result in insoluble fibers that are difficult to degrade. *Aspect 2:* When individual molecules of these carbohydrates align, bonds form between them and produce fibers or sheets that resist pulling and pushing forces. **(2)** apply Most are probably being broken down into glucose, some of which in turn is being broken down in reactions that lead to the synthesis of ATP. Some will be resistant to digestion, such as the insoluble cellulose that makes up dietary fiber. This will help retain water and support the digestion and passage of fecal material.

IF YOU UNDERSTAND . . .

5.1. understand Molecules have to interact in an extremely specific orientation in order for a reaction to occur. Changing the location of a functional group by even one carbon can mean that the molecule will undergo completely different types of reactions. **5.2** analyze Glycosidic linkages can vary more in location and geometry than linkages between amino acids and nucleotides do. This variability increases the structural diversity possible in carbohydrates compared to proteins and nucleic acids. **5.3** understand (1) Polysaccharides used for energy storage are formed entirely from glucose monomers joined by α-glycosidic linkages; structural polysaccharides are made up of glucose or other sugars joined by β-glycosidic linkages. (2) The monomers in energy-storage polysaccharides are linked in a helical arrangement; the monomers in structural polysaccharides are linked in a linear arrangement. (3) Energy-storage polysaccharides may branch; structural polysaccharides do not. (4) Individual chains of energy-storage polysaccharides do not associate with each other; adjacent chains of structural polysaccharides are linked by hydrogen bonds or covalent bonds.

YOU SHOULD BE ABLE TO . . .

✓ Test Your Knowledge

1. remember d **2.** remember Monosaccharides can differ from one another in three ways: (1) the location of their carbonyl group; (2) the number of carbon atoms they contain; and (3) the orientations of their hydroxyl groups. **3.** remember a **4.** remember c **5.** remember a **6.** understand The electrons in the C=O bonds of carbon dioxide molecules are held tightly by the highly electronegative oxygen atoms, so they have low potential energy. The electrons in the C−C and C−H bonds of carbohydrates are shared equally, so they have much higher potential energy.

✓ Test Your Understanding

7. understand c. **8.** apply a; lactose is a disaccharide formed from a β-1,4-glycosidic linkage, so if two glucose molecules were linked with this bond, they would resemble units of cellulose and not be digested by human infants or adults. **9.** understand Carbohydrates are ideal for displaying the identity of the cell because they are so diverse structurally. This diversity enables them to serve as very specific identity tags for cells. **10.** understand When you compare the glucose monomers in an α-1,4-glycosidic linkage versus in a β-1,4-glycosidic linkage, the linkages are located on opposite sides of the plane of the glucose rings, and the glucose monomers are linked in the same orientation versus having every other glucose flipped in orientation. β-1,4-glycosidic linkages are much more likely to form linear fibers and sheets, so they resist degradation. **11.** remember Because (1) no mechanism is

---

FIGURE A5.1

H−C=O
C−OH (H)
HO−C−H
H−C−OH
HO−C−H
C−H
HO

FIGURE A5.2

Start with a monosacchride. This one is a 3–carbon aldose (carbonyl group at end)

→

Variation 1: 3–carbon ketose (carbonyl group in middle)

Variation 2: 4–carbon aldose

Variation 3: 3–carbon aldose with different arrangement of hydroxyl group

known for the prebiotic polymerization of sugars; (2) no catalytic carbohydrates have been discovered that can perform polymerization reactions; and (3) sugar residues in a polysaccharide are not capable of complementary base pairing. **12.** [understand] Starch and glycogen both consist of glucose monomers joined by α-1,4-glycosidic linkages, and both function as storage carbohydrates. Starch is a mixture of unbranched and branched polysaccharides—called amylose and amylopectin, respectively. All glycogen polysaccharides are branched.

✔ Test Your Problem-Solving Skills

13. [analyze] Carbohydrates are energy-storage molecules, so minimizing their consumption may reduce total energy intake. Lack of available carbohydrate also forces the body to use fats for energy, reducing the amount of fat that is stored. **14.** [apply] d; lactose is a disaccharide of glucose and galactose, which can be cleaved by enzymes expressed in the human gut to release galactose. **15.** [analyze] Amylase breaks down the starch in the cracker into glucose monomers, which stimulate the sweet receptors in your tongue. **16.** [apply] When bacteria contact lysozyme, the peptidoglycan in their cell walls begins to degrade, leading to the death of the bacteria. Lysozyme therefore helps protect humans against bacterial infections.

APPENDIX B BioSkills

Scientists ask questions that can be answered by observing or measuring things—by collecting data. What units are used to make measurements? When measurements are reported, how can you tell how reliable the data are?

The Metric System

The metric system is the system of units of measure used in every country of the world but three (Liberia, Myanmar, and the United States). It is also the basis of the SI system—the International System of Units (abbreviated from the French, *Système international d'unités*)—used in scientific publications.

The popularity of the metric system is based on its consistency and ease of use. These attributes, in turn, arise from the system's use of the base 10. For example, each unit of length in the system is related to all other measures of length in the system by a multiple of 10. There are 10 millimeters in a centimeter; 100 centimeters in a meter; 1000 meters in a kilometer.

Measures of length in the English system, in contrast, do not relate to each other in a regular way. Inches are routinely divided into 16ths; there are 12 inches in a foot; 3 feet in a yard; 5280 feet (or 1760 yards) in a mile.

If you have grown up in the United States and are accustomed to using the English system, it is extremely important to begin developing a working familiarity with metric units and values. **Tables B1.1** and **B1.2** (see B:2) should help you get started with this process.

As an example, consider the following question: An American football field is 120 yards long, while rugby fields are 144 meters

TABLE B1.1 Metric System Units and Conversions

Measurement	Unit of Measurement and Abbreviation	Metric System Equivalent	Converting Metric Units to English Units
Length	kilometer (km)	1 km = 1000 m = 10^3 m	1 km = 0.62 mile
	meter (m)	1 m = 100 cm	1 m = 1.09 yards = 3.28 feet = 39.37 inches
	centimeter (cm)	1 cm = 0.01 m = 10^{-2} m	1 cm = 0.3937 inch
	millimeter (mm)	1 mm = 0.001 m = 10^{-3} m	1 mm = 0.039 inch
	micrometer (μm)	1 μm = 10^{-6} m = 10^{-3} mm	
	nanometer (nm)	1 nm = 10^{-9} m = 10^{-3} μm	
Area	hectare (ha)	1 ha = 10,000 m^2	1 ha = 2.47 acres
	square meter (m^2)	1 m^2 = 10,000 cm^2	1 m^2 = 1.196 square yards
	square centimeter (cm^2)	1 cm^2 = 100 mm^2 = 10^{-4} m^2	1 cm^2 = 0.155 square inch
Volume	liter (L)	1 L = 1000 mL	1 L = 1.06 quarts
	milliliter (mL)	1 mL = 1000 μL = 10^{-3} L	1 mL = 0.034 fluid ounce
	microliter (μL)	1 μL = 10^{-6} L	
Mass	kilogram (kg)	1 kg = 1000 g	1 kg = 2.20 pounds
	gram (g)	1 g = 1000 mg	1 g = 0.035 ounce
	milligram (mg)	1 mg = 1000 μg = 10^{-3} g	
	microgram (μg)	1 μg = 10^{-6} g	
Temperature	Kelvin (K)*		K = °C + 273.15
	degrees Celsius (°C)		°C = $\frac{5}{9}$ (°F − 32)
	degrees Fahrenheit (°F)		°F = $\frac{9}{5}$°C + 32

*Absolute zero is −273.15 °C = 0 K.

TABLE B1.2 Prefixes Used in the Metric System

Prefix	Abbreviation	Definition
nano–	n	$0.000\,000\,001 = 10^{-9}$
micro–	μ	$0.000\,001 = 10^{-6}$
milli–	m	$0.001 = 10^{-3}$
centi–	c	$0.01 = 10^{-2}$
deci–	d	$0.1 = 10^{-1}$
–	–	$1 = 10^{0}$
kilo–	k	$1000 = 10^{3}$
mega–	M	$1\,000\,000 = 10^{6}$
giga–	G	$1\,000\,000\,000 = 10^{9}$

long. In yards, how much longer is a rugby field than an American football field? To solve this problem, first convert meters to yards: 144 m × 1.09 yards/m = 157 yards (note that the unit "m" cancels out). The difference in yards is thus: 157 – 120 = 37 yards. If you did these calculations on a calculator, you might have come up with 36.96 yards. Why has the number of yards been rounded off? The answer lies in significant figures. Let's take a closer look.

Significant Figures

Significant figures or "sig figs"—the number of digits used to report the measurement—are critical when reporting scientific data. The number of significant figures in a measurement, such as 3.524, is the number of digits that are known with some degree of confidence (3, 5, and 2) plus the last digit (4), which is an estimate or approximation. How do scientists know how many digits to report?

Rules for Working with Significant Figures

The rules for counting significant figures are summarized here:

- All nonzero numbers are always significant.
- Leading zeros are never significant; these zeros do nothing but set the decimal point.
- Embedded zeros are always significant.

- Trailing zeros are significant *only* if the decimal point is specified (Hint: Change the number to scientific notation. It is easier to see the "trailing" zeros.)

Table B1.3 provides examples of how to apply these rules. The bottom line is that significant figures indicate the precision of measurements.

Precision versus Accuracy

If biologists count the number of bird eggs in a nest, they report the data as an exact number—say, 3 eggs. But if the same biologists are measuring the diameter of the eggs, the numbers will be inexact. Just how inexact they are depends on the equipment used to make the measurements. For example, if you measure the width of your textbook with a ruler several times, you'll get essentially the same measurement again and again. Precision refers to how closely individual measurements agree with each other. So, you have determined the length with precision, but how do you know if the ruler was accurate to begin with?

Accuracy refers to how closely a measured value agrees with the correct value. You don't know the accuracy of a measuring device unless you calibrate it, by comparing it against a ruler that is known to be accurate. As the sensitivity of equipment used to

check your understanding

If you understand BioSkill 1

✓ **You should be able to . . .**

1. **QUANTITATIVE** Calculate how many miles a runner completes in a 5.0-kilometer run.

2. **QUANTITATIVE** Calculate your normal body temperature in degrees Celsius (Normal body temperature is 98.6°F.).

3. **QUANTITATIVE** Calculate your current weight in kilograms.

4. **QUANTITATIVE** Calculate how many liters of milk you would need to buy to get approximately the same volume as a gallon of milk.

5. **QUANTITATIVE** Multiply the measurements 2.8723 and 1.6. How many significant figures does your answer have? Why?

TABLE B1.3 Rules for Working with Significant Figures

Example	Number of Significant Figures	Scientific Notation	Rule
35,200	5	3.52×10^{4}	All nonzero numbers are always significant
0.00352	3	3.52×10^{-3}	Leading zeros are not significant
1.035	4	$1.035\ (\times 10^{0})$	Imbedded zeros are always significant
200	1	2×10^{2}	Trailing zeros are significant only if the decimal point is specified
200.0	4	2.000×10^{2}	Trailing zeros are significant only if the decimal point is specified

make a measurement increases, the number of significant figures increases. For example, if you used a kitchen scale to weigh out some sodium chloride, it might be accurate to 3 ± 1 g (1 significant figure); but an analytical balance in the lab might be accurate to 3.524 ± 0.001 g (4 significant figures).

In science, only the numbers that have significance—that are obtained from measurement—are reported. It is important to follow the "sig fig rules" when reporting a measurement, so that data do not appear to be more accurate than the equipment allows.

Combining Measurements

How do you deal with combining measurements with different degrees of accuracy and precision? The simple rule to follow is that the accuracy of the final answer can be no greater than the least accurate measurement. So, when you multiply or divide measurements, the answer can have no more significant figures than the least accurate measurement. When you add or subtract measurements, the answer can have no more decimal places than the least accurate measurement.

As an example, consider that you are adding the following measurements: 5.9522, 2.065, and 1.06. If you plug these numbers into your calculator, the answer your calculator will give you is 9.0772. However, this is incorrect—you must round your answer off to the nearest value, 9.08, to the least number of decimal places in your data.

It is important to nail down the concept of significant figures and to practice working with metric units and values. The Check Your Understanding questions in this BioSkill should help you get started with this process.

BIOSKILL 2 some common Latin and Greek roots used in biology

Greek or Latin Root	English Translation	Example Term
a, an	not	anaerobic
aero	air	aerobic
allo	other	allopatric
amphi	on both sides	amphipathic
anti	against	antibody
auto	self	autotroph
bi	two	bilateral symmetry
bio	life, living	bioinformatics
blast	bud, sprout	blastula
co	with	cofactor
cyto	cell	cytoplasm
di	two	diploid
ecto	outer	ectoparasite
endo	inner, within	endoparasite
epi	outer, upon	epidermis
exo	outside	exothermic
glyco	sugary	glycolysis
hetero	different	heterozygous
homo	alike	homozygous
hydro	water	hydrolysis
hyper	over, more than	hypertonic
hypo	under, less than	hypotonic
inter	between	interspecific
intra	within	intraspecific
iso	same	isotonic
logo, logy	study of	morphology
lyse, lysis	loosen, burst	glycolysis
macro	large	macromolecule

Greek or Latin Root	English Translation	Example Term
meta	change, turning point	metamorphosis
micro	small	microfilament
morph	form	morphology
oligo	few	oligopeptide
para	beside	parathyroid gland
photo	light	photosynthesis
poly	many	polymer
soma	body	somatic cells
sym, syn	together	symbiotic, synapsis
trans	across	translation
tri	three	trisomy
zygo	yoked together	zygote

check your understanding

If you understand BioSkill 2

✔ **You should be able to . . .**

Provide literal translations of the following terms:

1. heterozygote
2. glycolysis
3. morphology
4. trisomy

Graphs are the most common way to report data, for a simple reason. Compared to reading raw numerical values in a table or list, a graph makes it much easier to understand what the data mean.

Learning how to read and interpret graphs is one of the most basic skills you'll need to acquire as a biology student. As when learning piano or soccer or anything else, you need to understand a few key ideas to get started and then have a chance to practice—a lot—with some guidance and feedback.

Getting Started

To start reading a graph, you need to do three things: read the axes, figure out what the data points represent—that is, where they came from—and think about the overall message of the data. Let's consider each step in turn.

What Do the Axes Represent?

Graphs have two axes: one horizontal and one vertical. The horizontal axis of a graph is also called the x-axis or the abscissa. The vertical axis of a graph is also called the y-axis or the ordinate. Each axis represents a variable that takes on a range of values. These values are indicated by the ticks and labels on the axis. Note that each axis should *always* be clearly labeled with the unit or treatment it represents.

FIGURE B3.1 shows a scatterplot—a type of graph where continuous data are graphed on each axis. Continuous data can take an array of values over a range. In contrast, discrete data can take only a restricted set of values. If you were graphing the average height of men and women in your class, height is a continuous variable, but gender is a discrete variable.

For the example in this figure, the x-axis represents time in units of generations of maize; the y-axis represents the average percentage of the dry weight of a maize kernel that is protein.

To create a graph, researchers plot the independent variable on the x-axis and the dependent variable on the y-axis (Figure B3.1a). The terms independent and dependent are used because the values on the y-axis depend on the x-axis values. In our example, the researchers wanted to show how the protein content of maize kernels in a study population changed over time. Thus, the protein concentration plotted on the y-axis depended on the year (generation) plotted on the x-axis. The value on the y-axis always depends on the value on the x-axis, but not vice versa.

In many graphs in biology, the independent variable is either time or the various treatments used in an experiment. In these cases, the y-axis records how some quantity changes as a function of time or as the outcome of the treatments applied to the experimental cells or organisms.

(a) Read the axes—what is being plotted?

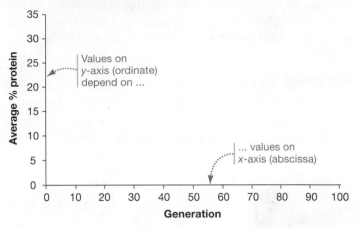

(b) Look at the bars or data points—what do they represent?

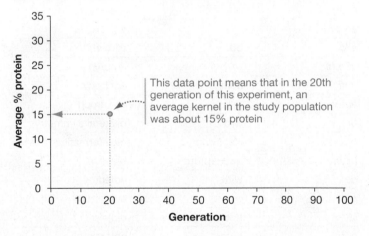

(c) What's the punchline?

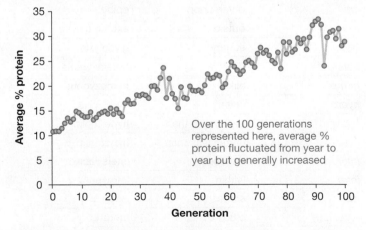

FIGURE B3.1 Scatterplots Are Used to Graph Continuous Data.

What Do the Data Points Represent?

Once you've read the axes, you need to figure out what each data point is. In our maize kernel example, the data point in Figure B3.1b represents the average percentage of protein found in a sample of kernels from a study population in a particular generation.

If it's difficult to figure out what the data points are, ask yourself where they came from—meaning, how the researchers got them. You can do this by understanding how the study was done and by understanding what is being plotted on each axis. The y-axis will tell you what they measured; the x-axis will usually tell you when they measured it or what group was measured. In some cases—for example, in a plot of average body size versus average brain size in primates—the x-axis will report a second variable that was measured.

In other cases, a data point on a graph may represent a relative or arbitrary unit of measurement. The data point shows the ratio of the amount of a substance, intensity, or other quantities, relative to a predetermined reference measurement. For example, the y-axis might show the percentage of relative activity of an enzyme—the rate of the enzyme-catalyzed reaction, scaled to the highest rate of activity observed (100 percent)—in experiments conducted under conditions that are identical except for one variable, such as pH or temperature (see Figure 10.14).

What Is the Overall Trend or Message?

Look at the data as a whole, and figure out what they mean. Figure B3.1c suggests an interpretation of the maize kernel example. If the graph shows how some quantity changes over time, ask yourself if that quantity is increasing, decreasing, fluctuating up and down, or staying the same. Then ask whether the pattern is the same over time or whether it changes over time.

When you're interpreting a graph, it's extremely important to limit your conclusions to the data presented. Don't extrapolate beyond the data, unless you are explicitly making a prediction based on the assumption that present trends will continue. For example, you can't say that the average percentage of protein content was increasing in the population before the experiment started, or that it will continue to increase in the future. You can say only what the data tell you.

Types of Graphs

Many of the graphs in this text are scatterplots like the one shown in Figure B3.1c, where individual data points are plotted. But you will also come across other types of graphs in this text.

Scatterplots, Lines, and Curves

Scatterplots sometimes have data points that are by themselves, but at other times data points will be connected by dot-to-dot lines to help make the overall trend clearer, as in Figure B3.1c, or may have a smooth line through them.

A *smooth line* through data points—sometimes straight, sometimes curved—is a mathematical "line of best fit." A line of best fit represents a mathematical function that summarizes the relationship between the x and y variables. It is "best" in the sense of fitting the data points most precisely. The line may pass through some of the points, none of the points, or all of the points.

Curved lines often take on characteristic shapes depending on the relationships between the x and y variable. For example, a bell-shaped curve depicts a normal distribution in which most data points are clumped near the middle, while a sigmoid or S-shaped curve exhibits small changes at first, which then accelerate and approach maximal value over time. Data from studies on population growth, enzyme kinetics (see Chapter 10), and oxygen–hemoglobin dissociation typically fall on a curved line.

Bar Charts, Histograms, and Box-and-Whisker Plots

Scatterplots, or line-of-best-fit graphs, are the most appropriate type of graph when the data have a continuous range of values and you want to show individual data points. But other types of graphs are used to represent different types of distributions:

- *Bar charts* plot data that have discrete or categorical values instead of a continuous range of values. In many cases the bars might represent different treatment groups in an experiment, as in **FIGURE B3.2a** (see B:6). In this graph, the height of the bar indicates the average value. Statistical tests can be used to determine whether a difference between treatment groups is significant (see **BIOSKILLS 4**).

- *Histograms* illustrate frequency data and can be plotted as numbers or percentages. **FIGURE B3.2b** shows an example where height is plotted on the x-axis, and the number of students in a population is plotted on the y-axis. Each rectangle indicates the number of individuals in each interval of height, which reflects the relative frequency, in this population, of people whose heights are in that interval. The measurements could also be recalculated so that the y-axis would report the proportion of people in each interval. Then the sum of all the bars would equal 100 percent. Note that if you were to draw a smooth curve connecting the top of the bars on this histogram, the smooth curve would represent the shape of a bell.

- *Box-and-whisker plots* allow you to easily see where most of the data fall. Each box indicates where half of the data numbers are. The whiskers indicate the lower extreme and the upper extreme of the data. The vertical line inside each box indicates the median—meaning that half of the data are above this value and half are below (see Figure 1.9 for an example).

When you are looking at a bar chart that plots values from different treatments in an experiment, ask yourself if these values are the same or different. If the bar chart reports averages over discrete ranges of values, ask what trend is implied—as you would for a scatterplot.

(a) Bar chart

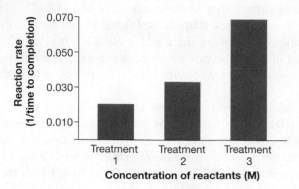

(b) Histogram

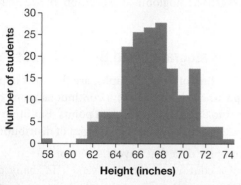

FIGURE B3.2 Bar Charts and Histograms. (a) Bar charts are used to graph data that are discontinuous or categorical. **(b)** Histograms show the distribution of frequencies or values in a population.

When you are looking at a histogram, ask whether there is a "hump" in the data—indicating a group of values that are more frequent than others. Is the hump in the center of the distribution of values, toward the left, or toward the right? If so, what does it mean?

Similarly, when you are looking at a box-and-whisker plot, ask yourself what information the graph gives you. What is the range of values for the data? Where are half the data points? Below what value is three quarters of the data?

Getting Practice

Working with this text will give you lots of practice with reading graphs—they appear in almost every chapter. In many cases we've inserted an arrow to represent your instructor's hand at the whiteboard, with a label that suggests an interpretation or draws your attention to an important point on the graph. In other cases, you should be able to figure out what the data mean on your own or with the help of other students or your instructor.

check your understanding

If you understand BioSkill 3

✔ **You should be able to . . .**

1. **QUANTITATIVE** Determine the total change in average percentage of protein in maize kernels, from the start of the experiment until the end.

2. **QUANTITATIVE** Determine the trend in average percentage of protein in maize kernels between generation 37 and generation 42.

3. Explain whether the conclusions from the bar chart in Figure B3.2a would be different if the data and label for Treatment 3 were put on the far left and the data and label for Treatment 1 on the far right.

4. **QUANTITATIVE** Determine approximately how many students in this class are 70 inches tall, by using Figure B3.2b.

5. **QUANTITATIVE** Determine the most common height in the class graphed in Figure B3.2b.

BIOSKILL 4 using statistical tests and interpreting standard error bars

When biologists do an experiment, they collect data on individuals in a treatment group and a control group, or several such comparison groups. Then they want to know whether the individuals in the two (or more) groups are different. For example, in one experiment student researchers measured how fast a product formed when they set up a reaction with three different concentrations of reactants (introduced in Chapter 10). Each treatment—meaning, each combination of reactant concentrations—was replicated many times.

FIGURE B4.1 graphs the average reaction rate for each of the three treatments in the experiment. Note that Treatments 1, 2, and 3 represent increasing concentrations of reactants. The thin

"I-beams" on each bar indicate the standard error of each average. The standard error is a quantity that indicates the uncertainty in the calculation of an average.

For example, if two trials with the same concentration of reactants had a reaction rate of 0.075 and two trials had a reaction rate of 0.025, then the average reaction rate would be 0.050. In this case, the standard error would be large. But if two trials had a reaction rate of 0.051 and two had a reaction rate of 0.049, the average would still be 0.050, but the standard error would be small.

In effect, the standard error quantifies how confident you are that the average you've calculated is the average you'd observe if

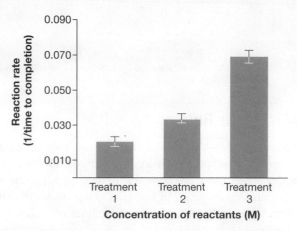

FIGURE B4.1 Standard Error Bars Indicate the Uncertainty in an Average.

you did the experiment under the same conditions an extremely large number of times. It is a measure of precision (see **BIOSKILLS 1**).

Once they had calculated these averages and standard errors, the students wanted to answer a question: Does reaction rate increase when reactant concentration increases?

After looking at the data, you might conclude that the answer is yes. But how could you come to a conclusion like this objectively, instead of subjectively?

The answer is to use a statistical test. This can be thought of as a three-step process.

1. Specify the null hypothesis, which is that reactant concentration has no effect on reaction rate.

2. Calculate a test statistic, which is a number that characterizes the size of the difference among the treatments. In this case, the test statistic compares the actual differences in reaction rates among treatments to the difference predicted by the null hypothesis. The null hypothesis predicts that there should be no difference.

3. The third step is to determine the probability of getting a test statistic at least as large as the one calculated just by chance. The answer comes from a reference distribution—a mathematical function that specifies the probability of getting various values of the test statistic if the null hypothesis is correct. (If you take a statistics course, you'll learn which test

statistics and reference distributions are relevant to different types of data.)

You are very likely to see small differences among treatment groups just by chance—even if no differences actually exist. If you flipped a coin 10 times, for example, you are unlikely to get exactly five heads and five tails, even if the coin is fair. A reference distribution tells you how likely you are to get each of the possible outcomes of the 10 flips if the coin is fair, just by chance.

In this case, the reference distribution indicated that if the null hypothesis of no actual difference in reaction rates is correct, you would see differences at least as large as those observed only 0.01 percent of the time just by chance. By convention, biologists consider a difference among treatment groups to be statistically significant if there is less than a 5 percent probability of observing it just by chance. Based on this convention, the student researchers were able to claim that the null hypothesis is not correct for reactant concentration. According to their data, the reaction they studied really does happen faster when reactant concentration increases.

You'll likely be doing actual statistical tests early in your undergraduate career. To use this text, though, you only need to know what statistical testing does. And you should take care to inspect the standard error bars on graphs in this book. As a *very* rough rule of thumb, averages often turn out to be significantly different, according to an appropriate statistical test, if there is no overlap between two times the standard errors.

check your understanding

If you understand BioSkill 4

✔ **You should be able to . . .**

QUANTITATIVE Determine which of the following tests used to estimate the average height of individuals in a class is likely to have the smallest standard error, and why.

• Measuring the height of two individuals chosen at random to estimate the average.

• Measuring the height of every student who showed up for class on a particular day to estimate the average.

In several cases in this text, you'll need to combine probabilities from different events in order to solve a problem. One of the most common applications is in genetics problems. For example, Punnett squares work because they are based on two fundamental rules of probability. Each rule pertains to a distinct situation.

The Both-And Rule

The both-and rule—also known as the product rule or multiplication rule—applies when you want to know the probability that two or more independent events occur together. Let's use the rolling of two dice as an example. What is the probability of rolling two sixes? These two events are independent, because the probability of rolling a six on one die has no effect on the probability of rolling a six on the other die. (In the same way, the probability of getting a gamete with allele R from one parent has no effect on the probability of getting a gamete with allele R from the other parent. Gametes fuse randomly.)

The probability of rolling a six on the first die is 1/6. The probability of rolling a six on the second die is also 1/6. The probability of rolling a six on *both* dice, then, is $1/6 \times 1/6 = 1/36$. In other words, if you rolled two dice 36 times, on average you would expect to roll two sixes once.

In the case of a cross between two parents heterozygous at the R gene, the probability of getting allele R from the father is 1/2 and the probability of getting R from the mother is 1/2. Thus, the probability of getting both alleles and creating an offspring with genotype RR is $1/2 \times 1/2 = 1/4$.

The Either-Or Rule

The either-or rule—also known as the sum rule or addition rule—applies when you want to know the probability of an event happening when there are several different ways for the same event or outcome to occur. In this case, the probability that the event will occur is the sum of the probabilities of each way that it can occur.

For example, suppose you wanted to know the probability of rolling either a one or a six when you toss a die. The probability of drawing each is 1/6, so the probability of getting one or the other is $1/6 + 1/6 = 1/3$. If you rolled a die three times, on average you'd expect to get a one or a six once.

In the case of a cross between two parents heterozygous at the R gene, the probability of getting an R allele from the father and an r allele from the mother is $1/2 \times 1/2 = 1/4$. Similarly, the probability of getting an r allele from the father and an R allele from the mother is $1/2 \times 1/2 = 1/4$. Thus, the combined probability of getting the Rr genotype in either of the two ways is $1/4 + 1/4 = 1/2$.

check your understanding

If you understand BioSkill 5

✔ **You should be able to . . .**

1. **QUANTITATIVE** Calculate the probability of getting four "tails" if four students each toss a coin.

2. **QUANTITATIVE** Calculate the probability of getting a two, a three, or a six after a single roll of a die.

You have probably been introduced to logarithms and logarithmic notation in algebra courses, and you will encounter logarithms at several points in this course. Logarithms are a way of working with powers—meaning, numbers that are multiplied by themselves one or more times.

Scientists use exponential notation to represent powers. For example,

$$a^x = y$$

means that if you multiply a by itself x times, you get y. In exponential notation, a is called the base and x is called the exponent. The entire expression is called an exponential function.

What if you know y and a, and you want to know x? This is where logarithms come in. You can solve for exponents using logarithms. For example,

$$x = \log_a y$$

This equation reads, x is equal to the logarithm of y to the base a. Logarithms are a way of working with exponential functions. They are important because so many processes in biology (and chemistry and physics, for that matter) are exponential. To understand what's going on, you have to describe the process with an exponential function and then use logarithms to work with that function.

Although a base can be any number, most scientists use just two bases when they employ logarithmic notation: 10 and e (sometimes called Euler's number after Swiss mathematician Leonhard Euler). What is e? It is a rate of exponential growth shared by many natural processes, where e is the limit of $(1 + \frac{1}{n})^n$ (as n tends to infinity). Mathematicians have shown that the base e is an irrational number (like π) that is approximately equal to 2.718. Like 10, e is just a number; $10^0 = 1$ and, likewise, $e^0 = 1$. But both 10 and e have qualities that make them convenient to use in biology (as well as chemistry and physics).

Logarithms to the base 10 are so common that they are usually symbolized in the form $\log y$ instead of $\log_{10} y$. A logarithm to the base e is called a natural logarithm and is symbolized ln (pronounced *EL-EN*) instead of log. You write "the natural logarithm of y" as $\ln y$.

Most scientific calculators have keys that allow you to solve problems involving base 10 and base e. For example, if you know y, they'll tell you what $\log y$ or $\ln y$ are—meaning that they'll solve for x in our first example equation. They'll also allow you to find a number when you know its logarithm to base 10 or base

e. Stated another way, they'll tell you what y is if you know x, and y is equal to e^x or 10^x. This is called taking an antilog. In most cases, you'll use the inverse or second function button on your calculator to find an antilog (above the log or ln key).

To get some practice with your calculator, consider this equation:

$$10^2 = 100$$

If you enter 100 in your calculator and then press the log key, the screen should say 2. The logarithm tells you what the exponent is. Now press the antilog key while 2 is on the screen. The calculator screen should return to 100. The antilog solves the exponential function, given the base and the exponent.

If your background in algebra isn't strong, you'll want to get more practice working with logarithms—you'll see them frequently during your undergraduate career. Remember that once you understand the basic notation, there's nothing mysterious about logarithms. They are simply a way of working with exponential functions, which describe what happens when something is multiplied by itself a number of times—like cells that divide and then divide again and then again.

Using logarithms will also come up when you are studying something that can have a large range of values, like the concentration of hydrogen ions in a solution or the intensity of sound that the human ear can detect. In cases like this, it's convenient to express the numbers involved as exponents. Using exponents makes a large range of numbers smaller and more manageable. For example, instead of saying that hydrogen ion concentration in a solution can range from 1 to 10^{-14}, the pH scale allows you to simply say that it ranges from 1 to 14. Instead of giving the actual value, you're expressing it as an exponent. It just simplifies things.

check your understanding

If you understand BioSkill 6

✔ **You should be able to . . .**

Use the equation $N_t = N_0 e^{rt}$.

1. Explain what type of function this equation describes.

2. **QUANTITATIVE** Determine how you would write the equation, after taking the natural logarithm of both sides.

Phylogenetic trees show the evolutionary relationships among species, just as a genealogy shows the relationships among people in your family. They are unusual diagrams, however, and it can take practice to interpret them correctly.

To understand how evolutionary trees work, consider **FIGURE B7.1**. Notice that a phylogenetic tree consists of a root (the most ancestral branch in the tree), branches, nodes, and tips.

- Branches represent populations through time. In this text, branches are drawn as horizontal lines. In most cases the length of the branch is arbitrary and has no meaning, but in some cases branch lengths are proportional to time or the extent of genetic difference among populations (if so, there will be a scale at the bottom of the tree). The vertical lines on the tree represent splitting events, where one group broke into two independent groups. Their length is arbitrary—chosen simply to make the tree more readable.

- Nodes (also called forks) occur where an ancestral group splits into two or more descendant groups (see point A in Figure B7.1). Thus, each node represents the most recent common ancestor of the two or more descendant populations that emerge from it. If more than two descendant groups emerge from a node, the node is called a polytomy (see node C). A polytomy usually means that the populations split from one another so quickly that it is not possible to tell which split off earlier or later.

- Tips (also called terminal nodes) are the tree's endpoints, which represent groups living today or a dead end—a branch

ending in extinction. The names at the tips can represent species or larger groups such as mammals or conifers.

Recall that a taxon (plural: taxa) is any named group of organisms (see Chapter 1). A taxon could be a single species, such as *Homo sapiens*, or a large group of species, such as Primates. Tips connected by a single node on a tree are called sister taxa.

The phylogenetic trees used in this text are all rooted. This means that the first, or most basal, node on the tree—the one on the far left in this book—is the most ancient. To determine where the root on a tree occurs, biologists include one or more outgroup species when they are collecting data to estimate a particular phylogeny. An outgroup is a taxonomic group that is known to have diverged before the rest of the taxa in the study. Outgroups are used to establish whether a trait is ancestral or derived. An ancestral trait is a characteristic that existed in an ancestor; a derived trait is a characteristic that is a modified form of the ancestral trait, found in a descendant.

In Figure B7.1, Taxon 1 is an outgroup to the monophyletic group consisting of taxa 2–6. A monophyletic group consists of an ancestral species and all of its descendants. The root of a tree is placed between the outgroup and the monophyletic group being studied. This position in Figure B7.1 is node A. Note that black hash marks are used to indicate a derived trait that is shared among the red branches, and another derived trait that is shared among the orange branches.

Understanding monophyletic groups is fundamental to reading and estimating phylogenetic trees. Monophyletic groups may also be called lineages or clades and can be identified using the "one-snip test": If you cut any branch on a phylogenetic tree, all of the branches and tips that fall off represent a monophyletic group. Using the one-snip test, you should be able to convince yourself that the monophyletic groups on a tree are nested. In Figure B7.1, for example, the monophyletic group comprising node A and taxa 1–6 contains a monophyletic group consisting of node B and taxa 2–6, which includes the monophyletic group represented by node C and taxa 4–6.

To put all these new terms and concepts to work, consider the phylogenetic tree in **FIGURE B7.2**, which shows the relationships between common chimpanzees and six human and humanlike species that lived over the past 5–6 million years. Chimps functioned as an outgroup in the analysis that led to this tree, so the root was placed at node A. The branches marked in red identify a monophyletic group called the hominins.

To practice how to read a tree, put your finger at the tree's root, at the far left, and work your way to the right. At node A, the ancestral population split into two descendant populations. One of these populations eventually evolved into today's chimps; the other gave rise to the six species of hominins pictured. Now

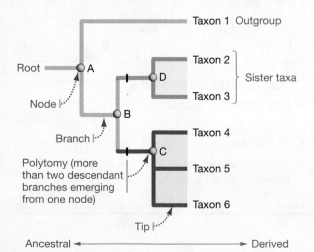

FIGURE B7.1 Phylogenetic Trees Have Roots, Branches, Nodes, and Tips.

✔**EXERCISE** Circle all four monophyletic groups present.

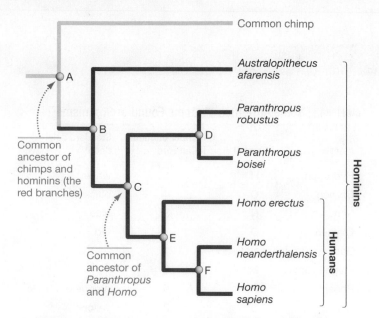

FIGURE B7.2 An Example of a Phylogenetic Tree. A phylogenetic tree showing the relationships of species in the monophyletic group called hominins.

✔**EXERCISE** All of the hominins walked on two legs—unlike chimps and all of the other primates. Add a mark on the phylogeny to show where upright posture evolved, and label it "origin of walking on two legs." Circle and label a pair of sister species. Label an outgroup to the monophyletic group called humans (species in the genus *Homo*).

continue moving your finger toward the tips of the tree until you hit node C. It should make sense to you that at this splitting event, one descendant population eventually gave rise to two *Paranthropus* species, while the other became the ancestor of humans—species in the genus *Homo*. As you study Figure B7.2, consider these two important points:

1. There are many equivalent ways of drawing this tree. For example, this version shows *Homo sapiens* on the bottom. But the tree would be identical if the two branches emerging from node E were rotated 180°, so that the species appeared in the order *Homo sapiens*, *Homo neanderthalensis*, *Homo erectus*. Trees are read from root to tips, not from top to bottom or bottom to top.

2. No species on any tree is any higher or lower than any other. Chimps and *Homo sapiens* have been evolving exactly the same amount of time since their divergence from a common ancestor—neither species is higher or lower than the other. It is legitimate to say that more ancient groups like *Australopithecus afarensis* have traits that are ancestral or more basal—meaning, that appeared earlier in evolution—compared to traits that appear in *Homo sapiens*, which are referred to as more derived.

FIGURE B7.3 presents a chance to test your tree-reading ability. Five of the six trees shown in this diagram are identical in terms of the evolutionary relationships they represent. One differs. The key to understanding the difference is to recognize that the ordering of tips does not matter in a tree—only the ordering of nodes (branch points) matters. You can think of a tree as being like a mobile: The tips can rotate without changing the underlying relationships.

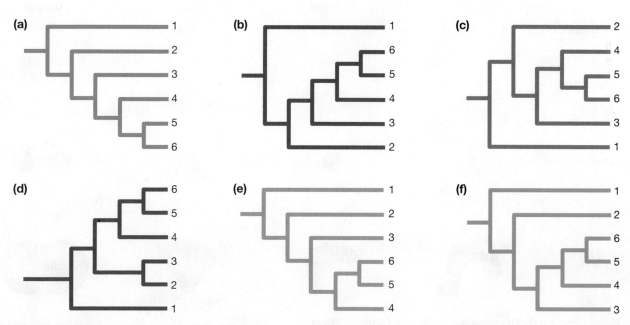

FIGURE B7.3 Alternative Ways of Drawing the Same Tree.

✔**QUESTION** Five of these six trees describe exactly the same relationships among taxa 1 through 6. Identify the tree that is different from the other five.

If you haven't had much chemistry yet, learning basic biological chemistry can be a challenge. One stumbling block is simply being able to read chemical structures efficiently and understand what they mean. This skill will come much easier once you have a little notation under your belt and you understand some basic symbols.

Atoms are the basic building blocks of everything in the universe, just as cells are the basic building blocks of your body. Every atom has a one- or two-letter symbol. **Table B8.1** shows the symbols for most of the atoms you'll encounter in this book. You should memorize these. The table also offers details on how the atoms form bonds as well as how they are represented in some visual models.

When atoms attach to each other by covalent bonding, a molecule forms. Biologists have a couple of different ways of representing molecules—you'll see each of these in the book and in class.

- Molecular formulas like those in **FIGURE B8.1a** simply list the atoms present in a molecule. Subscripts indicate how many of each atom are present. If the formula has no subscript, only one atom of that type is present. A methane (natural gas) molecule, for example, can be written as CH_4. It consists of one carbon atom and four hydrogen atoms.

TABLE B8.1 Some Attributes of Atoms Found in Organisms

Atom	Symbol	Number of Bonds It Can Form	Standard Color Code*
Hydrogen	H	1	white
Carbon	C	4	black
Nitrogen	N	3	blue
Oxygen	O	2	red
Sodium	Na	1	—
Magnesium	Mg	2	—
Phosphorus	P	5	orange or purple
Sulfur	S	2	yellow
Chlorine	Cl	1	—
Potassium	K	1	—
Calcium	Ca	2	—

*In ball-and-stick or space-filling models.

- Structural formulas like those in **FIGURE B8.1b** show which atoms in the molecule are bonded to each other. Each bond is indicated by a dash. The structural formula for methane in-

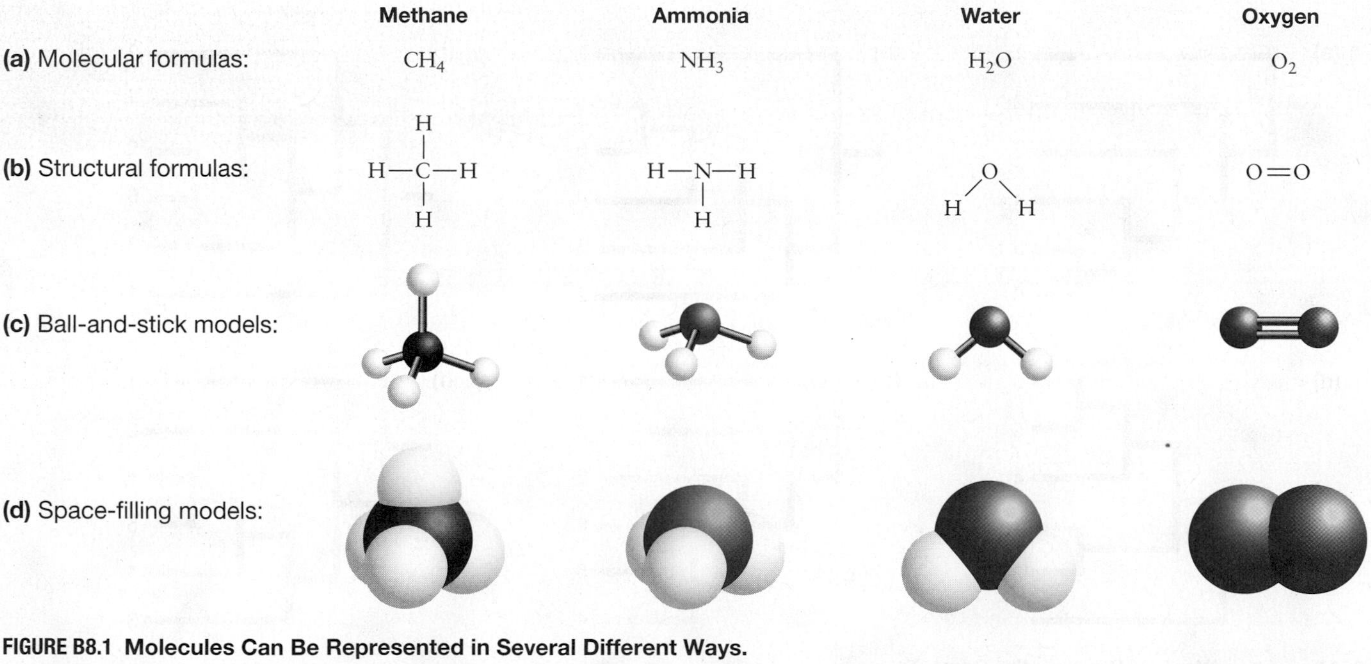

	Methane	Ammonia	Water	Oxygen
(a) Molecular formulas:	CH_4	NH_3	H_2O	O_2

(b) Structural formulas:

(c) Ball-and-stick models:

(d) Space-filling models:

FIGURE B8.1 Molecules Can Be Represented in Several Different Ways.

✔**EXERCISE** Carbon dioxide consists of a carbon atom that forms a double bond with each of two oxygen atoms, for a total of four bonds. It is a linear molecule. Write carbon dioxide's molecular formula and then draw its structural formula, a ball-and-stick model, and a space-filling model.

dicates that each of the four hydrogen atoms forms one covalent bond with carbon, and that carbon makes a total of four covalent bonds. Single covalent bonds are symbolized by a single dash; double bonds are indicated by two dashes.

Even simple molecules have distinctive shapes, because different atoms make covalent bonds at different angles. Ball-and-stick and space-filling models show the geometry of the bonds accurately.

- In a ball-and-stick model, a stick is used to represent each covalent bond (see **FIGURE B8.1c**).

- In space-filling models, the atoms are simply stuck onto each other in their proper places (see **FIGURE B8.1d**).

To learn more about a molecule when you look at a chemical structure, ask yourself three questions:

1. *Is the molecule polar—meaning that some parts are more negatively or positively charged than others?* Molecules that contain nitrogen or oxygen atoms are often polar, because these atoms have such high electronegativity (see Appendix D). This trait is important because polar molecules dissolve in water.

2. *Does the structural formula show atoms that might participate in chemical reactions?* For example, are there charged atoms or amino or carboxyl (−COOH) groups that might act as a base or an acid?

3. *In ball-and-stick and especially space-filling models of large molecules, are there interesting aspects of overall shape?* For example, is there a groove where a protein might bind to DNA, or a cleft where a substrate might undergo a reaction in an enzyme?

BIOSKILL 9 separating and visualizing molecules

To study a molecule, you have to be able to isolate it. Isolating a molecule is a two-step process: the molecule has to be separated from other molecules in a mixture and then physically picked out or located in a purified form. **BIOSKILLS 9** focuses on the techniques that biologists use to separate nucleic acids and proteins and then find the particular one they are interested in.

Using Electrophoresis to Separate Molecules

In molecular biology, the standard technique for separating proteins and nucleic acids is called gel electrophoresis or, simply, electrophoresis (literally, "electricity-moving"). You may be using electrophoresis in a lab for this course, and you will certainly be analyzing data derived from electrophoresis in this text.

The principle behind electrophoresis is simple. Proteins (when denatured and coated with a special detergent) and nucleic acids carry a charge. As a result, these molecules move when placed in an electric field. Negatively charged molecules move toward the positive electrode; positively charged molecules move toward the negative electrode.

To separate a mixture of macromolecules so that each one can be isolated and analyzed, researchers place the sample in a gelatinous substance. More specifically, the sample is placed in a "well"—a slot in a sheet or slab of the gelatinous substance. The "gel" itself consists of long molecules that form a matrix of fibers. The gelatinous matrix has pores that act like a sieve through which the molecules can pass.

When an electrical field is applied across the gel, the molecules in the well move through the gel toward an electrode. Molecules that are smaller or more highly charged for their size move faster than do larger or less highly charged molecules. As they move, then, the molecules separate by size and by charge. Small and highly charged molecules end up at the bottom of the gel; large, less-charged molecules remain near the top.

An Example "Run"

FIGURE B9.1 (see B:14) shows the electrophoresis setup used in an experiment investigating how RNA molecules polymerize. In this case, the investigators wanted to document how long RNA molecules became over time, when ribonucleoside triphosphates were present in a particular type of solution.

Step 1 shows how they loaded samples of macromolecules, taken on different days during the experiment, into wells at the top of the gel slab. This is a general observation: Each well holds a different sample. In this and many other cases, the researchers also filled a well with a sample containing fragments of known size, called a size standard or "ladder."

In step 2, the researchers immersed the gel in a solution that conducts electricity and applied a voltage across the gel. The molecules in each well started to run down the gel, forming a lane. After several hours of allowing the molecules to move, the researchers removed the electric field (step 3). By then, molecules of different size and charge had separated from one another. In this case, small RNA molecules had reached the bottom of the gel. Above them were larger RNA molecules, which had run more slowly.

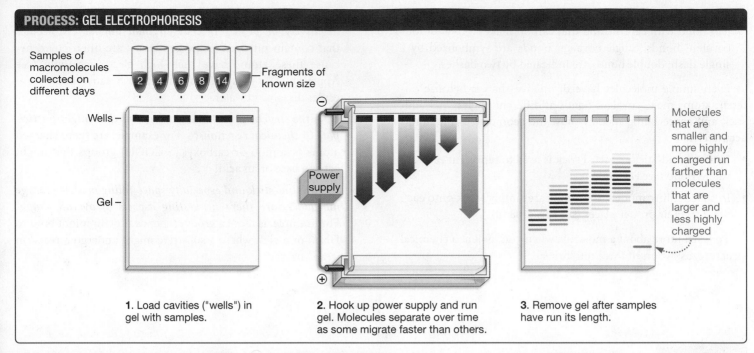

PROCESS: GEL ELECTROPHORESIS

Samples of macromolecules collected on different days

Fragments of known size

Wells —

Gel —

Power supply

⊖

⊕

Molecules that are smaller and more highly charged run farther than molecules that are larger and less highly charged

1. Load cavities ("wells") in gel with samples.

2. Hook up power supply and run gel. Molecules separate over time as some migrate faster than others.

3. Remove gel after samples have run its length.

FIGURE B9.1 Macromolecules Can Be Separated via Gel Electrophoresis.

✔**QUESTION** DNA and RNA run toward the positive electrode. Why are these molecules negatively charged?

Why Do Separated Molecules Form Bands?

When researchers visualize a particular molecule on a gel, using techniques described in this section, the image that results consists of bands: shallow lines that are as wide as a lane in the gel. Why?

To understand the answer, study **FIGURE B9.2**. The left panel shows the original mixture of molecules. In this cartoon, the size of each dot represents the size of each molecule. The key is to realize that the original sample contains many copies of each specific molecule, and that these copies run down the length of the gel together—meaning, at the same rate—because they have the same size and charge.

It's that simple: Molecules that are alike form a band because they stay together.

Using Thin Layer Chromatography to Separate Molecules

Gel electrophoresis is not the only way to separate molecules. Researchers also use a method called thin layer chromatography. This method was developed in the early 1900s by botanists who were analyzing the different-colored pigments from leaves of a plant (see Chapter 14), hence the name chromatography from the Greek words khroma for "color" and graphein, "to write."

In this method, rather than loading the sample into the well of a gel, the samples are deposited or "spotted" near the bottom of a stiff support, either glass or plastic, that is coated with a thin layer of silica gel, cellulose, or a similar porous material. The coated support is placed in a solvent solution. As the solvent

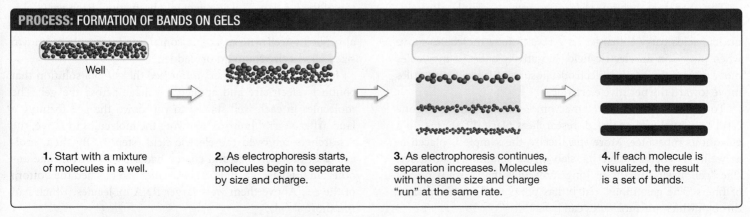

PROCESS: FORMATION OF BANDS ON GELS

Well

1. Start with a mixture of molecules in a well.

2. As electrophoresis starts, molecules begin to separate by size and charge.

3. As electrophoresis continues, separation increases. Molecules with the same size and charge "run" at the same rate.

4. If each molecule is visualized, the result is a set of bands.

FIGURE B9.2 On a Gel, Molecules That Are Alike Form Bands.

wicks upward through the coating by capillary action, it carries the molecules in the mixture with it. Molecules are carried at different rates, based on their size and solubility in the solvent.

Visualizing Molecules

Once molecules have been separated using electrophoresis or thin layer chromatography, they have to be detected. Unfortunately, although plant pigments are colored, proteins and nucleic acids are invisible unless they are tagged in some way. Let's first look at two of the most common tagging systems and then consider how researchers can tag and visualize specific molecules of interest and not others.

Using Radioactive Isotopes and Autoradiography

When molecular biology was getting under way, the first types of tags in common use were radioactive isotopes—forms of atoms that are unstable and release energy in the form of radiation.

In the polymerization experiment diagrammed in Figure B9.1, for example, the researchers had attached a radioactive phosphorus atom to the monomers—ribonucleoside triphosphates—used in the original reaction mix. Once polymers formed, they contained radioactive atoms. When electrophoresis was complete, the investigators visualized the polymers by laying X-ray film over the gel. Because radioactive emissions expose film, a black dot appears wherever a radioactive atom is located in the gel. So many black dots occur so close together that the collection forms a dark band.

This technique for visualizing macromolecules is called autoradiography. The autoradiograph that resulted from the polymerization experiment is shown in **FIGURE B9.3**. The samples, taken on days 2, 4, 6, 8, and 14 of the experiment, are noted along the bottom. The far right lane contains macromolecules of known size; this lane is used to estimate the size of the molecules in the experimental samples. The bands that appear in each sample lane represent the different polymers that had formed.

Reading a Gel

One of the keys to interpreting or "reading" a gel, or the corresponding autoradiograph, is to realize that darker bands contain more radioactive markers, indicating the presence of many radioactive molecules. Lighter bands contain fewer molecules.

To read a gel, then, you look for (**1**) the presence or absence of bands in some lanes—meaning, some experimental samples—versus others, and (**2**) contrasts in the darkness of the bands—meaning, differences in the number of molecules present.

For example, several conclusions can be drawn from the data in Figure B9.3. First, a variety of polymers formed at each stage. After the second day, for example, polymers from 12 to 18 monomers long had formed. Second, the overall length of polymers produced increased with time. At the end of the fourteenth day, most of the RNA molecules were between 20 and 40 monomers long.

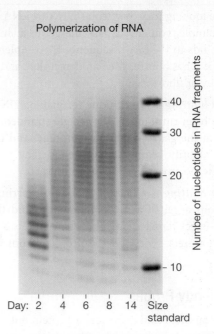

FIGURE B9.3 Autoradiography Is a Technique for Visualizing Macromolecules. The molecules in a gel can be visualized in a number of ways. In this case, the RNA molecules in the gel exposed an X-ray film because they had radioactive atoms attached. When developed, the film is called an autoradiograph.

Starting in the late 1990s and early 2000s, it became much more common to tag nucleic acids with fluorescent tags. Once electrophoresis is complete, fluorescence can be detected by exposing the gel to an appropriate wavelength of light; the fluorescent tag fluoresces or glows in response (fluorescence is explained in Chapter 14).

Fluorescent tags have important advantages over radioactive isotopes: (**1**) They are safer to handle. (**2**) They are faster—you don't have to wait hours or days for the radioactive isotope to expose a film. (**3**) They come in multiple colors, so you can tag several different molecules in the same experiment and detect them independently.

Using Nucleic Acid Probes

In many cases, researchers want to find one specific molecule—a certain DNA sequence, for example—in the collection of molecules on a gel. How is this possible? The answer hinges on using a particular molecule as a probe.

You'll learn in more detail about how probes work in this text. Here it's enough to get the general idea: A probe is a marked molecule that binds specifically to your molecule of interest. The "mark" is often a radioactive atom, a fluorescent tag, or an enzyme that catalyzes a color-forming or light-emitting reaction.

If you are looking for a particular DNA or RNA sequence on a gel, for example, you can expose the gel to a single-stranded probe that binds to the target sequence by complementary base pairing. Once it has bound, you can detect the band through autoradiography or fluorescence.

- **Southern blotting** is a technique for making DNA fragments that have been run out on a gel single stranded, transferring them from the gel to a nylon membrane, and then probing them to identify segments of interest. The technique was named after its inventor, Edwin Southern.

- **Northern blotting** is a technique for transferring RNA fragments from a gel to a nylon membrane and then probing them to detect target segments. The name is a lighthearted play on Southern blotting—the protocol from which it was derived.

Using Antibody Probes

How can researchers find a particular protein out of a large collection of different proteins? The answer is to use an antibody. An antibody is a protein that binds specifically to a section of a different protein.

To use an antibody as a probe, investigators attach a tag molecule—often an enzyme that catalyzes a color-forming reaction—to the antibody and allow it to react with proteins in a mixture. The antibody will stick to the specific protein that it binds to and then can be visualized thanks to the tag it carries.

If the proteins in question have been separated by gel electrophoresis and transferred to a membrane, the result is called a western blot. The name western is an extension of the Southern and northern patterns.

Using Radioimmunoassay and ELISA to Measure Amounts of Molecules

Another important method that makes use of antibodies is called a radioimmunoassay. This method is used when investigators want to measure tiny amounts of a molecule, such as a hormone in the blood. In this case, a known quantity of a hormone is labeled with a radioactive tag. This tagged hormone is then mixed with a known amount of antibody, and the two bind to one another. Next, a sample of blood, containing an unknown quantity of that same hormone, is added. The hormone from the blood and the radiolabeled hormone compete for antibody binding sites. As the concentration of unlabeled hormone increases, more of it binds to the antibody, displacing more of the radiolabeled hormone. The amount of unbound radiolabeled hormone is then measured. Using known standards as a reference, the amount of hormone in the blood can be determined.

Another commonly used technique based on similar principles is called ELISA (enzyme-linked immunosorbent assay). In this case, the amount of a particular molecule is measured using colorimetric signals instead of a radioactive signal.

check your understanding

If you understand BioSkill 9

✓**You should be able to . . .**

Interpret a gel that has been stained for "RNA X." One lane contains no bands. Two lanes have a band in the same location, even though one of the bands is barely visible and the other is extremely dark. The fourth lane has a faint band located below the bands in the other lanes.

Biologists use a technique called differential centrifugation to isolate specific cell components. Differential centrifugation is based on breaking cells apart to create a complex mixture and then separating components in a centrifuge. A centrifuge accomplishes this task by spinning cells in a solution that allows molecules and other cell components to separate according to their density or size and shape. The individual parts of the cell can then be purified and studied in detail, in isolation from other parts of the cell.

The first step in preparing a cell sample for centrifugation is to release the cell components by breaking the cells apart. This can be done by putting them in a hypotonic solution, by exposing them to high-frequency vibration, by treating cells with a detergent, or by grinding them up. Each of these methods breaks apart plasma membranes and releases the contents of the cells.

The resulting pieces of plasma membrane quickly reseal to form small vesicles, often trapping cell components inside. The

solution that results from the homogenization step is a mixture of these vesicles, free-floating macromolecules released from the cells, and organelles. A solution like this is called a cell extract or cell homogenate.

When a cell homogenate is placed in a centrifuge tube and spun at high speed, the components that are in solution tend to move outward, along the red arrow in **FIGURE B10.1a**. The effect is similar to a merry-go-round, which seems to push you outward in a straight line away from the spinning platform. In response to this outward-directed force, the cell homogenate exerts a centripetal (literally, "center-seeking") force that pushes the homogenate away from the bottom of the tube. Larger, denser molecules or particles resist this inward force more readily than do smaller, less dense ones and so reach the bottom of the centrifuge tube faster.

To separate the components of a cell extract, researchers often perform a series of centrifuge runs. Steps 1 and 2 of

(a) How a centrifuge works

When the centrifuge spins, the macromolecules tend to move toward the bottom of the centrifuge tube (red arrow)

The solution in the tube exerts a centripetal force, which resists movement of the molecules to the bottom of the tube (blue arrow)

Motor

Very large or dense molecules overcome the centripetal force more readily than smaller, less dense ones. As a result, larger, denser molecules move toward the bottom of the tube faster.

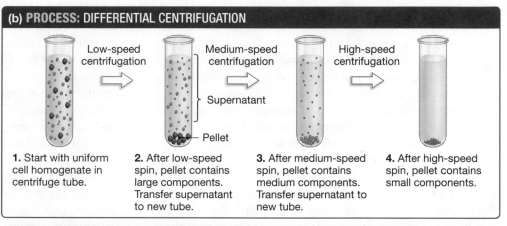

(b) PROCESS: DIFFERENTIAL CENTRIFUGATION

Low-speed centrifugation · Medium-speed centrifugation · High-speed centrifugation · Supernatant · Pellet

1. Start with uniform cell homogenate in centrifuge tube.

2. After low-speed spin, pellet contains large components. Transfer supernatant to new tube.

3. After medium-speed spin, pellet contains medium components. Transfer supernatant to new tube.

4. After high-speed spin, pellet contains small components.

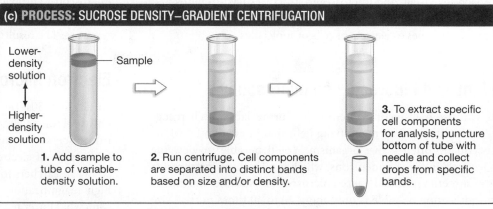

(c) PROCESS: SUCROSE DENSITY–GRADIENT CENTRIFUGATION

Lower-density solution · Higher-density solution · Sample

1. Add sample to tube of variable-density solution.

2. Run centrifuge. Cell components are separated into distinct bands based on size and/or density.

3. To extract specific cell components for analysis, puncture bottom of tube with needle and collect drops from specific bands.

FIGURE B10.1 Cell Components Can Be Separated by Centrifugation. (a) The forces inside a centrifuge tube allow cell components to be separated. **(b)** Through a series of centrifuge runs made at increasingly higher speeds, an investigator can separate fractions of a cell homogenate by size via differential centrifugation. **(c)** A high-speed centrifuge run can achieve extremely fine separation among cell components by sucrose density–gradient centrifugation.

FIGURE B10.1b illustrate how an initial treatment at low speed causes larger, heavier parts of the homogenate to move below smaller, lighter parts. The material that collects at the bottom of the tube is called the pellet, and the solution and solutes left behind form the supernatant ("above-swimming"). The supernatant is placed in a fresh tube and centrifuged at increasingly higher speeds and longer durations. Each centrifuge run continues to separate cell components based on their size and density.

To accomplish separation of macromolecules or organelles, researchers frequently follow up with centrifugation at extremely high speeds. One strategy is based on filling the centrifuge tube with a series of sucrose solutions of increasing density (**FIGURE B10.1c**). The density gradient allows cell components to separate on the basis of small differences in size, shape, and density. When the centrifuge run is complete, each cell component occupies a distinct band of material in the tube, based on how quickly each component moves through the increasingly dense gradient of sucrose solution during the centrifuge run. A researcher can then collect the material in each band for further study.

BIOSKILL 11 biological imaging: microscopy and x-ray crystallography

A lot of biology happens at levels that can't be detected with the naked eye. Biologists use an array of microscopes to study small multicellular organisms, individual cells, and the contents of cells. And to understand what individual macromolecules or macromolecular machines like ribosomes look like, researchers use data from a technique called X-ray crystallography.

You'll probably use dissecting microscopes and compound light microscopes to view specimens during your labs for this course, and throughout this text you'll be seeing images generated from other types of microscopy and from X-ray crystallographic data. Among the fundamental skills you'll be acquiring as an introductory student, then, is a basic understanding of how these techniques work. The key is to recognize that each approach for visualizing microscopic structures has strengths and weaknesses. As a result, each technique is appropriate for studying certain types or aspects of cells or molecules.

Light and Fluorescence Microscopy

If you use a dissecting microscope during labs, you'll recognize that it works by magnifying light that bounces off a whole specimen—often a live organism. You'll be able to view the specimen in three dimensions, which is why these instruments are sometimes called stereomicroscopes, but the maximum magnification possible is only about 20 to 40 times normal size (20× to 40×).

To view smaller objects, you'll probably use a compound microscope. Compound microscopes magnify light that is passed *through* a specimen. The instruments used in introductory labs are usually capable of 400× magnifications; the most sophisticated compound microscopes available can achieve magnifications of about 2000×. This is enough to view individual bacterial or eukaryotic cells and see large structures inside cells, like condensed chromosomes (see Chapter 4). To prepare a specimen for viewing under a compound light microscope, the tissues or cells are usually sliced to create a section thin enough for light to pass through efficiently. The section is then dyed to increase contrast and make structures visible. In many cases, different types of dyes are used to highlight different types of structures.

To visualize specific proteins, researchers use a technique called immunostaining. After preparing tissues or cells for viewing, the specimen is stained with fluorescently tagged antibodies. In this case, the cells are viewed under a fluorescence microscope. Ultraviolet or other wavelengths of light are passed through the specimen. The fluorescing tag emits visible light in response. The result? Beautiful cells that glow green, red, or blue.

Electron Microscopy

Until the 1950s, the compound microscope was the biologist's only tool for viewing cells directly. But the invention of the electron microscope provided a new way to view specimens. Two basic types of electron microscopy are now available: one that allows researchers to examine cross sections of cells at extremely high magnification, and one that offers a view of surfaces at somewhat lower magnification.

Transmission Electron Microscopy

The transmission electron microscope (TEM) is an extraordinarily effective tool for viewing cell structure at high magnification. TEM forms an image from electrons that pass through a specimen, just as a light microscope forms an image from light rays that pass through a specimen.

Biologists who want to view a cell under a transmission electron microscope begin by "fixing" the cell, meaning that they treat it with a chemical agent that stabilizes the cell's structure and contents while disturbing them as little as possible. Then the researcher permeates the cell with an epoxy plastic that stiffens the structure. Once this epoxy hardens, the cell can be cut into extremely thin sections with a glass or diamond knife. Finally, the sectioned specimens are impregnated with a metal—often lead. (The reason for this last step is explained shortly.)

FIGURE B11.1a outlines how the transmission electron microscope works. A beam of electrons is produced by a tungsten filament at the top of a column and directed downward. (All of the air is pumped out of the column, so that the electron beam isn't scattered by collisions with air molecules.) The electron beam passes through a series of lenses and through the specimen. The lenses are actually electromagnets, which alter the path of the beam much like a glass lens in a dissecting or compound microscope bends light. The electromagnet lenses magnify and focus the image on a screen at the bottom of the column. There the electrons strike a coating of fluorescent crystals, which emit visible light in response—just like a television screen. When the microscopist moves the screen out of the way and allows the electrons to expose a sheet of black-and-white film or to be detected by a digital camera, the result is a micrograph—a photograph of an image produced by microscopy.

The image itself is created by electrons that pass through the specimen. If no specimen were in place, all the electrons would pass through and the screen (and micrograph) would be uniformly bright. Unfortunately, cell materials by themselves would also appear fairly uniform and bright. This is because an atom's ability to deflect an electron depends on its mass. In turn, an atom's mass is a function of its atomic number. The hydrogen, carbon, oxygen, and nitrogen atoms that dominate biological molecules have low atomic numbers. This is why cell biologists must saturate cell sections with lead solutions. Lead has a high atomic number and scatters electrons effectively. Different macromolecules take up lead atoms in different amounts, so the metal acts as a "stain" that produces contrast. With TEM, areas of dense metal scatter the electron beam most, producing dark areas in micrographs.

The advantage of TEM is that it can magnify objects up to 250,000×—meaning that intracellular structures are clearly visible. The downsides are that researchers are restricted to observing dead, sectioned material, and they must take care that the preparation process does not distort the specimen.

Scanning Electron Microscopy

The scanning electron microscope (SEM) is the most useful tool biologists have for looking at the surfaces of structures. Materials are prepared for scanning electron microscopy by coating their surfaces with a layer of metal atoms. To create an image of this surface, the microscope scans the surface with a narrow beam of electrons. Electrons that are reflected back from the surface or that are emitted by the metal atoms in response to the beam then strike a detector. The signal from the detector controls a second electron beam, which scans a TV-like screen and forms an image magnified up to 50,000 times the object's size.

Because SEM records shadows and highlights, it provides images with a three-dimensional appearance (**FIGURE B11.1b**). It cannot magnify objects nearly as much as TEM can, however.

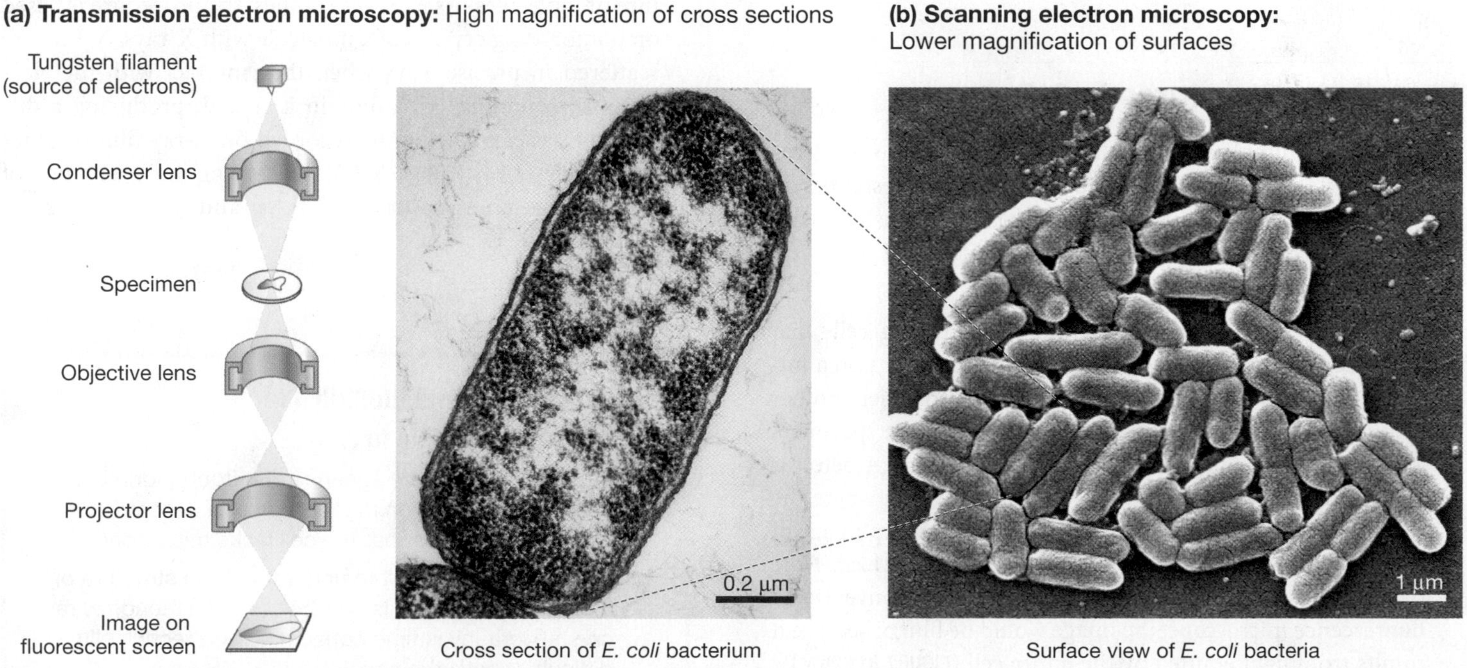

(a) Transmission electron microscopy: High magnification of cross sections

(b) Scanning electron microscopy: Lower magnification of surfaces

Tungsten filament (source of electrons)

Condenser lens

Specimen

Objective lens

Projector lens

Image on fluorescent screen

0.2 μm

Cross section of *E. coli* bacterium

1 μm

Surface view of *E. coli* bacteria

FIGURE B11.1 There Are Two Basic Types of Electron Microscopy.

Studying Live Cells and Real-Time Processes

Until the 1960s, biologists were unable to get clear, high-magnification images of living cells. But a series of innovations over the past 50 years has made it possible to observe organelles and subcellular structures in action.

The development of video microscopy, where the image from a light microscope is captured by a video camera instead of by an eye or a film camera, proved revolutionary. It allowed specimens to be viewed at higher magnification, because video cameras are more sensitive to small differences in contrast than are the human eye or still cameras. It also made it easier to keep live specimens functioning normally, because the increased light sensitivity of video cameras allows them to be used with low illumination, so specimens don't overheat. And when it became possible to digitize video images, researchers began using computers to remove out-of-focus background material and increase image clarity.

A more recent innovation was the use of a fluorescent molecule called green fluorescent protein, or GFP, which allows researchers to tag specific molecules or structures and follow their movement in live cells over time. This was a major advance over immunostaining, in which cells have to be fixed. GFP is naturally synthesized in jellyfish that fluoresce, or emit light. By affixing GFP to another protein and then inserting it into a live cell, investigators can follow the protein's fate over time and even videotape its movement. For example, researchers have videotaped GFP-tagged proteins being transported from the rough ER through the Golgi apparatus and out to the plasma membrane. This is cell biology: the movie.

GFP's influence has been so profound that the researchers who developed its use in microscopy were awarded the 2008 Nobel Prize in Chemistry.

Visualizing Structures in 3-D

The world is three-dimensional. To understand how microscopic structures and macromolecules work, it is essential to understand their shape and spatial relationships. Consider three techniques currently being used to reconstruct the 3-D structure of cells, organelles, and macromolecules.

- *Confocal microscopy* is carried out by mounting cells that have been treated with one or more fluorescing tags on a microscope slide and then focusing a beam of ultraviolet or other wavelengths of light at a specific depth within the specimen. The fluorescing tag emits visible light in response. A detector for this light is then set up at exactly the position where the emitted light comes into focus. The result is a sharp image of a precise plane in the cell being studied (**FIGURE B11.2a**). Note that if you viewed the same specimen under a conventional fluorescence microscope, the image would be blurry because it results from light emitted by the entire cell (**FIGURE B11.2b**). By altering the focal plane, a researcher can record images from

(a) Confocal fluorescence image of single cell

(b) Conventional fluorescence image of same cell

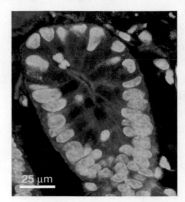 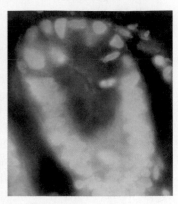

FIGURE B11.2 Confocal Microscopy Provides Sharp Images of Living Cells. (a) The confocal image of this mouse intestinal cell is sharp, because it results from light emitted at a single plane inside the cell. **(b)** The conventional image of this same cell is blurred, because it results from light emitted by the entire cell.

an array of depths in the specimen; a computer can then be used to generate a 3-D image of the cell.

- *Electron tomography* uses a transmission electron microscope to generate a 3-D image of an organelle or other subcellular structure. The specimen is rotated around a single axis while the researcher takes many "snapshots." The individual images are then pieced together with a computer. This technique has provided a much more accurate view of mitochondrial structure than was possible using traditional TEM (see Chapter 2).

- *X-ray crystallography, or X-ray diffraction analysis*, is the most widely used technique for reconstructing the 3-D structure of molecules. As its name implies, the procedure is based on bombarding crystals of a molecule with X-rays. X-rays are scattered in precise ways when they interact with the electrons surrounding the atoms in a crystal, producing a diffraction pattern that can be recorded on X-ray film or other types of detectors (**FIGURE B11.3**). By varying the orientation of the X-ray beam as it strikes a crystal and documenting the

check your understanding

If you understand BioSkill 11

✔ **You should be able to . . .**

1. Interpret whether the absence of mitochondria in a transmission electron micrograph of a cancerous human liver means that the cell lacks mitochondria.

2. Explain why the effort to understand the structure of biological molecules is worthwhile even though X-ray crystallography is time consuming and technically difficult. What's the payoff?

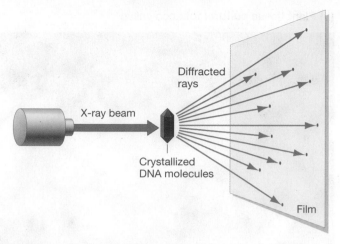

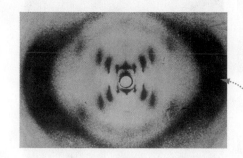

The patterns are determined by the structure of the molecules within the crystal

FIGURE B11.3 X-Ray Crystallography. When crystallized molecules are bombarded with X-rays, the radiation is scattered in distinctive patterns. The photograph at the right shows an X-ray film that recorded the pattern of scattered radiation from DNA molecules.

diffraction patterns that result, researchers can construct a map representing the density of electrons in the crystal. By relating these electron-density maps to information about the primary structure of the nucleic acid or protein, a 3-D model of the molecule can be built. Virtually all of the molecular models used in this book were built from X-ray crystallographic data.

BIOSKILL 12   cell and tissue culture methods

For researchers, there are important advantages to growing plant and animal cells and tissues outside the organism itself. Cell and tissue cultures provide large populations of a single type of cell or tissue and the opportunity to control experimental conditions precisely.

Animal Cell Culture

The first successful attempt to culture animal cells occurred in 1907, when a researcher cultivated amphibian nerve cells in a drop of fluid from the spinal cord. But it was not until the 1950s and 1960s that biologists could routinely culture plant and animal cells in the laboratory. The long lag time was due to the difficulty of re-creating conditions that exist in the intact organism precisely enough for cells to grow normally.

To grow in culture, animal cells must be provided with a liquid mixture containing the nutrients, vitamins, and hormones that stimulate growth. Initially, this mixture was serum, the liquid portion of blood; now, serum-free media are available for certain cell types. Serum-free media are preferred because they are much more precisely defined chemically than serum.

In addition, many types of animal cells will not grow in culture unless they are provided with a solid surface that mimics the types of surfaces that enable cells in the intact organisms to adhere. As a result, cells are typically cultured in flasks (**FIGURE B12.1a**, left; see B:22).

Even under optimal conditions, though, normal cells display a finite life span in culture. In contrast, many cultured cancerous cells grow indefinitely. This characteristic correlates with a key feature of cancerous cells in organisms: Their growth is continuous and uncontrolled.

Because of their immortality and relative ease of growth, cultured cancer cells are commonly used in research on basic aspects of cell structure and function. For example, the first human cell type to be grown in culture was isolated in 1951 from a malignant tumor of the uterine cervix. These cells are called HeLa cells in honor of their donor, Henrietta Lacks, who died soon thereafter from her cancer. HeLa cells continue to grow in laboratories around the world (Figure B12.1a, right).

Plant Tissue Culture

Certain cells found in plants are totipotent—meaning that they retain the ability to divide and differentiate into a complete, mature plant, including new types of tissue. These cells, called parenchyma cells, are important in wound healing and asexual reproduction. But they also allow researchers to grow complete adult plants in the laboratory, starting with a small number of parenchyma cells.

Biologists who grow plants in tissue culture begin by placing parenchyma cells in a liquid or solid medium containing all the

(a) Animal cell culture: immortal HeLa cancer cells

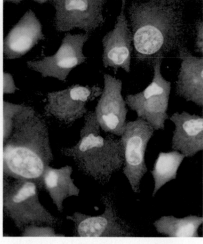

(b) Plant tissue culture: tobacco callus

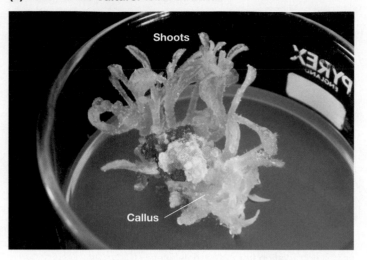

Shoots

Callus

FIGURE B12.1 Animal and Plant Cells Can Be Grown in the Lab.

nutrients required for cell maintenance and growth. In the early days of plant tissue culture, investigators found not only that specific growth signals called hormones were required for successful growth and differentiation but also that the relative abundance of hormones present was critical to success.

The earliest experiments on hormone interactions in tissue cultures were done with tobacco cells in the 1950s by Folke Skoog and co-workers. These researchers found that when the hormone called auxin was added to the culture by itself, the cells enlarged but did not divide. But if the team added roughly equal amounts of auxin and another growth signal called cytokinin to the cells, the cells began to divide and eventually formed a callus, or an undifferentiated mass of parenchyma cells.

By varying the proportion of auxin to cytokinins in different parts of the callus and through time, the team could stimulate the growth and differentiation of root and shoot systems and produce whole new plants (**FIGURE B12.1b**). A high ratio of auxin to cytokinin led to the differentiation of a root system, while a high ratio of cytokinin to auxin led to the development of a shoot system. Eventually Skoog's team was able to produce a complete plant from just one parenchyma cell.

The ability to grow whole new plants in tissue culture from just one cell has been instrumental in the development of genetic engineering. Researchers insert recombinant genes into target cells, test the cells to identify those that successfully express the recombinant genes, and then use tissue culture techniques to grow those cells into adult individuals with a novel genotype and phenotype.

check your understanding

If you understand BioSkill 12

✔ **You should be able to . . .**

1. Identify a limitation of how experiments on HeLa cells are interpreted.

2. State a disadvantage of doing experiments on plants that have been propagated from single cells growing in tissue culture.

Research in biological science starts with a question. In most cases, the question is inspired by an observation about a cell or an organism. To answer it, biologists have to study a particular species. Study organisms are often called model organisms, because investigators hope that they serve as a model for what is going on in a wide array of species.

Model organisms are chosen because they are convenient to study and because they have attributes that make them appropriate for the particular research proposed. They tend to have some common characteristics:

- *Short generation time and rapid reproduction* This trait is important because it makes it possible to produce offspring quickly and perform many experiments in a short amount of time—you don't have to wait long for individuals to grow.

- *Large numbers of offspring* This trait is particularly important in genetics, where many offspring phenotypes and genotypes need to be assessed to get a large sample size.

- *Small size, simple feeding and habitat requirements* These attributes make it relatively cheap and easy to maintain individuals in the lab.

The following notes highlight just a few model organisms supporting current work in biological science.

Escherichia coli

Of all model organisms in biology, perhaps none has been more important than the bacterium *Escherichia coli*—a common inhabitant of the human gut. The strain that is most commonly worked on today, called K-12 (**FIGURE B13.1a**; see B:24), was originally isolated from a hospital patient in 1922.

During the last half of the twentieth century, key results in molecular biology originated in studies of *E. coli*. These results include the discovery of enzymes such as DNA polymerase, RNA polymerase, DNA repair enzymes, and restriction endonucleases; the elucidation of ribosome structure and function; and the initial characterization of promoters, regulatory transcription factors, regulatory sites in DNA, and operons. In many cases, initial discoveries made in *E. coli* allowed researchers to confirm that homologous enzymes and processes existed in an array of organisms, often ranging from other bacteria to yeast, mice, and humans.

The success of *E. coli* as a model for other species inspired Jacques Monod's claim that "Once we understand the biology of *Escherichia coli*, we will understand the biology of an elephant." The genome of *E. coli* K-12 was sequenced in 1997, and the strain continues to be a workhorse in studies of gene function, biochemistry, and particularly biotechnology. Much remains to be learned, however. Despite over 60 years of intensive study, the function of about a third of the *E. coli* genome is still unknown.

In the lab, *E. coli* is usually grown in suspension culture, where cells are introduced to a liquid nutrient medium, or on plates containing agar—a gelatinous mix of polysaccharides. Under optimal growing conditions—meaning before cells begin to get crowded and compete for space and nutrients—a cell takes just 30 minutes on average to grow and divide. At this rate, a single cell can produce a population of over a million descendants in just 10 hours. Except for new mutations, all of the descendant cells are genetically identical.

Dictyostelium discoideum

The cellular slime mold *Dictyostelium discoideum* is not always slimy, and it is not a mold—meaning a type of fungus. Instead, it is an amoeba. Amoeba is a general term that biologists use to characterize a unicellular eukaryote that lacks a cell wall and is extremely flexible in shape. *Dictyostelium* has long fascinated biologists because it is a social organism. Independent cells sometimes aggregate to form a multicellular structure.

Under most conditions, *Dictyostelium* cells are haploid (n) and move about in decaying vegetation on forest floors or other habitats. They feed on bacteria by engulfing them whole. When these cells reproduce, they can do so sexually by fusing with another cell then undergoing meiosis, or asexually by mitosis, which is more common. If food begins to run out, the cells begin to aggregate. In many cases, tens of thousands of cells cohere to form a 2-mm-long mass called a slug (**FIGURE B13.1b**). (This is not the slug that is related to snails.)

After migrating to a sunlit location, the slug stops and individual cells differentiate according to their position in the slug. Some form a stalk; others form a mass of spores at the tip of the stalk. (A spore is a single cell that develops into an adult organism, but it is not formed from gamete fusion like a zygote is.) The entire structure, stalk plus mass of spores, is called a fruiting body. Cells that form spores secrete a tough coat and represent a durable resting stage. The fruiting body eventually dries out, and the wind disperses the spores to new locations, where more food might be available.

Dictyostelium has been an important model organism for investigating questions about eukaryotes:

- Cells in a slug are initially identical in morphology but then differentiate into distinctive stalk cells and spores. Studying this process helped biologists better understand how cells in plant and animal embryos differentiate into distinct cell types.

(a) Bacterium *Escherichia coli* (strain K-12)

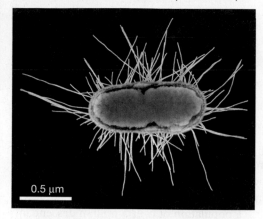

0.5 µm

(b) Slime mold *Dictyostelium discoideum*

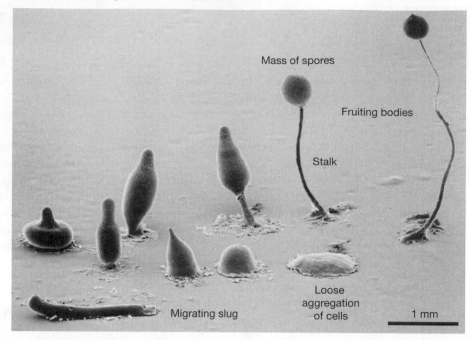

Mass of spores

Fruiting bodies

Stalk

Migrating slug

Loose aggregation of cells

1 mm

(c) Thale cress *Arabidopsis thaliana*

5 cm

(e) Fruit fly *Drosophila melanogaster*

0.5 mm

(f) Roundworm *Caenorhabditis elegans*

0.1 mm

(d) Yeast *Saccharomyces cerevisiae*

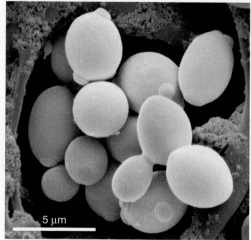

5 µm

(g) Mouse *Mus musculus*

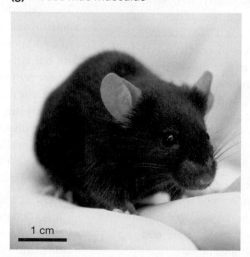

1 cm

FIGURE B13.1 Model Organisms.

✔ **QUESTION** *E. coli* is grown at a temperature of 37°C. Why?

- The process of slug formation has helped biologists study how animal cells move and how they aggregate as they form specific types of tissues.

- When *Dictyostelium* cells aggregate to form a slug, they stick to each other. The discovery of membrane proteins responsible for cell–cell adhesion helped biologists understand some of the general principles of multicellular life.

Arabidopsis thaliana

In the early days of biology, the best-studied plants were agricultural varieties such as maize (corn), rice, and garden peas. When biologists began to unravel the mechanisms responsible for oxygenic photosynthesis in the early to mid-1900s, they relied on green algae that were relatively easy to grow and manipulate in the lab—often the unicellular species *Chlamydomonas reinhardii*—as an experimental subject.

Although crop plants and green algae continue to be the subject of considerable research, a new model organism emerged in the 1980s and now serves as the preeminent experimental subject in plant biology. That organism is *Arabidopsis thaliana*, commonly known as thale cress or wall cress (**FIGURE B13.1c**).

Arabidopsis is a member of the mustard family, or Brassicaceae, so it is closely related to radishes and broccoli. In nature it is a weed—meaning a species that is adapted to thrive in habitats where soils have been disturbed.

One of the most attractive aspects of working with *Arabidopsis* is that individuals can grow from a seed into a mature, seed-producing plant in just four to six weeks. Several other attributes make it an effective subject for study: It has just five chromosomes, has a relatively small genome with limited numbers of repetitive sequences, can self-fertilize as well as undergo cross-fertilization, can be grown in a relatively small amount of space and with a minimum of care in the greenhouse, and produces up to 10,000 seeds per individual per generation.

Arabidopsis has been instrumental in a variety of studies in plant molecular genetics and development, and it is increasingly popular in ecological and evolutionary studies. In addition, the entire genome of the species has now been sequenced, and studies have benefited from the development of an international "*Arabidopsis* community"—a combination of informal and formal associations of investigators who work on *Arabidopsis* and use regular meetings, e-mail, and the Internet to share data, techniques, and seed stocks.

Saccharomyces cerevisiae

When biologists want to answer basic questions about how eukaryotic cells work, they often turn to the yeast *Saccharomyces cerevisiae*.

S. cerevisiae is unicellular and relatively easy to culture and manipulate in the lab (**FIGURE B13.1d**). In good conditions, yeast cells grow and divide almost as rapidly as bacteria. As a result,

the species has become the organism of choice for experiments on control of the cell cycle and regulation of gene expression in eukaryotes. For example, research has confirmed that several of the genes controlling cell division and DNA repair in yeast have homologs in humans; and when mutated, these genes contribute to cancer. Strains of yeast that carry these mutations are now being used to test drugs that might be effective against cancer.

S. cerevisiae has become even more important in efforts to interpret the genomes of organisms like rice, mice, zebrafish, and humans. It is much easier to investigate the function of particular genes in *S. cerevisiae* by creating mutants or transferring specific alleles among individuals than it is to do the same experiments in mice or zebrafish. Once the function of a gene has been established in yeast, biologists can look for the homologous gene in other eukaryotes. If such a gene exists, they can usually infer that it has a function similar to its role in *S. cerevisiae*. It was also the first eukaryote with a completely sequenced genome.

Drosophila melanogaster

If you walk into a biology building on any university campus around the world, you are almost certain to find at least one lab where the fruit fly *Drosophila melanogaster* is being studied (**FIGURE B13.1e**).

Drosophila has been a key experimental subject in genetics since the early 1900s. It was initially chosen as a focus for study by T. H. Morgan, because it can be reared in the laboratory easily and inexpensively, matings can be arranged, the life cycle is completed in less than two weeks, and females lay a large number of eggs. These traits made fruit flies valuable subjects for breeding experiments designed to test hypotheses about how traits are transmitted from parents to offspring (see Chapter 12).

More recently, *Drosophila* has also become a key model organism in the field of developmental biology. The use of flies in developmental studies was inspired largely by the work of Christianne Nüsslein-Volhard and Eric Wieschaus, who in the 1980s isolated flies with genetic defects in early embryonic development. By investigating the nature of these defects, researchers have gained valuable insights into how various gene products influence the development of eukaryotes. The complete genome sequence of *Drosophila* has been available to investigators since the year 2000.

Caenorhabditis elegans

The roundworm *Caenorhabditis elegans* emerged as a model organism in developmental biology in the 1970s, due largely to work by Sydney Brenner and colleagues. (*Caenorhabditis* is pronounced *see-no-rab-DIE-tiss*.)

C. elegans was chosen for three reasons: (1) Its cuticle (soft outer layer) is transparent, making individual cells relatively easy to observe (**FIGURE B13.1f**); (2) adults have exactly 959 nonreproductive cells; and, most important, (3) the fate of each cell in an embryo can be predicted because cell fates are invariant among individuals. For example, when researchers examine a 33-cell *C. elegans* embryo, they know exactly which of the 959 cells in the adult will be derived from each of those 33 embryonic cells.

In addition, *C. elegans* are small (less than 1 mm long), are able to self-fertilize or cross-fertilize, and undergo early development in just 16 hours. The entire genome of *C. elegans* has now been sequenced.

Mus musculus

The house mouse *Mus musculus* is the most important model organism among mammals. For this reason, it is especially prominent in biomedical research, where researchers need to work on individuals with strong genetic and developmental similarities to humans.

The house mouse was an intelligent choice of model organism in mammals because it is small and thus relatively inexpensive to maintain in captivity, and because it breeds rapidly. A litter can contain 10 offspring, and generation time is only 12 weeks—meaning that several generations can be produced in a year. Descendants of wild house mice have been selected for docility and other traits that make them easy to handle and rear; these populations are referred to as laboratory mice (**FIGURE B13.1g**).

Some of the most valuable laboratory mice are strains with distinctive, well-characterized genotypes. Inbred strains are

virtually homogenous genetically and are useful in experiments where gene-by-gene or gene-by-environment interactions have to be controlled. Other populations carry mutations that knock out genes and cause diseases similar to those observed in humans. These individuals are useful for identifying the cause of genetic diseases and testing drugs or other types of therapies.

check your understanding

If you understand BioSkill 13

✔ **You should be able to . . .**

Determine which model organisms described here would be the best choice for the following studies. In each case, explain your reasoning.

1. A study of why specific cells in an embryo die at certain points in normal development. One goal is to understand the consequences for the individual when programmed cell death does not occur when it should.

2. A study of proteins that are required for cell–cell adhesion.

3. Research on a gene suspected to be involved in the formation of breast cancer in humans.

BIOSKILL 14 primary literature and peer review

As part of the process of doing science, biologists communicate their results to the scientific community through publications in scientific journals that report on their original research discoveries (see Chapter 1). These published reports are referred to, interchangeably, as the primary literature, research papers, or primary research articles.

What Is the Primary Literature?

Scientists publish "peer-reviewed" papers. This means that several experts in the field have carefully read the paper and considered its strengths and weaknesses. Reviewers write a critique of the paper and make a recommendation to the journal editor as to whether the paper should be published. Often reviewers will suggest additional experiments that need to be completed before a paper is considered acceptable for publication. The peer review process means that research discoveries are carefully vetted before they go to press.

A primary research paper can be distinguished from secondary sources—such as review articles, textbooks, and magazine articles—by looking for key characteristics. A primary research paper includes a detailed description of methods and results,

written by the researchers who did the work. A typical paper contains a Title, Abstract, Introduction, Materials and Methods (or Experimental Design), Results and Discussion (**Table B14.1**), although the order and name of the sections varies among journals.

Getting Started

At first, trying to read the primary literature may seem like a daunting task. A paper may be peppered with unfamiliar terms and acronyms. If you tried to read a research paper from start to finish, like you might read a chapter in this textbook, it would be a frustrating experience. But, with practice, the scientific literature becomes approachable, and it is well worth the effort. The primary literature is the cutting edge, the place to read firsthand about the process of doing science. Becoming skilled at reading and evaluating scientific reports is a powerful way to learn how to think critically—to think like a biologist.

To get started, try breaking down reading the primary research article into a series of steps:

1. Read the authors' names. Where are they from? Are they working as a team or alone? After delving into the literature,

TABLE B14.1 Sections of a Primary Research Paper

Section	Characteristics
Title	Short, succinct, eye-catching
Abstract	Summary of Methods, Results, Discussion. Explains why the research was done and why the results are significant.
Introduction	Background information (what past work was done, why the work was important). States the objectives and hypotheses of the study and explains why the study is important.
Materials and Methods	Explains how the work was done and where it was done.
Results	Explains what the data show.
Discussion	Explains why the data show what they show, how the analysis relates to the objectives from the Introduction, and the significance of findings and how they advance the field.

certain familiar names will crop up again and again. You'll begin to recognize the experts in a particular field.

2. Read the title. It should summarize the key finding of the paper and tell you what you can expect to learn from the paper.

3. Read the abstract. The abstract summarizes the entire paper in a short paragraph. At this point, it might be tempting to stop reading. But sometimes authors understate or overstate the significance and conclusions of their work. You should never cite an article as a reference after having read only the abstract.

4. Read the Introduction. The first couple of paragraphs should make it clear what the objectives or hypotheses of the paper are; the remaining paragraphs will give you the background information you need to understand the point of the paper.

5. Flip through the article and look at the figures, illustrations, and tables, including reading the legends.

6. Read the Results section carefully. Ask yourself these questions: Do the results accurately describe the data presented in the paper? Were all the appropriate controls carried out in an experiment? Are there additional experiments that you think should have been performed? Are the figures and tables clearly labeled?

7. Consult the Materials and Methods section to help understand the research design and the techniques used.

8. Read the Discussion. The first and last paragraphs usually summarize the key findings and state their significance. The Discussion is the part of the paper where the results are explained in the context of the scientific literature. The authors should explain what their results mean.

Getting Practice

The best way to get practice is to start reading the scientific literature as often as possible. You could begin by reading some of the references cited in this textbook. You can get an electronic copy of most articles through online databases such as PubMed, ScienceDirect, or Google Scholar, or through your institution's library.

After reading a primary research paper, you should be able to paraphrase the significance of the paper in a few sentences, free of technical jargon. You should also be able to both praise and criticize several points of the paper. As you become more familiar with reading the scientific literature, you're likely to start thinking about what questions remain to be answered. And, you may even come up with "the next experiment."

check your understanding

If you understand BioSkill 14

✔ **You should be able to . . .**

After choosing a primary research paper on a topic in biology that you would like to know more about, select one figure in the Results section that reports on the experiment and construct a Research box (like the ones in this textbook) that depicts this experiment.

A concept map is a graphical device for organizing and expressing what you know about a topic. It has two main elements: **(1)** concepts that are identified by words or short phrases and placed in a box or circle, and **(2)** labeled arrows that physically link two concepts and explain the relationship between them. The concepts are arranged hierarchically on a page with the most general concepts at the top and the most specific ideas at the bottom.

The combination of a concept, a linking word, and a second concept is called a proposition. Good concept maps also have cross-links—meaning, labeled arrows that connect different elements in the hierarchy as you read down the page.

Concept maps, initially developed by Joseph Novak in the early 1970s, have proven to be an effective studying and learning tool. They can be particularly valuable if constructed by a group, or when different individuals exchange and critique concept maps they have created independently. Although concept maps vary widely in quality and can be graded using objective criteria, there are many equally valid ways of making a high-quality concept map on a particular topic.

When you are asked to make a concept map in this text, you will usually be given at least a partial list of concepts to use. As an example, suppose you were asked to create a concept map on experimental design and were given the following concepts: results, predictions, control treatment, experimental treatment, controlled (identical) conditions, conclusions, experiment, hypothesis to be tested, null hypothesis. One possible concept map is shown in **FIGURE B15.1**.

Good concept maps have four qualities:

1. They exhibit an organized hierarchy, indicating how each concept on the map relates to larger and smaller concepts.

2. The concept words are specific—not vague.

3. The propositions are accurate.

4. There is cross-linking between different elements in the hierarchy of concepts.

As you practice making concept maps, go through these criteria and use them to evaluate your own work as well as the work of fellow students.

check your understanding

If you understand BioSkill 15
✔ **You should be able to . . .**

1. Add an "Alternative hypothesis" concept to the map in Figure B15.1, along with other concepts and labeled linking arrows needed to indicate its relationship to other information on the map. (Hint: Recall that investigators often contrast a hypothesis being tested with an alternative hypothesis that does not qualify as a null hypothesis.)

2. Add a box for the concept "Statistical testing" (see **BIOSKILLS 4**) along with appropriately labeled linking arrows.

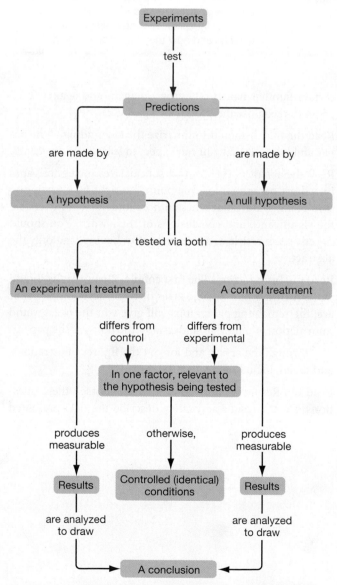

FIGURE B15.1 A Concept Map on Principles of Experimental Design.

Most students have at one time or another wondered why a particular question on an exam seemed so hard, while others seemed easy. The explanation lies in the type of cognitive skills required to answer the question. Let's take a closer look.

Categories of Human Cognition

Bloom's Taxonomy is a classification system that instructors use to identify the cognitive skill levels at which they are asking students to work, particularly on practice problems and exams. Bloom's Taxonomy is also a very useful tool for students to know—it can help you to figure out the appropriate level at which you should be studying to succeed in a course.

Bloom's Taxonomy distinguishes six different categories of human thinking: remember, understand, apply, analyze, evaluate, and create. One of the most useful distinctions lies not in the differences among the six categories, but rather in the difference between high-order cognitive (HOC) and low-order cognitive (LOC) skills. **FIGURE B16.1** shows how the different levels of the taxonomy can be broken into HOC and LOC skills.

Skills that hallmark LOCs include recall, explanation, or application of knowledge in the exact way that you have before (remember, understand, apply), while skills that typify HOCs include the application of knowledge in a new way, as well as the breakdown, critique, or creation of information (analyze, evaluate, and create). Most college instructors will assume students are proficient at solving LOC questions and will expect you to frequently work at the HOC levels. HOC problems usually require use of basic vocabulary and applying knowledge—working at this level helps students to master the LOC levels.

Six Study Steps to Success

Bloom's Taxonomy provides a useful guide for preparing for an exam, using the following six steps:

1. *Answer in-chapter questions while reading the chapter.* All questions in this book have been assigned Bloom's levels, so you can review the question answers and the Bloom's level while you study.

2. *Identify the Bloom's level(s) of the questions that you are having greatest difficulty answering.* While working through

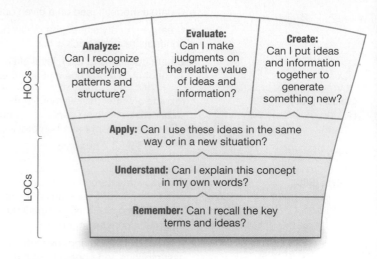

FIGURE B16.1 Bloom's Taxonomy.

the text, take note of the content and Bloom's level(s) that you find the most challenging.

3. *Use the Bloom's Taxonomy Study Guide* (**Table B16.1**; see B:30) *to focus your study efforts at the appropriate Bloom's level.* Table B16.1 lists specific study methods that can help you practice your understanding of the material at both the LOC and HOC levels, whether you are studying alone or with a study group.

4. *Complete the end-of-chapter questions as if you're taking an exam, without looking for the answers.* If you look at the chapter text or jump to the answers, then you really aren't testing your ability to work with the content and have reduced the questions to the lowest Bloom's level of remember.

5. *Grade your answers and note the Bloom's level of the questions you got wrong.* At what level of Bloom's Taxonomy were the questions you missed?

6. *Use the Bloom's Taxonomy Study Guide to focus your study efforts at the appropriate Bloom's level.* If you missed a lot of questions, then spend more time studying the material and find other resources for quizzing yourself.

By following these steps and studying at the HOC levels, you should succeed in answering questions on in-class exams.

	Individual Study Activities	Group Study Activities
Create (HOC) Generate something new	• Generate a hypothesis or design an experiment based on information you are studying • Create a model based on a given data set • Create summary sheets that show how facts and concepts relate to each other • Create questions at each level of Bloom's Taxonomy as a practice test and then take the test	• Each student puts forward a hypothesis about biological process and designs an experiment to test it. Peers critique the hypotheses and experiments • Create a new model/summary sheet/concept map that integrates each group member's ideas
Evaluate (HOC) Defend or judge a concept or idea	• Provide a written assessment of the strengths and weaknesses of your peers' work or understanding of a given concept based on previously determined criteria	• Provide a verbal assessment of the strengths and weaknesses of your peers' work or understanding of a given concept based on previously described criteria, and have your peers critique your assessment
Analyze (HOC) Distinguish parts and make inferences	• Analyze and interpret data in primary literature or a textbook without reading the author's interpretation and then compare the authors' interpretation with your own • Analyze a situation and then identify the assumptions and principles of the argument • Compare and contrast two ideas or concepts • Construct a map of the main concepts by defining the relationships of the concepts using one- or two-way arrows	• Work together to analyze and interpret data in primary literature or a textbook without reading the author's interpretation, and defend your analysis to your peers • Work together to identify all of the concepts in a paper or textbook chapter, construct individual maps linking the concepts together with arrows and words that relate the concepts, and then grade each other's concept maps
Apply (HOC or LOC) Use information or concepts in new ways (HOC) or in the same ways (LOC)	• Review each process you have learned and then ask yourself: What would happen if you increase or decrease a component in the system, or what would happen if you alter the activity of a component in the system? • If possible, graph a biological process and create scenarios that change the shape or slope of the graph	• Practice writing out answers to old exam questions on the board, and have your peers check to make sure you don't have too much or too little information in your answer • Take turns teaching your peers a biological process while the group critiques the content
Understand (LOC) Explain information or concepts	• Describe a biological process in your own words without copying it from a book or another source • Provide examples of a process • Write a sentence using the word • Give examples of a process	• Discuss content with peers • Take turns quizzing each other about definitions, and have your peers check your answer
Remember (LOC) Recall information	• Practice labeling diagrams • List characteristics • Identify biological objects or components from flash cards • Quiz yourself with flash cards • Take a self-made quiz on vocabulary • Draw, classify, select, or match items • Write out the textbook definitions	• Check a drawing that another student labeled • Create lists of concepts and processes that your peers can match • Place flash cards in a bag and take turns selecting one for which you must define a term • Do the preceding activities, and have peers check your answers

Periodic Table of Elements

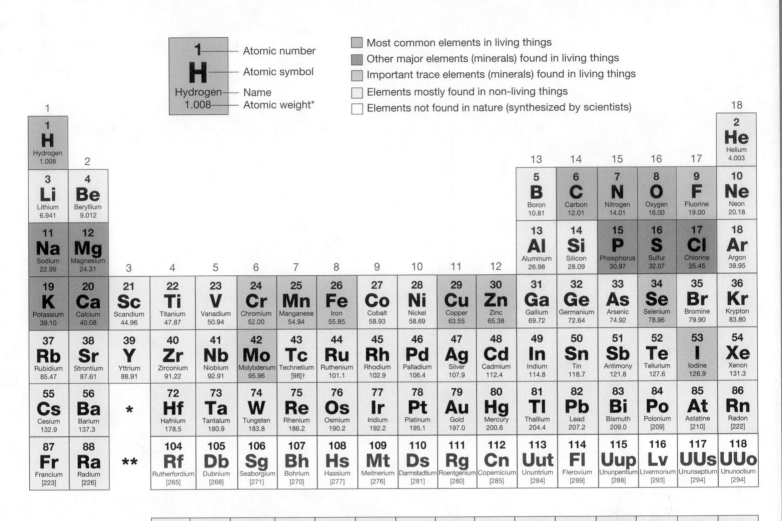

Key	
■	Most common elements in living things
■	Other major elements (minerals) found in living things
■	Important trace elements (minerals) found in living things
□	Elements mostly found in non-living things
□	Elements not found in nature (synthesized by scientists)

Legend box:
- 1 — Atomic number
- H — Atomic symbol
- Hydrogen — Name
- 1.008 — Atomic weight*

DATA: Wieser, M. E., and M. Berglund. 2009. *Pure and Applied Chemistry* 81: 2131–2156.

*Atomic weights are reported to four significant figures.

†For elements with a variable number of protons and/or neutrons, the mass number of the longest-lived isotope of the element is reported in brackets.

Water and Carbon: The Chemical Basis of Life

APPENDIX D

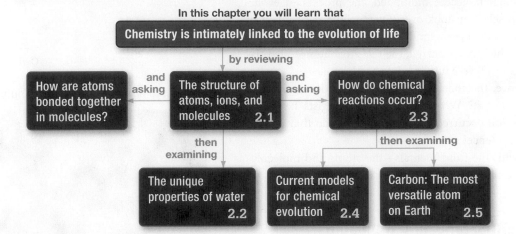

In this chapter you will learn that

Chemistry is intimately linked to the evolution of life

by reviewing

How are atoms bonded together in molecules? — and asking — The structure of atoms, ions, and molecules **2.1** — and asking — How do chemical reactions occur? **2.3**

then examining

The unique properties of water **2.2**

then examining

Current models for chemical evolution **2.4**

Carbon: The most versatile atom on Earth **2.5**

These deep-sea hydrothermal vents produce hydrogen-rich, highly basic fluids at temperatures that range from 40° to 90°C. It has been proposed that life emerged from similar seafloor chimneys early in Earth's history via chemical evolution.

A classic experiment on spontaneous generation by Louis Pasteur tested the idea that life arises from nonliving materials (see Chapter 1). This work helped build a consensus that spontaneous generation does not occur. But for life to exist, spontaneous generation must have occurred at least once, early in Earth's history.

How did life begin? This simple query has been called "the mother of all questions." This chapter examines a theory, called **chemical evolution,** that is the leading scientific explanation for the origin of life. Like all scientific theories, the theory of chemical evolution has a *pattern component* that makes a claim about the natural world and a *process component* that explains that pattern.

- *The pattern component* In addition to small molecules, complex carbon-containing substances exist and are required for life.

- *The process component* Early in Earth's history, simple chemical compounds combined to form more complex carbon-containing substances before the evolution of life.

This chapter is part of the Big Picture. See how on pages 68–69.

✔ When you see this checkmark, stop and test yourself. Answers are available in Appendix A.

The theory maintains that inputs of energy led to the formation of increasingly complex carbon-containing substances, culminating in a compound that could replicate itself. At this point, there was a switch from chemical evolution to biological evolution.

As the original molecule multiplied, the process of evolution by natural selection took over. Eventually a descendant of the original molecule became metabolically active and acquired a membrane. When this occurred, the five attributes of life (discussed in Chapter 1) were fulfilled. Life had begun.

At first glance, the theory of chemical evolution may seem implausible. But is it? What evidence do biologists have that chemical evolution occurred? What approaches do they take to gathering this evidence?

Let's start with the fundamentals—the atoms and molecules that would have combined to get chemical evolution started.

2.1 Atoms, Ions, and Molecules: The Building Blocks of Chemical Evolution

Just four types of atoms—hydrogen, carbon, nitrogen, and oxygen—make up 96 percent of all matter found in organisms today. Many of the molecules found in your cells contain thousands, or even millions, of these atoms bonded together. But early in Earth's history, these elements existed only in simple substances such as water and carbon dioxide, which contain just three atoms apiece.

Two questions are fundamental to understanding how elements could have evolved into the more complex substances found in living cells:

1. What is the physical structure of the hydrogen, carbon, nitrogen, and oxygen atoms found in living cells?

2. What is the structure of the simple molecules—water, carbon dioxide, and others—that served as the building blocks of chemical evolution?

The focus on structure follows from one of the most central themes in biology: *Structure affects function*. To understand how a molecule affects your body or the role it played in chemical evolution, you have to understand how it is put together.

Basic Atomic Structure

FIGURE 2.1a shows a simple way of depicting the structure of an atom, using hydrogen and carbon as examples. Extremely small particles called electrons orbit an atomic nucleus made up of larger particles called protons and neutrons. **FIGURE 2.1b** provides a sense of scale at the atomic level.

Protons have a positive electric charge (+1), neutrons are electrically neutral, and electrons have a negative electric charge (−1). When the number of protons and the number of electrons in an atom are the same, the charges balance and the atom is electrically neutral.

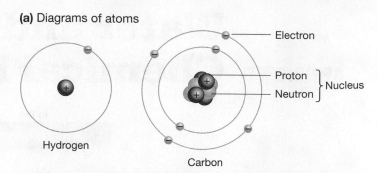

(a) Diagrams of atoms

(b) Most of an atom's volume is empty space.

If an atom occupied the same volume as this stadium, the nucleus would be about the size of a pea

FIGURE 2.1 Parts of an Atom. The atomic nucleus, made up of protons and neutrons, is surrounded by orbiting electrons. In reality, electrons do not orbit the nucleus in circles; their actual orbits are complex.

FIGURE 2.2 shows a segment of the periodic table of the elements. Notice that each atom of a given **element** contains a characteristic number of protons, called its **atomic number**. The atomic number is written as a subscript to the left of an element's symbol in Figure 2.2. The sum of the protons and neutrons in an atom is called its **mass number** and is written as a superscript to the left of its symbol.

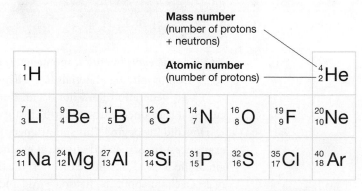

FIGURE 2.2 A Portion of the Periodic Table. Each element has a unique atomic number and is represented by a unique one- or two-letter symbol. The mass numbers given here are the most common for each element. (Appendix C provides a complete periodic table of elements.)

The number of protons in an element does not vary—if the atomic number of an atom changes, then it is no longer the same element. The number of neutrons present in an element can vary, however. Forms of an element with different numbers of neutrons are known as **isotopes** (literally, "equal-places" in regard to position in the periodic table).

Different isotopes have different masses, yet are the same element. For example, all atoms of the element carbon have 6 protons. But naturally occurring isotopes of carbon can have 6, 7, or even 8 neutrons, giving them a mass number of 12, 13, or 14, respectively. The **atomic weight** of an element is an average of all the mass numbers of the naturally occurring isotopes based on their abundance. This is why the atomic weights for elements are often slightly different from the mass numbers—the atomic weight of carbon, for example, is 12.01.

Most isotopes are stable, but not all. For example, ^{14}C, with 6 protons and 8 neutrons, represents an unstable **radioactive isotope.** Its nucleus will eventually decay and release energy (radiation). When ^{14}C decays, one of its neutrons changes into a proton, converting ^{14}C to the stable ^{14}N isotope of nitrogen, with 7 protons and 7 neutrons. Timing of decay is specific to each radioisotope, a fact that has been very useful in estimating the dates of key events in the fossil record.

Although the masses of protons, neutrons, and electrons can be measured in grams, the numbers involved are so small that biologists prefer to use a special unit called the **dalton.** The masses of protons and neutrons are virtually identical and are routinely rounded to 1 dalton. A carbon atom that contains 6 protons and 6 neutrons has a mass of 12 daltons, while a carbon atom with 6 protons and 7 neutrons would have a mass of 13 daltons. These isotopes would be written as ^{12}C and ^{13}C, respectively. The mass of an electron is so small that it is normally ignored.

To understand how the atoms involved in chemical evolution behave, focus on how electrons are arranged around the nucleus:

- Electrons move around atomic nuclei in specific regions called **orbitals.**
- Each orbital can hold up to two electrons.
- Orbitals are grouped into levels called **electron shells.**
- Electron shells are numbered 1, 2, 3, and so on, to indicate their relative distance from the nucleus. Smaller numbers are closer to the nucleus.
- Each electron shell contains a specific number of orbitals. An electron shell comprising a single orbital can hold up to two electrons; a shell with four orbitals can contain up to eight electrons.
- The electrons of an atom fill the innermost shells first, before filling outer shells.

To understand how the structures of atoms differ, take a moment to study **FIGURE 2.3**. This chart highlights the elements that are most abundant in living cells. The gray ball in the center of each box represents an atomic nucleus, and the orange circle or circles represent the electron shells around that nucleus. The small orange balls on the circles indicate the number of electrons that are distributed in the shells of each element. Electrons shown as pairs share the same orbital within a shell.

Now focus on the outermost shell of each atom. This is the element's **valence shell.** The electrons found in this shell are referred to as **valence electrons.** Two observations are important:

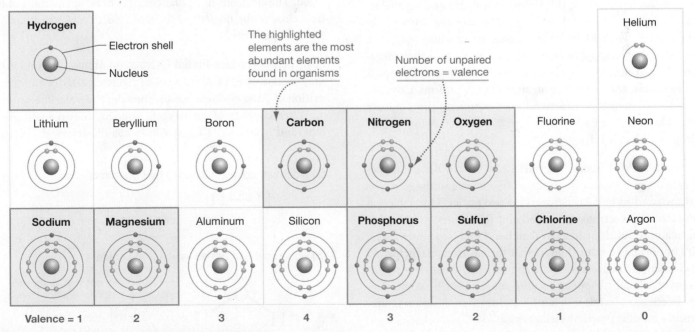

FIGURE 2.3 The Structure of Atoms Found in Organisms.

✔**QUESTION** If the mass number of phosphorus is 31, how many neutrons exist in the most common isotope of phosphorus?

1. In each of the highlighted elements, the outermost electron shell is not full—not all orbitals in the valence shell have two electrons. The highlighted elements have at least one unpaired valence electron—meaning at least one unfilled valence shell orbital.

2. The number of unpaired valence electrons varies among elements. Carbon, for example, has four valence electrons, all unpaired. Oxygen has six valence electrons; four are paired, two are not. The number of unpaired electrons found in an atom is called its **valence.** Carbon's valence is four, oxygen's is two.

These observations are significant because an atom is most stable when its valence shell is filled. One way that shells can be filled is through the formation of strong **chemical bonds**—attractions that bind atoms together. A strong attraction where two atoms share one or more pairs of electrons is called a **covalent bond.**

How Does Covalent Bonding Hold Molecules Together?

To understand how atoms can become more stable by making covalent bonds, consider hydrogen. The hydrogen atom has just one electron, which resides in a shell that can hold two electrons.

Because it has an unpaired valence electron, the hydrogen atom is not very stable. But when two atoms of hydrogen come into contact, the two electrons become shared by the two nuclei (**FIGURE 2.4**). Both atoms now have a completely filled outer shell. Together, the hydrogen atoms are more stable than the two individual hydrogen atoms.

Shared electrons "glue" two hydrogen atoms together. Substances held together by covalent bonds are called **molecules.** In the case of two hydrogen atoms, the bonded atoms form a single molecule of hydrogen, written as H—H or H_2.

It can also be helpful to think about covalent bonding as electrical attraction and repulsion. Opposite charges attract; like charges repel. As two hydrogen atoms move closer together, their positively charged nuclei repel each other and their negatively charged electrons repel each other. But each proton attracts both electrons, and each electron attracts both protons. Covalent bonds form when the attractive forces overcome the repulsive forces. This is the case when hydrogen atoms interact to form the hydrogen molecule (H_2).

Nonpolar and Polar Bonds   In **FIGURE 2.5a**, the covalent bond between hydrogen atoms is represented by a dash and the electrons are drawn as dots halfway between the two nuclei. This depiction shows that the electrons are shared equally between the two hydrogen atoms, resulting in a covalent bond that is symmetrical.

It's important to note, though, that the electrons participating in a covalent bond are not always shared equally between the atoms involved. This happens because some atoms hold the electrons in covalent bonds much more tightly than do other atoms. Chemists call this property **electronegativity.**

What is responsible for an atom's electronegativity? It's a combination of two things—the number of protons in the nucleus and the distance between the nucleus and the valence shell. If

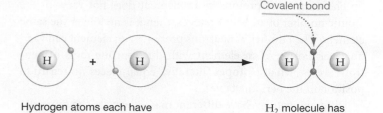

Hydrogen atoms each have one unpaired electron

H_2 molecule has two shared electrons

FIGURE 2.4 Covalent Bonds Result from Electron Sharing. When two hydrogen atoms come into contact, their electrons are attracted to the positive charge in each nucleus. As a result, their orbitals overlap, the electrons are shared by each nucleus, and a covalent bond forms.

you return to Figure 2.3 and move your finger along a row from left to right, you will be moving toward elements that increase in protons and in electronegativity (ignoring the elements in the far right column, which have full outer shells). Each row, however, represents shells of electrons, so if your finger moved down the table, the elements would decrease in electronegativity.

Oxygen, which has eight protons and only two electron shells, is among the most electronegative of all elements. It attracts covalently bonded electrons more strongly than does any other atom commonly found in organisms. Nitrogen's electronegativity is somewhat lower than oxygen's. Carbon and hydrogen, in turn, have relatively low and approximately equal electronegativities. Thus, the electronegativities of the four most abundant elements in organisms are related as follows: $O > N > C \cong H$.

Because carbon and hydrogen have approximately equal electronegativity, the electrons in a C—H bond are shared equally or symmetrically. The result is a **nonpolar covalent bond.** In contrast, asymmetric sharing of electrons results in a **polar covalent bond.** The electrons in a polar covalent bond spend most of their time close to the nucleus of the more electronegative atom. Why is this important?

Polar Bonds Produce Partial Charges on Atoms   To understand the consequences of differences in electronegativity and the formation of polar covalent bonds, consider the water molecule.

Water consists of an oxygen bonded to two hydrogen atoms, and is written H_2O. As **FIGURE 2.5b** illustrates, the electrons

(a) Nonpolar covalent bond in hydrogen molecule

Electrons are halfway between the two atoms, shared equally

(b) Polar covalent bonds in water molecule

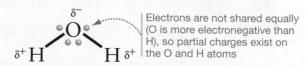

Electrons are not shared equally (O is more electronegative than H), so partial charges exist on the O and H atoms

FIGURE 2.5 Electron Sharing and Bond Polarity. Delta (δ) symbols in polar covalent bonds refer to partial positive and negative charges that arise owing to unequal electron sharing.

involved in the covalent bonds in water are not shared equally but are held much more tightly by the oxygen nucleus than by the hydrogen nuclei. Hence, water has two polar covalent bonds—one between the oxygen atom and each of the hydrogen atoms.

Here's the key observation: Because electrons are shared unequally in each O—H bond, they spend more time near the oxygen atom, giving it a partial negative charge, and less time near the hydrogen atoms, giving them a partial positive charge. These partial charges are symbolized by the lowercase Greek letter delta, δ.

As Section 2.2 shows, the partial charges on water molecules—due simply to the difference in electronegativity between oxygen and hydrogen—are one of the primary reasons that life exists.

Ionic Bonding, Ions, and the Electron-Sharing Continuum

Ionic bonds are similar in principle to covalent bonds, but instead of being shared between two atoms, the electrons in ionic bonds are completely transferred from one atom to the other. The electron transfer occurs because it gives the resulting atoms a full outermost shell.

Sodium atoms (Na), for example, tend to lose an electron, leaving them with a full second shell. This is a much more stable arrangement, energetically, than having a lone electron in their third shell (**FIGURE 2.6a**). The atom that results has a net electric charge of +1, because it has one more proton than it has electrons.

An atom or molecule that carries a full charge, rather than the partial charges that arise from polar covalent bonds, is called an **ion**. The sodium ion is written Na^+ and, like other positively charged ions, is called a **cation** (pronounced *KAT-eye-un*).

Chlorine atoms (Cl), in contrast, tend to gain an electron, filling their outermost shell (**FIGURE 2.6b**). The ion has a net charge of −1, because it has one more electron than protons. This

negatively charged ion, or **anion** (pronounced *AN-eye-un*), is written Cl^- and is called chlor*i*de.

When sodium and chlorine combine to form sodium chloride (NaCl, common table salt), they pack into a crystal structure consisting of sodium cations and chloride anions (**FIGURE 2.6c**). The electrical attraction between the ions is so strong that salt crystals are difficult to break apart.

This discussion of covalent and ionic bonding supports an important general observation: The degree to which electrons are shared in chemical bonds forms a continuum from equal sharing in nonpolar covalent bonds to unequal sharing in polar covalent bonds to the transfer of electrons in ionic bonds.

As the left-hand side of **FIGURE 2.7** shows, covalent bonds between atoms with exactly the same electronegativity—for example, between the atoms of hydrogen in H_2—represent one end of the continuum. The electrons in these nonpolar bonds are shared equally.

In the middle of the continuum are bonds where one atom is much more electronegative than the other. In these asymmetric bonds, substantial partial charges exist on each of the atoms. These types of polar covalent bonds occur when a highly electronegative atom such as oxygen or nitrogen is bonded to an atom with a lower affinity for electrons, such as carbon or hydrogen. Ammonia (NH_3) and water (H_2O) are examples of molecules with polar covalent bonds.

At the right-hand side of the continuum are molecules made up of atoms with extreme differences in their electronegativities. In this case, electrons are transferred rather than shared, the atoms have full charges, and the bonding is ionic. Sodium chloride (NaCl) is a familiar example of a molecule formed by ionic bonds.

Most chemical bonds that occur in biological molecules are on the left-hand side and the middle of the continuum; in the molecules found in organisms, ionic bonding is less common.

(a) A sodium ion being formed

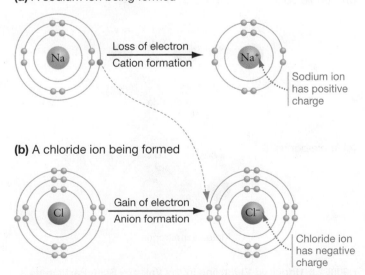

Loss of electron
Cation formation

Sodium ion has positive charge

(b) A chloride ion being formed

Gain of electron
Anion formation

Chloride ion has negative charge

(c) Table salt (NaCl) is a crystal composed of two ions.

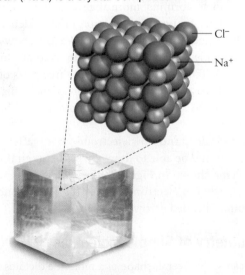

Cl^-

Na^+

FIGURE 2.6 Ion Formation and Ionic Bonding. The sodium ion (Na^+) and the chloride ion (Cl^-) are stable because they have full valence shells. In table salt (NaCl), sodium and chloride ions pack into a crystal structure held together by electrical attraction between their positive and negative charges.

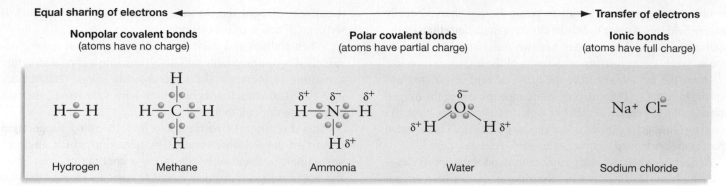

FIGURE 2.7 The Electron-Sharing Continuum. The degree of electron sharing in chemical bonds can be thought of as a continuum, from equal sharing in nonpolar covalent bonds to no sharing in ionic bonds.

✔QUESTION Why do most polar covalent bonds involve nitrogen or oxygen?

Some Simple Molecules Formed from C, H, N, and O

Look back at Figure 2.3 and count the number of unpaired electrons in the valence shells of carbon, nitrogen, oxygen, and hydrogen atoms. Each unpaired electron in a valence shell can make up half of a covalent bond. It should make sense to you that a carbon atom can form a total of four covalent bonds; nitrogen can form three; oxygen can form two; and hydrogen, one.

When each of the four unpaired electrons of a carbon atom covalently bonds with a hydrogen atom, the molecule that results is written CH_4 and is called methane (**FIGURE 2.8a**). Methane is the most common molecule found in natural gas. When a nitrogen atom's three unpaired electrons bond with three hydrogen atoms, the result is NH_3, or ammonia. Similarly, an atom of oxygen can form covalent bonds with two atoms of hydrogen, resulting in a water molecule (H_2O). As Figure 2.4 showed, a hydrogen atom can bond with another hydrogen atom to form hydrogen gas (H_2).

In addition to forming more than one single bond, atoms with more than one unpaired electron in the valence shell can form double bonds or triple bonds. **FIGURE 2.8b** shows how carbon forms double bonds with oxygen atoms to produce carbon dioxide (CO_2). Triple bonds result when three pairs of electrons are shared. **FIGURE 2.8c** shows the structure of molecular nitrogen (N_2), which forms when two nitrogen atoms establish a triple bond.

✔ If you understand how electronegativity affects covalent bonds, you should be able to draw arrows between the atoms in each molecule shown in Figure 2.8 to indicate the relative position of the shared electrons. If they are equally shared, then draw a double-headed arrow.

The Geometry of Simple Molecules

In many cases, the overall shape of a molecule dictates how it behaves. In chemistry and in biology, function is based on structure.

The shapes of the simple molecules you've just learned about are governed by the geometry of their bonds. Nitrogen (N_2) and

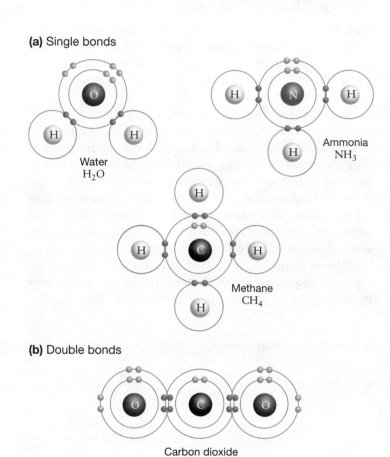

(a) Single bonds

Water
H_2O

Ammonia
NH_3

Methane
CH_4

(b) Double bonds

Carbon dioxide
CO_2

(c) Triple bonds

Molecular nitrogen
N_2

FIGURE 2.8 Unpaired Electrons in the Valence Shell Participate in Covalent Bonds. Covalent bonding is based on sharing of electrons in the outermost shell. Covalent bonds can be **(a)** single, **(b)** double, or **(c)** triple.

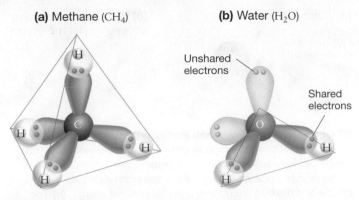

(a) Methane (CH₄) **(b)** Water (H₂O)

Unshared electrons

Shared electrons

FIGURE 2.9 The Geometry of Methane and Water.

	Methane	Ammonia	Water	Oxygen
(a) Molecular formulas:	CH₄	NH₃	H₂O	O₂

(b) Structural formulas:

H—C—H H—N—H $\overset{O}{\underset{H \quad H}{}}$ O=O

(c) Ball-and-stick models:

(d) Space-filling models:

FIGURE 2.10 Molecules Can Be Represented Several Ways. Each method of representing a molecule has particular advantages.

carbon dioxide (CO_2), for example, have linear structures (see Figure 2.8). Molecules with more complex geometries include

- Methane (CH_4)—which is tetrahedral, a structure with four triangular faces like a pyramid (**FIGURE 2.9a**). The tetrahedron forms because the electrons in the four C—H bonds repulse each other equally. The electron pairs are as far apart as they can get.

- Water (H_2O)—which is bent and two-dimensional, or planar (**FIGURE 2.9b**). Why? The electrons in the four orbitals of oxygen's valence shell repulse each other, just as they do in methane. But in water, two of the orbitals are filled with electron pairs from the oxygen atom, and two are filled with electron pairs from covalent bonds between oxygen and hydrogen. The shared electrons form a molecule that is V-shaped and flat.

Section 2.2 explores how water's shape, in combination with the partial charges on the oxygen and hydrogen atoms, makes it the most important molecule on Earth.

Representing Molecules

Molecules can be represented in a variety of increasingly complex ways—only some of which reflect their actual shape. Each method has advantages and disadvantages.

- **Molecular formulas** are compact, but don't contain a great deal of information—they indicate only the numbers and types of atoms in a molecule (**FIGURE 2.10a**).

- **Structural formulas** indicate which atoms in a molecule are bonded together. Single, double, and triple bonds are represented by single, double, and triple dashes, respectively. Structural formulas also indicate geometry in two dimensions (**FIGURE 2.10b**). This method is useful for planar molecules such as water and O_2.

- **Ball-and-stick models** take up more space than structural formulas, but provide information on the three-dimensional shape of molecules and indicate the relative sizes of the atoms involved (**FIGURE 2.10c**).

- **Space-filling models** are more difficult to read than ball-and-stick models but more accurately depict the spatial relationships between atoms. (**FIGURE 2.10d**).

In both ball-and-stick and space-filling models, biologists use certain colors to represent certain atoms. A black ball, for

example, always symbolizes carbon. (For more information on interpreting chemical structures, see **BioSkills 8** in Appendix B.)

Some of the small molecules you've just learned about are found in volcanic gases, the atmospheres of nearby planets, and in deep-sea hydrothermal vents, like those shown in the photograph at the start of this chapter. Based on these observations, researchers claim that they were important components of Earth's ancient atmosphere and oceans. If so, then they provided the building blocks for chemical evolution. The question is: How did these simple building blocks combine to form more complex products, early in Earth's history?

Researchers postulate that most of the critical reactions in chemical evolution occurred in an aqueous, or water-based, environment. To understand what happened and why, let's delve into the properties of water and then turn to analyzing the reactions that triggered chemical evolution.

check your understanding

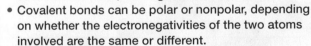

If you understand that . . .

- Covalent bonds are based on electron sharing. Electron sharing allows atoms to fill all the orbitals in their valence shell, making them more stable.
- Covalent bonds can be polar or nonpolar, depending on whether the electronegativities of the two atoms involved are the same or different.

✔ You should be able to . . .

Draw the structural formula of formaldehyde (CH_2O) and add dots to indicate the relative locations of the electrons being shared in each covalent bond, based on the relative electronegativities of C, H, and O.

Answers are available in Appendix A.

2.2 Properties of Water and the Early Oceans

Life is based on water. It arose in an aqueous environment and remains dependent on water today. In fact, 75 percent of the volume in a typical cell is water; water is the most abundant molecule in organisms (**FIGURE 2.11**). You can survive for weeks without eating, but you aren't likely to live more than 3 or 4 days without drinking.

Water is vital for a simple reason: It is an excellent **solvent**—that is, an agent for dissolving substances and getting them into **solution.** The reactions that were responsible for chemical evolution some 3.5 billion years ago, like those occurring inside your body right now, depend on direct, physical interaction between molecules. Substances are most likely to come into contact with one another and react as **solutes**—meaning, when they are dissolved in a solvent like water. The formation of Earth's first ocean, about 3.8 billion years ago, was a turning point in chemical evolution because it gave the process a place to happen.

Why Is Water Such an Efficient Solvent?

To understand why water is such an effective solvent, recall that

1. Both of the O—H bonds in a water molecule are polar, owing to the difference in the electronegativities of hydrogen and oxygen. As a result, the oxygen atom has a partial negative charge and each hydrogen atom has a partial positive charge.

2. The molecule is bent. Consequently, the partial negative charge on the oxygen atom sticks out, away from the partial positive charges on the hydrogen atoms, giving a water molecule an overall polarity (**FIGURE 2.12a**).

FIGURE 2.12b illustrates how water's structure affects its interactions with other water molecules. When two water molecules approach each other, the partial positive charge on hydrogen attracts the partial negative charge on oxygen. This weak electrical attraction forms a **hydrogen bond** between the molecules.

✔ If you understand how water's structure makes hydrogen bonding possible, you should be able to (1) draw a fictional version of Figure 2.12b that shows water as a linear (not bent)

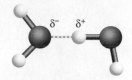

(a) Water is polar.

(b) Hydrogen bonds form between water molecules.

FIGURE 2.12 Water Is Polar and Participates in Hydrogen Bonds. (a) Because of oxygen's high electronegativity, the electrons that are shared between hydrogen and oxygen spend more time close to the oxygen nucleus, giving the oxygen atom a partial negative charge and the hydrogen atom a partial positive charge. **(b)** The electrical attraction that occurs between the partial positive and negative charges on water molecules forms a hydrogen bond.

molecule with partial charges on the oxygen and hydrogen atoms; and (2) explain why electrostatic attractions between such water molecules would be much weaker as a result.

In an aqueous solution, hydrogen bonds also form between water molecules and other polar molecules. Similar interactions occur between water and ions. Ions and polar molecules stay in solution because of their interactions with water's partial charges (**FIGURE 2.13**). Substances that interact with water in this way are said to be **hydrophilic** ("water-loving"). Hydrogen bonding makes it possible for almost any charged or polar molecule to dissolve in water.

In contrast, compounds that are uncharged and nonpolar do not interact with water through hydrogen bonding and do not dissolve in water. Substances that do not interact with water are said to be **hydrophobic** ("water-fearing"). Because their interactions with water are minimal or nonexistent, they are forced to interact with each other (**FIGURE 2.14**, see page D:9). The water molecules surrounding nonpolar molecules form hydrogen bonds with one another and increase the stability of these **hydrophobic interactions.**

Although individual hydrogen bonds are not as strong as covalent or ionic bonds, many of them occur in a solution. Hydrogen bonding is extremely important in biology owing to the

FIGURE 2.11 Fruits Shrink When They Are Dried Because They Consist Primarily of Water.

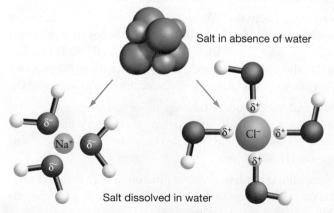

FIGURE 2.13 Polar Molecules and Ions Dissolve Readily in Water. Water's polarity makes it a superb solvent for polar molecules and ions.

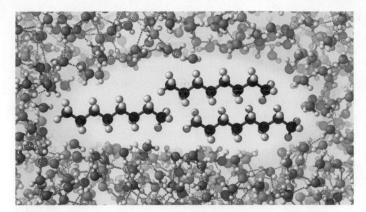

FIGURE 2.14 Nonpolar Molecules Do Not Dissolve in Water.
In aqueous solution, nonpolar molecules and compounds are
forced to interact with each other. This occurs because water is
much more stable when it interacts with itself rather than with the
nonpolar molecules.

✔**QUESTION** What is the physical basis of the expression, "Oil and
water don't mix"?

sheer number of hydrogen bonds that form between water and
hydrophilic molecules.

What Properties Are Correlated with Water's Structure?

Water's small size, highly polar covalent bonds, and bent shape
resulting in overall polarity are unique among molecules. Because the structure of molecules routinely correlates with their
function, it's not surprising that water has some remarkable
properties, in addition to its extraordinary capacity to act as a
solvent.

Cohesion, Adhesion, and Surface Tension Attraction between
like molecules is called **cohesion.** Water is cohesive—meaning
that it stays together—because of the hydrogen bonds that form
between individual molecules.

Attraction between unlike molecules, in contrast, is called
adhesion. Adhesion is usually analyzed in regard to interactions
between a liquid and a solid surface. Water adheres to surfaces
that have any polar or charged components.

Cohesion and adhesion are important in explaining how
water can move from the roots of plants to their leaves against
the force of gravity. But you can also see them in action in the
concave surface, or meniscus, that forms in a glass tube (**FIGURE
2.15a**). A meniscus forms as a result of two forces:

1. Water molecules at the perimeter of the surface adhere to the
   glass, resulting in an upward pull.

2. Water molecules at the surface hydrogen-bond with water
   molecules next to them and below them, resulting in a net
   lateral and downward pull that resists the upward pull of
   adhesion.

Cohesion is also instrumental in the phenomenon known as
surface tension. When water molecules are at the surface, there

(a) A meniscus forms where water meets a solid surface,
as a result of two forces.

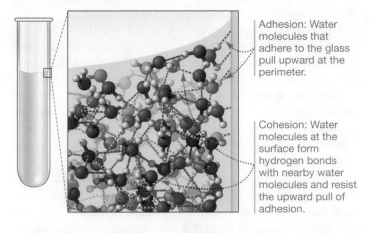

Adhesion: Water
molecules that
adhere to the glass
pull upward at the
perimeter.

Cohesion: Water
molecules at the
surface form
hydrogen bonds
with nearby water
molecules and resist
the upward pull of
adhesion.

(b) Water has high surface tension.

Because of surface
tension, light
objects do not
fall through the
water's surface

FIGURE 2.15 Cohesion, Adhesion, and Surface Tension.
(a) Meniscus formation is based on hydrogen bonding. **(b)** Water
resists forces—like the weight of a spider—that increase its surface
area. The resistance is great enough that light objects do not break
the surface.

are no water molecules above them for hydrogen bonding. As a
result, they exhibit stronger attractive forces between their nearest neighboring molecules. This enhanced attraction between the
surface water molecules results in tension that minimizes the total surface area.

This fact has an important consequence: Water resists any force
that increases its surface area. More specifically, any force that
depresses a water surface meets with resistance. This resistance
makes a water surface act like an elastic membrane (**FIGURE 2.15b**).

In water, the "elastic membrane" is stronger than it is in other
liquids. Water's surface tension is extraordinarily high because of
the stronger hydrogen bonding that occurs between molecules at
the surface. This explains why it is better to cut the water's surface with your fingertips when you dive into a pool, instead of
doing a belly flop.

Water Is Denser as a Liquid than as a Solid When factory workers pour molten metal or plastic into a mold and allow it to cool
to the solid state, the material shrinks. When molten lava pours

out of a volcano and cools to solid rock, it shrinks. But when you fill an ice tray with water and put it in the freezer to make ice, the water expands.

Unlike most substances, water is denser as a liquid than it is as a solid. In other words, there are more molecules of water in a given volume of liquid water than there are in the same volume of solid water, or ice. **FIGURE 2.16** illustrates why this is so.

Note that in ice, each water molecule participates in four hydrogen bonds. These hydrogen bonds cause the water molecules to form a regular and repeating structure, or crystal (Figure 2.16a). The crystal structure of ice is fairly open, meaning that there is a relatively large amount of space between molecules.

Now compare the extent of hydrogen bonding and the density of ice with that of liquid water, illustrated in Figure 2.16b. Note that the extent of hydrogen bonding in liquid water is much less than that found in ice, and that the hydrogen bonds in liquid water are constantly being formed and broken. As a result, molecules in the liquid phase are packed much more closely together than in the solid phase.

Normally, heating a substance causes it to expand because molecules begin moving faster and colliding more often and with greater force. But heating ice causes hydrogen bonds to break and the open crystal structure to collapse. In this way, hydrogen bonding explains why water is denser as a liquid than as a solid.

This property of water has an important result: Ice floats (Figure 2.16c). If it didn't, ice would sink to the bottom of lakes, ponds, and oceans soon after it formed. The ice would stay frozen in the cold depths. Instead, ice serves as a blanket, insulating the liquid below from the cold air above. If water weren't so unusual, it is almost certain that Earth's oceans would have frozen solid before life had a chance to start.

Water Has a High Capacity for Absorbing Energy Hydrogen bonding is also responsible for another of water's remarkable physical properties: Water has a high capacity for absorbing energy.

Specific heat, for example, is the amount of energy required to raise the temperature of 1 gram of a substance by 1°C. Water has a high specific heat because when a source of energy hits it, hydrogen bonds must be broken before heat can be transferred and the water molecules begin moving faster. As **TABLE 2.1** indicates, as molecules increase in overall polarity, and thus in their ability to form hydrogen bonds, it takes an extraordinarily large amount of energy to change their temperature.

TABLE 2.1 Specific Heats of Some Liquids

The specific heats reported in this table were measured at 25°C and are given in units of joules per gram of substance per degree Celsius. (The joule is a unit of energy.)

With extensive hydrogen bonding	Specific Heat
Water (H_2O)	4.18
With some hydrogen bonding	
Ethanol (C_2H_6O)	2.44
Glycerol ($C_3H_8O_3$)	2.38
With little or no hydrogen bonding	
Benzene (C_6H_6)	1.74
Xylene (C_8H_{10})	1.72

DATA: D. R. Lide (editor). 2008. *Standard Thermodynamic Properties of Chemical Substances*, in *CRC Handbook of Physics and Chemistry*. 89th ed. Boca Raton, FL: CRC Press.

(a) In ice, water molecules form a crystal lattice.

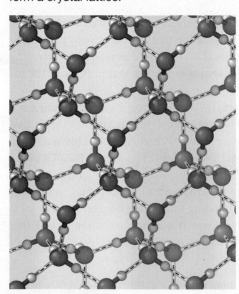

(b) In liquid water, no crystal lattice forms.

(c) Liquid water is denser than ice. As a result, ice floats.

FIGURE 2.16 Hydrogen Bonding Forms the Crystal Structure of Ice. In ice, each molecule can form four hydrogen bonds at one time. Each oxygen atom can form two; each hydrogen atom can form one.

Property	Cause	Biological Consequences
Solvent for charged or polar compounds	_____ _____ _____ _____	Most chemical reactions important for life take place in aqueous solution.
Denser as a liquid than a solid	As water freezes, each molecule forms a total of four hydrogen bonds, leading to the formation of the low-density crystal structure called ice.	_____ _____ _____
High specific heat	Water molecules must absorb lots of heat energy to break hydrogen bonds and experience increased movement (and thus temperature).	Oceans absorb and release heat slowly, moderating coastal climates.
High heat of vaporization	_____ _____	Evaporation of water from an organism cools the body.

✔**EXERCISE** You should be able to fill in the missing cells in this table.

Similarly, it takes a large amount of energy to break the hydrogen bonds in liquid water and change the molecules from the liquid phase to the gas phase. Water's **heat of vaporization**—the energy required to change 1 gram of it from a liquid to gas—is higher than that of most molecules that are liquid at room temperature. As a result, water has to absorb a great deal of energy to evaporate. Water's high heat of vaporization is the reason that sweating or dousing yourself with water is an effective way to cool off on a hot day. Water molecules absorb a great deal of energy from your body before they evaporate, so you lose heat.

Water's ability to absorb energy is critical to the theory of chemical evolution. Molecules that were formed in the ocean were well protected from sources of energy that could break them apart, such as intense sunlight. As a result, they would have persisted and slowly increased in concentration over time, making them more likely to react and continue the process.

TABLE 2.2 summarizes some of the key properties of water.

The Role of Water in Acid–Base Reactions

You've seen that water's high specific heat and heat of vaporization tend to keep its temperature and liquid form stable. One other aspect of water's chemistry is important for understanding chemical evolution and how organisms work: Water is not a completely stable molecule. In reality, water molecules continually undergo a chemical reaction with themselves. When a **chemical reaction** occurs, one substance is combined with others or broken down into another substance. Atoms may also be rearranged; in most cases, chemical bonds are broken and new bonds form. The chemical reaction that takes place between water molecules is called a "dissociation" reaction. It can be written as follows:

$$H_2O \rightleftharpoons H^+ + OH^-$$

The double arrow indicates that the reaction proceeds in both directions.

The substances on the right-hand side of the expression are the **hydrogen ion** (H^+) and the **hydroxide ion** (OH^-). A hydrogen ion is simply a proton. In reality, however, protons do not exist by themselves. In water, for example, protons associate with water molecules to form hydronium ions (H_3O^+). Thus, the dissociation of water is more accurately written as:

$$H_2O + H_2O \rightleftharpoons H_3O^+ + OH^-$$

One of the water molecules on the left-hand side of the expression has given up a proton, while the other water molecule has accepted a proton.

Substances that give up protons during chemical reactions and raise the hydronium ion concentration of water are called **acids;** molecules or ions that acquire protons during chemical reactions and lower the hydronium ion concentration of water are called **bases.** Most acids act only as acids, and most bases act only as bases; but water can act as both an acid and a base.

A chemical reaction that involves a transfer of protons is called an acid–base reaction. Every acid–base reaction requires a proton donor and a proton acceptor—an acid and a base, respectively.

Water is an extremely weak acid—very few water molecules dissociate to form hydronium ions and hydroxide ions. In contrast, strong acids like the hydrochloric acid (HCl) in your stomach readily give up a proton when they react with water.

$$HCl + H_2O \rightleftharpoons H_3O^+ + Cl^-$$

Strong bases readily acquire protons when they react with water. For example, sodium hydroxide (NaOH, commonly called lye) dissociates completely in water to form Na^+ and OH^-. The hydroxide ion produced by that reaction then accepts a proton from a hydronium ion in the water, forming two water molecules.

$$NaOH(aq) \longrightarrow Na^+ + OH^-$$
$$OH^- + H_3O^+ \rightleftharpoons 2 H_2O$$

(The "*aq*" in the first expression indicates that NaOH is in aqueous solution.)

To summarize, adding an acid to a solution increases the concentration of protons; adding a base to a solution lowers the concentration of protons. Water is both a weak acid and a weak base.

Determining the Concentration of Protons In a solution, the tendency for acid–base reactions to occur is largely a function of the number of protons present. The problem is, there's no simple way to count the actual number of protons present in a sample. Researchers solve this problem using the mole concept.

A **mole** refers to the number 6.022×10^{23}—just as the unit called the dozen refers to the number 12 or the unit million refers to the number 1×10^6. The mole is a useful unit because the mass of one mole of any substance is the same as its molecular weight expressed in grams. **Molecular weight** is the sum of the atomic weights of all the atoms in a molecule.

For example, to get the molecular weight of H_2O, you sum the atomic weights of two atoms of hydrogen and one atom of oxygen. Since the atomic weights of hydrogen and oxygen are very close to their mass numbers (see Figure 2.2), the molecular weight of water would be $1 + 1 + 16$, or a total of 18. Thus, if you weighed a sample of 18 grams of water, it would contain around 6×10^{23} water molecules, or about 1 mole of water molecules.

When substances are dissolved in water, their concentration is expressed in terms of molarity (symbolized by "M"). **Molarity** is the number of moles of the substance present per liter of solution. A 1-molar solution of protons in water, for example, means that 1 mole of protons is contained in 1 liter of solution.

Chemists can measure the concentration of protons in a solution directly using molarity and an instrument called a pH meter. In a sample of pure water at 25°C, the concentration of H^+ is 1.0×10^{-7}M, or 1 ten-millionth molar.

The pH of a Solution Reveals Whether It Is Acidic or Basic Because the concentration of protons in water is such a small number, exponential notation is cumbersome. So chemists and biologists prefer to express the concentration of protons in a solution, and thus whether it is acidic or basic, with a logarithmic notation called **pH**.[1]

By definition, the pH of a solution is the negative of the base-10 logarithm, or log, of the hydrogen ion concentration:

$$pH = -\log [H^+]$$

(To review logarithms, see **BioSkills 6** in Appendix B. The square brackets are a standard notation for indicating "concentration" of a substance in solution.)

Taking antilogs gives

$$[H^+] = \text{antilog}(-ph) = 10^{-ph}$$

Solutions that contain acids have a proton concentration larger than 1×10^{-7}M and thus a pH < 7. This is because acidic

molecules tend to release protons into solution. In contrast, solutions that contain bases have a proton concentration less than 1×10^{-7}M and thus a pH > 7. This is because basic molecules tend to accept protons from solution.

pH is a convenient way to indicate the concentration of protons in a solution, but take note of what the number represents. For example, if the concentration of H^+ in a sample of water is 1.0×10^{-7}M, then its pH is 7. If the pH changes to 5, then the sample contains 100 times more protons and has become 100 times more acidic. ✔ **QUANTITATIVE If you understand how pH is related to [H^+], you should be able to calculate the concentration of protons in a solution that has a pH of 8.5.**

FIGURE 2.17 shows the pH scale and reports the pH of some selected solutions. Pure water is used as a standard, or point of reference, for pH 7 on the pH scale. The solution inside living cells is about pH 7, which is considered neutral—neither acidic nor basic. The normal function of a cell is dependent on maintaining this neutral internal environment. What is responsible for regulating pH?

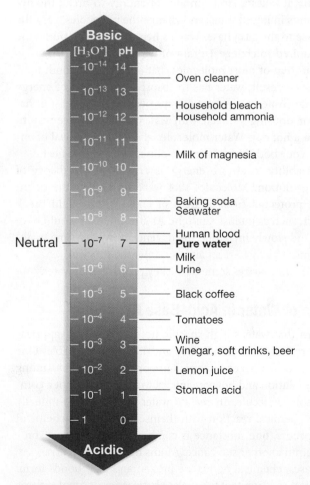

FIGURE 2.17 The pH Scale. Because the pH scale is logarithmic, a change in one unit of pH represents a change in the concentration of hydrogen ions equal to a factor of 10. Coffee has a hundred times more H^+ than pure water has.

✔ **QUESTION** What happens to the concentration of protons in black coffee after you add milk?

[1]The term pH is derived from the French *puissance d'hydrogéne*, or "power of hydrogen."

Buffers Protect Against Damaging Changes in pH Life is sensitive to changes in pH. Changes in proton concentration affect the structure and function of polar or charged substances as well as the tendency of acid–base reactions to occur.

Compounds that minimize changes in pH are called **buffers** because they reduce the impact of adding acids or bases on the overall pH of a solution. Buffers are important in maintaining relatively constant conditions, or **homeostasis,** in cells and tissues. In cells, a wide array of naturally occurring molecules act as buffers.

Most buffers are weak acids, meaning that they are somewhat likely to give up a proton in solution, but once the proton concentration rises, the acid is regenerated. To see how buffers work, consider the disassociation of carbonic acid in water to form bicarbonate ions and protons:

$$CH_2O_3 \rightleftharpoons CHO_3^- + H^+$$
$$\text{carbonic acid} \qquad \text{bicarbonate}$$

When carbonic acid and bicarbonate are present in about equal concentrations in a solution, they function as a buffering system. If the concentration of protons increases slightly, the protons react with bicarbonate ions to form carbonic acid and pH does not change. If the concentration of protons decreases slightly, carbonic acid gives up protons and pH does not change. ✔ **If you understand this concept, you should be able to predict what would happen to the concentration of bicarbonate ions if a base like sodium hydroxide (NaOH) were added to the solution of carbonic acid.**

As chemical evolution began, then, water provided the physical environment for key reactions to take place. In some cases water also acted as an important reactant. Although acid–base reactions were not critical to the initial stages of chemical evolution, they became extremely important once the process was under way. Now let's consider what happened in solution, some 3.5 billion years ago.

2.3 Chemical Reactions, Energy, and Chemical Evolution

Proponents of the theory of chemical evolution contend that simple molecules present in the atmosphere and oceans of early Earth participated in chemical reactions that eventually produced larger, more complex organic (carbon-containing) molecules—such as the proteins, nucleic acids, sugars, and lipids introduced in the next four chapters. Currently, researchers are investigating two environments where these reactions may have occurred:

1. *The atmosphere*, which was probably dominated by gases ejected from volcanoes. Water vapor, carbon dioxide (CO_2), and nitrogen (N_2) are the dominant gases ejected by volcanoes today; a small amount of molecular hydrogen (H_2) and carbon monoxide (CO) may also be present.

2. *Deep-sea hydrothermal vents*, where extremely hot rocks contact deep cracks in the seafloor. In addition to gases such as CO_2 and H_2, certain deep-sea vents are rich in minerals containing reactive metals such as nickel and iron.

When gases like CO_2, N_2, H_2, and CO are put together and allowed to interact on their own, however, very little happens. They do not suddenly link together to create large, complex substances like those found in living cells. Instead, their bonds remain intact. To understand why the bonds of these molecules remain unchanged, you must first learn about how chemical reactions proceed.

How Do Chemical Reactions Happen?

Chemical reactions are written in a format similar to mathematical equations: The initial, or **reactant,** molecules are shown on the left and the resulting reaction **product(s)** shown on the right. For example, the most common reaction in the mix of gases and water vapor that emerges from volcanoes results in the production of carbonic acid, which can be precipitated with water as acid rain:

$$CO_2(g) \; 1 \; H_2O(l) \rightleftharpoons CHO_2O_3(aq)$$
$$\text{carbonic acid}$$

The physical state of each reactant and product is indicated as gas (*g*), liquid (*l*), solid (*s*), or in aqueous solution (*aq*).

Note that the expression is balanced; that is, 1 carbon, 3 oxygen, and 2 hydrogen atoms are present on each side of the expression. This illustrates the conservation of mass in closed systems—mass cannot be created or destroyed, but it may be rearranged through chemical reactions.

Note also that the expression contains a double arrow, meaning that the reaction is reversible. When the forward and reverse reactions proceed at the same rate, the quantities of reactants and products remain constant, although not necessarily equal. A dynamic but stable state such as this is termed a **chemical equilibrium.**

Changing the concentration of reactants or products can disturb a chemical equilibrium. For example, adding more CO_2 to the mixture would drive the reaction to the right, creating more CH_2O_3 until the equilibrium proportions of reactants and products are reestablished. Removing CO_2 or adding more CH_2O_3 would drive the reaction to the left.

A chemical equilibrium can also be altered by changes in temperature. For example, the water molecules in the following set of interacting elements, or **system,** would be present as a combination of liquid water and water vapor:

$$H_2O(l) \rightleftharpoons H_2O(g)$$

If liquid water molecules absorb enough energy, like the heat released from a volcano, they transform to the gaseous state. (You may recall that water has a high heat of vaporization and requires a large amount of energy to change its state from liquid to gas.) As a result, this change is termed **endothermic** ("within heating") because heat is absorbed during the process. In contrast, the transformation of water vapor to liquid water releases heat and is **exothermic** ("outside heating"). Raising the temperature of this system drives the equilibrium to the right; cooling the system drives it to the left.

In relation to chemical evolution, though, these reactions and changes of physical state are not particularly interesting. Carbonic acid is not an important intermediate in the formation of more complex molecules. However, interesting things do begin to happen when energy is added to mixtures of volcanic gases.

What Is Energy?

Energy can be defined as the capacity to do work or to supply heat. This capacity exists in one of two ways—as a stored potential or as an active motion.

Stored energy is called **potential energy.** An object gains or loses its ability to store energy because of its position. An electron that resides in an outer electron shell will, if the opportunity arises, fall into a lower electron shell closer to the positive charges on the protons in the nucleus. Because of its position farther from the positive charges in the nucleus, an electron in an outer electron shell has more potential energy than does an electron in an inner shell (**FIGURE 2.18**). When stored in chemical bonds, this form of potential energy is called **chemical energy.**

Kinetic energy is energy of motion. Molecules have kinetic energy because they are constantly in motion.

- The kinetic energy of molecular motion is called **thermal energy.**

- The **temperature** of an object is a measure of how much thermal energy its molecules possess. If an object has a low temperature, its molecules are moving slowly. (We perceive this as "cold.") If an object has a high temperature, its molecules are moving rapidly. (We perceive this as "hot.")

- When two objects with different temperatures come into contact, thermal energy is transferred between them. This transferred energy is called **heat.**

There are many forms of potential energy and kinetic energy, and energy can change from one form into another. However, according to the **first law of thermodynamics,** energy is conserved—it cannot be created or destroyed, but only transferred and transformed. (A more thorough explanation of energy transformation is provided in Chapter 8 in the context of cellular metabolism.)

Energy transformation is the heart of chemical evolution. According to the best data available, molecules that were part of the early Earth were exposed to massive inputs of energy. Kinetic energy, in the form of heat, was present in the gradually cooling molten mass that initially formed the planet. The atmosphere and surface of the early Earth were also bombarded with electricity from lightening and radiation from the Sun. Energy stored as potential energy in the chemical bonds of small molecules was also abundant.

Now that you understand that energy transformations are involved in chemical reactions, a big question remains: What determines if a reaction will take place?

What Makes a Chemical Reaction Spontaneous?

When chemists say that a reaction is spontaneous, they have a precise meaning in mind: Chemical reactions are spontaneous if they are able to proceed on their own, without any continuous external influence, such as added energy. Two factors determine if a reaction will proceed spontaneously:

1. Reactions tend to be spontaneous when the product molecules are less ordered than the reactant molecules. For example, nitroglycerin is a single, highly ordered molecule. But when nitroglycerin explodes, it breaks up into gases like carbon dioxide, nitrogen, oxygen, and water vapor. These molecules are much less ordered than the reactant nitroglycerin molecules. The heat that is given off from this explosion also contributes to increasing disorder in the environment. The amount of disorder in a system is called **entropy.** When the products of a chemical reaction are less ordered than the reactant molecules are, entropy increases and the reaction tends to be spontaneous. The **second law of thermodynamics,** in fact, states that entropy always increases in an isolated system.

2. Reactions tend to be spontaneous if the products have lower potential energy than the reactants. If the electrons in the reaction products are held more tightly than those in the reactants, then they have lower potential energy. Recall that highly electronegative atoms such as oxygen or nitrogen hold electrons in covalent bonds much more tightly than do atoms with a lower electronegativity, such as hydrogen or carbon. For example, when hydrogen and oxygen gases react, water is produced spontaneously:

$$2\,H_2(g) + O_2(g) \longrightarrow 2\,H_2O(g)$$

The electrons involved in the O—H bonds of water are held much more tightly by the more electronegative oxygen atom than when they were shared equally in the H—H and O=O bonds of hydrogen and oxygen (see **FIGURE 2.19a** on page D:15). As a result, the products have much lower potential energy than the reactants. The difference in chemical energy between reactants and products is given off as heat, so the reaction is exothermic. And although the reaction between hydrogen and oxygen results in less entropy—three molecules of gas produce two molecules of water vapor—the reaction is still spontaneous due to the large drop in potential energy

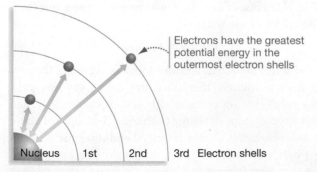

Electrons have the greatest potential energy in the outermost electron shells

Nucleus   1st   2nd   3rd Electron shells

FIGURE 2.18 Potential Energy as a Function of Electron Shells. Electrons in outer shells have more potential energy than do electrons in inner shells, because the negative charges of the electrons in outer shells are farther from the positive charges of the protons in the nucleus. Each shell represents a distinct level of potential energy.

(a) When hydrogen and oxygen gas react, the product has much lower potential energy than the reactants.

(b) The difference in potential energy is released as heat and light, which vaporizes the water produced.

Electrons are held "loosely" in bonds between atoms with equal electronegativities

Electrons are held tightly by highly electronegative atoms

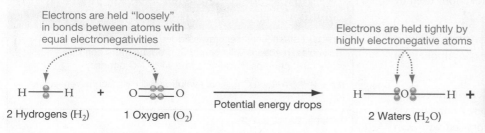

Potential energy drops →

2 Hydrogens (H₂)   1 Oxygen (O₂)   2 Waters (H₂O)

Heat and light

Released energy

FIGURE 2.19 Potential Energy May Change during Chemical Reactions. In the Hindenburg disaster of 1937, the hydrogen gas from this lighter-than-air craft reacted with oxygen in the atmosphere, with devastating results.

✔**EXERCISE** Label which electrons have relatively low potential energy and which electrons have relatively high potential energy.

released as heat. Since heat increases disorder in the environment, the second law of thermodynamics remains intact. The Hindenburg disaster of 1937 illustrates the large and terrifying amount of heat energy that is given off from this relatively simple reaction (**FIGURE 2.19b**).

To summarize: In general, physical and chemical processes proceed in the direction that results in increased entropy and lower potential energy (**FIGURE 2.20**). These two factors—potential energy and entropy—are used to figure out whether a reaction is spontaneous (see Chapter 10 for more detail). Were the reactions that led to chemical evolution spontaneous? Section 2.4 explores how researchers address this question.

Reactants:
• high potential energy
• more order (lower entropy)

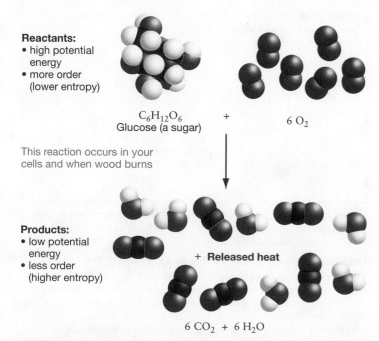

C₆H₁₂O₆
Glucose (a sugar)   +   6 O₂

This reaction occurs in your cells and when wood burns

Products:
• low potential energy
• less order (higher entropy)

+ **Released heat**

6 CO₂ + 6 H₂O

FIGURE 2.20 Spontaneous Processes Result in Lower Potential Energy, Increased Disorder, or Both.

check your understanding

Ⓒ Ⓨ Ⓤ

If you understand that . . .
• Chemical reactions result in the transformation of energy, either through the release of energy stored in chemical bonds or the uptake of energy from external sources.
• Chemical reactions tend to be spontaneous if they lead to lower potential energy and higher entropy (more disorder).

✔ **You should be able to . . .**

1. Determine if the reaction between methane (CH₄) and oxygen (O₂) shown here is spontaneous or not, addressing both potential energy and entropy:

$$CH_4 + 2 O_2 \longrightarrow CO_2 + 2 H_2O$$

2. Explain how the positions of the valence electrons in carbon and hydrogen change as methane is converted into carbon dioxide and water.

Answers are available in Appendix A.

2.4 Investigating Chemical Evolution: Approaches and Model Systems

To probe the kinds of reactions that may have set chemical evolution in motion, researchers have used two different approaches—one looking from the "top down" and the other from the "bottom up."

1. In the top-down approach, researchers examine modern cells to identify chemistry that is shared throughout the tree of life. Such ancient reactions are prime candidates for being involved in the chemical evolution that led up to **LUCA,** or last universal common ancestor (introduced in Chapter 1).

2. In the bottom-up approach, the primary focus is on the small molecules and environmental conditions that were present in

early Earth. Here, researchers attempt to identify reactions that could build the molecules found in life using only what was available at the time, without regard to reactions used by modern cells.

These approaches have been used to investigate two different model systems that attempt to explain the process component of the theory of chemical evolution:

1. The **prebiotic soup model** proposes that certain molecules were synthesized from gases in the atmosphere or arrived via meteorites. Afterward they would have condensed with rain and accumulated in oceans. This process would result in an "organic soup" that allowed for continued construction of larger, even more complex molecules.

2. The **surface metabolism model** suggests that dissolved gases came in contact with minerals lining the walls of deep-sea vents and formed more complex, organic molecules.

Since it is impossible to directly examine how and where chemical evolution occurred, the next best thing is to re-create the conditions in the lab and test predictions made by these models. In the following sections, you will learn about how biologists used the top-down and bottom-up approaches to identify reactions that support each of these models for chemical evolution.

Early Origin-of-Life Experiments

Chemical evolution was first taken seriously in 1953 when a graduate student named Stanley Miller performed a breakthrough experiment in the study of the prebiotic soup model.

Miller wanted to answer a simple question: Can complex organic compounds be synthesized from the simple molecules present in Earth's early atmosphere? In other words, is it possible to re-create the first steps in chemical evolution by simulating early-Earth conditions in the laboratory?

Miller's experimental setup (**FIGURE 2.21**) was designed to produce a microcosm of early Earth. The large glass flask represented the atmosphere and contained the gases methane (CH_4), ammonia (NH_3), and hydrogen (H_2), all of which have high potential energy. This large flask was connected to a smaller flask by glass tubing. The small flask held a tiny ocean—200 milliliters (mL) of liquid water.

To connect the mini-atmosphere with the mini-ocean, Miller boiled the water constantly. This added water vapor to the mix of gases in the large flask. As the vapor cooled and condensed, it flowed back into the smaller flask, where it boiled again. In this way, water vapor circulated continuously through the system. This was important: If the molecules in the simulated atmosphere reacted with one another, the "rain" would carry them into the mini-ocean, forming a simulated version of the prebiotic soup.

Had Miller stopped at merely boiling the molecules, little or nothing would have happened. Even at the boiling point of water (100°C), the starting molecules used in the experiment are stable and do not undergo spontaneous chemical reactions.

Something did start to happen in the apparatus, however, when Miller sent electrical discharges across the electrodes he'd inserted into the atmosphere. These miniature lightning bolts

RESEARCH

QUESTION: Can simple molecules and kinetic energy lead to chemical evolution?

HYPOTHESIS: If kinetic energy is added to a mix of simple molecules, reactions will occur that produce more complex molecules, perhaps including some with C–C bonds.

NULL HYPOTHESIS: Chemical evolution will not occur, even with an input of energy.

EXPERIMENTAL SETUP:

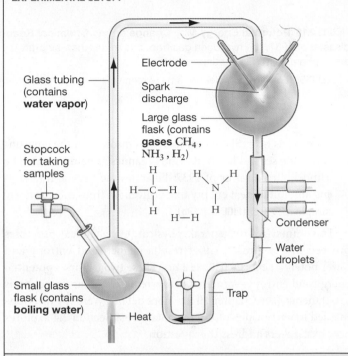

PREDICTION: Complex organic compounds will be found in the liquid water.

PREDICTION OF NULL HYPOTHESIS: Only the starting molecules will be found in the liquid water.

RESULTS

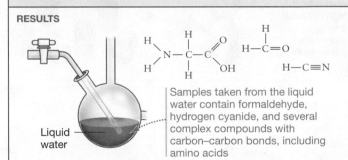

Samples taken from the liquid water contain formaldehyde, hydrogen cyanide, and several complex compounds with carbon–carbon bonds, including amino acids

CONCLUSION: Chemical evolution occurs readily if simple molecules with high free energy are exposed to a source of kinetic energy.

FIGURE 2.21 Miller's Spark-Discharge Experiment. The arrows in the "Experimental setup" diagram indicate the flow of water vapor or liquid. The condenser is a jacket with cold water flowing through it.

SOURCE: Miller, S. L. 1953. A production of amino acids under possible primitive Earth conditions. *Science* 117: 528–529.

✔ **QUESTION** Which parts of the apparatus mimic the ocean, atmosphere, rain, and lightning?

added a crucial element to the reaction mix—pulses of intense electrical energy. After a day of continuous boiling and sparking, the solution in the boiling flask began to turn pink. After a week, it was deep red and cloudy.

When Miller analyzed samples from the mini-ocean, he found large quantities of hydrogen cyanide and formaldehyde. Even more exciting, the sparks and heating had led to the synthesis of additional, more complex organic compounds, including amino acids, which are the building blocks of proteins (see Chapter 9).

Recent Origin-of-Life Experiments

The production of more complex molecules from simple molecules in Miller's experiment supported his claim that the formation of a prebiotic soup was possible. The results came under fire, however, when other researchers pointed out that the early atmosphere was dominated by volcanic gases like CO, CO_2, and H_2, not the CH_4 and NH_3 used in Miller's experiment.

This controversy stimulated a series of follow-up experiments, which showed that the assembly of small molecules into more complex molecules can also occur under more realistic early Earth conditions.

Synthesis of Precursors Using Light Energy One such reaction that may have played a role in chemical evolution is the synthesis of formaldehyde (CH_2O) from carbon dioxide and hydrogen:

$$CO_2(g) + H_2(g) \longrightarrow \underset{\text{formaldehyde}}{CH_2O(g)} + H_2O(g)$$

This reaction has not been observed in cells—like Miller's experiment, it represents the bottom-up approach. But researchers have shown that when molecules of formaldehyde are heated, they react with one another to produce larger organic compounds, including energy-rich molecules like sugars (see Appendix E). Note, however, that this reaction does not occur spontaneously—a large input of energy is required.

To explore the possibility of early formaldehyde synthesis, a research group constructed a computer model of the early atmosphere of Earth. The model consisted of a list of all possible chemical reactions that can occur among the molecules now thought to have dominated the early atmosphere: CO_2, H_2O, N_2, CO, and H_2. In this model, they included reactions that occur when these molecules are struck by sunlight. This was crucial because sunlight represents a source of energy.

The sunlight that strikes Earth is made up of packets of light energy called **photons.** Today, Earth is protected by a blanket of ozone (O_3) in the upper atmosphere that absorbs most of the higher-energy photons in sunlight. But since Earth's early atmosphere was filled with volcanic gases released as the molten planet cooled, and ozone is not among these gases, it is extremely unlikely that appreciable quantities of ozone existed. Based on this logic, researchers infer that when chemical evolution was occurring, large quantities of high-energy photons bombarded the planet.

To understand why this energy source was so important, recall that the atoms in hydrogen and carbon dioxide molecules have full valence shells through covalent bonding. This arrangement makes these molecules largely unreactive. However, energy from photons can break up molecules by knocking apart shared electrons. The fragments that result, called **free radicals,** have unpaired electrons in their outermost shells and are extremely reactive (**FIGURE 2.22**). To mimic the conditions on early Earth more accurately, the computer model included several reactions that produce highly reactive free radicals.

The result? The researchers calculated that, under conditions accepted as reasonable approximations of early Earth by most scientists, appreciable quantities of formaldehyde would have been produced. The energy in sunlight was converted to chemical energy in the form of new bonds in formaldehyde.

The complete reaction that results in the formation of formaldehyde is written as

$$CO_2(g) + 2\,H_2(g) + \text{sunlight} \longrightarrow CH_2O(g) + H_2O(g)$$

Notice that the reaction is balanced in terms of the atoms *and* the energy involved. The sunlight on the reactant side balances the higher energy required for the formation of formaldehyde and water. This result makes sense if you take a moment to think about it. Energy is the capacity to do work, and building larger, more complex molecules requires work to be done.

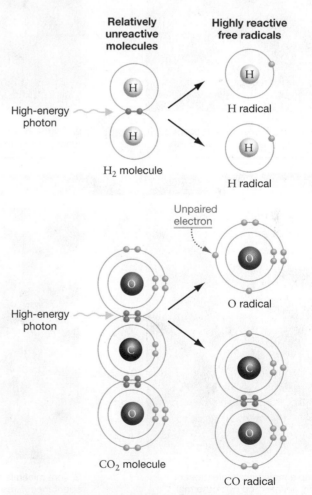

FIGURE 2.22 Free Radicals Are Extremely Reactive. When high-energy photons or pulses of intense electrical energy, such as lightning, strike molecules of hydrogen or carbon dioxide, free radicals can be created. Formation of free radicals is thought to be responsible for some key reactions in chemical evolution.

Using a similar model, other researchers have shown that hydrogen cyanide (HCN)—another important precursor of molecules required for life—could also have been produced in the early atmosphere. According to this research, large quantities of potential precursors for chemical evolution would have formed in the atmosphere and rained out into the early oceans. As a result, organic compounds with relatively high potential energy could have accumulated, and the groundwork would have been in place for the prebiotic soup model of chemical evolution to take off (FIGURE 2.23a).

Concentration and Catalysis in Hydrothermal Vents A major stumbling block in the prebiotic soup model is that precursor molecules would have become diluted when they entered the early oceans. Without some means of localized concentration, the formaldehyde and hydrogen cyanide mentioned in the previous section would have been unlikely to meet and react to form larger, more complex molecules. The surface metabolism model offers one possible solution to this dilution effect.

In the surface metabolism model, reactants are recruited to a defined space—a layer of reactive minerals deposited on the

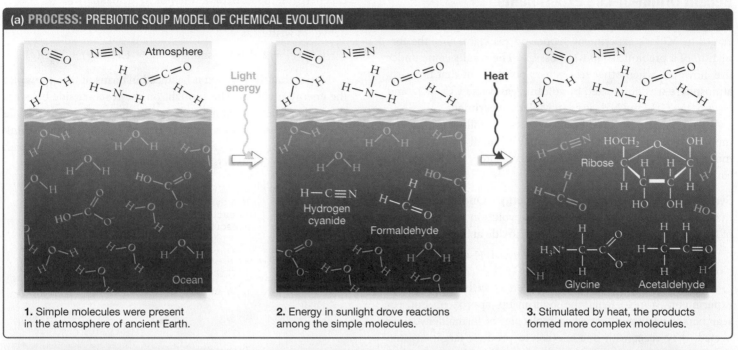

(a) PROCESS: PREBIOTIC SOUP MODEL OF CHEMICAL EVOLUTION

1. Simple molecules were present in the atmosphere of ancient Earth.

2. Energy in sunlight drove reactions among the simple molecules.

3. Stimulated by heat, the products formed more complex molecules.

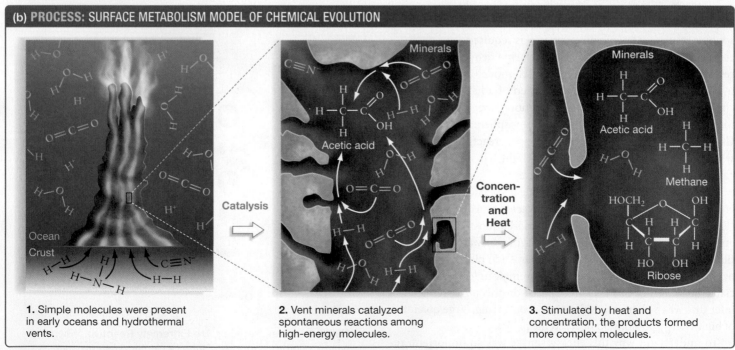

(b) PROCESS: SURFACE METABOLISM MODEL OF CHEMICAL EVOLUTION

1. Simple molecules were present in early oceans and hydrothermal vents.

2. Vent minerals catalyzed spontaneous reactions among high-energy molecules.

3. Stimulated by heat and concentration, the products formed more complex molecules.

FIGURE 2.23 The Start of Chemical Evolution—Two Models. The prebiotic soup and surface metabolism models illustrate how simple molecules containing C, H, O, and N reacted to form organic compounds that served as building blocks for more complex molecules.

walls of deep-sea vent chimneys. Dissolved gases would be attracted by the minerals and concentrated on vent-wall surfaces (**FIGURE 2.23b**).

Here's a key point of this model: Not only would vent-wall minerals bring reactants together, they would also be critical to the rate at which reaction products formed. Even if a potential reaction were spontaneous, it would probably not occur at a level useful for chemical evolution without the support of a **catalyst.** A catalyst provides the appropriate chemical environment for reactants to interact with one another effectively. (You will learn in Chapter 10 that a catalyst only influences the rate of a reaction—it does not provide energy or alter spontaneity.)

A reaction that provides an example of the role catalysts may have played during chemical evolution is the synthesis of acetic acid (CH_3COOH) from carbon dioxide and hydrogen:

$$2 CO_2(aq) + 4 H_2(aq) \longrightarrow CH_3COOH(aq) + 2 H_2O(l)$$
$$\text{acetic acid}$$

The reaction is driven by chemical energy stored in one of the reactants—H_2—and is spontaneous despite the apparent decrease in entropy. It is employed by certain groups of Bacteria and Archaea today as a step toward building even more complex organic molecules.

This reaction has grabbed wide attention among the chemical evolution research community, for two reasons in particular: (**1**) Acetic acid can be formed under conditions that simulate a hydrothermal vent environment (bottom-up approach). (**2**) It is a key intermediate in an ancient pathway that produces acetyl CoA, which is a molecule used by cells throughout the tree of life (top-down approach). (The role of acetyl CoA in modern cells is discussed in Chapter 13.)

Did vent minerals serve as catalysts in the synthesis of acetic acid in early Earth? Evidence from modern cells suggests the answer may be yes. The catalysts that perform the same reaction in modern cells contain minerals similar to those found in hydrothermal vents. These minerals may represent a form of molecular luggage taken from the deep-sea hydrothermal vents as LUCA evolved its independence.

Research is currently under way to establish laboratory systems to more closely mimic surface metabolism conditions in hydrothermal vents. Preliminary results show that in addition to the production of acetic acid, a variety of larger carbon-based molecules can be formed under early Earth conditions. Among these are precursors for the synthesis of nucleotides, the building blocks for the molecules of inheritance used by every living organism on Earth (see Chapter 5).

2.5 The Importance of Organic Molecules

Life has been called a carbon-based phenomenon, and with good reason. Except for water, almost all of the molecules found in organisms contain this atom. Molecules that contain carbon bonded to other elements, such as hydrogen, are called **organic** molecules. (Other types of molecules are referred to as *inorganic* compounds.)

Carbon has great importance in biology because it is the most versatile atom on Earth. Because of its four valence electrons, it will form four covalent bonds. This results in an almost limitless array of molecular shapes, made possible by different combinations of single and double bonds.

Linking Carbon Atoms Together

You have already examined the tetrahedral structure of methane and the linear shape of carbon dioxide. When molecules contain more than one carbon atom, these atoms can be bonded to one another in long chains, as in the component of gasoline called octane (C_8H_{18}; **FIGURE 2.24a**), or in a ring, as in the sugar glucose ($C_6H_{12}O_6$; **FIGURE 2.24b**). Carbon atoms provide the structural framework for virtually all the important compounds associated with life, with the exception of water.

The formation of carbon–carbon bonds was an important event in chemical evolution: It represented a crucial step toward the production of the types of molecules found in living organisms.

(a) Carbons linked in a chain

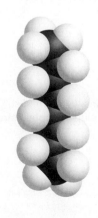

C_8H_{18} Octane

(b) Carbons linked in a ring

6 CH_2OH

$C_6H_{12}O_6$ Glucose

FIGURE 2.24 The Shapes of Carbon-Containing Molecules. (a) Octane is a hydrocarbon chain, and one of the primary ingredients in gasoline. **(b)** Glucose is a sugar that can form a ring-like structure.

Functional Groups

In general, the carbon atoms in an organic molecule furnish a skeleton that gives the molecule its overall shape. But the chemical behavior of the compound—meaning the types of reactions that it participates in—is dictated by groups of H, N, O, P, or S atoms that are bonded to one of the carbon atoms in a specific way.

The critically important H-, N-, O-, P-, and S-containing groups found in organic compounds are called **functional groups**. The composition and properties of six prominent functional groups that are commonly found in organic molecules and recognized by organic chemists are summarized in **TABLE 2.3**. To understand the role that organic compounds play in organisms, it is important to analyze how these functional groups behave.

SUMMARY TABLE 2.3 **Six Functional Groups Commonly Attached to Carbon Atoms**

Functional Group	Formula*	Family of Molecules	Properties of Functional Group	Example
Amino	$\begin{array}{c}H\\ {>}N{-}R\\ H\end{array}$	Amines	Acts as a base—tends to attract a proton to form: $H-{}^+N(H)(H)-R$	Glycine (an amino acid)
Carboxyl	$R-C(=O)OH$	Carboxylic acids	Acts as an acid—tends to lose a proton in solution to form: $R-C(=O)O^-$	Acetic acid
Carbonyl	$R-C(=O)H$	Aldehydes	Aldehydes, especially, react with certain compounds to produce larger molecules to form:	Acetaldehyde
	$R-C(=O)-R$	Ketones	$R1-C(=O)-H$ + $\begin{array}{c}H\\ R2\end{array}$ $\longrightarrow$ $R1-C(OH)(H)-R2$	Acetone
Hydroxyl	$R-OH$	Alcohols	Highly polar, so makes compounds more soluble through hydrogen bonding with water; may also act as a weak acid and drop a proton	Ethanol
Phosphate	$R-O-P(=O)(O^-)-O^-$	Organic phosphates	Molecules with more than one phosphate linked together store large amounts of chemical energy	3–Phosphoglyceric acid
Sulfhydryl	$R-SH$	Thiols	When present in proteins, can form disulfide (S–S) bonds that contribute to protein structure	Cysteine

*In these structural formulas, "R" stands for the rest of the molecule.

✔**EXERCISE** Based on the electronegativities of the atoms involved, predict whether each functional group is polar or nonpolar.

- *Amino and carboxyl functional groups* tend to attract or drop a proton, respectively, when in solution. Amino groups function as bases; carboxyl groups act as acids. During chemical evolution and in organisms today, the most important types of amino- and carboxyl-containing molecules are the amino acids (which Chapter 9 analyzes in detail). Amino acids contain both an amino group and a carboxyl group. (It's common for organic compounds to contain more than one functional group.) Amino acids can be linked together by covalent bonds that form between amino and carboxyl groups. In addition, both of these functional groups participate in hydrogen bonding.

- *Carbonyl groups* are found on aldehyde and ketone molecules such as formaldehyde, acetaldehyde, and acetone. This functional group is the site of reactions that link these molecules into larger, more complex organic compounds.

- *Hydroxyl groups* are important because they act as weak acids. In many cases, the protons involved in acid–base reactions that occur in cells come from hydroxyl groups on organic compounds. Because hydroxyl groups are polar, molecules containing hydroxyl groups will form hydrogen bonds and tend to be soluble in water.

- *Phosphate groups* carry two negative charges. When phosphate groups are transferred from one organic compound to another, the change in charge often dramatically affects the structure of the recipient molecule. In addition, phosphates that are bonded together store chemical energy that can be used in chemical reactions (some of these are discussed in Chapter 9).

- *Sulfhydryl groups* consist of a sulfur atom bonded to a hydrogen atom. They are important because sulfhydryl groups can link to one another via disulfide (S—S) bonds.

To summarize, functional groups make things happen. The number and types of functional groups attached to a framework of carbon atoms imply a great deal about how that molecule is going to behave.

When you encounter an organic compound that is new to you, it's important to do the following three things:

1. Examine the overall size and shape provided by the carbon framework.

2. Identify the types of covalent bonds present based on the electronegativities of the atoms. Use this information to estimate the polarity of the molecule and the amount of potential energy stored in its chemical bonds.

3. Locate any functional groups and note the properties these groups give to the molecule.

Understanding these three features will help you to predict the molecule's role in the chemistry of life.

Once carbon-containing molecules with functional groups had appeared early in Earth's history, what happened next? For chemical evolution to continue, small carbon-based molecules had to form still larger, more complex molecules like those found in living cells. How were the molecules of life—proteins, nucleic acids, carbohydrates, and lipids—formed, and how do they function in organisms today? The rest of this unit explores the next steps in chemical evolution, culminating in the formation of the first living cell.

If you understand . . .

2.1 Atoms, Ions, and Molecules: The Building Blocks of Chemical Evolution

- When atoms participate in chemical bonds to form molecules, the shared electrons give the atoms full valence shells and thus contribute to the atoms' stability.

- The electrons in a chemical bond may be shared equally or unequally, depending on the relative electronegativities of the two atoms involved.

- Nonpolar covalent bonds result from equal sharing; polar covalent bonds are due to unequal sharing. Ionic bonds form when an electron is completely transferred from one atom to another.

✓ **You should be able to compare and contrast the types of bonds found in methane (CH_4), ammonia (NH_3), and sodium chloride (NaCl).**

2.2 Properties of Water and the Early Oceans

- The chemical reactions required for life take place in water.

- Water is polar—meaning that it has partial positive and negative charges—because it is bent and has two polar covalent bonds.

- Polar molecules and charged substances, including ions, interact with water and stay in solution via hydrogen bonding and electrostatic attraction.

- Water's ability to participate in hydrogen bonding also gives it an extraordinarily high capacity to absorb heat and cohere to other water molecules.

- Water spontaneously dissociates into hydrogen ions (or protons, H^+) and hydroxide ions (OH^-). The concentration of protons in a solution determines the pH, which can be altered by acids and bases or stabilized by buffers.

✓ **You should be able to predict what part of water molecules would interact with amino, carboxyl, and hydroxyl functional groups in solution and the types of bonds that would be involved.**

2.3 Chemical Reactions, Energy, and Chemical Evolution

- The first step in chemical evolution was the formation of small organic compounds from molecules such as molecular hydrogen (H_2) and carbon dioxide (CO_2).

- Chemical reactions typically involve bonds being broken, atoms being rearranged, and new bonds being formed. This process involves energy, either from the reactants or external sources (e.g., heat).

- Energy comes in different forms. Although energy cannot be created or destroyed, one form of energy can be transformed into another.

✔ You should be able to explain how the energy in electricity can drive a reaction that is nonspontaneous.

2.4 Investigating Chemical Evolution: Approaches and Model Systems

- Experiments suggest that early in Earth's history, external sources of energy, such as sunlight or lightning, could have driven chemical reactions between simple molecules to form molecules with higher potential energy. In this way, energy in the form of radiation or electricity was transformed into chemical energy.

- The prebiotic soup and surface metabolism models for chemical evolution have been supported by the synthesis of organic molecules in laboratory simulations of the early Earth environment.

✔ You should be able to explain how the surface metabolism model is supported by both the top-down and bottom-up approaches used to investigate reactions involved in chemical evolution.

2.5 The Importance of Organic Molecules

- Carbon is the foundation of organic molecules based on its valence, which allows for the construction of molecules with complex shapes.

- Organic molecules are critical to life because they possess versatility of chemical behavior due to the presence of functional groups.

✔ You should be able to predict how adding hydroxyl groups to the octane molecule in Figure 2.24 would affect the properties of the molecule.

MB MasteringBiology

1. MasteringBiology Assignments

Tutorials and Activities Acids, Bases, and pH; Anatomy of Atoms; Atomic Number and Mass Number; BioSkill: Using Logarithms; Carbon Bonding and Functional Groups; Cohesion of Water; Covalent Bonds; Dissociation of Water Molecules; Diversity of Carbon-Based Molecules; Electron Arrangement; Energy Transformations; Functional Groups; Hydrogen Bonding and Water; Hydrogen Bonds; Ionic Bonds; Nonpolar and Polar Molecules; pH Scale; Polarity of Water; Properties of Water; Structure of the Atomic Nucleus

Questions Reading Quizzes, Blue-Thread Questions, Test Bank

2. eText Read your book online, search, take notes, highlight text, and more.

3. The Study Area Practice Test, Cumulative Test, BioFlix® 3-D Animations, Videos, Activities, Audio Glossary, Word Study Tools, Art

You should be able to . . .

✔ TEST YOUR KNOWLEDGE
Answers are available in Appendix A

1. Which of the following occurs when a covalent bond forms?
   a. The potential energy of electrons drops.
   b. Electrons in valence shells are shared between nuclei.
   c. Ions of opposite charge interact.
   d. Polar molecules interact.

2. If a reaction is exothermic, then which of the following statements is true?
   a. The products have lower potential energy than the reactants.
   b. Energy must be added for the reaction to proceed.
   c. The products have lower entropy (are more ordered) than the reactants.
   d. It occurs extremely quickly.

3. Which of the following is most likely to have been the energy source responsible for the formation of acetic acid in deep-sea hydrothermal vents?
   a. heat released from the vents
   b. solar radiation that passed through the ocean water
   c. chemical energy present in the reactants
   d. the increase in entropy in the products

4. What is thermal energy?
   a. a form of potential energy
   b. the temperature increase that occurs when any form of energy is added to a system
   c. mechanical energy
   d. the kinetic energy of molecular motion, measured as heat

5. What factors determine whether a chemical reaction is spontaneous or not?

6. What are the two models that have been proposed to explain the process component of chemical evolution?

7. Which of the following molecules would you predict to have the largest number of polar covalent bonds based on their molecular formulas?
   a. C_2H_6O (ethanol)
   b. C_2H_6 (ethane)
   c. $C_2H_4O_2$ (acetic acid)
   d. C_3H_8O (propanol)

8. Locate fluorine (F) on the partial periodic table provided in Figure 2.2. Predict its relative electronegativity compared to hydrogen, sodium, and oxygen. State the number and type of bond(s) you expect it would form if it reacted with sodium.

9. Oxygen is extremely electronegative, meaning that its nucleus pulls electrons shared in covalent bonds very strongly. Explain the changes in electron position that are illustrated in Figure 2.19 based on oxygen's electronegativity.

10. Draw the electron-sharing continuum and place molecular oxygen (O_2), magnesium chloride ($MgCl_2$), and carbon dioxide (CO_2) on it.

11. Consider the reaction between carbon dioxide and water, which forms carbonic acid:

$$CO_2(g) + H_2O(l) \rightleftharpoons CH_2O_3(aq)$$

In aqueous solution, carbonic acid immediately dissociates to form a proton and bicarbonate ion, as follows:

$$CH_2O_3(aq) \rightleftharpoons H^+(aq)\ 1\ CHO_3^-(aq)$$

If an underwater volcano bubbled additional CO_2 into the ocean, would this sequence of reactions be driven to the left or the right? How would this affect the pH of the ocean?

12. What is the relationship between the carbon framework in an organic molecule (the "R" in Table 2.3) and its functional groups?

13. When H_2 and CO_2 react, acetic acid can be formed spontaneously while the production of formaldehyde requires an input of energy. Which of the following conclusions may be drawn from this observation?
    a. More heat is released when formaldehyde is produced compared to the production of acetic acid.
    b. Compared to the reactants from which it is formed, formaldehyde has more potential energy than does acetic acid.
    c. Entropy decreases when acetic acid is produced and increases when formaldehyde is produced.
    d. The mineral catalyst involved in acetic acid production provides energy to make the reaction spontaneous.

14. When chemistry texts introduce the concept of electron shells, they emphasize that shells represent distinct potential energy levels. In introducing electron shells, this chapter also emphasizes that they represent distinct distances from the positive charges in the nucleus. Are these two points of view in conflict? Why or why not?

15. Draw a concept map relating water's structure to its properties. (For an introduction to concept mapping, see **BioSkills 15** in Appendix B.) Your concept map should include the following terms or phrases: polar covalent bonds, polarity (on the water molecule), hydrogen bonding, high heat of vaporization, high specific heat, less dense as a solid, effective solvent, unequal sharing of electrons, high energy input required to break bonds, high electronegativity of oxygen.

16. From what you have learned about water, why do coastal regions tend to have climates with lower annual variation in temperature than do inland areas at the same latitude?

An Introduction to Carbohydrates

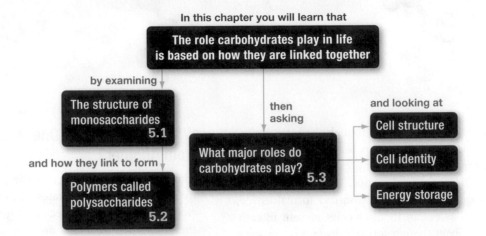

In this chapter you will learn that

The role carbohydrates play in life is based on how they are linked together

by examining →

The structure of monosaccharides 5.1

and how they link to form →

Polymers called polysaccharides 5.2

then asking

What major roles do carbohydrates play? 5.3

and looking at

Cell structure

Cell identity

Energy storage

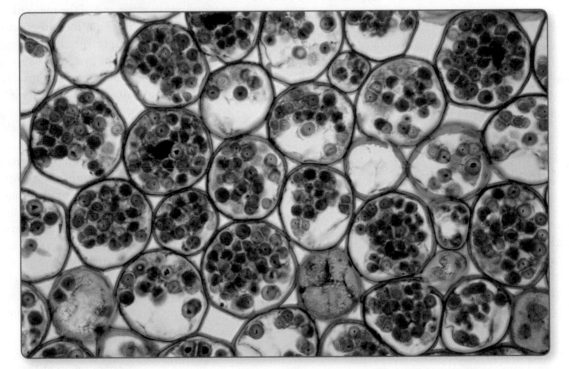

A cross section through a buttercup root. Cellulose-rich cell walls are stained green; starch-filled structures are stained purple. Cellulose is a structural carbohydrate; starch is an energy-storage carbohydrate.

This unit highlights the four types of macromolecules that were key to the evolution of the cell: proteins, nucleic acids, carbohydrates, and lipids. Understanding the structure and function of macromolecules is a basic requirement for exploring how life began and how organisms work. Recall that proteins and nucleic acids could satisfy only three of the five fundamental characteristics of life: information, replication, and evolution (Chapter 5). Carbohydrates, the subject of this chapter, play an important role in a fourth characteristic—energy.

The term **carbohydrate,** or **sugar,** encompasses the monomers called **monosaccharides** (literally, "one-sugar"), small polymers called **oligosaccharides** ("few-sugars"), and the large polymers called **polysaccharides** ("many-sugars"). The name carbohydrate is logical because the molecular formula of many of these molecules is $(CH_2O)_n$, where the n refers to the number of "carbohydrate" groups. The value of n can vary from 3, for the smallest sugar, to well over a thousand for some of the large polymers.

This chapter is part of the Big Picture. See how on pages 68–69.

✔ When you see this checkmark, stop and test yourself. Answers are available in Appendix A.

An aldose
Carbonyl group at
end of carbon chain

A ketose
Carbonyl group in
middle of carbon chain

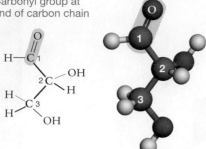

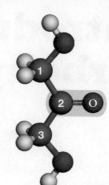

The name can also be misleading, though, because carbohydrates do not consist of carbon atoms bonded to water molecules. Instead, they are molecules with a carbonyl ($C=O$) and several hydroxyl ($-OH$) functional groups, along with several to many carbon–hydrogen ($C-H$) bonds. Consider formaldehyde, which was introduced as one of the molecules present in early Earth (Appendix D). Even though formaldehyde has the same molecular formula as the one given above (CH_2O), it is not a carbohydrate since it does not contain a hydroxyl group.

Let's begin with monosaccharides, put them together into polysaccharides, and then explore how carbohydrates figured in the origin of life and what they do in cells today. As you study this material, be sure to ask yourself the central question of biological chemistry: How does this molecule's structure relate to its properties and function?

5.1 Sugars as Monomers

Sugars are fundamental to life. They provide chemical energy in cells and furnish some of the molecular building blocks required for the synthesis of larger, more complex compounds. Monosaccharides were important during chemical evolution, early in Earth's history. For example, as you've seen, the sugar called ribose is required for the formation of the nucleotides that make up nucleic acids (Chapter 5).

What Distinguishes One Monosaccharide from Another?

Monosaccharides, or simple sugars, are the monomers of carbohydrates. **FIGURE 5.1** illustrates two of the smallest monosaccharides. Although their molecular formulas are identical ($C_3H_6O_3$), their molecular structures are different. The carbonyl group that serves as one of monosaccharides' distinguishing features can be found either at the end of the molecule, forming an aldehyde sugar (an aldose), or within the carbon chain, forming a ketone sugar (a ketose). The presence of a carbonyl group along with multiple hydroxyl groups provides sugars with an array of reactive and hydrophilic functional groups. Based on this observation, it's not surprising that sugars are able to participate in a large number of chemical reactions.

The number of carbon atoms present also varies in monosaccharides. By convention, the carbons in a monosaccharide are numbered consecutively, starting with the end nearest the carbonyl group. Figure 5.1 features three-carbon sugars, or **trioses**. Ribose, which acts as a building block for nucleotides, has five carbons and is called a **pentose;** the glucose that is coursing through your bloodstream right now is a six-carbon sugar, or a **hexose.**

Besides varying in the location of the carbonyl group and the total number of carbon atoms present, monosaccharides can vary in the spatial arrangement of their atoms. There is, for example, a wide array of pentoses and hexoses. Each is distinguished by the configuration of its hydroxyl functional groups. **FIGURE 5.2**

Glucose

Galactose

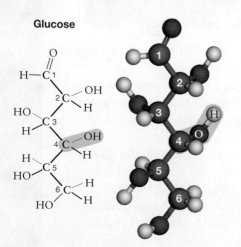

FIGURE 5.2 Sugars May Vary in the Configuration of Their Hydroxyl Groups. The two six-carbon sugars shown here vary only in the spatial orientation of their hydroxyl groups on carbon number 4.

✔**EXERCISE** Mannose is a six-carbon sugar that is identical to glucose, except that the hydroxyl (–OH) group on carbon number 2 is switched in orientation. Circle carbon number 2 in glucose and galactose; then draw the structural formula of mannose.

illustrates glucose and galactose, which are six-carbon sugars. Notice that the two molecules have the same molecular formula ($C_6H_{12}O_6$) but not the same structure. Both are aldose sugars with six carbons, but they differ in the spatial arrangement of the hydroxyl group at the fourth carbon (highlighted in Figure 5.2).

This is a key point: Because the structures of glucose and galactose differ, their functions differ. In cells, glucose is used as a source of carbons for the construction of other molecules and chemical energy that sustains life. But for galactose to be used in these roles, it first has to be converted to glucose via an enzyme-catalyzed reaction. This example underscores a general theme: Even seemingly simple changes in structure—like the location of a single hydroxyl group—can have enormous consequences for function. This is because molecules interact in precise ways, based on their shape.

It's rare for sugars consisting of five or more carbons to exist in the form of the linear chains illustrated in Figure 5.2, however. In aqueous solution they tend to form ring structures. The bond responsible for ring formation occurs only between the carbon containing the carbonyl group and one of the carbons with a hydroxyl group. Glucose serves as the example in **FIGURE 5.3**. When the cyclic structure forms in glucose, the C-1 carbon (the carbon numbered 1 in the linear chain) forms a bond with the oxygen atom of the C-5 hydroxyl and transfers its hydrogen to the C-1 carbonyl, turning it into a hydroxyl group.

Transfer of hydrogen between the C-5 and C-1 functional groups preserves the number of atoms and hydroxyls found in the ring and linear forms. The newly formed C-1 hydroxyl group can be oriented in two distinct ways: above or below the plane of the ring. The different configurations produce the molecules α-glucose and β-glucose.

To summarize, many distinct monosaccharides exist because so many aspects of their structure are variable: aldose or ketose placement of the carbonyl group, variation in carbon number, different arrangements of hydroxyl groups in space, and alternative ring forms. Each monosaccharide has a unique structure and function.

Monosaccharides and Chemical Evolution

Laboratory simulations, like those you read about in Appendix D, have shown that most monosaccharides are readily synthesized under conditions that mimic the conditions of early Earth. For example, when formaldehyde (CH_2O) molecules are heated in solution, they react with one another to form almost all the pentoses and hexoses.

In addition, researchers have discovered the three-carbon ketose illustrated in Figure 5.1, along with a wide array of compounds closely related to sugars, on a meteorite that struck Murchison, Australia, in 1969. Based on these observations, investigators suspect that sugars are synthesized on dust particles and other debris in interstellar space and could have rained down onto Earth as the planet was forming, as well as being synthesized in the hot water near ancient undersea volcanoes.

More recent evidence suggests that synthesis of sugars could have been catalyzed by minerals found in the walls of deep-sea hydrothermal vents. Most researchers interested in chemical evolution maintain that one or more of the above mechanisms led to the accumulation of monosaccharides in the early oceans.

Modern cells display a wide range of carbohydrates beyond monosaccharides. How do these monomers join together to form polymers? Is the process similar to how amino acids link together to form proteins and nucleotides join to form nucleic acids? Let's explore how the array of functional groups in monosaccharides influences the polymerization of carbohydrates.

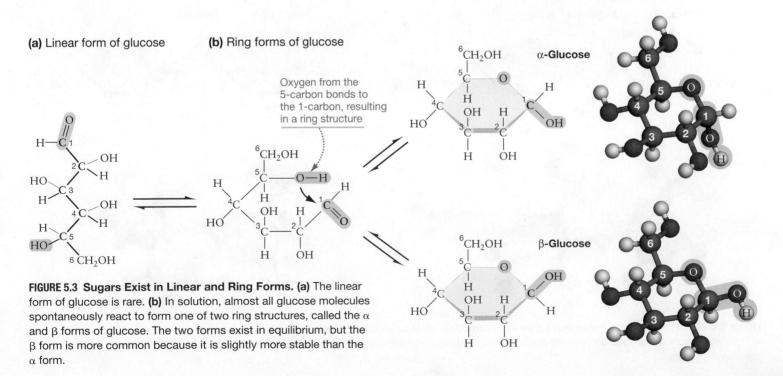

(a) Linear form of glucose   **(b)** Ring forms of glucose

FIGURE 5.3 Sugars Exist in Linear and Ring Forms. (a) The linear form of glucose is rare. **(b)** In solution, almost all glucose molecules spontaneously react to form one of two ring structures, called the α and β forms of glucose. The two forms exist in equilibrium, but the β form is more common because it is slightly more stable than the α form.

If you understand that . . .

- Simple sugars differ from each other in three respects:
  1. the location of their carbonyl group,
  2. the number of carbon atoms present, and
  3. the spatial arrangement of their atoms— particularly the relative positions of hydroxyl (−OH) groups.

✔ **You should be able to . . .**

Draw the structural formula of a three-carbon monosaccharide ($C_3H_6O_3$) in linear form and then draw three other sugars that illustrate the three differences listed above.

Answers are available in Appendix A.

5.2 The Structure of Polysaccharides

Simple sugars can be covalently linked into chains of varying lengths, also known as complex carbohydrates. These chains range in size from small oligomers, or oligosaccharides, to the large polymers called polysaccharides. When only two sugars are linked together, they are known as **disaccharides.**

Similar to proteins and nucleic acids, the structure and function of larger carbohydrates depends on the types of monomers involved and how they are linked together. For example, maltose, also known as malt sugar, and lactose, an important sugar in milk, are two disaccharides that differ by just one monosaccharide. Maltose consists of two identical glucose molecules (**FIGURE 5.4a**), while lactose is made up of glucose and galactose (**FIGURE 5.4b**).

Monosaccharides polymerize when a condensation reaction occurs between two hydroxyl groups, resulting in a covalent interaction called a **glycosidic linkage.** The inverse reaction, hydrolysis, cleaves these linkages. (To review condensation and hydrolysis reactions, see Chapter 9.)

(a) Formation of α-glycosidic linkage

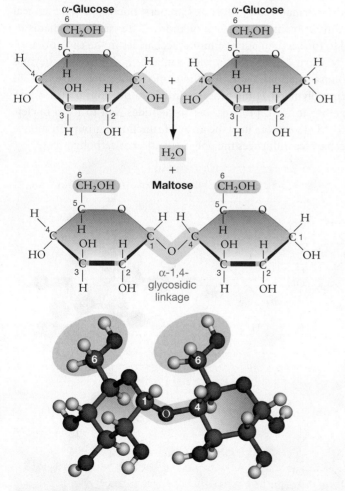

(b) Formation of β-glycosidic linkage

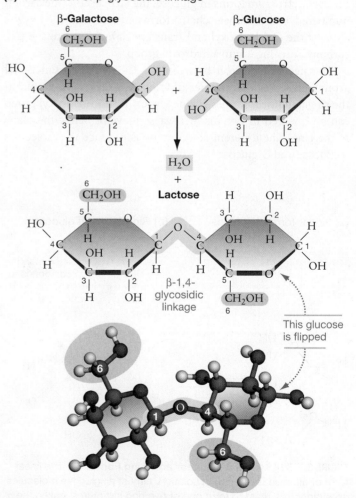

FIGURE 5.4 Monosaccharides Polymerize through Formation of Glycosidic Linkages. A glycosidic linkage occurs when hydroxyl groups on two monosaccharides undergo a condensation reaction. Maltose and lactose are disaccharides.

In that they hold monomers together, glycosidic linkages are analogous to the peptide bonds and phosphodiester linkages in proteins and nucleic acids. There is an important difference, however. Peptide bonds and phosphodiester linkages form between the same locations in their monomers, giving proteins and nucleic acids a standard backbone structure, but this is not the case for polysaccharides. Because glycosidic linkages form between hydroxyl groups, and because every monosaccharide contains at least two hydroxyls, the location and geometry of glycosidic linkages can vary widely among polysaccharides.

Maltose and lactose illustrate two of the most common glycosidic linkages, called the α-1,4-glycosidic linkage and the β-1,4-glycosidic linkage. The numbers refer to the carbons on either side of the linkage, indicating that both linkages are between the C-1 and C-4 carbons. Their geometry, however, is different: α and β refer to the contrasting orientations of the C-1 hydroxyls—on opposite sides of the plane of the glucose rings (i.e., "above" versus "below" the plane).

As Section 5.3 explains, the orientation of this hydroxyl in glycosidic linkages is particularly important in the structure, function, and durability of the molecules. In essence, the difference between polysaccharides used for storage and structural polysaccharides is a simple twist of a link.

To drive this point home, let's consider the structures of the most common polysaccharides found in organisms today: starch, glycogen, cellulose, and chitin, along with a modified polysaccharide called peptidoglycan. Each of these macromolecules is joined by particular α-1,4- or β-1,4-glycosidic linkages and can consist of a few hundred to many thousands of monomers.

Starch: A Storage Polysaccharide in Plants

In plant cells, some monosaccharides are stored for later use in the form of starch. **Starch** consists entirely of α-glucose monomers joined by glycosidic linkages. As the top panel in **TABLE 5.1** shows, the angle of the linkages between C-1 and C-4 carbons causes a chain of glucose subunits to coil into a helix.

Starch is actually a mixture of two such polysaccharides, however. One is an unbranched molecule called amylose, which contains only α-1,4-glycosidic linkages. The other is a branched molecule called amylopectin. The branching in amylopectin occurs when glycosidic linkages form between the C-1 carbon of a glucose monomer on one strand and the C-6 carbon of a glucose monomer on another strand. In amylopectin, branches occur at about one out of every 30 monomers.

Glycogen: A Highly Branched Storage Polysaccharide in Animals

Glycogen performs the same storage role in animals that starch performs in plants. In humans, for example, glycogen is stored in the liver and in muscles. When you start exercising, enzymes begin breaking glycogen into glucose monomers, which are then processed in muscle cells to supply energy. Glycogen is a polymer of α-glucose and is nearly identical to the branched form of starch. However, instead of an α-1,6-glycosidic linkage occurring

in about 1 out of every 30 monomers, a branch occurs in about 1 out of every 10 glucose subunits (see Table 5.1).

Cellulose: A Structural Polysaccharide in Plants

All cells are enclosed by a membrane (Chapter 1). In most organisms living today, the cell is also surrounded by a layer of material called a wall. A **cell wall** is a protective sheet that occurs outside the membrane. In plants, bacteria, fungi, and many other groups, the cell wall is composed primarily of one or more polysaccharides.

In plants, cellulose is the major component of the cell wall. **Cellulose** is a polymer of β-glucose monomers, joined by β-1,4-glycosidic linkages. As Table 5.1 shows, the geometry of the linkage is such that each glucose monomer in the chain is flipped in relation to the adjacent monomer. The flipped orientation is important because (1) it generates a linear molecule, rather than the helix seen in starch; and (2) it permits multiple hydrogen bonds to form between adjacent, parallel strands of cellulose. As a result, cellulose forms long, parallel strands that are joined by hydrogen bonds. The linked cellulose fibers are strong and give the cell structural support.

Chitin: A Structural Polysaccharide in Fungi and Animals

Chitin is a polysaccharide that stiffens the cell walls of fungi. It is also found in a few types of protists and in many animals. It is, for example, the most important component of the external skeletons of insects and crustaceans.

Chitin is similar to cellulose, but instead of consisting of glucose monomers, the monosaccharide involved is one called *N*-acetylglucosamine (abbreviated as NAG). These NAG monomers are joined by β-1,4-glycosidic linkages (see Table 5.1). As in cellulose, the geometry of these bonds results in every other residue being flipped in orientation.

Like the glucose monomers in cellulose, the NAG subunits in chitin form hydrogen bonds between adjacent strands. The result is a tough sheet that provides stiffness and protection.

Peptidoglycan: A Structural Polysaccharide in Bacteria

Most bacteria, like all plants, have cell walls. But unlike plants, in bacteria the ability to produce cellulose is extremely rare. Instead, a polysaccharide called **peptidoglycan** gives bacterial cell walls strength and firmness.

Peptidoglycan is the most complex of the polysaccharides discussed thus far. It has a long backbone formed by two types of monosaccharides that alternate with each other and are linked by β-1,4-glycosidic linkages (see Table 5.1). In addition, a short chain of amino acids is attached to one of the two sugar types. When molecules of peptidoglycan align, peptide bonds link the amino acid chains on adjacent strands. These links serve the same purpose as the hydrogen bonds between the parallel strands of cellulose and chitin in the cell walls of other organisms.

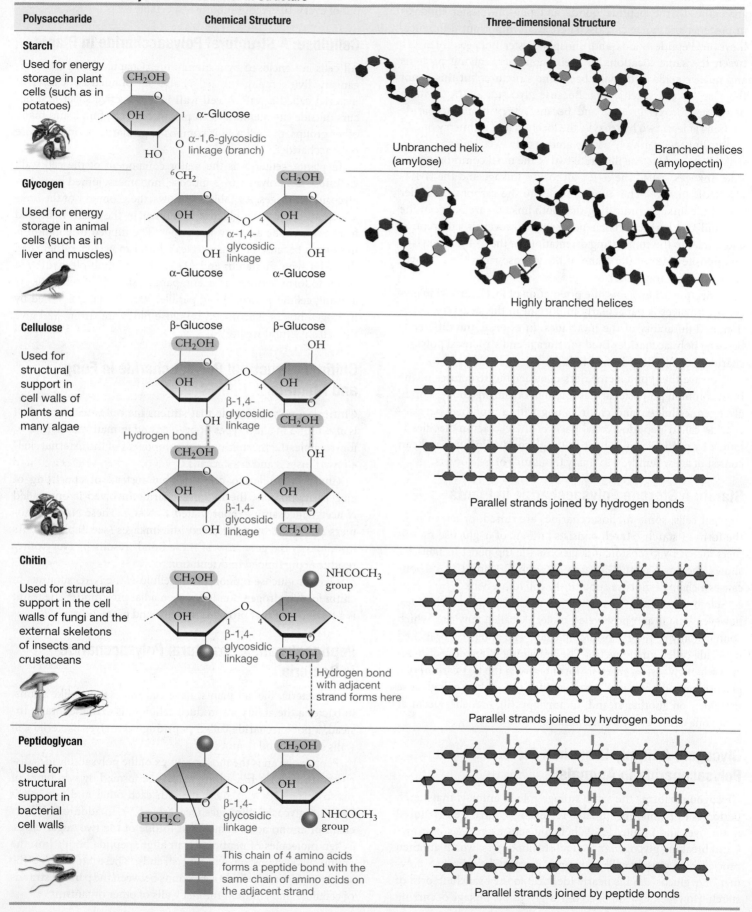

Polysaccharide	Chemical Structure	Three-dimensional Structure

Starch

Used for energy storage in plant cells (such as in potatoes)

α-Glucose

α-1,6-glycosidic linkage (branch)

Unbranched helix (amylose)

Branched helices (amylopectin)

Glycogen

Used for energy storage in animal cells (such as in liver and muscles)

α-1,4-glycosidic linkage

α-Glucose   α-Glucose

Highly branched helices

Cellulose

Used for structural support in cell walls of plants and many algae

β-Glucose   β-Glucose

β-1,4-glycosidic linkage

Hydrogen bond

β-1,4-glycosidic linkage

Parallel strands joined by hydrogen bonds

Chitin

Used for structural support in the cell walls of fungi and the external skeletons of insects and crustaceans

NHCOCH$_3$ group

β-1,4-glycosidic linkage

Hydrogen bond with adjacent strand forms here

Parallel strands joined by hydrogen bonds

Peptidoglycan

Used for structural support in bacterial cell walls

CH$_2$OH

β-1,4-glycosidic linkage

NHCOCH$_3$ group

This chain of 4 amino acids forms a peptide bond with the same chain of amino acids on the adjacent strand

Parallel strands joined by peptide bonds

Polysaccharides and Chemical Evolution

Cellulose is the most abundant organic compound on Earth today, and chitin is probably the second most abundant by weight. Virtually all organisms depend on glycogen or starch as an energy source. But despite their current importance to life, polysaccharides probably played little to no role in the origin of life. This conclusion is supported by several observations:

- *No plausible mechanism exists for the polymerization of monosaccharides under conditions that prevailed early in Earth's history.* In cells and in laboratory experiments, the glycosidic linkages illustrated in Figure 5.4 and Table 5.1 form only with the aid of protein enzymes. No enzyme-like RNAs are known to catalyze these reactions.

- *To date, no polysaccharide has been discovered that can catalyze polymerization reactions.* Even though polysaccharides contain reactive hydroxyl and carbonyl groups, they lack the structural and chemical complexity that makes proteins, and to a lesser extent RNA, effective catalysts.

- *The monomers in polysaccharides are not capable of complementary base pairing.* Like proteins, but unlike nucleic acids, polysaccharides cannot act as templates for their own replication.

Even though polysaccharides probably did not play a significant role in the earliest forms of life, they became enormously important once cellular life evolved. In the next section, let's take a detailed look at how they function in today's cells.

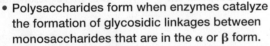

check your understanding

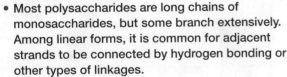

If you understand that . . .

- Polysaccharides form when enzymes catalyze the formation of glycosidic linkages between monosaccharides that are in the α or β form.
- Most polysaccharides are long chains of monosaccharides, but some branch extensively. Among linear forms, it is common for adjacent strands to be connected by hydrogen bonding or other types of linkages.

✔ You should be able to . . .

Provide four structural differences that could result in different oligosaccharides consisting of two glucose monomers and two galactose monomers.

Answers are available in Appendix A.

5.3 What Do Carbohydrates Do?

One of the basic functions that carbohydrates perform in organisms is to serve as a substrate for synthesizing more-complex molecules. For example, recall that RNA contains the five-carbon sugar ribose ($C_5H_{10}O_5$) and DNA contains the modified sugar deoxyribose ($C_5H_{10}O_4$). The nucleotides that make up these polymers consist of the ribose or deoxyribose sugar, a phosphate group, and a nitrogenous base (Chapter 4). The sugar itself acts as a subunit of each of these monomers.

In addition, sugars frequently furnish the raw "carbon skeletons" that are used as building blocks in the synthesis of important molecules. Your cells are producing amino acids right now, for example, using sugars as a starting point.

Carbohydrates have diverse functions in cells: In addition to serving as precursors to larger molecules, they **(1)** provide fibrous structural materials, **(2)** indicate cell identity, and **(3)** store chemical energy. Let's look at each function in turn.

Carbohydrates Can Provide Structural Support

Cellulose and chitin, along with the modified polysaccharide peptidoglycan, are key structural compounds. They form fibers that give cells and organisms strength and elasticity.

To appreciate why cellulose, chitin, and peptidoglycan are effective structural molecules, recall that they form long strands and that bonds can form between adjacent strands. In the cell walls of plants, for example, a collection of about 80 cellulose molecules are cross-linked by hydrogen bonding to create a tough fiber. These cellulose fibers, in turn, crisscross to form a tough sheet that is able to withstand pulling and pushing forces—what an engineer would call tension and compression.

Besides being stiff and strong, the structural carbohydrates are durable. Almost all organisms have the enzymes required to break the various α-glycosidic linkages that hold starch and glycogen molecules together, but only a few organisms have enzymes capable of hydrolyzing cellulose, chitin, and peptidoglycan. Due to the strong interactions between strands consisting of β-1,4-glycosidic linkages, water is excluded and the fibers tend to be insoluble. The absence of water within these fibers makes their hydrolysis more difficult. As a result, the structural polysaccharides are resistant to degradation and decay.

Ironically, the durability of cellulose supports digestion. The cellulose that you ingest when you eat plant cells—what biologists call dietary fiber—forms a porous mass that absorbs and retains water. This sponge-like mass adds moisture and bulk that helps fecal material move through the intestinal tract more quickly, preventing constipation and other problems.

The Role of Carbohydrates in Cell Identity

Structural polymers tend to be repetitive, with only one or two types of monosaccharides. The same is not true for all complex carbohydrates. Some types exhibit enormous structural diversity, because their component monomers—and the linkages between them—vary a lot. As a result, they are capable of displaying information to other cells through their structure. More specifically, polysaccharides act as an identification badge on the outer surface of the plasma membrane that surrounds a cell. (Chapter 3 describes plasma membranes in detail.)

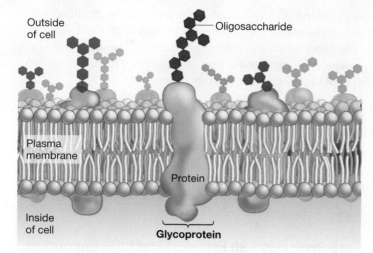

Outside of cell

Oligosaccharide

Plasma membrane

Protein

Inside of cell

Glycoprotein

FIGURE 5.5 Carbohydrates Are an Identification Badge for Cells. Glycoproteins contain sugar groups that project outside the cell from the surface of the plasma membrane enclosing the cell. These sugar groups have distinctive structures that identify the type or species of the cell.

FIGURE 5.5 shows how this information about cell identity is displayed. Molecules called glycoproteins project outward from the cell surface into the surrounding environment. A **glycoprotein** is a protein that has one or more carbohydrates covalently bonded to it—usually relatively short oligosaccharides.

Glycoproteins are key molecules in what biologists call cell–cell recognition and cell–cell signaling. Each cell in your body has glycoproteins on its surface that identify it as part of your body. Immune system cells use these glycoproteins to distinguish your body's cells from foreign cells, such as bacteria. In addition, each distinct type of cell in a multicellular organism—for example, the nerve cells and muscle cells in your body—displays a different set of glycoproteins on its surface.

The identification information displayed by glycoproteins helps cells recognize and communicate with each other.

The key point here is to recognize that the variety in the types of monosaccharides and how they can be linked together makes it possible for an enormous number of unique oligosaccharides to exist. As a result, each cell type and each species can display a unique identity.

During the 1980s, Paul Wassarman and colleagues investigated the role of glycoproteins in one of the most important cell–cell recognition events in the life of a plant or animal—the attachment of sperm to eggs during fertilization. This step guarantees specificity—sperm recognize and bind only to eggs of their own species.

In one experiment, the researchers mixed sperm with purified egg-surface glycoproteins and discovered that most of the sperm lost their ability to attach to eggs (**FIGURE 5.6**). Such loss of function is an example of what researchers call competitive inhibition. The glycoproteins had bound to—and thus blocked—the same structure on the sperm that it uses to bind to eggs. This result showed that sperm attach to eggs via egg glycoproteins.

QUESTION: What part of surface glycoproteins do sperm recognize when they attach to eggs?

HYPOTHESIS: Sperm attach to the carbohydrate component.

NULL HYPOTHESIS: Sperm attach to the protein component.

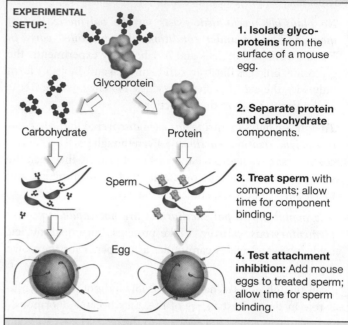

EXPERIMENTAL SETUP:

Glycoprotein

Carbohydrate

Protein

Sperm

Egg

1. **Isolate glyco-proteins** from the surface of a mouse egg.

2. **Separate protein and carbohydrate** components.

3. **Treat sperm** with components; allow time for component binding.

4. **Test attachment inhibition:** Add mouse eggs to treated sperm; allow time for sperm binding.

PREDICTION: The carbohydrate component of the glycoprotein will bind to sperm and block their attachment to eggs.

PREDICTION OF NULL HYPOTHESIS: The protein component of the glycoprotein will block sperm attachment to eggs.

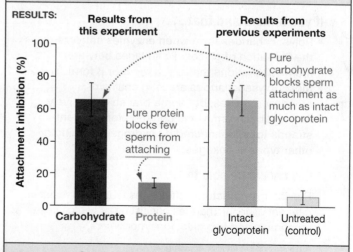

RESULTS:

Results from this experiment

Results from previous experiments

Attachment inhibition (%)

Pure protein blocks few sperm from attaching

Pure carbohydrate blocks sperm attachment as much as intact glycoprotein

Carbohydrate   Protein

Intact glycoprotein   Untreated (control)

CONCLUSION: Sperm recognize and bind to the carbohydrates of egg-surface glycoproteins when they attach to egg cells.

FIGURE 5.6 Carbohydrates Are Required for Cellular Recognition and Attachment.

SOURCES: Florman, H. M., K. B. Bechtol, and P. M. Wassarman. 1984. Enzymatic dissection of the functions of the mouse egg's receptor for sperm. *Developmental Biology* 106: 243–255. Also Florman, H. M., and P. M. Wassarman. 1985. O-linked oligosaccharides of mouse egg ZP3 account for its sperm receptor activity. *Cell* 41: 313–324.

✔**QUANTITATIVE** How would the bars change in the graph if sperm attachment required only the protein portion of egg glycoproteins?

But which part of the egg glycoproteins is essential for recognition and attachment—the protein or the carbohydrate? In follow-up experiments, Wassarman's group used the same type of competitive-binding assay to answer this question. When sperm were mixed with purified carbohydrates alone, most were unable to attach to eggs. In contrast, most sperm treated with purified protein alone were not inhibited and still attached to eggs. Both results show that the carbohydrate component plays a fundamental role in the process of egg-cell recognition.

Carbohydrates and Energy Storage

Candy-bar wrappers promise a quick energy boost, and ads for sports drinks claim that their products provide the "carbs" needed for peak activity. If you were to ask friends or family members what carbohydrates do in your body, they would probably say something like "They give you energy." And after pointing out that carbohydrates are also used in cell identity, as a structural material, and as a source of carbon skeletons for the synthesis of other complex molecules, you'd have to agree.

Carbohydrates store and provide chemical energy in cells. What aspect of carbohydrate structure makes this function possible?

Carbohydrates Store Sunlight as Chemical Energy Recall that the essence of chemical evolution was energy transformations (Appendix D). For example, it was proposed that the kinetic energy in sunlight may have been converted into chemical energy and stored in bonds of molecules such as formaldehyde (CH_2O).

This same type of transformation from light energy to chemical energy occurs in cells today, but instead of making formaldehyde, cells produce sugars. For example, plants harvest the kinetic energy in sunlight and store it in the bonds of carbohydrates by the process known as **photosynthesis.** (Photosynthesis is the focus of Chapter 14.)

Photosynthesis entails a complex set of reactions that can be summarized most simply as follows:

$$CO_2 + H_2O + sunlight \longrightarrow (CH_2O)_n + O_2$$

where $(CH_2O)_n$ represents a carbohydrate. The key to understanding the energy conversion that is taking place in this reaction is to compare the positions of the electrons in the reactants to those in the products.

1. The electrons in the C=O bonds of carbon dioxide and the C−O bonds of carbohydrates are held tightly because of oxygen's high electronegativity. Thus, they have relatively low potential energy.

2. The electrons involved in the C−H bonds of carbohydrates are shared equally because the electronegativity of carbon and hydrogen is about the same. Thus, these electrons have relatively high potential energy.

3. Electrons are also shared equally in the carbon–carbon C−C bonds of carbohydrates—meaning that they, too, have relatively high potential energy.

(a) Carbon dioxide

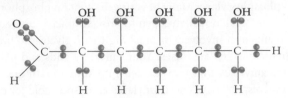

(b) A carbohydrate

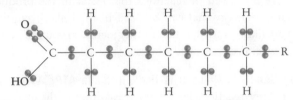

(c) A fatty acid (a component of fat molecules)

FIGURE 5.7 In Organisms, Potential Energy Is Stored in C−H and C−C Bonds. (a) In carbon dioxide, the electrons involved in covalent bonds are held tightly by oxygen atoms. **(b)** In carbohydrates such as the sugar shown here, many of the covalently bonded electrons are held equally between C and H atoms. **(c)** The fatty acids found in fat molecules have more C−H bonds and fewer C−O bonds than carbohydrates do. ("R" stands for the rest of the molecule.)

✔**EXERCISE** Circle the bonds in this diagram that have high potential energy.

C−C and C−H bonds have much higher potential energy than C−O bonds have. As a result, carbohydrates have much more chemical energy than carbon dioxide has.

FIGURE 5.7 summarizes and extends these points. Start by comparing the structure of carbon dioxide in Figure 5.7a with the carbohydrate in Figure 5.7b. The main difference is the presence of C−C and C−H bonds in the carbohydrate. Now compare the carbohydrate in Figure 5.7b with the fatty acid—a subunit of a fat molecule—in Figure 5.7c. Compared with carbohydrates, fats contain many more C−C and C−H bonds and many fewer C−O bonds.

This point is important. C−C and C−H bonds have high potential energy because the electrons are shared equally by atoms with low electronegativities. C−O bonds, in contrast, have low potential energy because the highly electronegative oxygen atom holds the electrons so tightly. Both carbohydrates and fats are used as fuel in cells, but fats store twice as much energy per gram compared with carbohydrates. (Fats are discussed in more detail in Chapter 3.)

Enzymes Hydrolyze Polysaccharides to Release Glucose Starch and glycogen are efficient energy-storage molecules because they polymerize via α-glycosidic linkages instead of the β-glycosidic linkages observed in the structural polysaccharides. The α-linkages in storage polysaccharides are readily hydrolyzed to release glucose, while the structural polysaccharides resist enzymatic degradation.

The most important enzyme involved in catalyzing the hydrolysis of α-glycosidic linkages in glycogen molecules is a protein called **phosphorylase.** Many of your cells contain phosphorylase, so they can break down glycogen to provide glucose on demand.

The enzymes involved in breaking the α-glycosidic linkages in starch are called **amylases.** Your salivary glands and pancreas produce amylases that are secreted into your mouth and small intestine, respectively. These amylases are responsible for digesting the starch that you eat.

The glucose subunits that are hydrolyzed from glycogen and starch are processed in reactions that result in the production of chemical energy that can be used in the cell. Glycogen and starch are like a candy bar that has segments, so you can break off chunks whenever you need a boost.

Energy Stored in Glucose is Used to Make ATP When a cell needs energy, reactions lead to the breakdown of the glucose and capture of the released energy through synthesis of the nucleotide adenosine triphosphate (ATP) (introduced in Chapter 5).

More specifically, the energy that is released when sugars are processed is used to synthesize ATP from a precursor called adenosine diphosphate (ADP) plus a free inorganic phosphate (P_i) molecule. The overall reaction can be written as follows:

$$(CH_2O)_n + O_2 + ADP + P_i \longrightarrow CO_2 + H_2O + ATP$$

To put this in words, the chemical energy stored in the C−H and C−C bonds of carbohydrate is transferred to a new bond linking a third phosphate group to ADP to form ATP.

How much energy does it take to form ATP? Consider this example: A cell can use the 10 calories of energy stored in a LifeSavers candy to produce approximately 2×10^{23} molecules of ATP. Although this sounds like a lot of ATP, an average human's energy needs would burn through all of this ATP energy in a little over a minute! The energy in ATP drives reactions like polymerization and cellular processes like moving your muscles.

Carbohydrates are like the water that piles up behind a dam; ATP is like the electricity generated at a dam, which lights up your home. Carbohydrates store chemical energy; ATP makes chemical energy useful to the cell.

Later chapters analyze in detail how cells capture and store energy in sugars and how these sugars are then broken down to provide cells with usable chemical energy in the form of ATP (Chapters 10, 13, and 14). For both of these processes to occur, however, a selectively permeable membrane barrier is required. The following chapter introduces the lipids needed to build these membranes and the role they played in the evolution of the first cell.

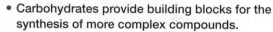

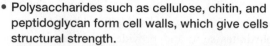

check your understanding

C Y U

If you understand that . . .

- Carbohydrates provide building blocks for the synthesis of more complex compounds.
- Polysaccharides such as cellulose, chitin, and peptidoglycan form cell walls, which give cells structural strength.
- Glycoproteins project from the surface of cells. They provide a molecular badge that identifies the cell's type or species.
- Starch and glycogen store sugars for later use in reactions that produce ATP. Sugars contain large amounts of chemical energy because they contain carbon atoms that are bonded to hydrogen atoms or other carbon atoms. The C−H and C−C bonds have high potential energy because the electrons are shared equally by atoms with low electronegativity.

✔ You should be able to . . .

1. Identify two aspects of the structures of cellulose, chitin, and peptidoglycan that correlate with their function as structural molecules.
2. Describe how the carbohydrates you ate during breakfast today are functioning in your body right now.

Answers are available in Appendix A.

APPENDIX E REVIEW

For media, go to MasteringBiology

If you understand . . .

5.1 Sugars as Monomers

- Monosaccharides are organic compounds that have a carbonyl group and several hydroxyl groups. The molecular formula for a sugar is typically $(CH_2O)_n$, but the number of "carbon-hydrate" groups may vary between sugars, as indicated by the n.

- Although some monosaccharides may have the same molecular formula, the arrangement of functional groups can lead to differences in the molecular structure of the sugars.

- Individual monosaccharides may form ring structures that differ from one another in the orientation of a hydroxyl group.

✔ You should be able to explain how a relatively small difference in the location of a carbonyl or hydroxyl group can lead to dramatic changes in the properties and function of a monosaccharide.

5.2 The Structure of Polysaccharides

- Monosaccharides can be covalently bonded to one another via glycosidic linkages, which join hydroxyl groups on adjacent molecules.

- In contrast to proteins and nucleic acids, polysaccharides do not always form a single uniform backbone structure. The numerous hydroxyls found in each monosaccharide allow glycosidic linkages to form at different sites and new strands to branch from existing chains.

- The types of monomers involved and the geometries of the glycosidic linkages between monomers distinguish different polysaccharides from one another.

- The most common polysaccharides in organisms today are starch, glycogen, cellulose, and chitin; peptidoglycan is an abundant polysaccharide that has short chains of amino acids attached.

✔ You should be able to compare and contrast glycosidic linkages in polysaccharides with the linkages between monomers in proteins and nucleic acids.

5.3 What Do Carbohydrates Do?

- In carbohydrates, as in proteins and nucleic acids, structure correlates with function.

- Cellulose, chitin, and peptidoglycan are polysaccharides that function in support. They are made up of monosaccharide monomers joined by β-1,4-glycosidic linkages. When individual molecules of these polysaccharides align side by side, bonds form between them—resulting in strong, flexible fibers or sheets that resist hydrolysis.

- The oligosaccharides on cell-surface glycoproteins can function as specific signposts or identity tags because their constituent monosaccharides are so diverse in geometry and composition.

- Both starch and glycogen function as energy-storage molecules. They are made up of glucose molecules that are joined by α-glycosidic linkages. These linkages are readily hydrolyzed to release glucose for the production of ATP.

✔ You should be able to describe four key differences in the structure of polysaccharides that function in energy storage versus structural support.

You should be able to . . .

✔ TEST YOUR KNOWLEDGE

Answers are available in Appendix A

1. What is the difference between a monosaccharide, an oligosaccharide, and a polysaccharide?
   a. the number of carbon atoms in the molecule
   b. the type of glycosidic linkage between monomers
   c. the spatial arrangement of the various hydroxyl residues in the molecule
   d. the number of monomers in the molecule

2. What are three ways monosaccharides differ from one another?

3. What type of bond is formed between two sugars in a disaccharide?
   a. glycosidic linkage
   b. phosphodiester bond
   c. peptide bond
   d. hydrogen bond

4. What holds cellulose molecules together in bundles large enough to form fibers?
   a. the cell wall
   b. peptide bonds
   c. hydrogen bonds
   d. hydrophobic interactions between different residues in the cellulose helix

5. What are the primary functions of carbohydrates in cells?
   a. energy storage, cell identity, structure, and building blocks for synthesis
   b. catalysis, structure, and energy storage
   c. information storage and catalysis
   d. source of carbon, information storage, and energy storage

6. What is responsible for the difference in potential energy between carbohydrates and carbon dioxide?

7. Which of the differences listed here could be found in the same monosaccharide?

a. different orientation of a hydroxyl in the linear form
b. different number of carbons
c. different orientation of a hydroxyl in the ring form
d. different position of the carbonyl group in the linear form

8. What would most likely occur if the galactose in lactose were replaced with glucose?
   a. It would not be digested by human infants or adults.
   b. It would be digested by most adult humans.
   c. It would be digested by human infants, but not adults.
   d. It would be digested by human adults, but not infants.

9. Explain how the structure of carbohydrates supports their function in displaying the identity of a cell.

10. What is the difference between linking glucose molecules with α-1,4-glycosidic linkages versus β-1,4-glycosidic linkages? What are the consequences?

11. Give three reasons why researchers have concluded that polysaccharides were unlikely to play a large role in the origin of life.

12. Compare and contrast the structures and functions of starch and glycogen. How are these molecules similar? How are they different?

13. A weight-loss program for humans that emphasized minimal consumption of carbohydrates was popular in some countries

in the early 2000s. What was the logic behind this diet? (Note: This diet plan caused controversy and is not endorsed by some physicians and researchers).

14. Galactosemia is a potentially fatal disease that occurs in humans who lack the enzyme that converts galactose to glucose. To treat this disease, physicians exclude the monosaccharide galactose from the diet. Which of the following would you also predict to be excluded from the diet?
    a. maltose   b. starch   c. mannose   d. lactose

15. If you hold a salty cracker in your mouth long enough, it will begin to taste sweet. What is responsible for this change in taste?

16. Lysozyme, an enzyme found in human saliva, tears, and other secretions, catalyzes the hydrolysis of the β-1,4-glycosidic linkages in peptidoglycan. Predict the effect of this enzyme on bacteria, and explain the role its activity plays in human health.

Credits

Photo Credits

Frontmatter p. v Anthony Bannister/Photo Researchers, Inc. **p. vi** R. B. Taylor/Photo Researchers, Inc. **p. vii** Brian Johnston

Chapter 1 Opener Thierry Montford/Biosphoto/Photo Researchers Inc. **1.1a** Biophoto Associates/Photo Researchers, Inc. **1.1b** Brian J. Ford **1.1c** The Print Collector/Alamy **1.6a** Steve Gschmeissner/Photo Researchers, Inc. **1.6b** Kwangshin Kim/Photo Researchers, Inc. **1.7** Corbis Premium RF/Alamy **1.10** Reproduced with permission from H. Wolf. 2011. Odometry and Insect Navigation. *Journal of Experimental Biology* 214: 1629–1641.

Chapter 2 Opener Dr. Torsten Wittmann/SPL/Photo Researchers, Inc. **2.1** SPL/Photo Researchers, Inc. **2.2a** Gopal Murti/Photo Researchers, Inc. **2.2b** Biology Pics/Photo Researchers, Inc. **2.3** Eye of Science/Photo Researchers, Inc. **2.4** Eye of Science/Photo Researchers, Inc. **2.7** Don W. Fawcett/Photo Researchers, Inc. **2.8** Omikron/Photo Researchers, Inc. **2.9LR** Don W. Fawcett/Photo Researchers, Inc. **2.10** Biophoto Associates/Photo Researchers, Inc. **2.11** Don W. Fawcett/Photo Researchers, Inc. **2.12** E.H. Newcomb & W.P Wergin/Biological Photo Service **2.13** Fawcett/Friend/Photo Researchers, Inc. **2.14** Don W. Fawcett/Photo Researchers, Inc. **2.15** E.H. Newcomb & W.P. Wergin/Biological Photo Service **2.16a** Dr. Don Fawcett/S. Ito & A. Like/Photo Researchers, Inc. **2.16b** Don W. Fawcett/Photo Researchers, Inc. **2.16c** Biophoto Associates/Photo Researchers, Inc. **2.16d** From "*Caveolin-1* expression is essential for proper nonshivering thermogenesis in brown adipose tissue." Cohen, A. W., Schubert, W., Brasaemle, D. L., Scherer, P. E., Lisanti, M. P. *Diabetes*. 2005 Mar; 54(3): 679–86, Fig. 6. **2.17** Don W. Fawcett/Photo Researchers, Inc. **2.26** Micrograph by Dr. Conly L. Rieder, Wadsworth Center, Albany, New York 12201-0509 **2.27ab** Reproduced by permission of the American Society for Cell Biology from *Molecular Biology of the Cell* 9 (12), December 1998, cover. ©1999 by the American Society for Cell Biology. Image courtesy of Bruce J. Schnapp, Oregon Health Sciences University. **2.28** John E. Heuser, M.D., Washington University School of Medicine, St. Louis, Missouri **2.29a** SPL/Photo Researchers, Inc. **2.29b** Biomedical Imaging Unit, Southampton General Hospital/Photo Researchers, Inc. **2.30** Don W. Fawcett/Photo Researchers, Inc.

Chapter 3 3.2a Multiart/iStockphoto **3.2b** lepas2004/iStockphoto **3.2c** ilker canikligil/Shutterstock **3.6L** Dr. rer. nat. Markus Drechsler **3.15** Jack W. Szostak **3.18** Don W. Fawcett/Photo Researchers, Inc.

Chapter 4 Opener G. Gimenz-Martin/SPL/Photo Researchers, Inc. **4.1T** Gopal Murti/Photo Researchers, Inc. **4.1B** Biophoto Associates/Photo Researchers, Inc. **4.5(1–7)** Micrographs by Conly L. Rieder, Department of Biology, Rensselaer Polytechnic Institute, Troy, New York. **4.8a** Ed Reschke/Getty **4.8b** Michael Danilchik

Chapter 5 Opener SSPL/The Image Works **5.5** National Cancer Institute

Chapter 6 Opener Dr. Gopal Murti/Science Photo Library/Photo Researchers, Inc. **6.1** Eye of Science/Photo Researchers, Inc. **6.5** Reproduced by permission of Matthew S. Meselson, Harvard University, from M. Meselson and F.W. Stahl, "The replication of DNA in Escherichia coli." *PNAS* 44(7): 671–682 (July 1958), p. 675, Fig. 4. **6.7** Dr. Gopal Murti/Science Photo Library/Photo Researchers, Inc.

Chapter 7 Opener J. Craig Venter Institute **7.4a** Rod Williams/Nature Picture Library **7.4b** Clint Cook & Janet P. Crossland, The Peromyscu Genetic Stock Center at the U. of South Carolina **7.9** Courtesy of Hesed M. Padilla-Nash and Thomas Ried. Affiliation is Section of Cancer Genomics, Genetics Branch, Center for Research, National Cancer Institute, National Institutes of Health, Bethesda, MD 20892

Chapter 8 Opener Oscar Miller/SPL/Photo Researchers, Inc. **8.5** Bert W. O'Malley, M.D., Baylor College of Medicine **8.8** From Hamkalo and Miller, "Electronmicroscopy of Genetic Material," Figure 6a, p. 379. Reproduced with permission, from *Annual Review of Biochemistry*, Volume 42. ©1973 by Annual Reviews, Inc. **8.9** Dr. Elena Kiseleva/Photo Researchers, Inc.

Chapter 9 9.9ab Janice Carr, CDC

Chapter 10 Opener Richard Megna/Fundamental Photographs **10.3** Thomas Eisner

Chapter 11 Opener David Phillips/The Population Council/Photo Researchers, Inc. **11.1** Look at Sciences/Photo Researchers, Inc. **11.6** Jupiterimages/Photos.com **11.7(1–9)** Warren Rosenberg/Fundamental Photographs **11.15** Dr. Rebecca Shulte

Chapter 12 Opener Brian Johnston **12.9a** Benjamin Prud'homme/Nicolas Gompel **12.9bLR** From "Learning to Fly: Phenotypic Markers in Drosophila." A poster of common phenotypic markers used in Drosophila genetics. Jennifer Childress, Richard Behringer, and Georg Halder. 2005. *Genesis* 43(1). Cover illustration. **12.16** Carla Fernanda Reis

Chapter 13 Opener Raiden32/Used under the Creative Commons license. http://creativecommons.org/licenses/by-sa/3.0/deed.en **13.1a** Oliver Hoffmann/Shutterstock **13.1b** Gergo Orban/Shutterstock **13.8** Terry Frey **13.16** Michael Delannoy

Chapter 14 Opener R.B. Taylor/Photo Researchers, Inc. **14.3T** John Durham/Science Photo Library/Photo Researchers, Inc. **14.3MB** Barbara Erienborn/Electron micrograph by Wm. P. Wergin, courtesy of E.H. Newcomb, University of Wisconsin **14.5b** Sinclair Stammers/Photo Researchers, Inc. **14.18LR** James A. Bassham, Lawrence Berkeley Laboratory, UCB (retired) **14.21ab** Dr. Jeremy Burgess/Science Photo Library/Photo Researchers, Inc.

Appendix A: Answers A7.1ab Don W. Fawcett/Photo Researchers, Inc. **A7.1c** Biophoto Associates/Photo Researchers, Inc. **A7.1d** From "*Caveolin-1* expression is essential for proper nonshivering thermogenesis in brown adipose tissue." Cohen, A. W., Schubert, W., Brasaemle, D. L., Scherer, P. E., Lisanti, M. P. *Diabetes*. 2005 Mar; 54(3): 679–86, Fig. 6.

Appendix B: BioSkills B9.3 Reproduced by permission from J. P. Ferris, et al. "Synthesis of long prebiotic oligomers on mineral surfaces." *Nature* 381: 59–61 (1996), Fig. 2. ©1996 Macmillan Magazines Ltd. Image courtesy of James P. Ferris, Rensselaer Polytechnic Institute. **B11.1a** Biology Media/Photo Researchers, Inc. **B11.1b** Janice Carr/Centers for Disease Control and Prevention (CDC) **B11.2ab** Michael W. Davidson/Molecular Expressions **B11.3** Rosalind Franklin/Photo Researchers, Inc. **B12.1aL** National Cancer Institute **B12.1aR** E.S. Anderson/Photo Researchers, Inc. **B12.1b** Sinclair Stammers/Photo Researchers, Inc. **B13.1a** Kwangshin Kim/Photo Researchers, Inc. **B13.1b** Richard L. (Larry) Blanton, Ph.D. **B13.1c** Holt Studios International/Photo Researchers, Inc. **B13.1d** Custom Medical Stock Photo, Inc. **B13.1e** Graphic Science/Alamy Images **B13.1f** Sinclair Stammers/Photo Researchers, Inc. **B13.1g** dra_schwartz/iStockphoto

Appendix D Opener IFE, URI-IAO, UW, Lost City Science Party; NOAA/OAR/OER; The Lost City 2005 Expedition **2.1** Dragan Trifunovic/Shutterstock **2.6c** Zedcor Wholly Owned/Photos.com **2.11** LianeM/Alamy **2.15b** Dietmar Nill/Getty Images **2.15c** John Sylvester/First Light/AGE fotostock **2.29** picture-alliance/Judaica-Samml/Newscom

Appendix E Opener Peter Arnold/Alamy

Illustration and Text Credits

Chapter 1 1.3 Based on S. P. Moose, J. W. Dudley, and T. R. Rocheford. 2004. Maize selection passes the century mark: A unique resource for 21st century genomics. *Trends in Plant Science* 9 (7): 358–364, Fig. 1a; and the Illinois long-term selection experiment for oil and protein in corn (University of Illinois at Urbana–Champaign). **1.7a** Based on T. P. Young and L. A. Isbell. 1991. Sex differences in giraffe feeding ecology: Energetic and social constraints. *Ethology* 87: 79–80, Figs. 5a, 6a. **1.9** Adapted by permission of AAAS and the author from M. Wittlinger, R. Wehner, and H. Wolf. 2006. The ant odometer: Stepping on stilts and stumps. *Science* 312: 1965–1967, Figs. 1, 2, 3. (http://www.sciencemag.org/content/312/5782/1965.short).

Chapter 2 2.5 Reprinted with kind permission from Springer Science+Business Media B.V. from David S. Goodsell, *The Machinery of Life*. 2nd ed., 2009.

Chapter 3 Opener CHARMM-GUI Archive—Library of Pure Lipid Bilayer (www.charmm-gui.org/?doc=archive&lib=lipid_pure), POPE Bilayer Library (pope_n256.pdb). Reference: S. Jo, T. Kim, and W. Im. 2007. Automated builder and database of protein/membrane complexes for molecular dynamics simulations. *PLoS ONE* 2 (9): e880. **3.10** Data: J. de Gier, J. G. Mandersloot, and L. L. van Deenen. 1968. Lipid composition and permeability of liposomes. *Biochimica et Biophysica Acta* 150: 666–675. **3.21** Data: C. E. Bear, F. Duguay, A. L. Naismith, et al. 1992. Purification and functional reconstitution of the cystic fibrosis transmembrane conductance regulator (CFTR). *Cell* 68: 809–818. **3.22** PDB ID: 2ZZ9. K. Tani, T. Mitsuma, Y. Hiroaki, et al. 2009. Mechanism of aquaporin-4's fast and highly selective water conduction and proton exclusion. *Journal of Molecular Biology* 389: 694–706. **3.23** PDB ID: 1K4C. Y. Zhou, J. H. Morais-Cabral, A. Kaufman, et al. 2001. Chemistry of ion coordination and hydration revealed by a K^+ channel–Fab complex at 2.0 Å resolution. *Nature* 414: 43–48. **3.23** PDB ID: 3FB7. L. G. Cuello, V. Jogini, D. M. Cortes, et al. Open KcsA potassium channel in the presence of Rb^+ ion. (To be published.) **7.18** A. D. Mills, R. A. Laskey, P. Black, et al. 1980. An acidic protein which assembles nucleosomes in vitro is the most abundant protein in *Xenopus* oocyte nuclei. *Journal of Molecular Biology* 139: 561–568. Also C. Dingwall, S. V.

Sharnick, and R. A. Laskey. 1982. A polypeptide domain that specifies migration of nucleoplasmin into the nucleus. *Cell* 30: 449–458.

Chapter 4 **4.6** G. J. Gorbsky, P. J. Sammack, and G. G. Borisey. 1987. Chromosomes move poleward during anaphase along stationary microtubules that coordinately dissemble from their kinetochore ends. *Journal of Cell Biology* 104: 9–18. **4.9** Based on J. L. Ptacin, S. F. Lee, E. C. Garner, et al. 2010. A spindle-like apparatus guides bacterial chromosome segregation. *Nature Cell Biology* 12: 791–798, Fig. 5. **4.10** Y. Masui and C. L. Markert. 1971. Cytoplasmic control of nuclear behavior during meiotic maturation of frog oocytes. *Journal of Experimental Zoology* 177: 129–145. **4.13** Data: the website of the National Cancer Institute (www.cancer.gov), Common Cancer Types, November 2010.

Chapter 5 **T5-1** PDB ID: 1EHZ. H. Shi and P. B. Moore. 2000. The crystal structure of yeast phenylalanine tRNA at 1.93 Å resolution: A classic structure revisited. *RNA* 6: 1091–1105. **5.11** PDB ID: 1X8W. F. Guo, A. R. Gooding, and T. R. Cech. 2004. Structure of the *Tetrahymena* ribozyme: Base triple sandwich and metal ion at the active site. *Molecular Cell* 16: 351–362.

Chapter 6 **6.2** A. D. Hershey and M. Chase. 1952. Independent functions of viral protein and nucleic acid in growth of bacteriophage. *Journal of General Physiology* 36: 39–56. **6.5** Adapted by permission of Dr. Matthew Meselson after M. Meselson and F. W. Stahl. 1958. The replication of DNA in *Escherichia coli*. *PNAS* 44: 671–682, Fig. 6. **6.14** Data: R. C. Allsopp, H. Vaziri, C. Patterson, et al. 1992. Telomere length predicts replicative capacity of human fibroblasts. *PNAS* 89: 10114–10118.
6.18a Data: J. E. Cleaver. 1970. DNA repair and radiation sensitivity in human (xeroderma pigmentosum) cells. *International Journal of Radiation Biology* 18: 557–565, Fig. 3. **6.18b** Data: J .E. Cleaver. 1972. Xeroderma pigmentosum: Variants with normal DNA repair and normal sensitivity to ultraviolet light. *Journal of Investigative Dermatology* 58: 124–128, Fig. 1. **6.UN2** Graph adapted by permission of the Radiation Research Society from P. Howard-Flanders and R. P. Boyce. 1966. DNA repair and genetic recombination: Studies on mutants of *Escherichia coli* defective in these processes. *Radiation Research Supplement* 6: 156–184, Fig. 8.

Chapter 7 **7.2** Data: A. M. Srb and N. H. Horowitz. 1944. The ornithine cycle in *Neurospora* and its genetic control. *Journal of Biological Chemistry* 154: 129–139.

Chapter 8 **8.2a** PDB ID: 3IYD. B. P. Hudson, J. Quispe, S. Lara-Gonzalez, et al. 2009. Three-dimensional EM structure of an intact activator-dependent transcription initiation complex. *PNAS* 106: 19830–19835. **8.11** Based on M. B. Hoagland, M. L. Stephenson, J. F. Scott, et al. 1958. A soluble ribonucleic acid intermediate in protein synthesis. *Journal of Biological Chemistry* 231: 241–257, Fig. 6. **8.13** PDB ID: 1ZJW: I. Gruic-Sovulj, N. Uter, T. Bullock, et al. 2005. tRNA-dependent aminoacyl-adenylate hydrolysis by a nonediting class I aminoacyl-tRNA synthetase. *Journal of Biological Chemistry* 280: 23978–23986. **8.14b** PDB IDs: 3FIK, 3FIH. E. Villa, J. Sengupta, L. G. Trabuco, et al. 2009. Ribosome-induced changes in elongation factor Tu conformation control GTP hydrolysis. *PNAS* 106: 1063–1068.

Chapter 9 **Opener** PDB ID: 2DN2. S. Y. Park, T. Yokoyama, N. Shibayama, et al. 2006. 1.25 Å resolution crystal structures of human hemoglobin in the oxy, deoxy and carbonmonoxy forms. *Journal of Molecular Biology* 360: 690–701. **9.8a** PDB ID: 1TGH. Z. S. Juo, T. K. Chiu, P. M. Leiberman, et al. 1996. How proteins recognize the TATA box. *Journal of Molecular Biology* 261: 239–254. **9.8b** PDB ID: 2X9K. F. Korkmaz-Ozkan, S. Koster, W. Kuhlbrandt, et al. 2010. Correlation between the OmpG secondary structure and its pH-dependent alterations monitored by FTIR. *Journal of Molecular Biology* 401: 56–67. **9.8c** PDB ID: 2PTC. M. Marquart, J. Walter, J. Deisenhofer, et al. 1983. The geometry of the reactive site and of the peptide groups in trypsin, trypsinogen and its complexes with inhibitors. *Acta Crystallographica* Section B39: 480–490. **9.8d** PDB ID: 1CLG. J. M. Chen, C. D. E. King, S. H. Feairheller, et al. 1991. An energetic evaluation of a "Smith" collagen microfibril model. *Journal of Protein Chemistry* 10: 535–552. **9.11b, left** PDB ID: 2MHR. S. Sheriff, W. A. Hendrickson, and J. L. Smith. 1987. Structure of myohemerythrin in the azidomet state at 1.7/1.3 resolution. *Journal of Molecular Biology* 197: 273–296. **9.11b, middle** PDB ID: 1FTP. N. H. Haunerland, B. L. Jacobson, G. Wesenberg, et al. 1994. Three-dimensional structure of the muscle fatty-acid-binding protein isolated from the desert locust *Schistocerca gregaria*. *Biochemistry* 33: 12378–12385. **9.11b, right** PDB ID: 1IXA. M. Baron, D. G. Norman, T. S. Harvey, et al. 1992. The three-dimensional structure of the first EGF-like module of human factor IX: Comparison with EGF and TGF-alpha. *Protein Science* 1: 81–90. **9.12a** PDB ID: 1D1L. P. B. Rupert, A. K. Mollah, M. C. Mossing, et al. 2000. The structural basis for enhanced stability and reduced DNA binding seen in engineered second-generation Cro monomers and dimers. *Journal of Molecular Biology* 296: 1079–1090. **9.12b** PDB ID: 2DN2. S.Y. Park, T. Yokoyama, N. Shibayama, et al. 2006. 1.25 Å resolution crystal structures of human hemoglobin in the oxy, deoxy and carbonmonoxy forms. *Journal of Molecular Biology* 360: 690–701. **9.14a** PDB ID: 1DMO. M. Zhang, T. Tanaka, and M. Ikura. 1995. Calcium-induced conformational transition revealed by the solution structure of apo calmodulin. *Nature Structural Biology* 2: 758–767. **9.14b** PDB ID: 3CLN. Y. S. Babu, C. E. Bugg, and W. J. Cook.

1988. Structure of calmodulin refined at 2.2 A resolution. *Journal of Molecular Biology* 204: 191–204. **9.16** PDB ID: 2PTC. M. Marquart, J. Walter, J. Deisenhofer, et al. 1983. The geometry of the reactive site and of the peptide groups in trypsin, trypsinogen and its complexes with inhibitors. *Acta Crystallographica* Section B39: 480–490.

Chapter 10 **10.8** PDB ID: 1Q18. V. V. Lunin, Y. Li, J. D. Schrag, et al. 2004. Crystal structures of *Escherichia coli* ATP-dependent glucokinase and its complex with glucose. *Journal of Bacteriology* 186: 6915–6927. **10.8** PDB ID: 2Q2R. A. T. Cordeiro, A. J. Caceres, D. Vertommen, et al. 2007. The crystal structure of *Trypanosoma cruzi* glucokinase reveals features determining oligomerization and anomer specificity of hexose-phosphorylating enzymes. *Journal of Molecular Biology* 372: 1215–1226. **10.14a&b** Data: N. N. Nawani, B. P. Kapadnis, A. D. Das, et al. 2002. Purification and characterization of a thermophilic and acidophilic chitinase from Microbispora sp. V2. *Journal of Applied Microbiology* 93: 865–975, Figs. 7, 8a. Also N. N. Nawani and B. P. Kapadnis. 2001. One-step purification of chitinase from *Serratia marcescens* NK1, a soil isolate. *Journal of Applied Microbiology* 90: 803–808, Figs. 3, 4. **10.15** PDB ID: 2ERK. B. J. Canagarajah, A. Khokhlatchev, M. H. Cobb, et al. 1997. Activation mechanism of the MAP kinase ERK2 by dual phosphorylation. *Cell* (Cambridge, MA) 90: 859–869. **10.15** PDB ID 3ERK. Z. Wang, B. J. Canagarajah, J. C. Boehm, et al. 1998. Structural basis of inhibitor selectivity in MAP kinases. *Structure* 6: 1117–1128.

Chapter 11 **11.13** Data: National Down Syndrome Society, 2012. **11.15** L. T. Morran, O. G. Schmidt, I. A. Gelarden, et al. 2011. Running with the red queen: Host-parasite coevolution selects for biparental sex. *Science* 333: 216–218.

Chapter 12 **12.3** G. Mendel. 1866. Versuche über Pflanzen-hybriden. *Verhandlungen des naturforschenden Vereines in Brünn* 4: 3–47. English translation available from Electronic Scholarly Publishing (www.esp.org). **T12.2** Data: G. Mendel. 1866. Versuche über Pflanzen-hybriden. *Verhandlungen des naturforschenden Vereines in Brünn* 4: 3–47. **12.13** Data: T. H. Morgan. 1911. An attempt to analyze the constitution of the chromosomes on the basis of sex-limited inheritance in *Drosophila*. *Journal of Experimental Zoology* 11: 365–414. **12.20** Data: Pan American Health Organization/WHO. 2004. *Epidemiological Bulletin* 25: 9–13, Graph 1.

Chapter 13 **13.7** PDB ID: 4PFK. P. R. Evans and P. J. Hudson. 1981. Phosphofructokinase: Structure and control. *Philosophical Transactions R. Soc. Lond. B: Biol. Sci.* 293: 53–62. **13.13** Data: X. Li, R. K. Dash, R. K. Pradhan, et al. 2010. A database of thermodynamic quantities for the reactions of glycolysis and the tricarboxylic acid cycle. *Journal of Physical Chemistry B* 114: 16068–16082, Table 4. **13.14** Data: D.F . Wilson, M. Erecinska, and P. L. Dutton. 1974. Thermodynamic relationships in mitochondrial oxidative phosphorylation. *Annual Review of Biophysics and Bioengineering* 3: 203–230, Tables 1, 3. Also V. D. Sled, N. I. Rudnitzky, Y. Hatefit, et al. 1994. Thermodynamic analysis of flavin in mitochondrial NADH: Ubiquinone oxidoreductase (complex I). *Biochemistry* 33: 10069–10075. **13.17** E. Racker and W. Stoeckenius. 1974. Reconstitution of purple membrane vesicles catalyzing light-driven proton uptake and adenosine triphosphate formation. *Journal of Biological Chemistry* 249: 662–663.

Chapter 14 **14.6** T. W. Engelmann. 1882. Oxygen excretion from plant cells in a microspectrum. *Botanische Zeitung* 40: 419–426. **14.7** Reprinted with kind permission from Springer Science+Business Media B.V. from The Photosynthetic Process. In *Concepts in Photobiology: Photosynthesis and Photomorphogenesis*, edited by G. S. Singhal, G. Renger, S. K. Sopory et al. Dordrecht: Kluwer Academic; co-published with Narosa Publishing House (New Delhi), pp. 11–51, Fig. 5. **14.11** R. Govindjee, Govindjee, and G. Hoch. 1964. Emerson enhancement effect in chloroplast reactions. *Plant Physiology* 39: 10–14. **14.18** A. A. Benson, J. A. Bassham, M. Calvin, et al. 1950. The path of carbon in photosynthesis. V. Paper chromatography and radioautography of the products. *Journal of the American Chemistry Society* 72: 1710–1718. **14.20a** PDB ID: 1RCX. T. C. Taylor and I. Andersson. 1997. The structure of the complex between rubisco and its natural substrate ribulose 1,5-bisphosphate. *Journal of Molecular Biology* 265: 432–444.

Appendix B: BioSkills **TB16.1** A. Crowe, C. Dicks, and M. P. Wenderoth. 2008. Biology in bloom: Implementing Bloom's Taxonomy to enhance student learning in Biology. *CBE–Life Sciences Education* 7: 368–381, Table 3.

Appendix D **T2-1** Data: D. R. Lide (editor). 2008. Standard thermodynamic properties of chemical substances. In *CRC Handbook of Physics and Chemistry*. 89th ed. Boca Raton, FL: CRC Press. **2.21** After S. L. Miller. 1953. A production of amino acids under possible primitive Earth conditions. *Science* 117 (3046): 528–529.

Appendix E **5.6** H. M. Florman, K. B. Bechtol, and P. M. Wassarman. 1984. Enzymatic dissection of the functions of the mouse egg's receptor for sperm. *Developmental Biology* 106: 243–255. Also H. M. Florman and P. M. Wassarman. 1985. O-linked oligosaccharides of mouse egg ZP3 account for its sperm receptor activity. *Cell* 41: 313–324; J. D. Bleil and P. M. Wassarman. 1988. Galactose at the nonreducing terminus of O-linked oligosaccharides of mouse egg zona pellucida glycoprotein ZP3 is essential for the glycoprotein's sperm receptor activity. *PNAS* 85: 6778–6782.

Index

Boldface page numbers indicate a glossary entry; page numbers followed by an f indicate a figure; those followed by t indicate a table.

Boldface page numbers indicate a glossary entry; page numbers followed by an
f indicate a figure; those followed by *t* indicate a table.

Boldface page numbers indicate a glossary entry; page numbers followed by an *f* indicate a figure; those followed by *t* indicate a table.

Boldface page numbers indicate a glossary entry; page numbers followed by an *f* indicate a figure; those followed by *t* indicate a table.

Boldface page numbers indicate a glossary entry; page numbers followed by an *f* indicate a figure; those followed by *t* indicate a table.